Sources of Vietnamese Tradition

INTRODUCTION TO ASIAN CIVILIZATIONS

Introduction to Asian Civilizations

Wm. Theodore de Bary, General Editor

Sources of Japanese Tradition,
1958; paperback ed., 2 vols., 1964. 2d ed., vol. 1, 2001, compiled by
Wm. Theodore de Bary, Donald Keene, George Tanabe, and Paul Varley;
vol. 2, 2005, compiled by Wm. Theodore de Bary, Carol Gluck, and Arthur
E. Tiedemann; vol. 2, abridged, 2 pts., 2006, compiled by Wm. Theodore
de Bary, Carol Gluck, and Arthur E. Tiedemann

Sources of Indian Tradition,
1958; paperback ed., 2 vols., 1964. 2d ed., 2 vols., 1988

Sources of Chinese Tradition,
1960, paperback ed., 2 vols., 1964. 2d ed., vol. 1, 1999, compiled by
Wm. Theodore de Bary and Irene Bloom; vol. 2, 2000, compiled
by Wm. Theodore de Bary and Richard Lufrano

Sources of Korean Tradition,
1997; 2 vols., vol. 1, 1997, compiled by Peter H. Lee and Wm. Theodore
de Bary; vol. 2, 2001, compiled by Yǒngho Ch'oe, Peter H. Lee, and
Wm. Theodore de Bary

Sources of East Asian Tradition,
2008, 2 vols., edited by Wm. Theodore de Bary

Sources of Vietnamese Tradition

*Edited by George E. Dutton, Jayne S. Werner,
and John K. Whitmore*

COLUMBIA UNIVERSITY PRESS

NEW YORK

Columbia University Press
Publishers Since 1893
New York   Chichester, West Sussex

Library of Congress Cataloging-in-Publication Data
Sources of Vietnamese tradition / edited by George E. Dutton, Jayne S. Werner,
and John K. Whitemore.
     p. cm. — (Introduction to Asian civilizations)
  Texts chiefly translated from Vietnamese, with some translated from Chinese and French;
commentary in English.
  Includes bibliographical references and index.
  ISBN 978-0-231-13862-8 (cloth : alk. paper)
  ISBN 978-0-231-13863-5 (pbk. : alk. paper)
  ISBN 978-0-231-51110-0 (e-book)
  1. Vietnam—Civilization—Sources.   2. Vietnam—History—Sources.   I. Dutton,
George Edson.   II. Werner, Jayne Susan.   III. Whitmore, John K.   IV. Title.
V. Series: Introduction to Asian civilizations.
  DS556.42.S69 2012
  959.7—dc23

2011033923

Columbia University Press books are printed on permanent and durable acid-free paper.
This book is printed on paper with recycled content.
Printed in the United States of America
c 10 9 8 7 6 5 4 3 2 1
p 10 9 8 7 6 5 4 3 2 1

COVER IMAGE: Detail of a badge, with a rooster, for third-rank civil official (silk- and metallic-thread embroidery), Vietnam, nineteenth century. (Dodi Fromson Collection; Maggie Smith Photography)

CONTENTS

PART TWO
Early Modern Vietnam

PART THREE
Modern Vietnam

With considerable trepidation we have undertaken a project that presumes to give substance to the conceptual sources of "Vietnamese tradition." We are acutely aware that in these postmodern (or perhaps post-postmodern) times, to speak of "tradition" is to embark on a discussion sure to provoke criticism from all sides. We are equally aware that what a previous generation largely accepted as "tradition" can no longer be taken up without intense examination. "Tradition," we acknowledge, is a concept invented, sometimes out of whole cloth, by scholars, politicians, religious leaders, and others to serve a wide range of agendas. Tradition is not "the way things have always been," for there is nothing so constant as change, and it is ahistorical in the extreme to suggest otherwise. Under these circumstances, it is perhaps better not to speak of a single, much less fixed, "tradition" but to think of multiple ideational threads, sometimes marked by continuity and sometimes by rupture.

The works that we classify as part of the Vietnamese "tradition" are not meant to be exhaustive, nor are they intended to be canonical (though, of course, we recognize that their inclusion in this volume runs the risk of their becoming so). Rather, and much more modestly, the excerpts in this anthology reveal some of the ways in which peoples living in the Vietnamese lands thought and wrote about their society over nearly two millennia. Any effort to understand the Vietnamese people must begin by thinking in a series of sometimes imperfect dichotomies that define elements of their cultural heritage.

These binaries include mountains and seas, China and Southeast Asia, war and peace, rice farming and trade, Buddhism and Confucianism, lowlands and uplands, men and women, scholars and soldiers. Among and between these dichotomous pairs, some geographical and others conceptual and even spiritual, we find the Vietnamese people. Although their heritage is confusing, it also is rewardingly heterogeneous, one whose essence cannot be distilled into a single volume or two. Because the "sources" of their "tradition" are many, they do not flow in a single stream but combine multiple streams to create admixtures viewed as "authentic" or "traditional." Both Vietnamese and non-Vietnamese scholars have long sought to reconcile these many sources, complex and sometimes antagonistic histories, into coherent narratives. Such efforts have sometimes served the purposes of the state, justifying their political actions, and sometimes they have enabled rulers to sway popular sentiment. These efforts themselves have shaped the understandings and meanings of the past, as court histories have been borrowed piecemeal by local historians and literati to produce particularistic visions of the past and its heritage. As one scholar noted, it is perhaps better to "make the past strange" so as to prevent its being used as a weapon by one side or another. Our sincere hope is that this volume will not be seen as a weapon or justification for exclusive interpretations of the origins of the Vietnamese people. Rather, our intent is to contribute to a better understanding of a cultural heritage that is still appreciated only dimly by most outside that country.

This is why, despite the numerous challenges, this book seems all the more necessary and, indeed, long overdue. The lack of such a volume was particularly glaring given the rapid development of the field of Vietnamese studies over the past decade in both Vietnam and the West. In addition, despite a decade-long lull following the end of the Vietnam War, Vietnamese studies has recently enjoyed a resurgence in the United States, with scholarly exchanges and research between the United States and Vietnam similarly expanding and flourishing. New research has generated new understandings of crucial periods, turning points, and conceptual frameworks in Vietnamese history. In the course of this rapidly evolving scholarship, new texts have emerged to enrich or revise our insights into, and understanding of, the Vietnamese past. In addition to the many known historical texts, new texts are being added to the canon. This book reflects these advances.

Many people contributed to the gestation, support, and preparation of this book. Wendy Lochner, senior executive editor at Columbia University Press, first proposed to Jayne Werner the idea of including Vietnam in the Introduction to Asian Civilizations series. Jayne Werner then asked John Whitmore and George Dutton to join her as coeditors. All three of us have been hampered by the lack of teaching materials in the form of readily accessible translations and textbooks for classroom use, and when we launched the project, we realized we faced a time-consuming task. We asked the Henry Luce Foundation for support for the project, having been encouraged to do so by officers of the foundation and also by David J. Steinberg, president of Long Island University and a noted scholar of Southeast Asia. We are very grateful to Dr. Terrill E. Lautz, vice president and secretary of the Henry Luce Foundation, for his intervention and personal interest in this project. Because he had served in Vietnam in the U.S. Army's Medical Service Corps from 1969 to 1970, he consequently had more than a passing interest in and appreciation for our project.

In assembling these texts, we relied on the talents and insights of many scholars in Vietnamese studies who generously contributed to shaping its final form. We are especially grateful to those who suggested texts and helped us narrow the list of readings, including Nguyen Ngoc, Alexander Woodside, Nguyen-vo Thu-huong, and Liam Kelley. In addition, we received commentary from members of the Vietnam Studies Group and two anonymous readers for Columbia University Press.

The organization of this book departs somewhat from that of the other *Sources* volumes. We divided Vietnamese history into three parts—"Premodern Vietnam," "Early Modern Vietnam," and "Modern Vietnam"—and we identified common themes for each period, around which the texts in each section are grouped. Although these themes vary somewhat from section to section, they generally follow the same pattern for each one. As a whole, the themes demonstrate the continuities in the texts from century to century and from section to section. Besides the more obvious categories of politics, economics, culture, and society, we added the category "The Land" at the beginning of each major section, as we believe it is a particularly strong historic theme in Vietnamese texts.

This book reflects the skills of numerous scholars in Vietnamese studies. We or other specialists translated many of the texts appearing in this volume for the first time. Other translations are from previously published sources, which we usually edited or updated. Several people helped us with the translations of texts from the seventeenth through nineteen centuries, most notably Liam Kelley, who also generously provided extensive, detailed feedback on a number of texts. Others who offered their expertise in reading classical Chinese include Joshua Herr, Hangmo Zhang, Yingzi Xu, Nathaniel Isaacson, and, especially, Matthew Cochran, who helped clarify a number of obscure passages. If an official translation by a governmental body, such as the Democratic Republic of Vietnam or the Republic of Vietnam, was available, we relied on that, checking it against the original Vietnamese if necessary. In some cases, several people worked on the texts, particularly those from the twentieth century. Both Pascal Bourdeaux and Jeremy Jammes helped with the modern texts in their areas of expertise. For twentieth-century poetry, Ton That Quynh Du and Kim N. B.

Ninh offered exceptionally helpful advice regarding the final selections, which they translated. We also thank Nha Ca, who currently lives in California, for permission to include the translation of her poem.

In addition, we thank the South Asia and Weatherhead East Asian Institutes at Columbia University, which provided facilities for preparation of the manuscript, as well as Cindy Middleton and the Center for Southeast Asian Studies at the University of Michigan for help with facilities for our editorial meetings in the middle of the country. Graduate students Lauren Meeker and Mai Lan Ha provided research assistance, and Joshua Herr created the chronology. C. Jon Delogu and Christoph Robert provided additional editorial help with a number of French and Vietnamese texts. Anandaroop Roy gave us excellent maps.

Prehistoric and Legendary Period

200,000–100,000 B.C.E.	*Homo erectus* and *Homo sapiens* exist in Indochina.
18,000 B.C.E.	Son Vi culture is thought to begin in northern Vietnam.
10,000 B.C.E.	Hoa Binh culture is thought to begin in northern Vietnam.
8000 B.C.E.	Bac Son culture is thought to begin.
3000 B.C.E.	Phung Nguyen culture is thought to begin.
1000 B.C.E.	Legendary kingdom of Van Lang or Lac Viet (Hung kings) is thought to begin. Traces of Bronze Age metallurgy are found.
500 B.C.E.	Dong Son culture begins: iron metallurgy, double cropping, chiefs. Proto-Cham culture in present-day central Vietnam begins.
400 B.C.E.	Iron-smelting and forging techniques appear in upper Red River valley.

Early History to End of Northern Period

257 B.C.E.	King An Duong of Tay Au tribes conquers Lac Viet and establishes Au Lac kingdom.
221 B.C.E.	Qin Shi Huang Di invades Yue lands.

207 B.C.E.	Trieu Da (Zhao Tuo), king of Nan Yue, conquers Au Lac.
111 B.C.E.	Han dynasty establishes suzerainty over Red River Delta.
9 C.E.	Wang Mang usurps the throne in China, triggering migrations to Red River Delta and coastal plain.
40	The Trung sisters overthrow Han administration.
42	Ma Yuan defeats the Trung sisters.
43	Ma Yuan institutes direct Han rule in Red River Delta.
150	"Funan" kingdom rises in Mekong River Delta.
180–226	Shi Xie rules northern Vietnam as the Han prefect and then in alliance with the Wu.
192	Lin Yi kingdom, precursor of Champa, is founded in present-day central Vietnam.
220	Han dynasty ends, and China is divided into three kingdoms, including the southern Wu kingdom.
248	Lin Yi invades Wu territories, and Lady Trieu leads rebellion against Wu.
280	Dao Huang consolidates power in Red River Delta and rebuilds Long Bien.
284	Lin Yi sends embassy to Jin court.
Mid-fourth century	Brahman religion and Sanskrit writing system spread in Funan.
Fourth–sixth centuries	Traders, scholars, and monks come from India, spreading Buddhism throughout Vietnamese lands.
446	Tan Hozhi, governor of Jiao, sacks Lin Yi capital.
494	Ly family strengthens its position in Jiao Province.
529	New dynasty with strong Brahman influences is established in Lin Yi.
541–546	Ly Bi leads revolt and rules independently until defeated by China's Liang dynasty.
570	Ly Phat Tu consolidates his position in Jiao Province and, under nominal Liang authority, promotes Buddhism.
580	Vinitaruci, a Brahman from southern India, is said to arrive in Jiao Province to teach Buddhism and establish a line of religious succession, beginning with his disciple Phap (dharma master) Hien.
590	Funan kingdom disintegrates; the middle and lower Mekong, now called Zhenla in Chinese texts, are ruled by Khmer monarchs.
602	Ly Phat Tu rebels against the new Sui dynasty in China but is defeated and captured.
605	Sui army sacks Lin Yi's capital.
622	New Tang dynasty divides Vietnamese lands into provinces under one administrator based near the modern-day Hanoi.

653	Vikrantavarman ascends Lin Yi throne and begins construction of major religious monuments at My Son and Tra Kieu in present-day Quang Nam.
679	Tang dynasty proclaims Protectorate of An Nan.
687	Dinh Kien leads a peasant rebellion.
700	Incomplete census of An Nan protectorate lists 148,431 "heads" in four provinces.
722	Mai Thuc Loan raises army in coastal Vietnam, seizes control of An Nan, and names himself the Black Emperor in present-day central Vietnam; the An Nan protector-general returns with reinforcements and destroys Mai Thuc Loan.
742	Census reveals substantial population growth.
750	Lin Yi shifts its center of gravity southward to modern-day Nha Trang.
767	Seaborne invaders from the south overrun the An Nan protectorate and destroy Cham sanctuary of Po Nagar.
782	Phung Hung seizes the capital of the protectorate and rules it independently of the Tang until his death in 789.
802	Jayavarman II establishes kingdom of Angkor.
808	The venerable Dinh Khong, a popular Buddhist figure in the Red River Delta, dies.
820	The Chinese monk Vo Ngon Thong is said to come to An Nan and found a new Buddhist school, which lasts until the thirteenth century.
863	Armies from the Nan Zhao kingdom attack and plunder An Nan.
867	The Chinese general Gao Pian defeats Nan Zhao forces and local allies in An Nan; the new capital of Dai La (Hanoi) is constructed and ushers in a period of peace.
875	Indravaman II, king of Champa, orders the construction of Buddhist monastery at Dong Duong.
906	The Tang dynasty disintegrates, and a local family, the Khuc, takes authority in the Red River Delta.
930	Southern Han army seizes Dai La.
938	Ngo Quyen defeats the Southern Han army and fleet on the Bach Dang River.

Independent Kingdoms: Early Regimes

939	Ngo Quyen names himself king, an act marking the traditional beginning of independence from the North.
950	Khmer armies invade Champa and steal a famous statue of Bhagavati.

959	Ngo Chan Luu is born; he becomes a famous Buddhist monk and dies in 1011.
968	Dinh Bo Linh defeats the twelve lords, establishes new capital at Hoa Lu, and proclaims himself king.
979	After Dinh Bo Linh is assassinated by a minor court official, Le Hoan takes the throne.
981	Le Hoan repels an invasion by the Song dynasty from the North.
982	Le Hoan invades Champa and destroys the capital of Indrapura.
Tenth century	Cheo theatrical form grows in popularity.
Tenth–twelfth centuries	Buddhism spreads across Dai Viet, with numerous pagodas, texts, and monks.

Ly Dynasty (1009–1225)

1009	Ly Cong Uan assumes throne, establishing Ly dynasty.
1010	The capital is moved to Thang Long (Hanoi).
1044	King Ly Thai Tong takes personal command of counterattack against Champa and seizes the Cham capital.
1054	Ly dynasty names its kingdom Dai Viet.
1069	Dai Viet demands three provinces of Champa (north-central Vietnam) in return for release of captured Cham king.
1070	Temple of Literature (Van Mieu) is constructed in Thang Long.
1075	Chinese-style examinations are first used to select scholars.
1076	Ly dynasty defeats invasion by China's Song dynasty.
1096	Ly Nhan Tong establishes Thien school of Buddhism in royal court.
1120s–1210s	Wars are fought among Dai Viet, Champa, and Angkor.
1159	Court minister Do Anh Vu dies.
1160	Champa recaptures Amaravati (Quang Nam); new religious monuments are built at My Son.
1177	Cham fleet takes Angkor by surprise, killing the monarch and pillaging the city.
1190	Jayavarman VII of Cambodia defeats Cham forces and gains complete control of Champa by 1203.
1200s	Dai Viet first uses kilns to produce monochrome and polychrome ceramic wares for export.
1220	Cambodian forces evacuate Champa, and Cham prince takes the throne in new capital of Vijaya, near modern-day Qui Nhon.
Thirteenth century	Tuong theatrical form grows in popularity.

Tran Dynasty (1225–1400)

1225	Tran Thu Do arranges for nephew to marry the Ly emperor's daughter, then puts him on the throne and establishes the Tran dynasty (1225–1400).
1242	Tran dynasty promulgates village administration procedures, which for the first time extend the court's attention to provinces and districts.
1248	Dinh Nhi dike is constructed in the Red River Delta.
1253	Tran court establishes the Royal Academy (Quoc Hoc Vien).
1258	The Mongols attack Dai Viet for the first time, burning the capital, but they soon withdraw under logistical and guerrilla pressure.
1272	Le Van Huu, Vietnam's first notable historian, completes writing the *Chronicle of Dai Viet* (*Dai Viet su ky*).
1282	A Mongol naval expedition captures the Cham capital, but the Cham resistance continues.
1284	The Mongols' second invasion of Dai Viet captures the capital, but in the following year, Tran Hung Dao leads a successful counteroffensive.
1287	The Mongols invade Dai Viet for the third time, but the Mongol fleet is destroyed at second battle of the Bach Dang River.
1293	King Tran Nhan Tong transfers throne to son, retires to Buddhist monastery, and, with two monks, founds the Bamboo Grove (Truc Lam) sect of Thien Buddhism.
1306	The king of Champa exchanges two provinces for the Tran monarch's sister in marriage.
1329	*Departed Spirits of the Viet Realm* (*Viet dien u linh tap*) is written.
1330s	Le Tac writes *A Brief Record of An Nan* (*An Nan chi luoc*) while in exile in China during the Yuan dynasty.
1335	Dai Viet campaign is launched against the Tai kingdom of Ai Lao.
1337	*Eminent Monks of the Thien Community* (*Thien uyen tap anh*) is written.
1360s	Che Bong Nga ascends the throne of Champa.
1369	The physician Tue Tinh dies, leaving behind treatises on medicinal plants and herbs.
1370s	Le Quy Ly gains power as court minister.
1371	Che Bong Nga sacks Thang Long.
1380	Nguyen Trai is born; he becomes a political adviser, scholar, and writer and dies in 1442.

Late fourteenth century	*Strange Tales from South of the Passes* (*Linh Nam chich quai*) is written.
1390	Che Bong Nga is killed during a naval reconnaissance, and Cham forces withdraw to Champa.
1397	Le Quy Ly builds the royal palace at Tay Do (Western capital).

Ho Dynasty (1400–1407)

1400	Le (Ho) Quy Ly, a powerful Tran minister, takes the throne and undertakes reforms.
1407	A Ming dynasty army invades Dai Viet, defeats the Ho forces, and makes Jiaozhi (Dai Viet) into a Chinese province.
1418	Le Loi begins revolt against Ming rule.

Le Dynasty (1428–1527)

1428	Ming forces withdraw from Dai Viet; Le Loi establishes Le dynasty (1428–1527), which is recognized by the Ming emperor.
	Nguyen Trai writes "Great Proclamation on the Defeat of the Ngo [Ming]" (Binh Ngo dai cao).
1430s	The Le dynasty's legal code is instituted.
1460	Le Thanh Tong begins his reign, which lasts until 1497.
1463	Le Thanh Tong initiates the standard triennial Confucian examinations and begins to adopt bureaucratic government.
1471	The Champa capital of Vijaya falls permanently to Vietnamese forces.
1479	Ngo Si Lien presents to the throne the *Complete Chronicle of Dai Viet* (*Dai Viet su ky toan thu*), a history of Vietnam from its mythological origins up to 1428.
1479–1480	Le armies invade the Lao territories.
1483	*Record of the Government Institutes of the South of Heaven* (*Thien Nam du ha tap*), along with a legal chronology, is compiled.
1516	The Tran Cao revolt against the Le court.
1527	Mac Dang Dung seizes the throne, forcing the Le emperor to commit suicide.

Mac Dynasty (1528–1592)

1535	The Portuguese Antonio da Faria establishes the first Western trading post at Faifo (Hoi An).
1541	The Mac reach an agreement with the Ming court.
1550s	Portuguese priest Gaspar da Cruz visits Dai Viet.

| 1558 | Nguyen Hoang is appointed governor-general of Thuan Hoa and Quang Nam, marking the beginning of the Nguyen political project in the southern frontier lands. |
| 1592 | The Mac flee the capital under attack from Nguyen and Trinh forces, who restore a member of the Le family to the throne. |

Restored Le Dynasty (1592–1788)

Sixteenth century	Christianity is introduced.
1600	Nguyen Hoang splits with his rival, the Trinh clan, in Thang Long and concentrates on building a separate domain in the south; the Trinh clan controls the royal Le family in the north.
1615	Jesuit Father Francis Buzomi builds the first Catholic church in Vietnam.

Divided Period: Trinh (North) and Nguyen (South)

1627	Civil war breaks out between Trinh and Nguyen. Father Alexander de Rhodes arrives in Ha Noi and plays a crucial role in developing the Latinized *quoc ngu* script.
1637	Dutch merchants establish a trading outpost in Pho Hien, northern Dai Viet.
1658	Rome appoints François Pallu to spearhead proselytizing efforts in the northern Vietnamese territories. Hostilities break out between the Nguyen state and Cambodia, and eventually the Nguyen court annexes territory in the Mekong Delta.
1672	Trinh and Nguyen arrive at a de facto truce, ending a half century of conflict.
1673	British merchants establish a trading office in Pho Hien.
1679	Three thousand Chinese refugees from the defeat of Ming dynasty forces arrive at Danang and receive Nguyen approval to settle in the Mekong Delta.
1692	The ruler of remaining small kingdom of Champa is put to death, and the Nguyen state annexes his territory.
1695	Chinese Buddhist monk Dashan visits the Nguyen court and later writes an account of his journey, *Overseas Journal* (*Hai wai ji shi*).
1705	Doan Thi Diem is born; she becomes a poet and teacher and dies in 1748.
1737–1769	The Le prince Duy Mat resists control by the Trinh from the western mountains of Thanh Hoa.

1741–1751	Nguyen Huu Cau leads a peasant revolt against the Trinh.
1744	Nguyen lord Nguyen Phuc Khoat declares autonomy from the Le dynasty as an independent ruler in the southern realm.
1749	Cambodia cedes the remainder of the lower Mekong Delta to the Nguyen state, which governs the region through its vassal, the ethnic Chinese Mac family, based in Ha Tien.
1750	The Nguyen court orders Christian missionaries to be deported, although several Jesuits with scientific skills are permitted to remain.
1763	Le Van Duyet is born; he becomes a Nguyen general and, later, the viceroy of the south in Gia Dinh; he dies in 1832.
1767	Pigneau de Béhaine, the bishop of Adran, arrives in the Mekong Delta.
1771	The Tay Son uprising in Qui Nhon Province begins.
1774	The Trinh invade and capture Phu Xuan, the Nguyen capital.
1776	Le Quy Don (1726–1784) writes *Chronicles of the Prefectural Borders (Phu bien tap luc)*.
1785	The Tay Son defeat the Siamese army allied with the Nguyen.
1786	Tay Son forces enter Thang Long, ousting the Trinh.
1787	Pigneau de Béhaine, on behalf of Prince Nguyen Anh, concludes a treaty of alliance between France and Cochinchina, but French aid fails to materialize.
1788	Qing dynasty forces invade Dai Viet in the name of protecting the Le dynasty but are defeated at Tet in 1789 by Nguyen Hue, the leader of the Tay Son.

Tay Son Dynasty (1788–1802)

1788	Nguyen Hue issues an edict proclaiming himself the Quang Trung emperor and establishes a new dynasty.
1790	The Quang Trung emperor issues an edict calling for a restoration of agriculture.
1792	Quang Trung dies suddenly and is succeeded by his young son; the Tay Son dynasty slowly begins to unravel.

Nguyen Dynasty (1802–1945, independent rule until 1885)

1802	Nguyen Anh defeats remnant Tay Son forces, establishes the Nguyen dynasty, names himself the Gia Long emperor, and reigns from 1802 to 1819.
1804	Gia Long and the Chinese court agree on Vietnam as the name of the country.
	Gia Long issues an edict "outlining propriety and ritual."
1807	Vietnam establishes a protectorate over Cambodia.

Ca. 1810	Nguyen Du composes epic poem *The Tale of Kieu* (*Kim Van Kieu*).
Early nineteenth century	Ho Xuan Huong writes her provocative poetry.
1812	Gia Long promulgates new legal code to replace the Le dynasty's code.
1820	Trinh Hoai Duc completes *Gia Dinh Citadel Records* (*Gia Dinh thanh thong chi*).
1820–1840	Reign of the Minh Mang emperor.
1821	John Crawford, representing the British East India Company, visits Vietnam to assess commercial prospects.
	Phan Huy Chu finishes writing *Categorized Records of the Institutions of Successive Dynasties* (*Lich trieu hien chuong loai chi*).
1825	Minh Mang refuses to conclude a commercial treaty with France and issues the first Nguyen dynasty decree outlawing the dissemination of Christianity.
1833–1835	Le Van Khoi, adopted son of Le Van Duyet, mounts a revolt in southern Vietnam against Minh Mang but is defeated and killed two years later.
1833–1845	Siam and Vietnam fight over Cambodia and in 1845 agree to joint control.
1834	Minh Mang issues "Ten Moral Precepts."
1835	Minh Mang issues edict of admonition to the literati and commoners of the six provinces of southern Vietnam in the aftermath of the Le Van Khoi revolt.
1838	Dai Nam becomes the official name of Vietnam.
1839	Minh Mang introduces a system of salaries and pensions for princes and mandarins, which is designed to replace the traditional assignment of fief estates.
1841–1847	Reign of the Thieu Tri emperor.
1846	A joint Vietnamese-Thai protectorate over Cambodia is established.
1847	Census records 1,024,338 male taxpayers.
	French warships sink five armored junks of the Vietnamese navy in Da Nang harbor.
1848–1883	Reign of the Tu Duc emperor.
1851	Vietnamese authorities execute two French missionaries and then a French bishop the following year.
1858	French and Spanish ships attack Da Nang, destroying the Vietnamese fleet and harbor defenses.
1859	The French conquest of the Mekong Delta begins with the seizure of the Gia Dinh fortress.

1862	The Nguyen dynasty cedes three provinces to France, opens three ports to French trade, and promises to pay a huge indemnity.
	The Complete Geographical Records of Dai Viet (Dai Viet dia du toan bien) is completed.
1863	Nguyen Truong To (1827–1871), a Confucian-educated Catholic, returns from overseas with a series of modernizing proposals to submit to the Tu Duc emperor, mostly without effect.
	Treaty of Hue affirms French territorial claims and makes further diplomatic concessions.
	Cambodia becomes a French protectorate.
1865	The first Vietnamese newspaper, *Gia Dinh News (Gia Dinh Bao)*, is published.
1866–1868	The Lagree-Garnier expedition travels up the Mekong River; Garnier's *Voyage d'exploration* is published in 1873.
1867	French forces seize three remaining southern Vietnamese provinces, creating the colony of Cochinchina.
1876	Truong Vinh Ky (1837–1898) completes writing *Tales from a Journey to the Northern Region (Truyen di Bac Ky)*.
1881	A major typhoon in Indochina kills 300,000 people.
	The French Society of Mines is formed to explore Tonkin coal resources.

French Period

1883	Tonkin and Annam become French protectorates.
1883–1885	Sino-French war over the issue of French protectorates begins; the Chinese concede and recognize the French protectorates of Tonkin and Annam.
1884	The Nguyen dynasty's history board releases *The Imperially Ordered Mirror and Commentary on the History of the Viet (Kham dinh Viet su thong giam cuong muc)*.
1885	The Nguyen Ham Nghi emperor issues the proclamation "Loyalty to the Emperor" (Can Vuong).
1887	France proclaims the Indochinese Union.
1890	Ho Chi Minh is born.
1893	Laos becomes a French protectorate.
1898	The Indochinese colonial administration is centralized in Hanoi.
1904	Phan Boi Chau forms the Modernization Society (Duy Tan Hoi).
1905	The Study in the East (Dong Du) movement commences, and Vietnamese students begin going to Japan to study.

Phan Boi Chau writes *The History of the Loss of the Country* (*Vietnam vong quoc su*) in Japan.

1906   The Tonkin Free School (Dong Kinh Nghia Thuc) is founded but the French close it in 1907.

1909   Japan expels Vietnamese students.

1912   Phan Boi Chau forms the Vietnam Restoration Society (Vietnam Quang Phuc Hoi).

1913   The first issue of the journal *Indochina Review* (*Dong Duong Tap Chi*) is published.

1915–1918   Civil service examinations are abolished in Tonkin (1915) and Annam (1918).

1917   The first issue of the monthly *Southern Ethos* (*Nam Phong Tap Chi*), edited by Pham Quynh, is published and runs until 1934.

1919   The Cao Dai religion is revealed to Ngo Van Chieu.

1920   Ho Chi Minh participates in founding the French Communist Party.

1923   The newspaper *La cloche felée* (*The Flawed Bell*) is first published in Saigon.

1924   Saigon and Paris are linked by direct transoceanic cable.

1925   Ho Chi Minh establishes the Vietnamese Revolutionary Youth Association.

1926   The Cao Dai religion is officially founded.
        The Women's Labor Study Association is established.

1927   The Vietnam Nationalist Party (VNQDD) is formed.

1929   The periodical *Women's News* (*Phu Nu Tan Van*) begins publishing in 1929 and runs until 1934.

1930   Ho Chi Minh unites Vietnamese Communist groups into one party, later named the Indochinese Communist Party (ICP).

1932   The Self-Reliance Literary Group (Tu Luc Van Doan) is founded.

1936   The Popular Front period in Vietnamese politics and publishing begins; it lasts until 1939.

1938   Popular literacy classes are organized by the Association for the Dissemination of Quoc Ngu Study.

1939   The Hoa Hao religious movement is formed.

1940   Japan occupies Vietnam, but French authorities are left in place.

1941   The Viet Minh (Viet Minh Doc Lap Dong Minh Hoi [League for the Independence of Vietnam]) is established.

1944   Vo Nguyen Giap forms the first units of the Vietnam Propaganda and Liberation Army.

1945, March 9	The Japanese overthrow the French colonial regime and install Tran Trong Kim as the prime minister of the Empire of Vietnam under the Bao Dai emperor.
1945, May	Vo Nguyen Giap's and Chu Van Tan's armed units are merged into the People's Liberation Armed Forces.
1945, August 13–15	Ho Chi Minh convenes an ICP conference at Tan Trao and plans the August Revolution.
1945, August 14	The Japanese surrender to Allied forces.
1945, August 25	The last Nguyen emperor, Bao Dai, renounces his throne.
1945, September 2	The Democratic Republic of Vietnam (DRV) is proclaimed in Hanoi.
1946–1954	The first Indochina War begins, lasting until 1954.

Postcolonial and Contemporary Period

1949	France recognizes the Associated State of Vietnam, with Bao Dai as the head of state; Vietnam joins the French Union.
1950	The People's Republic of China grants diplomatic recognition to the DRV.
1951	The Vietnam Workers' Party is formed after the dissolution of the ICP in 1945.
1954, May	The French defeat at Dien Bien Phu marks the end of the French–Viet Minh war.
1954, July	The Geneva Agreements temporarily divide Vietnam at the seventeenth parallel so the military can regroup; elections are to be held in two years to decide Vietnam's political future.
	Ngo Dinh Diem is appointed by Bao Dai as prime minister of the state of Vietnam.
1954, September	The United States forms the Southeast Asia Treaty Organization (SEATO), extending protection to the state of Vietnam.
1954, October	Viet Minh troops enter Hanoi, which becomes the capital of the DRV.
1955	The Republic of Vietnam is formed, with its capital in Saigon.
1955–1956	The DRV undertakes a land reform program.
1955–1958	The Nhan Van Giai Pham affair plays out in the north.
1958	The collectivization program begins in the north.
	Nguyen Thi Dinh and the southern Viet Minh launch the first armed uprisings against the Ngo Dinh Diem regime in Ben Tre Province.
1960	The National Front for the Liberation of South Vietnam (NLF) is formed.

1960, September	The Third Congress of the Vietnamese Workers' Party in the north decides to support the revolutionary struggle in the south.
1960, November	Military officials launch an abortive coup against the Ngo Dinh Diem regime.
1963, January	The battle of Ap Bac is fought in Dinh Tuong Province.
1963, summer	Buddhist protests challenge the Ngo Dinh Diem government.
1963, November	Ngo Dinh Diem is assassinated, and a succession of military governments take charge in the south.
1964	The United States begins bombing northern Vietnam.
1965	The United States sends ground troops into the Vietnamese conflict.
1968	The DRV/NLF launches the Tet Offensive.
1969	Ho Chi Minh dies.
	Nguyen Van Thieu, president of the Republic of Vietnam (RVN), signs the Land to the Tiller Program into law.
1973, January	The Paris Agreement leads to the withdrawal of U.S. forces from South Vietnam and the return of U.S. POWs.
1975, April 30	DRV forces occupy Saigon and accept the surrender of the Republic of Vietnam.
1976	A unified Vietnam is renamed the Socialist Republic of Vietnam (SRV), and the name of the party is changed to the Vietnam Communist Party.
1978	The SRV nationalizes commercial and manufacturing enterprises owned by Vietnamese of Chinese descent, leading to the exodus of several hundred thousand "boat people."
1978–1988	Vietnam overthrows the Khmer Rouge regime and occupies Cambodia.
1979	Chinese forces briefly invade Vietnam but begin withdrawing after a month.
1986	The Communist Party holds its Sixth National Congress; the failure of the socialist economy and agricultural cooperatives lead to *doi moi* (renovation) economic reforms.
	The decollectivization of the land begins.
1989	Vietnam withdraws from Cambodia.
1991	Vietnam normalizes its relations with China.
1994	The U.S. embargo of Vietnam is lifted.
1995	The United States and Vietnam establish diplomatic relations, and Vietnam joins the Association of Southeast Nations (ASEAN).

1999   Tran Do, an army general and party dissident, is expelled from the party.

2005   Thich Nhat Hanh, a prominent Buddhist activist, returns to Vietnam after thirty-eight years in exile.

CHRONICLES AND OTHER HISTORICAL SOURCES

Ca. 200   Mou Bo, a Southern Buddhist convert, writes *Master Mou* (*Mouzi*).

297   Chen Shou writes *Chronicle of the Three Kingdoms* (*San guo zhi*), a history of the three realms that divided the Chinese realm following the Han dynasty in the third century C.E., including the realm of Wu in the southeast, which controlled Jiaozhi.

445   Fan Ye writes *History of the Later Han Dynasty* (*Hou Han shu*), a history of the Later Han dynasty (25–220), including the Han control of Jiaozhi after the Trung sisters' rebellion.

945   Liu Xu writes *Old History of the Tang Dynasty* (*Jiu Tang shu*), the first history of the Tang dynasty (618–907), with references to the Protectorate of Annan in the south.

1250s   Tran Thai Tong, the first Tran ruler, writes *Exhortations on Resolution* (*Ngu khoa hu*), a Buddhist treatise.

1272   Le Van Huu writes *Chronicle of Dai Viet* (*Dai Viet su ky*), a history of Vietnam from the third century B.C.E. to 1225 C.E., the end of the Ly dynasty.

1329   Ly Te Xuyen writes *Departed Spirits of the Viet Realm* (*Viet dien u linh tap*), a collection of cultic tales about spirits that aided Dai Viet in the Mongol wars of the 1280s and then were used to protect the realm and Buddhism.

1333   Le Tac, a Southern scholar who fled to China with the defeated Mongols, writes *Short Record of Annan* (*An Nam chi luoc*), a work describing Dai Viet.

1337   *Eminent Monks of the Thien Community* (*Thien uyen tap anh*), a collection of biographies of famous monks in the Thien meditation school, is written.

1380s   *Short History of Dai Viet* (*Viet su luoc*), a history of Vietnam from its mythic beginnings to the end of the Ly dynasty (1225), is written.

        Strange Tales from South of the Passes (*Linh Nam chich quai*), tales that establish a new mythic pattern for Dai Viet in a time of cultural turmoil, is written.

1428   Nguyen Trai writes "Great Proclamation on the Defeat of the Ming" (*Binh Ngo dai cao*), Le Loi's proclamation on his victory over the Ming.

1431   Nguyen Trai writes *True Record of Mount Lam* (*Lam Son thuc luc*), the history of Le Loi's war against the Ming occupying forces and the foundation of the Le dynasty.

1435   Nguyen Trai writes *Geography* (*Du dia chi*), a study of each province of the land of Dai Viet.

1455   Phan Phu Tien writes (*Continued*) *Chronicle of Dai Viet* (*Dai Viet su ky*), covering the end of the Ly dynasty (1225) through the Tran and Ho dynasties to the defeat of the Ming (1427).

1479   Ngo Si Lien writes *Complete Chronicle of Dai Viet* (*Dai Viet su ky toan thu*), a new and revised edition of the *Chronicle*, covering the mythic past to the end of the Tran dynasty and the Ming occupation.

1483   Le dynasty officials write *Celestial South's [Records Made] at Leisure* (*Thien Nam du ha tap*), a collection of miscellaneous materials, including poetry, concerning the government of Dai Viet.

1492   Vu Quynh edits *Strange Tales from South of the Passes* (*Linh Nam chich quai*), a new and rearranged edition of the century-old tales.

1540s   Mac dynasty historians write (*Continued*) *Complete Chronicle of Dai Viet* (*Dai Viet su ky toan thu*), a continuation of the *Complete Chronicle* to the (temporary) end of the Le dynasty (1527).

        Book of Good Government of the Hong Duc Era (*Hong Duc thien chinh thu*), a compilation of laws and edicts from the 1430s onward, is written.

1553   Duong Van An writes *A Recent Record of O Chau* (*O Chau can luc*), a geography of the Hue region in the mid-sixteenth century.

1719   Nguyen Khoa Chiem writes *Recorded Tales of the Founding of the Country* (*Viet Nam khai quoc chi truyen*), an account of the Nguyen state's growth and development.

1767   *Laws of the State* (*Quoc trieu hinh luat*), the final edition of the Le dynasty's legal code, is drawn up.

1776   Le Quy Don writes *Chronicles of the Prefectural Borders* (*Phu bien tap luc*).

1777   Le Quy Don writes *Small Chronicle of Things Seen and Heard* (*Kien van tieu luc*), thoughts by a major scholar on various past and present aspects of Dai Viet.

Later 1700s Le Quy Don compiles *Anthology of Vietnamese Poetry* (*Toan Viet thi luc*), a collection of the poetry of Dai Viet up to that time.
            Bui Huy Bich writes *Selected Writings of the Imperial Viet* (*Hoang Viet van tuyen*), a collection of prose texts from Dai Viet's earlier centuries.

1780s   Le dynasty historians write *A Continuation of the Chronicle of Dai Viet* (*Dai Viet su ky tuc bien*).

1800s   Pham Dinh Ho writes *Following the Brush Amid the Rains* (*Vu trung tuy but*).

1811–   Nguyen dynasty historians write *The Veritable Records of Dai Nam* (*Dai Nam thuc luc*).

1820   Trinh Hoai Duc writes *Gia Dinh Citadel Records* (*Gia Dinh thanh thong chi*).

1821   Phan Huy Chu writes *Categorized Records of the Institutions of Successive Dynasties* (*Lich trieu hien chuong loai chi*).

1830s?   Ngo Cao Lang writes *Miscellaneous Records of Successive Dynasties* (*Lich trieu tap ky*).

1833   Phan Huy Chu writes *Records of the Imperial Viet Territories* (*Hoang Viet dia du chi*).
            Phan Huy Chu writes *Summary Record of an Overseas Journey* (*Hai trinh chi luoc*).

1837–   Nguyen dynasty historians write *Essential Records of Minh Menh* (*Minh Menh chinh yeu*).

1862   Nguyen Van Sieu writes *The Complete Compilation of the Geography of Dai Viet* (*Dai Viet dia du toan bien*).

1865   Nguyen dynasty historians write *The Unification Records of Dai Nam* (*Dai Nam nhat thong chi*).

1884   Nguyen dynasty historians write *The Imperially Ordered Mirror and Commentary on the History of the Viet* (*Kham dinh Viet su thong giam cuong muc*).

A NOTE ON NAMES AND DATES

A few clarifications regarding naming and transliteration are in order. First, the documents in this collection include many references to Vietnamese monarchs and dates within their reigns. Like the Chinese, the Vietnamese measured time cyclically by resetting their calendars with the ascension of each new emperor. Accordingly, many documents refer to years within a particular ruler's reign— for example, the fifth year of the Hong Duc reign (1474 C.E.). In addition, rulers are usually referred to by one of three names: their given name before taking the throne, the name (or names) under which they reigned, or the name bestowed after their death. The temple name is important because most historical documents were produced after the ruler's death and thus frequently refer to him by his temple name. For example, the three names of the founder of the Nguyen dynasty are his (1) given name, Nguyen Anh; (2) reign name, Gia Long; and (3) temple name, Nguyen Thai To. The year in the period during which this monarch ruled (1802–1819) typically is cited as, for example, "the fifth year of the Gia Long reign" (that is, 1806).

Second, in working on this project we were forced to make choices about the transliterations of names and places. Since most of our pre-twentieth-century texts are in classical Chinese, we had to decide whether to transliterate names and terms using the Chinese or the Vietnamese romanization. It could be argued that because Vietnamese writers would have pronounced Chinese names in their texts according to the Vietnamese romanization, we should use the *quoc ngu* forms of these names. But because most readers would be more familiar with the *pinyin* renderings of these names, we decided to use *pinyin* transliterations of the names of all Chinese persons in both Chinese and Vietnamese documents. In a number of cases we also provided, either parenthetically or in footnotes, the Vietnamese transliteration of the names of persons commonly referred to in that form. Similarly, for clarity's sake we used the *pinyin* transliteration for several common terms, notably *yin* and *yang*, rather than the Vietnamese romanizations, *am* and *duong*. The one notable exception to this general rule has been our use of the Vietnamese transliteration Thien for the Dhyana school of Buddhism, rather than Chan or Zen, to make clear that this is a distinct and localized form of the Dhyana school.

Sources of Vietnamese Tradition

INTRODUCTION

The reference in the title of this volume to "Vietnamese" suggests a common, albeit broad, society now bounded by the borders of the modern nation-state. Nonetheless, readers should bear in mind that it is anachronistic to use the term Vietnam to describe the territories inhabited by these peoples in the past. The reason is that the name Vietnam was not used until the early nineteenth century and that the territory so labeled did not reach its current size until around the same time.

Over the past two thousand years, the geographical expanse today known as Vietnam has had many labels, including Giao Chi, Lam Ap, Zhenla, Champa, Dai Viet, Van Lang, Van Xuan, Dai Nam, and Ai Lao. More recently, this area was separated into three territories—labeled by French colonial authorities as Tonkin, Annam, and Cochinchina—even after it was joined with the Lao and Khmer territories to form a new entity known as the Union of Indochina. Then, for nearly thirty years in the second half of the twentieth century, the Vietnamese territories were again divided, this time by the forces of Cold War politics, creating the Democratic Republic of Vietnam in the north and the Republic of Vietnam in the south. The geographies encompassed by these multiply termed places varied as well, some representing only small parts of what is today Vietnam and others representing large portions of this area. In this book, we hope to avert the all-too-common teleological perspective that views the Vietnamese past as an inevitable trajectory moving toward a unified modern state. We then must recognize that there are indeed multiple pasts, as well as what are now known as "regional" cultures, histories, and geographical realities bounded by a single, but still extremely diverse, modern state.

SELECTION AND ORGANIZATION OF TEXTS

We recognize that the sampling of texts in *Sources of Vietnamese Tradition* risks creating an artificial canon of readings that represent Vietnamese history and culture. This risk is particularly great in the Vietnamese case because of the very few existing translations of historical materials, especially those from before the twentieth century. But it is not our intention to create a canon of any kind, and we are not suggesting that the readings assembled here are the only significant ones or even that all of them are of equal importance. Instead, they may be viewed as representative of certain literary genres, ideas, or views.

Ten years from now, this project would be very different in different hands or, indeed, in our own. We caution, too, that these texts may not necessarily allow readers to arrive at some understanding of the "essential" Vietnamese cultural or social outlook. But the texts certainly do offer glimpses into the minds of certain Vietnamese individuals at particular moments, and they do suggest some of the many themes to be found over the long trajectory of Vietnamese history. What these (mostly) elite texts can tell us about the Vietnamese people is limited, however, since the vast majority of the Vietnamese population has historically been illiterate or semiliterate. Accordingly, their view of their world has been preserved to some extent in a rich tradition of folk stories, Buddhist tales, foundation myths, aphorisms, and songs, a few of which are included in this book.

In selecting the texts, we tried to cover a broad range of voices, time periods, regions, and issues. The voices are almost exclusively those of elites and lowland Vietnamese because only the elites were literate and, furthermore, their texts were preserved as part of official court histories or were passed down within literary lineages or even, in rare cases, were printed in woodblock form. Consequently, we seriously considered including materials from ethnic minority peoples living within the boundaries of modern Vietnam, for the histories of the Vietnamese are bound up with these groups in significant ways. But we finally decided that we could not do justice to the voices of these many groups, none of which could be said to "represent" the others, and therefore excluded them from the project. Thus when we speak of "Vietnamese" traditions, we are referring to the majority lowland Vietnamese populations, sometimes called the Kinh or, simply, the Viet. Our decision to limit our coverage to the lowland Vietnamese also was strongly shaped by the fact that the other volumes in the Introduction to Asian Civilizations series similarly restricted their coverage to the majority socioethnic groups in their countries.

Most of the documents we chose have not been previously translated into English, particularly those from the "early modern period," the early seventeenth through the mid-nineteenth century. Although many of these texts were translated from their original Chinese or vernacular Vietnamese characters into modern Vietnamese and were published and sometimes republished in Vietnam during the twentieth century, we based our translations on the original language in which the texts first appeared. Most of the pre-twentieth-century documents were written in either classical Chinese or *chu nom*, the demotic script used to represent the Vietnamese vernacular. A few texts from this period, all by Vietnamese Christians, were written in early forms of the romanized *quoc ngu* alphabet.

Tracking down the original texts was often a challenge, since most modern Vietnamese translations do not include a copy of the original, and many of the original texts have never been published. We consulted the originals in the Han-Nom archive in Hanoi, in Vietnamese journals from the early part of the twentieth century, or in microfilm versions when available. We also used texts from steles, on rubbings or on published versions of the stele texts, which was yet another challenge. Even many of the primary twentieth-century texts were difficult to locate in their original forms. Anthologies contain excerpts of some, while others appeared in short-lived Vietnamese newspapers or weeklies of the 1930s. Yet others we knew about only through references or even rough English translations but had trouble finding the original texts. Some texts that we wanted to include we ultimately could not because we could not find an original-language version and did not wish to work from a translation. The very few exceptions to this rule include some eighteenth-century texts that have survived in contemporary translations, into either French or Portuguese. Throughout our translations, we tried to minimize the use of footnotes. But at the same time, we recognized that certain texts, particularly classical references, needed an additional explication of terms, and in those cases we offer more extensive annotation.

We deliberately limited the number of literary texts that we would include. As a result, we have only a small number of poems and only a few excerpts from longer literary pieces, whether historical novels, modern novels, or short stories. We made this decision in part to limit the range of documents. Particularly with respect to poetry, English-language readers already are well served by a number of recent anthologies that offer a good sampling of Vietnamese poetry. Finally, we again followed the existing volumes in the Introduction to Asian Civilizations series, which focus mainly on nonliterary texts. We nonetheless hope that future scholars will translate more texts from Vietnam's rich literary tradition. For example, several significant historical "novels" from the seventeenth and eighteenth centuries offer compelling story lines and extremely useful insights into Vietnamese society at that time. The very brief excerpts we included from a few of the most important such texts can only hint at their rich content.

In organizing our materials, we decided to arrange our texts both chronologically and thematically. Chronologically, we divided the text into seven time periods, three in the premodern period and two each in the early modern and modern periods. The criteria we used to select the time periods were chiefly political and therefore a bit arbitrary. The documents' elite nature inevitably reflects political considerations, which helped justify this approach. The thematic divisions were more problematic, and we are aware that they sometimes appear arbitrary. Nonetheless, we felt that organizing readings under particular categories would make the book more accessible and more useful to readers interested in particular themes that they could trace through the various time periods. Moreover, our method of organizing anthologized materials is one with which the Vietnamese themselves are familiar. For example, Phan Huy Chu's famous early-nineteenth-century encyclopedia, *Categorized Records of the Institutions of Successive Dynasties* (*Lich trieu hien chuong loai chi*), organized its selected texts under such headings as geography, people, natural resources, and government.

The categories we settled on are both new and old. Some are those that the Vietnamese literati (like Phan Huy Chu) themselves used, particularly our geographical and economic classifications. Other categories, such as "Society and Culture" and "Philosophy and Religion," are modern inventions, which pre-twentieth-century Vietnamese would not have recognized. Nonetheless, we feel that such labels are useful, for our project is translation, which encompasses not merely words but also ideas. To translate is to build bridges between languages and between time periods, and our categories are part of this bridge-building process, enabling modern readers to find materials relevant to topics of interest. We understand that placing various practices, beliefs, and texts into the general category "Religion" narrows highly complex ideas, although our project is not about defining "religion" but providing some practical categories for modern readers. We could have used other categories, and some documents could well have been placed under several of our own headings. The chronological and thematic divisions that we selected largely guided our distribution of sources, as we sought to maintain some balance among time periods and across themes. Some time periods and themes contain a larger or smaller number of texts, reflecting various considerations, including the availability of suitable writings.

Finally, we note that nomenclature and labels can often become a stumbling point in a project spanning such a long history. Indeed, the terms China and Vietnam, whose modern territorial and political implications are readily apparent, are much less useful when discussing pre-twentieth-century geography. Accordingly, we tried not to use them in reference to earlier incarnations of what became China and Vietnam, unless doing so was either unavoidable or helped us avoid particularly awkward circumlocutions. Especially for earlier periods, we use the general geographical referents North and South to designate the peoples and polities of the Chinese and Vietnamese realms, respectively.

We hope that this volume will be the beginning of a much larger project to make the historical, cultural, and ideological heritage of an important civiliza-

tion available to an English-language audience. At the very least, the texts included here represent ideas and concepts and offer useful comparisons placing
Vietnamese civilization within a larger Asian or even global context. If this book
inspires another generation of students and researchers to explore more fully
the history and society of Vietnam we will consider our efforts to have been
worthwhile.

PART I

Premodern Vietnam

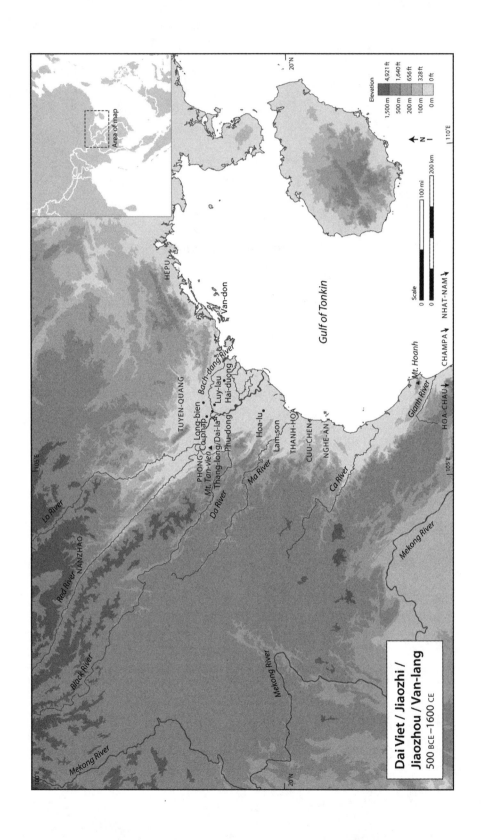

Dai Viet / Jiaozhi /
Jiaozhou / Van-lang
500 BCE –1600 CE

Chapter 1

THE PERIOD OF NORTHERN EMPIRE

The region of what is today north and north-central Vietnam entered the historical record as the Northern empire of the Qin (255–207 B.C.E.) expanded to the south into the land of the Yue (the Shanghai region and south). The rapid collapse of the Qin left a warlord family, the Zhao (V: Trieu), in control of what are now Guangdong and northern Vietnam (then referred to as Nan Yue [Southern Yue]; V: Nam Viet). From the beginning, the Qin forces met local armed resistance in a pattern that was periodically repeated throughout the centuries. What we now call guerrilla warfare originated in peripheral localities to contest the distant northern power.

When the Han dynasty took power in the North, the Zhao resisted its efforts at Southern control until their fall in 111 B.C.E. For the next century and a half, Han authority over the indigenous lords was loose and relatively unobtrusive. Despite greater contact with Northern influences, local society and culture remained the same. But when Wang Mang usurped power (9–25 C.E.) in the North, Northern refugees fled to the South, expanding the Sinic presence there. Led by the aristocratic Trung sisters, Nhac and Nhi, indigenous resisters drove out the Northern forces and kept them at bay for three years (40–42). The Han then sent General Ma Yuan to suppress the resistance. Establishing the Northern administrative system in the central Red River Delta, the general set the stage for almost nine centuries of Northern domination, during which Chinese power periodically waxed and waned.

During this time, there was a constant blending of incoming Northern families with the indigenous population, amid a growing sense of South and North, the local region and a more remote China proper. Besides the many Northern officials, merchants, and others who came south, carried out their business, and then returned north, some settled permanently in the South and adopted its way of life. Both groups brought with them their social, cultural, and intellectual habits and gradually began to remake the indigenous society. The Northerners had specific ideas about how to govern, via the prefecture/district system, and sought to apply them to their new homeland. The local economy was based on wet-rice agriculture, but it was the trade in exotic goods from the mountains and the seas as well as from the lands beyond them that attracted the Northerners, as explained by the Northern official Chen Shou's observations in "Riches of the South."

Others who came to Vietnam's Red River Delta during the first millennium C.E. arrived on the trade and communication routes stretching from the coastal Chinese seas all the way to the Middle East and the Mediterranean. Various merchants, monks, and travelers—Buddhist, Indian, Central Asian, and Arab— passed through the region's ports, bringing with them goods from their home regions, which stimulated local production and increased local wealth. In particular, Buddhists on the grand tour (India, Southeast Asia, China, Central Asia) entered the Red River Delta with their beliefs, texts, and need for temples and monasteries. Through these centuries, Buddhism increasingly permeated local society, especially in the central area of the Red River Delta, and its presence was noted by contemporary observers, including Tan Qian ("Buddhism in the South"), who wrote at the end of the fifth century, and Shen Quanqi ("Buddhism as It Existed in the South"), who wrote in the eighth century. Buddhism also served as a link to other societies, such as those in Champa (central Vietnam) and Srivijaya (southeast Sumatra) to the south, as well as to their Northern compatriots.

A variety of cultures thus took root across the Vietnamese lowlands, coast, and highlands. Locally diverse indigenous beliefs (such as those represented in the spirit cults), the standard Northern culture of the elite, the strong transnational Buddhist presence, and other ethnic patterns in the mountains and along the coast were included in the mix. During times of Northern political weakness, local patterns reasserted themselves and competed for dominance. In both the sixth and the tenth centuries, local chieftains used aspects of Northern rule, indigenous myth, and Buddhist claims of legitimacy to challenge Northern political control. Although the Sui and Tang dynasties were able to crush the first such effort at local autonomy in the sixth century, the Song dynasty was unable (or unwilling) to suppress the second effort in the tenth century.

From the seventh to the tenth century, forces outside the realm of Northern control vied in challenging it. To the south, Champa continuously raided up the coast, competing politically and economically with the Chinese territory. To the west, Nanzhao (in what is now Yunnan), on the southwestern fringe of the Tang empire, posed a threat down the Red River. Tai chieftains in the western and northern mountains sometimes allied with Nanzhao, and their political and economic relations with the lowlanders occasionally caused tensions. Throughout the eighth and ninth centuries, both coastal raiders from Champa and the islands of Southeast Asia and a strong Nanzhao and Tai invasion helped weaken the Tang's hold on this Southern territory.

Overall, the first millennium C.E. was a highly dynamic and transformative period for northern Vietnam. The indigenous society was stimulated externally by political, social, economic, religious, and cultural forces, and it responded by absorbing many of these elements into its own culture. A number of patterns for Vietnam in later periods were set during these centuries: the use of Chinese characters in writing, chopsticks for eating, money in the form of Chinese copper cash, and the Tang dynasty's poetry and laws. Nonetheless, the emerging Vietnamese polity did not become a replica of the Northern state, as the Vietnamese blended these internal and external influences to form their own style.

THE LAND

CHEN SHOU

SOUTH AND NORTH (297)

Shi Xie (V: Si Nhiep or Si Vuong [King Si]) was a local strongman of Northern descent in Jiaozhou/Jiaozhi (northern Vietnam) at the end of the Han dynasty (206 B.C.E.–220 C.E.). The following excerpt from his biography in the *Chronicle of the Wu Dynasty*, one of the books in Chen Shou's *Chronicle of the Three Kingdoms*, describes both the increasing chaos as the Han dynasty weakened and the sense of distance between this Southern border region and the capital far to the North. Such distance enabled the political mischief described here and a local family like the Shi to gain control in the South.

Xie's younger brother Shi Wu took sick and died first. After the death of Zhu Fu, the Han appointed Zhang Jin as Inspector of Jiaozhou. Jin was later assassinated by his own general, Qu Jing. Subsequently, the Governor of Jingzhou, Liu Biao, appointed Lai Gong from Lingling as Jin's replacement. At about the same time, the Grand Administrator of Cangwu, Shi Huang, passed away. Biao thereupon appointed Wu Ju to take his place. Along with Gong, he arrived to fill his post. The Han court, having learned of the death of Zhang Jin, sent an imperial proclamation to Xie, saying, "Jiaozhou is a very distant region, so far beyond the rivers and seas to the south, a place where our beneficence can barely reach and whence the gratitude of the people can hardly flow back. It has come to our attention that the rebellious Liu Biao, viceroy of Zhang province directly to the north, has had the effrontery to have appointed Lai Gong to office and that he has his ambitious eye on our southern lands. Thus we now charge you to become our

General of the Gentlemen of the Household Who Comforts the South, in charge
of all seven commanderies, maintaining as before your authority as Grand Administrator of Jiaozhi."

[Wu zhi, 4, in Chen Shu, *San guo zhi* (hereafter, SGZ); trans.
O'Harrow, "Men of Hu," 262]

SHEN QUANQI

LIFE IN THE SOUTH (EARLY EIGHTH CENTURY)

By the early eighth century, the Southern region had been fully absorbed into the
great cosmopolitan Tang dynasty as the Protectorate of Annan (V: Annam). In the
following poem, the poet Shen Quanqi describes a Northerner's sense of living and
growing old in the South. He evokes a sense of both space and time, the past and its
power, as represented by the spirits of the warlord Zhao Tuo (V: Trieu Da [second century B.C.E.]) and the local ruler, Shi Xie. Commissioner Tuo later became known as the
king of Nan Yue (V: Nam Viet). This poem was included in the *Short Record of Annan*
(1333), compiled by Le Tac, a Vietnamese living in China.

> I have heard it said of Jiaozhi
> That southern habits penetrate one's heart.
> Winter's portion is brief;
> Three seasons are partial to a brightly wheeling sun.
> Here Commissioner Tuo obtained a kingdom;
> Shi Xie has long been roaming the nether world.
> Village dwellings have been handed down through generations;
> Fish and salt have been produced since ancient times.
> In remote ages, the people of Yue [V: Viet] sent pheasants as tribute;
> The Han dynasty general pondered the sparrowhawk.
> The Northern Dipper hangs over Mount Chong;
> The south wind pulls at the Zhang Sea.
> Since I last left home, the months have swiftly come and gone;
> My hairline shows that I have grown old.
> My elder and younger brothers have yielded to their fates;
> My wife and children have departed to reap their destinies.
> An empty path, a ruined wall, tears;
> It is clear that my heart has not echoed Heaven's will.

[Le Tac, *An Nam chi luoc* (hereafter, ANCL), 157; trans. Taylor,
Birth of Vietnam, 185–86]

ZENG GUN

THE SPIRIT CAO LO (NINTH CENTURY)

Following the victory in the 860s over invaders from Nanzhao (present-day Yunnan) to the west, Gao Pian (V: Cao Bien or Cao Vuong [King Cao]), the Northern general stationed in the Protectorate of Annan (V: Annam, earlier known as Jiaozhi), was believed to have encountered the local spiritual power of the land. This was recounted in a document from the South written by a Northern official and later recorded in *Departed Spirits of the Viet Realm* (1329), a collection of cultic tales by Ly Te Xuyen. "The Spirit Cao Lo" describes the spirit world as viewed locally as well as Gao's view of the land's beauty. The so-called Dragon's Belly is an area in the center of the Red River Delta around the present-day Hanoi where Gao Pian established his capital of Dai La (Great Walled City).

Determinably Bold, Unyieldingly Orthodox, Majestically Gracious King

According to the Records of Jiaozhi as cited in Do Thien's *History*, the King was named Cao Lo and was a meritorious subordinate of King An Duong [r. 257?–179 B.C.E.].[1] He was commonly called Commander Lo or the Rock Spirit.

Long ago king Cao Bien pacified the Nanzhao enemy (866) and used troops to patrol Vu Ninh province. He reached the place and dreamed he saw a supernatural figure. His body stood nine feet tall and his dress was proper and solemn. His manner of speech was stern and severe. His hair was pinned up with a knife. He had a red stick and wore a belt. He said to king Cao (Bien), "My name is Cao Lo. Long ago, I assisted King An Duong as a great general. I had great merit in driving away the enemy. Afterwards, I served as a high official and was slandered by a great official and lord of Lac and killed. God on High pitied my loyalty and awarded me a stretch of river and mountain to govern as campaign commander-general. Whenever thieving enemies were quelled or punished, and in matters of sowing and reaping, I always managed these things as if I were the benevolent deity of the region. Now I have again followed Your Excellency in pacifying rebels and plunderers. The world is at great peace, and I have again returned to headquarters. If I did not thank you, it would be unceremonious."

King Cao Bien was taken aback and asked for what matter the lord of Lac despised him and which had absurdly provided a pretext for slander. The figure said, "Matters of the dark and obscure (the underworld) I am not desirous of disclosing." King Cao Bien questioned repeatedly, and the figure responded,

---

1. In these cultic tales, the "King" refers to the historical figure and to the spirit of the cult that he became; Do Thien was a Vietnamese historian in the first half of the twelfth century.

"King An Duong was a golden chicken spirit. The lord of Lac was a white ape spirit. I am a stone dragon spirit of the *giap mao* year.[2] Chicken and ape are mutually compatible. With dragon, they are each mutually destructive. Therefore, it was as it was." He finished speaking and vanished.

King Cao Bien awoke and spoke of this with his assistants. He joyfully intoned to himself.

> How beautiful is the land of Jiaozhou;
> So has it been for a long time, ten thousand years.
> Sages of yore can be encountered;
> Now I am not ungrateful to the mind of spirit.

Then he said,

> The Hundred Viet offered gifts to the empire;
> The two Han dynasties [Former and Later] defined
>   the mountains and rivers.
> Divine spirits all assisted obediently;
> The prospects of the Li Tang dynasty gave much prosperity.

Following this, Tang Con praised King Gao Pian, saying,

> The mountains and streams of the Viet land are old;
> Persons of the Tang house are new.
> The man called Cao Lo heard it had life-giving force,
> In action and inaction informing the dragon spirit.

Then he said,

> The Southern country's mountains and rivers are beautiful;
> The dragon spirit meets with a divine land.
> Jiao province has ceased knitting its brows in pain;
> From now on it will be an age of peace.
>
> [Ly Te Xuyen, *Viet dien u linh tap* (hereafter, *VDULT*); trans.
> Ostrowski and Zottoli, *Departed Spirits*, 57–59]

---

2. *Giap mao* refers to a particular year in the Chinese stem-and-branch, sixty-year calendrical cycle.

ECONOMICS AND TRADE

CHEN SHOU

RICHES OF THE SOUTH (297)

The prospect of exotic goods from the Southern seas and mountains and from their international trade routes, drew the Northerners to the South. The trade in goods from Southeast Asia, India, and even the Middle East and the Mediterranean joined agriculture as a major segment of the local economy, and by the second century, Northern officials sought to enrich themselves from the region's international trade. The goods available there were well represented in the items sent by the Shi family, who controlled Jiaozhi, to the Sun court of Wu (220–280) in the lower Yangzi valley to the north following the fall of the Han dynasty in the third century. This is depicted here in another excerpt from the biography of Shi Xie found in Chen Shou's *Chronicle of the Wu Dynasty.*

Each time Shi Xie sent officials to the Wu royal court of Sun Quan, he always presented as well different kinds of spices and the finest grass cloth and always by the thousand-fold, glossy pearls and great conches, Liuli pottery, emerald kingfisher feathers, shell of tortoise and horn of rhinoceros, elephant tusks and various valuables and strange fruits: bananas, coconuts, longans, and such like. And in no year did these things not come. Now and again, Xie's brother Yi would send horses in tribute, hundreds of head at a time. Quan would always send letters increasing royal favors to assuage them in reciprocation.

> [Wu zhi, 4, in Chen Shou, SGZ; trans. O'Harrow, "Men of Hu," 263]

XUE ZONG

ECONOMICS IN THE SOUTH (231)

Later in the third century, Xue Zong, an official from the North living in Jiaozhi, commented on Northern interests in the South, as noted in the *Chronicle of the Three Kingdoms* (297), by Chen Shou. The selection here also makes clear that the Northern regimes' wealth gained from the South was in the form of local exotica rather than tax revenues.

The local people easily become rebellious and are difficult to pacify; district officials act dignified but are careful not to provoke them. What can be obtained from field and household taxes is meager. On the other hand, this place is famous for precious rarities from afar: pearls, incense, drugs, elephant tusks, rhinoceros horn, tortoise shell, coral, lapis lazuli, parrots, kingfishers, peacocks, rare and abundant treasures enough to satisfy all desires. So it is not necessary to depend on what is received from regular taxes in order to profit the Central Kingdom.

[Chen Shou, SGZ, 53, 9b; trans. Taylor, *Birth of Vietnam*, 78]

LIU XU

MARITIME TRADE IN THE SOUTH (945)

With the Tang dynasty controlling the Protectorate of Annan from the seventh century onward, there was a continued need to keep order among the commercial interests, foreign and domestic, as briefly noted here in the *Old History of the Tang Dynasty*, by Liu Xu (887–946).

Chinese officials acted to control the barbarians of all the kingdoms in the southern seas, including those south and southwest of Jiao Province, and those who dwell on the islands of the great sea . . . arriving in boats after traveling unknown distances . . . bringing goods by the Jiaozhi route as they have done from the time of Emperor Wu of the Han [140–87 B.C.E.].

[Liu Xu, *Jiu Tang shu*, 41, 43a; trans. Taylor, *Birth of Vietnam*, 167]

PHILOSOPHY AND RELIGION

MOU BO

BELIEFS IN THE SOUTH (CA. 200)

In the late second century C.E., both Sinic and local thought were taking hold in the Southern region. Such thought included the ideas contained in the Five Classics of Confucianism and the classical thought that dominated the Han dynasty. Daoist influence was apparent in ideas about abstinence and the search for immortality. The following brief statement describing the intellectual scene before the author's conversion to Buddhism comes from the preface to a work by the early Buddhist monk Mou Bo.

At that time, after the death of [the Han] Emperor Ling [189], the empire was in disorder; only Jiao Province was relatively calm, and unusual men from the North came to live there. Many occupied themselves with the worship of gods and spirits, abstinence from cereals, and immortality. Many people of that time devoted themselves to these studies. Mou Bo unceasingly proposed objections based on the Five Classics; none of the Daoists and spiritualists dared argue with him.

[Mou Bo, *Li huo lun*, 1; trans. Taylor, *Birth of Vietnam*, 81]

CHEN SHOU

SCHOLARSHIP IN THE SOUTH (297)

The following excerpt is from the biography in the *Chronicle of the Wu Dynasty* of Shi Xie, a distinguished member of the elite Northern family who had settled in the South, as compiled by Chen Shou in the late third century. This passage describes his intellectual pursuits and shows the extent of local elite interest in the classical studies of the Han dynasty, even in the far distant South.

When Xie was young, he journeyed to the capital to study. He studied under Liu Ziqi of Yingchuan [commandery in Henan], and focused on *Zuo's Spring and Autumn Annals*.[3] He was recommended as filial and incorrupt and appointed a secretarial court gentleman. For reasons related to official business, he was dismissed from office. His father, Ci, passed away. After that, [Xie] became a cultivated talent. He was appointed magistrate of Wuyang, and then promoted to governor of Jiaozhi.

Xie was generous in nature and humble to his subordinates. Many scholars from the Central Kingdom went to rely on him [for protection]. He was extremely fond of the *Spring and Autumn Annals* and annotated them. Yuan Hui, from the Kingdom of Chen (Hui at that time was residing in Jiao Region) wrote to Director of the Imperial Secretariat Xun Yu and said, "The commandery governor of Jiaozhi has vast knowledge and excels at executing administrative matters. [Although] in the midst of unrest, he has held the commandery together for more than 20 years with no incidents on this frontier. The people have not lost their occupations [owing to warfare], and travelers have all benefited from this good fortune. Although Mr. Dou controlled Hexi, how could he have surpassed [Shi Xie]?

When taking a break from official matters, he reads texts, and is particularly well-versed in the *Spring and Autumn Annals* and *Mr. Zuo's Commentary*. I have queried him many times about questions I have [with these texts], and he has always offered model explanations, dense with meaning. He is also versed in the *Classic of Documents*, and knows all the ancient and current explanations.[4] Having heard of the debate at the capital concerning the study of new and old texts, he now wishes to list the most prominent points in *Mr. Zuo's [Commentary]* and the *Classic of Documents*, and to present this [to the emperor]." This reveals how he was praised.

[Chen Shu, SGZ, 2, 30b–31a; trans. Liam Kelley]

---

3. *Zuo's Spring and Autumn Annals* (*Zuoshi chunqiu*) is Zuo's commentary on the *Spring and Autumn Annals* (*Chunqiu zuozhuan*), one of the Five Classics. This is the only mention of Liu Ziqi in the standard histories.

4. The *Classic of Documents* is one of the Five Classics.

TAN QIAN

BUDDHISM IN THE SOUTH (CA. 480)

Along with Northern patterns of belief entering the South, international trade routes introduced a transnational Buddhism into the region. In the fifth century, Buddhism in the South already was recognized as being ahead of that found in the North. Tan Qian (542–607), a Buddhist master from Central Asia, reported this to the Chi court around 480 C.E. in this brief passage from Thong Bien's 1096 discussion of Buddhist history in Vietnam and recorded in *Eminent Monks of the Thien Community* (1337).

The area of Jiaozhou has long been in communication with Tianzhu [India]. Early on, when the Buddha-Dharma reached Jiangdong and still had not been established [there], in Luy Lau[5] more than twenty precious temples had [already] been built, more than five hundred monks had [already] been ordained, and fifteen volumes of scriptures had [already] been translated [from Sanskrit into Chinese].

[*Thien uyen tap anh* (hereafter, *TUTA*), 20b; trans. adapted from Nguyen Tu Cuong, *Zen in Medieval Vietnam*, 129]

SHEN QUANQI

BUDDHISM AS IT EXISTED IN THE SOUTH (EARLY EIGHTH CENTURY)

This poem, composed by a Northern scholar during the Tang period, reflects the establishment of Buddhist thought in the South. Le Quy Don, the great eighteenth-century Vietnamese scholar, later brought together such Northern Buddhist poems in his *Small Chronicle of Things Seen and Heard*. Shen Quanqi, who earlier described living in the South, here presents his poem to the Buddhist monk Vo Ngai Thuong Nhan.

Formerly the Buddha was born in Tianzhu [India],
Now he manifests himself here to convert the people of Rinan.[6]
Free from all defilements,
He built a temple at the foot of the mountain.
By the stream the fragrant branches are the standards,
The boulders on the mountaintop become his home.
Blue doves practice meditation,

---

5. Jiangdong was the capital of the state of Qi. Luy Lau, in the central Red River Delta, was the main port area of Jiaozhi at that time.
6. Rinan (V: Nhat-nam) comprised the north-central coast of Vietnam.

White monkeys listen to the sutras.
Creepers cover the cloud-high cliffs,
Flowers rise above the pond at the foot of the mountain.
The water in the streams is good for performing ritual,
The trees let him hang his clothes on them.
This disciple regrets that he is ignorant,
Not able to discuss the Buddha's doctrine.
Who one night crossed over the Tiger-stream,
Amidst mountain fog under a lonely tree.

[Le Quy Don, *Kien van tieu luc*, 1:193–94; trans.
Nguyen Tu Cuong, *Zen in Medieval Vietnam*, 335]

ZENG GUN

THE MOUNTAIN SPIRIT (LATE NINTH CENTURY)

Spirit cults continued to form a major part of Vietnam's early religious belief, with tales of the local spirits surfacing in records of the Tang period (618–907). The following is the tale of the rivalry between mountain and stream, the land and the water, first recorded by a Tang dynasty official and included in *Departed Spirits of the Viet Realm* (1329), compiled by Ly Te Xuyen. The event took place in mythic times among the local Lac people. Note the land and water products described.

Tan Vien Protecting Sacredness, Saving the Country, Manifesting Divinity, and Responding King

According to Duke Tang's *Records of Jiaozhi*, the Mountain Spirit enjoyed friendship with the Water Spirit. The Mountain Spirit lived hidden in the Gia Ninh cave in Phong Province where the Red River enters the lowlands.

King Hung had a daughter named My Nuong, who was of excellent appearance, her beauty great enough to fell cities. The king of Thuc sent an emissary to request a marriage.[7] King Hung was about to allow this when a great minister and lord of Lac disagreed, saying, "They only are spying on our country!" King Hung feared this would create a rift in relations.

The lord of Lac said, "Your Great Majesty's land is expansive and the people numerous. I beseech you to grant her to him who has strange talents and extraordinary abilities, making him your son-in-law. First, arrange your troops to wait in ambush. It is needless to imagine anything better." And so King Hung broke off negotiations with Thuc. Everywhere in the country, those with extraordinary abilities were sought after. Both the Mountain Spirit and the Water Spirit

---

7. Thuc (C: Shu) is the present-day region of Sichuan in southwestern China.

responded to the search, and King Hung ordered that they be investigated. The Mountain Spirit could penetrate jade and stone, and the Water Spirit could enter water and fire. They manifested their divine powers equally well. King Hung was greatly pleased and told the lord of Lac, "Both the two gentlemen are worthy matches. [But] I have only one daughter. Which of the two virtuous gentlemen shall be chosen?" The lord of Lac said, "Your Majesty should agree with them that whoever comes to marry her first shall be granted her hand." King Hung consented to do this. Each was bidden to return and prepare the ceremonial offerings.

The Mountain Spirit returned home overnight to bring local products, gold and silver, beautiful women, rhinoceroses, and elephants. There also were rare birds and beasts, all numbering in the hundreds. By sunrise the next day, he had already made his presentations to King Hung. The king was greatly pleased and thereby granted My Nuong in marriage. The Mountain Spirit met her in person and brought her back to live with him on Mount Loi.

That evening, the Water Spirit also prepared aquatic products, pearls, tortoise shells, valuables, and coral. There were great and fine fish as well, also numbering in the hundreds. The Water Spirit reached the royal city to present his offerings. Finding that My Nuong had already returned with the Mountain Spirit, the Water Spirit became very angry, leading a mob to pursue them and wanting to reduce Mount Loi to pieces.

The Mountain Spirit moved his residence to the peak of Mount Tan Vien.[8] And so later generations became enemies with the Water Spirit. Each year, the Water Spirit brought autumn rains (the monsoons) to strike Tan Vien. Together, the people on the mountain built a palisade to protect themselves, which the Water Spirit could not enter. Divine traces of the Mountain Spirit are so numerous that it is not possible to count all of them.

[Ly Te Xuyen, *VDULT*; trans. adapted from Ostrowski
and Zottoli, *Departed Spirits*, 75–77]

GOVERNANCE

FAN YE

MA YUAN'S ADMINISTRATION (445)

After the uprising of the indigenous aristocracy led by the Trung sisters (40–42), the new Northern regime needed to bring administrative order to Jiaozhi. Ma Yuan, the general sent south to crush the local resistance, immediately organized the new administration in the Northern fashion, as briefly described in his biography, which

---

8. Mount Tan Vien is a sacred site for the Vietnamese west of the capital Thang Long (Hanoi).

was recorded in the *History of the Later Han Dynasty*, by Fan Ye (398–445). The Yue (V: Viet) was a general term applied by the Han to the indigenous peoples on the far edge of civilization in the South. More specifically, the people of Jiaozhi were known as the Luo Yue (V: Lac Viet). The name Ma meant "horse," and the bronze figure was to remind the local people of his power, displacing the indigenous symbol of the bronze drum.

Ma Yuan sent up a memorial saying, "The prefecture of Xiyu holds 32,000 families. The distance from its borders to its administrative center is over 1,000 *li*. I beg permission to divide it into two prefectures by the names of Fengchi and Wanghai." Permission was granted. Wherever Ma Yuan went, he set up commanderies and prefectures, established fortified barracks, and dug irrigation channels in order to benefit the people. In a memorial to the throne, he itemized more than ten items of Yue (V: Viet) law that contradicted Han law, and he expounded the ancient traditions of the Yue people in order to discipline them. From that time on, the Luo Yue followed the ancient customs of General Ma Yuan. . . . In Jiaozhi, he took away the bronze drums of the Luo Yue and had them smelted into the form of a horse.

> [Fan Ye, *Hou Han shu*, 24/14, 14a; trans. Holmgren,
> *Chinese Colonisation of Northern Vietnam*, 16]

CHEN SHOU

GOVERNING THE SOUTH (297)

When the Han dynasty began to fall apart around 200 C.E., the powerful local Shi family of Northern descent, led by Xie (later called King Si by the Vietnamese), maintained a peaceful and prosperous regime in the South that included both foreigners from the international trading routes and those fleeing the chaos of the North. In another segment of his biography in the *Chronicle of the Wu Dynasty*, Xie, along with his brothers and his son, is described as controlling and maintaining the territory of Jiaozhi.

Shi Xie had the courtesy name of Weiyen. He was from the sub-prefecture of Guangxin in the commandery of Cangwu. His forebears were originally from the district of Wenyang in the state of Lu. At the time of the rebellion of Wang Mang [r. 9–25], his family had taken flight to Jiaozhou. Xie was one of the sixth generation thereafter. His father's name was Ci and during the reign of Emperor Huan of the Han [r. 147–167] he was Grand Administrator of Rinan [V: Nhat-nam].

Once the period of mourning for his father, Ci, had ended, Xie was titled Candidate of Accomplished Talent and named Prefect of Wu, whence he was transferred to become Grand Administrator of Jiaozhi. His younger brother, Yi, was at first Investigator in the commandery.

The Inspector of the province of Jiaozhou, one Zhu Fu, was killed by the Yi bandits and the provinces and commanderies rose up in rebellion. Xie thereupon recommended that [his brother] Yi take over as Grand Administrator of Hepu. His second brother, Hui, formerly the Prefect of Xuwen, was made Grand Administrator of Jiuzhen [V: Cuu-chan].[9]

And Hui's younger brother, Wu, was appointed Grand Administrator of Nanhai. Xie was a man of generous capacity and broad forbearance and he treated his subordinates with humility and open-mindedness. As for the Northern literati who fled to him from the troubles, they numbered in the hundreds.

In the midst of the great rebellions, Xie was able to preserve and protect the whole of the commandery; for more than twenty years there were no incidents within his borders. The people were not without employment; those who sojourn in their travels all receive his blessings.

Xie's brothers were all commandery notables and they occupied a dominant position throughout the province; ten thousand *li* away from the court, their majestic influence was incomparable. Whenever Xie entered and whenever he went out, the reverberation of bells and stone chimes was heard; pomp and decorum were fully observed and the flutes and pipes were sounded. Chariots and outriders filled the road while men of Hu by the dozen, with incense smoldering, marched close beside the wheels of his carriage.[10] Then there came the curtained coaches of his wives and concubines and then his sons and younger brothers, followed by the cavalry. All the while, his splendor awed the hundred Man [Southern barbarians] and kept them at bay; even Commander Zhao Tuo [V: Trieu Da] could not compare with him.[11]

Later, Xie sent out the official Zhang Min with the tribute to the capital. At that time there were revolts among the people everywhere and the road was cut off. Nevertheless, Xie did not cease sending tribute and so, exceptionally, the court again issued an imperial declaration of recognizance; he was bestowed the title of General who Brings Tranquillity to the Far Reaches and raised to the dignity of Marquis of the Commune of Long-do.

[Wu zhi, 4, in Chen Shou, SGZ; trans. O'Harrow,
"Men of Hu," 259–61]

---

9. Jiuzhen (V: Cuu-chan) covered present-day Thanh Hoa. Hepu was on the coast of present-day Guangxi Province, and Nanhai covered parts of present-day Guangdong Province.

10. Hu was the Sinic term applied to people of Indian and Central Asian origin.

11. In the second century B.C.E., Commander Zhao Tuo (V: Trieu Da) was the king of Nan Yue, now the two Chinese provinces of Guangdong and Guangxi and northern Vietnam.

ZHAO CHENG

In the late eighth century, an indigenous chief named Phung Hung led an uprising in the upper Red River Delta. He succeeded in taking control of the upriver area and declared himself king. His assumption of power shows the political pattern of local chiefs that was based on personal strength and charisma. This tale was originally recorded by a ninth-century Tang official and was collected by Ly Te Xuyen in *Departed Spirits of the Viet Realm* (1329).

The Great Father-and-Mother King

According to the *Records of Jiao Province* of Duke Zhao, the King was of the Phung line and was named Hung. For generations, his ancestors had passed down the tribal chieftainship of the Bien Kho barbarians of Duong Lam province. They were called "quan lang." A well-propertied family, they were powerful in their sphere. Hung was of extreme strength and courage, able to fight tigers and push buffalo. His younger brother, called Hai, was also of great strength, able to carry thirteen thousand pounds of stones or a small ten-thousand peck boat for over ten miles. The Di and the Lao all feared their names.

In the Tang Da Li era [766–780], because our army of Annan was in turmoil, the brothers went together to patrol the neighboring regions. These all fell to them, and wherever they went, there were none who did not scatter. Hung was satisfied and changed his name to Cu Lao; Hai changed his name to Cu Luc. Hung took the title of Metropolitan Lord; Hai took the title of Metropolitan Guardian. Using the strategy of Do Anh Luan of Duong Lam, they used troops to patrol the provinces of Duong Lam and Truong Phong. The people all followed them. Their power and reputation resounded greatly.

They released word of their desire to plot against the regional Tang headquarters. At that time, Protector General Gao Chengping brought troops to attack them, but he could not beat them. Melancholic and exasperated, he fell ill with a stomach ulcer and died. Hung entered the regional headquarters, overseeing affairs seven years before dying. The crowds wanted to install Hai. But the assistant chieftain, Bo Pha Can, who was strong enough to clear away mountains and lift up cauldrons, and whose courage and power were excellent, refused to accede and proceeded to install Hung's son, An, leading a mob against Hai. Hai fled from Bo Pha Can, moving to Chu Nham cave. It is not known what happened to him afterwards. Phung An honored Hung as the Bo Cai Great King, for it is the custom in the realm to call the father "bo" and call the mother "cai." For this reason, his name was given like this.

Phung An continued to rule for two years before Emperor Tang Dezong [780–805] appointed Zhao Cheng to serve as Annan Protector General. Cheng entered the scene, sending an envoy with gifts to instruct Phung An. Phung An duly set out the ceremonial guard and a crowd to meet them in surrender. The people of the Phung line were thus dispersed.

[Ly Te Xuyen, *VDULT*; trans. Ostrowski and Zottoli,
Departed Spirits, 11–12]

GAO PIAN

A NORTHERNER GOVERNING THE SOUTH (870)

After the Nanzhao wars of the 860s, Gao Pian, the victorious Northern general and high official (known to the Vietnamese as King Cao), commented, in a text recorded in the early fourteenth century, on the problems he faced in governing the territory. This text, *Short Record of Annan* (1333), was compiled by Le Tac, a Vietnamese scholar who had fled to China with the defeated Mongols.

Heaven and earth are boundless;
Man's strength is but a trifle.
Banish distress by bringing food;
Prosperity comes riding in boats.
Breaking free of this strange affair,
Not just defeat but prolonged destruction,
I devised plans against civil disorder,
For excavating mountains and splitting rocks,
For meritoriously caring for those in need,
Thus rousing the power of thunderbolts,
Causing the sea to form a channel,
Where boats can pass in safety,
With the deep sea stretching out peacefully,
A highway of supply for our city.
The way of Heaven is the foundation of prosperity;
The majesty of the spirits supports and maintains.

[Le Tac, ANCL, 104; trans. Taylor, *Birth of Vietnam*, 252]

SOCIETY AND CULTURE

FAN YE

HAN OFFICIALS IN THE SOUTH (445)

As the influx of Northerners increased in the first century C.E., they tried to persuade the peoples of the South to adopt their customs. Of particular note were the attempts of the Han officials Ren Yan, in Jiaozhi in the central Red River Delta, and Xi Guang, in Jiuzhen in what is now north-central Vietnam (Thanh Hoa), during the first century C.E., as recorded in the *History of the Later Han Dynasty*, by Fan Ye (398–445). The Northerners considered the indigenous peoples of the South to be "outside civilization" and hence barbarians.

Xi Guang gradually instructed the barbarians in feelings of respect and morality. His reputation in government was like that of Ren Yan. . . . The civilization of Lingnan began with these two men.[12]

Ren Yan ordered the casting of agricultural implements and taught the people land reclamation. Year by year the amount of arable land increased and the common people were provided for. . . . Yan sent out letters to all dependent prefectures commanding them to have married all men between 20 and 50 years of age and all women between 15 and 40 years. The poor being without betrothal gifts, he ordered all officials to put aside a portion of their salaries to help them. Over 2,000 people were married.

Xi Guang and Ren Yan taught the people agriculture, introduced hats and sandals, and correct betrothal and marriage procedures; they instructed the people in feelings of respect and morality.

[Fan Ye, *Hou Han shu*, 76/66, 6a–7a, 9a–9b; trans. Holmgren, *Chinese Colonisation of Northern Vietnam*, 5–6]

ZHOU CHENG

MEMORIAL ON THE SOUTH (SECOND CENTURY)

In the second century C.E., after the first-century rebellion led by the Trung sisters had been crushed, tensions lingered between the incoming Northern officials and local families, many of whom had originally come from the North. Included in the *Short Record of Annan* (1333), compiled by the Vietnamese Le Tac in China, was the following brief statement written by the official Zhou Cheng to the Northern court. Though short, it represents the Chinese style of critical remonstrance and memorial

---

12. Lingnan refers to the area "South of the Passes," comprising the present-day Chinese provinces of Guangdong and Guangxi and northern Vietnam.

presented by officials to their monarchs. In his memorial, Zhou presented a North-erner's view of Southern society.

Jiaozhi is a distant land; greed and corruption are customary practices; power-ful families connive in deceit; local officials are reckless and oppressive; the people are plundered and exploited. I have received great kindness and am pleased to be an imperial servant; my desire is that the throne allow me to clean up this one place.

[Le Tac, ANCL, 87–88; trans. Taylor, *Birth of Vietnam*, 66–67]

XUE ZONG

CUSTOMS OF THE SOUTH (231)

In the first half of the third century, the local official Xue Zong, a Northerner living in the South, was somewhat more measured in his own comments on local society as he pointed out its cultural variation. He believed that the distant Han presence had had little impact on local society. These random comments were recorded in the *Chronicle of the Three Kingdoms* (297), by Chen Shou.

Customs are not uniform and languages are mutually unintelligible, so that several interpreters are needed to communicate.

The people are like birds and beasts; they wear their hair tied up and go barefoot, while for clothing they simply cut a hole in a piece of cloth for their head or they fasten their garments on the left side in barbarian style.

If district-level officials are appointed, it is the same as if they were not.

Ren Yan taught the people to plow, established schools for instruction in the classics, and made everyone follow proper marriage ceremonies with designated matchmakers, public notification of officials, and parental invitations to formal betrothals.

Yet there is only a rude knowledge of letters here.

Those who came and went at the government posts could observe proper ways of doing things, and, according to the records, civilizing activities have been going on for over four hundred years, but, according to what I myself have seen during many years of travel since my arrival here, the actual situation is something else.

Concerning marriage in Zhuyai [Hainan Island], where all administration has been abandoned, in the eighth month family leaders assemble the people and men and women on their own volition take one another and become husband and wife with the parents having nothing to do with it. In the two districts of Me Linh [part of Phong to the west of present-day Hanoi] in Jiaozhi and Do Long in Jiuzhen, when an elder brother dies, a younger brother marries his widow; this has been going on for generations, thereby becoming an established custom, so district officials give in and allow it, not being able to stop it. In Rinan Prefecture, men and women go naked without shame. In short, it can be said that these people are on the same level as bugs.

[Chen Shou, SGZ, 53, 9a–9b; trans. Taylor, *Birth of Vietnam*, 75–76]

DAO HUANG

RELATIONS WITH CHAMPA (LATE THIRD CENTURY)

As the Northern dynasties worked to control and civilize peoples of the South—the area of present-day northern Vietnam—their officials in the South also had to contend with rival peoples living outside their territory. Dao Huang, an official appointed by the Wu dynasty, sent a report late in the third century C.E. to the now victorious Jin dynasty, which had replaced the Wu. In it, he speaks of the situation with the realm of Linyi, farther south, which controlled the territory along the coast of present-day central Vietnam, and discusses his thoughts on the matter. As the servant of the previous dynasty, Dao humbly acknowledges that his analysis has no bearing on the new dynasty, but in essence, he is cautioning the new court not to let down its guard against these barbarians on the frontier. In later centuries, Linyi came to be known as Champa. For its entire history, the people of the Red River Delta and the lowlands extending southward have had to contend with peoples of other cultures and ethnicities, in both the highlands and the lowlands. The *Chronicle of Dai Viet* (1272), by Le Van Huu, includes Dao's report.

Jiaozhou lies only several thousand leagues from Linyi [Champa]. The barbarian commander Fan Xung, a constant rebel, proclaimed himself king and proceeded to raid our people numerous times. That land, a neighbor of Funan [even farther south], consists of many tribes and rival groups and counts on the difficult access to itself so as to avoid submission to us. When Linyi was still in contact with the Wu, it frequently pillaged our peaceful people, destroyed our local administrative centers, and killed our officials.

While serving the former dynasty [Wu], I took over the defense of the South. It has been more than ten years now. I have eliminated their forces, yet fugitives still remain, hiding deeply in the wilderness. In the beginning, I had 8,000 troops under my command. But now, because the South has humidity and an unhealthy climate, the incessant campaigning and deaths from disease have proceeded to reduce my forces to 2,400. At this time, since the four seas [the world at large] are unified and there is no more insubordination to fear, is it time to hang up our armor and break our swords? Yet here uprisings can break out suddenly. My advice, though from one who served a lost realm [the Wu], doubtless does not merit being followed.

[Ngo Si Lien, *Dai Viet su ky toan thu*, *Outer Records*, 8a–8b; trans. John K. Whitmore]

Chapter 2

THE LY, TRAN, AND HO EPOCHS

As the Tang dynasty of the North crumbled and lost its control over various parts of the South, including northern Vietnam, a pattern of regionalism emerged. Local chiefs of what was now the land of Viet vied with one another for dominance, and from the mid-tenth to the mid-eleventh century, the monarchy of Dai Viet gradually took shape. During this time, the Vietnamese fought among themselves and also fended off regional rivals within the South of the old empire (the southeast coast of China). In the 960s, the chieftain Dinh Bo Linh conquered the "Twelve Warlords" and established his capital and court at Hoa Lu in the hills south of the Red River Delta. His successor, Le Hoan, was able to fight off both the Song dynasty's attempt to reconquer Annan and the effort by his southern rival, Champa, to achieve regional dominance.

In the early eleventh century, Ly Cong Uan ascended the throne. He was a military member of the royal court who had been mentored by the monk Van Hanh and supported by the Buddhist community. Ly Cong Uan moved the capital back to his home region in the central Red River Delta, situating it on the site of King Cao's (Gao Pian's) provincial seat of Dai La. He named his capital Thang Long (Ascending Dragon) and began what became the Ly dynasty (1009–1225). Using the Chinese concept of familial succession, Ly Cong Uan (also known as Thai To [r. 1009–1028]) and his two successors, son and grandson, created the monarchy of Dai Viet, invoking first the spirit cults of the localities, then the growing number of Buddhist temples, and finally the royal cult itself (involving the Buddhist gods Indra and Brahma). All were tied together by the annual oath of allegiance, and they saw themselves ruling the South, as opposed to the distant North.

Throughout the eleventh century, the lowland Vietnamese society grew and prospered in villages that were structured around bilateral kinship and an expanding wet-rice agriculture, mainly in the central Red River Delta region among numerous Buddhist temples and spirit shrines. At this time, Vietnamese society consisted of an aristocracy, a religious class (the Buddhist community), and peasants, along with a few scholars of Chinese texts. Successful wars with Champa down the coast to the south helped secure Dai Viet, in the middle of the Red River Delta, as did its defeat of a separate Tai realm in the northern mountains. Throughout this period, Dai Viet interacted with and borrowed from its Southeast Asian neighbors.

By the end of Dai Viet's first three reigns in the 1070s, the royal court and the realm had built a structure strong enough to survive without a mature and controlling monarch. Then after the establishment of a royal Buddhism by the fourth ruler, Ly Nhan Tong (r. 1072–1127), the court community of royal wives and mothers joined powerful ministers to rule Dai Viet during the twelfth century. Like their contemporaries at Angkor in Cambodia and Pagan in Myanmar (Burma), the Vietnamese kings governed the area immediately around the capital and cultivated relationships with local leaders farther away. The annual oath ceremony linked to the spirit cults bound the realm together, aided by the Buddhist community. The increasing population and prosperity of the midriver area of the Red River ensured a stable realm even as important changes were taking place. Social and economic growth led to greater trade with both the mountain regions (and their exotic goods) and the coast, where the great surge of international commerce with the Song dynasty had a major impact. Although the lower delta previously had been lightly populated, with the increase in trade the Ly rulers began to set up royal bases in the area. In addition, as Dai Viet's power grew, so did that of its southern rivals, Champa and Angkor. From the 1120s to the 1210s, warfare broke out among all three realms when each sought political and economic dominance, albeit not the cultural transformation of the other two.

With the twelfth century came a very different situation and new political configurations. The combination of the surge of maritime trade and the three-way competition brought about power shifts along the eastern coast of the Southeast Asian mainland. New ports were formed (Van Don in Dai Viet and Thi Nai in Champa) and, with them, newly powerful regions, notably the lower delta of Dai Viet and the central territory of Vijaya in Champa. The new Tran (C: Chen) dynasty (1225–1400) brought men to power in Thang Long who were descendants of settlers from Fujian Province on the southeast coast of China and who had settled in the lower Red River Delta. The Tran family was a tightly organized clan and, though of northern origin, considered the land of Dai Viet to be their home. In addition, they adopted the past of Dai Viet as their own, and the clan's literati forged this past into a tale of opposition to the North, notably citing the exploits of Zhao Tuo (V: Trieu Da) during the second century B.C.E.

The Tran dynasty kept the old inland capital of Thang Long while making its own base in the eastern delta the secondary capital, thereby integrating the upper and lower regions of the Red River Delta. The Tran also maintained the Ly's ritual aspects in the capital (such as the oath of allegiance and the royal worship of Indra, king of the gods) while at the same time introducing more Sinic elements into their central administration. This included moving coastal scholars of the Northern classical texts into the government and raising their status in Dai Viet society. These scholars began to advocate change by challenging Buddhist dominance as well as cultural interactions with foreigners on an equal plane while pressing for male dominance in society and for local schools to teach their beliefs. One aspect of this royal activism was, for the first time, coordination of the local diking systems and agricultural development in the lower delta.

The Tran royal house and its princes established a series of estates at strategic points across the Red River Delta, which served as local economic, religious, and defensive centers and also became bases for the resistance led by the princes against the major Mongol invasions of the 1280s. The skills of men like Tran Quoc Tuan, the Hung Dao prince, helped defeat the invaders. Warfare, however, led to a shift in power away from the growing civil administration of the scholar-officials to the central and local rule of the princes and their families.

While classical scholarship (Confucianism) was growing in Dai Viet under the Tran, the monarchs and their royal families also became strongly interested in Chan (V: Thien; J: Zen), a school of meditation of contemporary Northern Buddhism, which they blended with certain aspects of classical scholarship (the sage kings). The royal families also had contact with the Buddhism of Champa, an outgrowth of the alliance of Dai Viet and Champa against the Mongol threat. From the late thirteenth through the first third of the fourteenth century, the Tran monarchy sought to integrate the realm by bringing together various elements of Vietnamese Buddhist thought into an orthodox whole. The result was the Bamboo Grove (Truc Lam) school of Thien, created for the purpose of protecting the realm, the monarchy, and the Buddhist community and emphasizing the oneness of time and space.

By the mid-fourteenth century, socioeconomic problems and challenges from the Tai polities in the western mountains threatened Dai Viet. The ruler Tran Minh Tong (r. 1314–1357) switched from an emphasis on Buddhism to the classical Confucian texts and their focus on the antiquity of two millennia earlier.

Looking for answers to their current problems, the scholars rejected the Buddhist focus on timelessness. The king signaled this shift by bringing Chu Van An, a scholar of Northern descent, into the royal court at the capital. Over the next three generations, Chu Van An's school of thought formed. This school first emphasized the Northern Sinic antiquity before developing its own Southern antiquity, with its land of Van Lang and the eighteen Hung kings. During this process, Southern customs took precedence over Northern borrowings, and the people of Dai Viet began to reject aspects of the cultures of their Southeast Asian neighbors. At the same time, internal troubles and external pressures built up. Two decades of raids by Champa (1370–1390) brought the civilization of Dai Viet into a deep crisis. The Tran court repeatedly had to abandon Thang Long. The crisis led to the transformation of the Vietnamese past, now linked to the beginnings of Sinic myth and reinvented to rival that of the North.

During these years of crisis, Le Quy Ly, a new rival also of Northern descent, appeared from the south (from Thanh Hoa Province, south of the Red River Delta). Le Quy Ly, his family, and his southern associates took control of the royal court and formed the scholars' beliefs into a new royal ideology. First, as a powerful minister, Le Quy Ly built his own base in the south, undercutting the land and manpower resources of the Red River Delta's aristocracy. Then in 1400, he seized the throne for his family, changing the family name to Ho and the country's name to Dai Ngu, both referring to the Northern classical antiquity. But the Ho's activities greatly upset the newly powerful Ming dynasty to the north. In 1407, the Ming forces, with help from inside Dai Ngu, crushed the Ho and, for the next two decades, brought Dai Viet back into the Northern empire as the province of Jiaozhi (1407–1427).

The five hundred years of the Ly and Tran dynasties began the pattern of a Vietnam composed of different localities and regions brought together by a developing and transforming monarchy. Vietnamese society and culture continued to accumulate and incorporate internal and external influences. The ideologies of the spirit cults, Buddhism, and classical Confucianism continued to interact within the royal court and village society.

THE LAND

LY THAI TO

EDICT ON MOVING THE CAPITAL (1010)

With the collapse of the great Tang empire of the North in the early tenth century, the Southern portion of the empire (present-day northern Vietnam) began to splinter among local chieftains. In 938, a force led by Ngo Quyen, from the area near the middle of the Red River Delta, defeated another regional force, that of the Southern Han court in Guangzhou, which controlled the southeast coast of China. Through the mid-tenth century, other chiefs contested control of the central Red River Delta. Then in the 960s, a local chief from just south of the delta, Dinh Bo Linh, defeated the "Twelve Lords" and brought the localities together in what would become Dai Viet. After a brief period during which the Dinh and the Le families maintained military control from their capital of Hoa Lu in the hills south of the Red River Delta, a new military figure, Ly Cong Uan (King Ly Thai To [r. 1009–1028]), seized the throne and moved his court and capital back to the central Red River Delta, thus beginning the integration of the new realm. Like later statements by founders of Vietnamese dynasties (the Quang Trung and Gia Long emperors), Ly Thai To's edict, as recorded in Le Van Huu's *Chronicle of Dai Viet* (1272), justified his action as follows, using classical Chinese references and linking his monarchy to both indigenous forces and localized Sinic power.[1]

[In 1010, second month], the king felt that the Hoa Lu citadel was humid and tight, not satisfactory for the seat of royalty, so he wished to move it and put out a proclamation stating, "Of old, the house of Shang [in ancient China] in the age of Pan Geng [1401–1372 B.C.E.] moved five times, while the house of Zhou in the age of King Cheng [1115–1079 B.C.E.] made three moves. How many of the Three Dynasty rulers [of Chinese antiquity] followed personal and wild notions to move their royal seats? Utilizing one's own scheme to locate the great dwelling in the midst of everything is an artifice for myriad generations and descendants. Above we heed the will of Heaven; below we follow the wishes of the people. If the location is convenient, then make the change quickly. As a result, the land will be blessed, the royal court long lasting, and the customs rich and abundant. And yet the two families of the Dinh and the Le followed their own particularistic concerns, neglectful of Heaven's will, and did not take the paths of the Shang and the Zhou.

"Sitting securely in their home district, they allowed a great disturbance to fill the land. Their destiny was short, the people were wasted, ten thousand evil deeds were committed which do not bear retelling. I am a man of compassion; I have no choice but to move to another place. Especially is it impossible for me not to move when there exists the old capital of [General] Gao Pian at Dai La, in the region between Heaven and Earth where the dragon-coiled tiger is able to sit, between south and north and east and west, with a favorable view of the mountains behind and the river in front, where the earth is spacious and flat and high and clear, where the inhabitants are not oppressed by flooding, where the earth is fertile and prosperous, a location overlooking the entire land of

---

1. For an appreciation of the historical and geomantic significance of this location as it developed over subsequent centuries, see Nguyen Huy Luong's poem "Rhapsody on West Lake" (chap. 4) and Phan Huy Chu, "Hanoi/Son Nam" (chap. 5).

Viet; that spot is the best place imaginable. It is where the four directions meet, the location for a capital that will last ten thousand ages.

> [Ngo Si Lien, *Dai Viet su ky toan thu* (hereafter, *DVSKTT*), 2, 2a–2b; trans.
> John K. Whitmore (para. 1); Taylor, *Birth of Vietnam*, 173]

LY THUONG KIET

THE SOUTHERN LAND (1076)

In 1076, friction between Dai Viet and the Song court in the North, the latter being allied with Champa and Angkor (Cambodia), led to warfare along their mutual frontier. Here, as recorded in the *Chronicle of Dai Viet* (1272) and the *Departed Spirits of the Viet Realm* (1329), the famous Lord Ly Thuong Kiet arranged for a mysterious voice to recite the following verse from the temple of two famous spirits of martial valor, in an attempt to rally the defeated troops of Dai Viet. The result was victory over the Northerners. In this verse, the Vietnamese emperor implicitly juxtaposes the ruler of Dai Viet (the South) with the Song emperor of the North, as Nguyen Trai did with the Ming dynasty in the fifteenth century and as suggested in the reference to the "Celestial Script." Poetry as a means of stirring troops into action also was used during the late-eighteenth-century Tay Son wars, when the Nguyen military leader used the poem "Lament for the South" to rally his forces.

> The Southern mountains and rivers are the dwelling place
>   of the Southern emperor;
> The separation is allotted and fixed in the Celestial Script.
> How dare rebellious slaves come to invade?
> You will go out and see their utter defeat!

> [Ngo Si Lien, *DVSKTT*, 3, 9b; Ly Te Xuyen,
> *Viet dien u linh tap* (hereafter, *VDULT*);
> trans. adapted from Keith W. Taylor, introduction
> to Ostrowski and Zottoli, *Departed Spirits*, 51]

THE SPIRIT OF TO LICH (LATE ELEVENTH CENTURY)

Records Declaring the Ultimate, composed in the late eleventh century, was a major text of the early Ly dynasty. It expresses the royal tradition of that time, which joined the indigenous spirit beliefs with the continuity of localized Sinic power. This particular tale concerns the spirit of the capital region and links an earlier protector-general of Annan with Gao Pian and Ly Thai To. It was one of five tales from *Records Declaring the Ultimate* to be included in *Departed Spirits of the Viet Realm* (1329), compiled by Ly Te Xuyen.

Protector of the Country, Guarding Divinity, Fixing the State, God of the Capital of the Realm Great King

According to the *Records of Jiao Province* and the *Records Declaring the Ultimate*, the King was originally of the To line and named Lich.[2] He served as a magistrate in Long Do.[3] The King's forefathers had long resided in Long Do, with their village on the bank of a small river. The family was not overly wealthy, but lived by the rule of putting filial piety first. Three generations were benevolent and yielding and did not live apart.

In the Jin era [265–420], filial persons were nominated, and there was an edict to display a royal testimonial at the village gate. In years when the harvest failed and grain stores were empty, an edict was handed down to loan rice. For this reason, [the King's name] To Lich was taken as the name of the village.

In the third year of the Chang Qing era of Tang Muzong [823], Protector General Li Yuanxi saw that at the northern gate of Long Bien town [near To Lich] there was a stream flowing in reverse and the landscape was pleasing. He then went all around searching for a high, dry place and moved the prefectural town there. Its activities were regulated and there were several layers of gates and ramparts. There were houses and uneven rooftops in all four directions, including the King's old house from the time he was alive. Oxen were slaughtered and liquor was filtered; the village elders from all around were asked to come and tell stories of the King. They wished to petition the court to make the King the God of the City. All agreed to this, and their wish was satisfied. Scarcely a few days after construction of the temple was begun, completion was announced. As a matter of course, it was a crowded temple, solemn and imposing. On the day of inauguration, there were ceremonial dancing and singing, and the sounds of stringed instruments and flutes reached the sky. Because of the people, the land was a place of beauty, and because of virtue, the people were prosperous. Is that not right?

That night, Li Yuanxi was lying peacefully by a window. Suddenly there was a gust of cool wind that struck his nostrils as it came. Dirt kicked up and flew around. The curtains rustled and tables shook. There was a man riding a white deer who descended from the sky. His beard and brows were brilliantly white. His clothing was clear and distinct. He announced to Li Yuanxi, "Your Lord has appointed me King of the city. If you can teach and transform the people residing within these walls with complete purity and absolute loyalty, then you will fulfill the office of prefect and be worthy of the duty to follow excellence." Li Yuanxi bowed and made obeisance in consent. He asked the

---

2. The "King" refers to the historical figure and to the spirit of the cult that he became.

3. Long Do (Dragon's Belly) was the central portion of the Red River Delta around the capital (now Hanoi).

visitor's name, but there was no response. Suddenly he awoke. Then he knew it had been a dream.

When Gao Pian built the town of Dai La [ca. 866], he heard of To Lich's divine and supernatural powers. So he prepared offerings for a sacrifice and honored him as the Capital City Protector Spirit Lord.

When Ly Thai To was moving the capital [1010], he often dreamed he dimly saw an old white-haired man appearing in audience before the royal throne. The man kowtowed once, and then again, saying, "Long live the king!" The sovereign was taken aback and asked the man's name. The man set forth the whole story. The sovereign laughed and said, "Would the honorable spirit like incense kept for a hundred years?" The man replied, "I only hope that the royal fortunes are stable as a rock and prosperous, with endless saintly longevity, that in court and out in the districts there is great peace; and that servants like me will have incense kept not for just a hundred years." The sovereign awoke and ordered the chief priest to make an offering of liquor. The spirit was made Thang Long Capital City of the Realm God Great King. When the residents prayed and took oaths before him, a divine response was immediately observed.

> [Ly Te Xuyen, *VDULT*; trans. Ostrowski and Zottoli,
> *Departed Spirits*, 37–38]

LY NHAN TONG

POEMS ON A BUDDHIST LAND (CA. 1100)

The indigenous spirits and localized Sinic powers came to coexist in the broad Buddhist context of the land. The fourth ruler, Ly Nhan Tong (r. 1072–1127), composed the following two poems, which were included in *Eminent Monks of the Thien Community* (1337), about Vietnamese Buddhist monks and what he regarded as the inherent Buddhist nature of the Southern land. Van Hanh (d. 1025) helped Ly Nhan Tong's great-grandfather Ly Thai To seize the throne, and Pham Sung (1004–1087) was a famous monk who had studied in India for nine years.

> Van Hanh fused present, past, and future,
> He matched the workings of ancient prophecies.
> His native village was Co Phap,[4]
> He planted his staff there to guard the royal territory of the Ly.
>
> Sung Pham hailed from the Southern country,
> He returned home successful with mind empty.

---

4. Co Phap was the home of the Ly dynasty, just north of the capital, Thang Long, in the center of Dai Viet at that time.

Long ears reflect his auspicious quality,
He realized that all phenomena are inherently detached from all
    forms and extremely subtle.

> [*Thien uyen tap anh* (hereafter, *TUTA*), 51b, 53a; trans.
> Nguyen Tu Cuong, *Zen in Medieval Vietnam*, 64]

TRAN MINH TONG

ROYAL POEMS ON THE LAND (FIRST HALF
OF FOURTEENTH CENTURY)

In the first half of the fourteenth century, the ruler Tran Minh Tong (r. 1314–1357) wrote two poems on the nature of his land. The first speaks of the great victory over the Mongols on the Bach Dang River in 1287 (as well as over the Southern Han in 938), reflecting the ever present Northern threat to the Tran. The second poem addresses the vibrancy of the Southern land as defined by its mountains and rivers. Indeed, all the Tran kings recognized the need to separate the South and the North. This new style of poetry looked at nature and the past, reflecting the literati's growing influence during the Tran dynasty and their concern with the land. The eighteenth-century scholar Le Quy Don also included these poems in his *Complete Anthology of Vietnamese Poetry*,[5] for poetic reflections on the land and its historical echoes were standard fare among Vietnamese literati of this and later generations. The poem "Rhapsody on West Lake," composed by Nguyen Huy Luong in 1798, was a later and more elaborate example of this genre.

THE BACH DANG RIVER

The sharp-pointed jade green peaks thrusting at the clouds are
    like swords and lances.
The white-caps are like the sea serpent swallowing and churning
    the tide.
The aftermath of the spring rain resembles sparkling hair ornaments
    covering the ground like chain mail.
The cold evening wind sloughing through the pine trees makes
    the heavens shake.
Now as of old our mountains and rivers [our land] have learned
    from experience
That the fortunes of war for aliens and Vietnamese alike depend
    on natural barriers.
The river water has stopped flooding. The waning moon casts shadows.
The blood of battle that I see in error is not yet dry.

---

5. See Le Quy Don, "Introduction to *The Complete Anthology of Vietnamese Literature*" (chap. 4).

THE CHRYSANTHEMUM

As I sing my way into the yellow flowers, let wine be poured.
The chrysanthemum hedge is in autumn color. The evening is still
    fragrant.
Who can tell how many important persons there have been over time?
But as long as there is a drop of rain on the Southern hills, their
    greenness will never end.

> [Le Quy Don, *Toan Viet thi luc* (hereafter, *TVTL*), 19b–23a; trans.
> Wolters, *Two Essays*, 60–62]

LY TE XUYEN

THE CULT OF PHUNG HUNG (1329)

While Tran Minh Tong was the ruler, Ly Te Xuyen, a caretaker of Buddhist texts, compiled a collection of tales about the powerful spiritual forces of the land that were believed to have helped defeat the Mongol forces almost half a century earlier. Finished in 1329, this work, *Departed Spirits of the Viet Realm*, brought together mythic figures of earlier centuries who had served as protectors of the land, the throne, and the Buddhist community. Although this work included tales from the eleventh-century text *Records Declaring the Ultimate*, the two were quite different. Whereas the Ly dynasty's *Records Declaring the Ultimate* describes an integrated North and South continuing from the past into the present, the Tran dynasty's *Departed Spirits of the Viet Realm* makes explicit the Tran idea of Southern opposition to the North, in both the past and the present. From the second half of the late eighth century, this indigenous tale tells of Phung Hung, the Great Father and Mother King, and his supernatural aid to the tenth-century Ngo Quyen in bringing independence to the Vietnamese from Northern forces at the first battle of the Bach Dang River (938).

Soon after Phung Hung died in the late eighth century, his abilities were divinely manifested. He often appeared among the villagers. A thousand chariots and ten thousand horses flew up above the houses and amidst the trees. People in the crowds looked up to see something obscure like clouds forming the five colors of light. The sounds of strings and woodwinds carried far and echoed in the sky. Then there was a sound of shouts and cries, and flags and drums were seen in the distance. A fendered palanquin dazzled the eyes. All these things in the distance were clear to see. Whenever the region had fearful or joyous matters at hand, in the middle of the night the village notables would first see a supernatural figure announcing the tidings. The figure was made a deity by the crowds.

To the west of the regional headquarters, a shrine was built for worship. Prayers for clear skies and for rain were always divinely answered. Whenever there was suspicion over matters of theft or dispute, ceremonial items were brought before the temple to request an audience and oaths were sworn there.

Immediately, ill fortune or blessings were observed. Sellers offered gifts and prayed for large profits, and they were all answered. On every day of thanksgiving to the spirits, people gathered in great numbers and wheel tracks and footprints covered the roads. The appearance of the shrine was magnificent, and the incense has never been extinguished.

When First Lord Ngo Quyen founded the country in the tenth century, the Northern army came to pillage. The First Lord was distraught at this, and in the middle of the night he was dreaming when he suddenly saw an old gray-haired man in imposing, formal dress carrying a feather fan and bamboo cane. . . . The spirit declared his name and said, "I have sent ten thousand regiments of spirit soldiers to strategic places, where they are ready to lie in ambush. May Your Lord hasten to advance troops to oppose the enemy. You will have secret assistance and need not allow yourself to worry." Then, at the victory of Bach Dang [938], there indeed was witnessed the sound of chariots and horses in the sky, and the battle was in fact a great victory. The First Lord was taken aback and ordered the construction of a great temple, larger than on the former model. He supplied feather screens, royal banners, bronze gongs, deerskin drums, dancing and singing, and sacrificial oxen in show of gratitude. As things have changed over the successive royal reigns, this has gradually become an old ceremony.

[Ly Te Xuyen, *VDULT*; trans. Ostrowski and Zottoli, *Departed Spirits*, 13]

THE BUDDHIST MONK KHUONG VIET (1337)

In 1337, the Buddhist work *Eminent Monks of the Thien Community* harked back to the Buddhist monk Khuong Viet (933–1011) and the divine protection of both the land of Dai Viet and its Buddhist world. This tale describes the Tran's continued opposition to the North and how the South, with its Buddhist protection, thwarted the Song invasion of 981.

Khuong Viet often visited Mount Ve Linh in Binh Lo Prefecture and grew to love the elegant scenery there. He wanted to build a hermitage and settle down. One night he had a dream in which he saw a spirit wearing golden armor, holding a golden lance in his right hand and a jewel stupa in his left hand. He was accompanied by ten or more fearsome-looking attendants. The spirit came and told him: "I am the Celestial King Vaisravana, and all my attendants are *yaksas*.[6] The lord of Heaven has ordered us to come to this country to protect its border and enable the Buddha-Dharma to flourish. I have a karmic affinity with you, so I have come to entrust this task to you."

Khuong Viet woke up in astonishment. He heard the sound of shouting in the mountains. He thought the whole thing very strange. When dawn came, he

---

6. Vaisravana is the Indic god Kubera, king of the *yaksas* who guards Buddhism and the dharma.

went into the mountains and saw a great tree more than a hundred feet high, with many branches and luxuriant foliage. Above it was an auspicious cloud. Khuong Viet had some workmen cut down the tree, and he had it carved into the image of what he had seen in his dream. It was housed in a shrine.

In the first year of the Tianfu era [981]), the army of the Song regime invaded the South. King Le Hoan already had heard of Khuong Viet's story, so he ordered Khuong Viet to go to the shrine and pray for victory. The enemy took flight, escaping to the Ninh River in Bao Huu. Wild waves arose, raised by the wind, and flood-dragons appeared leaping and prancing about. The Northern army fled in complete disarray.

[*TUTA*, 8b–9a; trans. adapted from Nguyen Tu
Cuong, *Zen in Medieval Vietnam*, 72]

A VIETNAMESE ANTIQUITY (SECOND HALF OF FOURTEENTH CENTURY)

After studying the Northern classical antiquity, younger Vietnamese scholars began to imagine their own antiquity, the mythic land of Van Lang. By the 1360s, one such scholar-official, Pham Su Manh, wrote the following poem—which was included by Le Quy Don in his eighteenth-century *Complete Anthology of Vietnamese Poetry*— while serving on the northern border. The *Short History of Dai Viet*, written in the 1380s, further describes Van Lang and its significance. Van Lang was the land of Dai Viet's own antiquity, home of the newly conceived eighteen Hung kings and their indigenous Lac people, which was set to rival the classical antiquity of the North. Whereas the Ly had looked back to King Si of the second and third centuries C.E. and the Tran had emulated Trieu Da of the second century B.C.E., these scholars embraced a deeper past commensurate with the Northern classical antiquity, hundreds of years earlier, a pattern adopted by historians to this day.

> I moor my boat by a rock in the river facing the clear waves.
> The river guards race to hail the official's pennant as it goes by.
> Here were tribal stockades along the Lo River and the Thao
> River's settlements.
> Here were Van Lang's sage rulers and Thuc's land.[7]
> Then, when over ten thousand miles there were writing and chariots,
> the frontier soil was peaceful.[8]
> But for a thousand years there have been disorders in the world.

---

7. Thuc (C: Shu) is the region of Sichuan in southwestern China. Forces from there are believed to have conquered northern Vietnam in the third century B.C.E.

8. "Writing and chariots" represent standardized systems of written characters and roads and, hence, good governance.

I am favored with the royal order to control the border lands.
I shall expel and subdue robbers and bring warfare to an end.

Pham Su Manh

Van Lang's customs were of a simple and pure substance. For purposes of governance knotted cords were used.[9] There were eighteen generations of these Hung kings and they were all called Lac. The Yue ruler [in the North], Goujian, sent envoys with his commands, but the Lac king rejected them.

Short History of Dai Viet
[Le Quy Don, TVTL, 3, 10a; Viet su luoc (hereafter, VSL), 1, 2a;
trans. Wolters, Two Essays, 22, 25]

NGUYEN NHU THUYET

PROTEST ON MOVING THE CAPITAL (1397)

In the late fourteenth century as the Tran clan weakened, the Ho clan, also of Northern descent, took over in Thanh Hoa, then in the southern region of Dai Viet. Among other actions, the Ho moved the capital south, from Thang Long to Thanh Hoa, essentially reversing the movement carried out by the founder of the Ly dynasty nearly four centuries earlier. As with the earlier shift, the decision reflected significant regionalisms within the realm of Dai Viet, by transferring the state's center to an area outside the Red River Delta. In the following document, a court official counters the argument that Ly Thai To made when he first moved the capital to Thang Long. The official's statement was recorded in Ngo Si Lien's Complete Chronicle of Dai Viet (1479). In the nineteenth century, inhabitants of Hanoi probably had similar feelings when the capital was relocated to Hue.

In olden times, when the Zhou and the Wei [in the North] moved their capitals, it was seen as having been unfortunate. Today the land of Long-do,[10] with Mount Tan Vien standing high and the Lo and Nhi rivers running deep, lies flat and spacious. Since the kings and princes of old opened up their domain and established the state, there has never been a case of one who did not take this land as the place where his roots lay, deep and firm. Let us be in accord with the earlier situations. We have humbled and killed the Mongols; we have taken the heads of the Champa invaders. Think on these a moment and consider the indestructible [literally, "hard as rock"] nature of our country. The borderlands of An Ton [in northwestern Thanh Hoa], on the contrary, are closed in and miserable, lying as

---

9. "Knotted cords" represent a standardized system of record keeping and, thus, good governance.

10. Long Do (Dragon's Belly) was the central portion of the Red River Delta around the capital (now Hanoi).

they do at the end of the rivers and the beginnings of the mountains. It is a rebellious area, unable to be ruled, whose men may be trusted to be dangerous. There is an old saying that states, "Live in virtue; do not live in danger."

[Ngo Si Lien, *DVSKTT*, 8, 28b–29a; trans. Whitmore, *Vietnam*, 44]

ECONOMICS AND TRADE

LE VAN HUU

PRESERVING LIVESTOCK (1272)

The wet rice–growing economy of the Red River Delta was critically dependent on water buffalo and cattle, for both working the rice paddies and hauling. The Ly royal court—and the Le kings in later centuries—recognized the need to provide security for these beasts of burden and, by extension, for the farming families themselves. Accordingly, the court issued a formal edict establishing protection for livestock and stipulating punishments for those violating these protections. This episode was recorded in Le Van Huu's *Chronicle of Dai Viet*.

[In 1117], the second month, the king, Ly Nhan Tong [r. 1072–1127], spoke out about stealing or slaughtering cattle. The queen mother said, "Here, in both the capital city and the rural towns, many people often flee and take up cattle rustling. The people are destitute and suffering. Numerous families have to share a single head of cattle for plowing and so we make this statement." The royal court had already put out an order forbidding this. Today, there is much more slaughter of cattle than before. [Thus] in this matter, the king proclaimed that all who stole or killed cattle would receive eighty blows of the heavy stick and made to do hard labor. Their wives would also receive eighty blows and be made silkworm-breeding servants. They also would have to compensate the owners for the cattle. Those neighboring families who did not report such actions would also receive eighty blows.

[Ngo Si Lien, *DVSKTT*, 3, 17a–17b; trans. John K. Whitmore]

LE VAN HUU

FOREIGN TRADE (1272)

In the mid-twelfth century, the port of Van Don, located in the islands northeast of the Red River Delta (near Ha Long Bay), became an important trading entrepôt linked to trading routes along the southeastern coast of China, Hainan Island, and ports in Champa to the south. From these links, Van Don enabled Dai Viet to trade beyond Southeast Asia, across the Indian Ocean and as far as the Mediterranean. The lands mentioned in this excerpt from the *Chronicle of Dai Viet* were in Java, coastal Thailand,

and Sumatra. Such international commerce, frequently understated in Vietnamese historiography, continued into the nineteenth and twentieth centuries at different ports along the expanding coast.

Ly Anh Tong [r. 1138–1175], the tenth year of Dai Dinh [1149]. In the second month of spring, trading ships from the three countries of Qua Oa, Lo Ac, and Tiem La entered Hai Dong. They asked for a place to live and sell their wares. On an island they were allowed to establish a settlement, called Van Don, where they bought and sold precious commodities. They also presented tributary goods to the court.

Ly Cao Tong [r. 1176–1210], the ninth year of Trinh Phu [1184]. Traders from Tiem La, Tam Phat Te and other countries entered Van Don market town, presented tributary goods to the court, and asked to be allowed to trade.

[Ngo Si Lien, *DVSKTT*, 4, 6b, 20a; trans. Yamamoto, "Van-Don," 1]

NGO SI LIEN

THE DIKING SYSTEM (1479)

When the Tran dynasty came from the lower Red River Delta to take power in Thang Long, the rulers began to assert greater control over the countryside than had their Ly predecessors. One very important economic aspect of growing central control in the localities was the court's ability to strengthen the diking system throughout the Red River Delta, as well as in the Ma River valley just to the south in Thanh Hoa. For the first time, the central government was able to establish a stable set of dikes and a system for water control along the branches of the lower Red River. To do this, the court used the increasingly prominent group of literati officials and administrators, as recorded in Ngo Si Lien's *Complete Chronicle of Dai Viet*.

[In 1248], the third month, King Tran Thai Tong [r. 1225–1277] ordered all jurisdictions to construct dikes to control the water, calling them the Quai Vac system, from the headwaters to the seacoast, in order to hold back the floodwaters. He established river dike officers and assistant officers to supervise the construction sites, to inspect the lands and fields of the people, and to estimate what was needed for the construction. The Quai Vac construction began at this time.

[1255], second month, the king ordered Luu Mien to construct river dikes in the varied localities of Thanh Hoa Province [to the south].

Summer, fourth month, the king selected officials not currently in office as dike officers and assistant officers in all the jurisdictions. When they were not needed for agricultural matters, they were to direct the army in constructing the dikes and then to set up canals to guard against flood and drought.

[Ngo Si Lien, *DVSKTT*, 5, 15b, 20a–20b; trans. John K. Whitmore]

NGO SI LIEN

The coastal area in the lower Red River Delta around Van Don was linked through commerce with the southeastern coast of China. As a result, trading centers like Van Don often became multiethnic and polyglot entities reflecting the diversity of both transient and resident merchants. Among these multiethnic communities were the many Northerners who came down the coast to live, trade, and work in the thriving Southern economy. In the late thirteenth century, it was necessary to distinguish the inhabitants of the region around the port of Van Don, who wore Northern-style dress and maintained Northern customs, from the invading Mongol armies, which included ethnic Chinese troops. The Tran general, Prince Khanh Du, therefore ordered the locals to change their style of headgear (perhaps to a Champa style), which resulted in some sharp dealing and profit for him, as recorded in the *Complete Chronicle of Dai Viet.*

When Tran Khanh Du was first appointed to govern Van Don, the people there customarily depended on trade for their livelihoods. They relied on the "guests from the North" for whatever they ate, drank, and wore. And for this reason they customarily wore "Northern" clothing. After reviewing the militia of the villages, Tran Khanh Du issued an order which said that since Van Don's local troops were used for defense against the Northern barbarians [Mongols], they should not wear Northern-style hats, which made them hard to distinguish from their foes in the heat of battle. He commanded that they wear instead Ma Loi hats[11] and said that any who disobeyed this order would be punished. But Tran Khanh Du had first ordered his own family's people to buy Ma Loi hats and anchor their ship in the harbor. Then he had his servants secretly tell the villagers that the previous day they saw a ship selling these hats anchored in the bay. The villagers rushed to buy the hats, and the hats, which had been bought for only 100 cash, were then each sold for a whole bolt of cloth. This scheme gained Tran Khanh Du thousands of bolts of cloth and led the Northerners to make up a "congratulatory" poem which included the stanza: "chickens and dogs of Van Don were all astonished." Under the guise of admiring Tran Khanh Du's fame, this poem perhaps expressed satire instead.

> [Ngo Si Lien, *DVSKTT*, 5, 53a–53b; trans. adapted from Yamamoto, "Van-Don," 2–3]

---

11. Ma Loi hats, made of woven bamboo, are named after a village from Ma Loi commune in the mid–Red River Delta.

PHILOSOPHY AND RELIGION

POWER AND REDEMPTION (LATE TENTH CENTURY)

In the late tenth century, interfamily struggle among the sons of the ruler Dinh Bo
Linh (r. 968–980) led to the death of one prince at the hands of another. The first passage is from the *Chronicle of Dai Viet* (1272), by Le Van Huu, and describes what
happened. The second text is from a number of late-tenth-century Buddhist inscriptions on *ratnadhvaja* stone pillars in which the prince expresses his remorse and seeks
redemption. The single inscription on each of the pillars discloses how Buddhist action was thought to be able to redeem the brutality necessary in political struggle.

In the spring [of 979], the Nam Viet Prince Lien murdered the Crown Prince
Hang Lang. Lien, the elder son of king Dinh Bo Linh, underwent hardships in
serving his father's struggle for power. When the country was pacified, the king
intended to choose him to take the throne and gave him the title Nam Viet
Prince. Lien also requested the emperor of the Song dynasty to recognize his
status and confer a title. But when the king had another son, Hang Lang, Bo
Linh changed his mind and made the younger son the crown prince. In discontent, Lien murdered his younger brother.

Le Van Huu

Disciple Dinh Khuong Lien, granted the title Suy Thanh Thuan Hoa Cong
Than Tinh Hai Quan Tiet Do Su Dac Tien Kiem Hieu Thai Su Nam Viet
Prince and allotted land of 10,000 households, has a deceased younger brother,
the Highly Virtuous Dinh Noa Tang Noa, who strayed from the path of loyalty
and filial piety toward his king-father and his elder brother and thereby created
grave consequences. So I, Dinh Khuong Lien, had to bring doom to his life for
the sake of the land and family ethics. As the old saying puts it, "There is no
willingness to withdraw from the struggle for power, but the better way is first to
eliminate one's opponents." The affair has happened as it should. Now I have
made one hundred *ratnadhvaja* columns as offerings before the altar and pray
for the immediate release of the souls of my brother and others who died before
and after him, so that they can escape trials and judgments in hell. Most of all,
I wish the king Dai Thang Minh [his father, Dinh Bo Linh (r. 965–980)] to
reign forever over this Southern land, everlastingly on his throne.

Buddhist Inscription
[Ngo Si Lien, DVSKTT, 1, 5a; Épigraphie en chinois, nos. 5–9;
trans. Ha Van Tan, "Inscriptions," 52]

BUDDHIST POEMS (TENTH AND ELEVENTH CENTURIES)

Dai Viet's Buddhist community grew stronger with the emergence and growth of the state from the 960s to the 1060s. Its belief system is best expressed in the poetry written by religious figures. These poems, which are among the earliest recorded indigenous Vietnamese texts, stress the impermanence and complexity of existence, the Buddha nature (Dharma nature) in all people, and the possibility that humans could perceive this truth. Thien was the Vietnamese form of the meditation school of Dhyana. These poems were gathered in *Eminent Monks of the Thien Community* (1337).

The fire was already there in the wood,
Fire was there, then it came to life again.
If you say there is no fire in wood,
How could flames spring up when we drill for fire?

Khuong Viet (933–1011)

The body is like lightning; it's there and then it's not,
It is like myriad plants and trees—fresh in the spring but fading
    in autumn.
Trust in your destiny unafraid of ups and downs,
Because ups and downs are as evanescent as drops of dew on
    a blade of grass.

Van Hanh (d. 1025)

Prajna is really without a source,
It teaches the emptiness of both persons and phenomena.
The Buddhas of the past, present, and future,
Are identical in Dharma nature.

Ly Thai Tong (1000–1054)

Body and mind are fundamentally quiescent and still,
But through the transformations of spiritual powers, all forms are
    manifested.
Both created and uncreated phenomena come from this,
In worlds countless as the grains of sand on the banks of the Ganges,
Though they fill all space,
When contemplated one by one, they are formless.
For a thousand ages this has been difficult to describe,
But everywhere in every world it is always luminous and clear.

Cuu Chi (fl. 1050s)

Birth, old age, illness, and death,
Have always been the same.
If you wish to escape from them,
By trying to untie your bonds,
you add to your entanglement.
It's only when you are deluded
that you search for Buddha,
It's only when you are confused
that you look for Thien
I seek neither Buddha nor Thien,
I just close my mouth and keep silent.

The nun Dieu Nhan (1042–1113)
[*TUTA*, 9b, 52b, 17b, 19a, 67b; trans. Nguyen Tu Cuong,
Zen in Medieval Vietnam, 59–60, 62–63]

LE VAN HUU

BUDDHIST CULTS (1272)

The early Ly dynasty was closely connected to the Buddhist community, encouraging it to construct and consecrate temples. As the *Chronicle of Dai Viet* shows, for religious, political, and economic reasons, the kings and the aristocracy were heavily involved with this community. Accordingly, to strengthen itself, the Ly monarchy developed its own royal cult, a Buddhist ritual with the gods Brahma and Indra (king of the gods) at its core, reflecting how Dai Viet performed royal rituals similar to those of Angkor (Cambodia) and Pagan (Myanmar).

[In 1049], winter, tenth month, the king [Ly Thai Tong (r. 1028–1054)] built the Dien Huu [Prolonged Protection] Buddhist temple [now the Chua Mot Cot (Single Pillar Pagoda)]. At first, the king dreamed of the bodhisattva Quan Am [C: Guanyin], the goddess of mercy, sitting beautifully on a lotus flower pavilion, beckoning him to come up on the pavilion. Perceiving this, he spoke of it with all his ministers, about whether he should take the dream as an ill omen. The Buddhist monk Thien Tue advised the king to build a Buddhist temple by standing a stone pillar stuck into the earth and placing the Quan Am Lotus Flower Pavilion on top of it, just as the king had seen in his dream. The Buddhist monks and their acolytes encircled the king, chanting the sutras and praying for his prolonged life. Hence, the name of the temple became Dien Huu. . . .

[In 1057], twelfth month [early 1058], the king [Ly Thanh Tong (r. 1054–1072)] established two Buddhist temples, Thien Phuc [Heaven's Fortune] and Thien Tho [Heaven's Longevity], with gold cast images of King Phan [Brahma] and

De Thich [Indra] whom he attended in ritual. (Note: The Tran dynasty continued to perform these rituals at these two temples.)[12]

[Ngo Si Lien, *DVSKTT*, 2, 37a; 3, 2a; trans. John K. Whitmore]

LADY GOD OF THE EARTH (LATE ELEVENTH CENTURY)

Along with Buddhism, cults of local spirits offered magic, power, and protection. The following text illustrates how such local cults were brought into the capital of Thang Long to centralize power, as recorded in the late-eleventh-century work *Records Declaring the Ultimate*. It describes the cult to the spirit of the Lady God of the Earth, the spirit of the southern region of Dai Viet, and how the cult came to the capital. The tale is included in *Departed Spirits of the Viet Realm* (1329), compiled by Ly Te Xuyen.

Responding-to-Heaven, Transforming and Sustaining Force, Greatly Loyal, God of the Earth, Earth Deity Female Immortal

According to the *Records Declaring the Ultimate*, the Female Immortal was the Lord of the Southern Country [southern Dai Viet] and Great Earth Spirit.

Long ago Ly Thanh Tong [r. 1054–1072] made a punitive expedition to the south against Champa. He reached the Bay of Hoan [Nghe An] and suddenly met with violent winds and foul rains. The rains rushed and roared. The royal ship rocked to and fro, and the royal party wanted to turn around. Danger appeared unexpectedly. The king was in great fear. In his distress, the king suddenly saw a woman of around twenty years of age. Her appearance was like that of a peach blossom. Her brows were like willows, and her eyes like bright stars. Her smile was like a flower bed. On her body she wore a white robe and green trousers. She had fastened a belt over her light clothing. She came straight to the sovereign and explained, "I am the Great Earth spirit of this southern section of the country. I have long been reborn to live in a place of water and clouds, watching and waiting for a time at which to appear. Due to this opportune meeting and with the good reason of having fortune to come upon the royal countenance, my entire life's desire has truly been satisfied. Yet I still wish that your majesty on this trip proceed promptly and skillfully, achieving complete victory. Although I am only sedge and willow [a mere woman] and of light carriage, I hope to contribute my trifling strength, secretly giving support. On the day of your triumphant return, I shall be waiting here to pay my respects." She finished speaking and vanished.

The sovereign awoke with both fear and joy. He summoned all his assistants and told of everything he had seen in the dream. The general supervisor of the Buddhist monks, Hue Lam, said, "The spirit said it was reborn in a tree, living

---

12. This note is in the original text.

in a place of water and clouds. We should search for it in a tree, in an area with divine efficacy." The sovereign assented to this and ordered men to search all over the islets and riverbanks. They came up with a piece of timber very much resembling a human figure and of the sort of shape and color formerly seen. Indeed, this was in agreement with what had been seen in the dream. The sovereign, because of this, gave the spirit the title of Lady God of the Earth. He ordered the piece of timber put on a table and placed in the royal ship. Suddenly, at just that moment, the waves desisted and the grass and trees ceased shaking. Then, when the sovereign reached Champa and engaged in battle, it was as if there were the support of a spirit. The battle was indeed a great victory.

On the day of triumphant return, the royal ship anchored at the former place. An order was issued to erect a shrine. Again, there rose up wind and rain as before. Hue Lam petitioned, "If you invite the spirit to rest in the capital city, you will obtain your desire." The wind and rain were calmed. They went north to arrive at the capital. Outside the city, construction was begun on a temple in An Lang village. It has accumulated clear and wondrous signs. Those who slander and curse immediately witness misfortune.

> [Ly Te Xuyen, *VDULT*; trans. Ostrowski and Zottoli,
> *Departed Spirits*, 61–62]

THE QUEEN MOTHER AND THONG BIEN

THE ORIGINS OF BUDDHISM IN DAI VIET (1096)

In the late eleventh century, as recorded in the *Eminent Monks of the Thien Community* (1337), the queen mother, Phu Thanh Cam Linh Nhan, asked about the nature of Buddhism. She received this reply from the monk Thong Bien (Clear Communicator), in which he stated the view of the Thien meditational school of Buddhist thought and its transmission from India to China and Dai Viet. The monk laid out the basic tenets of Buddhism as seen by his school: constant change, the inner nature of the faith, and the contingent historical teachings of the religion in both time and space. The goal was nirvana, beyond all space, time, and contingencies. The truth was nonverbal and required instant understanding passed directly and personally from teacher to disciple. This marked the first royal acceptance of a particular school of Buddhist thought in Dai Viet. In the fifteenth century, the historian Ngo Si Lien issued a similar statement for Vietnamese Confucianism.

In the spring of the fifth year of the Hoi Phong era [1096], on the fifteenth day of the second month, the queen mother, Phu Thanh Cam Linh Nhan, gave a vegetarian feast for the Buddhist monks at the Opening the State [Khai Quoc] Temple. She inquired of the elders present: "What is the meaning of 'the Buddha' and 'the Patriarchs'? Which is superior? Where does the Buddha dwell? Where do the patriarchs live? When did they come to this country to pass on this

Path? Who came first, the Buddha or the patriarchs? What is the meaning of reciting the Buddha's name and teaching the mind of the patriarchs?"

No one in the assembly spoke. Thong Bien then replied to the queen mother: "The Buddha is the one who abides eternally in the world without birth or demise. The patriarchs are those who illuminate the source of the Buddha-mind and whose understanding and conduct are in accord. The Buddha and the patriarchs are one. Only undisciplined scholars would falsely assert that either is superior or inferior.

"'Buddha' means 'enlightened.' Fundamentally, enlightenment is profoundly clear and eternally present. All beings share this inner truth. Because they are covered over by sentiments and sensory experience, they drift according to their karma and revolve through the various planes of existence.

"Out of compassion, the Buddha appeared to be born in Tianzhu [India]. This is because Tianzhu [India] is the center of the world. At nineteen he left home. At thirty, he achieved enlightenment. He stayed in the world preaching the dharma for forty-nine years, setting forth all sorts of provisional teachings to enable sentient beings to awaken to the Path. This is what is called creating teachings for a certain period. When he was about to enter final nirvana, he was afraid that people attached to delusion would get stuck on his words, so he told Manjusri, 'In forty-nine years I have not spoken a single word. Will they think something was said?' So he held up a flower in front of the assembly on Vulture Peak. No one in the assembly knew what to say, except the Venerable Mahakasyapa, who cracked a slight smile. The Buddha knew that the latter had meshed with truth, so he entrusted the treasury of the eye of the true dharma to him, and he became the first patriarch of Chan. This is what is called the separate transmission of the mind-source outside the scriptural teachings.

"Later Moteng [Kasyapa Matanga] brought this teaching to Han China [ca. first century C.E.] and Bodhidharma traveled to the Northern kingdoms of Liang and Wei (ca. sixth century C.E.) with this message. The transmission of the teaching flourished with Tiantai: it is called the school of the scriptural teachings. The gist of the teachings became clear with the sixth patriarch of Chan Caoxi: this is called the Chan school. Both these schools reached our country [Dai Viet] many years ago. The scriptural teachings began with Mou Bo and Kang Senghui. The first stream of the Thien school began with Vinitaruci [Ty Ni Da Luu Chi]; the second with Vo Ngon Thong. Vinitaruci and Vo Ngon Thong are the ancestral teachers of these two streams of Thien."

The queen mother asked: "Leaving aside for now the school of the scriptural teaching, what has been accomplished by the two streams of Thien?"

Thong Bien said: "According to the biography of Dharma Master Tianqi [542–607], Emperor Sui Gaozu [r. 580–611] said, 'I am mindful of the compassionate teaching of the Buddha, whose benevolence I cannot repay. As monarch, I have supported the Three Jewels on a wide scale all over the country. I have had all the relics in the country collected, and I have built forty-nine precious stupas for them.

To show the world the way across [to enlightenment], I have built more than 150 temples and stupas. I have built them all across Jiaozhou, so that their sustaining power and fructifying merit can extend everywhere. Although Jiaozhou belongs to the Sui, we still need to bind it to us, so we ought to send monks renowned for their virtue to go there to convert everyone and let them all attain enlightenment.'

"Dharma Master Tan Qian had already said, 'The area of Jiaozhou has long been in communication with Tianzhu [India]. Early on, when the Buddha-Dharma came to the lower Yangzi region and still had not been established, yet in Luy Lau [in central Jiaozhi] more than twenty precious temples were built, more than five hundred monks were ordained, and fifteen volumes of scriptures were translated from Sanskrit into Chinese. Because of this earlier connection, there already were monks and nuns like Mo Luo Qi Yui, Kang Senghui, Zhi Jiang Liang, and Mou Bo there. In our time, there is the Venerable Phap [dharma master] Hien, who received the transmission from Vinitaruci and who is now spreading the school of the third patriarch [Sengcan]. Phap Hien is a bodhisattva living among humans; he receives disciples and preaches the dharma at Chung Thien Temple, and the congregation there numbers more than three hundred. Thus, Jiaozhou is no different from the Middle Kingdom [the North]. Your majesty, you are the compassionate father of all the world. Wishing to bestow your grace everywhere equally, you would send an emissary to spread Buddhism to Jiaozhou. But there are already Buddhist teachers there; we do not have to go to convert them.'"

Thong Bien continued: "Moreover, the Tang minister Quan Deyu composed a preface to transmit the dharma, which says, 'After Caoxi passed away, the teachings of Chan flourished and spread.' There are Chan schools everywhere. Chan Master Zhangjing Yun carried Mazu's essential teachings on mind to spread the teaching in Wu-Yue [southern China]. The Mahasattva [Great Hero] Vo Ngon Thong transmitted the essential message of Baizhang's teaching to spread enlightenment in Jiaozhou. So Your Highness, this is what has been accomplished by the Thien schools."

The queen mother also asked: "What is the order of succession in the two Thien schools?"

Thong Bien said: "The present representatives of the Vinitaruci stream are Lam Hue Sinh and Vuong Chan Khong. For the Vo Ngon Thong stream, they are Mai Vien Chieu and Nhan Quang Tri. The successor of Kang Senhui is Loi Ha Trac. The other side branches of these two streams are too numerous to mention them all."

The queen mother was very happy with Thong Bien's reply, so she honored him with the title Monk Scribe [Tang Luc] and gave him a purple robe. She gave him the sobriquet Thong Bien Quoc Su, which means "National Preceptor with Consummate Eloquence," and rewarded him munificently. Subsequently, she revered him so much that she summoned him into the palace and paid homage to him as the national preceptor. She asked about the essential teachings of Thien and had a deep appreciation of its message. The queen mother once composed a verse on enlightenment:

Form is emptiness, so emptiness equals form,
Emptiness is form, so form equals emptiness.
Only when you are not attached to either,
Do you mesh with the true source.

In his later years, Thong Bien moved to Pho Minh temple, where he opened
a great teaching center and showered down the rain of dharma on all. He often
taught people to practice by using the Lotus Sutra, so his contemporaries
spoke of him as Ngo Phap Hoa [Dharma Master Awakened to the Lotus]. In
the second year, Giap Dan, of the Thien Chuong Bao Tu era [1134], on the
twelfth day of the second month, Thong Bien announced that he was ill and
died.

[*TUTA*, 19a–21b; trans. adapted from Nguyen Tu Cuong,
Zen in Medieval Vietnam, 128–30]

FUNERAL INSCRIPTION OF A COURT MINISTER (1159)

While Buddhism thrived, Northern classical beliefs continued to develop, possibly with
the advocacy of coastal scholars in closer contact with the North. This segment of the
funeral inscription for Do Anh Vu (1114–1159) reflects this pattern of belief and demonstrates the presence of literati in Dai Viet, as seen in the references to Hou Chi and
Zhou Gong, figures from Northern antiquity. Zhou Gong, the famous Duke of Zhou,
remained a major influence throughout the history of Dai Viet. Curiously, this text does
not mention Buddhism. Nonetheless, the funeral inscription of this powerful minister
provides a strong sense of death and remembrance among Dai Viet's nobility, as they
intended the stone and its words to carry the memory of the man across the ages, as indeed it does. Note that here, aristocratic rank was designated by the number of households assigned an individual.

It has been said: "Among birds there is the phoenix and among fish there is the
leviathan." It is the same among human beings. Concentrating on the powers
of mountains and rivers, as happens but once in five hundred years, a man was
born predestined to occupy the position of general and minister of state and to
be the master of a hundred thousand households. With martial sternness worthy
of fear and ritual behavior worthy of emulation, manifesting orthodoxy and giving form to propriety, he [Do Anh Vu] assisted his age by establishing a foundation
for peace and order. At court he revealed a lofty and upright purpose, comparable
to Hau Tac and Chu Cong.[13] In life, he was honored; in death he was mourned.
From the time that people have appeared upon the earth, there has never been
anything like this.

---

13. Hau Tac (C: Hou Chi), Shun's minister of Shang, was famous for his righteousness. Chu
Cong (C: Zhou Gong, Duke of Zhou) was famous for his loyal service.

It was then that the queen and the king, considering that the Duke's literary accomplishments were sufficient to govern the kingdom and his virtue was sufficient to rouse demons and deities, and considering that his sense of purpose was as constant as a spring of water and that his doctrine was as precious as gold and jade, and further considering that he was able to be a teacher worthy of emulation, therefore commanded him to assume the responsibilities of overseeing the teachers and to discuss with them the principles for governing the country, to take charge of and to scrutinize the plans and criticisms in the memorials and dispatches of all the scholars, and to insure that everything be done with the utmost care and attention to detail with regard to the judging and recommendations for the three competitions in poetry composition.

He who is buried here is concealed and can no longer be seen. Years pass to eternity, ages shift and change; but an engraved stone will last a long time to make manifest these words so that readers can contemplate this man. That is why it is unthinkable to neglect raising this inscribed stone tablet at this man's tomb.

A god descended from a mountain peak;
Thereby was born this sage.
He carried himself with dignity.
He combined elegance with the essentials.
He had both wisdom and courage;
He assisted his generation and soothed the people.
He encouraged poetry and established good manners;
He trod the way of morality and dwelled in the house of humanity.
He descended from highest-ranking ministers of state;
He became the master of both humans and deities.
He went [into the court] to decide ten thousand affairs;
He went out to proclaim the Five Injunctions.
The Van Dan invaders were scattered and went back;
The border towns were swept of strange customs.
Thuong Suy was killed without delay.
Dust was no longer stirred up at the frontier passes.
His merit occupies the first place;
Among those of his rank, who has there been to equal him?
His vitals were suddenly struck with disease;
Drugs and acupuncture were without effect.
He flew far away to the palace of the immortals;
The king wept, soaking his handkerchief with tears.
Gifts presented at his funeral were abundant and excellent;
His burial ceremony was prepared with full honors.
This stone is engraved to record his merit;
For all eternity.

[*Épigraphie en chinois*, no. 19; trans. Taylor,
"Voices Within and Without," 60, 67, 70]

BUDDHISM AND THE SAGES
(MID-THIRTEENTH CENTURY)

The thirteenth-century Tran kings blended elements of Buddhist and Confucian (the sage's) thought, which were not seen to be in conflict with each other. The first Tran ruler, Thai Tong (r. 1225–1277), remarked on the closeness of his Buddhist and classical thought and followed this by calling the literati into the capital. The first passage comes from a Buddhist text written by the king, and the second is from the *Complete Chronicle of Dai Viet* (1479), by Ngo Si Lien. In the sixteenth and eighteenth centuries, there would again be a sense of closeness between Buddhism and Confucianism.[14]

Those who transmitted rules through the generations and laid guidelines were greatly honored by the former sages. For this reason Huineng, sixth patriarch of the Chan school of Buddhism in southern China, once said that there was no difference between these sages and the great Buddhist teachers. I can draw on the example of the former sages when I transmit the teachings of Buddhism. Cannot I make the responsibility of the sages my own responsibility in teaching Buddhism?

Tran Thai Tong

[In 1253], ninth month, the king ordered the classical scholars [V: *nho si*; C: *ru shi*] of the land to come to the Royal Academy to hear the Four Books and the Six Classics expounded.

Ngo Si Lien
[Tran Thai Tong, "Thien ton chi nam," 1, 27a; trans. Wolters,
"Historians and Emperors in Vietnam and China," 84;
Ngo Si Lien, *DVSKTT*, 5, 19a; trans. John K. Whitmore]

LITERATI ON BUDDHISM AND THE SPIRITS (1272, 1333)

The pattern of classical thought in Dai Viet at this time is best demonstrated by the *Chronicle of Dai Viet* (1272), in which the scholar Le Van Huu comments on events described in the text, offering his royally sanctioned opinions. In effect, his comments both helped his colleagues understand the past and served as position papers for the events of his time. Although he served a Buddhist court, Le Van Huu (like Truong Han Sieu later) felt strongly that the state should be run without undue Buddhist influence. Here he comments on the victory of Ly Than Tong (r. 1127–1137) over the invading Khmer in 1128, almost a century and a half earlier, pointing out that the soldiers, not the

14. See Nguyen Binh Khiem, "The Three Teachings" and "Good Government" (chap. 3), and Phan Huy Ich, "Preface to *The Sound of the True Great and Perfect Enlightenment from the Bamboo Grove*" (chap. 4).

religions, had won the battle. In contrast, Le Van Huu's fellow literatus Le Tac (who had fled North with the defeated Mongols in the 1280s) shows in his *Short Record of Annan* (1333) the literati's acceptance of the spiritual power of the cult of Phu Dong.[15]

Now, preparing plans in the tent, one definitely gains victory as far as a thousand *li* away. It is the achievement of excellent generals bringing the army to victory. The Court Minister Ly Cong Binh shattered the bandits from Zhenla [Angkor in Cambodia] in Nghe An Prefecture [to the south] and dispatched men to report back on the victory. Ly Than Tong then ought to have reported the victory at the Royal Ancestral temple [Thai Mieu] and to have announced the merit of the victory in the Royal Hall so as to award the service to the state by Ly Cong Binh and the other subduers of the enemy. Instead that day the king arranged to attribute these accomplishments to Buddhism and Daoism, going to Buddhist temples and Daoist shrines to give thanks to them. That is *not the way* to reward those with merit! It was the warriors who had the victorious energy [V: *khi*; C: *qi*].

Le Van Huu

The shrine of the Soaring-to-Heaven Spirit is located in Phu Dong village. In the past, the land was in chaos. Suddenly there appeared a prestigious and ethical person who commanded a popular following. This person led troops to suppress the rebellions. Finally, he flew up into the sky and disappeared. His name is the Soaring-to-Heaven King. The local people set up a shrine to worship him.

Le Tac

[Ngo Si Lien, DVSKTT, 3, 30b–31a; trans. John K. Whitmore;
Le Tac, An Nam chi luoc, 41; trans. Tran Quoc Vuong,
"Legend of Ong Giong," 25]

TUE TRUNG

THIEN BELIEFS (LATE THIRTEENTH CENTURY)

Even as literati thought was strengthening in Dai Viet, during the latter decades of the thirteenth century the Thien school of Buddhism sought to dominate and integrate the other strands of Buddhist thought in the kingdom. Here the key figure of Tue Trung (1230–1291), a major influence on the Tran aristocracy, expresses his views in two poems. Tue Trung was the teacher of King Tran Nhan Tong (r. 1278–1308), and his beliefs laid the foundation for the Bamboo Grove (Truc Lam) school of Thien Buddhism in the fourteenth century. Tue Trung stresses one's inner Buddhahood and the integration of time, past, present, and future. He believed that controlling the Two Wrong Views and establishing the Dharmadhatu (Realm of Ultimate

---

15. See Le Quy Don, "On *ly* and *khi*" (chap. 4).

Reality) were necessary for achieving this total oneness in time and space for the realm, beliefs that also were fundamental to the effort to achieve unity in Dai Viet by the Tran monarchy in the first third of the fourteenth century. In the late eighteenth century, this Truc Lam school of Thien Buddhism reappeared, this time with the literati's support.[16]

AN ORDINARY PERSON AND SAGE ARE NO DIFFERENT

The self is formless. It comes from the Void.
Illusory transformations and distinctions constitute the Two Wrong
    Views.
We humans are as transient as dew and frost.
Ordinary persons and sages are as transient as thunder and lightning.
Meritorious reputation and riches and honors, these are as transient as
    floating clouds.
Happenings in a lifetime are like flying arrows.
When one glances upward at the rising stars, they are as capricious
    as the emotions.
It is like searching for steamed bread and throwing away noodles.
Eyebrows taper horizontally and noses droop down.
Buddhas and all beings are the same.
Who is an ordinary person and who is a sage?
Even if one searches throughout the ages, the powers of the senses
    have no nature.
Mindlessness has neither being nor non-being.
Thought is neither about wrong nor about right views.

ILLUSION AND ENLIGHTENMENT ARE NO DIFFERENT

When illusion goes, there is formlessness and form.
When enlightenment comes, there is neither form nor formlessness.
Form and formlessness, illusion and enlightenment,
Are a single principle. Past and present are the same.
When false beliefs arise, the Three Paths arise.
When Reality is unimpeded, the Five Visions are unimpeded.
When it is extinguished, the Mind is peaceful.
The ocean of birth and death is endless.
When there is no birth, there is no extinction.
When nothing arises, nothing ends.

---

16. See Ngo Thi Nham, "The Sound of Emptiness," and Phan Huy Ich, "Preface to *The Sound of the True Great and Perfect Enlightenment from the Bamboo Grove*" (both in chap. 4).

If one is only able to forget the Two Wrong views,
The Dharmadhatu fuses entirely.

[Thuong Si, *Thuong Si ngu luc*, 23a–24a; trans.
Wolters, *Two Essays*, 130]

LY TE XUYEN

THE TRUNG SISTERS (1329)

The purpose of the royal Bamboo Grove sect of Thien Buddhism for the Tran kings in the aftermath of the Mongol wars was to establish a Buddhist orthodoxy for Dai Viet, one that fused the various strands of earlier thought and also united the kingdom itself. Just as Tran Minh Tong (r. 1314–1357) sought a unified belief system focused on the Bamboo Grove school of Thien Buddhism and based on Tue Trung's teachings, a new text, the *Departed Spirits of the Viet Realm*, was compiled in 1329 by the Buddhist official Ly Te Xuyen. This text organized the heroic spirit cults that had helped defeat the Mongols to protect the land, the monarchy, and the Buddhist world. As we saw in the earlier portions of this text, Ly Te Xuyen included tales from Chinese sources, *Records Declaring the Ultimate*, and Do Thien's *History*. This work, too, represented the unity of time and space for Dai Viet, as it brought together spirits from both the past and scattered localities of the land. One of Ly Te Xuyen's cultic tales is of the Trung sisters, the heroines of a revolt against Han China in the first century c.e. In this tale, Ly Te Xuyen stresses the efficacy of the cult and its strong connection to the Thien community.

The Two Trung Ladies

History records the elder sister's name as Trac and the younger sister's name as Nhi. They were originally of the Lac line and were daughters of Lac generals in our Jiao province. They were from the sub-prefecture of Me Linh in Phong province.

The elder sister was wedded to Thi Sach, a man from Chu Dien sub-prefecture who had courageous strength, as well as a heroic spirit, and who manifested an auspicious birth. Governor To Dinh arranged to use the law to bring Thi Sach down. The elder sister was furious. Together with her younger sister, she raised an army and ran out To Dinh, attacking and taking our province of Jiao. Because of this, Rinan, Hepu, and Jiuzhen looked to their fame and responded by taking more than sixty-five towns in Linh Ngoai [Beyond the Passes]. The sisters installed themselves as queens of [the land of] Viet, ruling from Chu Dien, and took the surname Rung. At that time, To Dinh fled to Nan Hai.

The Han ruler Guangwu [r. 25–58] heard of this and was furious. He banished Dinh to Dam Nhi and sent Ma Vien and Liu Long to bring a large army to strike them. When they reached Lang Bac, the ladies fought back. Their followers were few and did not withstand the attack; they retreated to defend Cam Khe. The band became more dispersed by the day. The ladies were isolated and died in battle.

The local people pitied them and built a temple for their worship. On many occasions its divine responsiveness has been manifest. Now the temple is in An Hat sub-prefecture. King Ly Anh Tong [r. 1138–1175], because of drought, ordered meditation Thien masters who strictly kept Buddhist principles to pray there for rain. The sought-for rain was obtained, and refreshing air spread among the people. The king was delighted to see this. Suddenly, when he was sleeping, he saw two women. Their faces were fair and their brows like willows. Their robes were green and their trousers red. Their hats were red and they wore belts. They rode atop steel horses with the rain to have an audience. The king was taken aback and asked who they were. They replied, "We are the two Trung Sisters. By the order of God on High, we have made rain." The king awoke and, being moved by this, he ordered the restoration of the temple and the preparation of ceremonial offerings for a sacrifice. He then sent an official to carry them in procession to the north of the city citadel, where the Vu So temple was built to worship the sisters. Later, they again appeared in a dream to the king, asking that a temple be built at Co Lai. The sovereign complied with this and appointed them Chaste Divine Ladies.

[Ly Te Xuyen, *VDULT*; trans. Ostrowski and Zottoli,
Departed Spirits, 22–23]

TRUONG HAN SIEU

A LITERATUS'S INSCRIPTION FOR A BUDDHIST TEMPLE (1339)

In the early fourteenth century, the literati continued to strengthen classical thought in Dai Viet, led by the scholar Chu Van An. Chu Van An founded his own school just south of the capital and was considered the first true Confucian teacher in Dai Viet. He was allied with a minister at the royal court, Truong Han Sieu, who composed the following inscription for the Khai Nghiem Buddhist temple as a favor for an official. As had Le Van Huu before him, Truong Han Sieu attacked what he viewed as an aberrant Buddhism and emphasized classical thought and schools.

Scoundrels who had lost all notion of Buddhist asceticism only thought of taking possession of beautiful monasteries and gardens, building for themselves luxurious residences, and surrounding themselves with a host of servants. . . . People became monks by the thousands so as to get food without having to plough and clothes without having to weave. Husbands and wives often left their families and villages. Alas! They have departed far from the sages! . . . In the provinces, villages, and hamlets, there are "no schools that discipline the people by teaching them the duties proper to parents and younger brothers." How can the people be other than disorderly?

I said, "Since the fact that Buddhist temples were ruined and later reconstructed is not my will, what do I have to say about the building and engraving of their stone steles?" On the other hand, our sagely court now wishes to develop majestic styles to rescue popular customs. Thus, heretical beliefs must be removed in order to revive the orthodox teachings. Those who are literati must not promote anything different from the classical way of Yao and Shun and should not write anything other than the teachings of Confucius and Mencius. Hence, if now I am going to present some Buddhist discourses, whom will I be deceiving?

However, Chu Tue served as an officer expert in official affairs on the Royal Council. At his late age, he had no further desire for official life and was fond of bestowing charity. Consequently, he refused generous official salaries and voluntarily retired. This is what I wish to learn from him, but have not been able to realize. Thus, I record the inscription for him on this stone.

[*Tho van Ly Tran*, 2, 1, 746–50; trans. Nguyen Nam,
"Being Confucian in Sixteenth Century Vietnam," 155]

THE LITERATI'S NEW WORLDVIEW
(LATE FOURTEENTH CENTURY)

By the second half of the fourteenth century, the school of classical thought was becoming rooted in the intellectual tradition of Dai Viet. Tran Nguyen Dan, a royal prince and scholar, composed the following poem (included in Le Quy Don's eighteenth-century *Complete Anthology of Vietnamese Poetry*) celebrating its founder, the scholar Chu Van An, as the Han Yu of his land. Han Yu had been a great scholar in the Tang dynasty who also had celebrated classical thought in his own land while living in an age in which Buddhism was predominant. The adoption of Chu Van An's school of classical thought led to the development of a notion of Vietnamese antiquity linked to that of the North, as recorded in the *Short History of Dai Viet* (1380s). By the end of the fourteenth century, this new school of thought had become the orthodoxy of the southern regime of Ho Quy Ly (r. 1400–1407), emphasizing Han Yu of the Tang dynasty rather than Zhu Xi and the Neo-Confucians of the Song dynasty (recorded in the *Complete Chronicle of Dai Viet* [1479], by Ngo Si Lien). Later histories, down to the present day, have deepened this sense of the far past for the Vietnamese.

The waves of the tide of the ocean of learning were renewed, and
customs were again simple and pure.

The highest college had found its proper man, a Mount Tai
    and Great Dipper.[17]
He plumbed the classics and was widely read in the histories.
His achievement was great.
As a result, old men were respected and scholars were honored.
Government and teaching were renewed.

Tran Nguyen Dan

In the time of King Zhuang of Zhou [696–682 B.C.E.], here in Gia Ninh [in
Phong, to the west of the Red River Delta], there was an extraordinary man
who was able to force the submission of all the aboriginal tribes by using the
magical arts. He styled himself King Hung, established his capital at Van
Lang, and named his realm the Kingdom of Van Lang. He used simplicity and
purity as the basis for customs and knotted cords for government. The realm
was handed down through eighteen generations and each ruler styled himself
King Hung.

Short History of Dai Viet

[In 1392, twelfth month, so early 1393], Le [later Ho] Quy Ly [1336–1407] composed "Clarifying the Way" [Minh Dao] in fourteen chapters, presenting it to
the throne. In summary, this work took the Duke of Zhou as the foremost sage
and Confucius as the foremost teacher. In the Temple of Literature, Le Quy Ly
placed the Duke of Zhou in the primary place, facing south, while Confucius
sat to the side, facing west. Le Quy Ly held that the *Analects of Confucius* had
four doubtful points: when the Master Confucius went to visit the young
woman Nanzi,[18] when Confucius ran short of provisions in the state of Chen
[V: Tran],[19] and the two occasions when the scoundrels Gong Shan and Fu Rao
called for him and Confucius wished to help them. Le Quy Ly took Han Yu [of
the Tang] as "plundering the Nho [classical learning]"[20] and stated that [the
Neo-Confucian intellectual lineage of] Zhou Dunyi, Cheng Hao and Cheng
Yi, Yang Shi, Luo Congyan, Li Tong, and Master Zhu [Xi] [during the Song]
may have had broad learning, but they were of little talent. They had little value
for contemporary affairs and focused on plagiarizing the past. The Senior Ruler
bestowed on Le Quy Ly a proclamation exhorting him further and had the
book promulgated widely.

---

17. The *New History of the Tang Dynasty* (*Xin Tang shu*, 1060) refers to Han Yu as Mount Tai
and the Big Dipper.

18. Nanzi was the beautiful and lascivious wife of the Duke of Wei.

19. This is a comment on the present Tran dynasty in Dai Viet.

20. This is a Tang dynasty phrase that refers to the achievement of the wisdom of the rulers
of antiquity.

An official in the Royal Academy, Doan Xuan Loi, thereupon presented a memorial stating that Le Quy Ly's position was untenable. Doan Xuan Loi was exiled.

Ngo Si Lien

[Le Quy Don, *TVTL*, 3, 20b–21a; trans. Wolters, *Two Essays*, 21; *VSL*, 1, 1a; trans. Taylor, *Birth of Vietnam*, 309; Ngo Si Lien, *DVSKTT*, 8, 22a–22b; trans. Whitmore, *Vietnam*, 34]

GOVERNANCE

PHAP THUAN

ADVISING THE KING (LATE TENTH CENTURY)

In the tenth century, as the Tang dynasty's control disintegrated and the area of what is now northern Vietnam loosened itself from Northern control, the personal leadership of chieftains was the primary source of political legitimacy. Carrying on that leadership from one generation to the next proved difficult because primogeniture was not fully established. Instead of sons being able to succeed and gain power, powerful men (among them Dinh Bo Linh, Le Hoan, and Ly Cong Uan) moved to seize the throne of the evolving Dai Viet. In the late tenth century, these chieftains competed for broader regional power and relied on the counsel of Buddhist monks. The strongman Le Hoan sought the advice of the dharma master (Phap) Thuan, who counseled the king to demonstrate awe and planned inaction—that is, to embody the royal role so effectively that action to sustain the throne would not be necessary. His advice is recounted in the collection *Eminent Monks of the Thien Community* (1337). This kind of counsel to rulers became an essential component of Vietnamese models of governance, manifested both in the ritual of presenting memorials to the throne and in the less formal, spoken advice offered by close confidants.

When the former Le dynasty started to establish itself, Phap Thuan was instrumental in deciding its political policies. When independence was gained and the country was at peace, he did not hold any office, nor did he accept any reward. King Le Hoan respected him more and more. He never called him by his name but always referred to him as Do Phap Su [Dharma Master Do] and entrusted him with literary responsibilities. Thuan told his Lord,

> The good fortune of the country is like a spreading vine,
> In the Southern land there is great peace.
> If Your Majesty stays in the palace without contrived activity,
> Then everywhere the clash of weapons will cease.

[*TUTA*, 49b; trans. Nguyen Tu Cuong, *Zen in Medieval Vietnam*, 77]

OMENS AND PROPHECIES (1337)

In the early eleventh century, another strongman, Ly Cong Uan (Ly Thai To [r. 1009–1028]), rose to power and, with omens paving the way for his ascent, closely associated himself with the Buddhist establishment. Prophecies predicted that the Ly would take the throne and that Dai Viet would become an independent country. Such omens and prophecies were a significant component of Vietnamese political culture, and records of such supernatural manifestations are frequently found in both official and unofficial texts. Omens, in particular, were important retrospective markers of dynastic change or other transitions of leadership. The occurrences described here were recorded in the Buddhist text *Eminent Monks of the Thien Community*.

At this time Le Ngoa Trieu, the son of Le Hoan who murdered his older brother, the crown prince, was on the throne, a cruel tyrant. Both Heaven and men detested his behavior. King Ly Thai To was then his bodyguard and had not ascended to the throne. During those years strange omens appeared incessantly in many forms: a white dog with hair on his back that looked like the characters *thien tu* [Son of Heaven] appeared in the Ham Thoai Hall, Ung Thai Tam temple, Co Phap Prefecture [Ly Thai To's home]; lightning struck a kapok tree and left writing on its trunk; sounds of chanting at night were heard around the grave of Great Lord Hien Khanh [Ly Thai To's father]; insects gnawed at the bark of a bastard banyan tree at Song Lam temple forming the character *quoc* [country]. All these events were interpreted as omens that the former Le dynasty was going to collapse and the Ly was going to flourish.

[*TUTA*, 53a; trans. Nguyen Tu Cuong, *Zen in Medieval Vietnam*, 421–22]

THE SPIRIT OF PHU DONG (LATE ELEVENTH CENTURY)

When Ly Cong Uan (Ly Thai To [r. 1009–1028]) took the throne at the start of the eleventh century, he established his capital in the center of the Red River Delta at Thang Long. He then began to integrate his realm in a spiritual/conceptual sense by joining the spirits of the localities with the Buddhist temples as protectors. By the late eleventh century, this episode had come to form part of the Ly royal tradition as defined in the *Records Declaring the Ultimate*. The cultic tale is of the famed spirit of Phu Dong village, not far from the capital, and can also be seen in the *Short Record of Annan* (1333), by Le Tac. The episode involving the magical appearance of writing on the bark of the tree was later mimicked by Nguyen Trai, the fifteenth-century adviser to Le Loi, the future founder of the later Le dynasty, when he forged such a divine message, anointing Le Loi as the future emperor of Dai Viet.

Soaring-to-Heaven, Eminently Courageous, Luminously Responding, Majestic and Responding Great King

According to the *Records Declaring the Ultimate* and the lore passed down over the generations, the King was the incarnation of the local earth spirit of the Kien So pagoda.[21]

Long ago, the Buddhist priest Chi Thanh [Cam Thanh (d. 860)] resided at the Kien So pagoda. In Phu Dong village he erected a house for the local earth spirit to the right side of the pagoda gate. It served as a clean place at which to recite prayers. Years and months went by, and the buildings gradually disappeared. Having lost its old form, spiritual truth-seekers and meditators had no way to authenticate the place. The local people were fond of ghosts, burning incense and bringing prayers there. They improperly called it a temple of obscenity.

After some time, the meditation Thien Master Da Bao repaired the Buddhist pagoda. Considering the temple a temple of obscenity, he wished to destroy it. One day on a tree at the spirit's temple, there was seen a prayer of eight lines which read,

> Whoever can protect the Buddha dharma,
> Be a pillar consenting to dwell in the Buddha's garden.
> If not of our seed,
> Be soon removed forthwith to another place.
> If you do not enroll in the Diamond Department of the spirits
> With Vajapani and Narayana [defending the Dharma],
> The masses, who are like the dust that fills the air,
> Will serve the Buddha only to bring about oppression and error.

Another day, after the prayer there appeared the spirit's response in a poem of eight lines that read,

> The Buddha dharma is greatly compassionate,
> Its majestic light covering the world.
> The ten thousand spirits all face it and are transformed;
> The three divisions of the world completely return and revolve
> around it.
> My teacher carries out the order;
> What demon dares come first?
> Desirous of always according with Buddhist discipline,
> Old and young guard the Buddha's garden.

The priest was taken aback at this and again had an altar set up to keep the Buddhist precepts and to make regular penance.

---

21. The "King" refers to the historical figure and to the spirit of the cult that he became.

When Ly Thai To was a hidden dragon [before he became king], he knew of Da Bao's high virtue, and together they made offerings. Once Ly Thai To had accepted the throne, he went on an excursion to visit the pagoda. The Buddhist priest greeted his carriage. Passing by the side of the pagoda, the priest raised his voice and asked, "Son of Buddha! Can you naturally congratulate the new Son of Heaven?" The response was seen in four lines on the bark of the tree:

> The king's virtue is as great as the Heavens and the Earth;
> His prestige calms the eight boundaries [that is, everywhere].
> Those in gloom and darkness receive favor,
> So inundated, they are given to soar to Heaven.

Thai To gazed on and recited this. He knew well its meaning and awarded the spirit the title Soaring-to-Heaven Spirit King. The writing suddenly vanished. The sovereign was amazed at this. He ordered laborers to fashion a statue of the spirit, eminent and lofty in appearance, as well as eight painted statues of attendants. Completion was announced, and again below the great tree there was seen a poem of four lines that read,

> A bowl of merit and virtue water,
> According with destiny, transforms the world.
> Brightly, how brightly and repeatedly shines the torch;
> The image is extinguished as the sun mounts the mountain.

The priest took this hymn and presented it.

> [Ly Te Xuyen, *VDULT*; trans. Ostrowski and Zottoli,
> *Departed Spirits*, 71–74]

FUNERAL INSCRIPTION OF A COURT MINISTER (1159)

Ministers like Do Anh Vu (1114–1159) dominated the aristocratic Ly court of Dai Viet throughout most of the twelfth century. In this selection, his rise to power and his work in governing the realm is described in a segment of his funeral inscription, as recorded in later documents.

From his youth, the Duke Do Anh Vu was slender and graceful with a snowy pure complexion and a radiant countenance. In the year of Giap Thin, the fifth year of the Thien Phuc Due Vu reign period [1124], King [Ly] Nhan Tong [r. 1072–1127], noticing Do Anh Vu's godlike demeanor and perceiving his intelligence, selected him to dwell in the royal compound. The Duke was eminent in dancing upon embroidered cushions with shields and battleaxe, and in singing "The Return of the Phoenix" while dancing with supple elegance. Merchants arriving from afar and those traveling for pleasure never failed to attend his performances.

In the *dinh mui* year [1127], [the new] king Than Tong's [r. 1127–1137] court chose Do Anh Vu to serve in the pavilion; he was ranked in a capped position[22] over the six lords-in-waiting to administer the women's apartments of the inner court. He governed every kind of affair; the king entrusted everything to him. When it came to writing, numerical calculation, archery, chariot driving, medicine, acupuncture, and diagnosing illness by taking the pulse, there was nothing in which he was not proficient. As for geomancy, military tactics, *hu bo*, and *bac dich*,[23] there was nothing about these that he did not study. It can be said: "The gentleman is without mere abilities."

In the *dinh ty* year, the ninth month of the first year of the Thieu Minh reign period [1137], the king was not well. He washed his face, leaned upon a table, and said: "There is no one but the Duke to whom we can entrust the Ly family." When the king died, the Duke, together with the Hien Chi Queen Mother, went to Thuong Thanh Lodge to greet [the new king] Ly Anh Tong [r. 1138–1175], the two-year-old son of the just-deceased king and the queen mother, and to advance him up the imperial stairs. The Duke upheld the laws of the court, and all the officials behaved with discipline and followed orders; he attended to the numerous affairs of the kingdom, and all the people looked up to him with respect. The queen mother rewarded him for his service to the state, commending his meritorious efforts. She promoted the Duke to Kiem Hieu Court Minister [Thai Pho]. Then, in the ninth month of the *mau ngo* year [1138], she promoted him to Phu Quoc Thai Uy [prime minister and generalissimo] and conferred on him the royal surname Ly. Military affairs were completely in his hands.

At that time, in the region of Ke Dong on the northern border, a strange lad called Suy Vi caused great excitement by declaring himself to be the orphaned son of Ly Nhan Tong, the deceased ruler; Suy Vi assembled his truculent partisans and usurped the title of Binh Nguyen Great General. The king commanded the minister Luu Cao Nhi to go out and subdue Suy Vi, but the rebels increased even more. During those days, the Duke lay down to sleep but could not rest; he went to meals but had no taste for food. So, he appealed to the king, saying: "I have heard it said that, when the sovereign worries, his minister is humiliated, and when the sovereign is humiliated, his minister is dead. When barbarians trouble the realm it is the fault of the minister."

The three jurisdictions of Nghe An, Thanh Hoa, and Phu Luong to the south of the Red River Delta were all bestowed upon the Duke in fief. The Duke prohibited barbarism and eradicated vulgarity, forcing violators to salute with

22. That is, he wore a cap marking him as an "adult."

23. *Hu bo* is a game that involves throwing pieces of wood, often used in gambling, and *bac dich* is a type of chess similar to Japanese *go*.

folded hands and to endure the punishment of being tattooed on their faces; pirates, rebels, and frontier people lost courage and returned to obedience to the imperial court.

[*Épigraphie en chinois*, no. 19; trans. Taylor, "Voices Within and Without," 64, 66–67]

NGO SI LIEN

THE OATH RITUAL (1479)

In 1225, the new Tran dynasty took power from the Ly, moving from the lower Red River Delta in the east to the capital of Thang Long and incorporating the lower and upper delta regions. The new dynasty continued the Ly dynasty's rituals, particularly the ceremony of the blood oath to the spirit of the Mountain of the Bronze Drum, in which lords from the different regions of the country swore allegiance to the throne. Elsewhere in Southeast Asia, such an oath was made after drinking sacral water; in Dai Viet, animals were sacrificed, and their blood became the sacral liquid. This ritual continued to be practiced in later centuries. The ceremony in Thang Long is described in the *Complete Chronicle of Dai Viet*, by Ngo Si Lien.

[In 1227], the throne announced the terms for the ceremony of swearing the oath of allegiance according to the old ways of the Ly court and began to set it up. These rites were as follows:

Each year on the fourth day of the fourth month, the lords and all the officials at cockcrow are to come straight outside the gate of the city. As the day brightens, they are to advance into the court. The king is to establish himself at the Huu Lang Gate of the Great Brightness Palace. All the officials in martial garb are to prostrate themselves twice, then step back. Each is to fall into martial rank according to the proper order, and all are to go out the Western Gate of the city to the Temple of the Spirit of the Bronze Drum. Together they are to take the oath before the spirit and drink the blood of the sacrificial victim. The court minister is to observe directly the pronouncement of the oath as they state: "May I be a subject totally loyal, and may I be an official pure and honest. If I should violate this oath, may the spirit strike me dead!"

The oath having been sworn, the lords order the gate to be closed. Those officials deficient in pronouncing the oath are to be fined five strings of cash. On the day of the oath ceremony, men and women from all over line the roads in order to see and hear the grand affair, as though they were of high status.

[Ngo Si Lien, *DVSKTT*, 5, 4a–4b; trans. John K. Whitmore]

NGO SI LIEN

OFFICIALS AND VILLAGE REGISTERS (1479)

The Tran dynasty maintained the major court ritual of the previous Ly dynasty but changed the administration of the realm. One change was better central control of resources through the maintenance of village registers of population and land, as the first text illustrates. The Tran rulers also began to assign literati-officials to local areas, thereby strengthening the capital's control over the outer areas, as the second text demonstrates. Both texts are from the *Complete Chronicle of Dai Viet*. Such registers formed a major element of governance in Dai Viet for many centuries, and these crucial records were periodically updated, particularly after a dynastic transition or internal disorder. The extent of state control over local resources through the use of these registers fluctuated with the power of the capital.[24]

[In 1242], the second month, throughout the land, there were twelve jurisdictions with protectors and captains, primary and secondary officials, to rule them. In all the village registers, offices will be established for large and small villages, with officials ranks five and up in the large village offices, and those ranks five and below in the small village offices. Where there are two, three, or four villages joined together, a main official, a clerk, and an administrator will serve as the officials of the community. They are to compile population figures for males: adults as healthy adult males, young men as young males, those sixty years of age as elderly, and the very old as infirm. Those adult males with land are to pay cash and grain, while those with no land owe nothing. Having two *mau* [1 *mau* is 3,600 square meters] of land, one pays one string [*quan*] of cash, with three or four *mau*, two strings of cash, with five *mau* and above, three strings. The rent for each *mau* of field is one hundred liters [*thang*] of grain. . . .

In 1244, the first month, the throne sent out orders to civil officials to serve throughout the land in all twelve jurisdictions and the prefectures. In the prefectures, there are to be prefects, and in the jurisdictions, administrators, while the districts will have water transport officers and assistants to take charge of river control.

[Ngo Si Lien, *DVSKTT*, 5, 13a, 14a; trans. John K. Whitmore]

LE VAN HUU

A LITERATUS'S CRITIQUE OF A PAST
COURT MINISTER (1272)

Literati voices from outside the royal court were included in the official chronicle of the thirteenth century when the new Tran dynasty arrived from the coast and brought

---

24. Another example of a ruler's ordering an updating of both population and field registers is Quang Trung Emperor, "Edict Encouraging Agriculture" (chap. 4).

scholars specializing in classical texts into the court and the government. In his *Chronicle of Dai Viet*, Le Van Huu, one of these coastal literati, expressed his intense dislike for Do Anh Vu's government of the preceding century while arguing for the proper procedure of memorializing the throne.

Do Anh Vu went in and out of the Forbidden Palace and had an intimate affair with the queen mother; there is no greater crime than this. Vu Dai and the others should have petitioned the throne with an accusation of wickedness against Do Anh Vu; then seizing, binding, imprisoning, and putting Do Anh Vu to death would have been correct. However, leading a crowd of men to rush suddenly and without authority through the Viet Thanh Gate, frightening and coercing an immature sovereign, violently demanding a royal edict to seize and imprison Do Anh Vu, and then accepting gold from the queen mother, and paying no heed to Nguyen Duong's words, ending up being killed by Do Anh Vu, and involving several tens of other men, this was simply a case of raising a tiger to bestow grief.

[Ngo Si Lien, *DVSKTT*, 4, 8b–9a; trans. Taylor, "Voices Within and Without," 76]

LE VAN HUU

UTILIZING THE PAST TO DEFINE THE PRESENT (1272)

In his official *Chronicle of Dai Viet*, Le Van Huu explained the Tran dynasty's new frame of reference, one that separated North and South. Unlike the Ly dynasty, which had accepted its Northern heritage by venerating the accomplishments and contributions of Shi Xie and Gao Pian, the Tran sought a Southern figure who had stood against the North. Reaching back to the second century B.C.E., Le Van Huu drew on Trieu Da, a Southern warlord of Northern descent, to express the dynasty's strong sense of the South standing against the North and of parity between the two courts. Later dynasties inherited and extended this deep sense of the Vietnamese past.

Martial Emperor Trieu Da, succeeding in opening up and developing our land of Viet, named himself emperor of the country and, contending with the Han dynasty, published a letter proclaiming himself emperor, thereby originating the imperial inheritance in our land of Viet; his achievement can be said to be great. If those who later were emperors in the land of Viet could have emulated Martial Emperor Trieu Da in carefully guarding the frontier, establishing the army and the country, and keeping friendly relations with neighboring countries in order to preserve the throne with humanity, then the borderlands would have been protected in perpetuity and the Northerners would not again have been to able to stare arrogantly at us.

[Ngo Si Lien, *DVSKTT*, *Outer Records*, 2, 8a–8b; trans. Taylor, *Birth of Vietnam*, 293]

LY TE XUYEN

THE IDEAL OFFICIAL (1329)

In the government of the early fourteenth century, ministers and officials were supposed to be extensions of the persona of the king, in this case Tran Minh Tong (r. 1314–1357). The text *Departed Spirits of the Viet Realm*, compiled by Ly Te Xuyen, expresses the ideal official in the cultic tale of Ly Hoang.

Majestically Enlightening, Ardently Courageous, Manifesting Loyalty, Assisting Sacredness, Believing and Assisting Great King

The prince was of the Ly line and was named Hoang. He was the eighth child of king Ly Thai Tong [r. 1028–1054], and his mother was queen Le Thi Trinh Minh. He was a loyal, filial, and carefully reverential person. Firm and daring in his actions, he was called the Eighth Son Prince.

In the first year of the Can Phu Huu Dao era [1039], he was chosen to serve as a tax collector in Nghe An province. He held that office for several years, not violating the smallest thing. He was famous for his fairness and honesty. The king loved him, granting him the title Majestically Enlightening Crown Prince and giving him control over the military and civil affairs in that province.

At that time, Ly Thai Tong wished to make a punitive attack against Champa. He ordered the prince separately to build a secret country estate called Fort Ba Hoa. It was to be secure and well-defended, with deep moats and high hedges on all four sides. The interior of the fort had to be large enough to hold thirty to forty thousand troops, and the treasury had to hold enough wages and provisions for three years. Then when the sovereign punished the south, indeed he scored a great victory. The Champa king, Sa Dau, was beheaded in battle [1044]. His wives and concubines, men and women, carriages, gold and silver, and other riches to be reckoned in the thousands were captured.

As the king returned in victory, he came to the military post in that province and saw that the prince had capably handled his tasks without fault, implementing official orders better each day. The king appointed the prince to administer the entire circuit and promoted him to the rank of high prince.

A royal order was then issued to bestow on the prince the registers of a circuit in that province, including six districts, four cantons, sixty communes, and all the inhabitants. In all, there were 46,450 households and 54,364 individuals [adult males?]. Furthermore, it was commanded by royal decree that each and every leader of a commune in a canton from then on could be installed only as high collector to govern the commune and must not, as at first, be excessively styled as Crown Prince Recordkeeper or Royal Palace Recordkeeper.

The prince, however, because most of the Di and Lao peoples from the coasts and mountains of Nghe An had not yet submitted, offered invitations for them to visit him as their superior, and he appealed for them to yield to his command, to grasp the royal insignia, and to patrol the royal frontier. The Di leaders all submitted to him, and thus five districts, twenty-two forts, and fifty-six bamboo palisades were taken. Then there was an edict to measure three borders of the province [north, west, south, with the sea on the east]. Stone steles were erected and engraved to record meritorious acts in these distant places.

In the second year of the Long Thuy Thai Binh era [1055] of Ly Thanh Tong [r. 1054–1072], the prince pacified the bandit groups of Ong Yet and Ly Bi. When he returned, a rumor reached the [new] king that [his brother] the prince was acting as a despot and independently using the troops for punitive expeditions. The king suspected him, and the prince resigned his offices. He had overseen provincial offices for sixteen years, and his good reputation was heard more widely every day. The people trusted and loved him. When they heard of his resignation, the people strove to hold on to his carriage and to push his horses, weeping with desire to detain him.

[Ly Te Xuyen, *VDULT*; trans. Ostrowski and
Zottoli, *Departed Spirits*, 28–31]

HOW TO GOVERN (1337)

King Tran Minh Tong tried hard to govern the land according to Buddhist precepts and thereby better unify it. *Eminent Monks of the Thien Community*, a Buddhist text, expressed the idea of governance in a way that brought together both the Buddhist and the sage kings' approaches. Its spokesman was the Buddhist monk Vien Thong (1080–1151). The "true gentleman/mean man" dichotomy came from classic Confucianism. The strong emphasis on upright officials was a prominent theme in Vietnamese ruminations on the successful administration of the state, and eighteenth- and nineteenth-century court memorials and edicts regularly emphasized the need for skilled and upright officials to ensure stability and successful governance.

The world is like an instrument. Put it in a safe place, and it is safe; put it in a perilous place, and it is in peril. It all depends on how the leader of the people behaves himself. If his benevolence is in harmony with the hearts and minds of the people, then they will love him as a parent and look up to him like the sun and the moon. This is putting people in a safe place.

Order or chaos depends on the behavior of the officials. If they can win the people over, then there is political order; if they lose the people's support, then there is upheaval. I have observed the activities of rulers of previous generations. No one succeeded without employing true gentlemen, or failed unless he employed petty men.

When we trace how these things come about, they do not happen overnight, but develop gradually. Just as Heaven and Earth cannot abruptly produce cold and hot weather, but must change gradually through the seasons like spring and autumn, kings cannot suddenly bring about prosperity or decline; rather it is a gradual process depending on their good or bad activities.

The sage kings of antiquity [to the North] knew this principle, and so they modeled themselves on Heaven and never ceased to rely on virtue to cultivate themselves; they modeled themselves on Earth and never ceased to rely on virtue to pacify the people. To cultivate oneself means to be cautious within, as cautious as if one were walking on thin ice. To pacify people means to respect those who are below, to be respectful as one riding a horse holding worn-out reins.

If one can be like that, one cannot but succeed; if not, one cannot but fail. The gradual process of prosperity or decline depends on this.

[*TUTA*, 69a–69b; trans. Nguyen Tu Cuong,
Zen in Medieval Vietnam, 82–83]

LITERATI POEMS, LITERATI CONCERNS
(LATE FOURTEENTH CENTURY)

Social and economic tensions across the land led to increasing problems for the Tran dynasty. During the mid-fourteenth century, literati for the first time expressed in their poetry concerns about the well-being of the countryside and the people's livelihood, referring to "carriages and script," the classical phrase meaning a well-regulated government. The following are selections from poems by various scholars who spoke of the increasingly desperate situation in which they found themselves. These poems reflect the literati-officials' sense of responsibility for the people and their efforts to call the problems to the ruler's attention, a pattern that continued into the nineteenth century. In later centuries, literati memorials to the throne served this purpose, but at this time, the poems were their best option. Le Quy Don gathered these poems in his *Complete Anthology of Vietnamese Poetry* in the latter half of the eighteenth century. Chu Van An (1292–1370) founded the activist school of classical thought. Nguyen Phi Khanh (1355–1408) was the father of the famous minister Nguyen Trai (1380–1442) and the son-in-law of the aristocratic scholar Tran Nguyen Dan (1320–1390).

Chu Van An remembered his late ruler, Tran Minh Tong:

> But just as the ancient cassia sways in the wind and perfumes
>   the stone path,
> And the tender moss, soaked with water, hides the pine gate,
> So my heart is still not yet dust,
> For, when I hear talk of my late king [Tran Minh Tong], I secretly
>   wipe away my tears.

Nguyen Phi Khanh spoke on the need for good officials:

> The country in former times was a realm with scholarly officials.
> Today ordinary men serve in the Secretariat.
> I disdain one who, promoted a grade, boasts to his country neighbors.
> Who is to say that he has a purifying character when he does not
>   relieve the poor?
> A thousand miles of paddy are red as if they were all burnt.
> The countryside is groaning and sighing. I am unhappy.
> The people are wailing. They wait to be fed and clothed.
> Which of these families have precious things piled in mounds?

Tran Nguyen Dan spoke of the scholar-official Le Quat:

> You are forgetful of yourself in the vicissitudes of fortune.
> Your mind is impregnable. Your position is at the center.

Nguyen Phi Khanh spoke to a scholar friend:

> Your plans will permit some display of your skill in affairs of state.
> Repulsing the enemy in the final reckoning depends on a "worthy"
>   [virtuous person] who saves the times.

Tran Nguyen Dan spoke in honor of Pham Su Manh as a scholar of high integrity:

> The waxing of the sun and moon, man can easily see.
> But wisdom and stupidity, failure and success, these phenomena are
>   difficult to control.

Addressed examination officials:

> When the ruler repeatedly asks for a large number of graduates,
> You must put first loyal advice and only afterwards put literary flourishes.

In 1362 spoke of the hard times:

> For some years the summers have been dry and, moreover, the autumns
>   have been very wet.
> The crops have withered and the sprouts have been damaged.
> The harm has been widespread and serious.
> Thirty thousand scrolls of writing are of no use.
> This white head vainly carries a mind that loves the people.

Spoke of the good times before:

> After the civil examinations were over, one beheld military arts.
> When can this old servant of the Tran dynasty expect the return
>   of those times?

Nguyen Phi Khanh remembered the heroics of the Red River valley a century earlier:

> For the heroes of a hundred years ago, here was a battlefield,
> For all time this territory has guaranteed the country's survival.
> I rely on my poem to record the scene,
> And suggest that you are observing a country of carriages and script.
>> [Le Quy Don, *TVTL*, 3, nos. 32, 114, 121, 137, 143, 147, 229, 263, 272–75;
>> trans. Wolters, "Possibilities for a Reading," 388–91, 395]

HO QUY LY

DAI NGU AND THE MING COURT
(EARLY FIFTEENTH CENTURY)

After seizing the throne of Dai Viet in 1400, Le Quy Ly (r. 1400–1407) changed the name of Dai Viet to Dai Ngu (C: Da Yu, a classical reference) and changed his family name to Ho (C: Hu, again a classical link). Using the old Northern name for Dai Viet, Annan, Ho Quy Ly spoke of his country and his government to the Ming envoy by means of a poem, in which he spoke of "simple and pure customs." Ho Quy Ly also referred to the Han and Tang dynasties, during which Dai Viet had been part of China, thus demonstrating to the Ming envoy a shared cultural status. The names used to designate the state remained of great importance to subsequent rulers, and two nineteenth-century edicts on this topic, by the Gia Long and Minh Mang emperors, reveal the historical background of the decisions to change the name of the kingdom.

> You inquire about the state of affairs in Annan.
> Annan's customs are simple and pure.
> Moreover, official clothing is according to the Tang system.
> The rites and music that control intercourse between the ruler
>   and the officials
> are those of the Han.
> The jade brush unfolds new laws.
> The gold sword slices the scales of armor.
> Every year in the second or third month
> Peach and plum seeds are planted in spring.
>> [Le Quy Don, *TVTL*, 1, 25a–25b; trans. Wolters, *Two Essays*, 29]

SOCIETY AND CULTURE

LY THANH TONG

LIFE IN JAIL (1055)

Few descriptions of everyday life in the early centuries of Dai Viet survive. In this selection, the third ruler, Ly Thanh Tong (r. 1054–1072), worries about the people in prison and, in his reflections, provides a sense of life at that time from the perspective of the royal court in Thang Long, a perspective preserved in chronicles of the thirteenth and fourteenth centuries.

I live in a palace; I have charcoal to burn and foxskin garments to wear in wintry weather like this. I think of the prisoners in jail, suffering in bonds, the rights and wrongs of their cases not yet judged, with not enough food for their stomachs and not enough clothing for their bodies; they feel the wintry wind, and perhaps some who are innocent will die. I deeply sympathize with them. So order the officers to issue them mats and quilts and give them cooked rice twice a day.

The love I have for my children is like the parental feelings I have toward the people. The people, without knowing, become trapped in the law. I deeply sympathize with them. From now on, let those guilty of crime, whether light or serious, be treated with lenience.

[Ngo Si Lien, *DVSKTT*, 3, 1b, 3b; *VSL*, 2, 10a–10b; trans. Taylor, "Looking Behind the Viet Annals," 52]

FUNERAL INSCRIPTION OF DO ANH VU: LIFE OF A COURT MINISTER (1159)

In the mid-twelfth century, the funeral inscription carved in stone that portrayed the aristocratic family, life, and career of the court minister Do Anh Vu (1114–1159) described how he rose in Ly court society. The text is useful for revealing gender roles, showing how the behavior of aristocratic men and women was expressed in what were undoubtedly ideal terms, and describing medical knowledge. A more detailed discussion of Vietnamese medical practices can be found in the preface to Le Huu Trac's eighteenth-century medical compendium.[25]

This man we recognize as none other than Do Anh Vu, styled Quan The, from the line of the Thai Uy [highest military court title] Duke of Quach from Lung Tay. His [Do Anh Vu's] ancestor was the Duke of Quach, originally from Cau

---

25. See Le Huu Trac, "Discourse on Medical Training" (chap. 4).

Lau District in Te Giang, who served as the Thai Uy at the court of Ly Thai Tong [r. 1028–1054] and begat Thuong Kiet who served the court of Ly Nhan Tong [r. 1072–1128] as Thai Uy and upon whom was bestowed the national surname of Ly. Do Anh Vu's deceased father was named Tuong of the Do family and was a sister's son of the Thai Uy Duke Ly Thuong Kiet; his family dwelled in Tay Du village. In his youth, Do Tuong went to the capital and saw the daughter of an honorable family; her thoughts were pure and dignified, her nature was gentle and chaste, her smile surpassed the blossoms of spring, and her behavior was like beautiful jade. Do Tuong loved her elegant beauty and accordingly sent bridal gifts and inquired of her name to fix a betrothal; they gave birth to two children. The son, Do Anh Vu, was called Duke; the Thai Su [highest nonmilitary court title] Duke of Truong, Le Ba Ngoc, observed his rare strength of character and recognized his ability to serve the kingdom, so Le Ba Ngoc brought him up as his own son. The daughter was called Do Quynh Anh and was given in marriage to the Thi Trung [a court title] of the Pham family.

In the *canh ngo* year [1150], the King Ly Anh Tong [r. 1138–1175] was not well, so the Duke [Do Anh Vu] fasted and bathed, selected a place to erect an altar, instituted ritual, lifted a jade tablet, and prayed that he be substituted.[26] The Emperor of Heaven was moved by his loyalty and filial devotion and graciously bestowed a divine potion; this elixir of immortality immediately yielded an efficacious result. The Duke was accordingly rewarded with one thousand strings of silver cash and thirty-four rolls of silk.

Also this year, the Duke's paternal cousin, the official with the surname Do, had two daughters: the eldest was named Thuy [a character is missing here], the younger was named Thuy Chau. The king at this time prepared festive ceremonies in order to receive them as wives. Both sisters were without jealousy and were zealous to increase in virtue. They worked together [cultivating] vegetables and were very industrious. They served at bathing and washing without weariness.

In the *giap tuat* year [1154], Thuy Chau gave birth to Crown Prince Thien Bao. In the *binh ty* year [1156], she gave birth to a third prince. Consequently, the Duke day by day increased in honor. His position excelled all other ministers. In the whole kingdom, seldom has there been anyone to equal him.

In the eighth month of the *mau dan* year [1158], the Duke was bedridden with illness at his private house in Dien Lenh village. The king and the queen mother daily summoned the eminent physicians of the kingdom to administer medicine and acupuncture, and they commanded the Trung Su [title of an officer] of the inner palace to inspect and taste his food; they emptied the inner storehouse of its treasures in search of a remedy. A sacrificial mound was raised for the Nguu Thu ceremony. Brush-and-ink men together with fierce warriors all assembled for the Thai Lao sacrifice and proceeded to the altars of state and the ancestral temple of the ruling family to beg for the Duke's life. But when it

---

26. That is, that the king's illness be placed on Do Anh Vu instead of the king.

was understood from consulting the Duke's pulse that recovery was unlikely, preparations were made for funeral rites.

On the twentieth day of the first month of 1159, the Duke died. He had assisted his sovereign for twenty-two years and had attained the age of forty-six. The king and the queen mother wept bitterly for seven days, lamenting the collapse of the ridgepole and roof tiles of the kingdom. Delicacies were banished from palace meals and court business was postponed. Gifts to assist with funeral expenses and rules of abstinence exceeded the usual custom. The Duke was buried at Sung Nhan lane in An Lac village on land belonging to the ancestors of the Duke's mother. The court minister and Duke To Hien Thanh in accordance with an imperial decree, assisted with the mourning [funeral and burial arrangements]. Chu Trung was in charge of the ceremonies.

[*Épigraphie en chinois*, no. 19; trans. Taylor, "Voices Within and Without," 62, 68–70]

FUNERAL INSCRIPTION OF THE PHUNG THANH LADY: LIFE OF A COURT LADY (1175)

Representations of women were fairly rare in earlier Vietnamese history. The following is the funeral inscription of a secondary wife of King Ly Than Tong (r. 1127–1137), the younger sister of the king's primary wife. It shows the social interconnections of the elite through women and embellishes the ideal portrayal of aristocratic women, as seen in the preceeding funeral inscription of Do Anh Vu.

Ly Than Tong (r. 1128–1137), Nhan Hieu king's lady of the Le family, with the taboo name Lan Xuan, was the youngest daughter of the Phu Thien great prince. Her mother was a Thuy Thanh princess, eldest daughter of the Du Tong member of the royal line. Her grandmother, also a Thuy Thanh princess, was the eldest daughter of the ruler Ly Thanh Tong (r. 1054–1072). Her grandfather was an official and Buddhist figure who was the adopted grandson of the Ngu Man great prince through his uncle. She was of the lineage of the Le family's Dai Hanh Hoang De [Le Hoan (r. 980–1005)]. Her father, the Phu Thien great prince, had twenty children in all, one a queen, three ladies of the court, four princesses, and twelve royal sons.

In the second year, *giap dan*, of the Thien Chuong Bao Tu era [1134], the king first received the youngest daughter of the Phu Thien great prince. Her eldest sister was the queen mother, Cam Thanh. Seeing the beauty of the lady who also possessed the Four Virtues, the king married her as his wife of the third rank. Shortly afterward, she entered the royal palace and brilliantly learned the way of a lady. As the foremost, she rose in the royal house and consistently maintained her feminine deportment. Her dress and usage were moderate, as were her words and her actions.

In the fourth year, *binh than* [1136], she was entered in the register as the Phung Thanh lady. At this time, her constant heart was in evidence, and she maintained her virtue in accord with the civilized tradition. She did not lose the duty of the *Classic of Poetry*, and the kindness of the same classic she extended down to the people. In accord with Huang and Ying, the wives of Shun,[27] how admirable and high was her counsel! Like the major support of the Zhou dynasty, the mothers of the rulers, she was foremost in making known the royal way! In the fifth year, *dinh ty* [1137], she received the title of escort for the royal vehicle upon Ly Than Tong's death and swore to care for the royal tombs and temples. Managing her diligent heart and thus manifesting it, she did not change the superior way and thereby taught the way of Shun of antiquity.

The lady's bearing was proper and sincere, and by nature she was most modest and soft spoken, displaying neither joy nor anger on her countenance. In employing men, she was pleasant and attentive, not argumentative, demanding, or difficult. When the new king [Ly Anh Tong (r. 1138–1175)] first took the throne, the queen mother, the lady's elder sister, was the pillar of the government. Every new and full moon, the lady came to court. The king genuinely respected her. Her words were extremely effective, with no missteps. When outside the court, she would come to one side for a private visit. The king and the queen mother constantly made royal processions to her palace, seeing her present and arrange matters. They admired her character and thus praised her, "You are a lady from the brilliant age of antiquity!"

The lady performed each ritual in a private, sincere, and reverent manner, totally in accord with the spiritual, and positioned herself secondary [in the phrase of the *Classic of Poetry*] to the royal clan. Her sense of family duty was, in all cases, true in its reverence. She was constantly able to recall the style of cloth of our ancestors, not neglecting to serve and willingly inform them of their victorious destiny in order to respond to the close familial ties of the former kings. . . . She had obtained a schema of *yin* and *yang*, the future and the past, and assisted in the dynasty's grand accumulated power. For this, she specially received a royal edict, bestowed for her humane accomplishments. She selected quality tile and set up the Jewel Establishment [a Buddhist temple]. Elegance says it all, and the incense and fire does not cease therein. The temple is venerated for its care.

In the ninth year of the Chinh Long Bao Ung era [1171], the ninth month, the lady became ill and took to her bed. The king personally checked on her medication. One hundred treatments, and yet she was not cured. On the eighteenth day of the following month, before daybreak, she passed away, aged sixty-three. The king was greatly affected by her death, ceasing all court business and cutting the delicacies from his meals. So the king sent down orders for the funeral expenses to be covered according to the usual arrangements. We can say that the wailing and the splendor of the ceremony were exceptional. The king

---

27. Shun (r. twenty-third to twenty-second century B.C.E.) was a legendary emperor of China.

proclaimed the court minister Tran and another official, Le, to take charge of the funeral arrangements. In the end, the ceremonies returned to the previous substantial style of the burial of the Chieu Thanh Queen Mother.[28]

In the eleventh year [1174], the winter twelfth month [early 1175], the eighth day, *binh dam*, at daybreak, by the grace of a royal decree, the lady was buried in the earth of her home village, on Mount Phac, to the west of Dien Linh Phuc Thanh Buddhist temple. Now the king commanded the country's history to tell the story of this virtuous gift in his life and to record it on her tombstone.

[*Épigraphie en chinois*, no. 22; trans. John K. Whitmore]

DAM DI MONG

CLEANING UP THE MONASTIC COMMUNITY (1194)

Buddhist temples and their lands formed an important part of Vietnamese society during the eleventh and twelfth centuries, resulting in a growing Buddhist population. In the late twelfth century, as the *Short History of Dai Viet* (1380s) describes, the sheer number of Buddhist monks, coupled with the growing corruption of the temples, started to present a problem, disrupting the social order. There was considerable concern that men were entering the monastic communities as a means of escaping the obligations imposed on them by the state, including taxation, labor, and military service. Concerns about this issue continued to plague Vietnamese royal courts through the centuries, as Buddhist centers remained significant sites of manpower and wealth, outside the state's immediate control.

[In 1194] Dam Di Mong reported to the king [Ly Cao Tong (r. 1176–1210)], "Monks are now as numerous as laborers. They form groups as they please, choosing their own leaders and flocking together in groups. They commit many odious acts, such as deliberately drinking wine and eating meat in austere places and monasteries or fornicating in monarchal alcoves and meditation halls. They disappear by day and appear at night like foxes and rats. Perverting morals and defiling religion is becoming a habit with them. It is time to put an end to such conduct, otherwise, they will only get worse in the long run." The king was in agreement. Dam Di Mong then summoned clergymen from all over the country to a public granary, chose some tens of them of repute as monks, and had the rest marked on the hand and sent back to lay life.

[*VSL*, 3, 12b–13a; trans. Nguyen Tu Cuong, *Zen in Medieval Vietnam*, 53]

---

28. The Chieu Thanh Queen Mother (d. 1108) was the queen of Ly Nhan Tong (r. 1072–1127).

NGO SI LIEN

SOCIAL CATEGORIES (1479)

In the first half of the thirteenth century, the new Tran dynasty provided continuity with the past by maintaining the Ly royal ritual and keeping the capital in Thang Long. At the same time, the Tran rulers emphasized stronger central power than that under the Ly, employing village registers.[29] These registers under the Tran provide a sense of Vietnamese society in these early centuries, as seen in this description from Ngo Si Lien's *Complete Chronicle of Dai Viet*.

[In 1228], in the old pattern of the Ly dynasty, every year at the beginning of spring, the village chief submitted a written report on the population of his village, calling it "Enumeration of Individuals" and consequently regarding the resulting account books as fixed, with all such individuals being placed in one of these categories: the royal clan, civil officials, civil ranks, military officers, military ranks, lesser officials, soldiers, officials of varied assignments, adult males, the infirm and elderly, the poor, those adopted or who entered their wife's families, and those scattered and drifting. Those descended from men of official rank will always have hereditary privileges, allowing them to enter the royal service. Those well-off, able-bodied, and with no rank are fit for the army. When the times require it, they will be taken as soldiers.

[Ngo Si Lien, *DVSKTT*, 5, 4b–5a; trans. John K. Whitmore]

NGO SI LIEN

ARISTOCRATIC LIFE (1479)

The aristocratic society that was a hallmark of thirteenth-century Dai Viet had a strong sense of rank and hierarchy. The Tran rulers were quite explicit about who had privilege and who did not, who was allowed which accoutrement and who was not, as the *Complete Chronicle of Dai Viet* lays out in detail. In this manner, the court visibly maintained its hierarchy, differentiating its ranks and ensuring that no one claimed a rank to which he was not entitled. Such painstaking concern with entitlements and rank persisted among subsequent Vietnamese rulers, who periodically issued regulations designed to restore idealized systems of differentiated sartorial and other accoutrements.[30]

---

29. See Ngo Si Lien, "Officials and Village Registers" (this chap.).

30. An eighteenth-century example of such a regulation is Trinh Cuong, "Edict Regarding Local Customs" (chap. 4).

[In 1254], summer, fifth month, the king [Tran Thai Tong (r. 1225–1277)] set out the vehicles, clothes, and mounted escorts for the royal clan and for all the officials, civil and military, according to rank. From the royal clan down to the fifth-rank official, all were to use sedan chairs, horses, and the "paper crow" [hammock]. For the royal clan, there was the Phoenix Front sedan chair with red varnish. For the high court ministers, there was the Parrot sedan chair with black varnish and a purple umbrella. Officials of the third rank and higher had a Cloud Front sedan chair and a blue umbrella. Those of the fourth to sixth ranks had a Normal Front sedan chair. Fifth rank and above had a blue umbrella, with the sixth and seventh ranks bearing black paper parasols. Many of the mounted escorts had a thousand men; a few, only a hundred.

At this time, the aristocracy would often fight with their fists and, acting independently, steal people away for their entourages. The Vu Uy prince, Tran Duy, son of the king, was one of these. One day the prince struck another with his hand at the capital's eastern landing. The king summoned the prince before him, saying, "Who are these fat, empty people? Apprehend them, and bring them here so that they may confess and receive my judgment." The prince heard [this] and fled.

[Ngo Si Lien, DVSKTT, 5, 19a–19b; trans. John K. Whitmore]

NGO SI LIEN

SCHOLARLY LIFE (1479)

As part of the Tran dynasty's reform of the government, the kings, wishing to strengthen the central government and gain stronger control over localities, gave greater precedence than before to scholars of classical texts and involved them in government office to a much greater extent. In fact, these scholar-officials gradually came to replace the Ly tradition of placing eunuchs in high court office. Prince Tran Ich Tac's school was the first in Dai Viet to emphasize the classical texts (though in the 1280s, the prince went to the North with the defeated Mongols). The *Complete Chronicle of Dai Viet* describes these changes.

[In 1267], summer, fourth month, the king [Tran Thanh Tong (r. 1258–1278)] chose to use those scholars who were able to *"van"* [apply texts] to staff the offices, the council chambers, the provinces, and the halls. At that time, Dang Ke became a scholar in the Han Lam [C: Hanlin] Academy, and Do Quoc Te, an official in the central administration. Both were scholars of classical texts. In the old system, "inner men" [eunuchs] became court ministers [*hanh khien*], and there was no use for such scholars of classical texts. Now, beginning at this time, those with a knowledge of these texts were so employed.

[In the] fifth month, the king made Tran Ich Tac, his younger brother, the Chieu Quoc prince. Tran Ich Tac was the second son of the senior ruler Tran Thai Tong [r. 1225–1277]. Tran Ich Tac was intelligent, studied well, comprehended the classics and histories as well as the Six Arts and was the brightest of his generation. Even though he had little talent in such areas as physical and board games, there was nothing else in which he was not skilled or well versed. He opened a school to the right of his home and assembled scholars of the classical texts from all directions. These scholars worked and studied with him and were provided clothes and food. The prince then prepared these scholars to perfect their talent, scholars like Mac Dinh Chi of Bang Ha and Bui Phong of Hoan Chau, and others, twenty of them in all, each of whom went on to assist the court and be used in the world.

[In 1272], tenth month, the king gave the order to seek out those who were good and virtuous and who clearly understood the classics to be scholars in the Royal Academy. If they could explicate the meaning of the Four Books and the Five Classics, they would enter and serve in the Royal Study for the Classics.

[Ngo Si Lien, *DVSKTT*, 5, 31a, 33b; trans. John K. Whitmore]

LE VAN HUU

THE TRUNG SISTERS (1272)

For us, the voice of the scholars is represented by the historian Le Van Huu. One aspect of literati thought in the thirteenth century was a stronger emphasis on masculine power and the male role in society. Here, in his *Chronicle of Dai Viet*, Le Van Huu voices this perspective in his comment on the Trung sisters of the first century C.E.

Trung Trac and Trung Nhi were women; they gave one shout and all the prefectures of Jiuzhen, Rinan, and Hepu, along with sixty-five strongholds in Lingwai [territory Beyond the Passes in the South], responded to them. Their establishment of a kingdom and declaration of themselves as monarchs was as easy as turning over one's hand, which shows that our land of Viet was able to establish the enterprise of a hegemon [ruler]. What a pity that from the Trieu to the Ngo family, a period of over a thousand years, the men of our land bowed their heads, folded their arms, and served the Northerners; how shameful this is in comparison with the two Trung sisters, who were women! Ah, it is enough to make one want to die!

[Ngo Si Lien, *DVSKTT, Outer Records*, 3, 1b; trans. adapted from Taylor, *Birth of Vietnam*, 334]

VIEWS ON NORTHERN INFLUENCE (1370, 1397)

During the fourteenth century, the literati increasingly advocated changing Vietnamese society so that it would be more in line with Northern social patterns. The following two passages from the *Complete Chronicle of Dai Viet* (1479), by Ngo Si Lien, show the different positions taken by the royal court in Thang Long on literati proposals for Vietnamese society. Tran Nghe Tong (r. 1370–1394) rejected literati influence, whereas Ho Quy Ly (r. 1400–1407) called for more of it. Whether or not to follow their Northern neighbor has remained a subject of debate among Vietnamese to the present day.

When the earlier reigns established the country, they had their own system of law and did not follow the system of the Song. This was because in the North and the South each ruler had his own land and no need to follow the other. During the Dai Tri reign [1358–1369], pale scholars were employed who did not understand the depth of the establishment of law in our state and who changed the old customs of our ancestors to follow the customs of the North entirely, as if these customs were clothes, music, or literature. We cannot choose anything of theirs.

Tran Nghe Tong

In antiquity, the state had colleges, social groups had halls, and everyone had public schools with the result that they clarified the civilizing mission and firmed up custom. In our view, this is most desirable. Today, however, while the educational system in the capital is quite sufficient, that in the subprefectures and districts is still lacking. How then can we spread widely the way of civilizing the people?

Ho Quy Ly
[Ngo Si Lien, *DVSKTT*, 7, 33a; 8, 30a–30b; trans.
Whitmore, *Vietnam*, 9–10, 49]

ETHNIC RELATIONS

THE NUNG AND THE CHAM (1039, 1043)

By the time of the second ruler, Ly Thai Tong (r. 1028–1054), the power of Dai Viet was quickly expanding, and the king became concerned about the prestige of his throne compared with that of his neighbors. He gloried in his power and did not like the idea of competing principalities on his borders, including both the Tai principalities to the north and the realm of Champa to the south. As a result, during the 1040s, Ly Thai Tong acted aggressively against both groups. In the northern mountains, he countered the effort of the Tai principality of the Nung to gain autonomy in the region between Dai Viet and the Song empire, as seen in a portion of his "Proclamation to Pacify the Nung." When Ly Thai Tong worried about Champa's perceived lack of respect for the throne of Dai Viet, his counselors instructed him that martial might meant more than a pacific approach and that, if the current situation were allowed to remain, it could also lead local powers within Dai Viet to rise up against the throne. Such concerns with neighboring countries and peoples continued into the modern age and were much discussed through the centuries. The following passages show the Vietnamese throne's concerns about external affairs and are included in Le Van Huu's *Chronicle of Dai Viet* (1272).

Proclamation to Pacify the Nung

Once I had come to possess All under Heaven, all my generals, ministers, and officials led a great celebration. From all foreign lands and special regions, there was no one who did not attend. Furthermore, according to precedent, the Nung clan for generations has protected our frontier, and they have frequently come to court bearing tribute. Today, Nung Ton Phuc is displaying a great arrogance by illicitly adopting a reign title and by issuing edicts as though he were a king. His followers are gathering like swarms of gadflies, and he has spread poisonous ideas among the people of the borderlands. With Heaven's authority, I will strike out and punish him. I have made five members of that group, Nung Ton Phuc among them, outlaws, and I will have them beheaded at the capital.

Ly Thai Tong

Champa

We counselors think the cause of this is that, although your virtue has reached Champa, your majesty has not yet spread far. The reason for this is that, ever since you ascended the throne, while they have rebelliously refused to come to court, you simply displayed virtue and bestowed favor in order to soothe them. You have not yet proven the truth of your majesty, glory, and military power by attacking them. This is not the way to show majesty to distant peoples. We fear that the different clans and nobles in our realm will all become like Champa. Why make an exception for Champa?

Lords of the Ly Court
[Le Quy Don, *TVTL*, 1, no. 31; trans. Anderson,
Rebel Den of Nung Tri Cao, 80–81; Ngo Si Lien,
DVSKTT, 2, 32a–32b; trans. Taylor, "Authority and Legitimacy," 162–63]

LE VAN HUU

MUSIC OF CHAMPA (1272)

The approach of the royal court of Dai Viet in Thang Long to the contending Southeast Asian realms around it, especially the Kingdom of Champa, was to dominate them politically and economically before these realms could do so to Dai Viet. Yet culturally and socially, all these realms were quite amenable to peaceful relationships among themselves. Princes, aristocrats, and religious figures of differing ethnicities circulated among these realms and absorbed one another's cultural elements. Thus while fighting the surrounding realms for political dominance, Dai Viet was still engaged in cultural interchanges with them, as the *Chronicle of Dai Viet* shows. Music from Champa was one such item that usually was welcomed in the Thang Long royal court. Reflecting the interpenetration of diverse dogmas in the Vietnamese ideological realm, the Buddhist monk quoted here who criticizes Cham music cites a Confucian classic in his memorial.

[In 1044, autumn, seventh month], the king [Ly Thai Tong (r. 1028–1054] led his forces into the Champa city of Phat The [Buddha's Oath], taking prisoner the Champa king Sa Dan's wives and palace women who were skilled in playing and dancing the Tay Thien Khuc Dieu [Western Heaven's Indian Tune]. He sent envoys out to all the communities to soothe, proclaim to, and leave his thoughts with their people. All their ministers quickly sent their congratulations.

   [In 1060], eighth month, the court [of Ly Thanh Tong (r. 1054–1072)] transcribed music and tunes of Champa and regulated its drumbeat so that the Vietnamese musicians could perform it.

   [In 1202], the king Ly Cao Tong [r. 1176–1210] gave an order to the musicians to compose a piece of music and called it "Cham Melody." Its sound was so mournful and sorrowful that it brought tears to listeners' eyes. The Buddhist monk and official Nguyen Thuong said: "I have heard that the Preface to the *Classic of Poetry* says that the sound of a disturbed country is mournful and angry. At the present time, the people are in an uproar and the country faces difficulties. Your majesty indulges himself in luxuries, court affairs are a mess, and the people's hearts are distressed: this is the omen of annihilation."

[Ngo Si Lien, *DVSKTT*, 2, 35a; 3, 2b; 4, 22b–23a; trans. John K. Whitmore (paras. 1 and 2); Nguyen Tu Cuong, *Zen in Medieval Vietnam*, 350]

EXTERNAL THREATS (1159, 1272)

The realms of Dai Viet, Champa, and Angkor (in Cambodia) competed for political and economic supremacy from the 1120s to the 1210s. During this time, the court minister Duke Do Anh Vu had to face both foreign forces, particularly those from Angkor to the southwest, and the challenge of the restive hill peoples on the edges of Dai Viet. His actions are described in this segment of his funeral inscription of 1159. The death of one ruler and the succession of the next, especially if a child, was a moment of weakness in Dai Viet, raising the possibility of both internal division and external invasion. In 1175, Do Anh Vu's king Ly Anh Tong (r. 1138–1175) died, and the young Ly Cao Tong (r. 1176–1210) took the throne. In the *Chronicle of Dai Viet* (1272), Le Van Huu describes how, after three years of mourning, the queen mother called for unity and support of Do Anh Vu's successor as court minister, To Hien Thanh, to ward off external threats. The three-year period of mourning was itself an innovation from China, as was starting the new king's reign the year after the death of his predecessor. These two changes in procedure might have been intended to mollify the Song court to the North.

In the first month of the third year of the Thien Chuong Bao Tu reign period [1135], in a time of long-lasting peace when the four directions were calm, Van Dan[31] invaded the southern border towns. The king sent the Duke [Do Anh Vu] and the general Ly Cong Binh to mobilize 300,000 soldiers; they followed the seacoast and arrived at Am Da in Nhat Nam [present-day north-central Vietnam]. The Duke gazed at the encampment of the invaders and said: "The soldiers of the Son of Heaven quell rebellion; they do not offer battle in contestation as between equals. The vulgarity of presenting oneself naked as the invaders do will surely be eradicated by Heaven." Thereupon, wind shook the mountains and the islands. The invaders were immediately thrown into a panic; they accordingly dispersed and went back the way they had come. The Duke with his soldiers pursued the routed foe, beheaded the enemy leaders, and took captives; they went as far as Vu On and returned.

Also in that same year the Duke received another command to punish rebels. The Son Lieu mountain dwellers held the passes and refused to come to court and submit. The king thereupon commanded the Duke and all the generals to lead soldiers out to subdue them. Only the Duke returned with captives; no one was equal to his stratagems. Consequently, people gave thought to his indomitable courage. All affairs both within and without the inner palace were accordingly entrusted to him.

Funeral Inscription

[In 1178], the mourning of the country for the king Ly Anh Tong [r. 1138–1175] ended. The Chieu Linh Queen Mother held a banquet for the officials in a separate palace and stated, "Today the former king Ly Anh Tong is a guest of Heaven and his successor [Ly Cao Tong (r. 1176–1210)] is young and immature. Champa has lost its propriety and the Northerners [Song] infringe on our borders. You nobles receive substantial favor from the country and must take the country's [royal] family as farsighted. The plan of today cannot be a repeat of before when we merely placed the crown prince on the throne and this led the other countries to honor him, thus bringing peace to the hearts of the people." All the ministers saluted, raising their hands and knocking their heads in prostration, stating, "Let the court minister receive the clear command of the king [Son of Heaven], and the throne will then constantly support him. As a consequence, the officials will not dare to oppose him." All thanked her and withdrew. The court minister To Hien Thanh took command of the Forbidden Palace troops, sternly called out

---

31. Van Dan here is Vientiane or is "Land Zhenla," in the middle Mekong valley (Laos), as distinguished from "Water Zhenla," in the lower Mekong valley (Cambodia).

the orders, and clearly dispensed reward and punishment. All under Heaven submitted in their hearts.

Le Van Huu

[*Épigraphie en chinois*, no. 19; trans. Taylor, "Voices Within and Without," 65;
Ngo Si Lien, *DVSKTT*, 4, 18a–18b; trans. John K. Whitmore]

LE VAN HUU

CRITIQUE ON HANDLING THE NUNG (1272)

As the new coastal Tran dynasty took control of the throne of Dai Viet from the Ly in 1225, it too perceived groups beyond its borders as a threat. The scholar Le Van Huu's official *Chronicle of Dai Viet* describes his fellow literati's feelings about how to deal with the peoples on Dai Viet's borders. Le Van Huu gave his forthright opinion about how the Ly had interacted with the Tai Nung two hundred years earlier and strongly criticized the second ruler, Ly Thai Tong (r. 1028–1054), for being too lenient in his handling of the situation in the northern mountains.

Previously, when Nung Tri Cao's father Nung Ton Phuc committed treason, usurped the title of king, and established a separate state, king Ly Thai Tong only punished the father and exempted the son Nung Tri Cao. Now that Nung Tri Cao followed the treasonous path of his father, he deserved, for his serious crime, the death penalty or at least the deprivation of title and land previously granted and demotion to the status of commoner. However, king Ly Thai Tong pardoned him, gave him additional districts to rule, conferred on him a seal and the noble title of Thai Bao. This is not a justifiable policy of punishment and reward. . . . All is due to the fact that king Ly Thai Tong was infatuated with the petty humanitarianism of the Buddhists and forgot about the great principles of being a king.

[Ngo Si Lien, *DVSKTT*, 2, 32b–33a; trans. Huy and Tai, *Le Code*, 1:11]

NGO SI LIEN

A TRAN PRINCE AND A MOUNTAIN CHIEF (1479)

Despite the feelings of literati like Le Van Huu toward other peoples and their cultures, the Tran princes of the thirteenth century were willing to recognize and work with (rather than scorn) these surrounding peoples. At the time of the Mongol threat, one of these princes went into the highlands to resolve a problem peacefully. Interestingly, Ngo Si Lien, the fifteenth-century compiler of the *Complete Chronicle of Dai Viet*, who strongly opposed such actions, included it, reflecting the essential trustworthiness of the chronicle itself.

[In 1280, tenth month], Trinh Giac Mat of the Da River region began a revolt. The king [Tran Nhan Tong (r. 1279–1308)] commanded the Chieu-van prince Tran Nhat Duat to talk Trinh Giac Mat back into line. At the time, Tran Nhat Duat commanded the Da River circuit. He secretly brought his troops into the area. Trinh Giac Mat sent a man to visit the camp and express his sincerity, saying, "Trinh Giac Mat would not dare to go against the royal command. If you will favor us by riding here alone, then Mat will return to his allegiance." Tran Nhat Duat did so, bringing five or six small boys with him. When a guard blocked him, Tran Nhat Duat said, "If that one goes against me, then the royal court will only have another prince come" and continued on toward Trinh Giac Mat's camp. Savage men surrounded him, several dozen deep, pointing their swords and spears at him. Nevertheless, Tran Nhat Duat kept going straight on and up to Trinh Giac Mat's camp. Mat invited in the prince. Tran Nhat Duat was thoroughly versed in numerous languages and knew the customs well. So he joined Trinh Giac Mat in eating the meal with his hand and drinking [with a straw] through his nose. The barbarians were greatly pleased. Tran Nhat Duat returned to his own camp, and Trinh Giac Mat led his clan to the camp to surrender. So everything went in good grace, without losing a single arrow, and the Da River region was at peace. On his return to the royal city, Tran Nhat Duat brought Trinh Giac Mat with the latter's wife and children to see it. The king found it very commendable. And so he allowed Trinh Giac Mat to return to his clan, keeping Mat's son in the capital.

[Ngo Si Lien, *DVSKTT*, 5, 40a–40b; trans. John K. Whitmore]

NGUYEN TRUNG NGAN

THE MA NHAI INSCRIPTION (1336)

Through the first decades of the fourteenth century, the mountains west of Dai Viet were the site of politically active Tai peoples who had begun to establish kingdoms in what are now Laos and Thailand. In the 1330s, armed forces of Dai Viet moved up into the hills west of Nghe An Province (in north-central Vietnam), southwest of the capital, to attack and control these groups. A stone inscription from that time gives us the Vietnamese perspective on the interaction of the two forces. Despite the bravado displayed in this inscription by the scholar-official Nguyen Trung Ngan (1289–1370), in the *Complete Chronicle of Dai Viet* (1479), Ngo Si Lien actually speaks of the defeat of the Vietnamese forces by these Tai. The feelings expressed in this inscription form the background for Vietnamese dealings with later foreigners who came across their borders.

Sixth ruler of the Tran dynasty of Imperial Viet [Dai Viet], the Chuong Nghieu Civilized and Sage Great Senior Ruler, Tran Minh Tong [r. 1314–1357], received the favored Mandate of Heaven and grandly held the Central Land,[32] extend-

---

32. Central Land refers to the Viet kingdom, regarded as similar to that of China.

ing across land and sea, so that there is no one within or without who does not serve and submit to us. But now it is very much the case that you, Ai Lao, scheme to obstruct the royal transformation. In the *at hoi* year, late autumn [September–October 1335], the ruler in person led the Six Armies on an expedition to the western region. The states of Champa with its heir apparent, Zhenla [Cambodia], and Siam, as well as the territories of the southern barbarian chiefs in the mountains, the delivered Quy Cam and Xa Lac [Tai peoples], the newly dependent Boi Bon, and the territory of the southern barbarian chief of Thanh Xa, of all these southern barbarian groups, each presents local products, competing to be the first to meet with us. Only the perverse Ai Lao chief, Bong, obstinately errs and dreads his punishment. He does not come immediately to our royal court. In late winter [early 1336], the king camped at the headwaters of Cu Don in Mat Chau and commanded all the generals and the barbarian troops to go into this country. The perverse Bong, seeing us coming, fled, skulking away from this territory and losing face. The order went out to withdraw the army.

In the seventh year of the Khai Huu reign, *at hoi*, first intercalary month [mid-January to mid-February 1336].

[Gaspardone, "L'inscription du Ma Nhai," 73–84;
trans. John K. Whitmore]

NGO SI LIEN

FOREIGN CULTURES (1374, 1390)

Scholars educated in the classical idiom continued to hold strong views about how the lowland Vietnamese should relate to their Southeast Asian neighbors, from both the lowlands and highlands. By the late fourteenth century, their view, which emphasized differentiating the Vietnamese from their neighbors, had begun to be accepted by the throne and aristocrats at court. Ngo Si Lien records this perspective in the *Complete Chronicle of Dai Viet* (1479). First, he summarizes the royal edict of 1374. Second, he describes the deathbed advice of the aristocratic scholar Tran Nguyen Dan (1320–1390), a member of the royal clan, court minister, and grandfather of the future scholar and minister Nguyen Trai, whose own geography closely echoes the sentiments of these two entries.

Royal Proclamation on Customs

The throne proclaimed to both the army and the people not to wear the clothes and hair styles of the Northerners [Ming] or to use Champa, Lao, or other foreign tongues.

Tran Nguyen Dan's Deathbed Advice to His Ruler, Tran Nghe Tong

[In 1390], eleventh month, fourteenth day, the court minister and Chuong Tuc high marquis, Tran Nguyen Dan, died.

Tran Nguyen Dan was a man of compassion and scholarly style who had the deportment of the superior man of antiquity. The senior ruler [Tran Nghe Tong (r. 1370–1394)] constantly went to Tran Nguyen Dan's home, inquiring after his health and what should be done with affairs after Tran Nguyen Dan's demise. Tran Nguyen Dan would say nothing but finally stated, "Your majesty should respect the Ming country [contemporary Ming dynasty] as a father and love Champa like a son, then our land will have no problems. Although your servant is dying, this advice will be lasting."

[Ngo Si Lien, *DVSKTT*, 7, 41b; 8, 19a–19b; trans. John K. Whitmore]

Chapter 3

THE LE AND MAC EPOCHS

The two decades of Ming occupation (1407–1427) brought to Dai Viet a much heavier layer of administration than the country had ever experienced before and introduced the Vietnamese to the full measure of contemporary Sinic bureaucracy. The Ming also set up schools (with libraries) and advanced the new Neo-Confucian orthodoxy just being developed in their own capital. For the Vietnamese, the occupation was a time of rapacious efficiency, although a number of local literati did flourish in the system. The Ming power was such that the Northerners were able to crush all resistance in the lowlands and the nearby highlands. Only in the distant mountains of Thanh Hoa to the southwest near the Lao hills was a resistance movement able to survive, just barely. Finally, between 1418 and 1428, Le Loi, a local chieftain based in the village of Mount Lam, led his local forces in a successful campaign to drive out the Ming.

In 1428, Le Loi (Le Thai To [r. 1428–1433]) became the king of a restored Dai Viet, whose capital was Thang Long, with his rough-hewn mountain soldiers forming the new aristocracy. Over the previous sixty years, the old Red River Delta aristocracy had been almost entirely eradicated by Champa, by the Ho, by the Ming, and finally by the Le. The new government of the Le (1428–1527, 1592–1789) continued certain aspects of the Ming rule, including its schools and the concept of a legal code, and quickly created a new fiscal foundation for itself. Now the emphasis was on individual villages and the newly created public lands within them. Revenue from the public lands went to the central government, not to local lords, and powerful families were now seen as a threat to the public domain. The new legal code stated, in no uncertain terms, its opposition to such private power. Yet the government and social structure still were aristocratic, as the lords of Mount Lam continued to dominate both the royal court and the countryside. Another set of laws in 1449 ensured the survival of existing social practices (especially the female ownership of property). The ideology of the monarchy changed, however, as the royal cults and Buddhism disappeared and Ho Quy Ly's brand of classical thought weakened. The Le royal ideology initially was based on their own parochial belief system, combined with some of the older literati thought. This provided an opening for a new, contemporary brand of Confucian thought, that of the Ming. This latter thought was advocated by a new generation of Vietnamese scholars, especially the younger ones who had most likely been educated in the Ming schools during the occupation and their local successors. Nonetheless, even though Buddhism had lost its place at court, it continued to be popular among the aristocracy and in the villages.

In the three decades after the death of the founder, Le Thai To, in 1433, a struggle ensued between the old aristocratic style of governance and the newly emerging style of contemporary East Asian bureaucracy. This was foreshadowed in the 1430s debate over the old and the new court ritual and music. Because the young Le rulers during this time tended to bring the younger literati over to the side of the throne against the lords of Mount Lam, the contemporary model of Ming rule gained ground, especially in ritual and music. When Le Loi's son Le Thai Tong (r. 1434–1442) and then the founder's third (Le Nhan Tong [r. 1442–1459]) and first (Le Nghi Dan [r. 1459–1460]) grandsons were murdered in conflict over the throne, the fourth grandson, Le Thanh Tong (r. 1460–1497), finally emerged to take the throne. Together with his literatus-official allies, the new emperor made the Ming bureaucratic state the new model of political control for Dai Viet. This entailed establishing the triennial Confucian examination system, a centralized administration based on the Northern six ministries model, a provincial system reaching down into the countryside, and a regime of paperwork that made "legible" the realm's human and material resources through the creation of written records.

In the process of transforming Dai Viet's political structures, Le Thanh Tong switched from the Tran emphasis on the South's holding off the aggressive North to an image of the South's forming part of the North's broader Sinic philosophical civilization. Le Thanh Tong adopted the term Thien Nam (South of Heaven) and joined Dai Viet to the North's "domain of manifest civility." During the fifteenth century, Dai Viet continued to underscore that the Vietnamese were *not* being influenced by their Southeast Asian neighbors' popular customs. In addition, as part of the administrative transformation, the king had Dai Viet mapped for the first time—a process described in the *Complete Chronicle of Dai Viet*—which explicitly marked off the land against the territory of its neighbors.

By the 1460s, Dai Viet had become a much stronger and more efficient state, and Le Thanh Tong and his literati advisers joined the remaining Mount Lam lords in a surge of Vietnamese power against their neighboring Southeast Asian rivals. This required not only greater military might but also a fundamental shift in foreign policy. The Vietnamese court no longer tolerated cultural equality and the acceptance of other peoples. Now such people were regarded as *hoa ngoai*, "outside civilization," and their capitals no longer would be merely captured, looted, and left for the next indigenous ruler. Instead, the Vietnamese would impose direct political control (the provincial administrative system) and civilization (the proper way of life) over newly conquered territories. In the 1470s, Dai Viet struck back against perceived threats on its borders while playing diplomatic games with the Ming court in Beijing. First, in 1470/1471, Le Thanh Tong's forces crushed Champa in a masterful campaign, split it up, and integrated its northern territories as Dai Viet's thirteenth province, a move that the emperor justified in his proclamation of 1470 on the eve of the attack. In this way, the Vietnamese state removed its southern rival and threat and opened the way for further expansion southward. Beginning in 1479, Le Thanh Tong attacked the restive Tai forces on his western borders, pushing all the way across what are now Laos and northern Thailand to the Irrawaddy River and Myanmar (Burma). This action quieted any possible threats from the west.

While pushing outward, Le Thanh Tong's government worked to consolidate administrative control of the villages and to bring its new philosophy and moral stance to them, all while striving to improve the people's economic situation. Local officials at the provincial and district levels engaged village headmen in a new way, urging proper behavior and ritual, especially in marriage and mourning; giving men precedence over women; and requiring the population and local resources (such as land) to be recorded in the village registers. The government also worked to maintain the dikes and to encourage the development of agriculture and commerce. Agriculture thrived, manufacturing (especially of ceramics) grew, and foreign trade expanded. The law code sought to provide regulation and standards for dealing with property and other economic transactions. Despite the government's unprecedented intrusion into the villages, no revolts are recorded, because of the increasing stability and prosperity of the land. Le Thanh Tong and his literati-officials saw their success in cosmic terms (Heaven was blessing their good efforts) and wrote much poetry celebrating this.

This bureaucratic regime lasted for roughly forty years, through the reign of Le Thanh Tong (1460–1497) and that of his son Le Hien Tong (1498–1504). Then, for almost a quarter century, aristocratic conflict and local rebellion badly shook the model of governance that Le Thanh Tong and his literati-officials had put in place. First, the maternal kin of Le Uy Muc De (r. 1505–1509) created havoc across the countryside and in the social and economic sectors, disrupting trade. Then the noble clans, particularly the Nguyen and the Trinh, began fighting, and in 1516 a revolt by Tran Cao, who claimed to be a descendant of the prior dynasty, threatened to end, once and for all, both the Le dynasty and its Sinic administrative model. Finally, the Mac family of the lower Red River Delta, which was led by the military strongman Mac Dang Dung (r. 1528–1541) and claimed its descent from more than two hundred years of literati-officials, seized power in 1528 and restored Le Thanh Tong's bureaucratic model.

The Mac regime (1528–1592) again emphasized proper Confucian relationships, stressing ritual land (*huong hoa*, the land set aside on the death of a male landowner to produce income to pay for his ancestral sacrifices) and the role of men. But at the same time, Confucian scholars and Buddhist temples coexisted peacefully in the villages and agriculture prospered.

Nevertheless, the Mac, like the Ming occupation before them, controlled only the lowlands. Once again, the Le and their supporters emerged from the highland base of Mount Lam on the edge of Lao territory, this time to contest the Mac hold on the throne. At the same time, the Mac also had to deal with the Ming court in Beijing and accepted a reduction in tributary status (no longer kings, but effectively just ministers). Nevertheless, by the mid-sixteenth century, the Red River Delta appears to have been prosperous and well governed.

After several decades, the Le Restoration forces, led by the Nguyen and another Trinh clan, intensified their pressure on the lowlands and the capital of Thang Long. Finally, in 1592 they swept across the Red River Delta and drove out the Mac, restoring the Le (1592–1789) to the throne. The rivalry between the Trinh and the Nguyen still had to be resolved. The Nguyen had established their base in the old territory of Champa on the southern border (in the vicinity of Hue) and had begun to link themselves to the new system of maritime trade system on the central Vietnamese coast. From that international contact, the Nguyen brought wealth and weapons to the Le cause, aiding the Trinh in the Restoration. Nonetheless, it was the Trinh who succeeded in holding power in Thong Long. By 1600, the Trinh lords *ruled* in the capital while the Le kings *reigned*; the Nguyen lords turned back to their southern maritime base, and the Mac survived on the northern border protected by the Ming court. In essence, two aristocratic military clans, the Trinh in the state of Dai Viet and the Nguyen on its southern fringe, ruled the land, stressing martial achievements, Buddhism, and personal loyalty. The literati had little influence in either regime and generally stayed in their villages, educating the youth.

During these two centuries, 1400 to 1600, Dai Viet's bureaucratic government took shape in the northern area, modeled on that of the Ming and clearly manifested in the Le Code, which regulated everything from the use of draft animals to the behavior of aristocratic families. Staffed by scholar-officials, the bureaucracy advocated Confucianism for both state and society, with patrilineality and rituals for marriage and mourning. This advocacy of Confucianism can be seen in various scholars' critical comments on Dai Viet's historical past, such as Ngo Si Lien's and Duong Van An's critiques of the failure of earlier monarchs to adhere to Confucian ideals. Scholar-officials' memorials and remonstrances to the throne demonstrated their sense of responsibility for the country's and society's well-being. In any case, power now lay in the hands of the aristocracy, specifically the Trinh and Nguyen families, and it was their choice whether or not to use the scholars as officials. The ideological juxtaposition of Buddhism, Confucianism, and the spirit cults continued, sometimes shifting in their relationship to one another. Regionalism emerged as a greater element in Vietnamese politics, and scholars' themes of loyalty to the proper authority became critical. The earlier relativistic approach to other Southeast Asian peoples increasingly became one of the civilized versus the barbarian, as suggested in Emperor Le Thanh Tong's order of 1472 requiring ethnic groups to conform to Vietnamese surname practices.

THE LAND

LE THAI TO AND NGUYEN TRAI

GREAT PROCLAMATION ON THE DEFEAT OF THE MING (1428)

The Le dynasty, with its new aristocracy from the southwestern mountains, adopted the Tran dynasty's conception of itself as the valiant South holding off the aggressive North. This was seen in the scholar-official Nguyen Trai's "Great Proclamation on the Defeat of the Ming," written on behalf of Le Loi (Le Thai To [r. 1428–1433]). In the first stanza, Nguyen Trai juxtaposes South and North in parallel terms. This proclamation of final victory, like Gia Long's almost four centuries later,[1] sought to bring the Vietnamese past to bear in integrating the newly conquered realm.

> Now, our Great Viet is truly a cultured country;
> The features of our mountains and our rivers [our land]
>   are different [from those of the North],
> Just as the customs of the South and the North are also different.
> From the time of the Viet, Trieu, Dinh, Ly, and Tran
>   dynasties' establishment of our state,
> And from the time of the Han, Tang, Song, and Yuan dynasties
>   [of the North],
> Each emperor has ruled over his own quarter.
> > [Ung Qua, *"Binh Ngo dai cao,"* 283; trans. Ungar,
> > "Vietnamese Leadership and Order," 96]

---

1. See Gia Long Emperor, "Commemoration of the Defeat of the Tay Son" (chap. 5).

MAPPING THE LAND (MID-SIXTEENTH CENTURY)

As described in the continuation of the *Complete Chronicle of Dai Viet* (1540s), the rise of the next generation of literati through the mid-fifteenth century and the transformation of Dai Viet's government in the 1460s produced a new conceptualization of the Vietnamese state, in the bureaucratic guise of the Ming dynasty. First, with the state's new administrative organization, Le Thanh Tong (r. 1460–1497) set about for the first time in the history of Dai Viet to map the land, focusing on the newly established provinces and their administrative boundaries. The addition of the thirteenth province in 1490 was the result of Dai Viet's victory over Champa in 1471.

[In 1467, sixth month], the king [Le Thanh Tong (r. 1460–1497)] ordered officials of the twelve provinces to investigate, within their jurisdictions, the mountains and the rivers, the dangerous points and the easily traversed, the ancient and the modern, and to draw a careful and detailed map of each province and then to send them to the Ministry of Finance. The ministry would then construct from them a map of the entire realm.

[In 1469, fourth month], the king created the map of the realm's twelve provinces, their prefectures, subprefectures, districts, villages, estates, and highland communities and then listed each province with the numbers of each of these, as well as of the capital region.

[In 1490], fourth month, the king set the new map of the realm, 13 provinces, 52 prefectures, 178 districts, 50 subprefectures, 20 subdistricts, 36 urban zones, 6,851 villages, 322 subvillages, 637 estates, 40 highland communities, 30 upriver communities, and 30 camps.

> [*Dai Viet su ky toan thu* (hereafter, *DVSKTT*), 12, 37a, 51a; 13, 63b;
> trans. John K. Whitmore]

HOANG DUC LUONG

A LITERATI VIEW OF THE LAND (1497)

Even as the Vietnamese maintained their strong sense of the heroic nature of their land and of being "South" against the "North" of the Ming, Dai Viet's growing literati community saw their country as being within the purview of Sinic civilization, or, in Liam Kelley's translation of the term, the "domain of manifest civility." Le Thanh Tong chose the term Thien Nam (South of Heaven) as the name of his realm, thus bringing it into the East Asian civilization's system of shared beliefs. In 1497, the scholar Hoang Duc Luong lamented the missing literary compositions that he felt had prevented the Vietnamese from being fully considered within that domain. He expressed his feelings in the preface to the collection of his poetry, *Selecting the Beautiful Poetry Collection*, which was preserved in *Small Chronicle of Things Seen and Heard* by the eighteenth-century scholar Le Quy Don.

There are reasons why not all poetry has been passed on to later generations. The ancients sometimes compared poetry to minced and broiled meat or to fine silk brocade. Minced and broiled meat is the most delicious object under Heaven, while silk brocade is the most beautiful object under Heaven. Anyone with eyes and a mouth knows that these objects are valuable and does not take them lightly. But poetry has a beauty beyond [all other kinds of] beauty and is of a flavor that surpasses [all other] flavors. You cannot view it with a normal set of eyes, nor can you taste it with a normal mouth. Only poets can appreciate it. This is the first reason why not all poetry has been passed on to later generations.

Ever since the Ly and the Tran established the kingdom, it has been called a domain of manifest civility. Poets and talents [during those two dynasties] all did their best to make a name for themselves, did they not? However, the great scholars and senior ministers all were too busy with official matters to take the time to compile anthologies. Meanwhile, those retired from office, lower officials, and scholars studying for exams paid no heed. This is the second reason why not all poetry has been passed on to later generations.

Among those lower officials and scholars studying for exams were those who attempted to make compilations. But they all eventually gave up when they found how difficult the task was and how insufficient their efforts were. This is the third reason why not all poetry has been passed on to later generations.

Of the books from the Ly and the Tran that we have today, most of them have to do with Thien Buddhism. Could it be that Confucianism was not revered as much as Thien? No, it is that the Thien monks were not subject to prohibitions. As a result, they could publish block-print editions of their works, thereby ensuring their longevity. And no one would dare publish non-Buddhist poetry and writing without first receiving the royal imprimatur. This is the fourth reason why not all poetry has been passed on to later generations.

These four factors have inhibited the dissemination of poetry for a long time, covering three dynasties. Consequently, even masterpieces that enjoyed the protection of the spirits have ended up piecemeal and scattered. Then there are the works recorded on thin parchment and left at the bottom of a chest or case; can we expect them to survive intact through times of turmoil?

When I go to study poetry, all I see are works by Tang poets. Writings from the Ly and the Tran cannot be verified. Sometimes when I come across half a couplet on some crumbling wall, I open a scroll [from the past to try to find the rest of the poem] but end up just sighing. I blame this on the worthies from previous generations.

Goodness! How can we call ourselves a domain of manifest civility, a kingdom that has been established for thousands of years, if we do not have a single scroll as proof and everyone goes back to reciting poetry from the Tang period? Is this not pitiful?!

[Le Quy Don, *Kien van tieu luc,* 4, 15a–16b; trans. Liam Kelley]

DUONG VAN AN

A COSMIC VIEW OF THE LAND (1553)

In the mid-sixteenth century, a more cosmic view of Dai Viet's geographical forma-tion appeared in the opening of Duong Van An's *Recent Record of O Chau* (region of Hue), written during the Mac dynasty (1528–1592). A very important aspect of this de-scription was regionalism, which became a matter of growing concern for the Vietnam-ese rulers from this time onward, as integrating the entire realm became increasingly difficult. The classification of regional populations using personality and other traits can be found in later Vietnamese geographical texts as well, notably in Trinh Hoai Duc's early-nineteenth-century gazetteer, *Gia Dinh Citadel Records*, which describes various attributes of the Vietnamese in the far southern reaches of the kingdom.[2]

There was this Heaven and this Earth, then there were these mountains and these streams, then there were these humans and these creatures. Now, naturally, Heaven and Earth opened and then the mountains and the streams emerged— the mountains piling up, and the streams flowing. And in this way, humans and creatures came into being. If there were no mountains or streams, we would not be able to see the achievement of Heaven's and Earth's creation. If there were no humans or creatures, we would not be able to see the forging force [*khi*] of the streams and mountains. So the cold and heat of Heaven differ and are suitable. Therefore, the mountains and the streams of Earth are finite and the waters and lands of Earth differ and are regular. Therefore, the practices of humans toward one another are difficult to change. Witness, therefore, the lands of Qing and Qi [in China] with their wiles, Chou and Lu [homes of Mencius and Confucius] practicing scholarly customs, with Yong and Yang being able to expand, Jing Han strong and fierce, Wu Han frivolous and shallow, and Yen and Zhao weighty and sincere. Southerners are volatile and careless; northerners are grave and generous.

All over the five places [the center and the four cardinal directions], there are different peoples, but human nature complies with the similarities of old. So, naturally, still more has Hoang Viet [Royal Viet = Dai Viet] established a coun-try. The Celestial Script has determined the lines for it. Beyond the four prov-inces of the northern Red River Delta immediately surrounding the capital, the people of Ai Chau [Thanh Hoa], individually and collectively, are good at *nghia*

---

2. For excerpts from the gazetteer, see Trinh Hoai Duc, "Climate and Geography of Gia Dinh," "Customs of Gia Dinh," and "Temple of the General of the Southern Seas" (all in chap. 5). The concern with regionalism may also be seen in the statements by Nguyen Hoang, "Deathbed Statement to His Son"; Nguyen Khoa Chiem, *The Enterprise of the Southern Court*; and Nguyen Phuc Khoat, "Edict Declaring Autonomy" (all in chap. 4). For a discussion of *khi*, see Le Quy Don, "On *ly* and *khi*" (chap. 4).

[or] righteous public consciousness, and the people of Hoan and Dien [Nghe An, Ha Tinh], blunt and real, love learning. Long ago, they came to what was the Good Way [Thien Dao]! Our Hoa Chau farther south is linked [by sea] to the Guang territory,[3] its land is rustic and rude, its customs simple and mean, its creatures sparse and scattered, separate and quite solitary. So they cannot be compared with those of Ai and Hoan.

[Duong Van An, *O Chau can luc*, 2a–2b; trans. John K. Whitmore]

ECONOMICS AND TRADE

LE THAI TO AND NGUYEN TRAI

EDICT ON CURRENCY (1430)

In 1427/1428, when the new Le dynasty took control of the capital, the government, and the entire country, the king and his officials quickly addressed the problem of economic liquidity. The court minister Nguyen Trai drafted an edict on this matter for his lord, Le Loi (Le Thai To [r. 1428–1433]), as recorded in the continuation of the *Complete Chronicle of Dai Viet* (1540s). The new regime needed a system of coinage in circulation in order to stimulate the economy after years of disruption and warfare during the Ho (1400–1407) and Ming (1407–1427) regimes, especially after the Ho regime's disastrous experimentation with paper money. Sufficient metal coinage for the growing economy continued to be a problem in the coming centuries,[4] as was the Vietnamese state's growing dependence on the importation of silver. Indeed, the kingdom's long-term economic and political health was closely bound up with currency issues.

[In 1430], autumn, on the fifth day of the seventh month, the king proclaimed to the lords and the officials, inner and outer, civil and military, subjects and underlings, and others, an edict for a conference on the rules of money, stating, "Now money is the lifeblood and pulse of the people. We cannot be without it! Our land by its nature produces copper veins but, in the past, the copper cash was largely melted down by men of the former Ho regime [1400–1407]. Out of one hundred, scarcely one remains. Today, [therefore,] it is absolutely necessary in the matters of the army and the country that we fill this lack [of copper cash] and seek its circulation for use so as to accord with the desires of the people. How can this lack not be difficult? Recently, Minister Tran spoke of using paper money to replace the copper cash. Morning and evening, we are concerned only with not being able to do this. Now, for those who advocate paper money, [remember that] useless things act on busy people. This is definitely *not* the idea of loving the people and employing wealth!

---

3. The provinces of Guangdong and Guangxi in southeastern China.
4. See Ngo The Lan, "Memorial on the Currency Crisis" (chap. 4).

"Thus, of old, people took gold and silver, skins and silk, as money. That there were no people who could together resolve this problem is alarming. Each of the lords, the officials, and the inner and outer scholars who grasp the times is deliberating on this edict's regulations for money. In order to accord with the desires of the people, we should not take one person's wishes over what a thousand, ten thousand, people do not want, applying it as good law for our generation. We cannot hastily decide this matter just in order to proclaim it. We shall personally select the best response and put it into action."

[*DVSKTT*, 10, 68a–68b; trans. John K. Whitmore]

LE CODE

PUBLIC AND PRIVATE LANDS (1430S)

The new Le law code of the 1430s had at its core both the ten military regulations and the thirty-two laws concerning property. As the Le regime moved away from the royal estates of the Tran era, it began to focus on the villages as the basis of its fiscal structure. In the following revolutionary articles, the Le established both land for the soldiers who had defeated the Ming and public lands within the villages. The capital then drew its revenue from these public lands, farmed locally. Private infringement on these lands was thus a serious and recurring problem for the Le government, which did not impose taxes on private holdings for almost three centuries. As Phan Huy Chu pointed out in 1821, resource control remained a major issue for the Vietnamese state.[5]

Article 342

Whoever sells officially granted land or soldiers' allotment land shall receive sixty strokes of the heavy stick and be demoted two grades. The scribe who drafts the sale agreement as well as the witnesses shall receive a penalty one degree lower. The sale proceeds and the land shall be forfeited to the state.

In the case of mortgage-sale of such land, the penalty shall be sixty strokes of the heavy stick, and the land must be redeemed from the mortgagee-purchaser.

Article 343

Whoever occupies public land beyond the amount authorized shall receive eighty strokes of the heavy stick for usurpation of one *mau* [3,600 square meters] of land, and a one-grade demotion for ten *mau*. In any case the penalty shall not

---

5. See Phan Huy Chu, "State Use of Resources" (chap. 5).

exceed a three-grade demotion. The income from such land shall be confiscated. Those who clear virgin land shall not be prosecuted.

Article 344

Whoever improperly claims to be proprietor of any piece of land belonging to another person shall be demoted one grade for a false claim of one *mau* of land or less, two grades for five *mau* or less, and three grades for ten *mau* or less. In any case, the penalty shall not exceed penal servitude as a heavy work menial.

Whoever encroaches on the boundaries of any piece of land belonging to others shall be demoted one grade.

The offenders in both cases shall return the income from such lands and pay punitive damages equal to the income from their false claims or encroachments.

If the false claim or encroachment involves public land, the penalty shall be increased one degree, and the punitive damages shall be equal to twice the income from such land. The supervisory official who fails to discover the wrongdoing shall be demoted one grade and removed from office.

Article 345

Whoever conceals public land and ponds shall be demoted for the concealment of one *mau* or more, condemned to penal servitude for five *mau* of land or more, and exiled for fifty *mau* or more. The penalty shall not exceed exile to a distant region. In all cases, the tax that should have been imposed on the land or ponds which have been concealed, shall be collected in conformity with tax regulations, together with punitive damages equal to twice the amount of the tax. Any informer shall be rewarded.

Article 346

Whoever cultivates public rice land but does not make grain payments within the time limit shall receive eighty strokes of the heavy stick and must deliver to the state granaries twice the amount of grain due. If the delay is protracted, the land shall be forfeited (completely if officially granted land, and in one part if soldiers' allotment land).

Article 347

After the equitable distribution of rice land by prefectural, district, and village officials, if some land has to be taken back from recipients who are degraded, are dishonorably charged, or die without heir, or, on the other hand, if some land has to be granted to newly promoted public servants or to taxable inhabitants coming of age, the officials at the prefectural, district, or village levels are allowed to make appropriate decisions after careful consideration. If in the equitable distribution of rice land there is some surplus, the regulations on public land shall apply; if there is a shortage, the public land of the village in question or of the ones at the nearest or most convenient location shall be taken for equitable distribution. The land registers shall be amended and submitted to the throne for approval. Every four years, they shall be revised.

Whenever the measurement and distribution of land are not done in timely fashion ("timely fashion" means autumn rice lands shall be measured in spring and distributed in autumn, and summer rice lands shall be measured in autumn and distributed in spring. For example, if an inhabitant reaches the age of fourteen in the current year, the summer rice land shall be measured in the autumn of this year and distributed in the spring of the next; the autumn rice land shall be measured in the spring of next year and distributed that autumn) or do not conform with the regulations on rice lands, the prefectural, district, and village officials shall be fined or demoted in accordance with the gravity of circumstances. If the rice land is not originally virgin land but has been left uncultivated because of a delay in measurement and distribution, the compensatory damages for lost income from land shall be collected from the responsible officials. If the land is misappropriated as private property, the offenders, in addition, shall have to pay to the state treasury punitive damages equal to twice the amount of the misappropriated income.

Article 348

Landowners who, without authority, establish estates where they harbor commoners in flight shall be punished with a fine of three hundred *quan* [strings of cash] if they are first- or second-rank officials. Their estate managers shall be condemned to penal servitude. Landowners who are third-rank or lower officials shall receive a penalty one degree higher. They shall all be required to pay the value of the missed corvée due from the commoners in flight and punitive damages equal to twice that value. Village officials who conceal and do not denounce these offenders shall be demoted. District officials who fail to discover the facts and to take appropriate measures shall be punished in proportion to the gravity of the circumstances. Informers shall be rewarded in accordance with the importance of the cases. Those officials who have reported the facts to the Throne shall not be prosecuted.

[Le Code (hereafter, LC), nos. 342–48; trans. Huy and Tai, *Le Code*, 1:191–93]

FOREIGN TRADE (MID-SIXTEENTH CENTURY)

Even though Dai Viet remained a heavily agricultural land, foreign trade continued, particularly at the port of Van Don in the islands beyond Ha Long Bay, as recorded in the continuation of the *Complete Chronicle of Dai Viet* (1540s). Ships from as far away as Java still came to trade, although, as indicated in the following passages, the government attempted to maintain control over the growing trade. In later centuries, this acceptance continued as the Vietnamese courts did business with a variety of foreigners.

Le Thai Tong [r. 1434–1442] the first year of the Thieu Binh reign [1434]. In the ninth month, Nguyen Ton Tu and Le Dao who were both managing officers of the province of Yen Bang were demoted three ranks and removed from office. The dynasty had prohibited both officials and common people from privately selling foreign goods. When ships from Qua Oa [Java] arrived in the Van Don trading post, Nguyen Ton Tu and others were in charge of investigating and making an accurate count of the ship's cargo. After they had once reported the actual amount, they schemed to alter the accounts and themselves privately sold goods worth more than nine hundred *man* [one *man* is one thousand cash]. Nguyen Ton Tu himself and Le Dao each took possession of one hundred *man*. They were punished, the facts being disclosed.

   Le Thanh Tong [r. 1460–1497], the eighth year of the Quang Thuan reign [1467]. Seafaring vessels of Tiem La [Siam] came to Van Don village and presented to the royal court a memorial of golden leaf and tributary goods. The King refused to accept them.

[DVSKTT, 11, 17a–17b; 12, 41a; trans. Yamamoto, "Van-Don," 4]

LE CODE

LAWS ON FOREIGN COMMERCE (FIFTEENTH CENTURY)

Four articles in the Le dynasty's law code attempted to bring Van Don's inherently loose maritime commerce under state control in ways similar to the official efforts of later ages.[6]

---

6. For seventeenth- and nineteenth-century imperial edicts, see Khanh Duc Emperor, "Edict Prohibiting Foreigners from Taking Up Residence Without Restrictions" (chap. 4), and Minh Mang Emperor, "Policy for Trading with Europeans" (chap. 5).

Article 612

Public servants who, without good reason, go to an estate in Van Don or to a frontier post in the military territories shall be condemned to penal servitude or be exiled. Any informer shall be rewarded with a grade in the honorary hierarchy.

Article 614

Any person serving at or living on a maritime estate or installation who receives a merchant vessel in order to transport goods fraudulently shall be demoted three grades. The *corpus delicti* shall be confiscated and punitive damages for transporting contraband in an amount equal to twice the value of the *corpus delicti* shall be collected for the benefit of the state treasury. Half the damages shall be used to reward any informer. The owner of the maritime estate or installation shall lose his ownership rights.

Article 615

Inhabitants of an estate in Van Don who transport goods of Northern origin to the capital and engage in clandestine trade, instead of obtaining the proper permission of the prefecture and presenting the goods upon arrival at Trieu Dong Bo to the inspection of the merchant marine service, shall be demoted one grade and fined one hundred *quan* [strings of cash]. Such inhabitants shall receive the same punishment if they clandestinely return to the maritime estate without obtaining the proper permission of the merchant marine service and without presenting themselves at the prefectural office for inspection upon arrival at the transit area. In all cases, one-third of the fine imposed on such offenders shall be used to reward informers.

If the offender stops in a village or hamlet to sell the same goods clandestinely, he shall be demoted three grades and fined two hundred *quan*. The reward granted to any informer shall follow the preceding rule.

The head of the prefecture or of the merchant marine service who fails to discover the wrongdoing shall be demoted one grade. In the case of condoning the offense, he shall receive the same demotion as the offender and shall be dismissed from public service.

Article 616

Whenever a foreign merchant vessel is heading toward an estate in Van Don for trading purposes, any maritime inspector who privately goes beyond the farthest limits of his maritime post to carry out his task of control and verification shall be demoted one grade. If a foreign merchant vessel must lie in port a long time, the owner of the estate concerned shall present a detailed application to the prefectural office, which shall take note thereof. Only then shall the vessel be permitted to lie in the port.

Any estate owner who privately harbors a vessel shall be demoted two grades and fined two hundred *quan*, one-third of which shall be used to reward any informer. If such an owner harbors an alien who has not yet reached the age required for registration, he shall be demoted one grade and fined fifty *quan*. Any informer shall be rewarded in accordance with the preceding rule.

[LC, nos. 612, 614–16; trans. Huy and Tai, *Le Code*, 1:263–64]

LE THANH TONG

GOVERNMENT AND THE ECONOMY (1461)

By the mid-fifteenth century, the influence of contemporary Ming thought (Confucianism) on Dai Viet was steadily increasing, which had a major impact on government policy with the ascension of Le Thanh Tong to the throne. Almost immediately, this young ruler expressed—perhaps for the first time by a Vietnamese ruler—the standard Sinic formula for the economy, which was the primacy of agriculture over commerce. The government's protection and encouragement of agriculture continued under this style of administration into the nineteenth century.[7]

[In 1461, the third month], the king [Le Thanh Tong] ordered the officials of the prefectures, the districts, and other jurisdictions down to the village level henceforth in agricultural matters to encourage and to admonish all civil and military personnel to work diligently at their callings so as to have enough to wear and to eat. "We must not cast aside the basic [agriculture] and follow the insignificant [commerce]. We need to put aside sharp dealing, wandering, and loafing. If those with land do not cultivate it diligently, the said administrative officials will forward an essay on the crime to the royal court."

[*DVSKTT*, 12, 7b; trans. John K. Whitmore]

LE CODE

DRAFT ANIMALS (FIFTEENTH CENTURY)

The significance of beasts of burden and vehicles described in the earlier edicts recorded in Le Van Huu's *Chronicle of Dai Viet* (1272) continued to be emphasized in the Le Code. The inclusion of boats in these articles confirms their importance to transportation and communication in the Red River Delta and along the coast.

---

7. An articulation of this principle in the late eighteenth century may be seen in Quang Trung Emperor, "Edict Encouraging Agriculture" (chap. 4).

Article 584

Whoever unwarrantedly appropriates a buffalo, ox, horse, or boat belonging to other people shall receive eighty strokes of the heavy stick. He shall return the animal or boat or its pecuniary equivalent to the lawful master or owner and pay as punitive damages an amount equal to its price.

Whoever forcibly takes such property from other people shall be demoted one grade. The restitution of the property as well as the payment of damages shall be governed by the preceding principle.

Whoever beats or stabs to death other people's cattle or horses shall receive seventy strokes of the heavy stick and be demoted three grades. He shall also pay compensatory and punitive damages as in the preceding cases.

Whoever damages a boat or injures one of the above animals shall receive fifty strokes of the light stick and a one-grade demotion. He shall pay damages commensurate with the degree of the damage or the injury.

Article 585

Whenever buffaloes or oxen owned by two families fight each other, these families shall be allowed to share the meat of the killed animal and use in common the surviving animal for land cultivation. Offenders shall receive eighty strokes of the heavy stick.

[LC, nos. 584–85; trans. Huy and Tai, *Le Code*, 1:258]

LE CODE

ELEPHANTS (FIFTEENTH CENTURY)

One aspect of Vietnamese warfare that followed the standard Southeast Asian pattern was the use of elephants in heavy fighting. Elephants served the Vietnamese well against Northern invaders, who lacked experience in handling these huge animals. The Le Code meted out severe punishment for mishandling or losing control over elephants, while it fined those responsible for any social or economic damage caused by these large beasts.

Article 583

Any person responsible for army elephant stables who releases these animals therefrom and lets them damage people's dwellings or the bamboos and trees in people's gardens shall receive the heavy stick penalty or a demotion. Supervisory officers shall be fined.

If the elephants rampage uncontrollably, thereby causing death or injury to a human being, the person responsible for the elephant stables shall be charged with the crime of unintentional killing or injuring, with a reduction in the penalty. In the case in which such person unleashes the animals for the purpose of causing death or injury to people, he shall receive a penalty two degrees lower than that imposed for ordinary killing or injuring. Owners of the property damaged by elephants must call on neighbors for an assessment of the losses and report such fact to the competent officials. Such owners may not thoughtlessly beat or stab the elephants. Offenders shall be demoted or condemned to penal servitude and shall pay damages amounting to fifty *quan* [strings of cash] in the case in which the animals are injured; if death ensues, they shall be exiled and shall pay damages amounting to three hundred *quan*.

[LC, no. 583; trans. Huy and Tai, *Le Code*, 1:258]

LE CODE

MARKET REGULATIONS (FIFTEENTH CENTURY)

Even though Le Thanh Tong's government was strongly Confucian and considered agriculture to be the root (the fundamental source of the state's economic well-being) and other economic forms to be extraneous, his officials were closely involved in other aspects of the local economy. The local marketplace was central to this effort, in which the government tried to be evenhanded. The efforts to standardize weights and measures were calculated to engender trust in market operations and to demonstrate the state's effort to keep the economy working smoothly, with minimal disruptions.

Article 186

Market supervisors within the capital city who improperly demand contributions for celebration of the New Year festival shall receive fifty strokes of the light stick and be demoted one grade. If they impose excessive taxes, they shall be demoted two grades and removed from their posts. They shall return the exacted money or goods to the people concerned and shall pay punitive damages equal to the value of the *corpus delicti*. In addition, they shall be subject to a fine designed to reward any informer as prescribed by law. Those who collect illegal taxes for the market supervisors shall receive eighty strokes of the heavy stick and shall be exposed at the market for three days as a warning to the people.

The collection of illegal taxes at the markets in the prefectures, districts, villages, and hamlets shall be subject to the same punishments increased one degree.

Article 187

In the markets of the capital, villages, or hamlets, those who disregard the official measurements of weight, length, or volume and privately modify measurement instruments used in the buying or selling of merchandise shall be demoted or condemned to penal servitude.

[LC, nos. 186–87; trans. Huy and Tai, *Le Code*, 1:155–56]

PHILOSOPHY AND RELIGION

PRAYING FOR RAIN (MID-SIXTEENTH CENTURY)

Although Buddhism no longer was recognized as the central religion of the Le dynasty's royal court, its temples and rituals remained spiritually significant across the realm. Especially in times of drought, all spiritual powers, Buddhist included, were mobilized in the effort to bring rain, as recorded in the continuation to the *Complete Chronicle of Dai Viet* (1540s).

[In 1448, the sixth month], the throne commanded all civil and military officials to fast, prepare themselves, and proceed to the Bao An temple in the Canh Linh palace to pray for rain. The king [Le Nhan Tong (r. 1442–1459)] personally performed the ritual of prayer and ordered the court minister Trinh Kha to travel to the village of Co Chau to greet the image of the Phap Van Buddha and to escort the image to the Bao Thien temple in the capital. The throne ordered Buddhist monks to chant the ritual and to pray. The king and the queen mother prayed and performed this ritual. They bestowed on the Buddhist monks and their disciples ten rolls of thin silk and twenty strings in new cash. That day, the throne released twenty-four suspected and difficult prisoners.

[*DVSKTT*, 11, 68b; trans. John K. Whitmore]

DEBATE OVER MUSIC AND RITUAL (MID-SIXTEENTH CENTURY)

Having abandoned the royal rituals of the Ly and the Tran courts, the new Le dynasty faced an ideological void. As courtiers and officials sought to fill it, a dispute arose over whether the old rituals should be brought back (as the minister Nguyen Trai argued) or the new rituals of the contemporary Ming dynasty should be adopted (as the new generation of scholars advised). The continuation of the *Complete Chronicle of Dai Viet* (1540s) illustrates how the young king, Le Thai Tong (r. 1434–1442), at first followed Nguyen Trai's advice to maintain the old rituals and then reversed himself, switching to the new Ming rituals and music. The rituals described here continued to be observed at the Vietnamese courts into the twentieth century.

[In 1437, the first month], the king ordered the court minister Nguyen Trai, with the official Luong Dang, to oversee the work on the bells and the carriages [royal protocol], the musical instruments, and the training in court music and dance.

Nguyen Trai proceeded to draw up and present to the throne a sketch of a stone chime and declared, "It is said, in times of strife, use military means; in times of peace, apply the proper civilized patterns. Now is precisely the time we need to perform the rites and the music. Yet we do not have the foundation for this and thus cannot establish it. Since we do not have the proper patterns, we cannot perform them correctly. Peace is the foundation of music, and sound forms its proper pattern. Your subject obeys your command to perform the music and does not dare not to give all his heart and effort to it. Yet, because the study and training is weak, I am afraid that it will be difficult to make the prosody harmonious. I request that the throne love and nourish the people so that those in the villages will not have discordant voices—that is the way *not* to lose the foundation of the music!"

The throne praised and accepted Nguyen Trai's proposal, ordering stone masons from Mount Giap district [in Thanh Hoa Province, to the south] to carve out stone from Mount Kinh Chu in order to make the stone chimes in the old way.

In the fifth month, Nguyen Trai reported to the throne, "Even though your subject and Luong Dang have worked on the proper music for the court, your subject's perceptions do not match those of Luong Dang. Your subject asks to withdraw from your mandate." Before this, Le Thai To [r. 1428–1433] had ordered Nguyen Trai to determine the system of court dress and headgear, but it had yet to be put in place. At this point, Luong Dang presented his own study that, in general, said, "In speaking of ritual, there are the ceremonies of the Great Court and the Common Court. To sacrifice to Heaven and report to the Temple of the Ancestors on sacred days and at Tet Nguyen Dan [New Year], then we do the Great Ceremonies. . . . We cannot merely use one single general pattern of music but must instead employ a music specific to each occasion. [Then he gave more detail about the carriages and implements for the rites and concluded,] your subject cannot put it all down in writing."

After this document had been presented, the throne again sent Luong Dang to prepare it. Luong Dang thereupon took the opportunity to present a new set of regulations regarding court clothing and music. In general, the proposals put forward by Luong Dang and Nguyen Trai contained many points that differed. Their discussions on large and small musical ensembles, heavy and light music, had many contradictory points, and their reports did not agree. Because of this, Nguyen Trai withdrew his proposal. The throne listened to Luong Dang's discussion and followed it. The king visited the ancestral temple where students performed a proper dance. There were no more performances of vulgar, lewd music and dance.

[In the eighth month], the official Bui Cam Ho presented a memorial to the throne, stating, "Since Your Majesty took the throne, there have been many changes in Le Thai To's institutions, such as those proposed by the official Luong Dang. The founding ruler employed those people with little literacy as his courtiers [that is, his lieutenants from the mountains of Thanh Hoa]. Yet we see that these men are ordinary and rustic, and we cannot work personally and closely with them, resulting in our remaining literati [and not becoming officials]. Today, the royal court also has taken these men as officials. Your subject wishes the throne to consider this."

In the ninth month, the official Luong Dang, now also officially in charge of the court music, presented the new music, modeled on the system of the Ming court, and began using it. Earlier Luong Dang and Nguyen Trai had obeyed the royal command to create the court music. Music at the upper level had the eight types of sound. . . .[8] Music at the lower level included . . . other patterns.

In the eleventh month, on the ritual occasions, specifically the days of Thanh Tiet [sacred sacrifices], Nguyen Dan [New Year], the new and full moons, ordinary court days, and great banquets, all were newly established. Before this, the king had ordered Luong Dang to set up the ritual for the Great Court events, and now he finished and presented it. The throne immediately had him record the annotations and post them outside the Thua Thien gate. The king visited and performed the new ritual at the ancestral temple. Beginning with this time, the officials wore the courtly garments and performed the new ritual.

[DVSKTT, 11, 35a–36a, 38a–39a, 45b–46b, 47b; trans. John K. Whitmore]

PHAN PHU TIEN

THE TEMPLE OF LITERATURE (1455)

When compiling the first continuation to the *Chronicle of Dai Viet*, covering the preceding Tran dynasty, in 1455, the scholar-official Phan Phu Tien added a variety of comments on the text. In the comment here, he discusses Confucian scholars (V: *nho*; C: *ru*) and the need to maintain continuity in thought through the centuries. The matter at hand was the Vietnamese Temple of Literature (Van Mieu) and who should be commemorated in it.[9] This temple was the central site for Confucian learning and ritual in Dai Viet and remained the focus of the public recognition of scholars' achievements until the early twentieth century when the civil service examinations were finally abandoned.

Those famous scholars through the ages who were able to put aside aberrant thought and transmit Dao Thong [linking ancient thought and the present age]

---

8. The eight types of sound are stone, metal, silk, bamboo, wood, hide, gourd, and earth.

9. For a mid-seventeenth-century example of the commemorative steles erected in honor of these scholars, see "Temple of Literature Stele for the Examination of 1623" (chap. 4).

have taken their places in the Temple of Literature. This showed clearly the origins of the Dao Hoc [study of the Way]. Tran Nghe Tong [r. 1370–1394] brought Chu Van An, Truong Han Sieu, and Do Tu Binh into the Temple. Truong Han Sieu was firm in his beliefs and put aside Buddhist thought, while Chu Van An set himself right through his writings, maintained this spirit, and did not seek personal success. These two scholars were fine. As to Do Tu Binh, he was lacking in scholarship and covetous. Now this villain who obstructed the affairs of state—how could he have been allowed into [the Temple]?

[*DVSKTT*, 8, 4a–4b; trans. Whitmore, "Text and Thought," 263]

LE THANH TONG

CHANGING THE REIGN NAME (1469)

Northern ritual was at the core of the state's activities in the new regime. Accordingly, when Le Thanh Tong changed the title of his reign from Quang Thuan (Broadly Conforming [to Heaven's Will]) to Hong Duc (Overflowing Virtue) in 1469, the continuation of the *Complete Chronicle of Dai Viet* (1540s) recorded his discussion of the significance of such ritual acts. The young emperor and his scholar-officials had completed the transformation of the government according to their bureaucratic style, and the crops were good, showing Heaven's favor for their actions. The emperor thus believed that this warranted a new name for his reign. Le Thanh Tong followed the Ming pattern of ritual, as argued in the 1430s, and quickly established the Sacrifice to Heaven (Nam Giao), which continued until the twentieth century. In the late eighteenth century, the scholar Pham Dinh Ho recorded a description of the Nam Giao ceremony.[10] Le Thanh Tong also greatly limited Buddhist activities (as did the Gia Long emperor in 1804).[11]

[In 1469], eleventh month, sixteenth day, the king proclaimed a great amnesty to mark the change in the name of the reign period [from Quang Thuan (Broadly Conforming [to Heaven's Will])] to Hong Duc, "Overflowing Virtue," making the next year the first of that reign period. On the eighteenth day, the king proclaimed to all civil and military officials and the people throughout the realm, "We are that which separates the human from the bestial. We do so by using rites as protective measures. If there are no rites, then reckless emotions will be let loose, and people will let their passions go, releasing mean and low feelings, depraved and extravagant desires—there will be no end to them! From today on, whenever all ranks of officials and their underlings are transferred or promoted, removed or given a position, the Ministry of Civil Service will send a letter to the prefecture, the district, and the village of the particular official, instructing the village

---

10. See Pham Dinh Ho, "Ritual for Venerating Heaven" (chap. 4).
11. See Gia Long Emperor, "Edict Outlining Propriety and Ritual" (chap. 5).

headman to prepare a statement on the official's proper offerings in ritual: Were the official and the people of his jurisdiction in the year past up to standard? Were the marriages performed in accordance with the proper ceremonies? Were the betrothals of the region celebrated and made known? The official will be promoted or removed according to regulation. If there are any men who do not do this and yet rise above their station, the local official shall mark them with ink and banish them."

[*DVSKTT*, 12, 51b–52a; trans. John K. Whitmore]

RULES OF BEHAVIOR (1471)

The *Book of Good Government of the Hong Duc Era* (1540s) includes the following summary of Confucian expectations for personal conduct in Dai Viet. These rules, drawn up in 1471, were conspicuously male oriented and worked against the assertion of women's authority in Vietnamese society. Their purpose was to guide society's behavior, especially that of the officials, and to form a model for future royal edicts that sought to impose the same values throughout society. These articles were measures of whether a scholar would be eligible for service, as the state made inquiries all the way down to the applicant's village. This was the first such set of behavioral expectations to appear in Dai Viet. In later centuries, others followed, and they were periodically reinforced when deemed necessary. In the early eighteenth century, the Trinh rulers drew up detailed guidelines for behavior and conduct, and in the nineteenth century, the Nguyen rulers laid out their expectations for conduct, most notably in the Minh Mang emperor's "Ten Moral Precepts," which were expounded in 1834.[12]

Article 1

Obligation of students toward their teachers: respect. If they show haughtiness and scorn, they shall be punished for lack of respect.

Article 2

Duties of brothers toward one another: mutual respect, love, and harmony. They should not listen to their wives at the expense of (male) blood relatives; if they do, they would attract shame on their family and shall be punished.

---

12. See Trinh Cuong, "Edict Regarding Local Customs" (chap. 4), and Minh Mang Emperor, "Ten Moral Precepts" (chap. 5).

Article 3

Obligations of children toward their parents: strict adherence to moral principles in serving them, feeding them, taking care of their funerals, and providing the ancestral sacrifice for them. No shortening of the mourning period shall be permitted.

Article 4

Duties of friends toward one another: maintain trust, have no jealousy, commit no damaging act. Violation shall lead to punishment.

Article 5

Obligations of men and women vis-à-vis one another: they shall not sit on the same mat, bathe at the same ford and directly hand over objects to each other.

Article 6

After the fiancé's family has conformed to the demands of the marriage rites and delivered the marriage gift, the fiancée shall, on the wedding day, go immediately to her husband's house to live. No one shall adhere to the corrupt ancient custom of compelling the husband to live and work in the fiancée's house for three years.

> [*Hong Duc thien chinh thu* (hereafter, *HDTCT*),
> nos. 95–100; trans. Huy and Tai, *Le Code*, 2:107–8]

NGO SI LIEN

LITERATI BELIEFS (1479)

In 1479, the historian Ngo Si Lien finished reworking the new edition of the *Complete Chronicle of Dai Viet* and, like Le Van Huu and Phan Phu Tien before him, added his own comments. He attacked the classical beliefs of the fourteenth-century scholars that had become embodied in the Ho regime when Ho Quy Ly used classical references to enhance his legitimacy. Ngo Si Lien instead emphasized Neo-Confucian values (those of the twelfth-century Chinese philosopher Zhu Xi) while also commenting favorably on the Trung sisters of the first century C.E. He stressed the continuing efficacy of the Trung sisters' spirit cult even as he masculinized the two women as scholars and warriors. Yet there was little philosophical discourse among Vietnamese

Confucians until the eighteenth century.[13] The accumulated practical lore of these northern scholar-officials was compiled by Phan Huy Chu in *Categorized Records of the Institutions of Successive Dynasties* (1821).

Confucianism

If, in the way of the ancients, there had been no Confucius, there would have been no one who understood it [the Way]. If, after the birth of the ancients, there had been no Confucius, there would have been no one who took it as regulating his life. Since mankind emerged, there has been no one as great as Confucius, yet Ho Quy Ly dared to take him lightly—truly, Ho Quy Ly did not know what was important!

Zhu Xi analyzed clearly and thoroughly and explained broadly. Indeed, he brought together the great accomplishments of the earlier scholars and is the model for later studies.

In the process, Zhu filled in the gaps and refined the results. All who follow need only to consult his work.

The Cult of the Trung Sisters

Trung Trac, angry with the tyrannical Han governor, raising her hand and shouting out, all but united and restored our country. Her heroic courage was not limited to her lifetime achievements of establishing the land and proclaiming herself queen, but after her death she also resisted misfortune, for, in times of flood or drought, prayers to her spirit have never gone unanswered. And it is the same with her younger sister. Because they had both the virtue of scholars and the temperament of warriors, there are no greater spirits in all Heaven and Earth. Should not all great heroes nurture an attitude of upright hauteur such as they had?

[Ngo Si Lien, *DVSKTT*, 8, 27b–28a, *Outer Records*, 3, 2a; trans. Whitmore, "Text and Thought," 265; Taylor, *Birth of Vietnam*, 336]

VU QUYNH

COLLECTING TALES (1492)

In the 1490s, the renowned scholar-official Vu Quynh edited the fourteenth-century *Strange Tales from South of the Passes* and adapted it to Le Thanh Tong's new state and society, with its Confucian morality.

---

13. See Le Quy Don, "On *ly* and *khi*" (chap. 4).

In ancient times there were not yet books of history to record the facts; therefore nearly all the old affairs have been forgotten and lost. Still, some items were not neglected, having been passed down orally [although] only among persons of special ability. . . . Now I do not know in which dynasty this collection of handed-down tales was written or by whom. My opinion is that it was initially drafted during the Ly or Tran dynasty [1009–1400], in rough form by an eminent scholar of broad learning, and then enriched and adorned by learned and accomplished gentlemen of the present day. . . . This material, though wonderful, does not reach the point of extravagance, and this literature, though unorthodox, does not reach the point of fantasy. Although [this literature was] passed down through an unverified tradition, not being found in the classics, it still has something that can be relied on, namely, to warn against evil and to exhort the people to reform, to discard the false and to follow the true, thereby encouraging public morality. . . . Alas! The wonders of Linh Nam [South of the Passes] are differently reported; these tales have not been engraved in stone or recorded in books but have been kept in the hearts of the people and inscribed in the tongues of men. The leader, able to do what is proper, cherishes and admonishes the young and the old alike, so their deeds will be bounded by principles and rules and enclosed in public morality. Is there not some small use in this?

I first encountered this manuscript in the spring of 1492. I opened it up and carefully read it. It did not lack confusions caused by clerical errors and obscure meanings. So, setting aside the low and vulgar, I revised and corrected it, arranged it into three chapters, and entitled it *Linh Nam chich quai liet truyen* [*Strange Tales from South of the Passes*]. I kept it in my home to read at my leisure and to improve it with a view toward publishing. I enriched and adorned it so that it might be brought to perfection; I examined its characters, refined its phrases, and expanded its meanings. All this I did for the benefit of future scholars fond of the past; is it possible that there will be such persons? Thus I have written this preface; autumn, 1492.

> [*Linh Nam chich quai liet truyen*; trans. adapted from Taylor,
> *Birth of Vietnam*, 355]

LITERATI AND BUDDHIST TEMPLE INSCRIPTIONS (SIXTEENTH CENTURY)

Most of the Vietnamese literati grew up and were educated in the villages, returning to them when not in service to the state. Vietnamese Confucianism thus was centered in the countryside rather than in the cities, and in the sixteenth century, Confucian scholars even composed texts for inscriptions at the local Buddhist temples. As members of the village community, these scholars felt an obligation to do so but also to explain why literati like themselves composed inscriptions for Buddhists.

Now how can Confucians be involved in Buddhist services? In addition, I've often heard that our Confucian predecessors did not write about Buddhist affairs. However, because of getting pleasure from the goodness of human beings, I'd like to join them [the Buddhists] in promoting goodness.

Inscription from the Linh Cam Temple (1557)

As a Confucian, I always remember the words of my predecessors, which state, "The rise and fall of Buddhist temples does not concern me." When Buddhist inscriptions are engraved or effaced, how does this require my words? Yet a true Confucian [superior man; V: *quan tu*; C: *junzi*] takes joy in the goodness of people of the Middle Path [Buddhism] and cannot limit himself to words. Consequently, I write this inscription to be engraved on the stone.

Inscription from the Thanh Quang Temple (1562)

As a Confucian I do not adore Buddhism. However, I am fond of joining people in doing good things, thus, I dare not reject their demands for an inscription.

I often hear the words "advocating goodness as the master did." So taught the *Shujing* [*Classic of Documents*]. How can those who want to do good things not seek the truth from these words?

Inscription from the Sung An Temple (1578)
[Han Nom Institute Library, nos. 2189, 5433, 8518–19; trans. Nguyen Nam, "Being
Confucian in Sixteenth Century Vietnam," 147, 149]

NGUYEN BINH KHIEM

THE THREE TEACHINGS (1578)

Even though the Mac government emphasized Confucian rule, Buddhist temples thrived in the villages, as the following temple inscription, written by the famous scholar Nguyen Binh Khiem (1491–1585), makes clear. In this case, the Buddhist temple also included elements of Daoist and Confucian beliefs. Indeed, the "Three Teachings" formed a syncretic belief system integrating the tenets of Buddhism, Confucianism, and Daoism, a system that could be found at all levels of Vietnamese society, with the balance among the three elements varying by time and location.

Stele Inscription with a Preface (Composed on the Occasion of) Building the Statues of the Three Teachings at Cao Duong

The ancient temple of Thuy Anh at Cao Duong has been renowned for its spiritual efficacy. The Buddhist hall is so dignified that it makes one look up with reverence. The bell tower is so lofty that it makes people all hear. All who pray here have their prayers answered. It is the most fortunate place in Thai Binh province. This village has enlightened gentlemen and benevolent ladies who, in the years of the Thuan Thien reign [Le Thai To (r. 1428–1433)], offered their seven *mau* of cultivated land to be the property of the Three Jewels. All people extol their attitude of taking joy in virtue. Now, the village literati Bui Tu Trang, Nguyen Le, Tong Moc, Nguyen Lam, together with monks and nuns, contributed money and directed craftsmen to cast the precious statues of the Three Teachings and of Miao Shan.[14]

After finishing the work, they asked me to compose the inscription to record the event. I also have a mind and heart fond of doing good and dare not refuse. However, I am a Confucian [V: *nho*; C: *ru*]. Although I am not well versed in Buddhism and the Daoism of Laozi [V: Lao Tu], I have read broadly and dispelled my doubts and learned something of their theories. Generally speaking, the Buddhist teaching is rooted in illuminating physical forms and the mind, and analyzing cause and effect. Daoism is based on concentrating on the vital energy [V: *khi*; C: *qi*) to make it supple, preserving oneness and keeping to genuineness. The sage Confucius rooted his teachings in morality, benevolence and righteousness, literature, life's realities, loyalty, and good faith. Aren't all of them the teachings that follow human nature in order to cultivate the Way?

Miao Shan got her reputation because of her goodness, which is nothing but the dwelling place of the mind/heart and human nature. All these virtuous ones were indeed able to spread the light of this Path of goodness, follow and preserve this teaching of goodness, establish themselves to be good examples for people, so that happiness and blessings would flow forever; their merits are inconceivable.

Accordingly, I have inscribed this on a solid piece of stone so that the transmission of their teaching shall endure through ages. The inscription reads as follows,

What Heaven imparts to man is called human nature,
To follow our nature is called the Way.
It is rooted in the Mind and lodged in the Teachings.
The forms through which it has been bequeathed to us are full of dignity,
Eternal and ageless as Heaven.

[Han Nom Institute Library, nos. 2696–97; trans. Nguyen Nam,
"Being Confucian in Sixteenth Century Vietnam," 143]

---

14. Miao Shan (V: Dieu Thien) was the Guan Yin (goddess of mercy) of the Southern Seas.

GOVERNANCE

LE THAI TO AND NGUYEN TRAI

HOW TO GOVERN (1430)

After the two decades of Ming occupation (1407–1427), the new Le dynasty sought to establish a more effective model of government for Dai Viet. The outcome was a blend of the leadership styles of the successful warrior chief Le Loi (Le Thai To [r. 1428–1433]), who was from the hills of Thanh Hoa southwest of the capital, and the famous literatus-minister Nguyen Trai (1380–1442). The new administration thus mixed aristocratic and literati rule. These two approaches are presented in *True Record of Mount Lam*, a description of the successful ten-year resistance against the Ming. Written from the new king's point of view, this work stresses his and his soldiers' warfare and suffering in their effort to set up the new government. This collaboration by royals and literati set the tone for later such partnerships, including that between Ngo Thi Nham and the Quang Trung emperor in the late eighteenth century. A similar remembrance can be found in the call for support by an eighteenth-century descendant of Le Loi's, the rebel prince Le Duy Mat.[15]

I consider that living things have their origins in Heaven and that man originates from his ancestors. Just as the tree must have its root and water its source, so from ancient times it was with the rise of emperors and kings. The Shang dynasty began with Yu Song, the Zhou with Yu Tai. . . . If the first generation's humaneness and kindness had not multiplied so thickly and if the gathering of blessings and favor had not been overwhelming, how could this not be the case?

During the troubled times, I met with many hardships; founding the state yet involved me in more difficulties. How fortunate that Heaven and men rallied to our cause. The fact that our meritorious achievement was completed is surely owing to the attainments of my ancestors in storing up virtue and accumulating goodness by their works of merit. I reflect on these things without cease and therefore have had them recorded in this book, entitled *The True Record of Mount Lam*, to give weight to the meaning of "origin" and further to describe the toll of my hardships and troubles so as to inform my children and grandchildren for generations to come.

The relationship between prince and subjects is that they dwell together in a great sense of obligation. Their kindness to each other is like that of flesh and blood: How can there be suspicion? How can there be jealousy among them? By this feeling of relationship, we have been able to win the heart of the masses, and people all happily follow us.

---

15. See Le Duy Mat, "Proclamation to Rally Troops" (chap. 4).

With respect to Heaven, it is difficult to make plans, for Heaven's Mandate is not constant. We must think about the difficulties in order to plan what is easy. With respect to merit, it is difficult to achieve, yet easily lost. We must be scrupulous about the beginnings and yet plan the conclusion.

When you think of delicious feasts, remember the months when I lacked food and went starving and thirsty. Wearing bright brocades and satins, you must think back to days past when my clothes were in tatters with no change be it winter or summer. Gazing on the splendid towers of the palace, remember how in times past I drank the rain and made a bed on sand, running and hiding in the mountain forests. Seeing the palace women, numerous and beautiful, think how, in the past, my fellow villagers were lost to me, wives and children scattered and dead.

We must guard against the causes of rebellion or they will arise from a life of ease. We must admonish all you ministers against pride and arrogance or they will arise from a life of indolence and pleasure.

Truly it is for my descendants to be able to see deeply [into the founder's principles].

> [Nguyen Trai, *Lam Son thuc luc*, 3, 33b–34a, 12; trans. Ungar,
> "Vietnamese Leadership and Order," 88–90, 92–94]

LE CODE

VILLAGE REGISTERS (1430S)

The new Le regime constructed an entirely new fiscal base for its government. Le Thai To used the idea of village registers from earlier centuries to set aside plots whose produce would fund the state. Then, in the 1430s, borrowing the idea of a law code from the Ming (though retaining the framework of the earlier Tang code), the Le compiled their own legal system. The initial portion of the new law code focuses on public land and an indigenous sense of property, reflecting very little influence from Northern law codes. The Vietnamese state continued using these village registers until modern times.

Article 368

If, in the registers of ponds and sandy tracts, and the registers of various taxes presented to the Throne, a large area is reported as a small one, productive as unproductive, a higher tax category as a lower tax category, or if there is any increase, decrease, or change resulting in a loss for the state or damage to the public, responsible prefectural, district, and village officials shall all be punished in proportion to the gravity of the increase, decrease, or change for the crime of concealment of state property. Officials of the departments and agencies in charge of endorsing these registers who negligently overlook such concealment shall be fined; but if they tolerate the fraud, they shall receive the same penalty as offenders.

Article 369

If there are natural resources usable by the armed forces or the state within an official's jurisdiction and yet he fails to survey them and memorialize the king, he shall be demoted one grade. Informers whose reports prove to be well founded shall be rewarded in proportion to the importance of the case.

[LC, nos. 368–69; trans. Huy and Tai, *Le Code*, 1:197]

DEMOTION OF THE QUEEN (MID-SIXTEENTH CENTURY)

Unlike the Tran and Ho dynasties, during the early Le era the royal family was quite weak and was confronted by the powerful new aristocracy from the hills of Mount Lam. The contest between these two political forces played out in numerous ways. Among them was a struggle in the royal women's quarters to determine which royal wife would be queen and produce the next ruler of Dai Viet. This issue was significant, since political alliances between powerful regional families and the central court were cemented through the marriages of daughters. In this case, Duong Thi Bi, the mother of the king's firstborn son, Nghi Dan, was from the Red River Delta, but she found herself being displaced by the Thanh Hoa aristocracy. She did not go quietly, as the continuation of the *Complete Chronicle of Dai Viet* (1540s) shows.

Duong Thi Bi produced a son, Le Nghi Dan. The king, Le Thai Tong [r. 1434–1442], made him crown prince. The queen, purposely and willfully, increased her haughtiness fourfold. The king was forbearing and patient, demoting her merely to Chieu Nghi Lady in the hope that she would change her ways. But Duong Thi Bi had become even more discontented and feared nothing. The king, seeing Duong Thi Bi become so distraught, felt that, though she had borne his son, she was of uncertain virtue, and so he demoted her to the status of a commoner. Consequently, he made a proclamation to the realm causing it to be clearly known that the position of crown prince had yet to be decided.

[DVSKTT, 11, 53b–54a; trans. Whitmore, "Establishment of Le Government," 34]

PHAN PHU TIEN

CONTINUITY IN GOVERNANCE (1455)

Phan Phu Tien, one of the older generation of scholars, began to compose the continuation of the *Chronicle of Dai Viet* in 1455, adding a section on the Tran dynasty to that on the earlier Ly. His comment on the death of the renowned ruler Tran Minh Tong (r. 1314–1357) a century earlier also may be construed as a comment to his own ruler, Le Nhan Tong (r. 1442–1459), on the politics of his own time when "noisy" officials influenced policy and, in his view, not necessarily for the better. Phan Phu Tien was arguing for continuity over change and the separation of North and South.

Tran Minh Tong was of a humane and generous disposition. Receiving the craft of great peace, which his ancestors had accomplished through their institutions, there was nothing he would have changed. At the time, some scholars proposed a memorial stating that there were many vagrants and wanderers among the people. There was no record of these people, even when they were old, so they [had not been recorded and] did not pay taxes and levies. The official runners did not reach these people. The king said, "If it is not like this, then how does one achieve the craft of great peace? You wish *us* to make this happen—[but] how will this accomplish anything?"

The court officials Le Quat and Pham Su Manh, each a scholar-official, wanted to change the administrative system. The king said, "This country itself has refined institutions. The South and the North each has a differing pattern. If we listen to white-faced, bookish students seeking to dispense with what we have established and devise new schemes, then disaster will definitely result."

The one occasion that we can deem regrettable was when King Tran Minh Tong listened to the crafty flattery of Tran Khac Chung and, as a result, killed the prime minister/father of the queen—isn't this the trouble with such cleverness, of listening to bright people?

[*DVSKTT*, 7, 21a–21b; trans. John K. Whitmore]

LE THANH TONG

LITERATI GOVERNMENT (1463)

Le Thanh Tong (r. 1460–1497) wanted a new approach to government. In 1463, he addressed his ministers, officials, and lords, stating that he wished the lords to accept his command, whereas the officials were to be quite open with him, as it was their responsibility to remonstrate and to present memorials to him. This was a reversal of Phan Phu Tien's advice a decade earlier to Le Thanh Tong's older brother Le Nhan Tong against change or listening to the scholar-officials. In later centuries, such memorials remained the standard for scholar-officials' action, and the eighteenth-century portion of this book offers several memorials by officials inspired by the scholar-bureaucrats' emphasis on candor. Le Thanh Tong also established the triennial examination system, for which a commemorative stone inscription was eventually written (1484) for each examination.[16] The following proclamation marks the transition from the aristocratic

---

16. See "Temple of Literature Stele for the Examination of 1623" (chap. 4).

style of government to the bureaucratic approach. It also is the first time that the six ministries of the North (minus Public Works) are described as a functioning entity in the administration of Dai Viet. Later regimes (the Le-Trinh, Tay Son, and Nguyen dynasties) also followed the pattern begun by Le Thanh Tong.[17] The continuation of the *Complete Chronicle of Dai Viet* (1540s) describes the new model.

[In 1463], winter, tenth month, the king proclaimed to all the ministers of the royal court, "Recently, the official Nguyen Phuc observed the great drought of the past spring and, in the third month, stated that we must do something, encouraging the throne to be serene while observing change and to be militant in protecting the royal person. The throne did not listen, and consequently nothing happened. So, the true sage examines the Heavenly Script in order to investigate the changing times and reads the writings of men so as to transform the realm. In the future, will we not be able to take this as a warning? Also, how can we doubt the defeat of such plots?"

[In the] twelfth month, the king proclaimed to the court minister Nguyen Xi and the other lords, "The safety or danger of the altars of the land lies with you, sirs! You need to contemplate this deeply and to apply it with your experience— report for me to hear! The power of the throne within the court will be quick to decide on matters of government. You, sirs, on the outside, will undertake them."

The king called together the minister of civil service, Nguyen Nhu Do, the minister of justice, Tran Phong, the minister of war, Nguyen Vinh Tich, the minister of finance, Nguyen Cu Phap, the minister of rites, Nguyen Dinh My, and quoted Sima Guang[18] to them, "'The Superior Man advances to the basis of good government; the Small Man leads to chaos.' Let us swear to Heaven and Earth to use superior men and to put aside small men. Day and night work diligently. Do not be inattentive to this!"

The king also proclaimed to the ministers and the officials of the Royal Study, "Today, among officials like Le Canh Huy, Nguyen Nhu Do, and Pham Du, some contribute to discussion in the court, [and] some add nothing to government business, whether they flatter and faun or stay silent and say nothing. Though there may be small errors, if you go by the rules, it is all right. Now, Nguyen Mau, Nguyen Vinh Tich, Nguyen Trac, and Nguyen Thien, among others, are able to be concerned about the ruler's well-being and to love the country. When pursuing matters, they exhaust all their words. While there are mistakes and errors in these words, if they are offered in a generous and concerned manner, this, too, is all right. In the past, the words of Nguyen Mau on matters were not true and did not follow the rules. Here the throne tells Nguyen Mau about the virtue of being able to speak."

[DVSKTT, 12, 13a–14a; trans. John K. Whitmore]

---

17. See Trinh Tac, "Edict Regarding Official Postions" (chap. 4).
18. Sima Guang (1019–1086) was a historian and scholar-official of the Song dynasty.

LE THANH TONG

THE PROPER MINISTER (1468)

Le Thanh Tong grew up during the 1440s and 1450s in the palace with his three older half brothers (including the king, Le Nhan Tong [r. 1442–1459], and the future king, Le Nghi Dan [r. 1459–1460]). When he was still a prince, Le Thanh Tong was educated with his brothers by younger scholars who advocated following the Ming model of governance. In the following, the young king, Le Thanh Tong, speaks in the 1460s about one of his tutors who later assisted him in the administrative transformation of Dai Viet. It shows the ideal relationship of ruler and official in the new government, as described in the continuation of the *Complete Chronicle of Dai Viet* (1540s).

Formerly, when I was little, you befriended me. You were a graduate of the Dai Bao days [1440–1442] and worked in the Royal Study. When you were a minister and I was beneath you, you were a close friend and exchanged learning and knowledge with me. When I became ruler and you were my minister, you were like the union of fish and water or the meeting of wind and clouds with me. You were able to exhaust your heart and unify your efforts in my cause. You encouraged the plan of repaying the state what was owed it. You achieved the public good with no private advantage. You blocked corruption. Thus I could be a ruler who knew men and you could be a minister who exhausted his loyalty. Illustrious in friendship, exalted in reputation, you gloried in correcting injustice and being dedicated, not pleasure-taking. If you had not been able to be like this, then I would be a ruler who did not know men and you would have been a minister who was dead [useless] to the throne! Of the two of us, it was you who chose what has been followed.

> [DVSKTT, 12, 48b–49a; trans. Whitmore, "Establishment of Le Government," 99–100]

NGO SI LIEN

SOUTH AND NORTH (1479)

In 1479, when Ngo Si Lien presented to the throne his *Complete Chronicle of Dai Viet*, he included comments on the events of the past that were described in the *Chronicle*. In so doing, he followed the Northern pattern of praise and blame in recounting the past, particularly the chronicle form of the eleventh-century Northern historian Sima Guang. As they had for the historian Phan Phu Tien about a quarter century earlier, these comments also acted as contemporary position papers and were directly relevant to current events. Even though his ruler saw a shared world of North and South within "the domain of manifest civility," Ngo Si Lien discussed the basic reality of the

Vietnamese state (the South) and its relationship to China (the North) in the surrender of Ly Phat Tu (Ly, Son of the Buddha) to the new Sui dynasty of China in 602. Military preparedness, as discussed by Phan Huy Chu in 1821, was always a key issue for the Vietnamese state.[19]

South and North, when strong or when weak, each has its time. When the North is weak, then we are strong, and when the North is strong, then we become weak; that is how things are. This being so, those who lead the country must train soldiers, repair transport, be prepared for surprise attacks, set up obstacles to defend the borders, use the ideas of a large country with the warriors of a small country. Days of leisure should be used to teach loyalty and respect for elders, so the people will clearly know their duty toward superiors and be willing to die for their leaders. If an invasion is imminent, take words and negotiate, or offer gems and silk as tribute; if this does not succeed, then, though dangers flood from every side, man the walls and fight the battles, vowing to resist until death and to die with the altars of the land; in that case one need be ashamed of nothing. But imagine someone who sees the enemy arrive on the border and, without a battle, grows afraid and begs to surrender! The king, Ly Phat Tu, was a coward and none of his officials spoke up; it can be said that there was no one in the country at that time.

[Ngo Si Lien, *DVSKTT, Outer Records*, 4, 22a–22b; trans.
Taylor, *Birth of Vietnam*, 301]

NGO SI LIEN

CRITIQUE OF A PAST COURT MINISTER (1479)

During the twelfth century, the rulers had weakened, and strong ministers, in alliance with the queen mothers, were running the state of Dai Viet. In his comment on that period, Ngo Si Lien expressed his intense dislike for the situation and specifically condemned the court minister Do Anh Vu for having usurped royal authority. As had Le Van Huu in the *Chronicle of Dai Viet* (1272), Ngo Si Lien castigated Do Anh Vu's opponents for their crude actions.

Do Anh Vu was very wicked. Vu Dai and the others, even including all the royal house, united in conspiracy; they were not able to be heard in the royal court and to deal with Do Anh Vu's crime clearly and correctly, so they used soldiers to frighten and coerce an immature sovereign, and this pleased Do Anh Vu by providing a pretext for speaking against Vu Dai. How can we know that Do Anh Vu did not calculate that he could depend upon his illicit affair with the queen

---

19. See Phan Huy Chu, "A Record of Military Systems" (chap. 5).

mother to make heavy use of bribes in order to facilitate his escape and then to proceed with his desire for revenge? It was fortunate for Vu Dai that Nguyen Duong clearly foretold the disaster to come, even to the point that when he saw that his words were not heeded by Vu Dai, he leaped into a well as an omen for Vu Dai. Even so, Vu Dai did not perceive the truth of Nguyen Duong's words and later suffered disaster, leading others into calamity as well! And as for the queen mother, was she without fault? No, her crime was extreme! When the talent, virtue, and authoritative position of Y Doan [C: Yi Yin] and Chu Cong [C: Zhou Gong, Duke of Zhou] are lacking, and there is a desire to resist what they stand for, it is difficult to escape from great and fateful errors.[20]

[Ngo Si Lien, *DVSKTT*, 4, 9a–9b; trans. Taylor,
"Voices Within and Without," 77]

LE THANH TONG

THE PURPOSE OF GOVERNMENT (1485)

During the 1480s, Le Thanh Tong repeatedly reminded his officials of their duties in the new age. For the king, their fundamental tasks were both ceremonial and practical, which he saw as equivalent in the framework of the new government system meant to keep his realm prosperous and in sync with Heaven. The continuation of the *Complete Chronicle of Dai Viet* (1540s) recorded his words to this effect. Two centuries later, in "History of the Country of Annam" (1659),[21] the author Bento Thien described some of the ritual practices that Le Thanh Tong referred to. In the eighteenth century, Le Quy Don wrote extensively about *ly*, the underlying principle of proper administration.[22]

[In 1485, eleventh month], twenty-sixth day, the king established the rites and ceremonies and issued the order for instructions on agriculture and sericulture. The throne proclaimed to the officials in each of the administrative jurisdictions[23] of the realm, "The purpose of ritual is to make good the hearts of the people; the purpose of agriculture is to provide sufficient food and clothing for them. These two matters are the urgent affairs of the government and the responsibility of each office. The throne itself does its utmost to bring this about, in all places transforming the people and refining their customs, through an administration that stresses the positive and removes the negative. In every case, it acts on all the royal instructions, honoring individual effort. Yet some of the people's

---

20. Y Doan (Yi Yin) and the Duke of Zhou were famous figures from classical antiquity.

21. See Bento Thien, "Regarding Festivals" (chap. 4).

22. See Le Quy Don, "On *ly* and *khi*" (chap. 4).

23. The administrative jurisdictions included the administrative and legal offices of each province as well as of the prefectures, the districts, and the subprefectures.

wealth does not contribute to the common surplus, and some of the people's customs do not contribute to great change. How can you all consider books to be an urgent matter and still consider my instructive orders to be merely empty words? How can you all believe that periodic gatherings are paramount and yet dismiss people's practices as beyond the pale, in order to cause what?

"From today, you will cease all your prior bad habits. You will unanimously accept and act on all orders issued by the royal court. The hunger and cold among the common people in many places need be managed by *ly* [proper principle], and so each year the officials of the prefectures, the districts, and the subprefectures will take the time to make observations together in the lowlands and the marshy regions and encourage the peasants in agriculture and sericulture. Where there is a tradition of profit, then follow the local patterns and see that they succeed. If people have a strong tradition, then follow it and urge them to work together. When people have a surplus and there are no abuses causing people to be cold or hungry or to flee, tour your jurisdictions each year—go out into the villages and alleyways where the people live. You must also read and consider the texts of the royal edicts of earlier ages, including the instructions for rites and music of the past and today, as well as the reports on the well-being of the adult population.

"To bring this about, follow the results of good governments in the past. If there are matters injurious to morality and ruinous to customs, you must warn against them. Men of loyalty and conviction, filial piety and brotherly duty, must use their hearts and minds to commend and encourage such behavior. The people will all then return to sincerity and abandon their evil and crafty ways. Who among you is able to honor the heritage, observing and fulfilling it? The two types of office [central and provincial] are to decide on awards for the renowned. In the event that you are merely looking for a steady job and are unwilling to put effort into this, you will be dismissed from office and put into the army."

[*DVSKTT*, 13, 48b–49a; trans. John K. Whitmore]

NGUYEN BINH KHIEM

GOOD GOVERNMENT (1542)

In 1542, Nguyen Binh Khiem, the principal intellect of the mid-sixteenth century, laid out his literati beliefs in the following inscription for a local Buddhist temple, in which he applied fundamental Confucian thought to government and society. For Nguyen Binh Khiem, this meant upholding the proper Confucian relationships (between ruler and subject, husband and wife, father and son, among brothers, and between friends). State and society should be ruled by goodness and the restraint of desire.[24]

---

24. See Le Quy Don, "On *ly* and *khi*" (chap. 4).

Human nature is rooted in goodness. Due to the restraint of the physical [V: *khi*; C: *qi*] endowment, or the concealment of human desires, the original goodness may become incomplete in comparison with its beginning, and one may turn out to be arrogant, miserly, wicked, and eccentric, and not hesitate to do anything. . . . Goodness has been uncultivated for a long time. The Heavenly principle is stored in the human mind and heart and is never destroyed. How nice it is to see the old people of my village encouraging one another to do good things: here and there bridges and temples are renovated! Since my mind is also fond of goodness, I always talk about it. . . . The building of the temple began on the third day of the eighth month and finished on the 29th. I inscribed the name "Centrality Shore" on its signboard. Someone asked me, "The edifice is named 'Centrality Shore,' what does it mean?" I replied, "The term *trung* means 'golden mean/exact fitness.' The completion of one's goodness is golden mean/exact fitness. The incompletion is not golden mean/exact fitness. Knowing limits is to realize crucial borders. Not knowing limits is to wander at the shore of delusion. The name of the temple is essentially based on these understandings. For instance, being loyal to the king, reverential to parents, responsive to siblings, congruous in the husband-wife relationship, and faithful to friends is the golden mean/exact fitness. Chancing upon wealth but having no greed for it, seeing profits but not striving for them, enjoying goodness and educating people, treating others with fidelity, these are also golden mean/exact fitness. The meaning of the golden mean/exact fitness is stored in perfect goodness; thus it is possible to use this as a delineation. Knowing the crucial delineation, one is able to pick up and handle everything with absolute goodness. How can the prosperity of his merits and virtues be measured approximately enough? Since the old people of the village take pleasure in my words about goodness, they ask me for an inscription to be engraved in stone in order to pass it on to later generations.

The Supreme Lord has given mankind goodness; all the people must hold it as their natural disposition.

Restrained by different endowment of material force, one will find oneself in danger if one follows one's desires.

> [Bui Huy Bich, *Hoang Viet van tuyen*, 13a–14a; adapted from Nguyen Nam, "Being Confucian in Sixteenth Century Vietnam," 151, 156–57]

DUONG VAN AN

DYNASTIC CHANGE (1553)

In his geography of what is now central Vietnam, *A Recent Record of O Chau* (region of Hue), written in 1553, Duong Van An explained his belief of why the Le dynasty fell. Written during the Mac dynasty's rule (1528–1592), he points out that the Le dynasty had failed in its administration of the land, leading to the succession of the Mac. Later dynasties also described their failed predecessors in such terms. At the core of Duong Van An's argument was the government's need for scholar-officials in order to gain Heaven's will. Accordingly, dynastic change now involved the loyalty of the literati, the question being whether they would be loyal to the old or the new dynasty.

During Le Chieu Tong's reign [1516–1522], the dynasty was beset with weakness and disaster, so that skilled and talented men slowly began to leave, as stars in the morning and leaves in autumn. In essence, Heaven did not continue the proper seasons, Earth did not continue the generations, and the people no longer prospered. . . . Thus, when Heaven's will had gone, the soil went bad, the fields cracked, and war appeared; when Heaven's will comes back, hillocks become solid ramparts, rubble becomes resplendent palaces, barbarian land becomes civilized. . . . With the Mac dynasty, the wise are established; Heaven and Earth are cared for; truly it is a time of prosperity. Heaven's will has returned.

[Duong Van An, *O Chau can luc*, 2b; trans. Whitmore,
"Chung-Hsing and Cheng-T'ung," 123]

SOCIETY AND CULTURE

LE CODE

LAW AND SOCIAL STATUS (1430S)

At the beginning of the Le dynasty in the 1430s, Vietnamese society had undergone a number of changes from the time of the Tran dynasty in the fourteenth century. The princely (and other) estates were mostly gone, victims of the chaos during the previous seventy years. The new Le regime established a law code, the first one in the history of Dai Viet, which theoretically would protect independent villages from being absorbed into larger private holdings. The Le Code, drawn up in the 1430s, attempted to keep social levels, such as those of dependents ("serfs") and commoners, stable and separate from private interests. In particular, the Le government wished to keep powerful individuals and families from gaining control of such individuals and forming their own independent followers and manpower. The property section, excerpts from which follow, was at the core of the new code.

Article 363

Whoever buys a serf but does not submit the sale contract to the authorities for endorsement, and privately takes the initiative to tattoo him or her, shall be fined ten *quan* [strings of cash].

Article 364

Serfs who reject their status and act as if they are commoners shall receive one hundred strokes of the heavy stick and be returned to their owner.

Article 365

Whoever tattoos other people's sons, daughters, wives, or serfs in order to change them into his own serfs shall be condemned to penal servitude. If he is not an official, he shall be exiled. The offender shall, in any case, pay to the parents, husbands, or masters fifty *quan* as reparation for taking away a person, and the sons, daughters, wives, or serfs shall be returned to them. The scribe who drafted the document and the witnesses who know about the illegality of the act shall be demoted two grades.

Whoever tattoos indentured laborers to change them into serfs shall be similarly punished.

In all cases, the offender shall be required to pay the cost for removing the marks or characters in conformity with the law.

Whoever sells a commoner as a serf to another person shall be demoted five grades and required to pay reparation for taking away a person, half the amount to the state treasury and half to the individual sold. The sale price shall be returned to the buyer and the victimized individual shall be reinstated in his status of commoner. If the buyer knows about the illegality of the sale, he shall be demoted three grades and the sale price confiscated. The scribe who drafted the sale document and the witnesses who knew about the illegality of the sale shall be demoted two grades.

[LC, nos. 363–65; trans. Huy and Tai, *Le Code*, 1:196]

LE CODE

CONTROLLING POWERFUL FAMILIES (1430S)

The Le government wished to restrain powerful families and individuals from accumulating land and resources. This was a long-standing problem for the monarchy of Dai Viet, competing with local powers for control over the resources of the countryside.

Article 370

Members of high-ranking and powerful families who take by force rice lands, dwellings, and ponds belonging to commoners shall be punished with a fine for illegal seizure of one *mau* [3,600 square meters] of land or more and demotion for five *mau* or more. If the offenders are third- or lower-rank officials, they shall receive a penalty two degrees higher. In all cases, the offenders shall return the seized property and pay punitive damages as prescribed by law. If a memorial has been submitted to the king, the case shall be treated differently.

Article 455

Princes and members of powerful families of the second rank upward who harbor thieves and robbers on their private estates and let them use these places as havens shall be fined five hundred *quan* [strings of cash]. In addition, their estates shall be confiscated. Estate managers shall receive a penalty one degree lower than that imposed for theft or robbery. Restitution of all *corpora delicti* and payment of damages shall be imposed on the estate owners. One-tenth of the confiscated lands shall be used to reward any accuser. Estate owners who, before their unlawful act is uncovered, take the initiative in arresting the thieves and robbers and turn them over to the authorities shall not be charged with any offense.

[LC, nos. 370, 455; trans. Huy and Tai, *Le Code*, 1:197, 222]

THE LITERATI AND LOCAL CUSTOM
(MID-SIXTEENTH CENTURY)

Through the mid-fifteenth century, a new generation of scholars increasingly advocated contemporary Ming practices for the government and the state. As recorded in the continuation of the *Complete Chronicle of Dai Viet* (1540s), the new morality of these scholar-officials conflicted with cultural patterns in the countryside. The following passage describes such a conflict when the royal procession moved through the countryside toward the royal home in Mount Lam.

[In 1448, second month], *giap tuat* day, the king [six-year-old Le Nhan Tong (r. 1442–1459)] traveled to Lam Kinh [his family home of Mount Lam, the new secondary capital] accompanied by the queen mother/regent, all three princes [his half brothers], and the lords attending him. The throne commanded the court minister Le Than and the capital official Le Bi to take charge of the capital in the king's absence. The people of Thanh Hoa Province came out to see the royal procession. Men and women at first led and then followed, dancing the Li Len and singing to the royal party in honor of the king. Equal numbers of men and women danced hand in hand and sang respectfully in the popular Li Len. Together, the men and women alternately crossed their feet and their throats in a dance called "Plant the Flowers, Braid the Flowers," a most vile display. The censor Dong Hanh Phat told the high lord Trinh Kha, "This is a lewd custom, an evil practice! Such an annoyance cannot be performed before the royal party." Trinh Kha thereupon banned and put a stop to it.

[DVSKTT, 11, 64a–64b; trans. John K. Whitmore]

LE CODE

PRIVATE PROPERTY (1449)

In 1449, fourteen articles were added to the Le Code's property section. This appears to have been the first time an effort was made to ensure that the code would protect the existing practices of private property and inheritance of land. These articles also were indigenous to the country and not of Northern origin. They detail property and inheritance arrangements and, in particular, show the relatively high position of women (compared with that of women in the North) in these arrangements. Women had the right to own and dispose of property; indeed, wills were very important to the Vietnamese.

Article 374

When a husband with children from his former principal wife and none by his later one, or a wife with children by her former husband but none by her later one, predeceases the later spouse intestate, if the distribution of real property between the children of the former wife or the children of the former husband on the one hand and the later wife or the later husband on the other, does not conform to the law, the persons responsible shall receive fifty strokes of the light stick and be demoted one grade.

The law provides: When the husband dies and the former wife has one child but the later wife none, the real property originating from the husband's clan shall be divided into three parts; two shall go to the child of the former wife and one to the later wife. However, when the former wife has two or more children, the part going to the later wife shall be equal to that of one child. In any case the part allocated to the later wife shall be used to support her during her lifetime, shall not become her own property, and shall be returned to the husband's children when she dies or remarries. When a wife dies, her later husband shall enjoy the same right, the only difference being that he shall not have to return the property after his remarriage.

Real property newly acquired during marriage with the former wife shall be in case the husband predeceases his later spouse divided into two parts: one shall be allotted to the former wife and shall be allocated to her children, and one to the deceased husband, to be divided in the proportions stated above.

Real property newly acquired during marriage with the later wife shall be divided into two parts: one shall go to the deceased husband, to be divided in the proportion stated above, and one to the later wife with full ownership.

In the case in which a wife predeceases, her later husband shall enjoy the same right.

However, if the parents of the deceased spouse are still living, the case shall be decided differently.

[LC, no. 374; trans. Huy and Tai, *Le Code*, 1:198–99]

LE CODE

IDEOLOGY AND SOCIAL STRUCTURE (1462)

By the 1460s, a new social pattern had begun to emerge in the Le state, promoted by scholar-officials influenced by Confucianism, as seen in new articles in the Le Code dealing with *huong hoa* (incense and fire) ritual land—that is, the land set aside on the death of a male landowner to produce income to pay for his ancestral sacrifices. These articles advanced the status of the male line (patrilineality) and the ideal of the eldest son as the inheritor (primogeniture). Although such concepts became elite ideals in Vietnamese society, they often conflicted with the realities of local social and cultural patterns, in which women continued to have property rights.

Article 388

When a father and a mother have died intestate and left land, the brothers and sisters who divide the property among themselves shall reserve one-twentieth of this property to constitute the *huong hoa* [incense and fire/ritual] property which shall be entrusted to the eldest brother. The remainder of the property shall be divided among them. Children of secondary wives or female serfs shall receive smaller parts than children of the principal wife.

In the case in which the father and mother have left an oral will or a testament, the relevant regulations concerning wills shall apply. Heirs who violate this provision shall be deprived of their parts.

(Decree of the third year of the Quang Thuan reign [1462])
[LC, no. 388; trans. Huy and Tai, *Le Code*, 1:203]

MOURNING (LATE FIFTEENTH CENTURY)

The new Confucian system emphasized correlation with the Heavenly principles. This meant the centrality of ritual, with death ceremonies at its core, binding together the paternal generations. Filial devotion also remained central to this behavior. By carrying out the mourning ritual, human society accorded with Heaven (the cosmos). This was the most important ritual in Dai Viet's new state system and continued into the modern age.[25] According to the Le Code, the punishment for violating mourning rites was as severe as that for violating the space of the royal palace. In addition, the key document of the Hong Duc reign (1470–1497), the *Celestial South's [Records Made] at Leisure,* called for burials to be carried out properly. Geomancy was important in this

---

25. The significance of proper mourning may be seen in the early nineteenth century in Nguyen Du, "A Dirge for All Ten Classes of Beings" (chap. 5).

regard, as its purpose was to keep one family from digging into (and blocking) another family's favorable tomb site and orientation.

Article 130

Persons knowing of the death of their grandparents, parents, or husband who conceal the news and do not publicly show grief shall be subjected to penal servitude as heavy work menials if they are male offenders and as silkworm-breeding menials if they are female. During the period of mourning for the said relatives or spouse, those who wear clothes other than the mourning garb or participate in musical or theatrical entertainments instead of remaining mournful shall be demoted two grades. Those who chance upon a musical party and join it or who attend celebration banquets shall receive eighty strokes of the heavy stick.

Article 131

Persons who participate in musical or theatrical entertainments while their grandparents, parents, or husband are detained for a crime punishable by death shall be demoted two grades.

Article 317

Persons who marry while they must observe the mourning period for their deceased parents or husband shall be condemned to penal servitude. Those who knowingly contract marriage with such persons shall be demoted three grades, and the marriage shall be dissolved.

Article 141

Whenever there are funerals and burials in a village, neighbors must help one another. The head of the family in mourning shall feed his guests in accordance with his financial situation. Those who adduce vile ancient customs to demand big trays of rice, wine, fish, and meat from the mourning family shall receive eighty strokes of the heavy stick.

Article 543

Whoever, upon the death of his parents, fraudulently asserts another kind of mourning and fails to wear the proper mourning garb shall be condemned to penal servitude as a heavy work menial. Whoever fraudulently alleges the death of his grandparents, parents, or husband in order to petition for a leave of absence or to avoid some obligation shall be demoted three grades. If the allegation of death concerns his uncles or their wives, his paternal aunts, his elder or younger brothers, or elder sisters, the penalty shall be a one-grade demotion.

Article 408

Fornication in the imperial city's Forbidden Area shall be punished by decapitation. The same penalty shall be inflicted on persons who commit fornication during the period of mourning for their deceased parents or husband.

Le Code

Decree of 1484

Those who carry out a burial cannot use the pretext that their burial ground is private in order to build a tomb next to a pre-existing one and thereby block the view of the latter. In case of violation of this provision, children and grandchildren of the person buried earlier shall be allowed to file a complaint with the local authorities. The family responsible for the later burial shall have to reinter the remains elsewhere and pay a reparation as prescribed by law.

Celestial South's [Records Made] at Leisure

[LC, nos. 130–31, 317, 141, 543, 408; trans. Huy and Tai, *Le Code*,
1:141–42, 185, 144, 248–49, 208; *Thien Nam du ha tap*, Legal Section,
31a–31b; trans. Huy and Tai, *Le Code*, 2:200]

PUBLIC LAND AND POWERFUL FAMILIES (1467)

The new regime under Le Thanh Tong sought to instill proper behavior in Vietnamese society at large while, at the same time, it had to contend with the private forces that sought to undercut the public (that is, state) domain. The continuation of the *Complete Chronicle of Dai Viet* (1540s) describes how Le Thanh Tong traveled to the homeland and tombs of his family (his second capital) in Mount Lam southwest of Thang Long and directly confronted efforts by powerful families to seize the public land meant for the royal family and the Meritorious Subjects who had helped establish the new dynasty, as well as the Subjects' descendants.

[In 1467, second month], the king commanded the minister of finance, Tran Phong, and other officials to investigate the public land of Mount Lam village. These lands were to be granted to the Meritorious Subjects[26] from the top rank

---

26. The Meritorious Subjects (Cong Than) were those who had fought beside Le Loi against the Ming forty years earlier.

down to the sixth and seventh ranks in accordance with these ranks. Then the king proclaimed to all the officials and the local elders, "Lam Kinh [Mount Lam as the secondary capital] is the root and the homeland of our kings and cannot be compared with any other capital. Now, powerful families [*the gia*] have opposed this, considering the common laws yet seizing land as their own, so that the princes and princesses do have not enough land to plant a stick! We wish to use the law to punish such crimes, to apply the ritual and righteousness previously proclaimed, and to allow the royal family to thrive and have a place to support itself. Now we have set the boundaries of those lands, so that any who dare to transgress them will be punished according to the law!"

[*DVSKTT*, 12, 27b–28a; trans. John K. Whitmore]

CHILDREN AND THE LAW (1474)

In order to maintain the desired social order, in 1474 Le Thanh Tong's government began emphasizing the education and control of children. The proper raising of children was fundamental to the social system and hence to the cosmic correlation between the state and Heaven. The *Book of Good Government of the Hong Duc Era* includes this edict, which applied to both male and female children.

Decree on Disowning Children Who Violate the Law

They shall be considered as belonging to the category of family-ruining offspring, those children and grandchildren who violate the law, who indulge in drinking, love-making, gambling, cock-fighting, hunting, chess-playing, sexual intercourse and vagrancy on public roads, who revile their parents, grandparents or relatives. The parents of such a child shall endeavor to educate him day and night. If he still refuses to follow the moral teachings, fails to correct his mistakes and continues to disobey his parents' orders, the latter shall enumerate all the grievances against him in a statement, for disowning him as a stranger, which statement shall be deposited for certification at the local government office and their native village. If later on, the child violates the law and is prosecuted, the parents shall not be held liable for his acts.

When becoming weakened with old age, the parents make a will to partition their estate among their sons and daughters, the disowned child shall not be entitled to any part thereof. If the partition of the estate, not determined by the parents, is later implemented by a distribution agreement among brothers, the latter shall conform to the parents' wishes in the settlement of the estate. Even though the disowned child has returned home to mourn for the parents, it was merely a formality of paying homage to his parents. The fact that he has been disowned bars him from making any claim against his relatives. If, revolting against the parents' wishes, he files a suit at the local government office, the latter shall not act upon his claim, in order to suppress any dispute and give a severe lesson to those guilty of lack of filial piety and discord.

[*HDTCT*, no. 269; trans. Huy and Tai, *Le Code*, 2:220–21]

THE KING ON BAD BEHAVIOR (1476)

Le Thanh Tong was determined to impose on his country and society what he saw as proper behavior. In order to control the wilder proclivities of his people, he ordered his officials and his people to put aside such risqué and destructive activities (and hence follow Heaven's dictates), as recorded in the continuation of the *Complete Chronicle of Dai Viet* (1540s).

[In 1476, first month], the king forbade debauchery [wine and women], proclaiming to the officials, their underlings, and the people, "From today, families that are not having guests or preparing a banquet may not party. Wives who are blameless may not be allowed to go out by themselves. Those who dare to indulge in alcohol are by nature reckless, the way of the family becomes quite irregular as a result, and as a consequence there are no words of the matchmaker [that is, you will never find a marriage partner!]. Hence there is the likelihood of 'jumping the wall' [committing adultery]. Resist such errors!"

[*DVSKTT*, 13, 1a; trans. John K. Whitmore]

LE CODE

MARRIAGE (LATE FIFTEENTH CENTURY)

Like the rites of mourning, those of marriage formed an important aspect of the new system and elicited comments for several centuries. Efforts were made to ensure that these rites, too, were properly carried out for the same cosmic reasons—that is, to keep in sync with the principles of Heaven. Formal guidelines were established between 1476 and 1478, eventually becoming part of the Le Code, and marriage practices were commonly commented on in discussions of local customs.

Article 314

Whoever, instead of bringing adequate gifts to the home of a girl's parents (if the parents are deceased, to the home of the paternal relatives' representative or that of the village chief) to celebrate a wedding ceremony, cohabits unlawfully with the girl, shall be demoted one grade and must pay the girl's parents reparation commensurate with the social standing of her family. (If the parents are deceased, the money shall be paid to the paternal relatives' representative or to the village chief.) The girl in question shall receive fifty strokes of the light stick.

Article 315

Whoever unwarrantedly breaks off an engagement after accepting the gifts offered by a man in return for his daughter's betrothal (such as money, silk, gold, silver, pork, or wine) shall receive eighty strokes of the heavy stick. If such father marries his daughter to a second man and the wedding is already celebrated, he shall be condemned to penal servitude as a heavy work menial. The second man shall be condemned to penal servitude if he knows about the original engagement but shall not be prosecuted if he does not. The female partner shall be returned to the first fiancé. If the latter refuses to marry her, the girl's parents must return the betrothal gifts and pay a sum equal to the value of said gifts as punitive damages. In this case, the girl shall remain with the second man as his wife.

When a fiancé's family refuses to celebrate the wedding after offering betrothal gifts, the responsible persons shall receive eighty strokes of the heavy stick and the gifts shall be forfeited.

[LC, nos. 314–15; trans. Huy and Tai, *Le Code*, 1:184–86]

MARRIAGE AND MOURNING (1494)

In 1494, near the end of Le Thanh Tong's reign, the king tried to resolve potential conflicts between marriage and mourning, as compiled in the *Book of Good Government of the Hong Duc Era*. The proper marriage ritual was very important to the regulation of society and hence the cosmos. But to Confucians, mourning one's ancestors was even more important. Nonetheless, for a planned marriage to proceed, some flexibility was needed.

Concerning mourning of all kinds, as on the day of death it is hoped that the deceased might still resurrect, it is permissible to get married in a hurry to be ahead of the mourning. From the third day, when the corpse is wrapped in shrouds and the deceased is unanimously deemed dead, it is no longer permissible to get married hurriedly to avoid the mourning period. Violation of this regulation shall be punished under the statute on cutting short the mourning period. The village or hamlet official who accepts the marriage fee would be punished for misapplication of the law.

[*HDTCT*, no. 111; trans. Huy and Tai, *Le Code*, 2:179]

RITUAL AND PATRILINEALITY (FIRST HALF
OF SIXTEENTH CENTURY)

During his reign, Le Thanh Tong continued to underscore the patrilineal clan, and especially the male head of the clan, as part of the new emphasis on men and patrilineality. Even so, local arrangements provided room for flexibility. This promotion of patrilineality continued after Le Thanh Tong's death in 1497 and was renewed during the Mac dynasty (1528–1592), as shown in the articles of the Le Code and the numbered item from the *Book of Good Government of the Hong Duc Era*.

Article 390

A father and a mother should make their testament when they feel themselves approaching old age.

When there is no testament, the patrilineal clan head may establish a distribution agreement on the basis of the land available. He shall follow the above-mentioned rule of reserving one-twentieth of the property as the *huong hoa* [incense and fire/ritual] property.

This clan head shall take into account all land for the constitution of the *huong hoa* portion. When one of his sons in turn becomes clan head, he shall combine the *huong hoa* land inherited from his father with all other land to be distributed to all sons and daughters and, after estimation of each child's part, reserve one-twentieth of all these lands as the new *huong hoa* portion. When a grandson in turn becomes clan head, he shall proceed in the same manner.

However, if the family members are numerous and the total land area is small, the family shall be allowed to distribute the land among the *huong hoa* portion and the other parts to be owned by the heirs in whatever proportion it finds appropriate, provided that there is unanimity and no dispute.

Article 391

The management of the *huong hoa* property shall be entrusted to the eldest son or, failing that, to the eldest daughter. Such property shall be one-twentieth of the total of the real property in the estate.

(Decree of the second year of the Quang
Thieu reign [1517])
Le Code

Number 47

When an eldest son neglects the ritual with which he is charged and does not stay in the locality where he is supposed to carry out the ritual, the paternal relatives shall be allowed to file a complaint against him. The offender shall lose the *huong hoa* property and shall be charged with lack of filial piety.

Book of Good Government
[LC, nos. 390–91; trans. Huy and Tai, *Le Code*, 1:204; *HDTCT*,
no. 47; trans. Huy and Tai, *Le Code*, 2:22]

ETHNIC RELATIONS

LE CODE

LAW AND ETHNIC GROUPS (FIFTEENTH CENTURY)

The Le regime's law code allowed ethnic groups other than the lowland Vietnamese to handle their own affairs. Only in cases in which more than one ethnic group was involved did state officials intervene. In earlier centuries, the chiefs of ethnic groups outside Dai Viet's political structure handled their own problems. But under the new bureaucratic system, solutions to these problems were laid out in law.

Article 40

Whenever persons of alien cultures belonging to the same ethnic group commit an offense against one another, justice shall be dispensed in accordance with their customs. If they come from different ethnic groups, the law code shall apply.

Article 451

Persons belonging to ethnic minorities who commit robbery or homicide against one another shall receive a penalty one degree lower than that imposed for ordinary robbery or homicide. However, if they reach a settlement between themselves before the trial, such settlement shall be authorized.

Responsible administrators and superintendents who improperly demand cattle or other domestic animals, money, or goods in return for toleration and concealment of the above offenses shall be demoted or condemned to penal servitude. They must turn over the *corpus delicti* to the state and pay punitive damages equal to twice its value. Moreover a fine shall be imposed on such officials to reward accusers in accordance with the law.

Article 452

Persons belonging to ethnic minorities living in military territories who rob or loot inhabitants of frontier areas shall be punished according to the general statute on robbery. If such persons pass through a village, responsible officials who do not arrest them shall be demoted or condemned to penal servitude.

Responsible administrators and superintendents who, though informed about the facts, fail to take appropriate measures to prevent such crimes shall be condemned to penal servitude or removed from their offices. If they take bribes to condone the offense, they shall receive the same penalty as the criminals.

[LC, nos. 40, 451–52; trans. Huy and Tai, *Le Code*, 1:119, 221]

NGUYEN TRAI AND OTHERS

REGARDING CULTURAL INFLUENCES (1435)

While he was helping to draft the law code in the 1430s, the court minister Nguyen Trai, a major scholar-official of the old school, was tutoring the crown prince, who then became the young king, Le Thai Tong (r. 1434–1442). In 1435, Nguyen Trai and his colleagues compiled the first *Geography* based on his lessons to the prince. The *Geography* reveals the intellectual developments of the late fourteenth century, including the growing sense by the lowland Vietnamese that they were different from their neighbors.

The people of our land should not adopt the languages or the clothing of the lands of the Wu [Ming], Champa, the Lao, Siam, or Zhenla [Cambodia], since doing so will bring chaos to the customs of our land.

Comment: The word "not to" means "it is forbidden." To speak Ngo [C: Wu = Northern] follows the tongue and needs to be translated, whereas to know Lao follows the throat, and Thai, Cham, and Khmer all follow the larynx, being like the sounds of the shrike. Thus none of these can be adopted because they do not resonate with the sounds of our land. The Northerners have been affected by Yuan [Mongol] customs—their hair hanging down the back, white teeth, short clothing, long sleeves, [and] caps and robes bright and lustrous as piles of leaves. Even though the people of the Ming have resumed the old ways of Han- and Tang-style dress, their customs have changed. The Lao use Western [Indian] cloth to wrap themselves in, patterned like the irrigated fields of dysfunctional families [robes of Buddhist monks]. The people of Champa use a piece of cloth that covers their thighs but exposes their bodies. The Thais and Khmer use a piece of cloth that joins and envelopes the hands and the knees like a shroud. None of these styles should be followed or worn, since they disregard our customs.

The scholar of the Ly family [Ly Tu Tan] said, "From the time that the Yuan [Mongols] entered the Middle Kingdom, all under Heaven [the empire] changed when the Hu [Central Asian] language and Hu dress alone were used. The only ones who did not change were our country, along with the Golden Tomb of the

Zhu family and the Golden Mountain of the Zhao family.[27] And when Ming Taizu was enthroned,[28] he sent Yi Jimin as ambassador to us to establish good relations. Our ruler, Tran Du Tong [r. 1341–1369], in turn sent Doan Thuan Than to inquire about the Ming. The Ming emperor, Taizu, rewarded and questioned our country's ambassador closely and then commended his garb and customs as being in accordance with the civilization of the Middle Kingdom. Taizu bestowed a poem of his own that said, "An Nan [Dai Viet] has the Tran clan, and its customs are not those of the Yuan [Mongols]. Its clothing and caps are in the classic pattern of the Zhou dynasty. Its rites and music follow the relationship between ruler and minister, as in the Song dynasty." Therefore he bestowed on the ambassador of Dai Viet in his own hand the four characters "domain of manifest civility" and promoted our ambassador three ranks to be equal to that of Chosŏn [Korea]. And when our ambassador was leaving, Ming Taizu sent Niu Liang to present the Dragon Phrase [imperial writing] Golden Seal and to reward and bestow favor upon us.

[Nguyen Trai, *Du dia chi*; trans. John K. Whitmore]

LE THANH TONG

EDICT ON CHAMPA (1470)

By 1470, Le Thanh Tong (r. 1460–1497) wearied of being attacked by Champa on the southern coast of Dai Viet. Given his new Sinic-style foreign policy, being "civilized" and standing against those "outside civilization" were additional reasons to fight back against his Southeast Asian neighbors. Earlier, the Le state had fought Tai groups to the west. Now the king turned his attention to Champa. Le Thanh Tong decided to lead a massive invasion and, this time, to crush Champa instead of invading, defeating, looting, and returning, as Dai Viet had done in the past. His forces would break up the Cham empire, paving the way for its integration into the Vietnamese realm. In the following proclamation, Le Thanh Tong articulates for the people of Dai Viet his rationale for deciding to invade Champa, as recorded in the continuation of the *Complete Chronicle of Dai Viet* (1540s). After defeating the Cham, Le Thanh Tong turned west to attack the Tai (1479) in another major expedition, which reached all the way to Myanmar (Burma).

[In 1470, eleventh month] In times past, our [grandfather] Le Thai To Cao Hoang De [r. 1428–1433] brought peace to hostilities, creating our land. Our father

27. This may refer to Zhu Yuanzhang (r. 1368–1398), the founder of the Ming dynasty, and Zhao Tuo (Trieu Da), regarded as the founder of independent Dai Viet.
28. Ming Taizu is the temple name of Zhu Yuanzhang.

Le Thai Tong Van Hoang De [r. 1434–1442] revered Heaven and felt compassion for the people, carrying on his father's [Le Thai To's] work. The small are anxious; the great are feared. Inside, we make improvements; outside, we quell troubles. Those whose garments are made of plants and whose dressed hair is like a mallet go up to the mountains and sail the seas to come here. Myriad peoples look to our virtue; the eight regions [entire world] respect our authority.

How slow-witted is Champa, unsure whether or not to emerge from its rabbit hole! Like a venomous bee, it has been able to nourish itself and sting again; like animals, they eat their fill and forget their moral debt. Of people without the Way and indifferent, each has little wit and is just hanging around. Its bad reputation spreads everywhere, and they forget that they do not have the land to bury anyone; their cruel hearts act secretly and still think that shooting at Heaven is a good strategy.

Our past rulers suddenly grew angry and worked out a distant strategy. But as a result of Le Thai Tong's death, not one act of great merit could be carried out against Champa. When our Le Nhan Tong [r. 1443–1459] took the throne, the activities of these tribes became even more numerous. The agricultural land of Co Luy in Champa is like a dog's den, and its citadel of Cha Ban [Vijaya] is like an anthill. Their insanity is thoughtless, and they dare to claim to be the superiors [elders] of our kings. Casting aside virtue as being prestigious, they declare themselves the Heavenly Buddha of the Vietnamese people. Their cruel crimes are many and cannot be hidden; their spoken words are obscene and set no good example. Gathering together their band, they dare to hinder our ways, like dogs sneaking in to steal; deceiving when apparently simple and open, they secretly bring troops in like a gathering flock of crows. Striking and seizing Hoa Chau [on the southern coast of Dai Viet], they kill the soldiers of our guard posts. Claiming the hand of Heaven for their cruel crimes, they speak of greater victories and control.

Yet their ruses have not succeeded, and their schemes have again failed, even more so. Death is about to arrive for them, and their destiny has been decided. Being blind, they do not see anything; opening their mouths, they speak wrongly. Their tricks have thus been foiled and are about to be blocked by us. Then they flattered like a fox in Beijing and twittered so as to disparage other peoples; they planned to invade like silkworms into Tuong Quan and in their guts, intended to strike both sides. They expected to take their old territories all the way to [the old southern border of Dai Viet at] Mount Hoanh, so that the Han army could come down to Bac Dao [in southwestern China]. Champa itself went to report in Beijing, falsely and ceaselessly slandering. They also slandered us for mobilizing soldiers and myriad people, being about to seize the border of the Northern coast, [and] then they said that we were like two suns in the sky rising together and that we revered the emperor of the Southern Country [and not that of the North]. Champa reported that we had seized their tribute of jade and gold and that we disputed the white elephant they sent. They scornfully consider our people as though we were garbage. With hearts deeply venomous, they dare to desire to harm our people; they think that taking our land will be as easy as playing chess—the bones of [the fourteenth-century ruler of Champa] Che Bong Nga still hope to come and take us! Look at the words they speak—they always want to harm our people. Thus, they shrewdly tighten their grip and do it constantly. In order to cause doubt about us in the Ming court, every few years they sharply ask for the Northerners to act immediately against us; only because the bandit officials are clearly arbitrary, the vehicles always follow the same tracks. They deserve both being placed in the cangue and being submerged; worrying about a burning gut is not wrong [that is, the evil will get their just deserts].

Dangerous times are like crows in a high nest, so they contemptuously dare to send embassies; seeing narrowly like a frog calling from the bottom of a well, they all bravely mock our royal edicts. One day past the first month, their people sing back and forth with one another. They follow the path of rebellion and imitate it, saying that cruelty does not harm anything. Taking the stink of a fish, the father of a dog, the mother of a pig, they seized and killed their king, expelling the offspring of King Bo De and usurping the throne; how costly to build the temples and construct the towers, creating catastrophe and fortune for the race of their [present] king, Tra Toan, to be able to follow their barbarian path. It is forbidden to kill and butcher so that people do not have enough to eat; it is forbidden to distill alcohol so that the spirits cannot receive offerings. Males and females alike serve and labor hard; officials apply cruel punishments. Consequently, the people of Champa are heavily taxed and pitifully punished. Those of the port of Thi Nai [present-day Quy Nhon] have high officials and important offices. Our men and women are captured and made slaves; the imprisonment or flight of our people has completely enveloped us. [Consequently, our] wandering people have to gather and suffer together.

Throughout the entire country, our people want to cry out to Heaven and yet cannot find the way. Although we dwell in a completed house that has burned, still we block their wicked ways that bring falsity to our people; Heaven does not leave in peace people who do cruel things, and they also follow their furious path and make policy. When people reach positions like that, the entire country is full of resentment. In their hearts, they always are furtively keeping an eye out; on the outside of their false faces, they pretend to accomplish something. Following the command, they call out to the capital and only then achieve a tranquil heart; it is obvious that they hope to establish and bring together the land and spirits of the capital so as to gain satisfaction. We release the hearts and move the flock to seize them; we urgently open up and, wagging our tail, entreat them. They are people who resent the possessions of our court and make trouble for our people. We think that the whip, though long, cannot reach the belly of the horse, that the wind has reached its end and cannot blow the feathers of the wild geese [that is, that Champa is too far away and cannot strike us]. They dare to grow hearts that love chaos and act arbitrarily; it is precisely such crimes that deserve to be attacked and must be killed. Heroes hear and believe, gnash their teeth, and are furious. Those who are loyal understand the situation and, in their guts, are saddened.

Examining before and after, the wit is small and the desire great. We have texts and regulations, and which laws will pardon those who go against them and revolt? If you do not go out with majesty, do not give up; if you kill cruelly, then the barbarians also will govern like that. We grasp the heart of God on High and connect with the will of the king and the father—to kill people who hate for nine generations according to the sense of the *Spring and Autumn Annals* [of Confucius], to employ stratagems that will bring peace to our land, to save the court and the people and avoid suffering and a topsy-turvy society, to bring order to the land that has been chaotic and contrary to the Way for a long time. To strike against revolt and rescue the people—a sage shows bravery, the good build up the earth, the bad tear it down, and Heaven and Earth take this as their heart.

. . . Although employing soldiers goes against the will of the sage, establishing rules for the foolish also is clear. Fog—how does it cover the brilliance of the rising sun? Your bed—do you allow a stranger to lie down on it and snore? Select generals of talent and raise a mass of soldiers. A billion tigers, ten thousand men, ships for hundreds of miles! An army a hundred times as strong, each man of one heart! Everyone turns the wing and heads for war and maintains discipline, waiting for the word to attack. The throne asks you to pile up the dunes to bury the enemy—hope to keep merit for the history books! Take the righteous way and volunteer—do not pardon those who have committed crimes. The throne shall personally command the martial banners and give the orders to the troops. Respectfully bring the Mandate of Heaven, and do the work of striking and killing those cruel people! The shadows of the banners will darken the plains like clouds roiling before the storm; hammers in an instant in the air, resembling the blazing sun or a dazzling star! It will be as easy as opening a bag, as simple as snapping a twig! The enemy is clearly on the lookout for us, and the sound of our thunder will cause them to cover their ears, but not in time. Our army will go out and project its force evenly; the strength of the fire will be hot and, thin as a hair, will burn rapidly. Attack once and that will finish them—the hatred of a hundred generations will be washed clean.

Again, because the people will rid themselves of this deep poison, we can never allow the enemy to exist for our descendants. Mocking the Han emperor Wu [r. 140–85 B.C.E.] for constant fighting without end, praising King Wen of Zhou for opening the land even more broadly—oi! The enemy in the end kills a goat and there is no blood, so when studying antiquity, in the sixth month we go out with the army. In the south, we see a pig wallowing in the mud. Champa should absolutely not wait two months to give up!

Announce this throughout the land so that each person will hear it!

[*DVSKTT*, 12, 55a–58a; trans. John K. Whitmore]

ORDERING ETHNIC GROUPS TO CONFORM
(MID-SIXTEENTH CENTURY)

After the conquest and dismemberment of Champa in 1471, Le Thanh Tong sought to ensure that Chams and other non-Vietnamese peoples living in his realm would follow the proper customs that he was establishing for Dai Viet. The king also wanted to make sure that these foreign peoples did not become part of private entourages, which might threaten the central state's monopoly on power, as the continuation of the *Complete Chronicle of Dai Viet* (1540s) records. As the Le Code regulations indicate, the state of Dai Viet was increasingly drawing other ethnic groups into its controlling framework instead of treating them as autonomous outsiders. This pattern continued in later centuries as the Vietnamese expanded their control southward.

[In 1472], ninth month, the king ordered a high official to examine the names, family and personal, of Chams, barbarians, and others dwelling in Dai Viet. For the surnames of the Chams, they were to start anew according to the Vietnamese system. The surnames of the barbarians were to be revived and preserved according to a standardized system. In renewing the names, the only requirement is that they have three characters, so that, for example, To Mon would become To Sa Mon and Sa Qua would become Sa Oa Qua.

   In the tenth month, the king forbade officials and the people from taking Chams into their entourages and concealing them from the state.

[*DVSKTT*, 12, 73b–74a; trans. John K. Whitmore]

RECEIVING FOREIGN ENVOYS
(MID-SIXTEENTH CENTURY)

Le Thanh Tong had an interest in dealing with foreign lands, and the state's economic initiatives attracted foreigners to trade with Dai Viet. During this age of increasing Sinification, the royal court in Thang Long modeled its foreign relations on those of the contemporary Ming dynasty. The following is a description in the continuation of the *Complete Chronicle of Dai Viet* (1540s) of how foreign political envoys should be handled. Later Vietnamese rulers were also concerned with regulating contacts with foreign commercial agents, as evidenced by the Khanh Duc emperor's 1650 edict regarding such contacts.[29]

[In 1485], eleventh month, the king set the regulations for all the emissaries of the lands who came to court to pay tribute in the capital. The envoys from lands like Champa, Lao Qua, Siam, Java, Melaka, and others, as well as the mountain

---

29. See Khanh Duc Emperor, "Edict Prohibiting Foreigners from Taking Up Residence Without Restrictions" (chap. 4).

chieftains in charge of the border regions, all will come together in the meeting hall. Strong men of the Cam Y Regiment, the Five Citadel soldiers and horses, the banner troops of the generals, and others, all of them must, following correct procedure, guard strictly and attentively, establish the defense so as to show the envoys how to enter the royal court and participate in the royal audience. These troops also must proceed and follow the envoys, leading the procession and chasing away all the lowly palace servants as well as public and private servants. They also are not to allow the envoys to get close to these people and make inquiries or speak with them, divulging matters and inducing them to do ill. Should the supervising officials not be able to follow the rules in providing strict precautions, following their private interests and allowing the envoys to make such contact, the banner- and placard-bearing strong men of the Xa Nhan Office in the Cam Y Regiment are to speak the truth and report what they hear, apprehending and bringing the miscreants for punishment.

[*DVSKTT*, 13, 48a; trans. John K. Whitmore]

PART II

Early Modern Vietnam

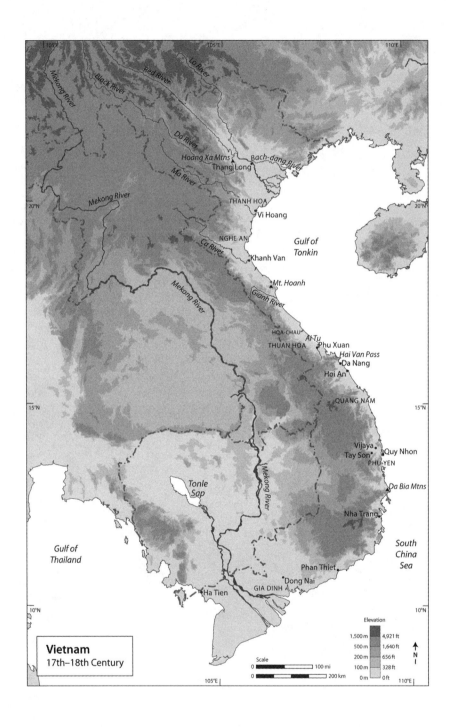

Mekong River
Black River
Red River
Lo River
Đà River
Hoàng Xa Mtns
Thang Long
Bach-dang River
Mã River
Mekong River
THANH HOA
Vi Hoang
Ca River
NGHE AN
Khanh Van
Gulf of Tonkin
Mt. Hoanh
Gianh River
Mekong River
HOA CHAU
Ai Tu
THUAN HOA
Phu Xuan
Hai Van Pass
Da Nang
Hoi An
QUANG NAM
Vijaya
Quy Nhon
Tay Son
PHU YEN
Da Bia Mtns
Tonle Sap
Mekong River
Nha Trang
South China Sea
Gulf of Thailand
Phan Thiet
Ha Tien
GIA DINH
Dong Nai

Vietnam
17th–18th Century

Elevation

1,500 m	4,921 ft
500 m	1,640 ft
200 m	656 ft
100 m	328 ft
0 m	0 ft

N

Scale
0 — 100 mi
0 — 200 km

Chapter 4

THE TRINH-NGUYEN PERIOD

In some respects, marking a historical break at the start of the seventeenth century might seem arbitrary and somewhat misplaced. It might seem more logical to view the year 1558 as the more obvious moment of historical rupture. It was in that year that Nguyen Hoang and a group of his supporters moved southward, escaping the substantial threat posed by the Trinh family, their erstwhile allies in the long-running defense of the Le court. Moreover, 1558 is the year later marked by nineteenth-century Nguyen court historians as the key moment in the rise of the southern realm. In many respects, the events of the seventeenth and eighteenth centuries in Vietnam were substantially shaped by that moment. And yet, before the seventeenth century it would have been less accurate to speak of two distinct political realms in the larger territories of Dai Viet. Despite his departure from the north, Nguyen Hoang and his followers continued to engage with the Trinh and to support them in the ongoing struggles to defeat the Mac and complete the Restoration of the Le dynasty. Indeed, Nguyen Hoang returned north in 1593 and spent the next seven years fighting with the Trinh army in campaigns that eroded the threat posed by the Mac.

In 1600, with the Mac largely defeated, Nguyen Hoang returned to his southern domains for the last time, signaling the start of a true break between the Nguyen and Trinh families. The dawn of the seventeenth century can thus be seen as marking the onset of a new era in Vietnamese history, one of increasingly tense political and eventually territorial division between the Nguyen and the Trinh families. At the same time, the fact of the north-south conflict represented a continuation of centuries-old patterns that pitted the cultural core of the Red River Delta against the ethnically diverse southern peripheries. Even though the Nguyen had taken over the Cham polities that had threatened earlier Vietnamese states, the geopolitical patterns were quite similar.

What had been an uneasy political balance between the Nguyen and Trinh gave way in 1627 to a military confrontation, which dragged on for forty-five years. The event precipitating the war was the refusal by Nguyen Hoang's successor, Nguyen Phuc Nguyen (r. 1613–1635), to continue the Nguyen practice of submitting taxes collected in Thuan Hoa and Quang Nam on behalf of the Le court. The protracted armed conflict between the two families in many ways became the defining feature of the seventeenth century. The conflict pitted a stronger, wealthier, and more populous Trinh polity against a much more sparsely populated and only loosely politically integrated Nguyen realm. Despite this seeming disparity, the succession of attacks and counterattacks did not lead to a decisive Trinh victory. The Nguyen were able to compensate for their disadvantages by using rugged terrain reinforced by a series of strategically placed defensive ramparts and walls, advanced artillery technologies, and a society that had been organized mainly along military lines. The result was a military stalemate, which ultimately was accepted by both sides after a last failed Trinh attack in 1672. Over the next century, the two sides went in separate directions, divided by a relatively rigid boundary along the Linh River, located in present-day Quang Binh Province.

This uneasy peace was shattered, however, in the early 1770s by the outbreak of the Tay Son uprising. Led by three brothers from a hamlet in the foothills west of coastal Qui Nhon, the rebel army was a complex coalition of lowland agriculturalists, uplanders, and ethnic Chinese merchants. The Tay Son soon had the Nguyen court on the run. Their uprising also created ideal circumstances for the Trinh to attempt to achieve the military success over the Nguyen that had eluded them in the seventeenth century. A large Trinh army swept into the northern Nguyen territories in 1774 and then reached an accommodation with the Tay Son armies, which continued to pursue the Nguyen survivors. The next three decades were dominated by fighting among these three armies. The Tay Son forces eventually turned on their Trinh allies and in 1786 overran them, subsequently ousting the Le rulers as well. In early 1789, the Tay Son rapidly and decisively defeated a Qing army that had invaded Tonkin on behalf of the ousted Le emperor. This was followed by a brief period of political consolidation by the Tay Son Quang Trung emperor (r. 1788–1792). He restored agricultural productivity and tried to promote trade with the Europeans, all while having to fend off challenges from survivors of the Nguyen court. These Nguyen remnants, led by Nguyen Anh, had retreated to the far southern Gia Dinh/Saigon region, where after twice taking refuge in Bangkok, they gradually built their own military machine. The deaths in rapid succession of the two principal Tay Son leaders in 1792 and 1793 paved the way for the Nguyen's ultimate victory over the short-lived Tay Son dynasty. The leader of the Nguyen forces and the future emperor of the new dynasty, Nguyen Anh, marched into Thang Long in the summer of 1802, bringing to an end the long, brutal, and destructive conflicts.

Although dramatic, these conflicts were not the only significant historical event between 1600 and 1802. This also was a period of considerable political, intellectual, and economic dynamism throughout the divided Vietnamese territories. This energy stemmed from various sources: tensions between the two ruling families, growing contact with European commerce and religious ideology, ongoing exposure to intellectual trends in China, the Nguyen family's extension of Vietnamese political and cultural influence southward into the realms of the Cham and Khmer peoples, and the arrival of immigrant refugees from southern China. The Nguyen expansion toward the far south later in the seventeenth century increased its engagement with Cambodia, which continued in the next century, eventually leading to direct conflict with Siam, which lasted into the mid-nineteenth century.

This period tested the limits of Vietnamese leaders' political control: in the north where popular unrest was a prominent feature of the eighteenth-century landscape and in the south where Nguyen authority was tempered by the challenges of governing a geographically and ethnically dispersed realm with relatively few soldiers and officials. But this was not merely a period of inevitable political decay. On the contrary, both realms attempted varying degrees of political transformation in the waning years and aftermath of their drawn-out wars. In the Trinh realm, there was a marked revival of literati influence during the latter half of the seventeenth century, a revival that echoes the Hong Duc period of the late fifteenth century. This transformation reached its high point during the Canh Tri reign era (1663–1672), when a substantial level of bureaucratic control had been extended through northern society.[1] This was in part an attempt by the northern lord Trinh Tac (r. 1657–1682) to counterbalance the power of relatively autonomous military leaders who had gained prestige and influence during the half century of conflict with the Nguyen. Although Trinh Tac eventually was forced to yield to a son with greater ability to control the military, the bureaucratic structures and their influence continued unchanged into the first decades of the eighteenth century.

The Nguyen realm also underwent a political transformation. In the aftermath of the wars, there was a gradual shift toward greater roles for civilian administration and attempts to create a more formalized administrative structure. While this did not greatly diminish the influence of the military and of military connections on those seeking to hold political power, it did mark a shift suggestive of a more permanently established state. In addition, the Nguyen lords moved toward asserting their autonomy from the Trinh and, to some degree, from the Le as

---

1. Taylor, "Literati Revival"; Whitmore, "Literati Culture in Dai Viet."

well. In 1703, the Nguyen ruler petitioned the Qing court to accept his realm as a tributary independent of the Le-Trinh polity. Although this request was refused, it illustrates the new path being charted by the Nguyen. The shift toward autonomy also was symbolized by the casting of royal seals and the gradual shift in titles claimed by the Nguyen rulers. This transformation reached its logical conclusion in 1744, the year in which Nguyen Phuc Khoat (r. 1738–1765), announced that he was ascending the kingly throne, thus establishing himself as royal ruler over the southern realm. This was followed by another series of administrative and sartorial changes designed to underscore this reconceptualization of the Nguyen polity.

This period was also one of economic change and periodic hardships. Trade had long been an important but complex part of Vietnamese economic life. Trade with the Chinese and the Chams, but also with more distant overseas merchants, had helped the Ly, Tran, and early Le dynasties prosper. Then, in the seventeenth century, the Vietnamese began new commercial interchanges with Europeans, with initially modest results, in addition to their ongoing, though slowly declining, trade with China and Japan. Both north and south suffered fiscal crises, partly because the courts were spending money faster than they could extract it from their populations, but also because of factors beyond the leaders' control. These included a series of droughts in the north and a decline in foreign trade in the south. To cover this gap in the north, internal commerce and handicraft production were taxed. At the same time, fiscal corruption in the form of extralegal fees imposed at various stages of the tax collection process, particularly in the 1750s and 1760s, developed in response to economic pressures in the south. The south was further beset by a currency crisis when its overseas sources for copper coinage dried up, forcing the Nguyen to begin producing their own coins from a zinc amalgam. The new zinc coins were of poor quality and easily counterfeited, causing a crisis of confidence in the official currency, which in turn led to inflation and contributed to economic uncertainty. A succession of officials warned about each of these economic problems, but their memorials for reform fell on deaf ears.

The seventeenth and eighteenth centuries were a time of economic vigor, reform, and some experimentation for the Trinh. The postwar climate enabled a return to economic stability and prosperity, and the state made some efforts to encourage this development. Among other things, a 1664 edict froze the household registers, bringing an end to the periodic population tabulations that had regularly updated state records. Although beneficial in the short run by making tax collection more predictable, over the next century the growing population meant a substantial disparity between the population and the population records. This hampered the state's ability to collect taxes in a manner that reflected demographic realities. As one scholar pointed out, the effect of freezing the villages' population records was to reduce their ability to negotiate their tax responsibilities in response to the changing circumstances, thereby strengthening the state's fiscal hand.[2]

Institutional Buddhism was revived during this time, owing to the increasing interest in Buddhism by both the courts and society at large. In the last decades of the seventeenth century, the Nguyen rulers brought a Chinese monk, Da Shan, to their capital to provide instruction to the court, and a Nguyen ruler was made a thirtieth-generation Thien master, thus reinforcing the legitimacy of the court.[3] Indeed, Buddhism rose to a prominence not seen since the early centuries of Vietnamese independence. This prominence symbolized the ideological freedom available to the Vietnamese far from their cultural core zone, as well as a means of asserting both leadership and distinctiveness from the northern polity. The reemergence of Vietnamese leaders as patrons of Buddhism in the south was followed by a more modest Buddhist revival in the north, where it attracted elite scholars, including Ngo Thi Nham. Ngo Thi Nham became active in reviving the Bamboo Grove (Truc Lam) school of Thien Buddhism, was named as the school's new patriarch, and wrote an important text on the major traditions and beliefs of the school and its adherents.

Finally, the late seventeenth and much of the eighteenth century was a time of intellectual vigor, the most dynamic since the Hong Duc era of the last decades of the fifteenth century. This dynamism can be seen in the substantial amount of philosophical, literary, and historical writings that have survived. We already have alluded to the economic and bureaucratic impact of the literati's revival during the Canh Tri period. This intellectual vigor also was reflected in efforts to restore social order and the influence of the Confucian classics, the former exemplified by public guidelines for appropriate behavior and the latter through regular discussions of the texts by court officials. Although the literati's bureaucratic influence faded by the early eighteenth century, intellectuals continued to flourish in Trinh society, in both public and private realms. Indeed, the latter half of the eighteenth century produced some of Vietnam's most distinguished intellects. Le Quy Don, Ngo Thi Si, and his son Ngo Thi Nham, Bui Huy Bich, and Phan Huy Ich were merely the most prominent among a major generation of scholar-officials. This period of scholastic energy was prompted in part by the political disorder that spawned numerous large-scale uprisings in the Trinh territory and the growing tension between the Trinh lords and the Le emperors. Scholars carried out extensive research into the classics and earlier Vietnamese texts in an effort to find ways of halting the disorder. Literati also reexamined the Confucianist canon and wrote commentaries on its texts, and the Tay Son Quang Trung emperor even initiated a project to make the Confucian classics more widely accessible by translating them into the vernacular script.

---

2. Taylor, "Literati Revival," 15–16.
3. Wheeler, "Buddhism in the Re-ordering of an Early Modern World," 323.

Such practical concerns did not prevent scholars from engaging in more esoteric studies as well. Le Quy Don, the preeminent scholar of premodern Vietnam, made major contributions to Vietnamese metaphysical thinking in his reflections on the concepts of *ly* and *khi*, or "principle" and "essence." At the same time, he and other scholars produced a wide range of what might be viewed as practical works. Le Quy Don wrote several histories, geographical texts, and noteworthy miscellanea. Ngo Thi Nham composed at least one gazetteer and a guide to learning Chinese and *nom* characters. Bui Duong Lich wrote histories, poetry, and guides to proper behavior. Pham Dinh Ho was another prolific scholar whose career spanned the late eighteenth and early nineteenth centuries and who wrote extensively in the "following the brush" genre. He produced several eclectic collections of essays on topics ranging from tea drinking to sartorial customs. Finally, the scholars of this era compiled extremely important anthologies of older literary and historical texts, thus ensuring their preservation for future generations. This undertaking reached its high point in the first part of the nineteenth century with Phan Huy Chu's encyclopedic work.

Although the Nguyen realm's outlook was less cerebral and more focused on practical matters relating to administration and economic management, it also made literary contributions. Noteworthy among these are the poems by Mac Thien Tu, a member of the ethnic Chinese family that ruled the port city of Ha Tien largely unfettered by Nguyen control. Hoang Quang, another prominent scholar, left as his legacy a lengthy paean to what he characterized as the golden age of the Nguyen lords that concluded with a lament about the precipitous decline of their rule in the latter eighteenth century. Other notable southern writers included Nguyen Cu Trinh, represented in this collection by one of his reform memorials but also noted for his poetry collections and his verse collaborations with Mac Thien Tu. A significant prose work from this period is Nguyen Khoa Chiem's *Recorded Tales of the Founding of the Country*, describing the establishment of the Nguyen realm from the mid-sixteenth through the seventeenth century. In short, even though the Nguyen south was not remembered for its many literary works, it did produce a number of notable talents.

The documents selected for this period touch on all these developments. They describe the origins of the divide between the Nguyen and the Trinh and the conflicts that ensued. The calls for reform and for more radical political change in these documents suggest the mind-set and justifications of those seeking to oust ruling powers. The documents also reveal the political confusions that increasingly came to define the eighteenth century as scholars became progressively more uncertain about where to direct their political allegiances. Political contests within the Nguyen and Trinh courts themselves and between the two ruling houses, plus the overarching challenge presented by the Tay Son uprising

(1771–1802), meant that decisions about political loyalties were no longer simple. In addition, these documents describe the worldview of these seventeenth- and eighteenth-century scholars, the civil service system, Confucian and Buddhist metaphysics and the relationship between these doctrines, as well as Vietnamese cultural practices by both commoners and elites.

Most of the documents are in prose, but we also included two noteworthy texts in verse that were composed during the Tay Son period and reflect the confusion of that era. Each of them was written in the Vietnamese vernacular using the demotic script, *chu nom*. The first, "Lament for the South," was composed to celebrate the so-called golden era of the southern Nguyen lords. The poem highlights that regime's success in spreading its authority through-out what became the southern realm of the Vietnamese peoples, as well as the decline of the Nguyen and the events that led to the Tay Son rebellion. Indeed, this poem became a rallying cry for the Nguyen survivors. In con-trast, the other verse selection in this section is Nguyen Huy Luong's famous *phu*-style poem "Rhapsody on West Lake," written as an ode to the prosperity and harmony said to characterize the northern Vietnamese realm under Tay Son rule.

THE LAND

NGO THI SI

ON VIETNAMESE GEOGRAPHY (1760S?)

Geography and its study were among Vietnamese scholars' principal concerns, for an understanding of geographical and topographical features, and the relationships among administrative units, was essential to the state's organization and administra-tion. Moreover, geographical writings were intertwined with historical memory, as places were closely linked to historical or quasi-historical events. The text excerpted here is by Ngo Thi Si (1726–1780), a member of one of northern Vietnam's most pro-minent literary lineages and an esteemed literatus. The Ngo Thi clan produced several generations of successful examination candidates in the seventeenth and eighteenth centuries, many of whom went on to serve as officials to the imperial court. This selec-tion reveals the relationship between the Vietnamese and their historical rivals and neighbors, to both the north and the south. It represents a part of the long-running project by Vietnamese scholars to highlight the prowess of their realm and its people and their efforts to challenge the Chinese domination of the Southern realm. Ngo Thi Si emphasizes the desirable resources and strategic location of the Vietnamese territo-ries, which attracted the Chinese and explain their great reluctance to surrender them. His words echo those of the early Chinese administrators, like Xue Zong, who similarly enumerated the many valuable products to be found in the South.

Note that at the beginning of the Tang era, all under Heaven was divided into fifteen circuits. This meant taking nine Han commanderies to establish the circuit of Linh Nam. An Nam, however, was established separately as a protectorate. All this was governed under Linh Nam. Until the fifth year of the Wu De era [618–626], this territory was called Giao Chau. Beginning with the Tiao Lu era [679–680], the territory was no longer called Giao Chau but was instead called An Nam. From the time of the martial emperor Trieu Da [second century B.C.E.] onward, our realm of An Nam was a dependency of the North for more than a thousand years.

Why is it that the trifling kingdoms of Linyi, Funan, Champa, and Ai Lao still had their leaders and never succumbed to anything like this? It was because all these kingdoms were located at the ends of seas or in mountain pockets and their people and natural resources were insufficient to bring any benefit to the Middle Kingdom [China]. Thus, when they revolted they would be attacked, but when they yielded they would be spared. And whether or not they provided tribute, they were not dealt with strictly. But An Nam, in the southern region, was a large urban center. Its fields were good for growing grains and its soils suitable for mulberry. The mountains produced silver and gold, and the seas produced pearls and jade. All the merchants and traders who came there became wealthy, and word of this abundance spread far and wide. As a consequence, they thought about establishing commanderies and districts and subordinating its people, and thus they remained for a very long time. Before they seized An Nam, they had thought about seizing it; once they had already taken it, how could they let it go?

Our majestic kingdom did not lack brave and heroic individuals. How was it that they could cover their eyes and bow their heads, content to do the bidding of protector-generals and regional inspectors? It was only because the country had been made a dependency for a long time and had been divided into commanderies in which officials were established and spread out along its borders. Therefore, the [Chinese] showed authority and good fortune, and as a consequence, everyone curried favor and obeyed and honored them. When a local tyrant emerged, the Chinese would bring their total force to overpower him. These uprisings included those by Ly Ton and Truong Thac in the Jin period [mid-third to early fifth century C.E.] and those of Duong Thanh, Ly Manh Thu, Huu Ngan, Mai Thuc Loan, and Vuong Thang Trieu in the Tang period, and they all were like this. Only two rulers succeeded, those of the Ly and Trieu courts [544–602], because the Liang and Chen dynasties [502–587] in China had taken refuge in a single place; the region south of the Yangtze was in turmoil; and no attention could be paid to Giao Chau. For this reason, these [local] rulers were able to establish their territories and take reign names lasting for fifty to sixty years. If the Han and Tang dynasties had truly been periods of great prosperity, then why would they have been willing to give up the borders and lands that they had already taken and from which they had received much tribute and contributions, to permit this land to be formed into a great kingdom beyond the territories of the [Ngu] Linh?[4] It was for this reason that each of these successive uprisings was put down and that the rebels were forced to accept authority. For more than one thousand years, these territories were divided into commanderies and districts to serve as dependencies. Most likely it was the circumstances that made it so, for how could it be that the will of Heaven did not yet wish for our kingdom to be governed peacefully but, rather, blamed these things on the actions of the people?

> [Phan Huy Chu, *Lich trieu hien chuong loai chi*, 6:13b–15a;
> trans. George Dutton]

NGUYEN HOANG

DEATHBED STATEMENT TO HIS SON (1613)

This brief excerpt from the later nineteenth-century *Veritable Records of Dai Nam* describes a crucial moment in the historical trajectory of the Nguyen clan. Even if the event itself is apocryphal, this short deathbed speech by Nguyen Hoang to his heir, Nguyen Phuc Nguyen, symbolizes a key political transition in early modern Vietnamese history. The position of governor-general of Thuan Hoa and Quang Nam, which had been bestowed on Nguyen Hoang, had effectively now become hereditary. Furthermore, the speech highlights the Nguyen determination to resist the Trinh militarily, suggesting the insuperable rift between the two clans. Finally, Nguyen Hoang enumerates the geographic and resource advantages that his clan's southern territory offers, which should enable the Nguyen to resist their northern rivals.

As a son you must be filial, and as a subject you must be loyal; brothers must, above all, have fraternal affection for one another. If you hold firm to these words of advice, I will have no regrets. [Nguyen Hoang also said]: To its north, the region of Thuan-Quang has Mount Hoanh[5] and the Linh River, which serve as [protective] barriers, while to the south lies the security provided by the Hai Van pass and the Da Bia mountains. The mountains give us gold and iron, and the seas give us fish and salt. Truly, this is a favorable land for heroes. If one knows how to teach the people to train as soldiers in order to resist the Trinh clan, this will be sufficient to establish a legacy that will endure for myriad generations. If it turns out that their powerful force cannot be overcome, then you must strive to guard and protect our territories and await a suitable opportunity. Do not forget these, my commands.

> [*Dai Nam thuc luc* (hereafter, *DNTL*) (1961–), 1:29;
> *DNTL* (2004–2007), 5:37; trans. George Dutton]

---

4. Literally, "the Five Ridges," referring to the territories below the mountains that constituted the traditional southern boundary of the Chinese realm.

5. Mount Hoanh was the traditional border between the northern and southern parts of Vietnam.

NGUYEN KHOA CHIEM

RECORDED TALES OF THE FOUNDING OF THE COUNTRY (1719)

Recorded Tales of the Founding of the Country is a semifictionalized, late-seventeenth-century account of the Nguyen clan's southward expansion. Its author, Nguyen Khoa Chiem (1659–1736), was a Nguyen court official whose grandfather had been part of Nguyen Hoang's entourage when he went south in the mid-sixteenth century. This tale provides one of the earliest extended southern accounts of this process. The excerpt translated here is from the beginning of the text and is a Nguyen version of their emergence as a political force. It also describes the Nguyen's growing conflict with their counterparts, the Trinh clan, and the eventual rupture between the two. This text is significant as one of the earliest surviving large-scale literary works produced in the Nguyen realm. In some respects, it can be seen as a southern analogue to the late-eighteenth-century *Unification Records of the Imperial Le*, a northern work of a similar genre and scale, which dealt with the Trinh clan and its eventual demise at the hands of the Tay Son armies.[6]

It is said that in the land of Viet Nam, the rise and fall of dynasties extended through the six houses of the Hung, Trieu, Dinh, Ly, Tran, and Le. When the Tran family's fortunes changed and the decadent period of their reign began, the land of Ming came to invade with ruthless generals and proud soldiers, and our people could not endure this great harm. Then Heaven begat Emperor Le Thai To, who used the cotton cloth [ordinary people] to rise up in righteousness from Mount Lam and who restored to us both our frontiers and the dignity of having an emperor, just as in the Middle Kingdom. He was succeeded by Emperors [Le] Thai Tong, [Le] Nhan Tong, [Le] Thanh Tong, and then [Le] Chieu Tong. Unfortunately, [Le] Chieu Tong was not sufficiently competent, so the powerful minister Mac Dang Dung usurped the throne [in 1527]. [Le] Chieu Tong fled and returned to his native area of Thanh Hoa. Constantly ashamed at having fallen to such miserable depths, he assembled his remaining troops at the mound of the national altar for the purpose of plotting to decimate the Mac and avenge his ancestors. In the definitive battle with [Mac] Dang Dung, he [Le Chieu Tong] suffered the misfortune of being taken captive, and after he had met with this disaster, the descendants of the Le and those with the imperial surname took flight. [Le] Chieu Tong's son, known as Ninh, was still an infant, and his mother feared that [Mac] Dang Dung would want to impose on them the great evil of "cutting the weeds and digging up the roots," so she took him away to Ai Lao.

At that time, all the old officials of the Le became allies of the Mac clan in the hope of gaining riches and honors. [There remained] only the old general,

---

6. See Ngo Family Literary Group, *The Unification Records of the Imperial Le* (this chap.)

the An Tinh marquis, Nguyen Kim, who was from the outer village of Gia Mieu in Tong Son District, Ha Trung Prefecture, in Thanh Hoa. Some years earlier in Thang Long, [Mac] Dang Dung had blocked his request for more soldiers, so [Nguyen] Kim would not cooperate with him. He had broken up his own regiment and withdrawn to his native region. He went to live in Nghe An, intending to pass his life at ease, but when he saw the Le family's royal influence shrinking by the day and their lack of capable and loyal ministers, he was deeply moved and shed tears both day and night. He traveled the length and breadth of Thanh [Hoa], Nghe [An], and other places, assembling a group of heroic men, whom he exhorted to support the Le and wipe out the Mac. Many came and joined him, so he devised a plan with [Le] Chieu Tong's relation, Trinh Duy San, and went off to find Le Ninh in the land of Ai Lao, installing him as emperor with the name of [Le] Trang Tong. They established a camp with a travel palace by the Tat Ma River and then at the forest hamlet of Van Lai. Constantly summoning soldiers and buying horses, inviting and accepting heroes, piling up straw and storing provisions, they all plotted together to restore the Le. Within a few weeks, they had a force numbering in the tens of thousands.

Although the An Tinh marquis regularly fought the Mac forces, they always kept him in check. Later, when he was fighting the Mac along a road in Son Nam, the Mac forces began losing, so they secretly ordered their general, the Trung Hau marquis, to feign surrender. The An Tinh marquis accepted him in good faith, and because of this, the Trung Hau marquis was able to give him poison. So very soon An Tinh died and was given the posthumous title of King Chieu Huan Tinh [King Tinh who displays meritorious conduct].

The An Tinh marquis had a son, Nguyen Hoang, who was naturally gifted with intelligence and stood above others with his wisdom. But he still was young and not yet capable of making decisions or leading the forces. His father's son-in-law Trinh Kiem was very talented and strong, and the soldiers liked him. At that time he belonged to the palace bodyguard, and Emperor [Le] Trang Tong gave him the authority to lead the troops and carry out military expeditions. By the time Nguyen Hoang came of age, he had been on campaigns with Kiem for many years and done some astounding soldiery. Emperor [Le] Trang Tong piled honors on [Hoang] and appointed him his right-hand minister. Kiem saw this and became more suspicious of Nguyen Hoang each day. Worried that Right-hand Minister Nguyen Hoang would at some time in the future outstrip him in deeds of valor, he petitioned the emperor to allow Nguyen Hoang to attack Thuan Hoa. But up to this point, the Mac troops and generals had had a firm hold on Thuan Hoa, and Kiem planned to send Nguyen Hoang there in order to use the Mac's power to kill him. Nevertheless, although people may wish for one thing, Heaven desires another. Afterward someone wrote a poem, which said:

Rise and fall, success and failure are truly overwhelming things,
The royal capital was a place submerged in these for many years.

Phoenixes nest in lone trees, only parrots frolic in flocks,
  A tiger will lie in forests of the plains, whereas ghosts are wont
    to moan in mobs.
There are none who tell of spiders weaving their webs in wells,
  But there are those who speak of horses whipped on into
    sandalwood gorges.
How could the heavenly dragon be content to lie low in a pond?
Just hearing the wind or thunder would have him soar skyward!

So it is said that in the *mau ngo* year, the eleventh year of Chinh Tri [1558], Nguyen Phuc Hoang, the son of the great preceptor King Chieu Huan Tinh and the Right-Hand minister and duke of the Doan commandary, had attacked the Mac many times and had had great success against them. All whom he [Nguyen Hoang] faced startled like roe deer or scurried away like mice, and everyone had the deepest admiration for him. Since the death of King Chieu Huan Tinh [Nguyen Kim], the grand preceptor Minh Khang—King Chieu Huan Tinh's adopted son-in-law [Trinh Kiem]—relied completely on his own power and authority and ignored all good graces. He thoroughly hated the Duke of Doan [Nguyen Hoang] and schemed to do him harm. Because of this, the Duke of Doan's nephew, who was the duke of the fiefdom of Thich, made a secret plan to have the Duke of Doan's fiancée go to the palace and ask the duke's elder sister, Lady Nguyen, for help in rescuing him. Lady Nguyen was Minh Khang's principal concubine, and she was very shocked when she heard of this. So she secretly plotted to deceive Minh Khang and went to plead with him, saying: "I, your lowly Nguyen concubine, have this contemptible younger brother, the Duke of Doan. He has suddenly been struck down with madness and has lost all his senses. He is not capable of entering the court to help with governing, and even I myself have suffered much ridicule at court. I have heard that the two places of Quang Nam and Thuan Hoa have poisonous peaks and evil waters, that they are the abode of wicked barbarians, and that they are hated by all. So I beg of you to consider compassionately his previous meritorious conduct, as well as my feelings, and permit my disgraced younger brother, the Duke of Doan, to serve as governor-general over these two places as his fiefdom. He can enjoy the rest of his life there, and I will have carried out some of my duties as an elder sister to a younger brother. I beseech you to take pity on him and allow this."

The grand preceptor Minh Khang [Trinh Kiem] replied, "Your brother Doan [Hoang] is a great hero and is very wise and knowledgeable in matters of strategy; he can bear heavy responsibilities and is certainly no fool. How could I bear to assign him to such a rotten place? You must not concern yourself with this. My opinion on the matter is firm." Upon hearing this, the Nguyen concubine knelt down and sobbed loudly, begging him again and again. The grand preceptor Minh Khang thought to himself, "Those places are the encampments of the Mac pretender's forces. I ought to let him go there, [for] then I can get the Mac to do all the work and avoid earning a reputation as one who does not know how to make use of people." So he permitted it to happen. The Nguyen concubine respectfully gave her thanks and the grand preceptor sent the throne a memorial that Nguyen Hoang was to be enfeoffed as the defender-in-chief Duke of Doan and that he was to serve as governor-general over the troops and people of the two areas of Quang Nam and Thuan Hoa and would have to collect taxes there and pay an annual tribute. The Duke of Doan gave thanks and returned to his residence. He then took leave of the Nguyen concubine, and on the very same day, with his sons; the grand guardians Hoa Quan, Thuy Quan, Van Nham, Thach Xuyen, Tien Trung, and Tuong Loc; and a naval force of one thousand men, he set off from the harbor for Thuan Hoa and Quang Nam. His warships sailed straight into the port of An Viet, and he stationed his troops on the Ai Tu plain in the county of Vo Xuong. From Vo Xuong he secretly sent people to Huong Tra and other counties to learn the geography of those areas. They observed that Phu Xuan village in Huong Tra County was encircled by rivers and mountains and that the people were attractive and the place was prosperous, and they returned to report this news. The duke was very pleased and decided to use virtuous government to conquer that place.

[Nguyen Khoa Chiem, Viet Nam khai quoc chi truyen,
8a–11a; trans. Catherine Churchman]

TRINH CAN

EDICT TO THE PEOPLES OF QUANG NAM (1672)

The "Edict to the Peoples of Quang Nam," by the leader of the northern armies, Trinh Can (1633–1709), son of the reigning Lord Trinh Tac (r. 1657–1682), outlines the Trinh government's view of its protracted conflict and military engagement with the Nguyen. Issued on the eve of the final (and ultimately unsuccessful) Trinh effort to overpower the Nguyen, this edict contains an extended comment on the circumstances that led to Nguyen Hoang's departure for the southern territories in 1558. The text charges the Nguyen leaders with having violated their promises and been disloyal to the Le emperors. Trinh Can argues that the Trinh campaigns represented an effort to reassert the emperor's authority over the southern lands and peoples, which had been usurped by Nguyen Hoang and his successors. There are echoes here of the Le dynasty's earlier military campaigns against the southern region, then under Cham control, which resulted in the extension of Vietnamese political control into the territories now governed by the Nguyen.

To attack despotic rulers and, in so doing, to rescue the people is the reason that kings raise troops. All who live in the two regions have their origins in the peoples and lands of the sagely ancestor [Le] Thanh Tong of our royal court. They do not belong to the Nguyen clan for their own exploitation. We have respect for the burden that produced the sagely king's thoughts that the Nguyen were related to him like reed stalks and shoots. Thus, we [the Trinh] memorialized and requested of the late emperor that he approve sending the Duke of Doan, Nguyen Hoang, to serve as governor-general for those two regions, where he would collect and submit the taxes so they might be used by the state. He swore an oath before Heaven and Earth that from the beginning to the end of his service, he would devote himself fully to serving as an official. At that time, the Great and Sagacious Ancestor king Trinh Kiem [d. 1570] was concentrating his efforts on restoring the royal family and eliminating the usurping Mac. The Duke of Doan lived in an outer province and took no part in the hardship of going into battle astride a sweat-drenched horse. Only when peace had been restored did the Duke of Doan finally return to the capital to offer his congratulations. The Great and Sagacious Ancestor king was magnanimous and forgiving and did not speak of the duke's lack of meritorious contributions but, rather, regarded him with righteousness as a relative. The Duke of Doan continued to memorialize the Le emperor, asking for more noble titles, and the emperor generously bestowed such favors in the form of positions and salaries.

It could not have been foreseen that the Duke of Doan would defy the emperor and break his oaths with dark schemes of rebellion and betrayal. In the *canh ty* year [1600], he incited a group of disloyal officials to create disorder and then fled to Thuan Hoa. He was now an official acting in a perverse fashion and deserved to be adjudicated according to the laws, but the Great and Sagacious Ancestor king was compassionate, pardoning him and forgiving his crimes. When the court ordered officials to bring the decrees and to present the proclamation to inform the Duke of Doan about the matter, he [the duke] had the envoys burned to death and schemed to seize the royal letter and then secretly used it to disgrace the envoy. Sedition was already beginning to take root in their hearts. From this time on, disloyal officials carried out these practices. We do not speak of this. In the following years, the court continued to send officials to bring decrees informing them of and making clear the sovereign's great righteousness, instructing them about the respective outcomes of misfortune and prosperity, and [expressing the sovereign's] desire that they change their hearts and return to the royal commands, so that the people of the two regions might be relieved of the hardships of warfare and might enjoy the prosperity and good fortune of a great peace. How could we anticipate that the mongrel would not come to understand this? Moreover, with arrogant and offensive words, he resisted and refused the imperial emissary. Can there be any more serious transgressions than these disrespectful and disloyal crimes?

Now then, this land is the land of the king, and the people are the people of the king, and yet the Nguyen clan has secretly seized this land. How is it that they do not understand that this is how things are? They have dug deep trenches and built high ramparts so as to resist [the court's] orders, and they have collected heavy taxes that have oppressed the people. They have forced the people to take up halberds and spears; how can such people constitute an organized rank of soldiers? They have caused the people to abandon the study of books and of ritual; how then will they achieve an illustrious name in the examinations? Looking at what they have done, we have seen that they have relied on a strategic location to act in a contrary fashion. They have also resisted and defied the imperial court and have continued to spread poison among the places and peoples. Because of such crimes, how can we be tolerant and permit them to go unpunished? The people have been hanged upside down in this fashion; how can we permit this and not rescue them? This is a matter on which we must act, and the troops are now being properly prepared.

Now, I [Trinh Can] have respectfully accepted the order of the generalissimo, the primary manager of national affairs, the supreme administrator, the great father, the western prince [Trinh Tac] who aids and supports the emperor, and [I] will personally go into battle. He has entrusted to me the overall task of raising the great army, giving orders to all the generals, and dividing my force along the routes to advance and suppress [the rebels]. I expect that this will be a complete success and that we will defeat and exterminate those who are disobedient, after which all will have been completed. So now, if the soldiers and the civilians in the two regions come to know this, they must turn their backs on darkness and turn to the light. They must return to humaneness and flee their tyrannical leaders. And they first must either put down their lances and surrender, or they must go to our troops' encampment and surrender there. If they are noted leaders, they will be pardoned and rewarded for their actions. If they are common people, they will be rewarded with lightened labor service and reduced taxes. And if there are people in other regions who fled for fear of being punished for their crimes, or if they were duped into acting as rebels and they now see the great army coming and return to the imperial commands, they also will be pardoned and put to work. If, however, they continue in their obstinate foolishness then even jade and stone will be burned up in the fires of Con Son.[7] When that point has been reached, there will be nowhere for them to flee.

> [Ngo Cao Lang, *Lich trieu tap ky* (hereafter, *LTTK*), vhv.
> 1321/1, 2b–5a; trans. George Dutton, with Matthew Cochran]

---

7. This refers to a phrase in the *Classic of Poetry* (*Shijing*): "In the fiery flames of Con Son, even jade and stone will burn up."

ECONOMICS AND TRADE

KHANH DUC EMPEROR

EDICT PROHIBITING FOREIGNERS FROM TAKING UP
RESIDENCE WITHOUT RESTRICTIONS (1650)

The "Edict Prohibiting Foreigners from Taking Up Residence Without Restrictions" was an early attempt by the Le rulers to regulate commercial contacts with the Europeans and with Asian traders, particularly from Japan and China. The edict shows the growing significance of trade, particularly with the Europeans, who were an important source of weaponry. It also suggests the northern court's ongoing concern with checking the expansion of commerce to the degree that it began to erode the powers of the central state. At the same time, the detailed regulations spelled out in this edict represent an elaboration of the commerce clauses found in the Le Code, which, since its promulgation in the mid-fifteenth century, sought to regulate trade, especially at the important northern port of Van Don. Also echoing issues contained in the Le Code, the Khanh Duc emperor's edict reveals the court's concern about the possibility of espionage by foreign visitors, a concern heightened by the ongoing Nguyen–Trinh conflict, which began in 1627.

When vessels from Portugal, Holland, Japan, and other places arrive at the entrance to the harbor, an inner emissary shall personally inquire into the situation in advance. [He shall] permit the [members of the delegation] to stay at Thanh Tri, Khuyen Luong, and other designated areas; select an official to ensure that they follow the regulations; and choose a local person to act as an interpreter to inform the captain and the sailors that they all must respect propriety and law and proceed to the capital to do obeisance. On the road, only the captain shall be permitted to ride a horse; when he passes the palace, government offices, or memorial halls to ancient sages, he must dismount. In places such as the inner-palace precincts, the delegates may not enter very far or come and go freely.

[The delegates shall] permit the superintending prefect to investigate those who disobey these orders, [to find out] whether it is true and, if it is, to punish the interpreter. If those from Portugal who study the Way [that is, Christianity] wish to practice within the palace city, the Ministry of Rites shall investigate and forbid them from doing so, and those who wish to practice outside shall not be allowed to do so, either. If they set up unorthodox temples, then, inside the palace city, the prefect and, outside the palace city, the surveillance commissioner are authorized to tear them down. If men or women of this country still carry weapons on their persons, all shall be collected and destroyed, and each person shall receive fifty strokes of the whip.

[Officials shall] make a precise inquiry of the ships from Fujian that arrive to engage in commerce, allow them to stay at Thanh Tri, Khuyen Luong and other designated areas, and regulate the transactions in their markets. The merchants from the arriving ships should not pressure the local merchants, and the local merchants also should not swindle the foreign merchants.

All the aforementioned are strictly forbidden from selling expensive goods, and they are not to conceal products and privately sell them elsewhere. If the intendant cannot strictly enforce this, then his punishment should be increased.

If envoys of the Northern kingdom [China] come with merchants overland by the northern road, they should be allowed to await orders at the An Thuong station so as to stringently enforce propriety and law and to prevent them from spying on us.

[*Le trieu chieu linh thien chinh*, 176–77; trans. Kate Baldanza]

LE QUY DON

WEALTH OF THE NGUYEN REALM (1776)

This excerpt from Le Quy Don's *Chronicles of the Prefectural Borders*, a report on the Nguyen realm in the mid-1770s, is noteworthy for revealing the substantial wealth enjoyed by the southern populations. This wealth was a product of active engagement in the far-flung commercial networks that linked Quang Nam to the rest of East and Southeast Asia and Europe beyond. The Nguyen capital's proximity to the coast facilitated its connections to seaborne trade, and its port cities served as entrepôts at river mouths where upland goods were regularly traded. Le Quy Don implicitly contrasts the degree of conspicuous consumption he sees in the Nguyen realm with the more austere society in the Trinh north with which he is familiar. This excerpt also includes an extended critique of the Nguyen regent, Truong Phuc Loan (d. 1776). It was Truong Phuc Loan's avarice and spendthrift ways that were widely seen by eighteenth-century commentators as responsible for the decline of the Nguyen polity. In this view, the Trinh invasion of 1774 was justified by a need to rescue the long-suffering southern populations and was widely welcomed by those long oppressed by Truong Phuc Loan.

Because the people in Thuan Hoa lived in peace for a long time, both officials and the common people were wealthy and accustomed to fancy things. Their lifestyles tended to be even fancier during the Nguyen Phuc Khoat period [1738–1765]. Because he himself liked luxury, his subjects followed him and luxury became the norm for them. No matter how high or low their positions, the officials all lived in ornamental buildings with gauze and satin as curtains and mosquito nets. Their pots were made of copper, their furniture of *trac*,[8] their cups and trays of porcelain, and their saddles of gold and silver. Dresses were made of brocade

---

8. *Trac* is a type of hardwood.

and colored silk, and mats of very good quality rattan. They showed off and competed with each other for richness and distinction.

The common people also wore satin shirts with flowers and damask trousers as their everyday garb. To be dressed in plain cotton was considered a disgrace.

The soldiers all enjoyed sitting on mats, with incense burners in their hands, receiving fine tea in silver or porcelain cups. Everything came from China, from spittoons to crockery, even the food. For every meal they had three big bowls of rice.

The women all dressed in gauze, ramie and silk, with embroidered flowers circling their round collars. People here looked upon gold and silver as sand, and milled rice as mud; their lives could not be more extravagant.

According to Nguyen Cong Binh, who used to be an official of the Nguyen, there were three officials on whom Nguyen Phuc Thuan [r. 1765–1777] relied. One was Truong Phuc Loan who was so greedy that he would never stop collecting money although he already had untold gold, silver, and valuable things at home. The other two persons were the Nguyen ruler's uncles: Nguyen Noan, in charge of the navy, a big drinker who was always drunk and knew nothing about life; and Nguyen Nghiem who was in charge of Huu Truong Co [that is, one of four high officials in the Nguyen army]. This man liked women; he kept 120 concubines, so women decorated with pearls and jade were all over his home. . . .

Truong Phuc Loan usurped authority for more than 30 years [during which he] collected a lot of money and killed many people. The taxes collected in the Sai, Thu Bon, Tra Van, and Dong Huong [river] villages were given to him as his salary, as much as 40 to 50 thousand *quan* per year. Moreover, as the official in charge of transportation and civil affairs he received another 30 to 40 thousand *quan* each year.

Thuan Hoa has very few products. All the valuable things were taken from Quang Nam which is the richest place in the world. The people in Thang Hoa and Dien Ban could weave, and the quality and beauty of the thin silk, satin, damask silk and gauze they produced were as good as those in Guangzhou.

Abundant rice was produced in Quy Nhon, Quang Ngai, and Gia Dinh. Chinese traders used to go there to buy rice, clicking their tongues as a sign of admiration.

There were as many elephants as oxen and horses in Ke Lanh, Thu Bon, and Phuong Tay in the Thang Hoa and Dien Ban prefectures. Every family there raised elephants and the same was true of Quy Nhon and Quang Ngai.

There were horses in Hat Co Dien and Hat Ke Thu in Quy Nhon. The horses were [wild] in the mountains; a herd could amount to hundreds or thousands. They stood 2.5 to 3 *thuoc* [3.3 to almost 4 feet] tall. The local people used to tame them and employ them to carry trade goods to Phu Yen. It was very common to see women go shopping or traveling on horseback.

[Le Quy Don, *Phu bien tap luc*; trans. Li and Reid,
Southern Vietnam Under the Nguyen, 124–25]

NGO THE LAN

MEMORIAL ON THE CURRENCY CRISIS (1771)

This "Memorial on the Currency Crisis" addresses a major economic issue facing the Nguyen rulers in the mid-eighteenth century: currency and its role in circulating commodities. This was an issue of periodic concern to Vietnamese rulers, as seen in the 1430 edict drafted by Nguyen Trai regarding the early Le transition from Ho Quy Ly's paper money to the use of copper cash.[9] By the mid-eighteenth century, the southern rulers had come to rely on the importation of copper coinage, primarily from Japan, to supplement their own, very limited copper production capabilities. When the Japanese curtailed the export of copper in the 1710s, the Nguyen were forced to find other means by which to produce coinage. Their solution was to use a mostly zinc alloy for their coins. As this memorial makes clear, these new coins were extremely unpopular with the Vietnamese, who saw this less durable currency as intrinsically less valuable than the earlier copper coinage. Ngo The Lan recommended taking steps to stabilize prices and to shift away from the unpopular zinc coinage. The Nguyen ruler accepted the memorial but did not act on it, and the *Veritable Records of Dai Nam* notes that Ngo The Lan later joined the Tay Son regime, which was established after 1775 in the south. For their part, the Tay Son were able to burnish their economic credentials by resuming the minting of copper coinage, having procured the metal from captured Nguyen cities and bells and drums seized from Buddhist temples.

Ngo The Lan, a retired official in Thuan Hoa, submitted a memorial discussing problems with currency. In summary, the memorial stated: "I have heard that when the first lord was developing [his realm], the land was still small and the people still scattered. To the south, we did not yet have Gia Dinh's great abundance. (Gia Dinh is land of the first order, as its soils are very suitable for cultivating paddy rice, and they also are suitable for cultivating areca palms. A popular saying is "First paddy rice, then areca palm.")[10] To the north, we still were on alert at Mount Hoanh, where there had been many years of warfare. Despite this, the people were not starving, and the state had a surplus of food. Now that under Heaven has been at peace for a long time, the lands are broad, and the population has grown. The areas for planting rice have already been fully cleared. The benefits that derive from the mountain regions have already been fully developed. Furthermore, the fields in Phien Tran and Long Ho have never suffered the misfortunes of droughts or floods.

Despite this, from the *mau ty* year [1768] until the present, the price of rice has soared upward, causing the people to suffer from famine. Why is this? It is not

---

9. See Le Thai To and Nguyen Trai, "Edict on Currency" (chap. 3).
10. This note is in the original text.

a shortage of rice. Rather, it stems from the distribution of zinc currency. Among the people, everyone prefers durable items and detests things that easily decay. Now we should replace bronze and zinc currency, which is decaying, with copper currency, which is more durable. In this way, the people will compete with one another to store rice and will not want to store money. Of course, we have had this zinc currency for a long time, and now that we wish to exchange it, it will be very difficult, but the hunger of the people makes this imperative. I venture to think that this is the expedient course for the present day and that there is nothing to be gained by imitating the actions of the Han dynasty.[11] Each prefecture should designate a specific warehouse, assign one responsible official, and set the price. Then, whenever there is cheaper paddy rice, it should be purchased at this price, and when the paddy price is expensive, we should [also] sell it at that price. In this way, the price of paddy rice will not become so cheap as to harm the farmers, and it also will not become so expensive that it is profitable for wealthy merchants. Then the exchange rate for the zinc currency will become fixed, and the price of goods will stabilize.

[*DNTL* (1961–), 1:156–57; *DNTL* (2004–2007), 1:238–39; trans. George Dutton]

QUANG TRUNG EMPEROR

EDICT ENCOURAGING AGRICULTURE (1789–1790)

The "Edict Encouraging Agriculture" was issued by the Tay Son Quang Trung emperor (r. 1788–1792) in an attempt to restore economic security through agricultural productivity after years of warfare and political turmoil. Widespread vagabondage had led to fields being entirely abandoned or underutilized. Through a combination of incentives and threats, this edict sought to induce people to return to their villages, reclaim their fields, and start to plow and plant them. Ensuring that the people remained in one place was of crucial importance to the state. It was only when peasants were in their villages that the state could count, supervise, tax, and extract military and labor service from them. Producing verifiable village registers thus was crucial to these sorts of projects, which had been undertaken by a succession of earlier dynasties. This edict also reveals the central importance of agriculture, both in classical formulations regarding statecraft and economics and in the realities of late-eighteenth-century Vietnam. Earlier policies focusing on agriculture can be seen in the edicts and laws of the early Le dynasty rulers, who, like the Tay Son, launched large-scale projects to rebuild a war-torn nation. Ultimately, this edict can be seen as a part of Quang Trung's larger economic recovery efforts, which included encouraging

---

11. This refers to the widespread circulation of poor-quality coins in the Han, as well as the frequent reduction in the weight of the coins being minted.

cross-border trade with China and reaching out to European trading communities in Macao and Manila.

A command to all under Heaven, the officials, the administrators, and the common people, that they might await and respectfully know the following:

The promotion by the emperor's administration of essentials and restriction of inessentials brought about achievements in transportation and agriculture, so that the state will no longer have wandering peoples, and the countryside will no longer contain neglected fields. From the time that disorder broke out until the present, warfare, as well as famine and starvation, has been common. The people wandered and shifted about, and fields were abandoned and left uncultivated. [Settled] villagers and cultivated fields now number no more than 40 or 50 percent of [those in] former times. We have accepted the intention of fate, which is that we clean up the four corners of our kingdom. At present, the great undertaking is just beginning, so we must set forth policies to stimulate and expand agriculture, and if we wish to achieve this, we must put them into action.

Alas! The recalcitrant drifters conceal their wealth, which is a common practice. To protect the people, nothing would be better than to return the vagabonds to work opening new fields, and thus making those with skillful hands and skills in agriculture return to working the land. In the past, certain people took up residence in a place other than their native village in order to avoid their corvée labor duties, or to take up residence in the village of their wife or mother, or to carry out commerce as a merchant. Except for those who have been enrolled as villagers for at least three generations, all others should be forced to return to their native place, and the village in which they took refuge will not be permitted to tolerate their [continued] residence. With respect to the various public and private fields, including those already abandoned, everyone must obey [the order to] return and accept the work of cultivation, and these fields certainly must not be permitted to remain uncultivated. The people who are actually cultivating fields are ordered to bear the assessment taxes. The village chiefs must examine the enrolled people to determine their residence and social status and what proportion of them are actually present, and look into the amount of acreage that is really being cultivated. The deadline for submitting these registers will be set at the tenth day of the ninth month, and they must be submitted to the *phan suat* and the *phan tri* county branch office officials, who will then forward this information. They must then await the viceroy's assessment of their accuracy and his consideration of their equity. And if any village permits outsiders to reside there and does not return them to their home villages, or if drifters hesitate and do not return home, then anyone who knows about this must report it. There will be an honest investigation to get the facts straight, and, both the village chief and the fleeing person will be judged on the basis of their place of residence.

If some villages contain abandoned fields that have not been claimed and cultivated by the deadline, then responsibility for the cultivation of public fields will lie with the offices of the village officials and the household heads in that village. They will be assessed in accordance with the original amount of field taxes. If this was private land, it will be confiscated, and the tax assessed will be the same as that for public lands.

Now first of all, we must establish policies for the aforementioned primary tasks of the people. This decree shall be presented and must be enacted.

Dear officials and people, each of you must strive to follow my virtuous intentions, return to your village gates, and exert yourselves to [restore] your fields and farmlands! Do not give in to emotions, which will hinder your means of livelihood. Do not flee or give in to weakness, or you will be arrested for your crimes.

To you of the hundred surnames, I offer the pleasures of abundance and accomplishments. Each of you must strictly strive to abide by this decree, and you may not act contrary to it!

[Ngo Thi Nham, *Ngo Thi Nham toan tap*, 2:623–26; trans. George Dutton]

QUANG TRUNG EMPEROR

LETTER TO THE GOVERNOR OF MACAO (JUNE 7, 1792)

While the Nguyen attempted to create alliances with the French,[12] the Tay Son looked for contacts with European outposts in Asia, including sending letters to European governors in Manila and Macao. After taking the imperial throne and driving out the occupying Qing army, the Quang Trung emperor turned his attention to restoring the Vietnamese economy while also attempting to limit his Nguyen opponent's access to European trade. This text is a letter from the Tay Son emperor to the Portuguese governor at Macao seeking to establish a trading relationship with the Portuguese. It contains criticisms of the Europeans for engaging in trade and providing armaments to the Nguyen, whom the emperor repeatedly denigrates. Quang Trung describes the strength and accomplishments of his armies, boasting of having attacked the two Quangs (Guangdong and Guangxi) in southern China. He also attempts to convince the Portuguese that the Nguyen territory is insignificant compared with his own and, moreover, that he is about to eradicate his southern rivals. The overall import is to persuade the Europeans to trade with him and not the Nguyen, hinting that there would be repercussions if they failed to do so. In some respects, the message echoes earlier rivalries between the northern and southern Vietnamese or Cham polities attempting to attract trade to their particular coastal ports.

12. See "Treaty of Versailles Between Nguyen Anh and King Louis XVI" (this chap.)

By this imperial letter, I hereby inform the European king of Macao that he might know exactly how events have unfolded. This year, in the fourth intercalary month [May–June 1792], two ships have arrived at my Kingdom of Quang Nam at the port of Thuchum. They were examined by the port guards, and they declared themselves to be ships from Macao, of which the captain's name was Joaquim António Milner. He had carried out commerce in Dong Nai and was returning to Macao, bearing letters of recognition from this lost family of the Nguyen. But alas! He was ignorant of the fact and unable to discern clearly that Dong Nai is nothing but a minor territory where the vanquished Nguyen family has taken refuge in order to hide themselves. That insignificant man [Nguyen Anh] will never regain his domains; those madmen of the Siamese king aided him with their armies, but they, too, were vanquished and exterminated in combat. Heaven has dispersed them; they are lost and have neither courage nor troops. For five years now, the French and those of your kingdom, and numerous merchants have given them boats and arms. Taking part in his tyranny, they have resisted my armies, fighting in the wars in which many have died by the blade of the sword; it is a fact known to all and should serve as an example. I, the emperor, have purified and pacified the kingdom out of this confusion. I have conquered all the southern provinces, not only in Tonkin, but also those of Cochinchina, where all the middle territories of Quang Nam were first pacified, after which all the major cities of these central regions of Quang Nam were made tributaries. However, this territory of Dong Nai is like a pearl; how is it that this lineage of the Nguyen has been able to elude me? For some years now, up to the present day, I have been at war in order to establish myself in the northern regions of Hinhing [Tonkin]. Moreover, I have made war on China and its provinces of Guangdong and Guangxi, where I put the Chinese to flight and carried out great massacres. These victories established peace, and I have been at rest for some time. My army is now on battle footing; my captains and soldiers are flush with courage and will take part wherever I command them.

As a consequence of this, you, the king of Macao, in truth but a small territory, should decide and send an edict in firm terms. I understand that not all those in Macao are supporters of the Nguyen in the outcome of this affair and were motivated to engage in commerce with Dong Nai only out of greed. They should not return there, so that they might no longer be marked by this wicked Nguyen lineage and no longer take part in their intrigues and criminal actions, under the pain of becoming, without any doubt, victims of my sword. My desire is to pacify all the neighboring princedoms, and I do not wish to be in discord with them. It is for this reason, king of Macao, that I admonish you and urge you to give rigorous instructions to your subjects that if they carry out commerce, it should be to Fuchum, a port in my kingdom, where they will find an accommodating anchorage, and that they no longer return to Dong Nai and its environs, in order that they no longer find themselves involved in those crimes with which they are unfamiliar. And if they do not wish to obey with good grace, they will regret it, but it will be too late. Consider all of this well, for on it depends fortune or misfortune, friendship or enmity.

[Manguin, *Les Nguyen, Macau et le Portugal*, 98–99, 236–37; trans. George Dutton]

PHILOSOPHY AND RELIGION

LE QUY DON

ON *LY* AND *KHI* (1773)

Le Quy Don was one of the few early modern Vietnamese literati to study Confucian metaphysics. His text *Categorized Sayings from the Van Terrace* includes a discussion of *ly* and *khi*, or "principle" and "essence," from which this excerpt is taken. This selection shows strong elements of Buddhist influence, and Le Quy Don makes several direct references to Buddhist beliefs in the text. The dualism of *ly* and *khi* was one of the central elements of Confucian metaphysics and is closely linked to other dualities such as *yin* and *yang*, Heaven and Earth, light and dark, and fullness and emptiness. Fundamentally, the conception of such dualities is based on harmony and balance, one of the core principles of Confucian thought and a central aspiration of both refined men and the states that they served as officials. The more applied approach to Confucianist thought reflected in Nguyen Binh Khiem's 1578 inscription discussing "goodness" is a useful contrast to Le Quy Don's approach.[13]

Heaven creates the Way from emptiness. The Earth creates the Way from stillness. Only when humans become empty and tranquil can they unite the Way of Heaven and Earth. This is because with emptiness, one comes to understand, and with stillness, one becomes established. The key to assisting Heaven and Earth is precisely in having one's mind illuminated and the principles established.

"How great is the fundamental nature of *kien*! The myriad things are provided their beginnings by it." This speaks of material force [*khi*]. How great is the fundamental nature of *khon*! The myriad things are provided their births by it."[14] This speaks of form [*hinh*]. From the perspective of Heaven and Earth, everything has material force and form. From the perspective of the myriad things, everything receives its material force from Heaven and takes its form from Earth.

---

13. See Nguyen Binh Khiem, "The Three Teachings" (chap. 3).

14. From, with minor modifications, *The Classic of Changes: A New Translation of the "I Ching" as Interpreted by Wang Bi*, trans. Richard John Lynn (New York: Columbia University Press, 1994), 129, 143.

The space between Heaven and Earth is filled with material force. Principle [*ly*] refers to something that truly exists and not to something that does not exist. Principles do not have visible forms but instead are revealed through material force. Principles are thus within material force. One can speak of *yin* and *yang* [*am* and *duong*], even and odd numbers, knowledge and action, and form and function as opposing elements in a pair, but one cannot do the same for principle and material force.

The Great Ultimate [*thai cuc*] is one. It is primordial material force. The one produced two, two produced four, and onward to create the myriad things. This is the oneness of the Great Ultimate. In divination, the number of yarrow stalks employed is fifty, but one is set aside and not used in order to signify the Great Ultimate. If it did not exist, then why do this?

To open and then close is called alternation. To go and come endlessly is called unobstructed movement. When closed, there is absence. When open, there is existence. When gone, there is absence. When coming, there is existence. Both existence and absence interact in succession with people and things. From antiquity to the present, this has never not been the case. This principle even holds in the vast emptiness. Can it be, then, that something is born from nothing?

Heaven belongs to *yang* and Earth belongs to *yin*. *Yang* takes charge of movement, and *yin* takes charge of stillness. This is what is called allocation. In its functioning, Heaven is always moving, but its substance (*the*) is never not still. Earth's substance is always still, but in its functioning it is never not moving. If Heaven were not still, then how could the four directions be secure, and to what would the sun, moon, and planets adhere? If Earth did not move, then it would just be a solitary object, and life on it would be exterminated. Heaven's form moves but its material force is still. Earth's form is still, but its material force is in movement. . . .

Below Heaven and above Earth are all the winds and vapors. If near where a person is there is no wind, then probably some objects are blocking it, or it is being dispersed by living forces.

High places are where wind is the strongest; the higher the place is, the stronger and drier the wind will be. Alternately, if one digs a meter or more into the ground at the foot of a mountain, at first the dirt will come up soft and wet, but after it is taken from the ground, it becomes hard as stone. Is it not the case that it becomes hard because it is exposed to wind?

When an infant is inside a woman's belly, it is just a blood-filled placenta, but it becomes firm when born. This is the same principle.

Heavenly material force descends, and Earthly material force ascends. The material force between Heaven and Earth is a life-producing force. When wind and vapors circulate in its midst, there is no time when it is not there. It is not the case that it is there when there is movement, and not there when there is stillness. *Plain Questions* talks of the five phases of circulation and the six climactic influences.[15] Zhu Cheng refuted this, arguing that the years, months, and days pass through sixty-year cycles and bring swift changes to Heaven and Earth, the five phases, cold and heat, and wind and rain. People encounter vapors [khi], and illness forms in their bodies. These vapors are difficult to predict; therefore illnesses are difficult to prevent. Vapors are not created by people, and therefore they are difficult for people to fathom. When examining matters, people can make many mistakes, and it therefore is easy to err in one's treatment.

This is not necessarily true. I humbly hold that the vapors of Heaven and Earth are nothing other than yin and yang and the five phases. Sometimes they conflict and at other times they harmonize; sometimes they serve as host, and at other times, as guest. They govern the years and months and change with the seasons, creating myriad alternations and transformations. And while there is not always a direct reaction from people to the effect of [these vapors] on them, this is nonetheless generally the case.

Smallpox is an example of this. Although the years are different, some hot and some cold, the form of this disease remains the same. However, just as sometimes the weather is dry and at other times it is wet, the symptoms of the disease differ. So how can one say that there is no evidence for the five phases of circulation and the six climactic influences? . . .

When someone is in a deep sleep, one has to call out for him to wake up. In this way, material force summons spirit [than].[16] During dreams, people speak, move about, become happy and angry. After they wake, this all becomes a memory. In this way, spirit activates material force.

People's spirit and material force is often like this. Heaven and Earth's spirit and material force have circulated from antiquity to the present, and there is no place where they cannot be found. Therefore, former worthies stated, "Heaven knows and Earth knows."

The mind of men is immense. Above, it can comprehend all between Heaven and Earth and can fathom ghosts and spirits. Below, it can examine the myriad things.

The marvel of the signs and numbers of the Classic of Changes is dispersed among form and material force. From where it is not, it emerges to be, and from where it is, it enters where it is not.

Between the unfathomable and the illuminated, there is nothing but the Way. After one rectifies one's mind, one can understand the Way. After one understands the Way, one can discover the subtle tendencies of all things. After one discovers the subtle tendencies of all things, one can comprehend how to adapt to all situations.

---

15. *Plain Questions*, structured as a dialogue between the Yellow Emperor and his ministers and physicians, is an ancient Chinese medical text, considered to be the source for Chinese medicine.

16. "Spirit" refers to a nimble state of mind enabled by the purest material force.

Fate is controlled by man. It cannot control man. The principle that Heaven and man are one is nothing more than this. . . .

There is only one principle in the universe; people believe what they regularly see and doubt what they do not see. In his *Bamboo Manual,* Dai Kaizhi of the Jin dynasty stated that "Heaven and Earth are boundless, the myriad living things are incalculable. What people see and hear is what they encounter. This is all they know. How can this be sufficient? If someone does not see or hear something and determines from this that it does not exist, is this not ignorant?"

During the Qi dynasty, Yan Zhitui stated in his *Family Instructions* that "Emperor Wu of the Han dynasty did not believe that there was a glue that could connect broken bow strings. The Civil Emperor of the Wei dynasty did not believe that there was a type of cloth that was resistant to fire. When a nomad saw silk brocade, he did not believe that it was made from a thread produced by insects that eat leaves. In the past in Jiangnan there was someone who did not believe that some tents can hold one thousand people, and when he came to the north he found that some people did not believe that some boats could hold twenty thousand bushels. This all is true."

From this argument, we can understand that one cannot know everything about material objects. In the void above and the earthly domains below are myriad odd forms and signs. If one uses one's mind to penetrate them, one will waste a lot of energy. If one uses words to discuss them, one will exhaust one's tongue and lips and still not get at the truth. So what can one do in such a case? This is why the learning of exemplary men applies only to norms.

In the past, people stated that sages emerged from the southern, northern, eastern, and western seas. This mind-set is the same, and this principle is the same.

The Muslim Mac Duc Na king [that is, Muhammad] established his realm during the first year of the Sui dynasty's Kaihuang era [589–600]. He created a calendar and compiled a book about his celestial calculations.

Loi Ma Dau [Matteo Ricci], Nam Hoai Nhan [Ferdinand Verbiest], and Ngai Nho Luoc [Giulio Aleni], from the Western Ocean's kingdom of Europa, went to the Middle Kingdom during the Ming Wanli era [1573–1619]. They engaged in deep discussions about Heaven and Earth and how to establish calendrical rules. There was much that the best scholars there had not discovered earlier. Although the Westerners' spoken language and written script were incomprehensible, their minds understood meaning and principle, and knowledge took form in their scholarship. How was this different from what transpires in the Middle Kingdom? . . .

Buddhist works talk of transmigration. Confucian scholars tend not to believe in this. However, people from the past to the present have truly seen and heard so much [regarding this issue] that is recorded in texts that this principle must exist.

Confucius said, "How great is the virtue of ghosts and spirits! We look for them but cannot see them. We listen for them but cannot hear them. In their great abundance, it is as if they are above us and to our left and right."

Ideas about the workings of officials of the underworld are ridiculous. In essence, the Creative force is mysterious and subtle. *Yin* and *yang* divide and cause people to be unable to see and hear certain things. That is all.

When it is time to make sacrifices, ghosts and spirits come. Although their bodies have disappeared, the consciousness of their spirit remains intact. When Buddhist texts talk about entering the cycle of reincarnation, they are referring to this same spirit consciousness.

The essence of the sun and moon descends to become water and fire. The material force of water and fire ascends to become wind and rain. The miraculous forms of the transformations of Heaven and Earth cannot be fathomed, let alone those of men.

[Le Quy Don, *Van dai loai ngu*, 1:8a–31a; trans. Liam Kelley]

PHAN HUY ICH

PREFACE TO *THE SOUND OF THE TRUE GREAT AND PERFECT ENLIGHTENMENT FROM THE BAMBOO GROVE* (1796)

This brief preface to a significant late-eighteenth-century Buddhist text is by the noted scholar Phan Huy Ich. The text to which the preface was contributed was written by Ich's brother-in-law and close friend Ngo Thi Nham. The Phan Huy and Ngo Thi clans were the most prominent intellectual families in the Trinh realms, each with several generations of successful examination candidates. Phan Huy Ich and Ngo Thi Nham were the most notable northern scholars to throw their lot in with the new Tay Son regime. *The Sound of the True Great and Perfect Enlightenment from the Bamboo Grove* was written in the late 1790s, after the death of the first Tay Son emperor, Quang Trung, and after Ngo Thi Nham had largely retreated from public service. In this period he became increasingly involved in Buddhism, particularly the Bamboo Grove (Truc Lam) sect. This sect originated in the Tran dynasty (as described in the early-fourteenth-century *Guiding Diagram to Zen Schools* [*Luoc Dan Thien Phai Do*]). As part of an attempted revival, Ngo Thi Nham became its new patriarch. Phan Huy Ich's preface is a concise statement of the view that Buddhism and Confucianism were not at odds but were complementary doctrines. Because both men were committed Confucianists, this view was important to them. Although historically many Vietnamese accepted the complementary nature of Confucianism, Buddhism, and Daoism, some did not subscribe to this view, and Phan Huy Ich's preface is clearly directed at Confucianists who criticized Buddhism as being a superstitious and antirational doctrine at odds with Confucianist beliefs. This preface echoes, to some degree, the sixteenth-century stele engravings written by Confucian scholars for the dedication of Buddhist temples, although Phan Huy Ich offers a more vigorous defense of the union of the two belief systems.

Sounds are to alert and inspire those who listen to them, awakening them from illusions to experience the enlightenment of wisdom, and making the Way eternally echo within the immense world. Generally, the essence of argumentation is expressed through words and speeches; similarly, the secret of nature is manifested in thunder and wind. How great the imagery of sounds is!

The great source of the Way originates from Heaven, flowing in the universe, spreading and revealing in myriad things that have the same root but different functions, sharing the same source but having many different manifestations.

Their realms seem divergent from one another, but they are unified by the same purpose and element. Thoroughly examined, they are not beyond the Way.

Although the Buddha's teaching discusses *emptiness, quiescence, voidness,* and *boundlessness,* it fundamentally removes and eliminates hindrances to an understanding of the *True Suchness,* concentrating on the task of enlightening the heart and mind in order to reveal the *True Nature.* Comparing it with our Confucian concept of "sincerity and extension of knowledge," we find no conflict between them. I learned the saying of our Confucius, "The west has a great sage"; thus, he never despises or upbraids Buddhist doctrine, neither does he consider it heterodoxy. Secular scholars adhere to vulgar traces, steadily create contradictions with Buddhists, and look at them askance for not being sectarians. Our teaching extensively circulates in the world and becomes the rival of Buddhism. This is only the superficial misunderstanding of things and not the convergence of researchable essential thoughts; this is to argue querulously for the sake of argument, just like a discussion about whether it is a duck or a swallow upon seeing a wild goose in the distance. Narrow-minded as they already are, these ideas are accumulating and have become innate for long time.

My brother-in-law, the Great Scholar in Attendance Hy Doan [Ngo Thi Nham], who has wide learning and outstanding knowledge, stands out as an exception from most of his peers. The more deeply he experiences the world, the more subtly he makes progress in his studies. He investigates and borrows from all schools, including the three teachings,[17] the nine classes of philosophy,[18] and the hundred schools of thought. Since his emotions are far-reaching, they are sufficient for him to direct all affairs and things nobly, as well as to amalgamate and penetrate the Three Mysteries.[19] His theory of the Twenty-four Sounds takes the subtlety of Buddhist words, divides it into phases, then reassembles these phases, regularizing and reconnecting them into sections, opening their fundamental implications, and publicizing them through block prints in order to expose them to those in the Thien [meditation] grove.

---

17. The three teachings are Confucianism, Buddhism, and Daoism.

18. The nine classes of philosophy are Confucian, Daoist, Divination, Law, Logic, Mozi, Politics, Miscellaneous, and Agriculture.

19. The Three Mysteries are the *Laozi, Zhuangzi,* and *Yijing.*

After the three patriarchs,[20] the inspiration of the Thien sect declined, but the purport of the cognitive acuity of five hundred years ago now has new sounds and is starting to radiate. It is certainly not untoward for disciples of the Truc Lam Thien sect to honor him as the fourth patriarch. Encountering his new sounds, some of us surely will comment as bystanders, saying that "Han Yu's [768–824] rationalization comes from Buddhism; Lu Jiuyuan's [1139–1192] advocacy of calmness flows into Chan [Thien]." Using common words like these to speak of him, how can one know him sufficiently? Based on the principles of "the complete development of the nature and the exhaustive study of principle" and "driving Buddhism into Confucianism," he frames the Buddha's eight collections of literature within the walls of the throneless king Confucius' palace. His sounds are truly the original ones that support the Way; vague, obscure, and baseless doctrines are no match for them. These sounds can be discussed only with those who understand the Way. Since my brother-in-law and I agree with each other formally and spiritually on many issues, I profoundly understand his aims in arranging these sounds. Thus, I must forthwith presume a few words at the beginning of his work, and I would like to consult them with profound persons who understand the Way. Please accept this as the preface to his work.

Written before the day of the beginning of winter, the *binh thin* year,
in the reign of Canh Thinh [1796], under the second emperor
of the Royal Nguyen

[Ngo Thi Nham, *Tho van Ngo Thi Nham*, 229–34;
trans. Nam Nguyen]

NGO THI NHAM

THE SOUND OF EMPTINESS (CA. 1796)

This excerpt from Ngo Thi Nham's collected reflections on Buddhist principles, *The Sound of the True Great and Perfect Enlightenment from the Bamboo Grove*, addresses one of the contemplative aspects of Thien Buddhist doctrine. It is taken from a volume whose focus is on sound and the ways in which one can use sounds to understand basic doctrinal principles. The Thien form of Buddhism came to Vietnam during the Ly dynasty in the eleventh century and was taken up by prominent Vietnamese scholars. Numerous Thien monasteries were established in and around the capital, Thang Long. Among the most noteworthy later Thien sects was the Bamboo Forest (Truc Lam) sect, which was established during the Tran dynasty and was initially led by a succession of Tran emperors. This school later went into decline but was revived during the late eighteenth century, with Ngo Thi Nham as its patriarch. Ngo Thi Nham's writings represent

---

20. The three patriarchs of the Truc Lam Thien sect are Emperor Tran Nhan Tong (1258–1308), Phap Loa (1284–1330), and Huyen Quang (1254–1334).

an effort to find different ways to address some of the difficulties presented by a time of turmoil, as well as an acknowledgment that Confucian doctrine alone could not offer solutions.

Sounds result from knocking. Heavy knocks create heavy sounds, soft knocks produce soft sounds, and all have their causes. As the produced sound has its cause, so too there is a time of silence. If a sound is made in emptiness, it comes from nowhere and has nowhere to go. One wants to receive it but does not know its origin; one wishes to follow it but has no idea about its end. It jingles and tinkles without halting even for an instant. When the earthly branches *ti* and *suu* had not yet opened,[21] sounds were in the primeval state of the universal chaos. When the *yang* had descended and the *yin* had risen, sounds were within the universe. In ancient and modern times, both dispositions and consciousness are in the sound of emptiness, which can be heard but cannot be found. Thus, it is called emptiness. Emptiness is what is in Heaven, or the soundless sound.

The great Thien Master Hai Luong[22] bows to the Three Patriarchs of the Truc Lam school in the Huyen Thien [Mysterious Heaven] temple. At his left-hand side is the monk Hai Hoa,[23] and at his right-hand side is the monk Hai Tinh, along with their twenty-four disciples. The disciples ask him, "Confucians speak about Principle. What does Principle mean?" The Master replies, "Principle is similar to the principle of the joints of this tree." They ask again, "People speak about desire. What is the so-called desire?" The Master responds, "Desire is similar to the wish of water to flow down or of fire to rise up." They query, "What if one follows the Principle?" The Master answers, "It is impossible to follow the Principle completely." Having listened to his words, the disciples turn their backs to the desk and are seated. The Master exhales and draws up one leg. The monk sitting at his left-hand side asks, "Why do you draw up only one leg?" The Master answers, "All waters stream east, but the Nhuoc River runs west. The chrysanthemum differs from other flowers." The monk from the left side steps forward and asserts, "All streams flow east or west: the windlass moves its axletree. Flowers blossom early or late: ants crawl in circles." The Master shouts, "Get up! Get up! Get up! Being beaten but never getting up. Sleep! Sleep! Sleep! Being cursed but continuing to sleep." The monk from the right side stands up, moves toward the front, and says, "Navigating the boat downstream and pulling back the reins in front of a dangerous path; one stops, one moves: they both are not what I pay attention to."

---

21. *Ti* and *suu* (C: *zi* and *chou*) are the first two of the twelve "earthly branches," which, in conjunction with the ten "heavenly stems," form the sexagenary cycle of time traditionally used in China, Korea, Japan, and Vietnam.

22. Hai Luong is the Buddhist name of Ngo Thi Nham.

23. Monk Hai Hoa is the Buddhist name of Nguyen Dang So (b. 1753).

In the past, the First Patriarch, Dieu Nguu Giac Hoang [Moderate and En-lightened Emperor] Tran Nhan Tong [1258–1308], sat under the *udumbara* tree, which was blooming with innumerable flowers. No matter whether or not the flowers were opened, their opening was because of the winds; no matter whether or not they were withered, their withering was because of the rains. There was a blue bird bringing a flower in its bill and flying away. The flower suddenly became one with the bird, and both of the bird's wings produced flowers. The Master observed the bird and recognized the flowers produced from its wings. He had a hymn as follows:

> The bird's body is not the bird,
> The flower's soul is not the flower.
> Moving or halting revolves with it.
> Why should I care?

The monk from the right presses his palms together and says, "This form is not form, this emptiness is not emptiness." The monk from the left steps for-ward, saying, "Encountering a level road, the horse runs without obstructions. Having reached the hard root of a tree, it is difficult to break it out." The monk from the right uncovers his right shoulder and replies, "The level road represents the fact that the horse follows the Principle. The hard root shows that one goes against the Principle when chopping the tree. The Principle consists of suitability and unsuitability. Thus, having no attachment, one can act in accord with the Principle without stepping over it." The Master turns the bamboo staff upside down, enters the temple, and pays respect to the world-honored Buddha.

Commentary by the Monk Hai Au[24]

The Principle is similar to the principle of the tree joints, which everything must have. Desire is similar to the wish of water and fire, which all things should possess. The Principle is only one. Generally speaking, the Principle cannot be two. The fact that in giving and taking things, men and women should not touch hands is the Principle. When a sister-in-law is drowning, her younger brother-in-law rescues her: can one judge this as going against the Principle? The gentle-man should stay away from the wicked. However, Chen Shi paid a condolence call to Zhang Rang in order to save his proscribed party,[25] and because Kang Hai

---

24. Hai Au is the Buddhist name of Vu Trinh (d. 1828).

25. Zhang Rang of the Eastern Han was a power-abusing eunuch under Emperor Ling. When Zhang's father died, Chen Shi was the only person from the local gentry class who at-tended his funeral. Zhang Rang was very grateful, and when Chen Shi was imprisoned, Zhang Rang protected and pardoned him and his family.

met Liu Qin, Mengyang was released.[26] None of them follows the Principle, and their specific cases can be shown as the Way only to enlightened people. All streams flow eastward, and all flowers blossom in the spring: these are the Principle. Because the East is an inhaling place, waters generally return there; because spring is the time of sterility, flowers normally blossom in this season. Even feathers can sink in the Nhuoc River, thus the river has its restrictions and cannot accommodate sturdy things. Chrysanthemums can overcome frost and snow, thus the flower has its pride and cannot be placed in the same rank with other substances. Indomitable, the river is self-restricted, gathering its branches in the west as its firm fortification. Durable, the flower proudly blooms in the difficult time of autumn. If the Nhuoc River is not the essential water, and if the chrysanthemum is not the essential flower, how can they rise as such, uniquely differing from other rivers and flowers, respectively? These examples roughly represent the inexhaustibility of the Principle. However, only people with great capabilities can follow the Principle inexhaustibly.

"Being beaten but never getting up; being cursed but continuing to sleep." These sentences develop the unfinished idea of the previously asserted words, "All streams flow east or west: the windlass moves its axletree; flowers blossom early or late: ants crawl in circles." They seem to catch the idea of following the Principle but have not yet attained the purport of the inexhaustibly explored Principle.

"Navigating the boat downstream and pulling back the reins in front of a dangerous path." These sentences successfully represent the idea that there is no interest in self-attachment to other things. However, those who navigate the boat downstream because of happily following the water or who draw the reins because of being afraid of a dangerous path have not yet established the realm of cognition either. Without a great conversion that people must go through once, isn't it true that the ignorant will likely become more ignorant?

The enlightened king turns into innumerable *udumbara* flowers that do not bloom or fall for thousands of years. However, their blooming is due to winds; and their falling is because of rains. The *udumbara* flowers, too, have their restricted times.

"The Principle cannot be explored exhaustively." This is the same Principle for those who respond to things and phenomena. Facing phenomena but not considering them within their limited scope; encountering things but not taking them within their restrained span—only the true-nature bodhisattva can do that. The bird flies away, bringing a flower in its bill. The flower becomes

---

26. The dramatist Kang Hai (1475–1540) persuaded the corrupt premier Liu Qin to release the imprisoned talented official Li Mengyang. Thanks to Kang Hai's persuasion, Li Mengyang was saved from execution.

one with the bird's feather. These illusory scenes are mixed, and they confuse the mind and the eye. Without spiritual nature and practical goodness resulting from wisdom, how many people are not bewildered by them? People respond to the scenes occurring in front of them and mix up the reality with the illusion of the feather and the flower.

The Great Thien Master observed the bird and distinguished the feather from the flower. He recognized that the bird's body is not the bird and that the flower's spirit is not the flower:

> Bringing a flower in its bill, the flying bird keeps flying away,
> The *udumbara* flowers are forever the flowers of sovereignty.

The bird is itself a bird, and the flower itself a flower. Passing by people's eyes, they have no relation to human affairs. Thanks to them, fellow monks apprehend the form and emptiness. Thanks to them, the monks also awaken to nonattachment. The Master turned his bamboo staff upside down, moving forward to the temple, and paying respect to the World-Honored One. The entire spirit is induced in the words "turning upside down" and "moving forward." The preceding chapter elucidates the discussion on the Principle and desires, directness and inversion. It also expounds the suitability of extending and contracting, moving and stopping: one should adapt himself to his encounters to be tranquil; he should also comply with things to acclimatize himself to them. Since his self does not attach to things and phenomena, his true nature is never concealed.

[Ngo Thi Nham, *Tho van Ngo Thi Nham*, 229–34; trans. Nam Nguyen]

THE CHILD-GIVING GUANYIN
(SIXTEENTH–SEVENTEENTH CENTURY)

The hagiography of Quan Am Thi Kinh, or the Child-Giving Quanyin, details the trials and tribulations of a devout maiden, Mang Thi Kinh, who endures earthly suffering to help others achieve enlightenment. While the Quan Am figure had a resonance for some Vietnamese elites—she is said to have appeared to a Ly dynasty ruler in the eleventh century—she had a stronger meaning for the larger Vietnamese population, as this tale reflects. It probably was started sometime in the sixteenth or seventeenth century and was performed in front of village pagodas, a practice known as "retelling good deeds" (*ke hanh*). In later centuries, this tale was written down and continues to be a popular morality tale for Vietnamese Buddhists, as it is in China. The tale describes the devout Mang Thi Kinh reluctantly marrying the son of a wealthy, influential man because of society's gender expectations. Soon after her marriage, she is accused of adultery and of attempting to murder her husband, after which she is banished from the village and enters a monastery, disguised as a young male novice.

There Mang Thi Kinh is accused of raping and impregnating the daughter of a wealthy local patron sent to live at the temple; Mang Thi Kinh is beaten and again ostracized from the community. Finding the baby abandoned, the supposedly male monk tends to it, begging for milk and enduring local derision for the child's sake. Then Mang Thi Kinh falls ill and, as she lays dying, sends her parents a letter, detailing her trials and tribulations. When the parents arrive to fetch their daughter, they find that she has died, and that while dressing her for the funeral, the villagers had discovered that she was a woman and had been improperly accused. Upon this realization, Mang Thi Kinh's spirit rises in the West (the Buddha's paradise). With her achievement of enlightenment, she saves her parents' spirits as well. The following excerpt details the trials and tribulations that Mang Thi Kinh endures in the earthly world to help others achieve enlightenment.

Imprint into your precious glands to transmit
Guanyin, the holy Mother embodies impermanent universality.
She is one who endured suffering in the world yet cultivated merit,
From the beginning, through twelve lives, she demonstrated
    compassion,
To the one who became illicitly pregnant, who falsely accused her
Pure and virtuous, she endured suffering and the injustice on her body
Her vestiges remain in the country of the Great Ming,
. . .
History shall transmit to a thousand countries to obey
The virtuous Buddhist path over hundreds of others.
There once was a man who was still enjoying good fortune,
Located in the northern district, his estate was next to the village
    entrance.
His wife was able to have three sons
And kept his reputation sweet and his home solid.
Fate had determined that his name would be so sweet-smelling!
Each grace brings about another grace.
The two eldest sons had decided to enter the monkhood
And the youngest remained home for the long run.
He put his efforts to lighting the books for tomorrow,
The father, in these five lines heard spoken
That there was a man named Mang in the same district,
Whose land, rumor had it, would soon be useless.
His wife had given birth to a child,
Named Thi Kinh [Venerable One], of round age and pure moon,
Of virtuous heart and virtuous soul, she followed custom,
Yet no one had erected a bridge to make her match.
Hearing this, Mr. Sung hurriedly devised a plan,
And entered the pagoda to tell his wife.

Arriving quickly, Mr. Sung entered the Mang house and followed custom
Mr. Mang welcomed him, asking,
"What brings you to visit us in such a rush?"
At that, Mr. Sung replied:
"Our two families have enjoyed the grace of the Buddha, Heaven, and the Waters.
I had three sons
The elder two have chosen the celibate Western Home,
There's just Thien Sy, who is now of age
To fulfill fate's course and establish grace for tomorrow.
I only hope you will allow me to have Thi Kinh
So our two families can become linked,
We must not waste time but resolve our hearts!"

Mr. Mang immediately informed the Mistress,
And young Thi Kinh of the veritable details,
"As your father, how should I reason?
"After all," he answered, "the Sung family lives nearby."
Compelled, the fair maiden reluctantly responded,
"Mother and Father, you have just me, not much to speak of.
Your deep love and loyalty are of utmost importance
And your labor of carrying me for nine months and ten days.
While in the household, how many roads do I have?
One path, to get married, and no other,
I'll obey and be true to the righteous teachings,
If I should become a wife, it is up to you, my mother and father."
A woman's life is like a drop of rain,
It flows into the garden and quickly flows out into the shallow paddy.
Hearing her words, Mr. Mang consoled,
"A flower that attracts numerous bees will, next spring, lose its roundness . . .
When a girl becomes a wife, she beautifies her destiny
And adheres to womanly duties and models."
Spring passed, summer came, fall arrived and then the winter.
Foot and pillow, together they lived happily to the third spring.
Mr. Sung then planned with his wife,
To build a house for Thien Sy near the Eastern roof,
Gave him 100 *mau* and ten *sao*
So they could raise silkworms, support each other, and study.
Obeying, Thien Sy established himself in the community,
Looked to open the door to a Confucian lifestyle,
And in the house, she tended to everything in the usual custom.
When she was unmarried, she obeyed her father, and followed custom,
Upon marriage she obeyed her husband, embodying righteousness to the core.

Lovingly, she tended the reading lamp for him each night,
Then, one moon, having studied little, he dozed in deep slumber.
She saw a single hair, growing on his back,
The hostile hair was growing in a backward direction,
Fearing that it portended bad things to come,
She opened the scissors in her hands
Looked down to cut the single hair.
Her heart was certainly true,
Who knows when Heaven's will makes its retribution?
Thien Sy, seeing the knife come toward his throat,
Hurriedly screamed, his voice echoing loudly.
Suspecting that his wife had habits of the moon,
He accused her of adultery, of bees and butterflies, and all kinds of things.

After hearing Thi Kinh's protestations the Master and Mistress asked their son,
"From beginning to end, how did all this start?"
At first hesitating, he fumed with anger,
"I'm grateful to you, my parents, but your efforts have not succeeded.
I require an effort to maintain my reputation
How could I know she would regard love, honor and womanly duties so thinly?
Tonight, one with a book, the other needle work,
I was fatigued, my body aching so I slept,
Oh, but if I hadn't awoken in time,
To see my wife's knife held in just the spot!"
Hearing this, the Master and Mistress became angry,
They immediately beckoned the in-laws.
Hearing the news, the Mangs immediately came.
Upon arriving they saw a crowd of relatives
Saw the maiden, sitting between two lines—the audience.

Mr. Sung then recounted all the details, the crowd passed judgment.

Thien Sy, exemplifying his fidelity to the teachings of Confucius,
"In matters of household and marriage, with regard to her, forevermore, I reject."

Abandoned, Thi Kinh disguised herself as a man, so none would bother,
And released herself from the duties attached to her birth body,
Murmuring, "The way of the Buddha will wash clean this filth."
Arriving at a monastery, asking the abbot to receive her,
Declared, "From the time I was born,
Whatever the teachings my desire was to meditate and to enter the monkhood,
To release myself from bodily worries,

I've heard that you, oh Abbot, can help my heart arrive at this goodness."
The Thien Abbot, hearing such earnestness,
Advised, "Child, you have embraced great intelligence and heart."
He then asked for more details,
"I have no mother, father, nor brothers or sisters," she responded.

Spring came, summer arrived, and then the fall,
And then the winter, until three winters passed.
In the village, there was a wealthy man named Duong,
Who had a daughter, by the name of Thi Mau.
Ordered a servant to accompany his daughter,
To bring offerings to the Buddha's house and live,
He had but little earnestness in the gesture!
The daughter obeyed, immediately left for the monastery,
Arrived, kowtowed to the Buddha and the Thien master,
Announcing, "Mr. Duong sends regards and these offerings,"
The Thien master, accepting the offerings from the maiden,
Called the young novice, "little Venerable One," to appear.
Obeying, the Venerable One appeared immediately,
Reached out her two hands to accept his instructions.
At that time, Thi Mau, caught a glance,
He was like a green spring, a full moon, full of righteousness!
Rumors abounded, people asked, "How can a family with a female child
Send her to live within the walls of a pagoda?
When will she become a Buddha a spirit,
Isn't it better for her to stay home, study and become a good person?"

The young monk just paid attention to his own work,
Completely unaware of another's intentions for him.

Three months passed, a small image had formed,
Mr. Duong, hearing rumors about the change
Ordered his daughter to tell him with whom she severed her innocence.
In front of the village, she responded, "I haven't disobeyed any teaching,
I don't know who caused this situation
I just found my body like this one day.

Perhaps the young monk desired some things one day
He had ten phrases, ten ways I followed him,
My parents, I've always venerated and followed your teachings,
I made the offerings as you instructed and now find myself like this."
Neither the abbot nor mother and father knew of this.

Hearing this, the entire village burst out in laughter,
Then gathered in front of the village temple.
The Abbot, hearing all the noise,
Called out, "Little Venerable One,
What reason does the village have to summon us?
Did you bring evil unto this sanctuary,
So that they would call us out to respond?"
The Little One responded, "From the time you took me in,
I've not a word with anyone,
Now I see that the village is ordering me out,
I beseech you to come with me, to see what awaits."
Villagers cried, "You, Little one, from whence did you come?
Why did you come to live in our pagoda, and pretend to be a monk?
Now, how will you explain, to what end? That you came down,
You, for whom it is forbidden, yet partook of the flowery moon?"

They took him out and beat him a hundred times,
"Why have you come with your licentiousness,
You poisoned monk, fake Thien, who has raped the Lady?"

In time, Thi Mau brought a baby to the exterior gates of the village,
Called out, "Little Venerable One! Here's your child, I've brought him to you."
Saying that, she put her son down,
The child she had in her stomach, she just turned and left.
The young novice came outside,
Saw a child from nowhere there.
He sat there, thinking to himself
"Who knows if there is someone to love this child?
No matter, I'll endure the rumors, so he can be released from his body!"
After Thi Kinh's funeral, villagers, now knowing the truth
Recounted her story, to fix her name,
"One hears of the White Bodhisattva who came,"
They said, "She loved a child, raised him when no one would,
The Buddha bestowed grace, when she left for the West,
A child appeared in her hands,
Her husband, too, appeared,
Upon her shoulder as a white parrot,
And as for her two parents, a step behind,
They were released from their bodies and became saints.
Now the teachings never allowed that,
But mother and father, they were released and went to the West."
Those are the details of the Bodhisattva.

Pagodas that hear, they keep and transmit them
Whether or not you have heart and believe,
Her image thus transmits fortune,
And thus we must make offerings to her spirit
And believe all that the Buddha's house offers us.

["Quan Am tong tu ban hanh" (1894), Han Nom Institute Library,
MS AB.639; trans. Nhung Tuyet Tran]

PHAM DINH HO

RITUAL FOR VENERATING HEAVEN (1790S)

The Giao Le (or Nam Giao) ceremony was the central imperial ritual linking the Vietnamese court with the forces of Heaven. Carried out at intervals that varied between one and three years, it required the emperor's direct participation in an elaborate ceremony whose performance sought to ensure the favors of Heaven while just as crucially serving to legitimate imperial rule. Proper observation of the Giao Le ritual was essential to ensuring suitable rainfall, good harvests, and peace and prosperity for the kingdom. In *Following the Brush Amid the Rains*, Pham Dinh Ho (1768–1839) describes the material aspects of the ritual as he observed it in the late eighteenth century. He also describes alterations in the ritual caused by political and personal circumstances of the rulers and the consequences of the Tay Son's seizure of power. This description highlights the importance that Vietnamese rulers placed on the proper enactment of ritual (meticulously spelled out in the Le legal code), as well as the consequences of failing to observe these rites appropriately. Whereas Pham Dinh Ho suggests that the ceremony began in the Ly and Tran periods, most sources suggest that its origins can be traced to Emperor Le Thanh Tong (r. 1460–1497), who began this ritual in the early 1460s as one of his first acts as emperor.

We have had the "sacrificing to Heaven and Earth" [*giao*] altar in our country since the time of the Ly dynasty. After the Restoration, succeeding dynasties were able to reconstruct it. In the exact center is the Chieu Su terrace, which is roughly one *truong* [twelve feet] in height. It has a throne made of stone and a finely carved stone balcony. Inside this are stone steps leading to a stone table for the joint worship of the Grand Heavenly [Jade] Emperor and the spirit of the Earth Empress. To its left and right are the halls of the prime minister. On both the left and right are corridors for worshipping the spirits of the Great Brightness and the Nighttime Brightness,[27] all the constellations of the heavens, the spirits below on the earth, as well as the successive generations of emperors, which are divided and arranged on subordinate spirit tables. Outside the first gate,

---

27. These are the spirits of the sun and the moon, respectively.

on the right-hand side, is the place where the emperor changes his robe. Next, to the left, going out through the second gate and turning to the southeast, one passes the king's place of imperial power. Arriving at the third gate, there are paired structures of seven compartments, and this is where the controlling official palace retainers are positioned.

The procedure for carrying out Heaven and Earth sacrifice rituals during the Ly and Tran periods cannot be investigated. But in the previous dynasty, during the three days of the New Year's festival, an auspicious day was selected on which to perform the Imperial Sacrifice to Heaven. From the time of the Restoration onward, political affairs fell entirely to the palaces of the lords, and for those inside the imperial palaces, the emperor was just an empty vessel. He emerged only on the first day of the spring to perform the Sacrifice to Heaven and then again during the metropolitan examinations when he resided in the Giang Vo palace. A few preparations were made for the imperial military training, and though in reality, it was weak and all about appearance, all the people considered this to be a great occasion.

When the ceremony according to the old ritual was held at the Nam Giao altar, it cost 145 *quan*, 5 *mach*, and 54 *van*. The head of the Ministry of Finance, the vice minister of rites, and the Receiving Edicts Department made preparations. In front of the earth god were placed the offering objects of the three realms,[28] along with plantain fruit to be eaten. From the left and right palace corridors, they descended in proper order, even though the ritual had been simplified, and there was no longer a ceremony for the burning sacrifice of livestock or jade. On the appointed day, the supreme emperor was positioned in the middle of the palace courtyard's carriage route. Then the superior king [that is, the lord] was positioned on the carriage route, just a bit after [the emperor], and the position of the assistant official was a bit lower still. And all those at and above the second grand official rank stood outside the first gate, while those of the third rank stood outside the second gate. During the ritual itself, they had to perform eight kowtows between the time of the incense burning and the time of the royal proclamation. This is the essence of it. From the time of the Great Ancestor Thinh Vuong's ascension to power [1767], the lord no longer accompanied him to participate in the ceremony. In the year that the Dai Hanh empress died, the supreme emperor had to inter her, and he ordered Prime Minister Nguyen Cong Hoan to act in his stead. Then, in the following year, [Lord] Thinh Vuong personally participated in the ceremony. In that year, there was a drought, and thieves were found everywhere, and consequently all under Heaven complained frequently. Thus, it can be seen that the people's hearts did not yet wish to abandon [the Le dynasty].

When the Tay Son seized power, they established the Northern Citadel military camp to the east of the capital, then used the Venerating Heaven Palace to

---

28. The three realms are Heaven, Earth, and man.

serve as a lookout tower, and finally took the Nam Giao altar to serve as the site for the summer rain sacrifice military camp. During each year in which a drought occurred, the provincial and prefectural officials would gather together at the Giao Phuong altar, obeying the command to pray for rain at this place, or they would take the image of the Four Rules Buddha outside the third gate. These ceremonies were very crude, and they are not worth discussing. In the summer of the *tan dau* year [1801], the young Tay Son lord abandoned Phu Xuan and fled to the north. He elevated the status of the Northern Citadel to serve as the capital of the north; he erected the altar on the Vien Khau hillock outside the area of O Cho Dua; and he excavated the brick wells of Phuong Dam at West Lake. On the days of the summer and winter solstices, he divided the holding of the ceremony for venerating Heaven and Earth between these places. The Nam Giao altar at the Chieu Su Palace imitated in form the Primary Great Quang Ming Palace of China, and it continued to be used as a place for ritual prayers and pronouncements. Then at the time of the change in reign name, a ritual of thanks was held, at which the ruler's hat fell off. People took this as an omen that the Tay Son would soon be toppled.

[Pham Dinh Ho, *Vu trung tuy but* (2003), 351–53; trans. George Dutton, with Matthew Cochran]

POLITICAL REFORM

BUI SI TIEM

TEN ITEMS FOR REFORM (1731)

"Ten Items for Reform" was a lengthy memorial presented to Lord Trinh Giang (r. 1729–1740) by Bui Si Tiem (b. 1690). Bui Si Tiem was a noted literatus who had passed the civil service examinations at the relatively young age of twenty-five and quickly risen through the ranks of the bureaucracy. In this memorial, he boldly offers far-ranging advice for steps that he considered necessary to take advantage of a period of political quiescence. In particular, he strongly advocates reforms in officialdom, military structures, and the civil service examinations, but he also touches on what he regarded as much-needed changes in the judicial apparatus and advised taking security measures to safeguard the villages.

Trinh Giang, however, took affront at what he viewed as a critique of his family's administration of the kingdom. He rejected the contents of the memorial, demoted Bui Si Tiem, and ordered him sent back to his home village. There Bui Si Tiem opened a library and a school and made a name for himself as a teacher. The following excerpt from this memorial is the introduction, in which Bui Si Tiem lays out the ten major issues, plus the first issue itself. In it, he offers a not very subtle critique of Trinh Giang's recent decision to replace the sitting Le ruler, which he suggests has brought about a multitude of dangerous omens. Such signs were seen as a mark of

Heaven's disapprobation of a particular dynasty, and this text echoes earlier scholars' references to omens, including Duong Van An's 1553 comment on the failings of the Le,[29] which served to justify the Mac capture of the throne. The memorial is also a good example of the literati's tradition of bravely offering unvarnished advice to the throne, a practice that began with the rise of literati government in the fifteenth century.

The country has now been at peace for a long time, and things are calm. The seas are tranquil and the borders are calm and secure, and consequently there are no matters to discuss. Nevertheless, during periods of great peace and judicious governance, the sages continue to give thought to various matters, as in the phrase "during times in which there is no rain, one should repair the house" and the phrase "one must bind and hold fast like the root of the mulberry."[30] This is just like the urgent matters of the present time. Your foolish and simple servant submits that in his humble opinion, the matters of the kingdom that need to be considered are the following:

1. We must diligently respect the matter of providing assistance in order to eliminate the problem of disorder.
2. We must eliminate the seeking of favors in order to correct the standards.
3. We must be generous to the people in order to make their livelihoods secure.
4. We must be circumspect in policies of using soldiers in order to prevent misdeeds.
5. We must reduce official positions in order to alleviate graft and harassment.
6. We must eliminate superfluous officials in order to halt seizures of property.
7. We must reorganize the literary examinations in order to encourage those with talent.
8. We must clearly examine the regulations in order to clarify the issue of lawsuits.
9. We must demonstrate honesty to know things thoroughly in order to differentiate virtue from villainy.
10. We must distinguish among categories of people in order to put a halt to spying.[31]

These ten matters are the most urgent at the present time. Your humble servant dares to forget his transgressions in venturing this, his gibberish, and respectfully

---

29. See Duong Van An, "Dynastic Change" (chap. 3).

30. Both phrases are references to the *Classic of Changes*.

31. This point addresses concerns about foreign residents potentially serving as agents for neighboring regimes.

submits and presents it. I prostrate myself and hope that I will be pardoned for my perverse foolishness and that you will discard what is false but keep what contains just a tiny bit of good, not omitting those laws and regulations that can be established and thus represent good fortune for the myriad clans.

The first matter [putting down rebellions]: In our kingdom for many generations, from the time of the Restoration [1592] to the present, all the ranks of sagacious kings have venerated and supported the imperial family with their efforts and with one heart provided enlightened assistance for the past two centuries. Truly, it was because of this that they were able to follow the outstanding figures who wisely oversaw the borders. They used the transmission of loyalty and filiality to secure their foundations, which could not be shaken. It was because of this that the family of the lords and the imperial family were like wheel and chariot, with the two able to rely on each other and able to undertake matters like an integrated whole, and thus did not eye each other with suspicion as did the countries of Qin and Yue, whose elites became fat while their commoners starved.[32]

Recently, in the *ky dau* year [1729], we saw the abdication of the throne, but we continue to follow the old regulations.[33] We truly do not know whether this stems from weariness or comes from a genuine commitment. These days, we speak of and indifferently pursue this matter, and we know that what we hear and see is not evidence, but we continue to speak of it as though it were important. Nevertheless, I venture that I have heard that when the venerated emperor [Le] Du Tong [r. 1705–1731] was on the throne, his countenance was angry at injustice and he spoke words and wrote edicts regarding this, and the officials and people could not possibly cover their ears and eyes to hide from them. Moreover, from the beginning of the summer of the *ky dau* year [1729] until the present, natural disasters have been occurring almost continuously. If the seers do not speak of matters concerning governance, then they are saying that policies are in error. I, your humble servant, have observed that in our kingdom, the rivers and streambeds are thirsty, and the river waters have dried up. For many years we feared drenching rain, and now we suddenly have had successive years of great flooding, and so we now know about Heaven and Earth. We now venerate the temples of supernatural spirits with their protective powers, so they would speak clearly for us to understand the omens of the rivers being wet or dry and of the skies being constantly overcast and [thus] be advised with respect to blessings or chastisements, so that these would not become so extreme that the emperor would be unable to venerate and assist. Moreover, this will bring about some turning of the Creative [Heaven] and shifting of the Receptive

---

32. This refers to the Qin dynasty (255–209 B.C.E.) and the Viet (Yue) state, which held out against it from a coastal position encompassing Fujian southward to Guangzhou.

33. This refers to the transition from Lord Trinh Cuong (r. 1709–1729) to Lord Trinh Giang (r. 1729–1740).

[Earth], and also cause a mending of skies and a washing of the sun,[34] and these responsibilities all lie with our lord. Oh! These strange omens of disaster are not a matter of chance. The great worth of sagely men lies in their ability to comprehend the will of Heaven, to examine the evidence, and then to repair the matters of men in order to return to the vital energies, to transform disaster into good fortune, and to transform evil into goodness. This is the most important matter at the present time. I bow and await the lord's thoughts about the tasks of cultivation and planting, but we must not now await an ultimate disaster. I respect and support the will of the ancestors, but not to the extent that there might be a decline in wealth and status. If a task must be done, then it should be done, and we should not be misled by the persistent hesitations voiced by petty men. This means that one must be brave, fearless, and determined, for then one will not stick to such formalities as the phrase "for three years there must be no change [of the things once done by the father]."[35] We must carry out these great tasks so that they are fully comprehended by the ruling powers and must reorganize in order to establish the way so that it cannot be altered. In so doing, we will hold back bursting waters that might seek to topple [the ruler] or attempt to pull back the setting sun. If it is thus, then natural disasters will gradually diminish, and fortune and prosperity will gradually increase. The undertakings of the emperor and lord are promises for ten thousand years that cannot be broken. This is what is called venerating and assisting in order to investigate and eliminate disorder.

[*Dai Viet su ky tuc bien* (hereafter, *DVSKTB*), A.1415, 6a–8a; Ngo Cao Lang, *LTTK*, 176–97; *DVSKTB* (1991), 121–33; trans. George Dutton]

NGUYEN CU TRINH

MEMORIAL DESCRIBING THE ECONOMIC CRISIS IN THE NGUYEN REALM (1751)

Nguyen Cu Trinh (1716–1767) was perhaps the most noted scholar-official serving the Nguyen lords in the mid-eighteenth century, and he was renowned for his integrity and administrative talents. This memorial, sent to the powerful ruler Nguyen Phuc Khoat (r. 1738–1765), represented a rare voice of dissent among court officials, as it questions the growing corruption and disregard for rural problems shown by the lords at Phu Xuan. Its frank critique is in the same tradition of literati criticism of a ruler's policies seen in Bui Si Tiem's memorial "Ten Items for Reform," presented to the

---

34. That is, a singular accomplishment.

35. This refers to a phrase in the *Analects* (1.11): "When his father is alive, you observe a man's intentions. It is when the father is dead that you observe the man's actions. If for three years, he makes no change from the ways of his father, he may be called filial."

Trinh rulers two decades earlier. In particular, Nguyen Cu Trinh laments the prolif-
eration of administrative positions, a frequent complaint from rural officials seeing
the burden that such a bureaucracy placed on villagers forced to make payments to
numerous levels of officialdom. *The Veritable Records of Dai Nam*, the later Nguyen
historical chronicle in which this memorial was recorded, noted laconically that
Nguyen Cu Trinh received no reply to his petition.

The people are the foundations of the country, and if the foundations are not
firm, then the country cannot be at peace. If we do not use compassion to bind
its inhabitants together during times of tranquility, on whom can we rely when
there is a task at hand? I venture to think that the people are being excessively
abused, and if we continue our current course of complacency and do not take
the opportunity to resolve our problems and to establish principles and regulations, then if we cannot control one city, how can we control the entire country?
At present, three matters are harming the people: providing for soldiers, caring
for elephants, and contributing money for judicial matters. Besides this are numerous matters of countless unnecessary expenditures. In regard to these various harmful matters at the capital, I do not dare to overstep my position, and I
wish only to bring up some matters pertaining to my office and state, as follows:

The peoples in the prefecture of Quang Ngai have accepted the commands
from all the guard offices that requisition and collect taxes and field rents and
have borne all the separate types of fees, such as those for transporting, for carrying, for private fields, and for oil. They also have endured orders from all the
local officials and the prefectural offices and from the various people who have
been ordered to go out hunting. This is clearly a case of "ten goats and nine
goatherds,"[36] which causes them great hardships and unemployment, and this
is truly piteous. If the people are not permitted to retain what they produce,
how then will it be possible to hold on to their hearts? If the people's hearts are
greatly disturbed during times of peace, how then in critical times will it be
possible to command them? I would like to lay out four matters that represent
the accumulated abuses.

The first matter is that in the prefectures and districts, those whose task is to
govern the people have no appointments for particular duties; they have only
permission to investigate legal cases. I request that henceforth any shortages or
surpluses of the field rents and other types of taxes be regulated so that all are
submitted to the county magistrate, who would then organize what they have
gathered and transmit it to the Quang Nam officials, so as to avoid there being
too many officials, which is harmful to the people.

The second matter is that up to the present, officials in the prefectures and
districts have used the money collected in their investigations as their regular
salaries. Because of this, the people's wealth has been steadily consumed while

---

36. This phrase refers to too many officials overseeing public matters.

their customs have become increasingly corrupted. Now I request that we establish the practice of fixed salaries so as to distinguish the honest from the corrupt, the industrious from the lazy, and use this as the basis for the [officials'] promotion or demotion.

The third matter pertains to the two types of vagabond villagers: drifting wastrels seeking to avoid conscription or taxation and those who drift and move about because hunger and cold directly affect their bodies. Now I will not distinguish between these groups but note only that it is essential that they all be entered into the books of duties and receipts [registers], so that officials can collect taxes from them. They surely are frightened and thus scatter and hide in the jungle. If the people of their village have to compensate for the vagabonds' share of the village taxes, how can they possibly endure such a fate? Now I ask you to investigate these vagabond villagers to see which ones are still earning a living and then collect taxes from them according to the regulations. Those who are hungry, cold, and facing hardships should be exempted from taxation, in accordance with the methods of providing comfort and nourishment, so as to revive the poor commoners.

The fourth matter is that the people should be permitted to be at peace. They should not be disturbed, for when they are disturbed it is too easy for them to rebel, whereas if they are calm, they are easy to govern. At present, we are sending people into the mountains and forests to go hunting and are sending others to look for birds. This [practice] is not based on virtuous intentions but instead harasses and harms respectable people. There are people who claim false identities as officials and travel about everywhere bullying and harassing the people, causing them to become resentful. I request that henceforth we send officials to perform tasks, with official seals as documentation they can present to local officials. These officials will investigate those who are harassing the people. They can then correct transgressions and impose punishments so that the hearts of the people can be at peace, and we can avoid these disturbances and careless movements that are not being reported.

[DNTL (1961–), 1:142–43; DVSKTB, A.1415, 96a–98b;
DVSKTB (1991), 232–33; DNTL (2004–2007), 1:156–57; trans. George Dutton]

NGUYEN THIEP

MEMORIAL REGARDING THE ECONOMIC CRISIS
IN NGHE AN (1789)

Nguyen Thiep (1723–1804) was a prominent and highly respected scholar in Nghe An. Although family circumstances prevented his achieving high academic titles, he became famous for his erudition and even more for his talents as a seer. Like the earlier recluse scholar and seer Nguyen Binh Khiem (1491–1585), Nguyen Thiep's advice was in great demand by political leaders. He was repeatedly summoned to the court by

Trinh Sam, each time declining to leave his place of seclusion. Later, Nguyen Thiep was actively courted by the Tay Son Quang Trung emperor. Although Nguyen Thiep was flattered by the attention, he was reluctant to join the Tay Son, and it took repeated summonses finally to convince him to serve and advise the new regime. He agreed to supervise a large-scale project to translate the Confucian classics into the Vietnamese vernacular, and as a concession to Nguyen Thiep, the project was based in Nghe An. However, Quang Trung died just as the project was getting under way, and Nguyen Thiep immediately returned home, ending his brief service to the Tay Son. As evidence of the important relationship between Nguyen Thiep and the emperor is a remarkable collection of letters exchanged between the two men from 1786 to 1792. This memorial is part of that exchange, and in it Nguyen Thiep describes the great hardships suffered by the people of Nghe An. The province lay along the major invasion route between north and south and thus was crossed and recrossed by a series of Tay Son armies, beginning in 1786. The memorial again reveals the willingness of a scholar to offer critiques of state policies and governmental structures while at the same time displaying the highly deferential and self-deprecating language used by literati in their missives to the throne.

I memorialize as a simple bureaucrat who concerns himself with crude and simple matters and who has hidden himself away in seclusion. I am a disgraceful, foolish one, while Your Majesty has broad power and learning, which I expect is both great and high. The falling fruit meets the springtime, truly an encounter of a thousand years.[37] Unfortunately, my physical constitution is weak and frail, and I am gradually becoming more decrepit. I can no longer follow along with the young and vigorous, although I offer to serve on [either] the left or the right. I fear that I am not much more than an empty husk, and thus my heart is extremely uneasy. For this reason, last fall I memorialized the throne, begging to repay the gift bestowed by the exalted emperor that my appointment might serve the public good. With utmost sincerity and tremendous attention I have received and seen the imperial instructions. At first, propriety prevented me from employing my strength. I bent down and read it over and over. My shame and fear grew even deeper. How could I dare again to speak these words, bringing offense with filth? However, what I presume to consider is this: the people alone are the roots of the state, and when the foundations are stable, the state will be tranquil.

In Nghe An, the earth is barren and the people are impoverished. Previously, there was only the frequent recruitment of soldiers but no collection of money or grains. Now both troops and provisions are being collected. Moreover, the number of soldiers has now doubled. Those who till the fields are few in number, and those who rely on others are numerous. What is needed for private consumption now exceeds the public taxes. One must pay serious attention to

---

37. "Falling fruit" alludes to Nguyen Thiep's being advanced in years, while "springtime" refers to Quang Trung's youthful vitality.

famine and epidemics, which cause people to die of hunger or to move and shift about. And of those who remain, there are perhaps only five or six out of ten. This winter there was an early dry spell, the farmlands were not cultivated, and those who went into the fields to plant were very few in number. One region has twelve districts, which have been further divided to create three or four markets, all of which are administered separately. The greater the number of officials is, the more harassment the people must endure. The matters of authority have not been centralized. Neither the generals and officers nor the bureaucrats and officials show any discipline or restraint. Even if there is loyalty and love, how can one use them to achieve their will? "No one knows his subjects as the sovereign does."

I prostrate myself and look to Your Imperial Highness regarding the selection of interior officials who are pure, hardworking, humane, and brave as members of an upright administration. For a long time, men of literary talent have been assistants. Appoint them, give them the appropriate power, and demand results. The people are suffering from illness and there must be a full investigation into the truth. Subsequently this trifling one [that is, Nguyen Thiep] consults and deliberates the reduction of punishments and the granting of pardons. The sly and artful ones should be removed, and the good and virtuous ones should be encouraged. If this is carried out, your imperial favor will be granted after all. The impoverished people will be revived. The people will always cherish this— they cherish the one who has humaneness. He is the one to whom the people will turn their hearts in allegiance, the one in whom the heavenly mandate resides. This opportunity must not be lost. I humbly offer these, the words of a dull and unlettered one, and respectfully look to your brilliance and exalted virtue. Please condescend to inspect this. Understand its circumstances thoroughly and clearly. Please bestow on it your respect, and grant that it be carried out. This is not only about the good fortune of the common people but also about the fortune of the state. Your humble subject looks up to you with extreme reverence and with great trepidation and presents this petition with all sincerity.

[*La Son Yen Ho Hoang Xuan Han*, 2:1199–1200; trans.
George Dutton, with Matthew Cochran]

TRINH TAC

EDICT REGARDING OFFICIAL POSITIONS (1674)

The "Edict Regarding Official Positions," issued by the northern lord Trinh Tac (r. 1657–1682), is a detailed explication of the numerous positions in the state bureaucracy and their ideal functioning. Such elucidations of government structure and its functions were one of the marks of political renewal, setting forth the order of the state and its claims to power. An earlier example of this type of edict is "The Collated and Established Imperial Court Regulations on the Administrative System" issued in

1471 by Emperor Le Thanh Tong (r. 1460–1497), which was similarly designed to suggest a new political course. In some respects, Trinh Tac's decree marks the culmination of a lengthy period in which Confucian literati reemerged and worked with the lord in order to place their stamp on a reordered bureaucratic structure. This period and, particularly, the Canh Tri reign era (1663–1672) have been remembered by later generations of scholars as the high watermark of this literati revival. This edict was a product of the work of Pham Cong Tru, one of Trinh Tac's closest Confucian advisers and among the most prominent scholar-officials of his generation.[38] But the edict was issued shortly before Trinh Tac was ousted in a mutiny led by disgruntled military units and was replaced by his son Trinh Can. Trinh Can's numerous military accomplishments in leading troops against the Nguyen made him a more likely candidate for regaining control over these renegade soldiers.

We must advance the worthy and discard the unworthy for the position of prime minister. When we see worthy people but are unable to promote them, this is concealing worthiness. When we know that people are unworthy but are incapable of removing them, this is tolerating dishonesty. We must have supplies of talent and must confer official positions on them and must determine their degree of virtuousness and then appoint them to high positions, ensuring that each great man serves in his appropriate position, and we may not act according to selfish private interests.

We must take care to discuss and weigh the candidates for the Civil Service Ministry; we must investigate and take notes regarding departments, and we must scrutinize their words and actions and how they have performed their tasks, whether they can be promoted to serve as an official in the capital or should be dismissed as capital officials, and whether they merit being appointed as prefects or should be dismissed as prefects. Private calculations may not be followed in appointing or dismissing them. If there are any open positions outside the capital, we should look at those in the two departments about whom reports have already been presented; then we should immediately select a person to appoint to that position within two days.

If the Justice Ministry inspection official sees a prisoner who has been heavily punished, his case shall be sent down for reexamination, and there shall be a joint examination of the case and the manner of its adjudication. The [official] shall strive to arrive at the truth of the circumstances and if the accused deserves to be redeemed, then this shall be done, and there shall be no delay in this matter that exceeds the deadline.

The imperial censor has the task of acting as the ears and eyes of the court and therefore must actively record the rules and regulations, so that acts contrary to public morality and law are suppressed. If generals or ministers have failed, or if any of the hundred officials have violated the law, or if any current

---

38. Taylor, "Literati Revival," 19.

policies have shortcomings, these all shall be presented so that their misdeeds can be made public.

Those legal cases that already have been sent to the offices of the provincial governors, the regents, and the judicial commission shall now be investigated. The investigating censor shall focus on detailed discussion and interrogation in order to determine guilt in the case and shall examine any misdeeds and record them in order to eliminate such incidents. The [censor] must not be permitted to present item by item any matters regarding current policies but, rather, is ordered to obey and carry them out.

In each circuit, the investigating censor also is responsible for investigating misdeeds. If he finds any faulty policies, or if any of the hundred officials have committed transgressions, they too shall confess these misdeeds. If cases of thievery or open robbery have already passed through the offices of the provincial governors, the regents, and the judicial commissions, then an examination shall be carried out. If it appears that the punishments in these cases have been too severe, permission is given to annul them and to expeditiously reexamine them.

The Office of Scrutiny for Personnel has the duty of appointing or dismissing officials. If it appears that the Civil Service Ministry has appointed people without talent, this shall be discussed, and these officials shall be dismissed and released to go home.

If the Office of Scrutiny for Justice sees that the Judicial Ministry has examined and decided a case unjustly, this too will be discussed, the original decision reversed, and the documents sent back.

The [responsibilities of the] superintendent of the capital city pertain to bridges and locks, roads and streets, dike dredging, water management, fire suppression, and security and police matters, all of which shall be kept in good order. [The superintendent] is permitted only to look into legal cases regarding such matters as theft, banditry, and open conflicts.

The prefectural governor is the official who deals with suppressing and quelling disturbances. If he sees anyone in the good families of the nobility or the ranks of ordinary people acting arrogantly in a vagabond fashion or not following the laws and regulations, he is permitted to look into this and to censure and punish him.

Those holding the positions of governor-general and regent shall concentrate on suppressing theft and plunder, as well as guarding against treachery, and they must conform to the official decrees. They shall maintain peace among the people of the countryside, and they may not act on their own accord to create positions that do not obey the regulations or recklessly harass the people.

If the judicial commissions in any of the regions see a natural disaster such as a flood or a drought, they shall present this information. And if the "undertaking and announcing" *yamens* [government offices] in the prefectures and districts commit acts of wanton venality and the governor-general and the regent are not able to curtail such treacherous profiting and all the officials and those of the hundred surnames are unable to comply with and preserve the rituals and regulations or the admonitions to their family members to the point that they become idle vagabonds with dissolute morals and customs, they all shall be punished for their misdeeds.[39]

Every year, the judicial commission officials shall travel throughout their jurisdictions and carefully investigate the people in each district and village and sincerely inquire into their hardships and sufferings as well as look into all the district officials' reports regarding theft and looting. Then at the end of each year, these matters shall be discussed and dealt with. The governors-general and regents who already have examined and decided on cases of theft and looting may reexamine them. Furthermore, they may reopen cases of oppressive actions brought by those in the offices of the governor-general, the regent, or among the families of nobles. Aside from this, they may not intervene in any other offices.

Those assuming the positions of *thua ty, thua su, tham chinh,* and *tham nghi* [in the provinces] must shoulder heavy responsibilities, maintaining offices that are honest in preserving the laws, compassionate with respect to the welfare of the people, and strict with respect to maintaining order among their officials.[40] If they see that any prefectural or district officials in their area have carried out just and equitable policies, these men should be recommended for praise and rewards. If, however, any officials have violated the regulations, they should be demoted and their cases investigated. People may be appointed temporarily to serve for one month in any offices with open positions. Then a rapid inquiry into their backgrounds shall be carried out publicly, and together with the judicial commission a report should be prepared and submitted to the Civil Service Ministry so that it may select people to fill these positions and may not hesitate in acting. All the legal cases in the various regions shall be dealt with according to their urgency and investigated with circumspection.

The prefectural magistrate is regarded by the common people as their teacher and moral exemplar. If he sees among his subordinates prefectural or district officials who have achieved praiseworthy feats, then he shall see that this information is acknowledged. Those who are not worthy with respect to their positions shall be censured and disciplined.

If [these officials] see that an accomplice has run off to ask for an investigation of a murder, they should immediately go directly to the place where it occurred in order to investigate it jointly with the county official to ascertain the truth. There should be no procrastination or delay beyond three days. All other legal cases shall follow in order and be investigated in their turn.

---

39. The "hundred surnames" is a synecdoche for the entire population.

40. These are a variety of lower-level administrative posts, including both aides and commissioners.

All the temple offerings used in temple rituals must be appropriate and pure and cannot cause hardships for the common people.

The county magistrate is the official closest to the common people, and he must cherish and treat them kindly. He should advise and teach them farming and sericulture, so that they may flourish and avoid harm and also teach the people the way of filial piety and fraternal duty. We give permission to the district chief to use the rod and cane to punish any person who is disobedient or disrespectful or who is a vagabond or adulterer or who spreads rumors, in order to teach them a lesson. People who engage in angry and resentful disputes or who initiate lawsuits about trifling matters that cause disputes but are harmless with respect to law and order shall be advised and instructed and shall be sent back, and they may not demand any ritual money. In addition, all the major cases of litigation must be examined and adjudicated in a manner that is correct for the circumstances.

Righteous wives and filial children also need to be reported and presented with imperial honors.

If any officials or offices are capable of complying appropriately with lessons and admonishments, they shall be praised and rewarded, and violators shall be punished by the imperial censors. If the [violators] are officials in the punishments section of the Judicial Ministry, their misdeeds shall be handled according to their severity.

Moreover, from now and into the future, if any official in any of the offices in the capital or out in the provinces has distinguished himself in his position, he shall be praised and rewarded. And if any officials in these offices have carried out tasks of civil justice and are honest and industrious, they also shall be promoted so that they might be put to good use. Any official involved in violations shall be dismissed from his post, and any official responsible for civil justice matters who acts greedily shall be driven out and forced to perform labor service just like a commoner. And no minor and subordinate officials may speak in the defense of any official who breaks the law, accepts bribes, or gives precedence to his own interests.

Finally, if any *yamen* officials in the capital or out in the provinces see any officials who act in a law-abiding manner and who are skilled, intelligent, honest, and industrious and who throughout the years and months have not committed any transgressions, we recommend that they be promptly appointed and put to use. If, however, they see anyone who acts in a self-satisfied manner and engages in corrupt practices, or focuses only on using the laws to enrich himself, and who is lazy and slow or who neglects his duties or who has committed crimes, then [that person] shall be censured. If his crimes are serious, he shall be tried for them, and if they are not serious, he shall be dismissed.

[Ngo Cao Lang, *LTTK*, vhv. 1321/1, 10b–13a; *LTTK*, 37–42;
trans. George Dutton]

TEMPLE OF LITERATURE STELE FOR
THE EXAMINATION OF 1623 (1653)

The Temple of Literature (Van Mieu) was built in Thang Long to honor the men who
had achieved academic success in the civil service examinations. These examinations
were designed to serve as the basis for appointment to high positions in the bureaucracy, although more generally they provided an avenue for social advancement and
prestige. The regular holding of examinations as a means of finding qualified officials
began in the fifteenth century, and the triennial examination system itself was initiated in 1463. According to tradition, the temple compound was established in 1070,
but its current form and structures date back to the late Ly and Tran dynasties. It was
a significant marker of imperial interest in the Confucian orthodoxy. Beginning in
1484, a stele was erected after each metropolitan examination, with a comment on the
exam and a list of the names and home villages of those who had passed. In periods of
political turmoil, however, there was often a substantial delay before such steles were
actually carved. In 1653, twenty-five steles were finally engraved and erected to address
the century-old backlog, but more important, they marked the court's renewed commitment to Confucianist principles. The stele translated here commemorated the
examination held in 1623. It is a good example of this literary genre, describing the
circumstances of the examination and the unusual features that distinguished it during a period when scholarship was less esteemed. It also extols the virtues of the ruler
and his adherence to Confucian principles in selecting officials to help him govern
the country.

Heaven brought about both the Restoration [in 1592] and an era of peace with
lords and sages.[41] We esteem only the imperial majesty, who was born to receive
the will of Heaven, who inherited the task of protecting the great undertaking,
and who honors the worthy, esteems the meritorious, is determined to carry out
his will, and strives to rule. Truly we recall the Great and Sagacious Ancestor
king [Trinh Tung (r. 1570–1623)], who continued the great undertaking of the
Great Generation Ancestor king [Trinh Kiem (r. 1545–1579)] and was the first to
establish institutions and regulations, put laws into order, make standards appropriate, and desire to gather all the world's worthy and talented men. For this
reason, at the doctoral examinations of the *qui hoi* year in the fifth year of the
reign of Emperor [Le] Vinh To [1623], there was a special command to Le
Nganh, the Minor Protector Eastern Prefecture duke, to serve as the supervisor,
and to Nguyen Danh The, the Auspicious Yang marquis and imperial censor at
the capital, to serve as the administrator of the recruitment section. He also appointed his subjects Nguyen Duy Thi, the Phuong Tuyen marquis and Ministry
of Rites left-hand waiting gentleman, and Luu Dinh Chat, the Nhan Linh
marquis and Ministry of Civil Service right-hand waiting gentleman, to proctor

41. The Restoration is of the Le dynasty after the Mac had been driven from power.

the metropolitan examinations. Out of all the scholarly men under Heaven, there were more than three thousand candidates, and from their ranks seven outstanding men were chosen.

In the summer, on the eighth day of the fourth month, the exalted emperor stood at the gate of the Respecting Heaven Palace and sent down the essay topics into the imperial courtyards. While the scholars were composing their essays, Nguyen Trat suddenly wrote an essay that substantially violated the required form, so he was prevented from completing the pretest. Thus only six examinations were graded. The officials collected the examination books, waited to present them, and then entered and read them aloud for the exalted emperor's inspection. The emperor selected Phung The Trung to pass at the highest position, while each of the other five was declared as a coequal Advanced Scholar Outstanding Subject. Moreover, in examining the test books according to the old standards, those who had prepared for the examinations beforehand were not disqualified, and so Nguyen Trat was permitted to pass in the auxiliary and lowest-ranking position, yielding seven men in total. There was, consequently, some delay in posting the list of names of the successful examination candidates. Also, the awarding of their gowns and caps and the congratulatory feasts for those who were returning in glory did not conform to the old traditions. During this time, all scholarly men under Heaven carried resentment and depression in their hearts.

Reaching summer, in the sixth month, just at the season for clouds and thunder, all the military and civil officials wisely assisted in the return of his majesty's carriage, in order to make secure the foundations and pacify the hearts of the people so that the kingdom might be made stronger and more radiantly brilliant.[42] Then, on reaching the Midautumn Festival, the emperor truly relied on the generalissimo, the head of the country's government, the supreme teacher, the Exalted and Meritorious, Humane and Sagely king to look to and rely on the awesomeness of Heaven and to put in order the righteous troops, including the infantry, the elephants, and the horses. All made a great noise like thunder, while on the water small vessels followed along. The might of the infantry was thus augmented, and it was able to eradicate the Mac rebels, regain the capital city, and clean and settle the forbidden palace. All under Heaven returned to unity, and the four seas became tranquil. All power was then entrusted to the generalissimo, the administrator of the national government, the Western Pacifying prince, to completely oversee and manage the hundred officials and to make plans for returning to the affairs of state.

During this period, in which all under Heaven experienced great peace, the exalted emperor placed his confidence in the Confucianist officials, and he sought out men of talent and virtue, knowing that the list of laureates should be valued and that the "advanced men" should be encouraged. Thus, he thought deeply

---

42. This passage refers to the Le and Trinh retaking Thang Long from the Mac family in 1592.

about the time that had passed since the reigning dynasty had been restored and of the examinations for "advanced men" for which a great many suitable men had been selected, thinking that if their names were not set forth and engraved in the great books describing their merits and accomplishments and lofty, enduring monuments were not erected, how then would it be possible to stimulate and encourage future generations? For this reason, in the tenth month of the first year of the Thinh Duc reign era [1653], all the literature-specialist officials were ordered to busy themselves with composing for the steles, carving them from emerald-green alabaster. These would be used to list the examination scholars' great accomplishments and to serve as a laudable deed of this prosperous reign. Although the many officials were clumsy and of limited talent, they still dared to offer congratulations to the refined scholars, sincerely bringing their hands together and bowing their heads in order to offer the following words:

> The examinations were frequently held through successive dynasties and continue to be held. It was in the time of the Zhou dynasty that the selection of "advanced scholars" began. Until the Tang and Song dynasties, they used either the subject examinations or the "advanced men" [examination], but in each case they relied on the examinations to select suitable men. This had benefits for governance and teaching, as can clearly be seen in the ancient texts. We respectfully reflect that in our current dynasty, when the Great Ancestral emperor [Le Thai To] had just regained control of the kingdom, he established education and sent for men of virtue, and he protected and preserved the system of the Way in order to open and further expand the great peace through the ten thousand generations.

During the periods in which [the subsequent] ranks of sagely emperors preserved the accomplishments of their predecessors, they also set examinations to select men of talent, to put in order a time of great peace so as to make grand the fine patterns of the hundred generations. From this time forth, the emperors maintained the transmission of the spirits and continued to abide by the old traditions. And we respectfully think:

> With respect to his restoration of the great undertaking, the virtuous emperor has had great successes in human affairs, has gathered the sages' great accomplishments, and has complied with the previous emperors' established laws and the various things that were set in motion by earlier generations, and he has followed and preserved them. He has increased and expanded those tasks that earlier rulers had not yet completed. Furthermore, we will post a list of names of those who have passed examinations up to the present time but whose names have not yet been set forth on the gilded roll so that they might be recorded and hung in the Quang Van

pavilion. Now is ordered the engraving in stone of the examination topic and their names, so that this might be erected at the Gate of Virtue to glorify the morals of our generation. Oh! Those scholars whose names are recorded on these stones, how can they not be glorified and made fortunate?

Now I would like to speak directly about this particular examination: All those who came forth from the royal compound were men of great talent as well as superb and extraordinary scholars. Some have the responsibility to speak out and inspire the court; some occupy the positions of supervising secretaries and secretariat drafters and maintain the correct treatises; some take part in military duty and praise strategies; some esteem the bridle and whip and deal with those in the hunt. Their writings have been transmitted everywhere under Heaven, and their undertakings are brilliant in their age, so how can they not serve as a standard that might be recorded and recalled for a long time to come?

If these were names only, without any realities, there first would be loyalty but later would come wantonness, which would give rise to pedantic scholars, which would in turn give rise to petty Confucianists. Those under Heaven would merely catalog them, and the people of that generation would despise them and consider them blemishes on the examinations. For this reason, these steles are chiefly the pillars of the names of the enlightened and the foundations of the Way of constant obligations of morality, and those who contemplate them will have some standards and also know what they must guard against. Truly this has benefits for the emperor's system of governance for a hundred million years, and it will mean that our country will be eternally stable and secure like the great stones of Mount Tai.[43]

[*Le trieu lich khoa tien si de danh bi ky*, 136–37;
Do Van Ninh, *Van bia Quoc Tu Giam Ha Noi*, 251–55;
trans. George Dutton, with Matthew Cochran]

GOVERNANCE

NGUYEN PHUC KHOAT

EDICT DECLARING AUTONOMY (1744)

The "Edict Declaring Autonomy" marked a crucial turning point in the political orientation of the Nguyen state. Before this date, the Nguyen rulers had maintained a stated allegiance to the Le court and had continued to style themselves as subjects of and officials serving the Le emperors. With this decree, however, the powerful mid-eighteenth-century lord Nguyen Phuc Khoat (r. 1737–1765) effectively declared an end to this subservience and announced the Nguyen rulers' autonomy. The edict formalized

---

43. Mount Tai is one of the sacred mountains of China.

what had long been practice, and it also gave the Nguyen rulers new scope for their own ambitions, particularly as reflected in their changes to titles and nomenclature. It also definitively marked a shift in the Nguyen gaze from north to south, away from their roots and toward the new frontiers into which their armies had already long been marching. At the same time, however, it also marked the Nguyen move toward the literati model, long in force in the north but largely absent in the more militarized and personal rule in the south. As with all such foundational edicts, this one contains a significant genealogical summary at the outset, followed by a justification for the actions being taken to assert a new political state. Similarly, like many edicts declaring the creation of new dynasties,[44] this one emphasizes the ruler's reluctance to take this step, which was taken only after considerable urging from the people.

Heaven and Earth extend benevolence, which brings relief to the people, spreading it to the farthest reaches where it creates great harmony. The king ascends the throne, beautifying the myriad things and bringing about renewal. [Let] the precious words of this royal decree be disseminated.

Our kingdom began its rise in O Chau, and by the great appointment the domain was established. Hoang To glared like a tiger over the region, a perfect crescent of mountains and rivers. Than Tong raised his power over the seven districts and brought in this territory of tremendous wealth. As the grand plan for hegemonic power was carried out, Heaven assisted, supplemented, and expanded. Minh Mieu displayed his military prowess and put fear into the Dong Phu rogues. Khao Vuong, so magnificent in favoring civility, roused the people of the south to great happiness.[45] The people of the four directions all admired his glorious rule. The richness of the successive generations of benevolence can be [recorded and] encased in a jade envelope, greatly enhancing the hope of these mountains and rivers. The *huan*-wood ceremonial tablet has never been changed, and our loyalty [to the Le monarch] remains constant.

I have been granted the task of carrying on this great enterprise. I have governed for only seven years and have yet to disseminate sixth-month awe.[46] I think deeply about the fact that the land has still not been unified and the bandits have not yet been pacified. I have exerted myself in the hopes of continuing in my ancestor's footsteps. Yet unexpectedly, the people, having consulted with the spirits and accorded with the auspicious, repeatedly requested that I take the glorious title [of king]. According to astrologists, the great and minor all are in accord, and everything has its correct and proper place. The dragon hesitates to leap when in the fourth line of *qian*, and one still flies the banner of modesty.

---

44. See Quang Trung Emperor, "Edict on Ascending the Throne" (this chap.).

45. Hoang To, Than Tong, Minh Mieu, and Khao Vuong are the posthumous honorific titles of Nguyen Phuc Khoat's predecessors as rulers of the Nguyen realm.

46. The "Sixth Month" is an ode in the *Classic of Poetry* commemorating a successful military campaign. Here, "sixth-month awe" is a reference to military success.

The fitness of the mare is her constancy, and the meaning of *kun* follows the third [line].⁴⁷ [But] together, people urged me to take power. I searched my moral virtue and repeatedly declined. Yet the united intent of three thousand people is difficult to hold back. Although this did not stem from my own desires, I agreed for the time being to follow the wishes of the people. Thereupon, on the twelfth day of the fourth lunar month of this year, I ascended to the position of king and granted amnesty to all within the realm, to propagate the joy of eight generations of accumulated moral virtue and to fulfill the desire of the people from the four directions to benefit from the sight [of a king on the throne].

[*DNTL* (1961–), 1:136–37; *DNTL* (2004–2007), 1:150–51; trans. Liam Kelley]

LE DUY MAT

PROCLAMATION TO RALLY TROOPS (1740)

The "Proclamation to Rally Troops" was issued by Le Duy Mat (d. 1769), the eleventh son of Emperor Le Du Tong (r. 1704–1728), when he sought support for his effort to overthrow the Trinh lords, who for a century and a half had been the power behind the throne. Le Duy Mat's uprising was just one of several very large-scale, and often long-lived, challenges to Trinh authority in northern Dai Viet during the mid-eighteenth century. Le Duy Mat managed to sustain his resistance for nearly three decades, from 1738 until his death in 1769, making it the longest lasting of these uprisings. It also was the most serious, periodically threatening the capital and controlling substantial amounts of territory. This proclamation was among numerous such appeals issued by rebel leaders looking for supporters. Like many such documents from the eighteenth century, it was issued in the demotic script, *chu nom*, which made its oral transmission easier. The proclamation explicitly recalls the heroic feats of Le Loi (Le Thai To [r. 1428–1433]), the founder of the Le dynasty who had driven out the Ming in the early fifteenth century. It also condemns the Trinh manipulation of the Le house and the injustices they are said to have visited on the Vietnamese population. Although rich in classical and historical allusions, some of which are quite obscure, the text's essential message is clear—it is a call to arms to defend the Le rulers against the Trinh.

We, the sons of the emperor, bearing resentment on behalf of our fathers, have been forced to go about with Heaven as our head covering. We are subjects of the emperor, dwelling on the soil of the emperor. Our hearts are loyal and righteous and must be so because of the country. We remember the beginnings of the Lam Son righteous uprising [1418–1427], during which the Great Ancestral

---

47. *Qian* and *kun* are trigrams found in the *Classic of Changes*, used for divination and prophecy.

Emperor set out with majesty, drawing his magical sword to cut off the head of Lieu Thang,[48] after which he ascended the precious throne to establish the matters of Nam Viet. Shaven hair once again grew long, and people were grateful for the endless and virtuous labors; white teeth once again were blackened, and mouths spoke words of great peace and generous circumstances. [The people] sang to welcome the Le and joined hands in happy spirits, [their songs recalling] the Yao era [third millennium B.C.E.] during which people patted their bellies with contentment and Tran Cao turned his face and departed, causing the people to turn their benevolent hearts toward thoughts of the Han.[49] The Mac had evil intentions, but even they found it difficult to prevent people from venerating the Zhou [dynasty]. In the South, Heaven's fate commenced the Restoration, and in the Tong [Son] territory, it borrowed the hand of the Nguyen general. And this Nguyen Cong was like the little crab that floats across the sand, and in all their work the Trinh were [like] black cuckoos bringing dependence. Earlier, they gave the appearance of seeking and then invading the branch, moving slowly like a mouse that has fallen into a container of rice. Later, they forgot the practice of pigeons fighting one another and instead acted belligerently like a water buffalo crashing into a spirit house. The eye of the *mang xa* [snake] spied on the western capital.[50] The salivating Thao demon coveted the throne of the Eastern Han.[51] The traces of the snake's belly revealed words of servile flattery, while heroes' mouths chanted about the soapberry. The growing hair of the eel bred worrisome troubles, while under Heaven people scratched their heads as disorder and chaos sprang up in their hearts.

What prolonged disaster! What miserable stinginess! Such lamentable hardships! Encountering flames, our hands are bound. The people and the territory within the former boundaries have fallen into the hands of cruel bandits. The *xa tac* [spirits] of the motherland are of the old order; how is it that they have fallen into the pockets of adulteresses? Now, though well into this disorder, who knows when these injustices can finally be repaid? Thus, we risk our lives to cross the seas and make great efforts to scale the mountains. The imperial commands will cause the frost to stain our banners; this band of the loyal and righteous will shake their knives with great fierceness. We slowly collect and seize a single citadel, a single brigade, and the ashes from the stoves of the kitchens of the Xia [dynasty] will blow and drift about; we open the hearts of the land and the

---

48. Lieu Thang was the commanding general of the occupying Ming force.

49. The "Yao era" refers to the time of the legendary Chinese emperor Yao; Tran Cao was a rebel who attacked the capital of Thang Long in 1516; and the reference to the Han dynasty is to suggest that the people are thinking of the Le rulers who had been attacked.

50. A *mang xa* is a large snake. The reference is to Wang Mang, the official who usurped the Han throne early in the Common Era and briefly established the Xin dynasty.

51. Tao Thao (C: Cao Cao) was a warlord who seized power toward the end of the Eastern Han dynasty in the early third century C.E.

hearts of the people, and the old sword of Luu will be honed to a fine edge.[52] Through nine autumns, Heaven has been longing, and through five changes of the moon, it also has dreamed. The throngs who trampled about during the Qin dynasty in search of the deer with the unbroken antlers are entering the net that was empty of heroic people;[53] they are bathing in the So River while the monkey wearing the hat stretches forth its hand, since it lacks heroic people.[54]

Our ancestors' public virtue assisted everyone, so how could the loyalty and righteousness of the hearts of the people be denied? People accepted the responsibility of royal favor when they undertook to establish the throne; there was Heaven and there was Earth, and there were the two sons. People relied on the great blessing for the time of the Restoration; there was still the water, and there were still the mountains, and there were still positions and salaries. The people were originally those of the borders of Viet; and any land [within these] was the land of the Le dynasty. With regard to the divine throne, the phoenix's feathers were short, and those who looked could see its falling tears. The enemy soldiers were on the opposite side; in their mouths, silkworms chewed on leaves, but when looking inside them, no flaming liver was found. Just as a small snake sheds its skin to become a dragon, so too the lightning bug makes its way toward the sun. Transplanted paddy rice cannot tolerate nourishing a different mother; so when one eats its fruits, one must remember those who plowed the fields. That La Chicken is stubborn and cannot be stirred by anyone, and the blood of La San brings disgrace to the markets of the Han.[55] Those dogs of the Ho, wrinkled and with canine teeth, bite their master, and the stomach of [An] Lushan adds to the misfortunes of the Tang sword.[56]

I ask that we not rely on the power of the snowy mountains, that we make preparations together with the hearts of the truly righteous. The house of the "great below" has crumbled and collapsed, and we try to support its pillars and beams; the lineage of the loyal flows along carried by the rolling [waves], and we reach out a hand to grab the tiller and steer. The purse on the horse does not covet the possessions of Thao; the Peach Garden gathering is not ungrateful for

---

52. This possibly is a reference to Lu Dongbing, a Tang dynasty Daoist figure noted for using his sword to fight for justice and against evil.

53. During the Qin dynasty, tradition had it that whoever succeeded in capturing such a deer would become the new ruler of the state.

54. The phrase was a scoffing one made by an official about the Chu dynasty ruler Xiang Yu (r. 232–202), whom he called "a monkey wearing a hat."

55. "La Chicken" is a reference to the wife of Emperor Han Gaozu (r. 202–195 B.C.E.), noted for her power-hungry cruelty; "La San" was a relative of the empress, also involved in schemes to seize the Han throne.

56. An Lushan (V: An Loc Son) was a Tang dynasty general who led a rebellion against the Tang in the mid-eighth century.

the righteousness of Luu.[57] Gathering together the kilns, the countries of Chuan and Qin encountered times of adversity and cuts to the abdomen.[58] The people of Feng and Deng lit their stoves while hurrying with their golden bile.[59] Sometimes we advance our troops and followers; sometimes we send [only] news and envoys. Ban and Dang point to the Hoang River and the Thai Mountains,[60] so everyone helps everyone else, casting darkness on the demons and giving light to the spirits; pacifying and restoring order while transmitting regulations of iron and documents in vermilion script, virtue announcing virtue but setting it forth so that Heaven and Earth would know of it. With these loyal words, my saliva is at an end, and I ask that superior men reflect on them together.[61]

["Tai lieu tham khao: Hich cua Le Duy Mat ke toi ho Trinh," 58–59;
trans. George Dutton]

NGO FAMILY LITERARY GROUP

THE UNIFICATION RECORDS OF THE IMPERIAL LE
(1780s–1800s)

The Unification Records of the Imperial Le is a major late-eighteenth-century prose work recounting the political developments and intrigues of that era. In particular, it describes the events leading to the fall of the Trinh rulers and the eventual demise of the Le emperors. Even though it usually is classified as historical fiction, much of its content can be confirmed by other sources, suggesting that it was based substantially on fact. The Unification Records is invaluable as a near-contemporary northern account of the arrival and impact of the Tay Son armies, which had overthrown the Nguyen lords in the southern regions in the early 1770s. There is considerable debate about the work's author(s). It was probably written by at least two men from the Ngo clan, one of whom was almost certainly Ngo Thi Chi (1753–1788), the younger brother of Ngo Thi Nham. The following lengthy excerpt is from the fourth of seventeen chapters and focuses on the summer of 1786 when a key Trinh defector, Nguyen Huu Chinh, helps the Tay Son brothers in a scheme to attack the Trinh and recapture the

---

57. This refers to a brotherhood oath taken in a peach garden by three main characters in the *Romance of the Three Kingdoms*.

58. Chuan and Qin were two vassal states that helped a ruler regain his throne during the Xia dynasty.

59. Feng and Deng were generals for the Han emperor Guangwu (r. 36–57) who assisted their ruler by lighting fires to dry his drenched clothing after a battle.

60. Ban and Dang are references to hexagrams from the *Classic of Changes* that indicate times of chaos; the Hoang River and Thai Mountains are synecdoches for all Chinese rivers and mountains.

61. I am indebted to the notes to the translation of this document in the *Dai Viet Su Ky Tuc Bien* (1991), 280–83, translated by Ngo The Long and Nguyen Kim Hung and edited by Nguyen Dong Chi.

former Nguyen capital at Phu Xuan. This chapter depicts the younger Tay Son brother, Nguyen Hue (in the text referred to as Binh), being goaded by Nguyen Huu Chinh into extending his campaign into the heart of Trinh territory and capturing Thang Long itself. This attack works nearly flawlessly, and in short order the Tay Son forces gain control of the entire Trinh-Le realm. This is a key moment in Vietnamese history. Territories stretching from China to the Gulf of Siam were broadly integrated for the first time. More immediately for the Tay Son leaders, it meant a dramatic increase in the territory under their control, thereby complicating their political position. The northern campaign was followed by conflict between the Tay Son brothers, eventually creating a rift that resulted in their dividing the enlarged territories between themselves.

Taking Revenge for His Master, Nguyen Chinh Leads His Army

FOR PROCEEDING INTO NATIONAL CALAMITY, DUKE LY DIES FOR HIS LORD

It is said that starting in the *giap ngo* year [1774] when Thuan Hoa was returned to our territory, the court designated Phu Xuan as the area of the main outpost for the extreme frontier and established a garrison of three thousand troops to be camped there, plus a rotating guard of thirty thousand troops. A general in chief and a vice general were appointed there, along with an inspector of the armies and a vice inspector of the armies. Encampments were placed in all the strategic areas from Hai Van pass northward, and the people of those areas were registered in order to boost troop numbers. The land was cultivated to increase provisions, trading in goods was commenced, and the benefits of the mountains and seas were exploited. Examinations were held to select men of talent, and titles were given to gain the people's hearts. Absolutely everything was properly controlled and regulated. The only problem was the general in chief, Duke of Tao Quan. By nature he was an easygoing person and would just give verbal orders to people, but being adaptable with strategy when facing battle was not his forte. Before this, the inspector of the armies, Nguyen Linh Tan, had often said that the possibility of quickly suppressing the Tay Son rebels had been lost because of Tao Quan. Linh Tan addressed the court saying, "Because of his cowardice, Tao Quan has thwarted the national plan, and Thuan Hoa will surely fall if left in Tao Quan's hands. Please dismiss him and promote the vice general to general in chief. If we do so, then we will probably be able to hold Thuan Hoa." But the king took into account the fact that Thuan Hoa had just been pacified and was happy with the way that Tao Quan was keeping the peace in such a strategic area, so instead he removed Inspector of the Armies Linh Tan and replaced him with another official.

The second graduate in the palace examination, Le Quy Don, investigated the prophecies concerning the area where the Tay Son rebellion had begun and addressed the king, saying, "In Tay Son there is a place, which by virtue of its geomancy can create a Son of Heaven. In twelve years no one will be able to resist this land's power, and I fear that Thuan Hoa's general in chief is no match for it. I beg Your Majesty to consider this." The king thought that he was overreacting and did not pay much attention to him.

Thereafter, there were no troubles in the border areas, and both north and south were at peace. Thuan Hoa was a tranquil and happy place. But then in the fourth lunar month of the *binh ngo* year [1786], a Chinese trading ship unexpectedly arrived, and its captain went to have an audience with Tao Quan. Using various techniques, he predicted that His Excellency would enjoy unbelievable prosperity and fortune in his latter years and, because he was facing some difficulties, should be careful to ward off illness. The Chinese also told him that at the height of summer, everything would become auspicious if he performed the proper rituals and prayed. Tao Quan believed all this and then arranged to sponsor a huge vegetarian feast and to pray for seven days and nights.

For days, all the soldiers served at this feast day and night, until suddenly they heard that the rebels' infantry had taken Hai Van, that the general protecting it, the Quyen Trung marquis, had died in battle, and that all the enemy sailors had gone to sea and were expected to arrive in the evening. Tao Quan returned to his citadel in distress, with no idea of what he should do. All the troops had been working at the feast for a long time, and when they suddenly heard this news about the enemy, they were disheartened and demoralized. Tao Quan sent someone to look for the Chinese merchant, but no one knew where he had gone, and it was only then that Tao Quan realized that the man had been a spy who had come to deceive him.

While Nguyen [Huu] Chinh was with the Tay Son, he learned that Tao Quan was cowardly and very sneaky and that an announcement of surrender [by Tao Quan] could not necessarily be believed. So he secretly sent a man with a sealed letter to Vice General The Quan, saying that the Tay Son troops were very skillful and that their advance could not be stopped. It also said that since The Quan and [Nguyen Huu] Chinh had once served together as retainers of Huy Quan, if the city were surrendered, its noble and rich inhabitants could be protected. He also secretly instructed the bearer of the letter to deliberately deliver it to the area controlled by Tao Quan. [Accordingly,] Tao Quan got hold of the letter but did not show it to anyone, as he was secretly harboring thoughts of surrender. Shortly after this, enemy troops arrived in great numbers, and the general in chief and vice general met to discuss how to resist them. The citadel of Phu Xuan was on the river; from the middle of the river, the base of the city wall was more than two *truong* [twenty-four feet] above it. The naval forces of the enemy arrived from downriver and fired [their guns] upward but could not reach the citadel. Inside the city, the gates were shut and the walls fortified, and all its forces resisted the enemy. The enemy infantry retreated to their ships and were chased by arrows. One ship was sunk, which boosted the spirits of the troops [in the citadel]. That evening the tide suddenly rose, and the water in the river reached up to and surrounded the base of the city wall. The enemy sent its naval forces to go and fire directly at the citadel and sent its infantry to besiege the city gates.

The general in chief sent the vice general and his subordinate, the Kien Kim marquis, and others to leave the citadel and face the enemy. The vice general had two sons who were commandants, and they both followed their father into battle. In formation behind the ramparts, the soldiers fought a defensive battle for more than two hours. When they used up all their poisoned arrows, the vice general sent a man into the citadel to ask for more. Sitting up in the citadel tower, the general in chief ordered people to close the doors and refused their request, saying: "Besides salaries and provisions, each of my companies has already received its poisoned projectiles, so who are you to ask for more?" The vice general was enraged and announced to all his troops: "Tao Quan has rebelled. I'm going to break down the gate and go in to cut off that blackguard's head, then I will come back out to fight!" Then he turned to his two sons and said, "You two hold them off at the front, and I will come out shortly."

He turned around his elephant's head and went in. As the elephant retreated, it disturbed the troops' formation, which the enemy troops used to advantage and advanced. The vice general's two sons galloped ahead of the rest of the formation brandishing their swords and managing to kill hundreds of men. Then more enemy troops came and hacked at their horses' legs. The horses fell to the ground, and the two brothers fought on foot still killing dozens of men. Heavily wounded and losing strength, they called out to their father to save them. The vice general turned his elephant around to rescue them, but they already had been cut down at the front line. The Kien Kim marquis also had been killed in the battle on the front line. The vice general collected his troops and prepared to deploy them in another formation, but looking back he saw that a white flag had already been hoisted over the citadel. His elephant boy dismounted and fled. The rebel troops pursued the elephant and fired, and the vice general died in his saddle.

The general in chief opened the citadel gate and came out in a carriage with a coffin.[62] Binh [that is, Nguyen Hue] then led his troops into the citadel, where they went on a rampage of slaughter. Superintendent Inspector of the Armies Nguyen Trong Dang died during this. The defending troops fled from the citadel, and the locals killed all of them. After this battle, out of the tens of thousands of people of Phu Xuan there was not a sole survivor.

Now that Phu Xuan had been taken, Binh extended his victory by sending some troops to capture the Dong Hai garrison. The commanding officer of the garrison, Vice Commandant Ninh Thon, the Vi Phai marquis, considered the situation and then fled. Thuan Hoa was entirely lost. That was on the fourteenth day of the fifth lunar month of the Canh Hung reign, a *binh ngo* year [1786].

Having taken Thuan Hoa, Binh then met with all his generals to discuss restoring the old border along the La River and sent a proclamation of his victory

---

62. This indicates that he was aware of having committed a crime punishable by death.

to the Tay Son king [his brother, Nguyen Nhac]. [Nguyen Huu] Chinh said, "Your Honor, you were commanded to take Thuan Hoa, and you did it in a single campaign. Your magnificence has impressed all under Heaven. Commanding troops entails timing, position, and opportunity. If one can take advantage of these three, one will always be victorious. Now in Bac Ha, the generals are lazy, the soldiers are overly proud, and the court has not had firm control for a long time.[63] We should take advantage of our position of strength. This is what is meant by the saying 'Annex the weak and attack the blind; take [kingdoms] in chaos and deal summarily with those going to ruin.' This opportunity and this timing must not be lost."

Binh replied, "Bac Ha is a large country, and many talented people live there. There is an old proverb that says, 'Bees have poison, so one should never treat them lightly.'" [Nguyen Huu] Chinh said, "Only one person in Bac Ha had talent, and that was I. Now that I have left, it is an empty country, so I urge you not to worry." Binh had always been good at speaking eloquently to humble himself, so he answered in jest: "My doubts aren't about the people there but about myself." [Nguyen Huu] Chinh's face lost a little of its color, and he apologized, saying, "If you think of yourself as mediocre and dim-witted, that means this country truly has no men of talent!" Binh then calmed him down again by saying, "If I can take on and conquer a four-hundred-year-old country in one morning, what will its people call me?" [Nguyen Huu] Chinh replied, "The country has an emperor and a king, and this is the result of the insurrections of the past and the present. Although the Trinh lords have always said they support the Le, the reality is that they have control over the emperor by coercion. What really makes the people of this land unhappy is that in the past whenever a strongman has wanted to make trouble, he has always done it in the name of respect for the Le. But the fate of the Trinh clan is still not at an end, and thus all the undertakings of these people have failed. Now, Trung's *Local Records* say that if one does not make kings or earls and a single ruler controls all the land for two centuries, it will lead to conflict in the imperial house. In calculating the length of time from King Thai to King Tinh,[64] it is already more than two hundred years. So if you take as your justification [the slogan] "Eradicate the Trinh, and support the Le," there would be no one under Heaven who would not respond to this. This would be a great achievement unparalleled in this age." Binh replied, "This would truly be a great thing, but I have received orders to take Thuan Hoa, not to attack other provinces. What would happen if I were to violate my orders?" [Nguyen Huu] Chinh replied, "The *Spring and Autumn Annals* say, 'If one oversteps in a small way but has great success, it will be considered a success,' how then could it be considered a transgression?' Moreover, you must have heard the expression 'when a general is out on campaign he cannot receive orders from his lord,' haven't you?"

---

63. Bac Ha (literally, "north of the river") refers to the Trinh-governed territory north of the Linh River.

64. This refers to the seigneurial lords Trinh Kiem (r. 1545–1570) and Trinh Sam (r. 1767–1782).

Binh had a bold and determined temperament, and he accepted [Nguyen Huu] Chinh's words, which were precisely in keeping with his own ideas. He sent off [Nguyen Huu] Chinh to choose his vanguard troops and then set out for the port of Dai An, where he was first to capture the grain yard at Vi Hoang. After that Binh would lead out his naval forces. They had agreed that [Nguyen Huu] Chinh would light the beacon at Vi Hoang first as a signal. All the arrangements had been made, and [Nguyen Huu] Chinh commanded his troops to go out first. They sailed past Nghe An and Thanh Hoa, each commanding a naval force of hundreds. Their majesty raced ahead of them, and both the guards of Nghe An and Thanh Hoa, the Dang Trung marquis and the Thuy Trung marquis, had abandoned their citadels and fled. On the sixth day of the sixth month, [Nguyen Huu] Chinh reached Vi Hoang; the general of the encampment there considered the situation and then fled, so [Nguyen Huu] Chinh took all the millions of pecks of grain stored there. He then lit the beacon as a signal. Binh saw this and led his thousand ships out over the sea. The common folk of Nghe An climbed up the hills to look out on the sea at the turreted ships with their flags and pennants. They sighed, saying, "There's a proverb about 'a lying snake biting a chicken.' They really are guilty of a crime, but these are deeds unrivaled by their contemporaries." [Nguyen Huu] Chinh joined forces with Binh at Vi Hoang, and their magnificence shook the land.

At the royal court, advisers were continually reporting to the throne about [Nguyen Huu] Chinh's army, but they always spoke of the affairs of state in a way to make it seem as if the enemy had been defeated, so the court was confused and ignorant of the true situation. Before this, when Phu Xuan had fallen and the report from the border had reached the capital, many councillors said that Thuan Hoa was not originally a part of the realm to begin with and that its conquest by a previous dynasty was an extravagance far too costly for the central provinces. Moreover, it had taken a great deal of military power to hold but was not of any genuine benefit to the country, so losing it now was actually a blessing. They said that the only important endeavor was to make encampments at Nghe An and to extend and secure the old border. They also said that if their side considered losing Thuan Hoa to be a blessing, then the enemy would certainly consider attacking their side as a warning to them.

Having thus fixed a general plan, the minds of all the people were at rest. Then came the sudden news of the fall of the Nghe An regiment and the imminent arrival of the enemy troops, and at this the people were stricken with panic. So the Thai Dinh marquis was sent as a commandant to lead the twenty-seven special regiments to resist the enemy at Nghe An. Ten days after he had received the order to go, Thai Dinh still had not finished organizing and packing his equipment. By the time he left the city, the enemy troops had already reached Vi Hoang, so Thai Dinh was commanded to lead his soldiers to hold them off at Son Nam, and in addition the Lien Trung marquis, Dinh Tich Nhuong, was sent to oversee the naval route, along with the left- and right-hand guards, the five marquises, the five experts, the five middle selected cavalry divisions, and others. With the dispatch of the Thai Dinh marquis's forces, both the land and sea forces were sent at the same time. At this time, [Nguyen Huu] Chinh's forces had been fighting pirates at Hai Duong, which led the pirates to ally with the southern troops; thus, the court selected Nhuong Hoi to defend the southern front. Nhuong [Hoi], who was from Ham Giang, was a famous general with an illustrious reputation; the court had given him the responsibility for naval warfare. Nhuong [Hoi]'s force arrived at Luc Mon to deal with the enemy there.

Soon a strong wind blew in from the southwest, and the rebels sent five ships up the river as a vanguard. They went against the current of the river at full sail, and the royal fleet advanced slowly on them from behind. Nhuong Hoi saw that the rebels had sent a vanguard of ships, so he organized his boats across the river to line up in a formation shaped like the character "one" and ordered the loading of the precious unicorn cannon, aiming it toward the rebels and firing. After one shot had been fired, the rebels did not move, so Nhuong Hoi ordered a second shot, at which the rebels furled their sails. All in the fleet were very pleased at what they thought was the enemy's fear. After Nhuong Hoi had ordered a third shot, the rebels replied with a thunderlike shot from a huge gun. Its projectile flew into the crown of an old tree, splitting it in two. By this time the Truong Trong marquis had led his troops out onto both banks of the river, but when they saw the shot coming, they all wanted to flee, and the enemy seized the advantage, leaving their ships and climbing onto the riverbanks. All of Truong Trong's troops ran away, and the enemy advanced directly to Hien Doanh. Truong Trong and the joint commander [*doc dong*], Nguyen Huy Binh, were able to escape by hiding in the water. The Thai Dinh marquis advanced to the mouth of the Kim Dong River, but his troops, too, were routed.

The reports from the front spoke of an emergency, but the military and civil officials in the capital were making plans only for keeping their wives and children safe and hiding their goods and riches, and no one dared to take on the task of fighting the rebels. The king had decided that his official Bui Huy Bich had been prime minister for too long and thought him very ill-mannered. Furthermore, at this time [Bui Huy Bich] had not come up with a policy for defending against the rebels, and in his heart the king detested him. Those around Bui [Huy Bich] stepped up their attacks on his character, so he was dismissed as prime minister and demoted to the position of military supervisor. With the prime minister gone, the people's minds were even more uneasy, so the king summoned Cong Xan to discuss in secret whether it would be better to run from the enemy or to fight them. Cong Xan said, "If the rebel army is deep in our territory and cut off from outside assistance, then there is nothing to fear. We should lead them into an area close by and destroy them in a single battle. In the deployment of soldiers, this is a very good strategy. Moreover, the capital is the center of all under Heaven, and if you were to leave it, where would you go? If you leave the capital in distress in a sedan chair, the people's hearts will be lost, and this would be just like offering up the country to the enemy. For now, you should just temporarily send the imperial concubines and the six palace authorities out of the city." The king followed this advice.

[Ngo Gia Van Phai, *Hoang Le nhat thong chi*, 5:61–71; trans. Catherine Churchman, with Liam Kelley]

NGO THI NHAM

LETTER TO NGO TUONG DAO (CA. 1788)

The letter to Ngo Tuong Dao was one in a series written around 1788 by Ngo Thi Nham after he decided to serve the new Tay Son dynasty. These letters were addressed to friends and family members who were actively resisting the Tay Son regime or who had simply chosen to retire after the fall of the Le dynasty. The Tay Son era was one of considerable interfamilial tension among northern literati, as clans disagreed over whether to serve or resist the Tay Son. Indeed, Ngo Thi Nham may have written these letters to justify his own difficult decision to transfer his loyalty from the Le. Written to an uncle, the letter explores the issue of acting versus temporizing under certain circumstances. Ngo Thi Nham argues along Neo-Confucian lines that it is better to act according to principle than it is to hesitate and ponder issues of gaining fortune or consequence. Put another way, he suggests that appropriate change sometimes may be a better course of action than continued advocacy for established patterns.

In late autumn and early winter I received two letters in succession from you. The first discussed the two-character expression "state of affairs" and referred to the fact that in military matters, the sage took direct responsibility with regard to the Lai [people] and [the men of] Bi but that he exhausted his provisions in the Kingdom of Chen and had to proceed again for a while to the Kingdom of Song.[65] You noted thus that truly nothing is impossible and that this must be considered. Your point is very clear and logical, and I take it to heart.

The second letter discussed the two-character expression "calamity and [good] fortune." I have gone over this back and forth in my mind. The basic point is that scholars use calamity and fortune to appraise others, and in the process there is much room for error. I have seen Master Zhu's discussion of the

---

65. In 500 B.C.E., Confucius, advising the ruler of the Kingdom of Lu, prevented a rival kingdom, Qi, from arming and using non-Chinese people, the Lai, against Lu. Then in 498 B.C.E., Confucius ordered an attack on a group of men from the town of Bi who were rebelling. But in 493 B.C.E., while working for the Kingdom of Wei, he refused to offer military advice to its ruler and left, nearly starving to death in the Kingdom of Chen, before eventually going to the Kingdom of Song.

Zuo Commentary. He said that [Zuo] was a person who knew how to recognize benefit and harm and that he generally just talked about the difference between calamity and fortune, and benefit and harm.[66] He also said [Zuo] liked to use success and failure to judge people. If he saw that someone did something well, he would say that this person was good. If someone did not do something well, he would say that this person was not good. He never judged people based on what was right or wrong on principle. This was his great defect.

[Zhu Xi] also discussed the "bend an inch and extend a foot" passage in the *Mencius* and said that whenever a person does something, he inclines toward benefit and avoids harm but that he does not understand that whenever there is benefit, there is also harm. Although I might be in a position in which I gain plenty of benefit, harm will follow. It is thus better to proceed according to principle. This is why the sages put aside [the issue of] the calamity and fortune of calamity and fortune and looked at calamity and fortune only from the perspective of principle. Sovereigns who are benevolent, officials who are loyal, the three relationships in correct form, and the nine categories in order—these constitute the good fortune of a kingdom. Fathers who are compassionate, sons who are filial, elder brothers who are friendly, younger brothers who are reverent, husbands who are righteous, and wives who comply—this is the good fortune of a family. To oppose this is calamity. We scholars must embody this [principle], and then what it means to avoid calamity and seek fortune will be completely clear. The illusoriness of gain and loss, the illusoriness of mundane matters, the inevitability of life and death, and the inevitability of day and night—all this is completely clear. It is only recently that I have come out of the darkness to understand this principle.

Our family has encountered misfortune, a terrible time when uncles and nephews and older and younger brothers are contending with one another. The *Classic of Poetry* states: "In seeking fortune do not defy." This is profound. Your letter stated that "the establishment of a family tradition of cultivation should serve as a foundation." To expand on this, to be sincere and just is what you are teaching now. There is nothing precious about losing someone, whereas being benevolent to kin is precious. That is what I am now learning. To love one's kin, to respect one's elders, to reverently study, to manifest goodness in keeping one's promises—these are the activities that we brothers are now engaged in. If members of a family encourage one another in these ways, then amidst this there is good fortune.

In the *Classic of Changes*, the "not yet across" [hexagram] comes after the "already across" [hexagram].[67] Its judgment states: "Not yet across, prevalence

---

66. Master Zhu is the Neo-Confucian philosopher Zhu Xi (1130–1200). The *Zuo Commentary* (*Zuozhuan*) is the main commentary for an early historical chronicle known as the *Spring and Autumn Annals* (*Chunqiu*) and covers the years 805 to 453 B.C.E.

67. The two hexagrams, "already across" and "not yet across," make their point by reference to the crossing of a river. Ngo Thi Nham appears to be following Zhu Xi's explanation of these

[may be had]." The meaning of prevalence is broad. One should not privilege the prevalence of "already across" over the prevalence of "not yet across." Here I humbly offer my ignorant views for your correction.

[Ngo Thi Nham, *Ngo Thi Nham toan tap*, 1:810–11; trans. Liam Kelley]

QUANG TRUNG EMPEROR

EDICT ON ASCENDING THE THRONE (1788)

In the summer of 1788, the Le emperor had fled his capital, taken refuge with the Qing governor-general in southern China, and successfully appealed for assistance in recapturing his kingdom from the Tay Son. At the urging of his ambitious governor-general, Sun Shi Yi (Ton Si Nghi), the Chinese emperor, Qianlong, agreed to provide an army to oust the Tay Son and restore Emperor Le Chieu Thong to his throne. As the Qing armies—numbering anywhere between 50,000 and 200,000 soldiers—advanced, the Tay Son troops undertook a strategic retreat. At this juncture, Nguyen Hue still claimed only the title of lord in Phu Xuan but decided that laying claim to the imperial throne abandoned by the Le would be the most effective way to unite his followers in advance of a campaign to drive out the Qing. Thus in late 1788, Ngo Thi Nham drafted the "Edict on Ascending the Throne." In it, Nguyen Hue describes his reluctance to name himself emperor, explaining that his final decision was prompted by a combination of fate and the desperate straits of the people who had suffered chaos and warfare for too many years. Like previous public statements by founders of new dynasties, this edict is concerned with laying out a genealogy of dynasties and the failings of the new rulers' immediate predecessors. Also echoing earlier foundation edicts, such as that by Nguyen Phuc Khoat in 1744,[68] this edict emphasizes the emperor's reluctance to take the throne, doing so only at the repeated urging of the people. Although the form of the edict is quite conventional, it is significant as marking the first successful claim to the Vietnamese imperial throne since Mac Dang Dung (r. 1527–1541) more than two and a half centuries earlier.

I have considered how the Five Emperors received the Mandate of Heaven and replaced the existing dynastic house, and how the Three Kings began their

---

two hexagrams, which argues that if everyone has been ferried across a river, then the action is complete and there is little room for change or for someone to gain prevalence. When a river has not yet been completely crossed, however, someone could try to gain prevalence, if he did so in an appropriate manner. Hence, what Ngo Thi Nham appears to be saying to his uncle is that he should not privilege the set order over the possibility of change, as change can be good at certain times when it is brought about appropriately.

68. See Nguyen Phuc Khoat, "Edict Declaring Autonomy" (this chap.).

destinies by taking advantage of unstable times.[69] When there are changes in the Way, the times must adjust. These sage rulers respected the Way of Heaven; they considered the acts of ruling over their domain and treating the people as their children as the same kind of duty.

From the time that our country of Viet was founded by the Dinh, through the Le, Ly, and Tran families up to the present, sagely rulers have produced bright good fortune, and they did not have the same surname. Moreover, a country's prosperity, duration, and destiny are truly conferred by Heaven; they are not something that can be accomplished by man.

In the past, the Le house lost control of governing the country, and the land was divided between the Trinh clan and the former Nguyen. For more than two hundred years, the people's livelihoods were in disarray; rulers could only cling to false authority, while private families granted themselves fiefs. The pillars connecting Heaven and Earth fell and were not raised; never before had there been such a time. Furthermore, for these past few years, north and south have been at war and have sunk into a morass. I am a cotton-cloth [ordinary] person from Tay Son, without an inch of land to rely on and initially did not have imperial ambitions. Since in their hearts, the people abhor disorder, they longed for an enlightened ruler to benefit the age and settle the people. Therefore, I gathered together a righteous force. We assiduously cleared mountain and forest to aid my elder brother the king, and we rushed forward with our war horses, setting up our base on western ground. In the south, we pacified land belonging to Siam and Cambodia, and then we captured Phu Xuan and took Thang Long. Initially, I wanted to stamp out the rebellion, save the people from the midst of their distress, and then restore the country to the Le clan and return the land to my elder brother. I then could have roamed about in court robes and red slippers, only looking after the joys of the two territories.

But because of the vicissitudes of the times, it could not be as I wished.

No matter how I supported the Le family, the Le heir failed to take care of the gods of land and grain;[70] he abandoned the country and fled. The people of Bac Ha did not see the Le ancestral lineage as worthy of allegiance; the one they rely on is me. My elder brother Nhac was weary of hard toil, so he was willing to maintain the one prefecture of Qui Nhon and consented to be called the western king. The thousands of *li* of land that we had subdued in the south belonged entirely to me. I thought to myself: my talent and virtue are paltry, as they cannot approach that of the ancients. Moreover, the land is vast and the people numerous.

69. The Five Emperors are the Yellow Emperor, Emperor Zhuanxu, Emperor Ku, Emperor Yao, and Emperor Shun. The Three Kings are Fuxin, Suiren, and Shennong. All are legendary wise rulers of ancient China.

70. This is a synecdoche for the country.

I quietly reflected on how to govern and, in trepidation, likened it to driving a car-riage of six horses with rotted reins.[71] Previously, civil officials and military officers inside and outside the court all wanted me to take the throne even earlier. In order to comply with the people's aspirations, they sent up a memorial urging me for-ward; in fact, they repeatedly sent up memorials. Their precious memorials—with-out having planned it—even wrote the same words!

Alas! Regarding imperial power to be the most grave, and the heavenly throne to be arduous, I truly fear that I am not worthy. However, the countless people within the four seas flock to me alone. This is the will of Heaven; how could it be an affair of man? I assent to Heaven and submit to man, I cannot stubbornly decline. Therefore, this year, on the twenty-second day of the eleventh month, I ascend the throne, and mark it as the first year of the Quang Trung reign.

For all of you common people, I think that of the rules disseminated by the throne for your observance; those concerning morality and law, humaneness, justice, equilibrium, and correctness are the main aspects of humanity. Today, the people and I start anew, respecting the enlightened methods of the sages of the past in order to govern and civilize all under Heaven.

In every place in the thirteen circuits, the winter's ordinary labor and tax ob-ligations shall be reduced 50 percent this year. For those affected by the ravages of war, I will listen to the reports of the local administrator and waive all taxes.

Some officials of the old dynasty have been implicated in wrongdoing, and many have been reported several times. Except for those who committed seri-ous crimes, the rest shall be pardoned.

[Ngo Thi Nham, *Ngo Thi Nham toan tap*, 2:648–50; trans. Kate Baldanza]

TREATY OF VERSAILLES BETWEEN NGUYEN ANH AND KING LOUIS XVI (1787)

In 1785, Nguyen Anh entrusted his young son Prince Canh (1780–1801) to the care of a missionary, Pierre Pigneau de Béhaine, for an embassy to the French court of Louis XVI. The mission was intended to conclude an agreement with the French court that would trade Nguyen territorial and commercial concessions for French military support in the ongoing Nguyen battles with the Tay Son. But the treaty was never implemented, because the French official in Pondicherry (India) charged with seeing to its completion decided not to pursue the matter, and the French Revolution soon rendered French aid moot. Despite its never having been carried out, the treaty is of considerable signifi-cance because it became one of the touchstones of France's popular legitimation of its nineteenth-century colonial conquest. It was periodically cited as one of the bases of French territorial claims, conveniently overlooking France's failure to fulfill its own

---

71. This is a reference to the *Classic of Documents* (*Shujing*).

obligations under the terms of the treaty. It nonetheless foreshadowed the types of concessions that the Vietnamese courts would eventually make in the second half of the nineteenth century under French military pressure. The treaty was originally written in French.

Nguyen-Anh, the king of Cochinchina, having been dispossessed of his states and needing to employ an armed force to recover them, has sent to France Seigneur Pierre-Joseph-Georges Pigneau de Béhaine, the bishop of Adran, with a view to calling for the support and assistance of His Majesty, the Most Christian King. This said majesty, convinced of the justice of this prince's cause and wishing to give him a sign to indicate his friendship as well as his love of justice, is determined to respond favorably to this request made in his name. Consequently, he has authorized Count Émile de Montmorin, the marshal of his camps and armies, chevalier of his orders and that of the Golden Fleece, his counselor and all his counsels, minister and secretary of state of his commandments and finances, including the Department of Foreign Affairs, to discuss and settle, with the said bishop of Adran, the nature, scope, and conditions of the assistance he will provide. And the two recognized plenipotentiaries make it known that in communicating his complete authority, the count of Montmorin, and in producing the grand seal of the Kingdom of Cochinchina, the bishop of Adran, as well as a resolution of the grand council of said kingdom, have agreed on these points and the following articles.

Article 1

The Very Christian King promises and engages to second in the most efficacious manner the efforts that the king of Cochinchina is resolved to make in order to reenter into the possession and enjoyment of his states.

Article 2

To this effect, His Very Christian Majesty himself will immediately send to the coasts of Cochinchina and, at his own expense, four frigates, along with a body of troops of 1,200 infantrymen, 200 artillerymen, and 250 kafirs [non-European soldiers]. These troops will be supplied with all their articles of war, particularly artillery appropriate to these campaigns.

Article 3

In awaiting the important service that the Very Christian King has dispatched and sent to him, the king of Cochinchina will eventually cede to him and to the crown of France, the absolute control of and sovereignty over the island that forms the principal port of Cochinchina called Hoi Nan [Hoi An] and, by the Europeans, Touron.

Article 4

It is further agreed that the Very Christian King also will, in conjunction with that of Cochinchina, ensure the suitability of the above-named port and that the French will be permitted to make on the mainland all the establishments that they judge to be necessary. . . .[72]

Article 5

The Very Christian King furthermore also takes control of and sovereignty over the island of Poulo Condore.

Article 6

The subjects of the Very Christian King will enjoy complete liberty to engage in commerce in all the lands of the king of Cochinchina, to the exclusion of all other European nations. To this effect, they will be allowed to come and go and travel freely, without any obstacles and without paying for any rights of any sort for their persons, on the condition that they are always provided with a passport by the commander of the island of Hoi Nan. They will be permitted to import all kinds of merchandise from Europe and other parts of the world, with the exception of what is prohibited by the laws of the land. They will be permitted as well to export all the resources and merchandise of the country and of the neighboring countries, without exception; they will not be required to pay any import or export duties except for those normally assessed on local persons, and these rights shall not be increased in any case or under any different designation that exists under this power. It is agreed, furthermore, that any foreign ship, whether commercial or military, shall not be admitted into the states of the king of Cochinchina, except under the umbrella of the French and with a French passport.

Article 7

The government of Cochinchina accords to the subjects of the Very Christian King the most efficacious protection for the liberty and security of all their persons and effects and, in case of difficulty or conflict, will render them the most precise and prompt justice.

---

72. The ellipses are in the original text.

Article 8

If the Very Christian King is attacked or threatened by any power, regardless of what this power might be, relative to his possession of the islands of Hoi Nan and Poulo Condore, and if His Very Christian Majesty is engaged in a conflict with some power, whether it be European or Asian, the king of Cochinchina commits to send him aid in the form of soldiers, sailors, supplies, vessels, and galleys. This assistance shall be furnished three months after being requested, but it shall not be employed beyond the islands of the Moluccas or the Straits of Sunda or Malacca. Their upkeep will fall on the sovereign who has furnished them.

Article 9

The Very Christian King is obliged to assist the king of Cochinchina when he has trouble with respect to the possession of his states. This assistance will be proportionate to the necessity of the circumstances; however, it will in no case exceed those statements in the second article of the present treaty.

Article 10

The present treaty will be ratified by the two contracting sovereigns, and their ratifications will be exchanged within the space of one year, or sooner if possible. In the faith of which we, the plenipotentiaries, have signed the present treaty and have affixed the seal of our arms.

Made at Versailles, the twenty-eighth of November 1787

Separate Article

With a view to preventing all difficulties and misunderstandings relative to the establishments that the Very Christian King has authorized to be carried out on the Continent for the utility of navigation and commerce, he has agreed with the king of Cochinchina that the same establishments will appertain in all properness to His Very Christian Majesty and that the jurisdiction, the police, and the guard, and all the acts of authority, without exception, are exercised privately in his name. In order to prevent the abuses that the aforementioned cases might cause, it is agreed that he will not take any Cochinchinese being pursued for a crime and that those who are there will be extradited at the first request of the government. It also is agreed that any French fugitives will be extradited at the first request of the commander of Hoi Nan or that of Poulo Condore.

Made at Versailles, the twenty-eighth of November 1787

[Taboulet, *La geste française en Indochine*, 1:186–88; trans. George Dutton]

SOCIETY AND CULTURE

BENTO THIEN

REGARDING FESTIVALS (1659)

This excerpt from "History of the Country of Annam" belongs to the small but significant body of writings in the romanized script (*quoc ngu*) produced by Vietnamese Catholics in the early modern period. *Quoc ngu* was developed by early European missionaries as a means to facilitate the transmission of their religious message, and it was soon taken up by their literate converts. Indeed, from its inception until the late nineteenth century, the romanized script was used almost exclusively by Vietnamese Catholics. Although much of the early *quoc ngu* literature is religious in nature—prayers, sermons, rituals, confessions of faith, hagiographies—there are some notable secular writings. The following excerpt comes from a brief history of Vietnam written by a man named Bento Thien. We know little about him and not much about the background to this text, except that it was written in 1659. It is a description of Vietnamese ritual practices as they were carried out throughout the year, starting with the New Year ceremonies. It details the practices of every level of society, from elite rituals like the Nam Giao ceremony[73] to more popular events. It is a rare and quite early account of such events, offering insights into Vietnamese social structures, the expectations of rulers, and the origins of these rituals.

The custom of the country of Annam is that the first day of the first month of the new year is called Tet. Everyone goes to bow before the king, and then they bow before the lord,[74] and then they bow before their grandparents and their ancestors, and finally their parents and anyone else who ranks above them. All the officials in power go to bow before the king and the lord, while the ranks of ordinary people go, first of all, to bow before the Buddha. The feasting for Tet lasts three days; there is the first day, which is followed by a second and a third, and all of them are auspicious days. Then the king and the lord go to the *giao*, which is known as the Temple of Heaven and also as the realm of the Supreme Heavenly Emperor. There both the king and the lord bow down and ask that all under Heaven will have rain and that the people will have peace. Then, by the seventh or eighth day, the festival is over, and feasts also are set out for everyone to eat for ten days. Once an auspicious day is identified, arrangements are made so that everyone may go to the feast and also to visit government officials and to ask about all matters; this is done as it was in former times when the country was first

---

73. See Pham Dinh Ho, "Ritual for Venerating Heaven" (this chap.).

74. The "king" is the Le emperor, and the "lord" is the Trinh Chua, the power behind the throne.

established, when anyone could have an audience with the king. It was at that time that the notion of going into a royal audience first appeared. Whether at the interior tower, the exterior office, or among officials of the prefectures and districts, people could come forward to present their lawsuits. Then, in the middle of the week, there was the birthday celebration and the informing of the spirits so that all under Heaven might offer their congratulations to the king. Anyone who practiced any type of profession would then demonstrate it for the king to observe. Then, during the last week of the first month, the Virtuous Lord [the Trinh ruler] would again offer sacrifices to the "Ky Dao" down by the sandbanks and would build a sacrificial altar.[75] First there would be an altar for the Heavenly Lord Supreme Emperor, then an altar for all the kings from Le Thai To to the present, and finally one altar to worship the Ky Dao spirit. Then the Virtuous Lord would bow at these three altars. Next the Virtuous Lord would go to the altar of the Ky Dao spirit and bow there, after which he would pull out his sword and swing it and then take his bow and shoot it. Then he would again strike the gong and take out the sword as a signal for everyone to fire their guns, and then he would turn and go, and this was called examining the troops. Then he would go directly to drilling the elephants and horses, and this would mark the end of the new year [ceremonies]. There would then be another Tet feast on the second day of the second month. . . . Then on the third day of the third month there would be yet another Tet feast, and this was called the *an uoi*.

In the past it was said that a respectful court official sought to dissuade the king from doing one or two things; the king, however, did not listen to him, so the official fled into the forest. The king then summoned the man, and when he did not return, the king burned down the forest in an effort to force him to come back. The official did not come out, however, but remained there and the fire burned until he died.[76] All the people admired him and so they established a death anniversary on that day, and this was called the Tet of the third month, and they ate marble [rock sugar–filled] dumplings until they were full. Then there was the festival of the fifth day of the fifth month, and this was also a Tet and it was called the "Double Five Tet," and there are numerous ideas concerning this festival. One is that everyone should go to bow before the king and the lord and then also bow to the ancestors of their lineage, and the king and the lord would give out fans to everyone, and these were to be white and inscribed with characters.

Also, [there is a story] that in ancient times, a person in the king's palace offered advice, but because he was not given an official position, he threw him-

---

75. Ky Dao refers to a military flag, and it is linked to the commemoration of the spirits of semilegendary military leaders.

76. This is a retelling of the tale of Jin Wen Gong, a ruler during the Zhou era, who sought to force state service on every capable man in his realm. One official refused, insisting on remaining at home to care for his mother and thus placing filial duty above state service. The king's reply was to burn the forest in order to drive the man out.

self into the ocean and died. This person's name was Quat Nguyen, and when everyone celebrates this Tet, they go to sail boats, and this is called going to look for this person under the seas, and it included the singing of *hat boi*.[77]

The third tale tells of a person who made bronze pillars, and the diviners and all the sorcerers taught that anyone who had any kind of problem should go to celebrate this Tet, and they would trap fairies on that day. In the sixth month, everyone, including the various ranks of people who worked in the fields, would hold a feast to honor the death anniversary of the Agricultural Spirit King, the one who had created all the types of rice found in the world. On the day of the highest tide, the Virtuous Lord would row a boat and also fire a large gun to mark it, and this would be called competing with the water.

Then, in the seventh month, there was the autumn Tet, and anyone who had parents or siblings or a wife or children who had recently died would, in this seventh month, hold a feast for the village. If it was a wealthy family, they would also arrange a reading of the sutras for many days and then would be satisfied, and they would [also] pray to the Dia Tang buddha, Muc Lien, that their souls might have a safe journey to the Buddha paradise land, and they would also burn a mandarin's gown and hat along with all types of other items for their father and mother.[78] Then, on the fifteenth day of the seventh month, they would hold a ritual burning of their grandparents' clothing. The Virtuous Lord would also distribute money to the sons and nephews of various people who had provided service to the king and had died; then every year on that day, ritual money would be burned for the spirits. On that day, called All Souls Day [Trung Nguyen] transgressions are forgiven, and no one goes to the market on that day, so that the ghosts and spirits can come together. On that day, all who have committed any small transgression for which they have been detained in prison will be set free to return to their homes. Then in the eighth month there is the autumn Tet, and everyone eats, sings, and plays together. Then, on the festival of the tenth day of the tenth month, no one celebrates a Tet festival. On that day, there are instead a sorcerer and a witch who celebrate that Tet together.

Then, in the last month of the year, everyone plants more grass on the grave of a father or mother, a brother or a spouse, repairs it, and then also cleans it; he or she also sets out a complete feast. Then, as the Tet day approaches, the king and the lord issue a calendar for everyone to see. On the thirtieth day, the Virtuous Lord goes to pour out water, and this is called discarding old things and taking on new things. Then, on the first day [of the feast], a New Year's pole is erected in front of each house to prevent mischievous spirits from stealing things. Thus, the home of anyone who has a New Year's pole belongs to the

---

77. The word *quat* is homophonous with the Vietnamese word for "fan"—hence the distribution of fans. *Hat boi* is a Vietnamese sung, staged performance.

78. The Dia Tang buddha is a bodhisattva who protects believers from suffering. The "Buddha paradise land" is a reference to the paradise where practitioners of Pure Land Buddhism believe they will go when they die.

land of the Buddha, and any house that does not have a New Year's pole belongs to the land of the spirits. In ancient times, our people told the story of a Buddha and a spirit who fought over the land. The Buddha said: "I have this 'Casa' tunic, and I can go where I wish, and that is how far my land stretches." Saying this, the Buddha took the shirt and went out to claim all the land, so the spirit had to go into the sea. Every time we reach the last day of the year, the spirits return to try to take the land. The house or its land of those who do not have a New Year's pole will revert to the spirit, and for this reason all under Heaven must have a New Year's pole. All these things vary widely.

[Bento Thien, "Lich su nuoc Annam," 119–21;
trans. George Dutton]

TRINH CUONG

EDICT REGARDING LOCAL CUSTOMS (1720)

The "Edict Regarding Local Customs," issued by Trinh Cuong (r. 1709–1729), was part of an attempt by the northern rulers to restore social and cultural propriety. It spells out a range of reforms to be implemented at the village level, from educational practices to sartorial habits to consumption patterns. The regulations elaborated here suggest both the elite concern about harmony deriving from adherence to formal guidelines for behavior, as well as what amounted to a substantial gulf between official regulations and daily practices. The meticulous delineation of dress, expenditure, and sumptuary rights and obligations indicates the importance of hierarchy to Vietnamese courts, a concern found in the records as far back as the early Tran dynasty. Regulations regarding the types of sedan chairs and parasols allotted to various official ranks had already been spelled out in 1254.[79] This edict also echoes the regulations issued by Emperor Le Thanh Tong in the latter part of the fifteenth century regarding the proper practices for marriage and mourning, two rituals seen as critical to upholding public morality.[80]

On the seventh day of the eighth month, the Trinh lord sent down an edict that stated the following:

In order to follow the essentials of governing in accord with enlightened civilization, the rectification of customs, and the provision of good government to the nation, the following clauses supersede all existing provisions, which have long since become degraded and obsolete. As such, this new edict goes beyond and replaces the previous regulations in its comprehensiveness and the extent of its clauses. It is wholly efficacious and correct to act in this manner. Crises commonly arise from abuses, and, having called for deliberation on this, we have put

---

79. See Ngo Si Lien, "Aristocratic Life" (chap. 2).
80. See "Marriage and Mourning" (chap. 3).

together the following ten clauses that we proclaim and promulgate here and beyond. All should give their utmost respect to them. By thus taking this opportunity for setting out to reform customs and practices, we further increase the people's morals and return them to what is genuine.

1. Each prefecture shall establish schools, and we authorize education officials to reside in these schools in order that they might carry out their lessons. Whether scholars or commoners, they shall esteem achieving enlightenment and shall be devoted and industrious in their study of the way of propriety, righteousness, modesty, humility, filiality, loyalty, and trustworthiness.

2. In their personal conduct, people shall clearly understand moral principles. Current marriage practices have frequently failed to adhere to the [proper] rites, the practice of marriages between the children of maternal cousins having become a common one. Henceforth, this polluting custom may not be carried out as before. Those who violate these rules will be seized for having committed a crime against ethics and morality. Members of clans of the same lineage, even though they have obeyed to the utmost and have complied with the rituals, are also prohibited from marrying each other.

3. When petty officials, soldiers, common people, servants, and the like encounter an official, they must, if they are sitting, stand up, and, if walking, yield or back up. They must not act in an arrogant, haughty, or impertinent fashion. Transgressors will be seized and taken before the authorities to be punished in accordance with the statutes governing their crimes.

4. Among the ranks of commoners, all garments must be made of silk gauze, cotton, or silk cloth. Food trays and boxes must be of black lacquer. Bowls and porcelain must be of Southern manufacture [that is, Vietnamese]. When people pray for good fortune, make supplications, or present congratulations in village shrines, they are permitted to wear dark blue-green festival clothing and hats, but the garments must not be lined or pleated. They may not transgress restrictions by using the color purple, using expensive items of gold and jade, or wearing festooned sandals, walking shoes, stockings, or slippers. When they go to present incense at large Buddhist assemblies, they also are not allowed to transgress restrictions about the usage of each type of article, including horsetail caps, parasols, umbrellas, sedan chairs, and the wheels of vehicles, as well as swords, guns, and other types of military weapons.

5. When taking a wife, in stretching the cord across the street, one should comply with precedent, paying out one string of cash and one bottle of wine. If a wealthy family wishes to make private gifts of wine or meat, the value of these items may not exceed three strings of cash, and they must not forget to follow village customs or make excessive demands. Ordinary people should hold simple and inexpensive celebrations of scholars' examination successes. No large festival may expend more than five strings of cash for wine and meat, no small one may expend more than two strings, and they may not fall back on the old ways.

6. Buddhist temples and monasteries henceforth may not, on their own accord, manufacture or cast bells or images. Only those monks and nuns who at childhood left their families to follow their aspirations to observe the Buddhist tenets [at a monastery] shall be permitted to reside there. Only those enrolled villager adult males already fifty years of age or older will be permitted to become monks. Historical vestiges and famous sites should await the receipt of formal documentation. We will permit each of the remaining Buddhist temples to have only one or two monks, and any beyond that number must be eliminated and sent home. Those who had previously followed a vegetarian diet for more than a year and shaved their heads will no longer be investigated. From now into the future, this must be complied with, and those who are in violation will be open to investigation by local officials and can be subjected to labor service among the people, so as to reduce the number of lazy idlers.

7. When prayers are offered, they should accord with the solemnity of the occasion. Only one or two head of sacrificial oxen or cattle should be offered. Discharging firearms or following other such customs, which also are transgressions whose expenses are harmful to the people, is not permitted. In regard to the items used in marriage, good fortune, or commemorative rituals, officeholders of the first rank may have no more than a total of ten head of oxen or cattle and no more than twenty settings of serving vessels. Allotments for those of the second rank and below shall be reduced proportionately: Each rank will have an additional decrease of one head of cattle and two serving vessels. The utilization of cattle by scholars and common people shall be less than that used by those of the ranked officialdom. Furthermore, ritual gifts to bereaved families may not cost more than ten strings of common cash and, for ordinary people, may not cost more than ten strings of old-style cash. Officials may use banners of woven silk or gauze as items to be used in cremations. Those of other ranks, like scholars and common people, may use only paper and are not permitted to use patterned brocade secretly.

8. During the Midautumn Festival, families in bereavement are not permitted to undertake the funerary offerings but must instead exchange chanted respects.

9. Creditors may not seize any debts from families in mourning or make any demands of them, [or] make inquiries that would hinder their filial responsibilities. Only when the mourning period is over may they press claims in accord with clear and sincere customs.

10. When a family in a village community is dealing with death and burial matters, it is not permitted to use the excuse of following local custom to inquire into issues of outstanding debts, to insist on banquets or meals, or to sign contracts requiring the sale of farm fields. Anyone who violates these stipulations will be reported to government authorities for punishment.

[Ngo Cao Lang, *LTTK*, vhv. 1321/1, 59a–61a; *LTTK*, 286–88; trans. William Pore and George Dutton]

HOANG QUANG

LAMENT FOR THE SOUTH (1777)

"Lament for the South," an epic poem of more than 860 lines, was written by the Nguyen loyalist Hoang Quang (d. 1803), a noted scholar from the Nguyen capital region around Phu Xuan. It is a literary response to the chaos surrounding the Tay Son uprising and the overthrow of the Nguyen rulers. The poem surveys the history of the Nguyen family and the evolution of the southern polity under its leadership. It then details the decline of the Nguyen, which Hoang Quang attributes to the machinations of the regent Truong Phuc Loan, who oversaw the transition to a new ruler after 1765 and continued to dominate the state into the early 1770s. The text is titled a lament and as such could be and was recited orally, simplifying its transmission within the Nguyen territories during the Tay Son years. The Nguyen dynasty's *Veritable Records of Dai Nam* reports that Nguyen Anh's sister heard a recitation of this lament and was so moved by it that she told her brother about it. Equally impressed by the poem, Nguyen Anh actively promoted its recitation among his troops. It became something of a rallying cry for the Nguyen thereafter. The excerpts here are a comment on the decline of the Nguyen and then a critique of the Tay Son brothers and their uprising.

As one eats rice, one suddenly thinks of former things,
And reflects on the patrimony of the Nguyen lords with increasing fondness.
One's feelings are moved, thinking of the virtue of our first king
    [Nguyen Hoang]
Who labored to open the roads to come down to this place.
He divided the frontier at the place of the Thay ramparts.
North and south shared a mutual boundary, [simply] changing the flag,[81]
Guarding against even the smallest crack or crevice.[82]
The warming pond's heat has already reheated the gold.
On high there are the Dao Duong [Nguyen] lords,
Below their subjects still have the heroes Gao and Gui.[83]
The ladders in the mountains and the boats at the docks all have been
    pulled back,
As long as there are people, Heaven and Earth will continue to protect them.
The title "lord" has already been transmitted through seven generations,
Fortunately, we continually wore the Heaven of Tang and Wen.[84]

---

81. "North" and "south" refer to the Trinh and Nguyen territories.

82. This is an allusion to the phrase *kim thanh thang tri*, describing strong and stable moats and walls.

83. Gao and Gui were two loyal officials who served the legendary Chinese emperor Yao.

84. Tang (V: Thang) was the first ruler of the Shang dynasty, and Wen (V: Van) was a ruler in the Zhou dynasty. Here, their names stand in for earlier Nguyen rulers.

The eighth transmission [of leadership] had recently passed to the late king.

Sash and turban had been altered; shirts and trousers also were changed.

One school of ritual music constituted a happy reunion.

People competed to cover the world in embroidered silk and to erect palace walls.

Everywhere there was peace and there was no conflict,

The gates of power were a purple red and the huts, a beautiful satin.

Mouths had rice and people patted their stomachs and all sang.

Looking at the south of Viet, one might have mistaken it for [the era of]
    Tang [and] Yu.[85]

*After having depicted what he saw as a golden age of harmony and prosperity under the
guidance of a succession of Nguyen rulers, Hoang Quang turned to an attack on those
who had contributed to undoing this idyllic time, specifically the rebellious Tay Son.*

Entering the *quy ti* year [1774], nine years had already quickly passed.

The rebellious people rose up in the region of Champa.

The lowly Tay Son official Nhac thought to take for himself the position of
    Tang and Wen.

"Aid the bright, destroy the dark" was their echoing cry.

Recklessly, they gathered iron, hammer, sword, gold, and gun.

From inside the mountains warfare burned black.

For banners they hung out tunics, and as for soldiers they pulled them from
    the trees.

They urged each other on, like packs of rats and bands of foxes,

With claws and fangs these interlopers labored side by side with the rabble of
    merchants.[86]

It was funny to see grasshoppers attacking carriages.

As for those who expected the grasshoppers to fall, who could have foreseen it
    would be the carriages that were toppled?

The great prestige that followed them was without a capital.

At their head was still a dog, nipping from behind and continually fighting and
    gobbling up.

Everywhere they went, the precious jade stones disappeared,

Officials reported that in [the prefectures of] Thang and Dien the people had
    suffered all manner of crimes.

The court was far distant and it was not easy to get news,

Resigned to escape, it departed like a wounded animal in flight.

Why is it that there were no heroes who stepped forth?

---

85. The names of two legendary Chinese emperors, Tang (V. Duong) and Yu (V: Ngu)
(ca. 2300 B.C.E.), allude to the putative "golden age" of ancient China.

86. Ethnic Chinese merchants aided the Tay Son in the early years of their uprising.

It was because mouths were full of steamed rice and because of gluttonous and greedy Buddhist pagodas.

There being no paddy rice to pour out to hinder them, the three armies attacking the rebels had to eat rice from their own homes.

Why is it that there was no order for shields and spears?

Even with shields and spears sharpened, who was there to sue for peace or lead an attack?

Never mind the hundred battles lost, or their capture of storehouses full of silver and gold.

Crack troops, frontier soldiers, coastal patrols,

We brought out but weakened troops along the Tay Son routes.

Beyond the pass, we sent them into great difficulties,

The foundations of houses and military outposts returned to the part of the offspring.

Battles spread in lowlands along the shores and in highlands among the headwaters.

Scooping up people, money, and possessions, they built up ramparts as people's reluctance grew.

As a result of deviousness, they'd assented to inhumane treatment.

Alone they wished to live, while the myriad peoples were forced to hope in vain.

If it is the case that below there is arrogance and above there is a throne, then there is none who cannot easily achieve fame and fortune.

Recalling more than any, the losses we have seen,

The country has lost half its dukes and marquis and others.

Why is it that there are no lineages of strength who bring out their talents,

Who take their livers to build ramparts and use their shoulders to construct citadels.

Only thus could we render the "hissing rebels" nameless nobodies,[87]

Spluttering spears, and frogs in wells, who boast of themselves in a deplorable plight?

Heroes have already had to come forth to aid the generation,

How is it that their talents have not yet been able to clean up this rebellion?

Despite their clever military strategies amidst a fate that puts them inside mosquito nettings,

They do not concern themselves with attacking the rebels, instead thoughtlessly attacking the people.

[Nguyen Cam Thuy and Nguyen Pham Hung, *Van tho nom thoi Tay Son*, 379–80, 386–87; trans. George Dutton]

---

87. The Tay Son rebels were sometimes called "hissing armies" because of the loud noises they made to intimidate their enemies as they traveled about the countryside.

LE HUU TRAC

DISCOURSE ON MEDICAL TRAINING (1783)

Le Huu Trac (1720–1791), whose pen name was Hai Thuong Lan Ong (Lazy Master of Hai Thuong), is among the most celebrated figures in the history of Vietnamese medicine. Family circumstances forced him to abandon the more conventional track of officialdom to return home to care for an ailing mother. During this time, he was tutored by a local doctor, and soon Le Huu Trac had earned a widespread reputation, attracting students of his own. He produced an extensive corpus of medical writings detailing many aspects of the etiology of disease, treatments, medicines, and general medical practices. These, the most important early modern Vietnamese medical texts, reflect a combination of Chinese influences and local healing arts. Le Huu Trac also was well known for his account of Vietnamese urban society and culture written during a visit to Hanoi in 1782 when Trinh Sam summoned him to treat the ruler's son, the crown prince. The following excerpt is from the introduction to *The Medical Practices of the Lazy Master of Hai Thuong*, one of his medical compendia. It describes some of the fundamental aspects of practicing the medical profession, particularly the ethics of encounters with patients.

When you study the vocation of medicine, you must adhere to and thoroughly understand Confucianist principles. Once you completely understand these principles, the study of medicine will be much easier. During my leisure time, I take out books by brilliant doctors of past and present, studying them and refusing to put them down. I can find and understand in great detail the parts written brightly and clearly and presented so skillfully and concisely. What I learn I keep in my heart, for if what I understand I have before my eyes, I can respond more naturally with my hands.

When families ask you to examine ill members, you must consider the urgency of each patient's condition in deciding when you will attend to them. First, you must not consider their wealth or status or their poverty or humble rank. Furthermore, the proper sequence should be followed when examining a patient, and when prescribing medicines, you must not distinguish between the superior and the inferior. If your heart is not entirely sincere, this will cause difficulties, for your emotions will limit the effectiveness of your efforts.

When you attend to a married woman, a widow, or a Buddhist nun, you should have an attendant close at hand; only then should you enter the bed chamber to see the ill person. The reason for this is to avoid raising any suspicions, and the same holds true even for the households of singers and prostitutes. It is essential that you guard your heart and maintain propriety, and you should regard [these people] just as if they were children of respectable and honest families and must not take advantage of them in the slightest way, as this would harm your reputation and surely result in reports of licentiousness on your part.

Once you have become a doctor, your primary concern must be to help people. You cannot pursue amusements on a whim, whether climbing mountains with alcohol in hand or going out for pleasure to see the countryside. Even when you are far from home, if people come to seek your help with a serious illness, you must accept your responsibility and yield to their wishes, and you must not be late in case the patient's life is in danger. Thus, it is essential that you recognize your responsibilities.

Encountering a critical illness and wanting to devote all your strength to curing it is a worthy intention, but you must fully explain [the situation] to the patient and his family so they understand that they must both pay for the medicine and administer it to the patient. If the medicine helps the patient, then people will realize your good intentions, but if it does not help, then they will be suspicious and resentful of you. In either case, you have nothing to be ashamed of. When preparing medications, you must place great value on selecting and purchasing the best ingredients, and you must carefully observe Lei Gong's rules[88] for pharmaceuticals and follow them correctly with respect to the season, their manufacture, and their storage. Sometimes you should stringently follow the usual methods for preparation, and at other times you must adapt to the circumstances of the illness and make the necessary adjustments. When mixing medicines, you should be careful to adhere to the ancient wisdom and ideas and not combine ingredients and test them on people. Although you should prepare medicinal potions and medical powders in advance, pills and salves are best made fresh. You then can use those that would be the most effective for the particular illness. Avoid finding yourself in a situation in which you need medicines and do not have them at hand.

When you encounter people in the same profession, it is appropriate to be modest and amiable toward them, as well as circumspect, and you must not disparage or insult them. Be respectful of those of advanced years, and treat educated people as you would your teachers. Be modest and yielding toward arrogant people. Recommend and promote your inferiors. Acting in this fashion will permit you to maintain a virtuous and magnanimous heart and enable you to enjoy benefits and blessings.

When you examine a patient from a poor family, or a widow or orphan, or someone living alone, you should pay particular and careful attention. People of wealth and rank do not worry about not having someone to look after them. But what harm would there be in giving those who cannot employ a renowned physician a single dose [of medicine], sincerely hoping that they will enjoy a life of good health? And if poverty has caused the illness of those who are filial sons

---

88. Lei Gong was the Chinese god of thunder.

or virtuous wives, then besides prescribing medicine, you should offer any assistance you can, for if they have medicine but no food or drink, they will die anyway, so you must concern yourself with all aspects of their lives in order to show your benevolent skills. However, you need not pity idle loafers or careless wanderers who are impoverished by illness.

After the ill person recovers, you must not demand generous gifts, because if you accept them, people will fear you; [this is just as true for] wealthy people whose gratitude or anger can be overwhelming. Also, if you seek glory, you are likely to have many problems. Seeking to please people only to gain substantial benefits for yourself can produce many harmful consequences. For this reason, to have the most refined techniques, you must establish for yourself moral integrity of the highest order.

By heeding the wisdom of the great sages of the past, I avail myself of their instructions to keep a heart that is compassionate and helpful, and the virtue that this produces will be sufficient. The path of medicine is a humane calling, and you must concentrate on human life. You must take pleasure from people's happiness and must accept as your only duty the task of caring for people's lives and not scheme for personal gain or calculate your achievements. Even though you may receive no worldly recompense, you will still gain the blessings that accrue to good works done in secret. A proverb says: "For three generations there will be physicians, thereafter people will surely serve as officials." Is it not true that when you do that, this will occur? I have often seen physicians of my generation or that of my parents who blackmailed the relatives of people who were dangerously ill or urgently summoned them for difficult cases in the middle of a rainy night. When the [patient] has a mild illness, they declare it to be a serious one, and when the [patient] has a serious illness, they announce that it is life threatening, and thus they deceive people to obtain benefits for themselves; this is very harmful. These physicians seriously contemplate taking advantage of wealthy people to seek profits, whereas they are completely indifferent to the poor and destitute, insensible to life or death. Alas! We must replace these ruses and deceptions with benevolent practices and must replace hearts that are humane and virtuous for these hearts of commerce. Patients who survive should reproach them, and [the souls of] those who die should be bitter toward them; they cannot be pardoned under any circumstances.

As for the matchless ambition of public recognition, I am happy to feel the clouds and water. The ancients said: "If one cannot be a wise prime minister, one can still be a good physician." For this reason, it was my intention to put all my energy into worthwhile matters, strongly emphasizing philanthropic matters and taking up medicine to serve as my heart's aspiration, so that I would not be ashamed when I raised my head [to look at the heavens] or when I bent my head [to look at the earth]. But when I encounter illnesses that lie beyond my power to cure, this is the fate of Heaven. In situations where I can act despite contrary forces but where my hands are tied, I can only watch the patient's declining strength. If I have not exerted myself with all my heart, I should not receive any reward, and there is nothing else I can do but complain and lament, which achieves nothing whatsoever. Master Yue said: "To regard the body lightly while giving great weight to riches are two incurable matters. Lacking sufficient food and clothing is the third incurable matter."[89] I have met such people; they treat others with scant regard, whereas I regard others as important, and even when I am not capable of acting suitably, I still deal with them. Oh! It is difficult to maintain both one's prosperity and one's compassion. Moreover, it is hard to exert one's strength but not be able to follow one's heart, for one can give only half of one's abilities to the medical arts.

[Le Huu Trac, "Y huan cach ngon," 1a–3b; trans. George Dutton]

LE QUY DON

INTRODUCTION TO *THE COMPLETE ANTHOLOGY OF VIETNAMESE LITERATURE* (1770S)

This excerpt is taken from the introductory essay to Le Quy Don's compilation *The Complete Anthology of Vietnamese Literature*, a volume that includes nearly 1,800 poems representing 175 poets. This text provides a useful comment on the importance of literature to the Vietnamese elite. In it, Le Quy Don examines the literary pursuits of a range of people in Vietnamese society, from rulers to monks to women. He describes the kinds of poetry being composed and the nature of these different compositions. The larger project to which this text is a preface was one in a long line of literary anthologies created by Vietnamese literati throughout the centuries. Indeed, contemporary Vietnamese scholars continue to compile such volumes. In earlier periods, such compilations were essential to the preservation of a relatively fragile literary heritage whose transmission depended on periodic recompilations. The scholars who created these compendia regularly complained that much had been lost because of Chinese invasions or simply the vicissitudes of time, though much also was destroyed by the Vietnamese themselves through domestic warfare or deliberate action. Several of the poems translated earlier in this volume are included in Le Quy Don's anthology.[90]

Emperors' education concerns the illumination of principles and the establishment of rule. Florid words are not necessary. Yet in moments of leisure, the emperor may express his sentiments by reciting verse to create harmony. Shun thus had the "Clear Cloud" ode and Yu, the lyric of the "Jade Documents." The

---

89. Master Yue is Tai Yue Ren (Bian Que), a noted Chinese physician in the Zhou dynasty.

90. See Tran Minh Tong, "Royal Poems on the Land"; "A Vietnamese Antiquity"; "The Literati's New Worldview"; "Literati Poems, Literati Concerns"; and Ho Quy Ly, "Dai Ngu and the Ming Court" (all in chap. 2).

ornateness of these works established the tradition of poetic teaching. They were followed by Han Gaozu's "Great Wind" ode, Han Wudi's "Autumn Wind" lyric, Tang Taizong's "Imperial Capital" chapter, and Song Taizong's "New Moon" verse. Their heroic talent and exceptional thoughts have moved everyone, from the past to the present.

The Viet domain has demonstrated its civility in a manner not inferior to that of the Middle Kingdom [China]. The verse that Le Tien Hoang sent to the Song dynasty's envoy, Li Jue, has a gentle beauty. Although Ly Thanh Tong and Ly Nhan Tong [apparently] could both write well and were adept at poetry, we cannot verify this at the present time, as the *Collection of Outstanding Figures of the Thien Community* has only two poems by [Ly] Thai Tong and one by [Ly] Nhan Tong.

The various emperors of the Tran dynasty greatly enjoyed reciting verse. Each had his own poetry collection, but these have scattered and disappeared. The *Collection of Viet Verse* contains only a few dozen [of their poems]. Nonetheless, the expansiveness and refinement of their verses can still be discerned. Despite the Thien terminology, we still can gain a sense of the government's standard for a moral education.

The current [Le] dynasty has expanded the empire. While Emperor Cao Hoang [Le Thai To] was working on horseback to do so, the spirit of the three poems that he composed dominated the age, and so he is comparable to Han Gaozu.[91] Le Thanh Tong preserved this inheritance; he loved to compose poetry, producing as many as one thousand [poems]. He ordered each to be capped by prominent officials, and today, these works can be found in collections. Heroic and exacting, they exhibit the brilliant spirit of an emperor and are in no way inferior to the poetry of Emperor Wu of the Han.

Since the Restoration [1592], all the emperors have displayed civil virtue. They have embellished their peaceful rule by composing lines about the landscape and offering verses to departing officials. The valiant tones and harmonious rhymes of their verses are in the same category as the Song [dynasty] master's verse about appreciating flowers and the Tang emperor's work about journeying to his residence.

Poetry and odes are composed by sages during their leisure times. I dare not offer my own praise but merely carry out the order to compile this collection. This work is divided into chapters that follow each age in succession. The initial [chapters] contain the poetry of monarchs and officials from the Ly and Tran [dynasties]. The fifth and sixth chapters respectfully record the writings of emperors from the current dynasty, and the poetry of officials and prominent literati from the current dynasty is appended to the seventh chapter onward.

Works from the Han, Wei, Qi, and Liang [dynasties], such as four-, five-, six-, and seven-line verses, odes, and Music Bureau poems all are referred to as [being

---

91. Han Gaozu was the founder of the Han dynasty.

in the] ancient style. The five-, six-, and seven-character [per line] regulated verse and quatrains dating from the Tang are called the new style. Old-style verse must have movement, while new-style verse must have parallelism. Old-style verse values loftiness and smoothness, while new-style verse values clarity and beauty. Their temperaments are therefore very different. Accordingly, people in the past said, "Regulated verse does not mix with ancient-style verse, and ancient-style verse cannot mix with regulated verse."

Following the *Complete Tang Poetry*, this work is divided for ease of reading into two sections, one [made up] of old-style and one of new-style verse. The seven-character regulated poems in the new style are listed first, followed by five-character regulated verses, six-character regulated verses, seven-character quatrains, and five-character quatrains.

Poetry was first collected during the Qi and Liang dynasties. Only [the poet's] name was appended to the poem. Information about his hometown and official position was not investigated. [In contrast,] the *Complete Tang Poetry* and the *Compiled Poetry of the Song and Yuan* provide personal information about each poet, like a small biography, in order to enhance readers' appreciation. We will respectfully follow this model.

The poetry of emperors comes first, and here is respectfully recorded information about their sagely virtue. The names of officials and Confucian scholars are listed, and information about their families, their villages, and famous sites nearby, as well as their writings, has been researched and included. Information that cannot be verified is omitted. The poetry from the Tran period also is dealt with in this manner.

Lu Donglai's *Mirror of Song Literature* categorizes writers in five ways: (1) those whose writings are strong in both form and principle; (2) those whose writings are beautiful in form; (3) those whose writings are acceptable but that people consider beautiful in form; (4) those whose writings are not beautiful in form but who themselves are virtuous in character but not well known, and out of fear that such works will be lost, a few have been included; and (5) those whose writings are not beautiful in form but from which good principles can be learned. In compiling this work, we also have humbly followed this model.

Each poet has his own style. Ministers and those who attend to the emperor write poetry that is gentle and rich. Officers and those guarding the border compose works that are austere and heroic. Poetry about scenery and the seasons favors a pure beauty. Poetry about a life of retreat in the mountains values leisureliness. Declarations of purpose must be solemn. Laments about the past must be moving. Verse offered as a departing gift must be supple and attractive. The intent must be expressed first, with tone following next. It is impossible to use such a poem in other contexts, as it is too precise.

The great poets of the past all excelled at their task, which one can see in their verse. But poetry that deals only with love or curiosities and that dwells on certain words or phrases is vulgar.

During the Hong Duc era [1470–1497], Hoang Duc Luong compiled the fifteen-chapter *Selecting the Beautiful Poetry Collection*. Its preface states,

> There are reasons why not all poetry has been passed on to later generations. Minced and broiled meat is the most delicious object under Heaven, and silk brocade is the most beautiful object under Heaven. Anyone with eyes and a mouth knows that these objects are valuable. Poetry has a beauty beyond other kinds of beauty and has a flavor that surpasses other flavors. You cannot view it with ordinary eyes, nor can you taste it with an ordinary mouth. Only poets can appreciate it. This is the first reason why not all poetry has been passed on to later generations.

> Ever since the Ly and the Tran established the kingdom, talents in each age made a name for themselves. Were such people ever lacking? Those in high government positions, however, were all too busy with official matters to take the time to compile anthologies. Meanwhile, those who had retired from office, lower officials, and scholars studying for exams paid no heed. This is a second reason why not all poetry has been passed on to later generations.

> Among these people were those who tried to make compilations. But they all eventually gave up when they found how difficult the task was and how insufficient their efforts were. This is a third reason why not all poetry has been passed on to later generations.

> During the Tran [dynasty], if poetry and prose did not obtain the royal imprimatur, it could not be published. This is a fourth reason why not all poetry has been passed on to later generations.

> These four factors have inhibited the dissemination of poetry for a long period of time, covering three dynasties. This is why even masterpieces that enjoyed the protection of the spirits have ended up piecemeal and scattered. Then some works were recorded on thin parchment and left at the bottom of a chest or case; how can we expect them to have survived intact through times of turmoil?

> The preface to Duong Duc Nhan's fifteen-chapter *Essential Poetry Collection* states, "Among the materials that I have not found are poems by top officials of the Tran dynasty. We therefore cannot follow their words in order to understand their hearts. [But] we hope that later gentlemen will collect and record them, so that we will not lose these jewels."

> The collections of both these gentlemen were like this, and now we have only half of what they collected. The rest has been scattered and lost. Oh, how regrettable this is!

> I have compiled this collection based on what I have seen and heard. This includes material from torn scrolls and abandoned stelae, which I copied and included. When compiling the best writings from a period of more than five hundred years, including the fine lines of several dozen great writers, I used all

my energy. But I still am not confident that I found everything, and hope that later generations will be able to fill in what I omitted.

Some Thien monks were good at reciting verse, such as Huizong Tangxiu. Since ancient times, people have spoken highly of them. Buddhist teachings were deeply appreciated during the Ly and Tran [dynasties], and exams often were held to test Buddhist knowledge. As a result, for a time there were quite a few literate Buddhists. Van Chieu Khanh Thien was skilled at composing verse, while both [Masters] Phap Loa and Huyen Quang produced poetry collections.

By the time of the current dynasty, Buddhist ways had dissipated. And while monks like Tung Gian early in the dynasty, or Huong Hai at the time of the Restoration, did not delve deeply into Buddhist teachings, even their writings are hard to find, so I have appended such works at the end of this collection.

While verse is not supposed to be recited in the bedroom, out of the three hundred poems in the *Classic of Songs* are quite a few by women and girls. Later, women like Yi'an [that is, Li Qingzhao] and Ximeng were praised in poetry collections, so there is no harm in collecting their poetry.

Information about the Front Palace's Kim Hoa female scholar [Ngo Chi Lan] can be found in recorded tales. Even though she was the most outstanding poet of her age, her poetry was not saved for later ages. More recently, there have been a few women who have been fairly good at composing verse and whose poetry is somewhat readable. It definitely does not have a womanly feel to it. I have appended here three such poems.

During times of peace between the South and North, poetry and prose were exchanged. During the previous dynasty, when envoys arrived, they presented poems, and the emperor responded in verse. When the envoys from this dynasty cross the border on their 10,000-league journey, they often impress scholars in the Middle Kingdom. They also exchange verse with envoys from Chosen [Korea], creating deep and lasting bonds as well as fame for themselves. Therefore, I also have appended here verse from Northerners and foreigners.

[Bui Huy Bich, *Hoang Viet van tuyen*, 3:246–59; trans. Liam Kelley]

LE QUY DON

PREFACE TO THE LITERATURE SECTION OF *GENERAL HISTORY OF DAI VIET* (1749)

To Confucian scholars, the preservation and transmission of ideas by means of the written word was of paramount importance. The *General History of Dai Viet* was an important historical summary of the early Le dynasty. In it, Le Quy Don comments on both the importance of Vietnam's literary tradition and the factors that influenced its creation and preservation. He compares the Vietnamese tradition unfavorably with the Chinese, noting that the Vietnamese produced only a fraction of the enormous output of their Northern counterparts. Le Quy Don is particularly interested in the issues related to the preservation and compilation of literary collections and notes the numerous physical and political challenges that make such efforts very difficult. In his view, this preservation is crucial, precisely because future historians and officials need to be able to examine the thoughts and experiences of those who came before them in order to be able to learn from them.

The *Classic of Changes* states, "By observing the patterns in the heavens, one can discern temporal changes. By observing the patterns in human society, one can transform all under Heaven." Lu Wen of the Tang dynasty commented on these lines by stating, "Those who wish to observe temporal changes must first establish their moral being in order to be able to discern the [correct] signs. Those who wish to transform all under Heaven must first choose words that will assist in this meritorious enterprise." How great literature is! The Five Classics and the Four Books all are masterpieces! They complement the five planets and the four celestial houses, serving respectively as the inner and the outer, the beginning and the end.

After this time [of the writing of the Five Classics and Four Books] great ministers and eminent [Confucian] scholars produced works in each age. Although some of them did not achieve complete purity, they all nonetheless resonate with the refined essence of *khi/qi* and find their source in the virtuous heart of the [correct] Way. Each has based his own teachings on what he knows. The wise and virtuous have given us writings that can broaden our understanding of myriad things, allowing us to better ourselves. Can such works then be disregarded and not read?

I have often examined the bibliographies from the Han, Sui, Tang, and Song dynasties and have seen that the number of books they produced easily exceeded a million volumes. What richness! What abundance! At that time, the palace library was extremely detailed and complete. Scholars also carefully maintained their own private collections, and works were distributed widely. Therefore, even when [the North] endured periods of war and turmoil, not much was lost.

Our kingdom calls itself [a domain of] manifest civility. Above is the emperor and below are his officials. All have engaged in writing. But when we compile their works, [we find that] these number just over one hundred volumes. Compared with writers in the Middle Kingdom, we have not produced even one-tenth of what they did. Not only is the volume of works we produced small, but our preservation efforts also have been haphazard. We do not have a central library to hold works or an official in charge of collection. The collating, copying, sun drying, and storage of books all are done without following any set rules. The scholars of each age have been concerned only with following established standards as a means to examination success. Should they come across a work from an earlier dynasty that is unrelated to their studies for the civil service examination, they put it aside and make no note of it. Or if they do copy it down, they neglect to collate it carefully. Those who are fond of collecting old books keep for themselves the works they possess and do not show them to others. Therefore, it is difficult to obtain old books and when one does, one finds that the errors and lacunae are so numerous that the works are impossible to correct. This is profoundly regrettable!

The Tran dynasty was a time of prosperity; its literature was refined and its institutional records complete. Then at the beginning of the Tran Nghe Tong reign [r. 1370–1372], the Chams invaded, burning and pillaging almost everything. For a time after that, a few works were collected again. Then when the Ho lost power, the Ming general Zhang Fu sent all books, past and present, to Jinling.[92]

Our dynasty [the Le] dispelled turmoil and established order. The famous [Confucian] scholars Nguyen Trai [1380–1442], Ly Tu Tan [b. 1378], and Phan Phu Tien [fifteenth century] together collected ancient works and lost writings. Given the destruction caused by years of war, they could obtain only four- or five-tenths of what had been written. Le Thanh Tong [r. 1460–1497] was especially fond of the [Confucian] classics and ancient texts. During the beginning of his Quang Thuan reign [1460–1469], he ordered unofficial histories, as well as works in private collections, to be collected. All were to be presented for his perusal. Then in his Hong Duc reign period [1470–1497], he ordered that lost books be found and preserved in the palace library. Those who presented rare works were generously rewarded, so books from the past gradually began to reappear.

When, however, Tran Cao created disorder [1516], and the capital was lost, people raced into the palace in search of valuables. Books and scrolls were left scattered about the streets. The Mac usurpers then collected and recopied some works. However, when our kingdom retook the capital again [1592], all the books were destroyed in the fighting. Only a few scholars who had their own collections were able to preserve them [through these times]. Oh, how unbearably regrettable!

During the more than three hundred years of the Ly and Tran dynasties, how many decrees, orders, elegies, songs, compositions, essays, memorials, regulations, and laws there must have been. Today, however, they all have been lost. The *Celestial South's [Records Made] at Leisure* records the laws, regulations, literary works, and administrative orders from our dynasty, much like the *Complete [Record of] Institutions* or a [compendium of] "important documents." But it contains only about one- or two-tenths of what there once was. Of the works compiled by erudite gentlemen, like the *Selecting the Beautiful Poetry Collection*, which was an anthology of the literary output of wise and virtuous men, we have today only the title. Its contents are nowhere to be found.

Oh, my goodness! When our sage [that is, Confucius] wanted to view the teachings of the Xia and Yin dynasties, he lamented that what remained in the

---

92. This occurred around 1406 or 1407. At that time, Jinling (present-day Nanjing) was the capital of the Ming dynasty.

kingdoms of Qi and Song was insufficient to verify [his statements]. This is only what happened to very ancient institutional records. But the abundant and flourishing records of the Western Zhou remain brilliant and verifiable. How is it then that the works from before the time of our dynasty's restoration [1592] and those of the Ly and Tran have all come to naught?

[Le Quy Don, *Dai Viet thong su*, A.1389, 63a–65a; trans. Liam Kelley]

NGUYEN HUY LUONG

RHAPSODY ON WEST LAKE (1800)

This poem, "Rhapsody on West Lake," by Nguyen Huy Luong (1740s–1808), describes a large lake in the western part of the capital, Thang Long. It was written in the vernacular script *chu nom* around the year 1800 as an ode to the prosperity and harmony said to characterize the northern Vietnamese realm under Tay Son rule. Some sources suggest that the poem was commissioned by the Tay Son emperor, Nguyen Quang Toan, rather than constituting a scholar's spontaneous reaction to the Tay Son era. Whatever the case, Nguyen Huy Luong's poem prompted a scathing reply by a fellow scholar, Pham Thai, who in "Against the Phu Poem in Praise of West Lake" mimicked the meter and rhyme of this poem to reverse its imagery and paint a bleak portrait of life under the Tay Son. This confrontation in verse reflects the divisions created by the new Tay Son regime, in which some scholars shifted their allegiance to the new dynasty while many others chose to remain loyal to the toppled Le regime in the hope that it might somehow be restored. The poem's language echoes earlier works that discuss the beauty of the Vietnamese lands. Its association of particular geographical features with historical figures and mythical spirits recalls Ly Thai To's 1010 edict regarding the establishment of the new capital at Thang Long.[93] It also includes references to the many tales of places and spirits found in Ly Te Xuyen's compilation *Departed Spirits of the Viet Realm* (1329).

How beautiful the landscape of the West Lake!
How strange the scenery of the West Lake!
Venturing to recall the time when the earth was divided into nine regions,[94]
One knows that here existed a stony hill.
Previously a white fox came and dwelled there as its den;
The Dragon King broke out and turned the hill into a large swamp.[95]

---

93. See Ly Thai To, "Edict on Moving the Capital" (chap. 2).
94. According to the *Classic of Documents*, after regulating rivers and watercourses, the legendary Chinese emperor Yu divided the land into nine regions.
95. *Tales of the Strange Collected from Linh Nam* (fifteenth century) tells the story of a thousand-year-old, nine-tailed white fox living in a cave in the mountain at the present West Lake. When the demon fox harmed local people, the king of the Water Realm dispatched his army to kill it and destroy its den, which was turned into an immense swamp.

Later, a golden ox ran into it, and it became an abyss,[96]
Where King Gao Pian disturbed the artery of the royal capital;[97]
Formerly named Dam Dam [Lake of Heavy Rains] and Lang Bac [Anchoring
   upon the Waves],[98] the lake's landscape looks as if it were an islet of stars or
   a bottle of ice.
Deeply dyed in royal blue, it looks like limpid waters emerging from an
   emerald cave;
Sinuously shaped like a silver hook, it invites an association with a silvery piece
   dropped from the moon.
More than a thousand hectares of the mixed color of water and sky are
   surrounded by flowers and grass of all seasons.
As the trace of the phoenix's beak remains observable on the hillock, one calls
   it the tower of the rising moon.
An estuary so deep a dragon could not drink it dry, people name it the bowl
   of milk.
The stone stupa is the site where immortals hide their treasures,
The mound is the place where the Chinese alien buried talismans.[99]
The temple of Gentleman Muc is always filled with burning incenses,
   commemorating his victory in capturing the tiger with his magic net.[100]
The shrine of the spirit Tran Vuu remains intact through the rainfall and
   sunshine of temporal changes, preserving the trace of his divine sword
   on the turtle.[101]
Near that wharf scintillates the temple of Thien Nien and, separated from the
   lake by forests, heaves the rapid of Van Bao.[102]
The fragrance from the Kim Lien temple flows on the ripples of the lake; the
   shadow of the Tran Quoc temple seems to imprint itself on the heavenly realm.

---

96. *Tales of the Strange* describes a golden ox spirit in the mountains of Tien Du. Since the spirit often appeared at night, a monk exorcised it by pointing his metal staff at its forehead. The golden ox ran wild and butted several places, which created ponds. Finally, it jumped into the swamp, which turned it into an abyss.

97. Gao Pian of the Tang dynasty (618–907) was the governor of the Tang protectorate of An Nam and was well versed in geomancy.

98. The lake was named Dam Dam in the time of the Trung sisters (ca. 40) and Lang Bac during the Ly dynasty (1009–1225).

99. Acknowledging the geomantic royal channels of West Lake, the Chinese general Gao Pian buried talismans there to block them.

100. It is said that during his excursion on West Lake in 1096, King Ly Nhan Tong was suddenly attacked by a tiger. At this threatening moment, the fisherman Muc Than threw his magic net and captured the tiger, which turned out to be Le Van Thinh. Le Van Thinh was an exiled official who had learned black magic and wanted to kill the king.

101. Tran Vuu is a composite Sino-Vietnamese spirit. In China, he is the god of the north. In Vietnam, he helped Thuc Phan (the would-be king An Duong) wipe out evil spirits during the construction of Co Loa citadel. It is said that his metamorphosis took place at West Lake.

102. The temple of Thien Nien is located in the Trich Sai area near West Lake, and the Van Bao rapids are east of the lake.

The shadows of the lines of old trees reflected in the water are stirred by winds,
and the school of Phung Thien[103] intuitively combines the pleasures of the
Yi River and rain altars.[104]

King Bo Cai's traces on the temple's foundation are overgrown with moss;[105]
the landscape of the temple of Ba Danh is adorned with flowers blossoming
in front of its entrance gate.[106]

This place looks dreamily like the Vulture Peak,[107] and at the edge of Hoa
village, chirping sounds can be heard from magpie nests.[108]

Those roofs give the impression of being the Peach Blossom valley[109] and,
from farms, echoes the crowing of a few roosters.

Smokes rise in curls from the Thach Khoi village's hearths, and waves rise
languidly from the rapids of Nhat Chieu.

Coming in flocks to the edge of the riverbank, merchants' boats are in full sail,
jostling like butterflies.

Resting quietly on the shores of the Co Ngua pond, the Cao Tang stupa's vault
windows are still ajar.

The pounding sounds of the Yen Thai ward's pestles clatter in frosty air,[110] and
the fishing nets of Nghi Tam village strain the winding stream.

On the other lakeshore willow branches fly idly; darting back and forth like
shuttles, orioles flirt with the two brocade-weaving wards.[111]

In the estuary rise scattered parasol-like lotus leaves; fireflies envy the fires
burning in the five villages.[112]

---

103. Located in Quang Ba, the school of Phung Thien was where the regional examinations
were held.

104. Confucius asked his disciples, "If some ruler were to know you, what would you like to
do?" Zeng Xi (Dian) replied, "I would wash in the Yi, enjoy the breeze among the rain altars,
and return home singing" (*Analects* 6:25). The custom of washing one's hands and clothes at a
river during the third month is believed to remove evil influences.

105. King Bo Cai is the popular title of Phung Hung (r. 791–799), who defeated the Chinese
Tang army in 791. The term "Bo Cai" can be translated literally as "Father and Mother," suggesting his originary role.

106. The temple of Ba Danh (Lady Danh) is located in the Thuy Chuong ward. It is said that
Lady Danh was a princess of the Ly dynasty and the founder of the ward.

107. Vulture Peak is a small mountain outside the ancient city of Rajgir, India, where the
Buddha preached.

108. In the commune An Hoa, north of West Lake, there is a temple surrounded by trees in
which magpies build their nests.

109. Tao Yuanming of the Eastern Jin dynasty (317–420) composed *The Peach Blossom
Spring (Taohuayuan ji)*, in which a fisherman accidentally discovers a valley completely isolated
from the rest of the world whose inhabitants fled the political chaos of the Qin dynasty and led
a simple and pastoral life.

110. Early in the morning, residents of Yen Thai village, north of West Lake, often pounded
paper powder to produce traditional handicraft paper.

111. The "two brocade-weaving wards" Tich Sai and Bai An are located near West Lake.

112. The five villages (*ngu xa*) are well known for bronze casting.

Cicadas sound shrilly like lutes being played,

Cuckoos' calls resonate rhythmically like the beating of wooden bells.

As breezes blow past the hill of Chau Long,[113] time-keeping drums echo along Truc Bach Lake.

When the half moon peers over Mount Phuc Tuong,[114] cold sounds of cloth beating are heard from a distance over the To River.[115]

Sightseers loiter at several places,

And idle visitors gather in groups here and there.

. . .

Now Heaven gladly blesses orthodoxy, and the kingdom opens to great examples.

The Creator's mechanism pervades every movement, and the vital force of Heaven and Earth operates as if in the auspicious time of Yao and Shun.[116]

The foundation of the royal citadel is established steadily in Long Bien, and everywhere people turn toward the throne.

The altar of Trung Trach laid the groundwork for the temple of Nguu Chu, and now all elements in West Lake's scene expose their fragrances.

Bushes of decayed grass have not yet transformed into fireflies,[117] but pink clouds have already passed the time of "grain in ear."[118]

Drawing on monthly divinations and the symbolism of the hexagram *cau*, starting from its first horizontal line, [one knows that] Heaven is sweeping all dusts away.[119]

Watching the annual natural principles, and waiting for the seven-decimeter Tuy Tan pipe to be used during the fifth month,[120] [people will see] the earth cast off the pipe's ashes.[121]

---

113. The hill of Chau Long is located by the Truc Bach pond.

114. Mount Phuc Tuong is on the south side of West Lake.

115. People washed their clothes, beating them with a pestle, on the banks of the To Lich River, which begins at West Lake.

116. Yao and Shun are two legendary emperors of China.

117. According to the *Classic of Rites* (*Liji*), decayed grass changes into fireflies from the end of the third month to the beginning of the fourth month of the lunar calendar.

118. The "time of 'grain in ear'" was from the end of third month to the beginning of the fourth month of the lunar calendar.

119. The hexagram *cau* (C: *gou* [coupling]) is the forty-fourth of sixty-four in the *Classic of Changes*. Here, it refers to the fifth lunar month. See also note 122.

120. In ancient China, the Chinese divided music into twelve tunes, with six *yin* and six *yang*, and created a series of standard bamboo pitch pipes used in ancient music. Starting from the time of the *Master Lu's Spring and Autumn Annals* (*Lushi chunqiu*, ca. 239 B.C.E.), these twelve tunes represented the twelve months of the lunar calendar. The pipe Tuy Tan (C: *ruibin*) belongs to the *yang* group and stands for the fifth lunar month.

121. According to the "Records on Regulated Calendar" (Luli zhi) in the *History of the Han*

Based on the concepts of reciprocity, when cold ends, warmth will take its place;
According to the principle of fullness and emptiness, when insufficiency is at
    an end, sufficiency will follow.
When a *yin* line appears under five lines of *yang*,[122] all beings will have
    received the favor of having been born.
As the seven rulers of the times and seasons have been settled around the
    nine-step throne, the four seasons operate in accordance with the Dubhe
    star of the Big Dipper.[123]
Reverent incense fragrances fly up to great heaven; ritual wine permeates the
    responsive earth.
As splendid auspicious five-color clouds expose themselves like two lines
    of gems and silks, let grass and trees praise the merits of Kings Tang
    and Wu.[124]
When panpipes resound from time to time below the nine-step throne, birds
    and beasts all dance to honor the power of Tang and Yu.[125]
Flowers are intermingled with five-color flags,[126] and the three-pompom
    spears are mirrored on the water surface.
When southerly breezes blow, one seems to hear harps being played, and
    species from deep waters appear as if willing to come up to pay respects.[127]
On the fifth day of the fifth lunar month, we hear resounding good wishes,
    and images of distant mountains seem to be taking a bow with three cheers.
Such rituals and music have but rarely been experienced for thousands of years,
And very few things in history can compare with this scene.
From both above and below, the leader and people find themselves in
    appropriate circumstances, just as a dragon flies through the clouds or a
    fish swims in the stream; officials gather in good order like two ranks of
    mandarin ducks and egrets watered by congratulatory wine.
All near and remote places are now united within the kingdom's territory; the

---

Dynasty (Hanshu), in order to monitor seasonal changes, people filled the pipes with reed ashes. Then, on the day marking one of the twenty-four divisions of the solar year in the traditional Chinese calendar, the ash would fly out of the pipe because of the seasonal change.

122. According to the twelve hexagrams of growth and decay (twelve *xiaoxi gua*), the hexagram *cau*, represented by five unbroken *yang* lines on the top and one broken *yin* line at the bottom (☰), stands for the fifth lunar month.

123. The sun, moon, and five planets are the seven rulers of times and seasons.

124. In ancient China, Cheng Tang (ca. sixteenth century B.C.E.) defeated the Xia and established the Shang dynasty, and King Wu destroyed the Shang and established the Zhou dynasty (ca. tenth century B.C.E.).

125. Tang and Yu are two prosperous dynasties of ancient China's two legendary emperors, Yao (ca. 2356 B.C.E.) and Shun (2255 B.C.E.), respectively.

126. The five colors of flags are correlated with the five elements and directions: green, wood, east; red, fire, south; yellow, earth, center; white, metal, west; and blue, water, north.

127. It is said that King Shun composed the poem "Southerly Wind," praising the wind for bringing peace to his people.

[king's] sincere and devout mind-and-heart makes allowances even for grass cutters and wood collectors.

Demonic air is swept away under blue banners,

Propitious light flows in front of hanging braziers.

Clearing their throats, at the rapids' end, people borrow the phrase "directing the rearing of the walls" and send it to wild geese.[128]

Singing at the end of the estuary, one chants the phrase "being on the islets" and leaves the words to wild ducks and wigeons.[129]

Similar praises seem to be found in the "Greater Odes of the Kingdom,"[130]

And the chanting tunes we hear appear as if coming from Yao's thoroughfare.[131]

We reflect on people enjoying the happiness of digging wells and plowing fields; everywhere, the young sing and the elderly dance.

We observe that animals and plants have been pacified; nowhere do we see pilfering, as by rats or foxes.

Gladly time now appears with peaceful omens; we would like the sage king to be more cautious during entertaining periods.

The streams overflow at the other side of the rapids; the water-illuminating lantern distinguishes the Jing from the Wei waters.[132]

Bushes of grass overgrow beside that temple; every sound of the drum beating that speeds up the full bloom of flowers separates fragrant grass from stinking weeds.

Surveying the scenery of the open country, one can examine the diligence or laziness of people's practices;

Looking at the water's brightness, one can scrutinize the purity or filthiness of the nature of things.

By observing swimming fish and flying birds at the fishpond and on the tower terrace, [the king] can understand the circulation and stagnation along the path of the literati.

---

128. The phrase "directing the rearing of the walls" (C: *vu vien* or *yuyuan*) is from the poem "Wild Geese" (Hongyan) in the *Classic of Poetry* ("Xiaoya," II.3.181). The phrase is cited here to indicate people's return to their hometown after the war's end.

129. The phrase "being on the islets" (C: *tai chu* or *zaizhu*) is from the poem "Fuyi" (Ducks and Wigeons) in the *Classic of Poetry* ("Daya," III.2.248). In this context, the phrase describes people's enjoyment of peace.

130. The "Greater Odes of the Kingdom" (Chu Nha [C: Daya]) is a section in the *Classic of Poetry*.

131. According to the "Chronicle of the Five Emperors" in Sima Qian's *Records of the Grand Historian (Shiji)*, during the reign of Emperor Yao, an old man was standing on a street, striking the ground, and singing in praise of the peaceful life of the time.

132. The Jing and Wei rivers in Shanxi Province differ in that the Jing is clear and the Wei is muddy. At the site of their confluence, near Xian, these two streams appear unmixed for a stretch after their junction. Analogously, the author hopes that the king will be able to distinguish the good from the bad.

Listening to singing birds and crowing roosters in villages, [the king] can tell
  which places are becoming crowded, and which deserted.
All hidden emotions have been displayed visibly and audibly;
Peaceful efficacy must start from the regulation of the family and
  self-cultivation.
When people plant rice in these paddy fields and regard them as heavenly
  sources, they should be cautious with mouse holes covered by grass;
As people have built up dikes planted with willows and solidified their
  foundation, they must be careful about ants' cracks in the dikes during
  times of high tides.
Although beautiful landscapes gather around the lake as a small complex, the
  merit of spreading out peace from here to all corners of the world is truly
  great.
I now feel shame for the shallowness of my knowledge and for the vulgarity of
  my premature nature;
I see myself as useless wood like timber of ailanthus or chestnut-leafed oak,
  and in my fifties I feel ashamed when facing the dying rays of the sun
  lighting upon the mulberry and elm.
In front of the fragrant altar, I dare not stand in the same rank with mandarin
  officials, but admiring the stunning scenery of the lake, I venture to submit
  a rhapsody in national language.
Standing by the imperial path, I face the sun, and following the rustic sounds
  of folk songs, I celebrate the long life of the precious kingly way.

  [Nguyen Cam Thuy and Nguyen Pham Hung, *Van tho nom thoi Tay Son*, 125–47;
  trans. Nam Nguyen]

PHAM DINH HO

ON MARRIAGE (LATE EIGHTEENTH CENTURY)

Pham Dinh Ho was a noted scholar and a prolific author whose life spanned the Le,
Tay Son, and early Nguyen regimes. He wrote several historical works and some geographical texts but is best known for his two compendia of stories, myths, and comments on various popular practices: *Following the Brush Amid the Rains* and *Mundane
and Random Records*, the latter co-written with a friend, Nguyen An. The *tuy but*
genre was a free-form prose style used by both Chinese and Vietnamese literati that
allowed them to compile miscellaneous information in a single volume. Pham Dinh
Ho's works are excellent examples of these kinds of freewheeling texts, and they cover
a wide range of historical anecdotes and strange tales. This excerpt on marriage rituals from *Following the Brush Amid the Rains* is representative of Ho's observations
about ideal cultural practices and the realities as they existed in late-eighteenth-century
Vietnam. Here and elsewhere, he lamented the cultural decay all around him, contrasting ancient rituals with those he witnessed, in which shortcuts and distortions of

ideals had become commonplace. While the Le Code of the fifteenth century had delineated very specific regulations for marriage practices,[133] this commentary suggests that they were frequently ignored and probably not enforced. Indeed, there are faint echoes here of Xue Zong's third-century criticisms of marriage practices on Hainan Island, which he viewed as reflecting the barbarism of the distant southern lands under Chinese authority.[134]

The ritual of marriage has been established since the time of Fu Xi, and a succession of sagely officials has fully elaborated its details, which can be seen in the *Classic of Rites*.[135] Later, Wen Gong collected these texts, deemphasizing the exchange of wealth and emphasizing the ritual of betrothal.[136] He set forth the "six rituals," and although the list of requirements was extensive, all people from the middle ranks downward carried out these tasks according to their capabilities.

In our country, those from the ranks of the higher nobility to local notables to the families of scholars performed only the three rituals of asking the bride's name and horoscope, paying the bride price, and exchanging visits. Broadly speaking, this meant using the dowry as the primary ritual and clothing as the secondary [ritual]. Finally, rarely did people choose a match and discuss the notion of virtue. The Wen Zhong master said: "A marriage that is determined by money is one that follows in the way of the barbarians, and men of refinement do not set foot into that village."[137] Oh, how true that is! In ancient times, the families of boys would send out engagement queries, and the families of girls would send letters of reply. And the only one who went back and forth between them was the matchmaker. But now the custom is no longer like this. From the time that the process begins until the time that the marriage has been completed, the bridegroom's family usually invites the entire clan to participate, and when the bride returns to her husband's family, her entire clan also comes along. The rituals concerning money, clothing, and food are carried out only as formalities. Thus, even before the wedding rites have been completed, the family fields have already been mortgaged.

In earlier times, families marrying off daughters to their new husbands would not extinguish the torch for three days while thinking about one another and their separation. Those families to whom the new daughter-in-law was

---

133. See Le Code, "Marriage" (chap. 3).

134. See Xue Zong, "Customs of the South" (chap. 1).

135. Fu Xi is the legendary Chinese founder of the writing system and other cultural practices.

136. Wen Gong was a ruler in the Zhu era best known for making heavy demands on the people under his control, to the point of setting fire to a forest to force a reluctant official to come into service rather than care for his parents.

137. Wen Zhong was a Sui dynasty ruler in the late sixth and early seventh century noted for his commentaries on the *Analects*.

returning, would not play music for three days as they worried about carrying on their family name. The ancients considered this the roots of human relations and the sources of civilization: they worked simply so as not to forget the correct way of [doing] things. How could one perform them only to please the senses?

[In ancient times], the rituals would involve the use of animal hides, and then in the time of the Zhou dynasty, people began to use marriage contracts. Later generations also had rituals for bringing the horoscope card and for exchanging names and ages and letters, all of which increased this event's cultured nature. In this respect, too, our predecessors' intentions have begun to decline.

In our kingdom, we do not have the letters of invitation, but we do have the custom of blocking the path with a reed. We have abandoned the ritual of numbers but use money and grains, and in this way [the ritual] has already become quite vulgar, even though people consider it very important. Furthermore, the folk customs are quite varied. In some places, children from neighboring villages block the road and make demands, even to the point that people must stop their carriages and identify themselves. Sometimes they are held hostage and not permitted to continue their journey until they pawn their possessions. This is truly not something that makes for a flourishing age. I often think of the two characters for "orchids and reeds," which are completely without meaning. I looked for but could not find any written references to them. Then in my readings I came across an imperial edict from the Mac dynasty's Ming Duc period [1527–1529] and then understood that "orchids and reeds" had mistakenly been rewritten as "block the road." In recent times, this has been mistakenly passed on, even though it is not true to the original. Local officials continue to circulate and use this edict, but without understanding it. One cannot help but laugh aloud.

In accordance with ritual, maternally related cousins may not marry each other. It also is true, as recorded in the *Ngoc Kinh Dai* [*Terrace of the Jade Mirror*] that since the Jin dynasty this ritual instruction has fallen into disuse. This [practice] cannot be very common, because such cousins are, in fact, first cousins on the maternal side of the family. In our kingdom, the offspring of first cousins also may not marry each other; only more distant relations may marry each other, and these customs continue to be upheld through their oral transmission. But this being the case, interactions between in-laws continue to be in dispute. Now, marriage serves as the basis for maintaining human relations, and as long as things continue in this way, it will produce chaos in all the ranks and status of the external lineage. There is no way that civilized men of great refinement in the future will be able to stand to listen to this tale.

Recently, some people have stopped mourning in order to continue with the marriage ritual of betrothal, which is extremely damaging to morality and already has been sternly rejected by the sages. When betrothal dowries are insufficient, a marriage contract is drawn up. Some cases even end up with lawsuits being filed, at which point the discussions about wealth have gone too far. How could we not end up like criminals or barbarians!

In ancient times, there was no ceremony for admitting the woman into the family, and so the *jiao* sacrifice was performed in the central hall. The family would then say their farewells. After three months, [the new wife] would return [to her family of origin], but afterward, it was improper for her to return again.

According to the *Classic of Rites*, an adoptee should wear mourning clothing for his father and mother. The ancient worthies' commentaries interpreted this to refer to males being adopted and females being married off. Thus, when his parents die, [the adopted son] must go into mourning for his adoptive father, just as he also must go into mourning for his mother. This is what this [commentary] is talking about.

[Pham Dinh Ho, *Vu trung tuy but* (2003), 92–95, 346–49;
trans. George Dutton, with Matthew Cochran et al.]

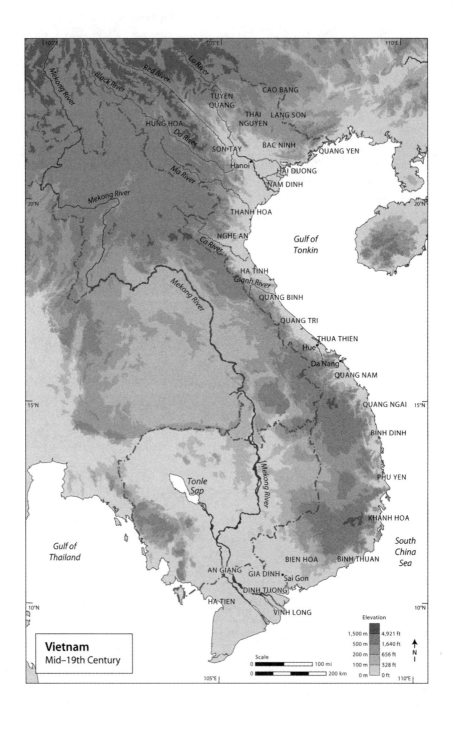

Red River

Lo River

Black River

Mekong River

TUYEN QUANG

CAO BANG

THAI NGUYEN

LANG SON

HUNG HOA

Da River

SON TAY

BAC NINH

QUANG YEN

Hanoi

HAI DUONG

Ma River

NAM DINH

20°N

Mekong River

THANH HOA

NGHE AN

Gulf of Tonkin

Ca River

HA TINH

Gianh River

QUANG BINH

QUANG TRI

Mekong River

THUA THIEN

Hue

Da Nang

QUANG NAM

15°N

QUANG NGAI

15°N

BINH DINH

PHU YEN

Tonle Sap

Mekong River

KHANH HOA

Gulf of Thailand

South China Sea

BIEN HOA

BINH THUAN

AN GIANG

GIA DINH

Sai Gon

DINH TUONG

HA TIEN

VINH LONG

10°N

10°N

Vietnam
Mid–19th Century

Scale

0 ___ 100 mi

0 ___ 200 km

Elevation

1,500 m	4,921 ft
500 m	1,640 ft
200 m	656 ft
100 m	328 ft
0 m	0 ft

N

105°E

110°E

Chapter 5

THE EARLY NGUYEN DYNASTY

The Nguyen imperial dynasty (1802–1945) emerged from the ashes of a brutal civil war fought over the last three decades of the eighteenth century. On taking power, its rulers faced enormous difficulties in establishing their authority. Thirty years of warfare had drained the country's resources and exhausted its people. Moreover, at the outset of their reign, the Nguyen rulers' legitimacy remained tenuous, and they repeatedly tried to secure a greater base of political support. Both partisans of the defeated Tay Son regime and, even more significantly, those remaining loyal to the Le dynasty in the north initially resisted switching their allegiance. Some actively organized armed resistance, while many others simply refused to offer their services to the new rulers. Socioeconomic problems also eroded the strength of the early Nguyen, as large-scale rural uprisings were a major problem into the 1830s. Finally, the Nguyen rulers needed to control the largest expanse of territory ever governed by a Vietnamese court.

The challenge of controlling a large territory was particularly intractable and, in some ways, was never fully resolved. The compromise by the first Nguyen ruler, the Gia Long emperor (r. 1802–1820), was to permit the northern and southern sections of the country, centered on Thang Long and Gia Dinh, respectively, to temporarily maintain some political autonomy under the authority of warlords answerable to the imperial court at Hue. This arrangement gave the Nguyen rulers breathing space to consolidate their authority at the center and to work on building up the court institutions. But in other respects, it merely deferred issues of regionalism, which continued to fester until the rule of Gia Long's successor, the Minh Mang emperor (r. 1820–1840).

Gia Long was succeeded not by his eldest son, Prince Canh, who had died in 1801, but by another son, by a favored concubine. The choice of Prince Chi Dam was announced in 1816 and met with considerable opposition from a court faction that favored Prince Canh's son, the emperor's grandson. The selection of Prince Chi Dam may have been based on his being eight years older than the other prince but was surely determined partly by his considerable training in Confucian learning. Some scholars argue that Gia Long also selected the prince because he was known to be hostile to Christianity and that as founder of the dynasty, he wanted a successor who would confront any challenge from the Europeans. Whatever Gia Long's reasoning, elements within the court continued to resist the choice of Chi Dam. As a result, the first years of Chi Dam's reign as the Minh Mang emperor were spent consolidating his authority while confronting opposition within the court, as well as some distrust by the largely autonomous warlord Le Van Duyet (1763–1832), who governed in the south. Another consequence of this preoccupation with court matters was that the system of political autonomy for the southern and northern reaches of the kingdom continued into the first decade of the Minh Mang reign.

Once Minh Mang had consolidated his authority, however, he began to turn his efforts to integrating the realm more fully and directly. This attempt was met with substantial resistance in the southern provinces, eventually exploding into the Le Van Khoi rebellion of 1833, in which Le Van Duyet's adopted son led an uprising against the central court in Hue. Le Van Khoi's challenge was the most dramatic manifestation of the regionalisms that underlay the new Nguyen imperial regime. Minh Mang's successful suppression of the Le Van Khoi rebellion in 1834 marked a significant turning point in the rise of centralized authority. Thereafter, Minh Mang worked aggressively to impose direct court control over the previously autonomous regions, and his edict of 1835 to the southern populations demonstrates this assertive policy. The last five years of Minh Mang's reign thus might be regarded as the apex of the Nguyen dynasty's power.

In the nineteenth century, the political commitment to Confucianist doctrine strengthened substantially, although the extent to which this permeated Vietnamese society at large is debatable. Both Gia Long and his successor sought to establish a government and a society substantially shaped by Confucian orthodoxy. This restructuring along Chinese and Confucian lines took place on a scale not seen since the height of the Le dynasty's Hong Duc reign in the last three decades of the fifteenth century. The Vietnamese court sought both to emulate and to surpass its Chinese neighbors in its efforts, which were driven partly by a desire to legitimate itself in the eyes of the literati and partly by a need to restore order to a society emerging from years of warfare and dynastic decline. This commitment to Confucian doctrine is also reflected in the Nguyen restoration of the civil service examinations, in court rituals and commemorations, and in the Nguyen rulers' paternalistic reiteration of behavioral and cultural guidelines. The rulers made an extensive effort to stamp out unorthodox religious practices as well as excessive expenditures on village and family celebrations. Early in his reign, Gia Long issued a lengthy edict (1804) in which he offered a detailed survey of various cultural excesses and improprieties and announced new regulations to curtail these practices. The edict also sought to curb lavish spending for local rituals and to halt the practice of what were regarded as unorthodox religious observances. Three decades later, in 1834, as part of his consolidation of central authority, Minh Mang issued another edict in which he standardized the state's expectations of proper behavior and conduct through ten moral maxims. These maxims were to be read each year to all villagers, as a reminder of what the court expected from them.

While internal stability was a chief concern of the Nguyen rulers, Europe's growing attention to the Asian mainland became a problem as well. In the nineteenth century, the Vietnamese court was characterized by a peculiar combination of engagement with and distancing from the European powers. The early Nguyen rulers kept a number of Europeans in their employ, including several holdovers from among the French missionaries and mercenaries who had helped the Nguyen defeat their Tay Son rivals. At the same time, Hue was concerned about Europe's increasing interest in various parts of Southeast Asia. Both Britain's colonial conquest of Burma (Myanmar) and its challenges along the Chinese coast were seen as possible signs of danger. While not entirely closing off their country to foreign trade and influence, the Nguyen rulers nonetheless sought to keep the Europeans at bay. In 1840, Minh Mang issued an edict in which he noted the plight of the Qing court, which was forced to yield to European demands for ports and trading access in the aftermath of the First Opium War. The Vietnamese ruler observed that the Chinese had been too lenient in permitting the Europeans access to their country, a mistake the Vietnamese would try to avoid, thus steering clear of the Qing court's problems.

Although this stance was in some ways naïve, the Nguyen rulers had not merely buried their heads in the sand. Indeed, Minh Mang and his successors made numerous efforts to learn more about the Europeans, including sending officials to visit European colonial outposts in Southeast Asia. The literatus Phan Huy Chu, for instance, traveled to Singapore and Batavia in 1833 and wrote a report of his impressions of the European colonies there ("Summary Record of a Sea Journey"). In 1847, the Thieu Tri emperor (r. 1840–1847) sent a diplomatic mission to Paris, partly as an attempt to negotiate with the French, but also to gain information about challenges faced by his court. Then, in the 1860s, the Tu Duc emperor (r. 1848–1883) sent several missions to France, one of which included Nguyen Truong To (1828–1871), a noted advocate of reform, who drafted numerous memorials urging radical political and social changes based on what he had seen and read while abroad. Although Nguyen Truong To's was a lonely voice for reform in Tu Duc's court, it represented a singular perspective, for he was both a trained Confucian scholar and a Catholic who had received some education in mission schools. Nguyen Truong To's sweeping advocation of the implementation of a new vernacular writing system, the transformation of the educational system, and greater freedom of religion, among other matters, was well ahead of its time. But even if the emperor had wanted to carry out any of these changes, there was a strong sense that their implementation would remove the very underpinnings of the court's legitimacy, which were strongly tied to conventional Confucian education and ritual.

The nexus of Vietnamese engagement with the Europeans was the French missionaries, whose numbers and determination increased during the 1830s and 1840s. Even though Gia Long had tolerated the missionaries' presence, he had done so in the Napoleonic years, during which France was preoccupied with events in Europe and few missionaries went to Vietnam. Then, both the post-Napoleonic peace in Europe and the rise of French religious fervor in the mid-nineteenth century contributed to the growing missionary activity in Asia, including Vietnam. Although Christianity was perceived as corroding Confucian bonds and familial relationships, the Nguyen rulers were not as concerned about its doctrines as about its contribution to political factionalism. Their concern stemmed from a feeling of weakness and fear of Christians' participation in internal politics, in particular their siding with court factions or regional forces allied against the emperor. Despite the court's pragmatic concern, imperial edicts opposing the religion were couched in ideological terms, invoking Christianity's contributions to disrupting the social order. We have included here an extended critique of Christianity by the Minh Mang emperor after two officials refused to renounce their faith, arguing that to do so would be unfilial to their Christian fathers.

The increasing persecution of Christians, in the form of both edicts and, in some cases, the execution of missionaries, provoked outrage in France, which in turn served to justify more aggressive French imperial actions against Vietnam. Persecution of missionaries, however, was little more than a convenient rationale for French intervention. Although subsequent French demands did include the protection of missionaries and their freedom to preach, these appear almost as afterthoughts in long lists of other demands focused on trade, unfettered access to the Vietnamese territories, and the establishment of military installations. Moreover, the French dusted off the never-fulfilled treaty between Nguyen Anh and Louis XVI as evidence of French territorial claims in Vietnam.[1] Even though the French claim rested on spurious legal grounds, the treaty nonetheless proved to be a useful tool during the internal French debates about whether and why to intervene. Meanwhile, there were fierce debates at the Nguyen court as well, regarding how best to respond to the French encroachment. The rationale of the so-called peace faction is central to the 1862

---

1. See "Treaty of Versailles Between Nguyen Anh and King Louis XVI" (chap. 4).

text "Debating French Demands," arguing that resistance to the French would be futile and a temporary accommodation to French demands would be a more pragmatic response.

The independent dynasty of the Nguyen came to an end during the lengthy reign of the Tu Duc emperor (r. 1848–1883), who came to power only to face an uprising from court factions loyal to another member of the royal family. Even though Tu Duc succeeded in suppressing the uprising, it was an inauspicious start to his reign. Moreover, there had been suspicions that the rebels had been in contact with Vietnamese Christians, once again raising concerns about Christian involvement in political actions that challenged the throne. This, not surprisingly, led to additional crackdowns on Catholic missionaries and their Christian followers, a move that further fueled French antagonisms.

Despite the political turmoil it faced, the Nguyen dynasty saw a remarkable outpouring of literary texts, at both the official and private levels. At the private level, a wide range of scholars across the country produced historical accounts and local gazetteers. In fact, gazetteers became very popular in the nineteenth century, examples of which survey the entire realm and individual provinces or regions. These texts are particularly valuable for having preserved many local tales and traditions and for providing information about prominent local figures, whether military heroes, notable scholars, or even the mothers of important historical figures, as in Tran Dam Trai's "Two Noteworthy Women." The Nguyen court itself oversaw the production of numerous large-scale projects to compile histories, biographies, ritual manuals, and geographies, all the while keeping detailed records of daily court affairs. Indeed, the outpouring of texts in the nineteenth century represents a remarkably rich written legacy of the Nguyen dynasty. The wealth of material from the nineteenth century reflects its greater proximity to our own time, but it also reflects a period in which the Nguyen court was intent on establishing its legitimacy. Its production of these texts was a significant part of this legitimation project.

The early Nguyen period is, regrettably, often viewed as merely a prelude to European intervention and French colonization. The readings selected here attest to the European presence and include texts relating to Christianity, encounters with Europeans, and the negotiations that resulted in the loss of the six southern provinces. Most, however, focus on other issues, from the significant writings of the greatest nineteenth-century literatus Phan Huy Chu on taxation and natural resources, to the edicts concerning domestic politics issued by the Gia Long and Minh Mang emperors. Other texts deal with imperial concerns about morality and behavior. We also offer several extended excerpts from Trinh Hoai Duc's *Gia Dinh Citadel Records*, a detailed gazetteer of the Gia Dinh region that describes customs and cultural practices in the southern realm. This we contrast with selections from Truong Vinh Ky's description of his 1876 trip to the northern reaches of the country, in which he comments on cultural and social practices in and around Hanoi. These two readings, in particular, bring

to life Vietnamese daily practices and beliefs, making concrete what often remains abstract in the more rarified documents produced by emperors and other
elites. In both instances, the accounts are produced by scholar elites, but it should
be fairly clear that their descriptions ring true, reflecting firsthand knowledge of
ordinary people's daily lives. We hope that the documents selected for inclusion
here make clear that in the nineteenth century, the presence of Europeans and
their increasing interest in Vietnam were not yet defining features of the Vietnamese worldview. Although Vietnamese rulers had to contend with these challenges, until the 1870s or early 1880s a great many other issues concerned them
and attracted the attention of the Vietnamese literati.

THE LAND

GIA LONG EMPEROR

NAMING THE COUNTRY VIET NAM (1804)

Although touching only on a brief episode in the history of the early Nguyen dynasty,
the following edict deals with a significant element of Vietnamese national identity. It
marks the moment at which the court formally adopted the name by which the country is known today. Before the early nineteenth century, the country called itself Dai
Viet (Great Viet). This term of self-reference was not, however, adopted by its neighbors, most notably the Chinese court, which persisted in calling the Vietnamese state
An Nam (Pacified South). Ironically, the very name Viet Nam set forth by the Nguyen
emperor in this edict was bestowed by the Chinese themselves. Immediately after
coming to power in 1802, the Nguyen had sent a diplomatic delegation to the Qing
court, requesting permission to call their country Nam Viet (Southern Viet). To the
Chinese court, however, this name had defiant historical overtones, for it recalled a
third-century B.C.E. southern kingdom that had resisted Chinese authority. It seemed
to suggest that there might be "Viets" both north and south of their mutual border,
hinting at the possibility of Vietnamese territorial claims on Chinese lands. Moreover, the Quang Trung emperor had recently threatened a military campaign to "recapture" the two southern Chinese provinces of Guangdong and Guangxi, which
also made the Chinese particularly sensitive to this possibility. Consequently, the
Qing court insisted that the Nguyen reverse the order of the terms to Viet Nam, the
present-day name of the country. Interestingly, the term was largely ignored by both
the Vietnamese and the Chinese through most of the nineteenth century, with the
Chinese continuing to use the name An Nam, and the Vietnamese reverting to Dai
Viet in 1813 and later adopting Dai Nam, a name formalized under the Minh Mang
emperor.

On the *dinh suu* day, the matter of establishing the national name as Viet Nam
was brought before the imperial court. At the imperial palace, the emperor accepted the court's congratulations and then issued a proclamation to be distrib-

uted to inform those both inside and outside [the court]. The edict stated: "When the ancestral emperors founded the country, they first had to decide on a name for the nation in order to clearly express its unity. In examining our lineage of ancestral sage kings, we see that they established the foundations and, in the beginning, devised the earth and fire sacrifices, and opened the territory of Viem Bang, which comprised the lands from Viet Thuong southward.[2] At that time they used the character 'Viet' to serve as the name of the country. For more than two hundred years, continuous harmony and great brilliance in abundance were recorded. The gods and spirits transmitted, continued, and protected these foundations, and both inside and out all was calm because of this good fortune. Then suddenly, the country's fortunes encountered hardship, and at this time, although we regarded ourselves as small in person, we were concerned with pacifying rebels and disorderly attacks. Relying on the help granted us by the spirits, we have been able to continue our mandate after the interregnum, and the entirety of our enfeoffed territories of Giao Nam has been returned to our domain. The extreme difficulties are obvious, so we intend to make intense efforts at upright conduct to bring about renewal. Accordingly, we chose the seventeenth day of the second month of this year to respectfully announce at the temples of the imperial palace a change in the country's name to 'Viet Nam' in order to establish the great foundations, which will be bequeathed to the distant future. All matters of state pertaining to the name of the kingdom and all the documents that we send to inform foreign countries will use Viet Nam to serve as the name of the country, and they are no longer to use the old name of An Nam." [The emperor] also sent down this edict to be announced to the countries of Siam and Luzon and to the dependent states of Cambodia and Laos so that they might all know of it.

[*Dai Nam thuc luc* (hereafter, *DNTL*) (1961–), 3:646–47; *DNTL* (2004–2007), 1:588; trans. George Dutton]

MINH MANG EMPEROR

NAMING THE COUNTRY DAI NAM (1838)

By 1838, the Minh Mang emperor had fully consolidated his authority and had brought the previously semiautonomous northern and southern parts of the country under his direct authority. The decision to adopt a new name for the country was made in part to reflect this new era of unity. It also was a way to underscore the reality that the realm's southward expansion had reconfigured its geographical orientation. The emperor justified this action by noting that Chinese courts had similarly changed the terms used

2. Viet Thuong is a term for the Vietnamese territories, derived from the name of a southern people who presented tribute to the Zhou dynasty court. It was appropriated by Vietnamese historians to refer to the pre–Han dynasty Vietnamese realm and is used in the *Short Record of Annan* and later texts.

to describe their realm, in part to reflect changing times. As the decree points out, the term "Viet," which had been part of the national name since the tenth century, would remain at least an implicit part of the nation's name. In contrast, the shift to using the name Dai Nam allowed the Vietnamese court to step away from Viet Nam, which it had adopted reluctantly in 1804 after it was bestowed on it by the Chinese court. Although the Vietnamese shifted to using the name Dai Nam on internal official documents and texts, the court retained Viet Nam for its official interactions with the Chinese court.

Since the time of the Great Ancestor, the Gia Du emperor [Nguyen Hoang (r. 1558–1613)], our state was able to establish its foundations in the southern regions. And the succession of sagely rulers steadily enlarged the realm, governing and controlling the lands of the Viet Thuong;[3] previously, the country was called "Dai Viet" by the Central Plains [that is, China], and the calendars and books also gave precedence to these two characters. In the past, the characters "An Nam" were used to distinguish them from [those] for the name "Dai Viet." Upon reaching the era in which our Exalted Ancestor emperor brought the country of An Nam under his control, he chose "Dai Viet Nam" as the name of the country, but the calendars and books still used the two-character simplification "Dai Viet," which, on principle, did no harm. Only the ignorant who, seeing the calendars of the An Nam kingdom of the successive Tran and Le dynasties featuring the words "Dai Viet," erroneously saw the two terms as interchangeable, which provoked perplexity and astonishment. This was not a trifling matter for the state's prestige. We examined all the past eras, such as the Tang and Song dynasties and even earlier ones, which used the territory under the king's control to serve as the name of the [governed] realm under Heaven. The Yuan and the Ming, both of which disliked following the old names, selected beautiful words to serve as their states' name. Finally, during the era of the great Qing, the original name, "Manchu," was later changed to "great Qing." In all these instances, the names of the country responded to the needs of the times, and all were derived from a sense of righteousness. Now our court has put the southern regions under its control and is constantly expanding these territories. From the shores of the seas to the feet of the mountains, all these lands are being brought under our command. Earlier the territory was called "Viet Nam," but now we shall call it "Dai Nam," which will increasingly clarify and expand its righteous name while implicitly keeping the character "Viet" in the name. The kingdom thus shall be known as "Dai Nam," so the records and calendars must be changed to use the characters "Dai Nam."

[*Minh Mang chinh yeu* (hereafter, MMCY) (1972), 1:44a–45a;
MMCY (1994), 1:61; trans. George Dutton, with Joshua Herr]

---

3. Both Viet Thuong and Trung Nguyen described ancient or mythical realms associated with Vietnamese and Chinese territories, respectively.

LE QUANG DINH

VIETNAMESE GEOGRAPHICAL EXPANSION (1806)

The Geographical Records of the Unified Imperial South was produced early in the Nguyen dynasty by Le Quang Dinh (1759–1813), a close confidant of the Gia Long emperor. He had actively supported Nguyen Anh during his campaigns against the Tay Son in the 1780s and 1790s. Le Quang Dinh had also served as a member of the Nguyen embassy to China in 1802, which had sought recognition of the new Vietnamese rulers. This gazetteer provides detailed measurements between localities throughout the realm rather than the conventional practice of focusing on geographical features, cultural monuments, and prominent local residents. Thus it is a very practical guide for the Vietnamese court or others calculating distances, borders, and administrative boundaries. This excerpt is from the introduction to the text and expresses an early-nineteenth-century scholar's view of the territorial expansion of the Vietnamese state, an expansion that reached its apogee under unified Nguyen rule.

I observe that the *Rites of Zhou* records that Zhi Fangshi preserved the registers and prepared records of the distances of that under Heaven and that these were presented to the ruler. The lower officials complied with the king's decree to receive them. This [practice] has continued since the Han and Tang dynasties and through successive generations that kept records. Consequently, how can one exaggerate the extensiveness of the lands and peoples? Now that the people already are many, we must determine which mountain and river routes are difficult and which ones easy and whether each route is long or short. We must determine the boundaries of the borders and cities and discover all the details concerning the rivers and seas. Then the ruler will gradually be able to comprehend everything by unrolling a single map, and all will be arranged in his grasp. Once he fully controls all under Heaven, there will be no deficiencies.

From the time of the state's founding by the Dinh clan, our Viet emperor has stood together side by side with the Northern court. The Southern country's rivers and mountains already had been divided and settled in the registers of Heaven. As the Ly and the Tran dynasties followed each other, the imperium was very broad. To the north, our national boundaries abutted the interior territory [China], and to the extreme south they reached as far as Nghe An. To the south of Thanh Ha lay Champa, and to its south lay Zhenla [Cambodia]. During the middle of the Tran period, there was a further expansion incorporating the two counties of O and Ly, although these were held in name only. Then during the Le dynasty's Quang Thuan and Hong Duc reigns [1460–1497], there was a great attack on Champa, invading as far as the northern edge of the Thach Bi mountains. Prefectures and districts were established, and an effort was made to resettle people from the north in this area. The land from the Thach Bi mountains southward remained the territory of Champa and Zhenla. Then, from the time of our Great Ancestor emperor [Nguyen Hoang], the ruler's true foundations were marked by the flooded fields of the southern region, and from Thanh Ha southward these were separated to become a single country. The ranks of talented and virtuous ministers followed in succession, and the attributes of civilization flourished while military feats continued to increase. Our first ancestral emperor belonged to the ranks of great military leaders and began to open Champa's territories. He moved his people into the mountainous regions of Binh Thuan. He reorganized the towns in Thuan and Thanh and enfeoffed their tribal chiefs as hereditary kings in order to provide comfort to their common people. The sounds of Heaven resonated in all four directions, and the neighboring realms were greatly frightened as we succeeded in unifying the lands of Water Zhenla [Mekong Delta region] to create the prefecture of Gia Dinh. At that time, although our territory to the south was gradually expanding, to the north, the Le family remained, whose country was our close neighboring state. During the great disorder of the *giap ngo* year [1774], the country went into decline. Our subjects from Tay Son took this opportunity to rise up and attack, and they usurped authority and then seized the territory. Furthermore, they attacked and drove out the Le family. All the land, from its damasks and brocades to its rivers and mountains, was seized by rebellious bandits, who made it their own. Our supreme emperor was forced to submit to a time of wandering, sojourning to foreign lands while continuing to plan his restoration and return. In the *dinh mui* year [1787], he came back from Siam and, in the *mau than* year [1788], was able to recover Gia Dinh. Then, in the *tan dau* year [1801], he restored the old capital [Phu Xuan]. Then, under the reign title of Gia Long, in the *nham tuat* year [1802], he attacked to the north, captured the false rulers, and completed the pacification of the northern region. Now, after more than two hundred years, those borders and edges have all been brought together, in the north as far as Lang Son and in the south as far as Ha Tien. There are large and small units, market towns and military encampments: thirty in all, unified as one, all becoming units of imperial cultural enlightenment. It is true that in our country of Viet, from ancient times to the present, this territory had never before been as broad and vast as this.

[Le Quang Dinh, *Hoang Viet nhat thong du dia chi*, 1836–28, 11–12;
trans. George Dutton]

NGUYEN VAN SIEU

TALES OF THE COUNTRY OF CAMBODIA (1862)

The expansion of Vietnamese political authority into the southern reaches of the Indochinese peninsula led to a growing need for information about this region and its people. The number of gazetteers grew during the nineteenth century. They gathered information about all parts of the country and the histories of the peoples whose territories had been taken over by the Vietnamese, especially the Chams and the Khmers. The following excerpt from *The Complete Compilation of the Geography of Dai Viet* recounts one of the Khmer foundation myths describing the origins of the Cambodian state when it was known to the Vietnamese as Zhenla and relates some of the earlier history of this region. Nguyen Van Sieu (1796–1872) was a noted scholar and native of the Hanoi region who filled a series of high-level posts in the Nguyen state's educational hierarchy. He also was part of an embassy to China in 1849. Nguyen Van Sieu submitted a number of recommendations for administrative reforms, and when they were ignored he left his position to spend the rest of his life researching and writing. *The Complete Compilation* is probably his best-known text, although he also wrote a number of pedagogical works.

In ancient times, Cao Man, which also is called Zhenla [Cambodia], originally belonged to the country of Funan. In the Qin period, the people of Funan were the barbarians beyond the southern boundaries of the territory of the Tuong commandary and, during the Han period, of the commandary of Nhat Nam. Then it was a neighbor of Lam Ap and was in the region of the great waters of the Western Sea to the south of the commandary of Nhat Nam. That country was several thousand *li* [one *li* is approximately one-third mile] in circumference, and the capital was five hundred *li* [175 miles] from the ocean. It had a large river that was more than ten *li* [3.5 miles] wide and flowed toward the sea from the northwest to the east. The land was low, flat, and broad, and the climate was warm in the winter, with many clouds. For this reason, the mountains were called the Misty Warm mountains, and broadly speaking, the land was quite similar to that of Lam Ap.

There is a tale as follows: A woman named Lieu Diep was the first ruler of this country. A man from the country of Khich named Hon Dien dreamed that a spirit had given him a bow. When he awoke, he found the bow under a tree in the temple to this spirit. He went directly across the sea to a place outside the capital of Funan, where Lieu Diep summoned all her troops to attack him. Hon Dien took his spirit bow and shot an arrow that squarely struck the enemy boat's commander. Lieu Diep became frightened and surrendered, and Hon Dien took her as his wife and seized control of her country. They produced seven sons, each of whom ruled over the country's cities, and they and their heirs succeeded one another for six generations. Then a general named Pham Tam emerged as the king of Funan. From the Han period onward, Funan was cut off by the country of Lam Ap, so envoys from Giao Chau could not reach it. Then in the Sun Wu era [Eastern Wu (222–280)], a palace attendant named Khanh Thai traveled as an envoy to that country, where he studied its people, whom he ridiculed because all of them were naked. After this, Tam ordered his sons to wear long gowns; wealthy people wore brocade; and the poor wore cotton. In the time of the Jin dynasty's martial emperor, during the Tai Kang reign period [280–289] that country sent an envoy to offer tribute, and in return its ruler was enfeoffed as the king of Funan. Later, a Brahman from India named Kieu Tran Nhu dreamed that the spirits told him that he should become the king of Funan. So he traveled south to the land of Ban Ban, and when Funan heard of his reputation, he was welcomed and installed to serve as their king. They then changed their practices to follow the laws of India, and through the [earlier] Song, Qi, and the Liang dynasties, India regularly sent tribute. In the third year of the Dai Dong reign [538 C.E.], the king heard that [Funan] had a Buddha whose hair was one *truong* and two *thuoc* [fifteen feet] long, so he sent an envoy to go there to look at it. Because Funan venerated the Buddha, during the Liang [502–557] era the court sent many decrees praising it. Thereafter, Funan gradually became weaker and was finally taken over by Zhenla.

The country of Zhenla was also called the country of Wendan and was known too as the country of Cat Miet. The name of its founding clan was Sat Loi, and the clan leader was named Chat Da Tu Na. Starting with this ancestor, the country gradually had become strong and prosperous. By the time of Chat Da Tu Na in the era of the Chen and the Sui dynasties [557–618], it had already invaded and taken control of Funan. During the Tang dynasty, at beginning of the Zhenguan reign era [627–649], it had taken all the lands of Funan. And all the neighboring principalities, including Tham Ban, Chu Giang, Thu Mai, Can Da Loi, and Sich Tho, became frontier outposts of Zhenla. (The *Sui Dynasty History* [*Sui shu*] states that "the country of Can Da Loi is on the edges of the Southern Sea, and its customs are like those of Funan and Lam Ap. Its local products include cotton and areca palm, with its areca palm being of the highest quality of all countries. To reach the country of Ba Loi, [one must go] from Giao Chi across the ocean and across all the countries of Dan Dan, Ban Ban, and Sich Pho to reach its border; and then stretching from east to west, it takes two months, and from south to north, it takes forty-five days.")[4] According to the histories, Ba Loi is the Siam of the present time, or essentially its equivalent. Trinh Hoai Duc's work [*Gia Dinh Citadel Records*] states that the territory of Ba Dia is the country once known as Ba Loi, but it is not yet certain if this is true. Perhaps it was the country of Can Da Loi, and Sich Tho was the present-day province of Bien Hoa.

After the Than Long reign period [705–707], this country was divided into two parts. The very mountainous northern part was called Land Zhenla; its territory stretched for more than seven hundred *li* [245 miles]; and its king was called Dat Khuat. And the southern half, which was directly on the ocean and had many sloping, watery fields, was called Water Zhenla; it stretched for more than eight hundred *li* [280 miles]; and the king resided at the capital of Ba La De Bat. During the Tang dynasty, these two countries came to present ritual tribute, and both their rulers were enfeoffed as kings. Around the time of the Zhenyuan

---

4. This parenthetical note is in the original text.

reign era [785–805], they regularly sent several dozen tame elephants from the southern Kinh Son mountains to serve as tribute. In the Song period, these two countries came together to form a single country called Zhenla [Cambodia].

[Nguyen Van Sieu, *Dai Viet dia du toan bien* (n.d.), A.72, no. 53; *Dai Viet dia du toan bien* (1997), 312–30; trans. George Dutton]

PHAN HUY CHU

HA NOI / SON NAM (1833)

Phan Huy Chu (1782–1840) was a scion of one of the most illustrious literary lineages of northern Vietnam. His father, Phan Huy Ich, was a noted pro–Tay Son literatus. Phan Huy Chu is best known for his *Categorized Records of the Institutions of Successive Dynasties*, but he also wrote other significant works. The three sections here, from the *Records of the Imperial Viet Territories*, written in the 1820s, are examples of the genre of geographical compendia, which became quite popular in the nineteenth century. The first excerpt contains a geographical and historical description of the northern capital—Hanoi—and its numerous subdistricts. The text focuses on the area's lakes, rivers, and mountains, all of which played important mythical and historical roles in the development of Ha Noi. Besides tracing the changing names used for the capital and its topography, the text describes significant historical events associated with particular locales. It relates, as well, important legends linked to the capital region, including that of the founder of the Le dynasty's use and later return of a magical sword to a giant turtle living in a lake in the center of the capital, now called Hoan Kiem (Restored Sword) Lake.

In earlier times, Ha Noi was called the city of Thang Long. The capital of many dynasties, it lies in the territory of Phung Thien Prefecture. At present, this place is referred to as the Thang Long city area. It has 11 military districts, 31 prefectures, 115 districts, 29 counties, and 1,053 cantons, each consisting of several villages, as well as 7,413 smaller divisions of territory, including villages, urban wards, and upland settlements.

Long ago, the area around Ha Noi belonged to the Kingdom of Lac Long. During the Qin dynasty [221–209 B.C.E.], it became the Department of Nam Hai. In the Han dynasty [206 or 209 B.C.E.–220 C.E.] the area became the Department of Giao Chi, and during the Tang dynasty [618–907] was changed to Giao Chau, or Giao County. Up to the Dinh and earlier Le dynasties [968–1008], it was sometimes called a circuit and sometimes a prefecture. The villages of Lam Dong, Duong Lam, and Phu Liet all were part of this area. During the Ly dynasty [1009–1224], the area was split up to create several circuits, [and extending] into the Tran dynasty [1225–1400], these circuits were known as Thien Truong, Kien Xuong, Ung Thien, Ly Nhan, Tan Hung, Khoai Chau, Truong An, Long Hung, Dai Hoang, and An Xiem. Sometime in the middle of the Quang Thuan reign of the Emperor Le Thanh Tong [1460–1469], Le dynasty [officials] mandated that Thien Truong serve as the seat for governing and managing all prefectures and districts. When they drew the map, they changed the name of this area to Son Nam, consisting of nine prefectures and thirty-six districts. Around the beginning of the Canh Hung reign of Emperor Le Hien Tong [1740–1786], Le dynasty [officials] divided Son Nam's prefectures, districts, and villages into two circuits, upper and lower.

Tri Mountain lies in the western part of Son Nam. To the east, Son Nam borders the sea. Kinh Bac and Hai Duong border Son Nam to the north and northeast. Thanh Hoa lies to the south. The terrain is broad and expansive, the people's circumstances flourish and prosper, and thus this area ranks the highest of the four provinces.

All Son Nam has an outstanding natural beauty. The inhabitants of the upper circuit have a reputation for being cultured, although lately they seem to be in decline. The lower circuit has many material things, but its people are rough and superficial. One could say that cultural/literary pursuits thrive in the upper circuit while rather attractive material riches prosper in the lower circuit. These represent the capital city's protection and support, and the country's storehouse.

Hoai Duc Prefecture (excerpt)

Thuong Phuc is the most lively of the three districts in the area of Thanh Tri renowned for its literary achievement. At present, twelve degree holders come from Thanh Tri, fifty from Thuong Phuc, and six from Phu Xuyen. Many famous officials are from Thuong Phuc, including a second-place finisher in the metropolitan examinations from the Nguyen lineage of Lan Xuyen, who himself was a first-place finisher when the country was founded, as well as the first-place metropolitan examination candidate from the Nguyen family of Nguyet Ang. At the time of the [Le] Restoration, many outstanding learned people came from this region, including members of the Bui family of Dinh Cong.

The great lineages of Son Nam have produced many notable laureates. The region, including Long Hoang and Nhi Khe, has been the most productive in regard to examination candidates. Thinh Duc and Linh Duong each have produced learned and skilled people up to the present day. The popular customs of the people of this region are, on the whole, distinctively civilized. In industry and small handicrafts, they have increasingly demonstrated their dexterity and expertise. Whether it is carpentry in Nhi Khe, lacquerware in Van Giap, hat weaving in Vinh Hung, or aquaculture in Ngoc Nu, it seems that whatever Son Nam people do, they always prove to be clever and sophisticated.

At Cung Hoang village in the district of Thanh Tri, Chu Van An (later honored with the title of duke) built a thatched dwelling facing the riverbank, a place to which many scholars and students were drawn. After [his death], a temple to honor him was built in the village, and it survives to this day. Nhi Khe village in the district of Thuong Phuc is the home of Nguyen Trai's father, who used to build houses there. He later raised Nguyen Trai, a man of talent and ability who helped Le Thai To's righteous uprising. [Nguyen Trai] was enfeoffed as the Kai duke of state and appointed as an official. When he died, the people of the village built a temple to honor him. Thinh Duc village in Phu Xuyen District has many storied lineages. The villages of Cuong Duc and Lang Xa also have been noteworthy in this regard through many dynasties.

Next to Linh Duong village in Thanh Tri District is a lake with water as clear as glass. In that village lived a woman of the Nguyen family who became a wife of Lord Trinh Nghi To. She gave birth to Trinh Thanh To.[5]

Bo Dau temple in Bo Dau village, Thuong Phuc District, was built in honor of the great saint Huyen Thien. According to local legend, the mother of the Celestial King had been abducted by the water dragon. The king then descended from Heaven to catch and kill the dragon. Although the creature had already fled, it left behind footprints. The villages of Huu Dinh, Nhue Giang, and Hop Kham erected a commemorative temple, which was recorded in the *Records of Upper Son Nam*.

In the winter and spring, the rivers of Son Nam become quite dry. But in the fall and summer, they can be navigated by a small boat. During the Tang era [dynasty] while Gao Pian controlled the area of La Thanh, he saw a gray-haired person with a very strange demeanor. Gao Pian followed him to a small river and asked him who he was. The man responded: "My surname is To and my given name is Lich," after which he disappeared. Gao Pian realized that this was a spirit so named it the To Lich River. This tale is recorded in *Strange Tales from South of the Passes* [*Linh Nam Chich Quai*]. During the Ming rule, in the eleventh year of the Yongle reign [1413], Huang Fu, the minister of the board of public works, led his troops in an expedition against [our] people. When passing the To Lich River, he stopped his armies in order to change the name of the river to To Giang. This is recorded in *Summary Records of Our Land* [*Ban Quoc Chi Luoc*].

West Lake has also been called Lang Bac [during the Han dynasty] or Dam Dam [during the Tran dynasty]. It lies in Vinh Thuan District, Hoai Duc Prefecture. To the west, it borders the districts of Son Tay and Tu Liem. To the north, it is enveloped by the Nhi River. The To Lich River surrounds it to the south. According to legend, long ago a stone mountain stood there. In the middle of the mountain was a nine-tailed ghost fox. All who lived there were frequently troubled by [the fox], which made their lives very difficult. The divine dragon king heard of this and reported it to the head of the spirits. The head of the spirits became angry when told what was happening. He ordered the dragon king to take revenge. The dragon king then created a sea creature in the Nhi River to vanquish the ghost fox. The sea creature captured the ghost fox alive and then drowned it. As a result of this fight between the sea creature and the ghost fox, a lake was formed. This tale is recorded in *Strange Tales from South of the Passes*.

---

5. Trinh Thanh To is the temple name of Lord Trinh Tung (r. 1570–1623).

During the Han dynasty, Ma Yuan commanded his armies to attack here. During the Xian Tong reign of the Tang dynasty [860s], Gao Pian declared that this was a scenic place of the South. It was said that a phoenix came to drink the lake's waters, at which the mountains to the south glowed brightly and, in that luminous light, had the appearance of a coiled dragon. Other stories told of a golden ox, which escaped from the mountain valleys and concealed itself in the middle of the lake, where it left marks as its eternal spirit.

One day, Emperor Ly Nhan Tong [r. 1072–1127] went for a leisurely outing on the lake, piloting a boat. His tutor, Le Van Thinh, disguised himself as a tiger and rowed out in another boat to attack the emperor. But a fisherman named Muc Chan used an arrow to kill Thinh, thereby foiling his plot. A temple to Muc Chan still stands at the lakeshore today.

During the Le dynasty, certain names were forbidden, so the name of the lake was changed to West Lake. Later, the Trinh lords, who enjoyed beautiful words, again changed the name to Doai Lake. The Trinh lords cultivated lotus blossoms in the middle of the lake and built a small temple to visit for pleasure, frequently ordering the court officials to compose poetry there. But during the reign of Canh Hung [1740–1786], the color of the lake suddenly changed. Stinking vapors appeared, forcing people to stay away, and the flowers soon withered away. In the end, the court's splendor, as well as the scenery and its spiritual influence, declined because of these omens.

Ung Thien Prefecture

Ung Thien Prefecture is on the western side of Son Nam. Thanh Oai is the district that sits in the middle of the prefecture. From Chuong Duc southward, there is nothing but mountains. The forested hills of Son Minh and Hoai An districts border a vast and beautiful plain. Scenic locations include Tuyet Mountain, Huong Tich Mountain, Hinh Bong Mountain, and Tien Mountain, as well as other unusual sites like Tuong Son, Ninh Son, and Chuc Son. Very prosperous in regard to literary achievements, the land of Thanh Oai has produced many scholars and many degree holders, such as those from Chi Ne.

Hoan Kiem Lake sits in the center of Dai La city [Ha Noi]. An old story records that Emperor Le Thai To [r. 1428–1433] was rowing on the lake when he suddenly saw a large turtle break the surface. He unsheathed his precious saber and pointed at the turtle. The turtle snatched the sword and disappeared. For this reason, this place is called Hoan Kiem [Restored Sword] Lake. Later it was also called Navy Lake, because the court would use it to drill the royal navy. In the middle of the lake, a houselike structure rises up from the lakebed. With north as its left side and south as its right, it faces the middle of the city.

Tu Uyen Lake lies to the southwest, outside the city and in the ward of Bich Cau. In the middle of the lake is a pagoda called the Pagoda of the Southern Kingdom. According to legend, a young scholar named Tu Uyen was preparing for his exams when he encountered a fairy on the shores of the lake. For this reason, the lake is named for him.

The Ly court constructed the Temple to Literary Sages outside and south of the capital. During the Le dynasty, the court repaired the main chamber as well as each of the altars, left and right, front and back. The wooden rafters received a fresh coat of varnish. Stone walls surround the temple. In front of the main gate, an inscription once read "Gate of Great Learning." It now has been changed to read "Gate of the Temple of Literature." To the rear of the temple, the Minh Luan [Bright Discourse] Hall has steles on which successive dynasties carved the names of those who passed the highest level of the civil service examinations, and each placed steles there engraved with their names. Today, people still respectfully maintain the site, having added to it the Pavilion of Literature and decorative fringes in front of the interior altars. The architecture is quite elegant. Every spring and autumn, on "fourth stem" days, the court orders officials to make an offering at the temple. Also, in the summer, civil service examinations for scholars are held there.

Tuyet Mountain in Hoai An has a peak that stretches on endlessly and on which there is a pagoda. In it is a very strange cave containing hanging stones in, the shape of a coiled dragon. Looking toward the summit, one sees a stone Buddha whose gilded body is clearly visible from the immense pine forest below. The trees spread their branches as if a gusty wind had blown them apart.

Huong Tich Mountain, to the west of Tuyet Mountain, has a clear-blue arroyo that runs deep into its base. Inside the mountain is a cave of such depth and unimaginable magical qualities that it seems as if the spirits themselves carved it. It truly deserves being called the finest cave in Son Nam. According to legend, the bodhisattva Guanyin [Quan Am] once went south to banish a monk to exile in Huong Tich's cave. A very imposing Buddha statue stood in the cave. The monks filled the air with incense and smoke, but the imposing statue never ceased to fill them with dread. Then, in the spring, a group of Buddhist monks and nuns came by on pilgrimage. The sounds of their prayers to the Buddha calmed the entire mountain and surrounding forest, which represented a grand and triumphant gathering.

[Phan Huy Chu, *Hoang Viet dia du chi*, 231–45;
trans. Bradley Camp Davis]

TRINH HOAI DUC

CLIMATE AND GEOGRAPHY OF GIA DINH (1820)

Trinh Hoai Duc (1765–1825) was an ethnic Chinese (Minh Huong) scholar and poet from the Gia Dinh region who served the Nguyen during their lengthy struggle against the Tay Son in the last decades of the eighteenth century. For his loyalty and contributions, Trinh Hoai Duc was rewarded with posts in the new Nguyen court, serving both the Gia Long and Minh Mang emperors. He traveled several times as an envoy to China, including on the first Nguyen mission of 1802. Among his most significant prose works is the *Gia Dinh Citadel Records*, a geographical gazetteer summarizing the history, geography, climate, and culture of his native region. Gia Dinh was an important southern trading hub and had served as the Nguyen base during their wars against the Tay Son. The following excerpt is a close examination of the geography and climate of the region, looking at its features from both a material and a metaphysical perspective. It shows the importance of geomancy and astrology in the Vietnamese worldview and a sense of the correspondence between Heaven and Earth, which was often manifested in a belief that omens in the natural world were portents of change. The section on climate is a detailed description of the winds and waters as they combine to create weather conditions for the southern regions.

The south belongs to the diagram *ly* [in the *Classic of Changes*] and is sunny and fiery hot. The people who live near the sea in Gia Dinh always see the sun rise before others do, and it appears to be of great size; this is because Nam Dien is not far from the Valley of the Sun,[6] so the sun appears to be large; moreover, its corona also is visible, thus making it appear large. The corona is the emanation of light, and the core is the light itself. When the sun first begins to rise, the corona already is visible but the light source is not, and thus there is *yin* but not yet *yang*. The sun is pressed down by the vapors from the mountains, forests, rivers, and swamps, and so it appears large but remains azure in color and still is cool. The climate of Gia Dinh always is hot. The first rains come at the end of spring and last until the summer. In the autumn there is some seasonal rain. There are frequent and heavy showers, during which the power of the water is as if it had been poured out of a bowl, and it is like this for one or two hours, after which the sky suddenly clears. Longer torrential rains last for a day or two; this happens only occasionally, and it never rains constantly for weeks or months. Even though there is rain during all four seasons, it is only around the winter solstice that it becomes somewhat cool. The climate is inconsistent, and flowers bloom in all seasons; there are many of them and they are pure in fragrance. Once the cool nights have arrived and the moon is bright, it is truly autumn, and one need not consider the day and month to determine it. Su Shih's record says: "All seasons are like summer, but as soon as it rains, it becomes autumn."[7] It also says: "South of the passes are ten thousand households, and all appear cheerful." This certainly seems to be the case.

The air of Viet is flaming hot, and the ground is low-lying and damp in places. When struck by phosphorescence, the sea vapors rush and surge, often clashing together and creating thunder, which is why rain is accompanied by

---

6. Valley of the Sun (Yanggu), from the *Classic of History* (*Shang shu*), is a geographical reference to the cardinal point where the sun sets and rises.

7. Su Shih (Su Dongpo [1037–1101]) was a Song dynasty scholar and poet.

thunder and lightning. Along the coast, the soil is very poor and cannot store up the fire of the lightning; being too full of *yang* essence, it sometimes strikes against the *yin* essence, and stagnant air and steam issue into each other, often resulting in a lightning bolt. Masts and trees and other tall things can be blown over by this harmful air, which forces, shakes, and hits them. But even if people or creatures are shaken by it, they seldom are killed. Lightning in winter is also very common.

Gia Dinh is a remote place where there is much *yang* and not much *yin*, and [it has] frequent southerly winds. Because the sun is in the south and the wind comes from the south, too, southerly storm winds are quite common, but one need not worry about typhoons. This is probably because typhoons contain winds from all four directions. Those that blow from the northeast are certain to come from the north and move west, while those that blow over from the northwest will certainly come from the north and move east, but they disperse when they reach the south. Moreover, the winds of Gia Dinh blow directly southward, and all typhoons cease when they move south, which is why there are no typhoons in Gia Dinh.

The mountains and swamps of Gia Dinh have been dredged and are well ventilated by many winds so there is no buildup of swamp gases or mountain mists. Also, it [Gia Dinh] lies beyond the Five Passes, so there is neither ice nor snow. Dew is the vapor from pure metal, and in the south the fire element is strong, but the metal element is weak. In the late autumn, it is particularly hot, and the vapor of the metal element cannot liquefy. As a result, there is little dew, and because there is so little dew, it cannot freeze to form frost. Not until the winter solstice do the leaves wither and turn yellow, and only then can one tell that some frost has formed.

The vapor from mountain marshes begins as steam, then changes into clouds, and finally becomes rain. Rain is formed by the clouds, and many clouds come from the mountains. When it is dark, much of the rain comes from the sea. In Gia Dinh there are many red clouds, and these come from the fire element. Other clouds rise up from the ground. Dark and misty, dusky black, the clouds and mists leap up for one or two *li* [one- to two-thirds of a mile]. In the middle of this, what look like the heads or tails of dragons flicker in and out of sight. The wind makes the water curl up in waves, and when the rivers have ceased flowing and the swamps are dry, the trees and houses rock in the wind; mists swirl around and rise up; then suddenly the rain begins to pour down in torrents. The common folk call this phenomenon "the dragon collecting water," but people rarely see this.

Water is like a system of blood vessels for the land, and it ebbs and flows in accordance with the essence of the earth. The morning water is called the *ebb*, and that of the evening, the *flow*, and together they can be referred to as the *tides*. The tides correspond to the movement of the moon. *Yin* and *yang* fluctuate, always keeping time, which is why we say "as trustworthy as the tides." It is often observed that when the tides are high, the wind is strong and that when the tides are low, the wind stops. In the two or three days around the first and fifteenth of each month, when the tides begin to rise, there is certain to be a strong wind. During the two or three days around the time of the crescent moon, the tides diminish and the wind is sure to be light. This is probably because wind is the mother of water and water is born from wind.

The tides in Gia Dinh are different from those in other places. For two or three days each month, there is no ebb or flow of the tides at all. In winter, this happens for three or four days but in the eighth or ninth month, the power of the tides is singularly great. In summer, it is greatest during the daytime, and in winter, during the night. On the twenty-fifth or twenty-sixth day of each month, the tides are high and rise to a peak on the last day of the month. On the third day of the new month, the tides peak again but gradually diminish thereafter. They rise again on the eleventh and twelfth days, strengthening once more on the fifteenth day. On the eighteenth day, the tides are at their highest and then recede again.

Everyone observes the waxing and waning of the moon in order to keep time. The high tide is commonly called the "water head" (in the tongue of the common folk, *con dau nuoc* or *nuoc rong*), and the low tide, the "water tail" (the common folk say *cuoi con nuoc*, and another name is *nuoc khiem*). The fisherfolk always observe the times of the high and the low tides while fishing. When there is a "water head," the fish are plentiful, and when there is a "water tail," fish are sparse. Also in autumn and summer, when the morning flow still has not yet receded, the evening flow overtakes it; it rides on the east wind, and the ebb and flow contract together. The sea waters splash and spurt upward; this is known as the "joining of the tides" (the common name is *nuoc uong*) and is caused by the water's not being able to keep up with the change of the tide. Gia Dinh is near the ocean, and in the waters along the coast are many underflows. Because of this, the tides come in like a galloping steed, swiftly swell up, flood the beach, and hit the cliffs and shore. In addition, the lay of the land is very high in the north and west and very low in the south and east, so the tides go out very rapidly, returning to the east in an overwhelming rush. When this happens, all the streams and sandbanks empty and dry up. Once, someone waited and measured [the tide], to find out the level after it had gone out, and it was said to have a depth of thirteen *thuoc* [eighteen feet]!

All along the coast in the counties and districts of Gia Dinh, the soil is thin and the earth poor. The burning heat of the *yang* vapor often leaks out; the damp *yin* vapor often issues forth in steam. People's circulation frequently blocks up, their pores become sore and restricted, and sweat collects on their backs. So in the summer they often drink cool, clear drinks, and in autumn and winter they often get malaria. This probably is caused by the cold vapor entering their spleen, and because the spleen is subordinate to the earth element, there surely is a connection here. Therefore malarial fever always breaks out in seasons when it is not warm.

Gia Dinh has prolonged *yang*, so it accumulates, and heat and humidity are stored up. During the year the wind and rain, cold and heat, rarely arrive at the expected times. So there are many wayward winds. When people's pores are restricted, it is easy for them to catch diseases. Sicknesses often arise from the wind, and the bad air is polluted. It can even cause people to go mad, which is why the Chinese term for madness contains the character for wind, to indicate the origins of the affliction.

> [Trinh Hoai Duc, *Gia Dinh thanh thong chi* (hereafter, GDTTC), 5–11 (3a–6a), 15–18; trans. Catherine Churchman]

ECONOMICS AND TRADE

PHAN HUY CHU

STATE USE OF RESOURCES (1821)

Taxation and the government's extraction of resources from its population were among the state's central concerns and among the major causes of tension in the realm. During the eighteenth century, unhappiness with tax obligations that proliferated into many aspects of commercial and daily life was a chief cause of popular uprisings in both the Trinh and Nguyen territories. Indeed, the imperial court's awareness of the importance of carefully calibrating taxes led to the detailed guidelines spelled out in the Le Code. In this excerpt from his *Categorized Records of the Institutions of Successive Dynasties*, Phan Huy Chu discusses the ideals of government control and management of natural resources and the need to tap into these resources, principally through moderate and systematic taxes on agricultural output, with secondary taxes on other natural resources. A harmonious relationship between rulers and subjects is the ideal, whereby tax rates are kept at manageable levels and taxes are collected and expended strictly according to the state's need. By adhering to such practices, he concludes, resources will continue to remain abundant and taxation will not in any way harm people or hinder their livelihood.

None of the most important concerns of governing a country compares with the utilization of resources. Besides the gold and paddy rice in the six storehouses described in the Five Classics, which must be accounted for, are the eight policies, of which those concerning food and commodities are regarded as the most urgent. Since ancient times, emperors have governed that under Heaven, and all have managed [the earth's] wealth in order to bring the people together. Our Kingdom of Viet has been expanding since the time of Guijiao [Giao Chi], when the bronze pillars marked the extent of the borders. Our styles and manners were already set in motion, and all the hundred goods had been gathered. The number of people and creatures increases by the day, and the products of the seas and mountains are infinite. We rely on benefits from the three riches to serve the country and truly have no worries about any kind of shortages.[8] Nonetheless, even though these resources originate in Heaven and Earth, their management lies with men. If the [Confucian classics] had not put us on the correct course, how could we have circulated and sufficiently utilized these resources?

Now I want to discuss several important matters. The primary tax should be collected from the people and should reflect whether the number of households is growing or shrinking and whether their wealth is increasing or decreasing. Thus, the census records must be examined and checked very carefully. If there are fields, there must be field taxes; if there are registered villagers, there must be head taxes; and if there are households, there must be household taxes; and they should frequently be adjusted to be sufficient for the country's needs. Thus, the regulations for levying taxes must be fixed and standardized. Money and coinage are necessary so people can exchange them for merchandise, and places that either have or lack certain goods can trade them. For this reason, the circulation of money should not be impeded. Fields exist [to supply] common benefits from the earth, and if their boundaries are not accurate, then the amount of food supplies cannot be determined. For this reason, the system of field land must be kept in balance. In addition, goods from the four quarters include those from the mountains and the seas, and the regulations on taxing these products should be spelled out. Merchants who travel to and fro should pay taxes for ferry crossings and market openings, which also must be scrutinized.

Those who govern that under Heaven must fully understand these financial policies and whether they can meet the country's needs. Some officials must be responsible for taking from those below in order to give to those above, and the regulations for confiscation must be appropriate. The calculated capacities and amounts collected must stay in balance, and the rules for managing their use must remain constant. This is how the regulations for taking from the people are determined, and the implementation of this system must be cautious and restrained. Earlier kings' systems for the use of the country's resources have prevailed and did not overstep [their boundaries]. From the time of the Ly and Tran, the rules for using the country's resources survive only in summary form. In the Le dynasty, these regulations began to be more thorough. The taxes were calculated to remain balanced and never to reach a point that they harmed the people. [The Le dynasty] had a very detailed and regulated system for expenditures, and our country experienced a time of great wealth. Thus, over the past three hundred years, despite changes and particular concerns, the system has been considered and organized very clearly.

[Phan Huy Chu, *Lich trieu hien chuong loai chi* (hereafter, *LTHCLC*), 6:1a–2a; trans. George Dutton]

---

8. The "three riches" are Heaven, Earth, and people.

MINH MANG EMPEROR

POLICY FOR TRADING WITH EUROPEANS (1840)

In 1840, Vu Duc Khue, a court official, submitted a memorial to the throne arguing for a policy of isolationism to protect the Vietnamese from the dangers posed by the Western "barbarians." Minh Mang answered with a lengthy reply in which he rejected the course of isolation, contending that proper management of interactions with Europeans would be sufficient to prevent the difficulties that the Chinese had encountered. In his response, Minh Mang describes the sequence of events that led to China's Opium Wars with the British in 1839. Ostensibly having learned from the Qing court's overly accommodating trade policies, the Vietnamese court sought to realize the benefits of trade while minimizing the opportunities for Europeans to gain any kind of foothold in its realm. In this respect, the emperor's approach was similar to the Le ruler's edict nearly two centuries earlier (1650), which also had sought to regulate and restrict the Europeans' access to Vietnamese territory for trading purposes.[9] Even though Minh Mang's approach shows an awareness of the challenge posed by foreign traders, it does not fully acknowledge the extent of the threat. French missionaries were already proving that Europeans could penetrate the Vietnamese territories, and the Vietnamese military defenses that Minh Mang boasts of were no longer as effective as they had been earlier in the century. In any case, the court's decision to treat the Europeans as simply another among many "barbarians" was an indication of its failure to appreciate the strength and complexity of their challenge.

Your memorial contains nothing that we have not already seen with our own eyes, [namely,] the Hong Mao [British] provoking hostilities with the Qing and their excessive precautions against the unexpected. This is being unaware of the roots of one's limitations and being able to see only a matter's unessential details. Besides those engaged in farming and sericulture, many of the people in our country cook and manufacture granulated sugar for their livelihood. But granulated sugar cannot be used as food when one is hungry, and it cannot be used as clothing when one is cold. Thus, the court thinks very seriously about the issue of food, and so every year during temporary shortages, the court uses disbursements from the public treasury to create harmony by giving rice to all the merchants to trade for sugar. In this way, the people will have enough food, which is the greatest benefit this [money] provides.

Accordingly, when official vessels are sent out on maneuvers, they take [sugar] in their holds, so that when they reach foreign lands they can trade it for firearms, gunpowder, cottons, satins, and such items. On the one hand, this [trade] supplies our military needs, and on the other hand, it provides supplies for the

---

9. See Khanh Duc Emperor, "Edict Prohibiting Foreigners from Taking Up Residence Without Restrictions" (chap. 4).

state's use. Trade is a convenient means of procuring these things. Moreover, some of our country's territory lies along the coast, and because the coastal route has both easy and difficult passages, we have expertise in navigation. In the past, delegations from the capital were dispatched to come and go by sea. They all were capable of handling waves on the open ocean, sailing, and anchoring, and this was necessary to be able to depart and return. Thus they were clearly prepared. But when people were dispatched to nearby seas, many were unfamiliar with setting out or anchoring their boats, and because of their haste, there have been repeated accidents. Therefore we must determine which officials and sailors have become skilled and which have not, which ones have succeeded and which have failed.

In fact, we have our own techniques for defending against barbarians, and if we take precautions to ward off disputes, then conflicts should not arise. The Ming permitted barbarians to come every year and to engage in commerce inside their country and also to live among the people. Thus, everywhere [the barbarians] went, they drew maps of those places, covering all parts of the Ming coastal areas and territorial seas and their dangerous or safe points; they knew every place well. Throughout the entire Ming dynasty, Japanese pirates were a worry, so no one paid attention to [other matters]. The Qing people benefited the most from the tax on silver and therefore permitted foreigners to come ashore at the thirteen *cohang* [authorized trading guilds] in order to trade. This was a great mistake. Recently, they have been confronted with the widespread use of opium, which has been very difficult to contain. Local officials again engaged in deceit, collecting the opium and promising that they would pay the British in silver at the set price. In the end, however, the officials did not repay them anything, so the foreigners incurred losses and withdrew. They used their warships to blockade the Qing coast. Therefore, when we examine the origins of this troublesome event, it is clear that the Qing brought it upon themselves.

Our own court treats foreigners as follows: we do not reject them when they arrive, and we do not chase them when they depart; we truly regard them as barbarians and deal with them as such. Occasionally foreign vessels come to trade, and we allow them to anchor only temporarily at Tra Son Bay, to exchange their goods, and then we force them to leave. We do not permit them to come ashore, much less allow them to live here. We do not permit the local people to trade privately with the foreigners, thus nipping the problem in the bud. Of course, [the foreigners'] intentions are not good, but if we leave no openings [for them to enter], how could they create any problems?

[*DNTL* (1961–), 12:359–60; *DNTL* (2004–2007), 5:828–29; trans. George Dutton]

GOVERNANCE

PHAN HUY CHU

PREFACE TO *CATEGORIZED RECORDS OF
THE INSTITUTIONS OF SUCCESSIVE DYNASTIES* (1821)

The *Categorized Records of the Institutions of Successive Dynasties* is the single most important privately compiled encyclopedic work of the nineteenth century. Phan Huy Chu's text, which took a decade to compile, is a wide-ranging examination of the pre–Nguyen dynasty historical record divided into ten sections, ranging from geography to biography and from natural resource management and taxation to literature. The text was designed as a guide and resource for the new Nguyen rulers. This excerpt, the preface, includes a discussion of the importance of economic and political record keeping. Phan Huy Chu notes the problems of maintaining good records and preserving texts in the face of warfare and political turmoil, echoing Le Quy Don's comments in his introduction to *The Complete Anthology of Vietnamese Literature*.[10] The text shows a scholar's view of his role as a record keeper and the ways in which this serves the state and the rulers. The preface concludes with a reflection on Phan Huy Chu's struggles in bringing the work to fruition and of its considerable limitations—a result of his "modest skills"—and of the hardships of compiling scattered texts. Despite the requisite humility expressed at the end of this introduction, the Minh Mang emperor interpreted the overall text as a criticism of Nguyen rule. Phan Huy Chu's magnum opus was thus coolly received, and its author only modestly rewarded for his labors.

I have heard that in the pursuit of knowledge, institutions are what is most important. The Master [Confucius] stated, "Those who have a broad learning in the literary arts, are called cultivated." This is because they have found a congruence between the past and present. In arriving at the essentials of state statutes and rituals, the Confucian literati, beyond having read the classics and histories, have had to look broadly and deeply, searching and collecting near and far, investigating fastidiously, and selecting carefully among these [materials] so they might have a clear conscience and broad learning. How can one refer to these works, which extracted chapters and sections and cleaned up words, as literature?

Only when the emperor established the Viet state during the Dinh and then from the Le and the Ly to the Tran [dynasty] were common practices gradually expanded, with each generation having its own system. By the Le era, laws and rules were established, drawn up in detail, and announced. The famed reputation of these documents, they [literati] concede, is nothing compared with those of the Middle Kingdom. The regulations controlling all aspects of governance—the

---

10. See Le Quy Don, "Introduction to *The Complete Anthology of Vietnamese Literature*" (chap. 4).

appointment of officials, the method for choosing scholars, the method for ordering the military, the regulations regarding finances, the rites pertaining to the state's relations with its neighbors—all have their own chapter and articles, and all have their own standards. These regulations have been in force ever since the Hong Duc era [1470–1497]; all subsequent generations have conformed to them; and over this time, they have been consulted by brave rulers and upright leaders and supported by noted officials. Their reputation has been established, and for more than three hundred years, the preservation and observance of what are called statutes and rituals have been carried out continuously, although we know that there have been some additions and subtractions.

Before this, the collected laws of earlier dynasties had not yet been compiled into a book. Moreover, all the volumes of historical chronicles still had many inaccuracies. Then in the *binh ngo* year [1786], even with the raising of armies and the breakdown of the old statutes, which were scattered and lost, some people made plans for their preservation, and families of officials and other long-influential families concealed and stored them. But these texts were abbreviated or were missing parts, and some were mixed up or contained errors, and there even were some about which no clues have been found. So those who spoke about the past dynasties' regulations had no concrete evidence to rely on. Consequently, I have compiled what I have seen and heard and separated [this information] into various categories in order to create a single work of institutions and regulations. Such is the responsibility of the scholar, is it not?

For the time being, I would like to summarize some essential matters like the determination and establishment of frontiers, which sometimes were divided and other times were brought together, and thus have varied; the selection and gathering of men of talent, which in earlier and later times was done differently; the appointment of officials whose ranks and duties differed over time; the establishment of rituals, with a system for the Mieu, Tu, Giao, and Xa rituals; the system for setting examinations and the rules for selecting the scholars, which sometimes was detailed and other times was less so; the regulations for using state resources and collecting from the people, which sometimes required large and at other times small contributions; a system of laws to help in governance with fixed regulations that varied over time; and an army to protect the state, whose name changed over time, even in the books and works narrating the successive dynasties and the rituals and our correspondence with the Northern dynasties. All these included the statutes and regulations that had a bearing on this [enterprise]. Thus, researchers should pay close attention to the past to find precise evidence.

The statutes from the Ly and Tran periods and earlier have been lost; only their broad outlines could be found in the histories. During the period of the Le dynasty's founding and, later, its restoration, rules and regulations still existed but were scattered among the literary volumes that survived and were not properly organized. Certainly, we must not be ashamed to study and to seek out, to differentiate, and to classify the categories and minor details, for then they will be easy to verify.

I, your subject, have studied since my youth and, since then, have had the aspiration [to undertake this task]. I have had the good fortune of the accumulation of previous generations' knowledge and have hurried to follow their teachings with regard to decrees and regulations. And yet, even this feels incomplete, and it is like looking through a narrow tube, so that I have only an inkling of their brilliance. The historical records have been scattered, and the people did not compile [complete] narratives. After I retreated to the mountains and closed my door, I worked hard to collect and gather the books. Then in my free time, I studied their methodologies and dared to return and follow their categories to examine and correct them, thereby enabling me to find hidden meanings. Thus, over the course of [many] discussions and deliberations, the days accumulated and the months piled up, and ten years passed before I finished my project. The edited records consist of ten sections: geography, biography, official positions, rites and protocol, examinations, state expenditures, legal structures, military systems, literature, and diplomatic relations. Each of these records has a summary and then a narrative of the main ideas. And each section has subsections and a table of contents, which is divided into different articles. I have called this work *The Categorized Institutions of the Successive Dynasties*. There are forty-nine books in all.

[Phan Huy Chu, *LTHCLC*, 1:4b–13b; trans. Will Pore and George Dutton]

PHAN HUY CHU

RECORDS OF MEN (1821)

The *Categorized Records of the Institutions of Successive Dynasties* is broken into ten sections, ranging from geography to foreign relations. Each section includes a general introduction in which Phan Huy Chu highlights the fundamental aspects of that particular sphere of knowledge. In the following excerpt, he is reflecting on the role of men in supporting and serving the state. He describes the differences in individual moral qualities and capacities, emphasizing the importance of recognizing worthy, talented, and heroic individuals. Such men must be remembered for their accomplishments and contributions, he argues, for this is a debt that the state owes them for their service. In turn, Phan Huy Chu also sees that his responsibility as a historian is to highlight those individuals who might otherwise not enter the historical record. This echoes the thoughts of Duong Van An, which were set forth in the sixteenth century.

States use men to serve as their foundations, and men can be divided according to their qualities, for they range from high to low and are not uniform. At the top is the emperor, who relies on officials to arrange and organize matters of state, while below him are the scholarly men, some of whom participate in outside affairs, while others remain in private life. Men's virtue also varies; consequently, whether a country is under stable rule or in chaos varies as well. Thus when one speaks about the matters of each era, one must single out the men of talent. When we collect ancient tales, we must look for details as we examine the historical mirror. These records have helped in the preparation of dynastic annals and biographies. The records show the classification of clans as having nine different ranks of men, and each has a detailed record of their affairs in order to distinguish among them.

The quintessence of the airs and vapors in our country of Viet has already been developed and brought together. There was a period in which virtuous emperors and shining lords frequently appeared and in which noteworthy and upright officials were common. And each generation produced heroic men capable of producing outstanding accomplishments, as well as great achievements in administration. Some people performed labors with the sword or the woolen banner; other people were renowned as writers; and still other people revealed great courage during times of need. All of them were people who had many outstanding talents worthy of being recorded and who had accomplished feats, both above and below, for whom praise will endure for more than a thousand years and will be displayed for the generations yet to come. Therefore, aside from the historical records and biographies, there still are some omissions, and people who investigate the past must be able to distinguish clearly among them.

I often muse that when people and creatures are born, they need someone to watch over and nurture them, and thus the emperor must teach and also examine them systematically. Each dynasty has people who accept its commands, so the meritorious achievements of generals or noted officials should be recorded. Moreover, cultured men and Confucianists who display scholarship and moral conduct, and loyal officials who disregard their own situations when times are bad all are linked to the fate of their generation and are truly linked to the emperor's rule. Thus, we must record everything from the beginning to the end and write down events in detail, for only then can we research and compare all the persons from the past to the present without leaving out anyone.

[Phan Huy Chu, *LTHCLC*, 2:1a–2a; trans. George Dutton]

MINH MANG EMPEROR

EDICT TO THE LITERATI AND COMMONERS OF
THE SIX PROVINCES OF SOUTHERN VIETNAM (1835)

In 1833, tensions between the imperial capital at Hue and the largely autonomous southern region culminated in an uprising by Le Van Khoi (d. 1834). Le Van Khoi was the adopted son of the long-ruling southern warlord Le Van Duyet (1763–1832). Based in Gia Dinh, Le Van Duyet had governed the southern provinces on behalf of the Nguyen court from 1813 to 1816 and then again from 1820 to his death in 1832. By the time of Le Van Duyet's death, the Minh Mang emperor had already begun his project of consolidating the central court's authority over the autonomous southern and northern parts of the kingdom. Le Van Duyet's death provided an excellent opportunity to implement this process in the south. There was, however, a strong southern reaction to these efforts, led by Le Van Khoi and supported by various groups, including Vietnamese Christians and exiled convicts. The rebellion lasted for two and a half years before finally being suppressed by imperial troops. The edict translated here, which was issued after the rebellion had been put down, represents Minh Mang's reassertion of control over the south. It conveys in particular the emperor's sense that the region and its people had strayed from cultural and political ideals, which he had to restore. The document has echoes of earlier regional tensions, such as those in expressed in Trinh Can's 1672 edict to the peoples of Quang Nam on the eve of the last Trinh invasion of the defiant southern Nguyen realm.[11] In each case, the edicts chastise wayward populations for following renegade leaders while promising compassion for the contrite and strict punishment for the recalcitrant.

The people of the six [southern] provinces have enjoyed the consideration of our saintly ancestors, which for a long time permitted them to lead comfortable lives accompanied by great appreciation and benevolence. The people have enjoyed virtue and harmony for more than two hundred years. When our imperial father, the Great Exalted Ancestral emperor [Gia Long], was rising like a dragon, they, also with a single mind and common strength, contributed materials and labor in the face of great difficulty. At the time, there were only gentle and honest customs and neither lecherous nor cunning practices.

In recent times, the officials in charge of this region have been voracious and dirty. For example, Huynh Cong Ly was arrogant, while Le Van Duyet did not think about the proper ways to instruct the people. All this led the people to become accustomed to ill manners, causing them to violate the higher path and gradually leading to the literati's becoming accustomed to idleness, while the people's customs degenerated into arrogance and luxuriousness. Lecherous musical plays were performed, and people became addicted to opium. They regarded the value of grain as trifling but at the same time wore only extravagant clothes. They cunningly violated laws repeatedly, sometimes resulting in their being executed.

More seriously still, the region had become accustomed to practices and customs in which they claimed about themselves that the "remote and distant people know only the existence of the local leader but do not know the existence of the central court." The hearts of the people did not follow the past, and Heaven's teaching was full of hatred toward this. This was the reason for the rebellion by Le Van Khoi. Although it was caused by the inferior man Nguyen Van Que and the cruel man Bach Xuan Nguyen, if we examine its spread, the

---

11. See Trinh Can, "Edict to the Peoples of Quang Nam" (chap. 4).

manner in which it became a disaster, and also its origins, it was clearly the unavoidable consequence of such circumstances.

At the time the rebellion broke out, the southern people, inspired by their good nature and encouraged by loyal anger, gathered a righteous army, made a common enemy with the central court, and contributed their strength, which was in no way inferior to that shown by others. There also was, however, a group of wicked people who regarded this disaster as their own good fortune, enjoying it and carrying out cunning deeds by following and praising the revolt. Some of them destroyed or stole the stores of government offices during the rebellious episodes, and some of them threatened the local villages by relying on the power of bandits. And some even cooperated with the rebels by contributing elephants, while others captured the heads of the government offices and turned them over to the rebels. Chinese settlers and groups of Christians also contributed to these vicious deeds. The mobs were like foxes, and the bands were like dogs, and they grew larger by the day, finally leading to the formation of this exceptionally large incident. For three years, it caused suffering for generals and soldiers, and only now have they finally reported success.

When I think of this, it fills me with great anger. I think about when the bandits had just started this rebellion. The number of Hoi Luong's and Bac Thuan's rebel soldiers was only between thirty and fifty, and the number of convicts helping them was also only between one hundred and two hundred. If only a few people had followed them, the weak power of such a gathering of ravens could easily have been scattered and the flames of these fireflies easily extinguished. How, then, could this have led to such a disaster that it engulfed the Six Provinces and resisted the court's orders for three years?

Moreover, the groups of those who supported Hoi Luong and Bac Thuan must have anticipated that their crimes could not be pardoned and so readily defended themselves at the expense of their lives. But what gives me mixed feelings is the southern people. In the past, they said that fierce cruelty forced them to act and that they could not escape this threat. But when the court's army arrived to put down the revolt, why did they not immediately surrender to us but [instead] persisted for a long time in defending their walls and attacking the besiegers? It is greatly regrettable that they had to die along with the bandits.

It is unfortunate that whereas previously the air of loyalty and generosity was fulfilling, there came a time of extreme foolishness, in which the people waited until the lonely castle had already fallen and these violations of the state's laws were difficult to forgive. We have now reached the point at which we must kill them all to appease the fury of the gods and people and to console the hearts of the generals and soldiers. This is truly unavoidable, but when my consideration extends to thoughts of the people's foolishness, I truly feel troubled and a sense of pity.

Now, this calamity has been brought to an end. I cannot avoid teaching and advising you again to repent the past and be cautious in the future, and so I expect you to return to a state of purity and honesty. Previously, I enlightened and ordered you to move in the direction of justice and to rectify your mistakes, to be cautious, not to be arrogant and ostentatious, and to respect thriftiness. I repeated it again and again, and it is without tiring that I repeat it yet again.

Truly, all my people have enough knowledge and understanding that any claims not to comprehend and repent their errors are nonsense. Henceforth, be assured that you will give up your erroneous ways. Although the land of the southern region is distant, it cannot be compared with hidden valleys and remote forests, thus the rays of the central court's light do not remain distant, and its mirror-like warning remains very bright.

As we think about the time when this disturbance took place, the persons who followed the path of righteousness were compensated with official ranks; those who contributed materials also were rewarded; and anyone who had been threatened but who then changed the direction of his spear to kill the rebels was recorded in the list of the contributors. Those who had loyalty and righteousness and did not yield but instead scolded the rebels and were killed for doing so were posthumously promoted and generously rewarded. Although they have died, they have glorious names; so why did you continue to follow the rebels, to the point that this led to your being beheaded along with the barbarian herds and your being given pejorative names, and why did you permit this disaster to reach your wives and children? The causes and consequences regarding disaster or good fortune, which depend on betrayal or obedience, are already clear. The chance of going or escaping according to one's goodness or wickedness can serve as a bright mirror.

Each of you must repent and acknowledge your errors and should be mindful of our common laws. Refine yourself to make your name only by piety, sympathy, loyalty, and trust, and regard justice and common sense as being of paramount importance. If you are scholars, cleanse your bodies and bathe your virtue, so that you might make yourselves talented men capable of governing the state and aiding the world. If you are peasants, make efforts in farming and working in the fields so that you have stores and your bins are full. If you are craftsmen, stay in the workshops and carry out your trade, and make an effort to achieve even greater skills. If you specialize in trade, you should strive to enrich your stocks by working diligently. All who are commoners should know how to preserve their duties and abide by the laws. Whoever belongs to the army must not again act deceptively by fleeing.

As a rule, if something lies outside the correct cause and effect, then you should certainly cut it off and stop doing it. If there already is a law forbidding such actions, you should respect it and avoid breaking it. Fathers and elder brothers should lead sons and younger brothers harmoniously to practice this teaching without violating it. Everybody must obey it with dignity, and every generation must not lose it. Therefore, you should push yourselves to return to the ancient customs, and then you will receive the coming good fortune. This is what I, in fact, desire greatly. I have great love for the people of the southern area and also have great expectations of them, and that is why I do not hesitate to speak so extensively.

[DNTL (1961–), 10:223–25; DNTL (2004–2007), 4:742–44;
trans. Choi Byung Wook]

NGUYEN TRUONG TO

A PLAN FOR MAKING THE PEOPLE WEALTHY
AND THE COUNTRY STRONG (1867?)

Nguyen Truong To (1827–1871) was the rare intellectual who combined Confucian training with a Catholic education received both in Vietnam and abroad. He learned French from missionary priests and then traveled to Italy and France, gaining first-hand insights into Europe's colonial ambitions. When he returned to Vietnam, he became a voice for political reform at the court of the Tu Duc emperor. Between 1863 and 1871, Nguyen Truong To submitted at least fourteen lengthy memorials to the emperor suggesting numerous and wide-ranging reforms of political institutions and, indeed, of the entire method of governance. He strongly emphasized the need for European-style practical education, with a focus on scientific knowledge and a departure from the traditional Confucian-style instruction and examination system. He urged the adoption of a modified vernacular script to facilitate this educational reform. The kinds of changes being urged in his memorials were again echoed in the early twentieth century, particularly in the textbooks of the Dong Kinh Nghia Thuc.[12] The excerpt here is the introduction to one of Nguyen Truong To's prominent appeals, in which he lays out the sources of Vietnamese shortcomings and discusses the changes necessary to overcome them. This document is noteworthy for showing some awareness of world historical trends and of Europe's exploration and exploitation of the Americas. Reflecting his Confucian training and his audience, Nguyen Truong To's memorial begins with references to the *Mencius* and other ancient texts before launching into its wide-ranging contemporary analysis. This memorial parallels a contemporary discourse in China that regarded the East as the origin of civilization and cultivation, a primacy that it eventually lost to a formerly barbaric but rapidly developing West.

In my humble opinion, there are many troubles in the country. Men urgently worry about matters concerning their lives, and Heaven's will is to help them. This stemmed from something unforeseen. It is for this reason that Mencius set forth the maxim "Hostile powers carry out foreign aggression." The ancient literati had the phrase "The will of Heaven has humaneness and compassion." Thus, looking at this from the perspective of the affairs of men, this is common

---

12. See Tonkin Free School, "A Civilization of New Learning" (chap. 6).

to each and every country in the world. All have had times of trouble but have [also] had men capable of driving the carriage over great distances. Viewed from the perspective of the Way of Heaven, we have had even more wonderful things. Nature has provided blessings to people. These blessings have come only gradually and have only slowly been discovered and only then could they be seen. People do not understand Nature because of the misery they see but, rather, because of the sorrows conveyed by Heaven. Because of this, Nature has given birth to the myriad creatures for people to rely on, and yet there is no love for the Way, but only for wealth.

Many people stubbornly remain idle, unwilling to search out and develop what has been hidden from them. Consequently, the precious treasures that Heaven has hidden in the mountains and seas have not yet been fully exploited. Since people and creatures first appeared seven thousand years ago, calculating in accordance with Heaven's system, not even 40 percent of the benefits found on the earth's surface have been exploited. Moreover, it is Nature that has brought people into existence, and they all are from a single source. Nowadays, however, across the face of the earth, civilized people are few in number, while barbarians are numerous. How has Nature [caused] such a gap between the well-off and the indigent? It is because the time has not yet come. This is just as it is with fathers and mothers with respect to their numerous children. The older ones are sent out to create businesses in order to earn a living. The younger children are taught their numbers and how to reply appropriately and are also held back because of their birth order. And even though it is contrary to Nature's intentions that they be pushed to take steps on their own, [children] inevitably make careful calculations. But Nature desires that people broaden their knowledge and learning in order to clarify and open up the quintessence of Heaven and Earth, so as to provide humankind with countless aspirations, to search out the marvelous, and to strive for success. Nature also fears that people have become content with the ordinary and are consequently unwilling to communicate with one another. Each person has suitable land, and each has some things in abundance while lacking others, and this will cause them to open communications and contacts so that these visionaries can later transform and civilize the barbarians. This [process] is necessary to provide what Nature has not yet fully provided, and this will produce changes in a timely fashion, as well as demonstrating all the marvelous uses of humankind's intelligence.

If we consider the issue of people's seeing and hearing and eating and breathing, and just let Nature take its course, this would be acting like creatures who do not have souls and lack the power to control their own movements. How, then, can we differentiate people with souls from the myriad creatures? Thus, the five continents have four directions that are surrounded by and lie inside the great seas and that are in turn transected by the great rivers that link up and connect the flatlands and that flow and connect the boats and carriages. These continents also are separated by mountain ravines and passes that block routes, which force people to open the passes and roads themselves in order to reach the places where the precious veins [of minerals] can be found. Throughout the earth it is like this; the wonderful arrangements of Nature are innumerable.

To summarize, then, what has been discussed: all these races of people are covered by a single heaven and carried on a single earth. A single sun shines on them. A single moon illuminates them. A single atmosphere fills them. A single water source moistens them. A single breeze perfumes them. A single principle channels them. A single nature binds them. This all began from one, and then divided, and in the end it all must be brought back together, for only then will it have created Heaven and Earth's great usefulness. For this purpose, the Creator could not bear having Heaven and Earth's great principles end up somewhere obscured and obstructed and also could not bear to think that the daily necessities of the earth's people would end up being limited by territorial divisions, and so he set forth many ways to inspire and induce people to move along the path toward achieving the Great Harmony.

The East, 3,500 years ago, was the first place in which people began to clear fertile land, and in this secret place they gradually established their common practices. Furthermore, they used the hundred tasks in order to achieve prosperity, and so by the time of the Middle Ages, prosperity was increasing day by day. During this time, the West was a place of wilderness and beasts and had not yet been transformed, and for this reason all the barbarians of the northwestern regions of the East repeatedly invaded these territories. Consequently, the West was gradually transformed by the East. Because of military actions on both sides, there was movement in both directions, which caused each side to seek out information about the other. Each side did not have certain things, so each thought about crossing its borders to seize these things. Thus, each was humiliated by the other and so thought about various ways of capturing, defeating, and taking the enemy.

This looked not unlike ancient times when our country was invaded by China and was cut and broken apart. Although this looked like Nature had sown misfortune, it also provided benefits. It was because of this that ours became a civilized country. In the region of the Southern Seas there were three countries: ours, Burma, and Siam. But those two [other] countries still preserve the dark and vulgar and are far behind and inferior to our country. Isn't this because of the reasons I have already described? During the time of the Zhou dynasty, a scholar from the country of Phat Lam [Fu Lin] had already traveled to China,[13] and during the time of Emperor Wu of the Han dynasty [r. 141–86 B.C.E.], some had already come from India and gone to Bactria [in Central Asia]. Then, during the time of the Northern and Southern dynasties, the northern barbarians

---

13. Phat Lam (Fu Lin) has been the subject of much scholarly speculation but has not been definitively identified. It may have been Byzantium.

had already seized all four directions. And in the time of the founding emperor of the Yuan dynasty, when they had not yet finished looting the Jurchen, they already were opening up the northwestern part of the eastern region, the southwestern part of the eastern region, the northeastern part of the western region, and the northern part of the southern region. Every place had productive and advantageous terrain, and none was able to avoid being overrun, and because of this the overland routes between East and West made contact with each other. At the end of the Yuan dynasty, the imperial horse escort commander Tat Ma Nhi Tu Thien of the country of the Khazaks spread his majesty as far as the Western citadels, and some Westerners joined him and became a part of his army. Because of this they were already bringing back firearms and all sorts of other unusual instruments. Westerners had long been in chaos, but now they thought about restoring order and so they imitated [Eastern] methods of manufacturing to make firearms, and they used these in warfare and also took all the various types of ingenious technologies that were from the East to serve as their models. From then on, studying the skills for making these instruments became increasingly in demand, which gave birth to ingenuity. And this ingenuity reached a point that it produced bravery, and this brought about changes regarding the earlier weaknesses and ignorance.

Consequently, by the time of the Ming dynasty, the [Westerners'] rising and flourishing was increasing daily, and there was no place that tested their bravery. For this reason, they moved to the West for their search, suddenly discovered the Western Continent (that is, the New World),[14] seized it, and made it their land. They cleared the grand lands that had lain uncultivated for many thousands of years, changing the customs and habits that had been barbaric for many thousands of years. In the beginning, the native people grasped their swords as they faced them, but gradually they became like relatives. They studied exhaustively to obtain the Western region's ingenuity, and after less than a hundred years, they were able to brandish weapons and to expel [the barbarians]. Countries that had once been colonized by the West, instead became allied with the West. Countries that had relied on the West changed their old habits and became wealthy and strong, and the Westerners relied on the benefits of these lands in order to become self-sufficient. Where formerly there had been teeth-gnashing animosity, now there were enduring good feelings like those among brothers.

After the Western people's access to the benefits of these lands declined, their greedy hearts still were not satisfied. They repaired their boats and inspected their weapons and then turned them toward the East. Although the people of the countries of the East were the ancestors of the hundred skills, their basic nature was to be absorbed in leisure and pleasure, and they did not welcome change. Moreover, in earlier times, they had already asserted control over that

---

14. The parenthetical phrase is in the original text.

under Heaven and had become contented and self-sufficient and thought that no one under Heaven could triumph over them. Consequently, they focused on esteeming empty writings and venerated the study of the enchanting, and gradually they had an abundance worthy of great esteem; in the end, their fate was of the worst kind (this is something that can be said of all countries). Thus, when foreign enemies suddenly arrived, they regarded them merely as a different kind of people, with a different type of wisdom and cleverness, and they did not know that the other's current ingenuity came from the surplus from earlier times in our Eastern region. Earlier, Nature's Creator had given this to us, but we had not yet made full use of it, so Nature used our misfortune to take it from us and give it to them. They took our surpluses and regarded them as highly valuable; every day they increased and embellished them, and then sold them back to us to collect a substantial profit.

I reflect on the fact that Nature has created the Earth, which is primarily for the common use and the benefit of all the races of people and not for the private use of a single person. Therefore, when the wildernesses had not yet been cleared, the races of people scattered and settled in places where each established their own power and leaders, cultivated land, established governments, and expanded their territory. When there was contact across the mountains and rivers, and the dangers and difficulties had been overcome, trade developed between those who had and those who did not have certain resources, helping the people prosper. When examining their history, people gradually came to realize that in the beginning they had been like close brothers and were of a common root and had a mutual and deep affection. So they used their surpluses to supplement those who had shortages; this was like a division of labor, each gaining a mutual benefit. Thereafter, all under Heaven could come together to form a single family to balance the use of the wonderful resources of those under Heaven. If it is not like this, then the people of the mountains would lack fish and salt; the people of the coast would lack animals and wood; some places in our country would lack medicines; other places in the Central Plains [China] would lack rice. Nature is such that sagely men have love for all, regarding all children as their own children. When, then, cannot they use one country's self-sufficiency to help another country? And why can't one person's self-sufficiency aid other people out of friendship rather than for money in order to stop going back and forth in ways that create problems?

The earlier feelings were uncongenial, but later changed to beneficial relations. The hardships of earlier generations led to successes in human affairs, and these successes will surely be enduring. For this reason, at the inception of future cooperation and future successes, there surely will be misgivings that will cause people to pause and think about possible harmful consequences, and only then will they be able to achieve enduring and eternal mutual benefits. If there are misgivings, they must seek to understand them, since there is usually a reason to pause and rest. But soon they will clearly understand them and will know Nature's plans for dividing and distributing its bounty, which they must not oppose or change. At first, it seems as if all creatures have [someone] who is master over them, and all are frightened of one another. But if we look further, we see that all provide mutual assistance to one another, with appropriate levels for each type. Not all types of people are equal children of Nature. If they are big and powerful, they will always gain benefits; if they are *yin*, they will be weak and small, and consequently a great divide will be produced between them with respect to their benefits, which will cause great harm. How can we call this just?

This discussion is from one part of an essay in the *Theory of the General Trends and Synthesis and Analysis of That Under Heaven*. All these are the actual circumstances and the true principles in heaven and on earth. From the beginning of creation until the present, it has always only been like this. Although strong people have been able to distinguish themselves temporarily, they have not been able to do so forever.

Now I would like to highlight parts of my earlier discussion, because at present, the majority of scholars in our country hold onto the old and not the new; their methods of discussion cause disorder and chaos in governance; and their noisy discussions encourage the formation of cliques that then dare to slander the imperial court. They can hardly understand the changing circumstances of the current period. The old methods are no longer practical in the current age. The ancient sages had the saying "Heroic individuals are those who take note of the current situation, not those who take note of past circumstances." To ignore a crisis by not putting down disorder is not wisdom but a lack of ability. This is just like praising those of former times, even if they were extremely foolish. Therefore, when discussing the events of their generation, the sages would examine these specific plans and make whatever changes were necessary for that particular period in order that men might be in accord with Heaven. This is just like nowadays, when all men of character inquire into the various matters of the common people, with no concern for the common patterns.

[Nguyen Truong To, "A Plan for Making the People Wealthy and the Country Strong," *Nam Phong*, no. 119 (1926): 3–11; trans. George Dutton]

NGUYEN DYNASTY HISTORY BOARD

NGUYEN COMMENT ON THE FATE OF THE LE (1884)

Writing histories of its predecessors was one of the imperatives of a new dynasty. This gave the new rulers an opportunity to comment on the past, noting both the successes and the failures that necessitated the establishment of a new dynasty, thus legitimating their authority. Earlier generations of court historians, perhaps most famously Ngo Si

Lien in the latter half of the fifteenth century, had carefully scrutinized the past and noted the shortcomings of previous generations of rulers and their advisers. Given the circumstances under which they came to power, the Nguyen paid particular attention to the reasons for the final collapse of the Le dynasty. Despite their interest in this project, it was more than fifty years before it was initiated, and then another twenty-eight years before the Nguyen record of their imperial antecedents was completed. *The Imperially Ordered Mirror and Commentary on the History of the Viet* contains the Nguyen dynasty's official historical record of the rise and fall of the Le dynasty, which the new dynasty viewed as its immediate predecessor, pointedly ignoring the Tay Son interlude. This excerpt is the concluding comment in the work, which offers a critical assessment of the Le court's rocky trajectory. The commentary praises the Le dynasty's founder, Le Thai To (r. 1428–1433), as well as emperor, Le Thanh Tong (r. 1460–1497), but then describes the dynasty's descent into chaos and its only partial recovery under the Trinh. It also includes a critique of the Trinh lords' oppressive rule, which is contrasted with the enlightened and humane rule of the Nguyen lords who governed the southern realm. Finally, the commentary touches on the important question of why the Trinh never formally displaced the Le, noting the Le dynasty's great reputation, which the lords continued to fear and respect.

From the time of its founding by the Great Ancestor, the Le dynasty did not follow an unbroken succession through many generations. Only Emperor [Le] Thanh Tong can be said to have been truly wise, whereas many other rulers were slow-witted and incapable and unworthy of consideration. From the time of the Restoration [1592], formal power had devolved entirely to the Trinh clan, and the Le dynasty survived only as a useless word. At the time of its founding, this dynasty's course was straightforward and direct, but later the throne's transmission became confused, stunted, and disorderly, and one could not know whether the matters being reported were really true. How could it be that the standards for establishing the country still were not in good order? Despite these problems, the Le dynasty's authority was transmitted through many generations, longer than that of the Ly dynasty and the earlier Tran dynasty, which must be attributed to the labors and virtue of the Great Ancestor [Le Thai To (r. 1428–1433)]. . . .

The Le dynasty began with the Great Ancestor, who rose up in righteousness from Lam Son, destroyed the Ming, established the kingdom, and triumphed over the barbarians. He did away with killing and was magnanimous toward the common people, and his virtues were profound and his accomplishments lofty. Compared with the earlier Ly and Tran dynasties, there had never been anything like this. Rule was then transmitted to Emperor [Le] Thanh Tong [r. 1460–1497]. Inside the country he developed civil administration, while outside it he vigorously used his military. His splendid brilliance and increasing efflorescence exceeded that of earlier generations. It can also be said that this was an era of great prosperity.

From the time of the Uy Muc emperor [r. 1505–1509], there were continual challenges, seizures [of the throne], and regicides. So it was that the blessings of the Le began to decline, and the Mac family overstepped its authority with false accusations. The Mandate of Heaven, however, had not changed, and so to help the emperor, our founding ancestor [Nguyen Kim] initiated a righteous uprising and then found Le Trang Tong [r. 1533–1548] and put him on the throne. In this manner, orthodoxy had again been restored; the former guiding principles had once again been made correct; and the restoration of order could then inspire and encourage for a thousand generations. The Trinh clan, however, took advantage of the disorder and seized political power. The Le emperor merely held empty ritual vessels and dared not demand anything of anyone. His only consolation was that he was still regarded by all under Heaven as the joint ruler.[15] During the reign eras of Chinh Hoa [1680–1705] and Vinh Thinh [1705–1719], there were no problems in the four directions; things in the country were calm, just as things had been during the reign of Emperor Shaokang [of the Xia dynasty].

Then there was [Le] Hien Tong [1740–1786], who, after having been imprisoned, undertook the great enterprise of unifying the country. He concealed his clear-sightedness and followed the course of events. He was calm and silent and did not carry out any actions. He arranged for Trinh Sam's accession to power, even though Trinh Sam was arrogant, rash, and unrestrained, and he dared not act forcefully despite Trinh Sam's cruelty. Consequently, Le Hien Tong was able to remain on the throne for more than forty years.

The Trinh clan ignored the Way, so Heaven forced it to reflect a desolate wall. Hostilities rose within their family, and the soldiers and officers became arrogant and overbearing. The rebel Nguyen Huu Chinh took this opportunity to lead external troops [the Tay Son] to destroy the country. As a consequence, the Trinh were defeated, and the Le then also followed them.

When the Le dynasty began to decline, they never were able to restore order, and the Trinh lineage, in that and subsequent generations, continually acted with cruelty and oppression toward the imperial tombs. In the end, however, they never dared to seize the throne, and so they permitted the Le throne to remain for more than two hundred years. It may be that this was because of our court's lineage of sagely kings, who in the southern regions had begun acting with benevolence and establishing righteousness, and their sacred reputation spread everywhere. Therefore, despite the covetousness of their hearts, the Trinh were fearful and did not dare to displace them.

The Man De emperor [r. 1787–1789] encountered a period of disaster, and the officials who assisted were nothing like those of earlier eras of the Restoration. Consequently, even though they did not wish to suffer destruction and loss, how

---

15. That is, the one ruler recognized by the lords in both the northern and southern realms of the country.

could they avoid it? But during his exile, the emperor manifested righteousness, and his officials showed unswerving loyalty. This moved the hearts of the Chinese, which is made clear in the historical records. Is it not thanks to our ancestors' benevolence and generosity in founding the country that kindness and charity continue to flow and be transmitted up to the present time?

[*Kham dinh Viet su thong giam cuong muc* (1884), 49:49–51; trans. George Dutton, with Matthew Cochran]

SOCIETY AND CULTURE

TRAN DAM TRAI

TWO NOTEWORTHY WOMEN (1811)

The following excerpts are from the *Records of the Customs and People of Hai Duong*, a local history and geography written by Tran Dam Trai, a minor literatus from Hai Duong Province. Besides describing geographical features, these texts typically contain brief biographical sketches, including figures of national prominence as well as locally important individuals. This volume contains several tales of significant local women from Hai Duong Province who distinguished themselves through their intellectual prowess and accomplishments. The first tale is about the mother of Nguyen Binh Khiem, a famous scholar-adviser of the sixteenth century, and suggests that he inherited from her his own abilities as a noted seer. The second tale is about a brilliant young woman, Nguyen Thi Du, who was forced to disguise herself as a man in order to sit for the examinations, which were restricted to men. Stories about her already had appeared in eighteenth-century biographical compilations and were later included in the Nguyen court's gazetteers. The stories of these two women are significant, too, because both are connected with the Mac dynasty, which was regarded by subsequent official histories as having usurped Le imperial authority.

An Intelligent Matriarch

In the hamlet of lower An Tu, in the district of Tien Minh, there was an off-spring of the Nhu clan, who was the daughter of a Ministry of Public Works official. She was very intelligent, had read the Confucian classics and histories, and was skilled in composing essays. She also was expert in the arts of fortune-telling and divination. While the Hong Duc reign was flourishing [1470–1497], she foresaw its collapse in forty years, but she also predicted that the eastern region would prosper. Even though she exerted her will just as a man would, she had not yet married. Several decades later when she first saw Van Dinh, she realized that he had a favorable appearance, and only then did she agree to marry. Then one day while she was crossing on the Tuyet Giang ferry, she met a young man and, sighing deeply, said, "Why is it that we did not chance to meet sooner?"

When she asked his name, it was none other than Mac Dang Dung [r. 1528–1541],[16] and she then was moved by regrets for the rest of the day. After that, she gave birth to the future duke, Nguyen Trinh [Nguyen Binh Kiem].

A Girl of Talent

In the hamlet of Kiet Dac, in Chi Linh District, there was a young woman named Nguyen Thi Du. The graves of her ancestors had been in the Tri Ngu mountains, and according to a [local] tale, "A geomancer prophesied: 'A single mirror will reflect three kings.'" After this, her mother had a dream in which she saw a star come down and enter her womb. She then gave birth to a girl who was very beautiful and unusually intelligent. When she was twelve years old, the Mac dynasty ended, and her father brought [the girl] to Cao Bang [which the Mac still controlled]. There she dressed to disguise herself as a boy in order to find a teacher with whom she could study. She gained broad knowledge, and her writing became very skilled.

At that time, the northeastern region was supporting the Mac family, which organized a metropolitan civil service examination in Cao Bang. A huge number of people came to take the examination, in which the young woman placed at the very top and her teacher finished second. When she entered the court to pay her respects to the Mac lord, he saw through her disguise and realized that she was a woman. He asked her about this and then invited her into the palace. After the Mac were defeated, the girl went to live alone in the mountain valleys until she was captured by the Trinh lord's soldiers. She asked the soldiers to take her to pay tribute to the lord but told them she would not become his concubine. All the scholars regarded this as strange but immediately took her into an audience. In her later years she became a Buddhist nun, and when a new ruler ascended the throne, he searched for a female scholar to teach those in the palace. Everyone tried to persuade the woman [to accept the position] and summoned her to enter the palace. She accepted the command to teach in the palace and was called the "instructor of rituals." The woman served two dynasties, and her writings were used to help the court, and when a metropolitan civil service examination was held, this woman served as the censor. During the examination in the *tan vi* year of the Duc Long reign era [1631], Nguyen Minh Triet passed at the top of the lists, but few people fully understood his essays. The Nghi Chua [Lord Trinh Trang] asked the woman to explain them, which clearly revealed her remarkably wide knowledge.

[Tran Dam Trai, *Hai Duong phong vat chi*, 155–59; trans. George Dutton]

---

16. Mac Dang Dung (r. 1527–1541) was the founder of the Mac dynasty.

TRINH HOAI DUC

CUSTOMS OF GIA DINH (1820)

Descriptions by Vietnamese of early modern Vietnamese social and other daily practices are relatively rare, which makes Trinh Hoai Duc's gazetteer *Gia Dinh Citadel Records* a particularly valuable document. It combines elements of Confucian and Sinic textual references with what amount to ethnographic descriptions of a wide range of social, religious, and cultural habits of the peoples of the southern Vietnamese territories. The account was written by a particularly sympathetic insider, a native of Gia Dinh, who became familiar with many popular practices through his residence, travel, and official service in the region. This series of excerpts examines such issues as the status of women, religious practices, marriage and clothing customs, birth practices, New Year and other rituals, the written vernacular language, and the influence of rivers on the southern peoples. It is interesting to compare Trinh Hoai Duc's description of marriage rituals with those of his near contemporary and northern counterpart Pham Dinh Ho.[17] The importance of ritual in various stages of the life cycle, as well as the seasons of the year, also reasserts the age-old concern with proper behavior that can be traced to ancient Chinese practices and that was periodically reinforced by Vietnamese courts and scholars. As did Nguyen Trai and Luong Dang, his predecessors who debated appropriate musical forms in the 1430s,[18] Trinh Hoai Duc discusses scholars' concerns with the need for appropriate music and dress to ensure ritual efficacy.

The chapter of the *Zhou Rituals* entitled "Duties of Regional Clans" says: For every two men in the southeast, there are five women, and the land has little *yin* but much *yang*. Its people have only rudimentary customs, and its birds and beasts have sparse feathers and fur but, because of these qualities, can endure the hot weather." The Gia Dinh region of the country of Viet has many broad regions with abundant amounts of food, and its people need not worry about want or disease. For this reason, few people set aside supplies, the customs are extravagant, and its scholars compete with one another to display their talents. The peoples of the four directions are mixed in with one another, and each family has its own, distinct customs. . . .

The Gia Dinh region lies in the southern realm, in a place with bright sunlight. Many of its people are loyal, brave, and righteous. They, including the women and girls, place greater importance on righteousness than on wealth. Many of its beautiful women are single, and the majority of those who are wealthy, long-lived, astute, and cunning are women as well. They venerate the Buddha and believe in sorcery, and many of them admire such female spirits as the Lady

---

17. See Pham Dinh Ho, "On Marriage" (chap. 4).
18. See "Debate over Music and Ritual" (chap. 3).

of Jade, the Lady of the Grotto (the common term for women who are held in such esteem is *ba*), the Lady of the Fire Spirit, the Lady of the Water Dragon, the Red Miss and the Apricot Miss, and so on. This practice is contrary to the "broken line trigram" [of the *Classic of Changes*] and can cause mishaps. These people also worship the [Daoist] kitchen god with the image of two men on either side and an image of a woman in the middle. This, too, contradicts [the *Classic of Changes*] in that there are two *yangs* but the *yin* is taken to serve as lord in the place of honor. . . .

The rituals for marriage rely on a matchmaker, and the use of baskets of betel nuts and hibiscus is important for preparing the six rituals, which can be performed only by scholars. Sometimes a man takes up residence in his fiancée's home before actually getting married. Families with both boys and girls may sell their rice fields and buffalo to one another in order to cover their marriage expenses. To carry out funeral rites, people study the *Family Rituals of Wen Gong [Van Cong Gia Le]*[19] and the *Kham Clan Book of Protocol [Kham Thi Nghi Tiet]*. Most funeral rituals entail music. People wear either dark-blue or green silk clothing to funerals, in accordance with Su Dongpo [To Dong Pha]'s instructions: "The sounds of bell and drum cannot be distinguished in matters of sorrow or happiness, [just as] the gowns and hats of people who are in mourning and those who are not cannot be differentiated." At present, ritual regulations are starting to be followed, and customs have completely changed. Because they now are so refined and elegant, they have become the state's accepted rituals. . . .

I think that our Viet people are continuing to practice the old customs of Giao Chi. People in official positions wear the cap of Cao Son; their clothing is a kind of cloak; and they wear leather shoes. Commoners leave their hair loose and go barefoot. Both men and women wear stiff-collared, short-sleeved tunics whose sleeves are sewn directly to the tunic, and they do not wear skirts or trousers. Instead, the men wear a long cotton turban that stretches from their back down to their buttocks and is knotted at the end. These are called *kho pants*. Girls wear an unlined skirt and, on their heads, a large, conical bamboo hat. People smoke pipes. Their houses are built low to the ground; people sleep directly on the floor; and they have neither chairs nor tables. In the *mau ngo* year [1738], Nguyen The Tong's[20] first year as the Hieu Vu emperor [the fourth year of the Le emperor Y Tong Vinh; and the third year of the Qing emperor Qianlong], the color of clothing was changed, and the outfits of all civil and military officials had to conform to the regulations of the dynasties from the Han and Tang to the Ming. Accordingly, they had to create a new pattern, which was just like the mandarin's outfit of all the officials in those days. These rules and regulations concerning both ornamental

---

19. The *Family Rituals of Wen Gong* was written by Zhu Xi during the Song period.
20. Nguyen The Tong is the posthumous name of Nguyen Phuc Khoat (r. 1738–1765).

and substantive [matters] were then disseminated.[21] The commoners' clothing and their tools also had to conform to the styles of the Ming, and the people were supposed to abandon the corrupted customs of the Bac Ha [northern] region, in order to create a country with civilized styles of dress. . . .

In Nong Nai (that is Dong Nai), on the evening of the twenty-eighth day of the last lunar month, a troublemaker (popularly known as Nau Sac Bua),[22] beats the barbarian drum, shakes the castanets, and assembles fifteen people to form a group. They circle the canals, looking for the homes of the rich and powerful. They then open the gate without ceremony and enter, attaching amulets to all the doorways. They read and chant incantations to the spirits, still beating the drums and castanets, and follow this by singing words of well-wishing. The master of the house then sets out plates of meats and cakes, as well as tea and wine, and also distributes envelopes with money as rewards and expressions of thanks. Then the group goes to another house and does the same thing. They do this until New Year's Eve and then stop. The idea behind all this is to chase off the evil spirits and discard the old year while welcoming the new. . . .

The people in each village build a village hall for the sacrificial rituals. An auspicious day is selected in advance for the veneration ritual. On that day, as the sun begins to set, older and younger people all gather together, spending the night [in the village hall], which is called "staying the night to pay one's respects." Early in the morning of the following day, the people put on their tunics and hats, beat the gong, and go in pairs to perform the ritual of veneration. On the day after that, they carry out continuous sacrifices, which is called the "great gathering." When this ritual is completed, the people return home. They follow the customs of each village for setting the times in which they hold these ceremonies, which usually differ from one another. Some villages hold the ceremony in the first month, regarding spring as the most appropriate time to pray for good fortune, while others hold the ceremony in the eighth or ninth month, seeing the fall as the most appropriate time. Yet others hold the ceremony during the three winter months, seeing this as an appropriate time to celebrate the success of their labors. All, however, understand that the reason for celebrating the twelfth month ritual is to give thanks to the spirits. All of these are referred to as "praying for tranquillity." In addition to these rituals, there also might be a water buffalo sacrifice or ritual singing, depending on the particular village's customs. When carrying out the rituals, once the seating order has been suitably arranged, everyone in the village is allowed to participate, with the local official serving at the head. If there is a village scholar, he will perform the "village wine-drinking ritual,"[23] recite the national laws, and explain the local village regulations. This is a praiseworthy

---

21. "Ornamental and substantive" comes from the *Analects*. Here, it suggests that these changes were not merely superficial.
22. The parenthetical phrases are in the original text.
23. This practice was derived from the *Classic of Rites* (*Liji*).

village. These days, generally without exception, each village annually gathers and submits paddy rice money and taxes for cultivating new fields and for labor service. They examine the surpluses or deficits, the number of people, the amount of field land, and whether and why these have increased or decreased. Then they all gather to examine and calculate this [information]. They also select someone to manage the village affairs. There are regulations determining the date on which this transfer of duties must take place. . . .

In Gia Dinh, people use the end of the year to clean [their homes] and offer sacrifices at the graves of their ancestors, which are tasks regulated by the state. Mindful of the approaching days of Tet, everyone makes things ready and puts them in order at the beginning of the year. When there are children and grandchildren, they wait upon the dead with the same courtesy due them when they were still alive, for how can one sit and look complacently at collapsed, decaying, and weed-infested tombs and not repair and redecorate them? In the old days, graves were not ritually venerated, but this began out of necessity. It can be compared with the ritual sweeping of the graves on the Thanh Minh date in China,[24] although our country regards the last month of the year as having greater meaning. . . .

In Gia Dinh, when guests arrive, they enter the house and are offered betel [nuts]. They then are offered tea, rice, and cakes, for it is essential to follow the correct customs. It does not matter whether [the guests] are close or distant relatives, whether they are strangers or acquaintances, or what their origins are; once they have arrived, they must be treated very generously. For this reason, when people travel, the majority do not take along provisions. Because so many places provide nourishment to guests, the number of people avoiding the village registers or fleeing [their native villages] is quite large. . . .

In the past, the Chinese [Tang] people regarded the people of Gia Dinh as those who go barefoot. Previously, only officials and powerful individuals and people who circulated in the markets and streets wore shoes and socks. Nowadays, under the imperceptible influence of the Chinese, it has become common practice to wear either leather or cotton shoes, whether one is a wage earner or a servant girl. . . .

[The territory of Gia Dinh] has many rivers with islands in them, [so] nine out of ten people are good swimmers and know something about piloting boats. They like to eat salted fish. They eat three meals a day, and everyone eats rice but very few eat congée [rice porridge]. . . .

Just before a baby is born into a family, according to custom some firewood is cut into rods, which are wedged in front of the door. If the baby is a boy, the cut wood is pointed toward the inside, and if a girl is expected, it is pointed toward the outside. This is used as an indicator. It is absolutely forbidden for inauspicious women who are having a difficult pregnancy, are not able to produce

---

24. Thanh Minh (C: Qing ming) is the traditional Tomb-Sweeping Day.

a child, are dizzy, or have an illness of the uterus to enter [this house]. When the pregnant woman lies down on the bed, a blazing hot charcoal brazier is placed at her side and burns both day and night. A hot pot is used to press down on her abdomen once or twice a day. She eats various kinds of hot, salty, and dried foods and drinks soup. In general, pregnant women follow the customs of their village and their family and commonly take frequent doses of Southern [Vietnamese] medicine made from root plants, which are usually chopped and boiled in water. After a month, the mother and child are permitted to go outside. Anywhere they go, they are supposed to sit and rest for half an hour. When the child turns one month old, a noodle soup is made and given to the spirits of the twelve mothers as thanks for the birth. If the baby is a boy, the people calculate one month and subtract one day; and if it is a girl, they subtract two days to determine the day for the offering. For the one-year birthday, they take a tray, as is done in China.[25] No matter whether the husband is a soldier or a civilian, he is exempted from labor service for one month, which is called "irrigating the auspicious." This is considered important to preserving good health. . . .

In the past, groups of shameless people would sometimes fight among themselves or with other people, regardless of whether they were in the right or not. They would throw themselves to the ground and tear one another's clothing. They would scratch and injure each other's bodies and moan and scream. This would bring disaster to a thousand people, which they would use to demand money and apologies. This was called "lying down for misfortune." Recently, governmental regulations have become very strict, and every locality must suppress and punish this practice. . . .

All the people in the country study Chinese books, which included, from time to time, aphorisms in the national tongue or a local dialect. From the books of Chinese characters, they find one that is phonetically similar and then add something to it. [For example], if a word has something to do with gold, they add the character for "gold"; if it is related to wood, they add the character for "wood"; or if it deals with speech, they add the character for "mouth," and so forth. They imitate the methods of the six categories of [Chinese] characters or combine them to create compounds that have harmonious sounds as well as being mutually recognizable from their origins, even though they are not native to this country. When the people write characters in other scripts, they spread out the paper on a table and write in grass or *zhuan-li* characters, supplying the answer in whatever characters they see fit. When they write, some people take the paper in their left hand and the pen in their right and then write very quickly, using the broad, comma-like, and transverse strokes as in China, even though these structures have been modified and are no longer similar and people use only those that are convenient. As in China, the hundred families all use completely different methods of writing grass-style characters, and their

---

25. A tray containing various objects is presented to the child, and the first object picked up is seen to symbolize his or her future career or financial prospects.

meanings differ from one another as well. For this reason, [personalized] grass-style characters are not often used in administrative matters. . . .

In Gia Dinh there are boats everywhere. People use boats as their homes or to go to market or to visit their relatives. Other people transport firewood and rice or engage in itinerant commerce, which is particularly profitable. The boats fill the rivers both day and night, and in coming and going, their sterns get so close that they are in contact with one another. For this reason, many of them collide, causing damage, leading to lawsuits. When determining who was at fault, each person blames the other, so it is very difficult to decide what really happened. Eventually, the Nghi Bieu marquis, the military counselor overseeing the military region, issued an order stating: "No matter what time of day and whether going upstream or downstream, whenever one boat approaches another [boat], each must shout out *bat* (or, more precisely, those passing on the left side shall call out *cay*, and those passing on the right shall call out *bat*).[26] If a boat is traveling on the right side and another boat also is traveling on the right side, then depending on which is more convenient, they should steer and row so as to avoid a collision. If one [captain] has already called out *bat* and the other boat continues to travel to the left side and they are not able to avoid a collision, damaging their boats, then the second boat is at fault." Nonetheless, some people refuse to follow this rule, using any convenient boat to transport light-weight items with the [flow of the] stream, and they do go more quickly. For this reason, people who pilot boats who wish to avoid one another usually just call out *bat*. They call out *cay* [only] when their boats approach their docks, if they have encountered a wind that might cause them to run aground, or if they have an accident that causes them to call out like this. Thus the shout of *cay* is seldom heard. This is a settled law.

[Trinh Hoai Duc, GDTTC, 363–89, 141–49; trans. George Dutton]

NGUYEN DU

A DIRGE FOR ALL TEN CLASSES OF BEINGS (1815?)

"A Dirge for All Ten Classes of Beings" is arguably Nguyen Du's best-known literary work after *The Tale of Kieu*. Written sometime in the 1810s, "A Dirge" is a useful contrast to the celebratory rhetoric found in state-sponsored verse, such as Gia Long's "Commemoration of the Defeat of the Tay Son." It is an extended reflection on the miseries of those who have died untimely deaths away from their homes. Such deaths are viewed as particularly inauspicious, since the body cannot be given a proper burial in the family plot and therefore cannot be properly mourned or visited in subsequent commemorative rituals. In particular, "A Dirge" reflects on the recently ended Tay Son wars and the great hardships and killings visited on the Vietnamese. Rather than a critique of either

---

26. The parenthetical phrase is in the original text.

the Tay Son or their Nguyen rivals, the poem comments on the brutality and inhuman-
ity of war itself and offers compassion to the soldiers and the suffering they faced. The
poem is surprisingly critical of the Nguyen for a scholar who avoided serving the Tay
Son court and who then was part of the Nguyen embassies to China. Like *The Tale of
Kieu*, "A Dirge" is full of Buddhist elements, reflecting the strong Buddhist revival
among scholars in the late eighteenth and nineteenth centuries.

> Throughout the seventh month, rain sobs and wails.
> The chill of wind gnaws into aged bones.
> An autumn evening—what dismal scene!
> Reeds drown in silver, plane trees strew gold leaves.
> Among the poplars twilight lingers still.
> Upon the pear trees, drop by drop, dew falls.
> Whose heart would not feel sorrow at this sight?
> And if the living mourn, what of the dead?
> Out of the darkness shrouding sky and earth,
> let specters, ghosts, and phantoms all appear!
> All creatures of ten classes, pity them!
> Lost, lonely souls, they wander in strange lands.
> They find no home where votive incense burns—
> forlorn, they prowl and prowl from night to night.
> They once sat high or low—what matter now?
> Can you now tell the sages from the fools?
>
> As autumn starts, let's set up an altar.
> Pure water sprinkles from the willow branch.
> May Buddha's mercy heal those suffering souls,
> save them and guide them toward the Promised West.
>
> There were proud men who followed glory's path—
> they warred and hoped to conquer all the world.
> Why talk about the heyday of their might?
> Remember their decline, their fall, and grieve.
> A storm broke forth—their roofs came crashing down:
> could they trade places with the meanest boor?
> For pride and pomp breed hatred and revenge—
> blood flowed in streams, bones crumbled into bits.
> Killed young, they've left no heir—they drift unmourned
> as headless ghosts that moan on nights of rain.
> Defeat or triumph lies in Heaven's scheme—
> will ever those lost souls escape their fate?
>
> Where are those ladies, veiled by flowered drapes,
> who reigned supreme in cassia-scented bowers?

Once more the realm changed masters—hapless leaves,
did they know where they'd go, swept off by winds?
From lofty towers they toppled into waves—
the hairpin snapped in two, the pitcher sank!
A merry court had flocked round them in life—
once their eyes closed, none gathered up their bones.
Alas, no incense burns to keep them warm:
they hide in thickets, or they skulk near brooks.
Oh, pity their soft hands, their tender feet!
They wilt night after night, rot year by year.

Those who once wore tall hats and waved broad sleeves
meted out life and death with their red brush.
To rule—they did know how; their pockets stuck
with statecraft handbooks like so many knives:
they'd read Yi Yin, the Duke of Zhou by day,
study Guan Chong or Zhuge Liang at night.
Higher they climbed, more hatred they inspired,
creating all around more tombs, more ghosts.
No gold on earth can ransom back their lives.
Their halls lie shattered where gay sounds once rang.
No kinsfolk stay close by to offer them
a bowl of water or an incense stick.
Deserted souls, they stagger here and there,
far from salvation, loaded down with guilt.

There were those who mapped plans and marshaled troops.
They rushed to battle, seized batons and seals.
They raged like windstorms, roared like thunderbolts:
many laid down their lives for one man's sake.
Stray arrows, errant bullets spelled their doom—
they squandered flesh and blood on battlegrounds.
Stranded and waifed upon some distant shore,
where could they find a grave, poor bones none claimed?
All through the sky's abyss, rain wails, wind howls:
the mists of darkness blur and dim the world.
Forests and fields wear mourning shades of gray—
the cast-off dead receive no sacrifice.

There were those who once hankered after wealth.
They traded, losing sleep and appetite.
Estranged from kith and kin, they had no friend:
to whom could they bequeath their hard-earned goods?
Who would be there to hear their dying words?

All earthly riches come and go like clouds—
now dead, they could not take one coin with them.
The neighbors, squeezing out some ritual tears,
dumped them in coffins made of banyan wood
and buried them by torchlight after dark.
Bewildered, at a loss, they roam the fields—
where is an incense stick, a drop of drink?

There were those scholars chasing post and rank—
they'd all trek into town and try their luck.
In fall they would pack up and leave their homes
to go and measure pens with fellow scribes.
But was officialdom, their cherished goal,
a cause worth risking body and soul for?
When they took sick, bedridden at some inn,
they lacked their wives' and children's loving care.
Without ado, they were consigned to earth,
while strangers, and no brothers, would look on.
Far, far away from their ancestral soil,
their corpses dot unhallowed burial grounds.
Unarmed by fire and incense, exiled souls
must shiver as winds blow beneath the moon.

There were those travelers roving streams and seas,
whose sails unfurled and dared the east's fierce gusts.
A tempest rose and struck them in midcourse—
they met their end inside the maws of sharks.
There were those who strolled round and peddled wares,
their shoulders mangled by the carrying pole.
As they fell victim to harsh sun or rain,
where did they wend their way, souls turned adrift?

There were those who, enlisted by main force,
left their beloved to go to serve the state.
With water scooped from brooks, rice kept in tubes,
they trudged along rain-swept, wind-beaten trails.
In wartime human life is cheap as trash—
stray bullets and chance arrows smote them down.
Will-o'-the-wisps, they flutter to and fro,
as night skies echo with their piteous moans.

There were poor girls whom fortune failed in need:
they sold their charms and threw their youth away.

Old age caught them alone and desolate—
unmarried, childless, where could they seek help?
Alive, they drained the cup of bitter dregs;
and dead, they eat rice mush from banyan leaves.
How sorrowful is women's destiny!
Who can explain why they were born to grief?

There were those wretches tramping all year—
a bridge served as their roof, hard ground their bed.
They too belonged to humankind—alas,
they lived on alms and died beside back roads.
Some got locked up in jail for no offense—
they languished, clad in tattered mats, and died.
Their bones were tucked in nooks of prison camps.
When will they ever have their wrongs set right?
Some children, newborn at a baleful hour,
had to forsake their parents and pass on.
Who's to hold them, walk and play with them?
Their strangled cries and wails distress the heart.

And there were those who drowned in streams or lakes,
those who climbed trees and fell when their foot slipped.
Some tumbled down deep wells when their rope broke.
Some washed away in floods, some burned in fires.
Some perished by wolves' fangs or elephants' tusks,
a prey to monsters of the hills or seas.
Some women bore a child, but left it soon;
and some, alas, miscarried of their babe.

Along the way, all tripped and fell head first
to cross the Bridge of No Return, one after one.
Those persons bound for separate destinies,
stray souls and vagrant ghosts—where are they now?
They crouch against a dike, behind a bush.
They dwell where rivers spring, where earth meets sky.
They lurk in clumps of grass, in shades of trees.
They hover near this hostel, haunt that bridge.
They find asylum at some shrine, some church.
They make abode in market town and ports.

They clamber up and down some mounds or knolls.
They wade all through the mire of bogs or swamps.
After a life of agonies and woes,

bowels and guts have shriveled, numb with cold.
For scores of years they've suffered gales and storms;
moaning, they eat and sleep on dirt or dew.
By cockcrow frightened, they all flee and hide—
at sunset they all venture forth again.
In rage they all slink out, hugging their young
or steering by the hand their tottery old.
All wandering, damned souls, both old and young!
For your salvation come and hear a prayer.
May Buddha rescue you from life and death
and ferry you to his Pure Land of Bliss.
Let his effulgent light dispel such gloom
as clouds the mind in ignorance and sin.
Then over all four seas his peace shall reign
to soothe all griefs and purge all enmity.
May Buddha's power send the Wheel of the Law
through all three realms, to all ten cardinal points.
The Burnt-Faced King shall raise his holy flag
and lead all creatures on their joyous march.
May Buddha work his magic and awake
all beings from the dream of self-deceit.

All creatures of ten classes, are you there?
Women and men, young and old, all come!
All enter Buddha's house and hear his word!
This life is just a bubble or a flash.
O friends, make room for Buddha in your hearts,
and you'll escape the cycle of rebirths!
At his behest, we set a bowl of gruel
and incense candles on the hallowed board.
We offer paper gold and paper clothes
to help you speed your heavenward ascent!

All who have come, be seated and partake:
spurn not these trifles, gifts of our goodwill.
By Buddha's grace they'll grow a millionfold,
and all of you shall get your even share.
To all he brings compassion release:
no longer fear the curse of life and death.
Buddha, the Law, the Order—all be praised!
Glory to those who sit on lotus thrones!

[Huynh Sanh Thong, *Anthology of Vietnamese Poems*, 77–83]

HO XUAN HUONG

SELECTED POEMS (EARLY NINETEENTH CENTURY)

Ho Xuan Huong (fl. early nineteenth century) is one of a small number of pre-twentieth-century Vietnamese female authors whose works have survived. Ho Xuan Huong's poetry is noted for its biting criticisms of elements of Vietnamese society, from concubinage to Buddhism. Her poems, including "Ode to the Fan," are often filled with sexual innuendos, barely skirting Confucian taboos regarding the open discussion of sex. Very little concrete information about her life has been preserved; most of what we know about Ho Xuan Huong comes from her poems themselves. Indeed, there is considerable uncertainty about when she lived, although the current consensus is that she most likely wrote in the early nineteenth century and not the late eighteenth, as has sometimes been argued. Because so little is known about her life, Ho Xuan Huong has been the subject of much speculation regarding her family origins and possible relationships with various scholars, including the noted literatus Pham Dinh Ho. The following three poems exemplify the nature and themes of her work, revealing a strong critical voice unafraid to engage in sexual banter.

ON BEING A CONCUBINE

One wife gets quilts, the other wife must freeze.
To share a husband—damn it, what a fate!
I'd settle for just ten, nay, just five times.
But fancy, it's not even twice a month!
I take it all for rice: some musty rice.
I labor as a maid: a wageless maid.
Had I but known I should end up like this,
I would have sooner stayed the way I was.

ODE TO THE FAN

One hole can fit just any number in.
But fate's glued me to you since days long past.
Stretch out three corners—creased remains the skin.
Close up both sides—some jutting flesh still shows.
I cool the hero's face when winds die down.
I cap the gentleman's head as rains descend.
While coddling him, I'll ask the man in bed:
"Are you pleased yet with my flip-flap inside?"

Are you eighteen or only seventeen?
Let me love you, kept always in my hand.
Slender or thick, you stretch three corners out.
Narrow or broad, you stick one rivet in.
You cool me all the better when in heat.
I fondle you at night, love you by day.
A wild persimmon lends your cheeks pink charm.
Lords cherish, kings adore this single thing.

POKING FUN AT A BONZE

No Chinaman nor one of us is he:
a head without one hair, an unhemmed frock.
Under his nose lie three or five rice cakes;
behind his back lurk six or seven nuns.
Now he claps cymbals, now he clangs the gong;
he hees, he haws, he hee-haws all the time.
Keeping that up, he'll rise to be top bonze:
he'll mount the lotus throne and sit in state.

[Huynh Sanh Thong, *Anthology of Vietnamese
Poems*, 214, 217–18, 220]

MINH MANG EMPEROR

TEN MORAL PRECEPTS (1834)

Minh Mang, the strongest of the Nguyen monarchs, ruled from 1820 to 1840, his reign marking the high point of Confucian influence on Vietnamese governance and political philosophy. This influence contained a strong element of state-sponsored paternalism, which is nowhere better demonstrated than in Minh Mang's edict "Ten Moral Precepts." Issued in 1834, shortly after his centralization of power in Hue, the edict was an attempt to impose social order and proper behavior on his subjects throughout the realm. This practice was in keeping with Chinese precedent, exemplified in similar precepts issued by the Ming dynasty's Hungwu emperor (r. 1368–1398) and the Qing dynasty's Kangxi emperor (r. 1661–1722). In a general sense, however, the edict reflects the Vietnamese state's long-standing involvement in dictating morality and behavior, a role whose apogee may have been in the fifteenth-century Le Code, which criminalized a wide range of moral misdeeds.[27] Minh Mang's moral precepts and explications of their importance were widely disseminated throughout the kingdom. Village leaders were to ensure that they were publicly recited each year. Popular

---

27. For more on the Le Code, see chapter 3.

attitudes toward this practice can be summed up in the village saying "To go to the theater, what joy! A swimming contest is a poor second. A procession? We might go and have a look. And even a burial passes the time if there is nothing better. But to go and listen to the ten precepts—one must have lost all sense and reason!"[28]

The emperor sent an order to the Ministry of Rites that stated: The stability of the country is bound up with the hearts of the people, and the beauty of their customs is connected to their education. Recently, groups of good-for-nothings have been goading one another into depraved practices and have been seducing people into drinking and gambling. The number of dull and stupid "little people" is great because of this poison that deludes them. They become thieves and bandits because they do not know what is proper. Every time we think of the people's affairs we are not pleased, and we cannot help but speak of educating them. We think about the chaos that the people have endured and that their hearts must have become somewhat aware of this. We must instruct them in this matter, which will be easy because of our strength. Only the Ministry of Rites can set forth the important ideas contained in the Qing country's "Sagely Edict to Broadly Teach," each of whose admonitions is clear. We must devote ourselves to understanding the meanings of these ideas in a serious and refined manner, and not in a superficial and merely decorative manner. And we must provide guidance to the foolish men and foolish women who do not know this. Then we can reverse the disdainful and return to the pure, and the customs will once again be virtuous. This has long been the country's highest objective, and to achieve this I have composed ten moral precepts:

1. Be sincere in all that you do.
2. Maintain an upright heart.
3. Hold fast to your proper profession.
4. Always practice frugality.
5. Keep to virtuous customs.
6. Educate your children.
7. Respect the correct [Confucian] teachings.
8. Guard against licentiousness and evil.
9. Prudently adhere to the rules and laws.
10. Be generous in doing good.

The emperor ordered that this be made public in the people's native villages.
[MMCY (1972), 3:chap. 13, 24a–24b; trans. George Dutton]

---

28. This version of the edict contains only the outline of the precepts. The full text of the lengthy edict, in *The Veritable Records of Dai Nam*, includes extensive commentary on each of the precepts and the reasoning behind it.

TRUONG VINH KY

TALES FROM A JOURNEY TO THE
NORTHERN REGION (1876)

Truong Vinh Ky (1837–1898) was a noted polymath and polyglot (he spoke fifteen Asian and European languages) who had been trained in missionary schools in both Vietnam and other parts of Southeast Asia. Shortly after the French conquest of Cochinchina in the early 1860s, he began to work with the French naval administration in Saigon as an instructor in the newly established schools for colonial officials. In 1876, Ky traveled from Saigon to Hanoi on a fact-finding tour, from which this report is derived. The text is reminiscent of the geographical gazetteers written by scholars during the early Nguyen years, which also included details about geography, distances, customs, and noted historical sites. This report is a useful bookend to Le Quy Don's account of his visit from the north to the Nguyen realms in the south a century earlier,[29] and it also can be compared with Trinh Hoai Duc's survey of southern Vietnamese customs a half century earlier.[30] The following excerpt looks at issues of gender relations, sartorial habits, feasting rituals, and festival games in the region around Hanoi. It is an evocative description of everyday life among ordinary people: how they lived, how they dressed, and how they enjoyed themselves.

Customs

Among the four social classes, each has its particular occupation, with peasants constituting the majority. The city is the place where artisans and merchants congregate, and there are Chinese who intermingle with them. Men and boys usually sit in shops and cafés, leisurely drinking tea or alcohol, while women and girls are the ones who carry out the working of the land.

The clothing of the men is also quite ordinary; it is a kind of short tunic that hangs to their knees, and on their heads they usually wear a conical "horse hat" or a black kerchief.

Women wear a tunic around which they tie a piece of cloth as a carrying belt. They wear a red bodice whose buttons are not fastened, leaving one shoulder flap unattached. On their heads, they wear a three-tasseled palm-leaf hat, nearly the size of a winnowing basket. This [hat] has a cord attached on both sides, and the two straps are pulled tight under the chin. The cord is wound through their braided hair, which is then wound around their heads. (There is one hamlet called Ke-loi in which women tie their hair in a bun.) On the lower

---

29. See Le Quy Don, "Wealth of the Nguyen Realm" (chap. 4).
30. See Trinh Hoai Duc, "Customs of Gia Dinh" (this chap.).

half of their body, they wear a skirt and on their feet, lacquered slippers. Their complexions are smooth as silk and fair, and their cheeks are rosy. Their skin has a bit of color, they have the pink heels of beautiful girls, and they are somewhat plump. Their teeth are dyed with a black lacquer.

The custom of leaving their tunic belts untied comes from the cold winter weather. Women with young children who wish to nurse them would otherwise have to undo many layers, which would be quite awkward, and so they wear their tunics in this fashion. And as for the waist belt, it is also worn because of the cold. Seeing women dressed this way, girls have naturally imitated them. Thus, regardless of the season, they dress in this fashion, and it has become the accepted custom.

On feast and festival days, or when venerating spirits or their ancestors, [the people] hold feasts, host games, engage in singing and theatrical performances, and seek assistance to divine the future or ask favors of spirits. The matter of mourning is taken very seriously and is carried out in very formal and ostentatious fashion. Thus the Chinese have a saying: "Be born in Guangdong, die in Hanoi, and grow up in Korea."

Geisha

When there are village feasts, social gatherings, weddings, prayers for peace, or death anniversaries, singing girls are usually hired. Singing girls are women of a sweet and pleasant disposition who are trained in the arts of singing and chanting. They are commonly referred to as *co dao*. When there is a festival, they are usually brought in to sing, typically in the *ca-tru* style, to act out *The Tale of Kieu*, to chant sung verse, to recite *phu* poems, or to tell stories. When they sing, they sometimes sit and sometimes stand, using their hands to beat the rhythm on a piece of wood. They sing both high notes and low ones in ways that resonate most beautifully and delicately upon the ear. Sitting to one side is a musician plucking on an instrument called a *don day*, and there is a person beating time on a small tom-tom. At times, the singing girls also stand up to act, dance, or sing. When the guests are there, the host has the singing girls pour the wine. At such times, they lift the [wine] bowls in both hands while chanting verses about passion or lovers to urge the guests to drink. . . .

There is a common expression, "girls in the second month, boys in the eighth month," which refers to the fact that it is usually in the second month that villages hold a festival at which girls vie in a beauty contest, while in the eighth month there is a feast at which boys compete in displaying their talents.

Feasts

In the eighth month, the custom is to hold a feast in the village communal house, at which villagers sacrifice to the spirits and pray for peace. They compete with one another in readying the feast, which is first offered to the spirits, after which the food is eaten by the people sitting together in the communal hall. The food for the feast is arrayed on stacked trays, which are arranged in several layers. They use sugarcane with the bark removed and replaced by red paper wrapped around it to separate the displayed trays of food. On top of this are placed the figures of a phoenix, a dragon, a unicorn, and a turtle, which stand arrayed on either side. The villagers wait until the evening before they divide the food among themselves. At such events, they usually listen to singing girls; watch fighting with staffs (including boxing and martial arts), wrestling, marionettes, water puppets, and rope climbing; or play card games and human chess. There are also contests in rice cooking, cotton weaving, eel catching, and statue carving. Prizes are awarded to the winners of each of these competitions.

In the cooking contest, contestants must boil the rice, with the winner being the one whose rice is first ready to be eaten and also who is best at keeping the rice from burning or overcooking. The contestants are provided with a small amount of kindling and crushed sugarcane or some thatch, which they must light and then hold the pot over the fire until the rice is cooked.

For the weaving contest, a platform is constructed in the middle of a pond, and looms are placed on it. The weaving girls go out and climb onto the platform, where they sit down to weave. At the signal to begin, they thrust their shuttles back and forth through the warp as fast as they can. Anyone who misses the flying shuttle and drops it into the pond is eliminated.

The eel-catching contest features one boy and one girl, each of whom uses one arm to embrace the other around the neck. They then stick their free arms into a deep jar into which an eel has been released, and the first to catch the eel is awarded the prize.

For the sculpture-carving contest, a beautiful and charming singing girl who is wearing a sheer silk dress and shiny satin trousers sits on a platform erected in the middle of a pond. The boys competing in the contest put on loincloths made of paper and then pretend to be sculpting the sitting girl. Each time a contestant is no longer able to contain his passion, his penis rises in an erection, shredding his loincloth and eliminating him from the contest. When this happens, he dives headfirst into the pond to hide his shame. These are just a few words of summary about customs [in Tonkin], so that you might know about them.

[Truong Vinh Ky, *Voyage au Tonking en 1876*, 14–16;
trans. George Dutton]

FOREIGN RELATIONS AND WARFARE

GIA LONG EMPEROR

COMMEMORATION OF THE DEFEAT OF THE TAY SON (1802)

In 1802, Nguyen Anh finally succeeded in his long-running campaign to defeat the Tay Son. Aided by the premature deaths of the two most powerful Tay Son leaders and the succession of a young son to the Quang Trung emperor's throne, Nguyen Anh gradually extended his territorial control from his southern base in Gia Dinh. After the young Tay Son emperor was captured, the newly named Gia Long emperor had him torn limb from limb by elephants. Not satisfied with this vengeance, he ordered the exhumation of the deceased Tay Son rulers' bones and their desecration by his troops. The following commemorative poem was issued publicly shortly after these events. It is a brief summary of the Tay Son conflict, with an emphasis on the alleged cruelty of the Tay Son rebels and the contrasting humanity and virtue of the Nguyen leader. The genre of official commemorative poetry is significant, and there are numerous surviving examples, particularly from the Le dynasty. Le Thai To and Nguyen Trai's famous fifteenth-century declaration on the defeat of the Ming (Binh Ngo dai cao) is perhaps the most notable example, containing both a description of events and a commentary on the responses of the righteous Vietnamese armies.[31] This prose translation does not attempt to capture the poetic feel of the original but focuses on its essential meaning.

Thanks to the nine preceding generations [going back to Nguyen Hoang (r. 1558–1613)], we were unified against our enemy; this is the fundamental principle of the *Spring and Autumn Annals.*

Pitying the myriad people, we attacked despots, the mark of a ruler's great benevolence.

Early difficulties nourished our profound sorrow.

We used our imperial edicts to set forth and make clear the great commands.

Thus it was in our country.

Ha Trung nourished excellence; Mieu Ngoai produced auspiciousness. (This was seen and recorded by Emperor Le Trang Tong.)[32]

The great achievements of the first Viet rulers established the vast foundation, while benevolence and generosity have been transmitted along a single artery.

Through the succession of sagely rulers who had gloriously made outstanding achievements, we enjoyed a great peace for two hundred years.

---

31. See Le Thai To and Nguyen Trai, "Great Proclamation on the Defeat of the Ming" (chap. 3).

32. Ha Trung was the home prefecture and Mieu Ngoai, the natal village, of the Nguyen clan, from which they emerged to help restore the Le dynasty.

But during this undertaking, we met with disaster, leading rebellious men to cause chaos.

They seized and occupied our citadels and hamlets;

They poisoned and tormented our people.

From Hue and Nhac onward, from Nguyen Trat[33] backward, they created evil, which extended far beyond a single day.

From Thuan [Hoa] and Quang [Nam] southward and from the Linh River northward, disaster and calamity spread everywhere.

I gnashed my teeth at the country's enemies, heartbroken at the sufferings of the people.

I moved about on foot, blown by the wind away from stability, just like Xia Shaokang from the land of You Reng.[34]

I was cautious and disciplined as I plotted my return, more so even than was Han Guangwu of the land of Bai Shui.[35]

It was the will of Heaven that I assumed this position, and so I waited patiently for the [right] time.

Then the opportunity to prevail appeared once again, and I led the army to attack on foot in order to restore the state.

In the *mau than* year [1788], I set out from Siam and, before long, recaptured the city of Gia Dinh.

In the *ky vi* year [1799], I entered Qui Nhon.

In the fifth month of the *tan dau* year [1801], I entered and subdued Phu Xuan.

The cruel usurper fled in a panic, going northward alone on horseback.

After that, Mount Hoanh was taken, and I exhausted myself restoring the old boundaries.

Only the isolated forces of the traitorous Dieu remained, still clinging to their old strongholds.[36]

I decided that to eliminate their evil, I first had to clean out their caves; and to punish the enemy, I first had to repair our halberds.

Only then could our attacking troops overrun and cut off their ramparts,

Only then could we catch and punish the enemy who would be forced out of Ban Thanh.[37]

---

33. Nguyen Trat was another name for Nguyen Quang Toan, the son and successor of the Quang Trung emperor.

34. This refers to the exile of the restorer and future emperor of the Xia dynasty, Xia Shaokang, in the third millennium B.C.E.

35. This refers to the exile of the future emperor Han Guangwu, who restored the Han dynasty after the Wang Mang uprising in the first century C.E.

36. This refers to the noted female Tay Son general Bui Thi Xuan, the wife of General Tran Quang Dieu.

37. This refers to the Tay Son's long-standing imperial center at Cha Ban (the former Cham capital of Vijaya).

They had already fled the fates and hidden in the forests;

We chased after their troops, attacking them toward the north.

Finally, in the fifth month of the *nham tuat* year [1802], I personally guided the great masses in the ferry across the Linh River.

Riding the winds, the circumstances inspired us, and the task was easily accomplished.

The sun pointing out the way, our triumph was achieved as easily as destroying bamboo.

All the paths of Hoan and Ai [Nghe An and Thanh Hoa] directly witnessed the crumbling mountainsides;

Dieu and Dung were in a hopeless situation, following each other to take refuge in ditches.[38]

The entire journey resembled thunder and lightning;

Their ranks of citadels were all falling tile and flying ash.

All the false and rebellious [ranks] were captured;

The guilty ones had now been taken.

The forces of darkness had been swept away, and all the lands under Heaven had been cleaned up.

The six creatures with their songs of triumphant return fill the roads while the mountains and rivers add their colors.

For this we truly relied on the assistance of exalted Heaven and on the nine temples,[39] which are unified in their sacrality; the generals, too, contributed, and the three armies also used their strength to achieve this result.

[Phan Thuc Truc, *Quoc su di bien*, 91–97; trans. George Dutton]

PHAN HUY CHU

SUMMARY RECORD OF AN OVERSEAS JOURNEY (1833)

Summary Record of an Overseas Journey describes a voyage to Singapore and Batavia (present-day Jakarta, Indonesia) that the noted scholar Phan Huy Chu made in 1833 on behalf of the Nguyen court. It recounts the course of the journey and its various ports of call, as well as observations of European culture and social structure in the Dutch East Indies. In the following excerpts, Phan Huy Chu compares European calendar systems with those of Vietnam and China and comments on the structures and forms of Dutch military and judicial systems. Collecting information about Europeans was one of the Minh Mang court's objectives, which it did through such voyages and discussions with arriving European traders. What is striking is that this information seems to have hardly altered Vietnamese awareness of the threat posed by European colonial

---

38. Tran Quang Dieu and Dung were noted Tay Son generals.
39. This refers to the nine generations of Nguyen lords in the south.

ambitions or resulted in any substantive policy responses. By the time strong arguments for reform were being made in the 1860s,[40] the court's position was already extremely precarious.

The Westerners' method for calculating calendars:

The system of the Great West does not use reign names, and it does not record the years in which the kings of those countries came to the throne. Every time they record something, at the end of the document they record only that it was, for example, the Hoa Lan [Dutch] year of 1833, along with the day and the month. This is the method used by the Western barbarians and the Dutch. All the documents translated by the local Chinese residents into Chinese also are written in this manner. Perhaps this records the year that the Dutch people first established their country. Now if we use this to calculate backward eighteen hundred years, it is roughly around the beginning of the Han dynasty in China. And in our country of Viet, it would be approximately during the era of [King] An Duong. By the Chinese system of reckoning, who knows how many dynasties have existed in its history, and Holland has thus existed as a country for this length of time. The laws and regulations of all the powerful foreign countries must have originated in Holland. For this reason, all the records of time periods are like this, so we do not have any idea of their beginnings.

The regulation of the Westerners' weeks:

The custom of the Westerners is that once every seven days, they all gather together to go out for pleasure, to eat and drink, and they call this "going to banquets." On the afternoon of that day, the government offices halt their work, and the markets are closed. The idea behind this is similar to the ancient custom of resting and bathing once every ten days. But the custom among the Westerners is to go to attend banquets in order to enjoy themselves. Speaking of their customs, when they eat food, they do not use chopsticks but rather use a spoon. And when they drink water, they all like it sweetened and cold. The meat that they eat for their meals fills the tables, and most of them use their hands to tear it up. They pour their wine into tankards, which makes it appear as though they are drinking with their noses. The forms of their banquets are very much different from those found in China.

The military system:

The military regulations of the Dutch are very strict, correct, and systematic. All the soldiers wear long shirts made of a bluish-black wool; they wear a blue cotton sash and a copper insignia. At their back is tied a red velvet sash embroidered with flowers. They wear cotton trousers and leather shoes. The style of their clothing is extremely detailed. Their military weapons are both guns and swords, each of which is very sharp. Their banners are distinctive, and their length does not exceed six *thuoc* [nearly eight feet]. Broadly speaking, they look like Qing-

40. See "Debating French Demands" (this chap.).

court soldiers, except that they do not carry bows and arrows. When they go out to drill, one general holds the banner of command, and he gives orders and shouts out commands in a loud voice, which all the troops must follow very precisely: about face, step together, advance, and then all stop together. The military regulations and military deployment give the impression of being very strict. The number of Dutch soldiers does not exceed one thousand men, and the Javanese troops, who are used only as laborers do not appear to equal this number.

The judicial system:

I do not know in any detail the stipulations and patterns of the Westerners' judicial regulations, so I can speak only about those that I have witnessed at first hand. Minor violators are punished by being beaten with a cane. First the person is tied to a wooden shelf, then once his punishment is determined, he is immediately struck a certain number of times with the cane and then released. Major violators are shackled with iron chains tied around the waist as well as both legs, and they are forced to perform manual labor. They often are seen constructing ramparts. An official wearing a tunic and red hat supervises several dozen shackled prisoners. They are forced to carry the soil to bank up the ramparts. Although they are not subjected to caning, they compete with one another in their efforts. Along the roads are people who carry various goods, sometimes seven or eight of them and occasionally more than ten, and among them is only one soldier, who holds a stick to urge them on. They converse directly with one another as they travel, and generally speaking, there is no need to restrain them. According to the regulations for arresting criminals, only a cord is used to tie up the ringleaders, on whom a rattan cane is used freely. Even though there may be several dozen [criminals], none attempts to escape. I have heard that [the Dutch] legal codes are very strict. Thus those who charge excessive interest rates or abuse their authority are punished. Some overseas Chinese residents say that the legal institutions of the country of Batavia [location of present-day Jakarta] are well established and their precedents are firmly fixed. The laws have no biases, and those who act as judges make impartial decisions. The scales of justice are balanced. Consequently, it is very easy to control the people.

[Phan Huy Chu, *Hai trinh chi luoc*, 153–54, 161–63; trans. George Dutton]

PHAN HUY CHU

A RECORD OF MILITARY SYSTEMS (1821)

This introduction to the military affairs section of the *Categorized Records of the Institutions of Successive Dynasties* provides a brief history of the ways in which Vietnamese courts organized and deployed their soldiers. The introduction also is a prelude to a more detailed examination of the problems encountered by the declining Le rulers, in which uncontrolled units of soldiers terrorized civilian authorities, contributing to the collapse of the dynasty. As such, the text is a warning to the new Nguyen regime about the need to tightly supervise the military. This warning is directed at a regime that came to power through military means and that maintained the military's strong role in state building in the aftermath of the Tay Son wars.

Heaven issued the five elements, among which one cannot ignore military matters. Under "systems," the *Classic of Changes* states that "one must repair weaponry," whereas the *Classic of Documents* states that "one must put in order military affairs," and they both state that the arts of preparing the kingdom cannot be neglected. In earlier times, soldiers were taken from the peasantry and used in times of danger. Since the Qin and Han dynasties, soldiers and peasants have been distinguished from each other, and the military systems were structured differently from earlier times. The main problems were suppressing rebellions and preventing treachery, although each generation had military policies specific to its era. We have no evidence of the early military systems in our kingdom of Viet. From the time of the ten circuits of the Dinh and earlier Le dynasties when they founded [the country], we can discern only the general outlines, but we know much more about the Ly and Tran dynasties' establishment of military nomenclature. The Ly had ten specialized military units, and the Tran had troop quotas for all the [provincial] capitals. The imperial city had permanent military specialist units, as well as detachments of intimidating troops. [The Tran] maintained the earlier practices for troops established outside the imperial city, so during peacetime the soldiers returned to farming their fields, and when necessary, they were summoned according to the registers. This made it possible to keep a fixed number of soldiers at a reasonable cost while maintaining [an offensive posture] toward their enemies. The [Tran] succeeded in pacifying the Cham and destroying the Song armies (Ly Thai Tong pacified the Cham, while [Ly] Nhan Tong destroyed the Song army), and they were able twice to attack and defeat the Yuan [Mongol] troops. (Both times it was Tran Nhan Tong who destroyed the Yuan troops.) Thus, the armed forces of two generations brought strength and prosperity.

Then came the time when the Le rose up in Thanh Hoa [against the Ming], and for the ten specialized units they relied completely on their own troops. Thus, the circumstances of their establishment of a new dynasty were different from those of earlier generations. They used only local troops from the regions of Nghe An, Tan Binh, and Thuan Hoa. After they had pacified the Ngo [Ming], they began to use troops from the five circuits throughout the country. During the Restoration [1592], they used only ordinary soldiers from the three prefectures in Thanh Hoa and the twelve districts in Nghe An. Only after the Mac had been eliminated did they begin to use the unified troops from the four military regions. Because these two regions [Thanh Hoa and Nghe An] were where the dynasty originated and with whose troops it had endured hardships and suffering, the dynasty drew [these soldiers] close as their "talons and teeth" and treated them as their close confidants, giving them preference over the unified soldiers; this was, of course, quite natural under these circumstances.

But these troops came to rely on coercion and began to disregard the laws. They had been supported for a long time, which gave birth to arrogance. Starting in the middle of the Restoration era, the troops became difficult to control, to the point of killing officials and stealing their possessions. They did not change their old habits, became arrogant toward the emperor, and could not be removed. Then, near the end of the Canh Hung period [1740–1786], they helped Prince Doan [Trinh Khai] take power. Claiming credit for this, [the troops] became even more arrogant, disregarded all laws and regulations, defied everyone, and intimidated [even] government officials. (During that period the soldiers arrogantly abused power, and entreaties had no impact on them. They would urge one another to destroy the home of any great official or ordinary person who was unsympathetic to them and chase him away, and none of the officials in the court knew how to restrain them.) The officials were united in despairing of this. (The soldiers spoke very clearly of wishing to kill the [Trinh] lord's nephew, and the principal concubine had to go out to cry and ask to be able to pay them off. Only then was [this problem] resolved.)[41] Finally, [the lack of control over the soldiers] caused the court to fall into decline, all while its foreign enemies were becoming stronger. [Consequently,] when the southern troops arrived, the gates of the capital could not be defended.[42]

In my investigation of the Le Restoration, I found that [the Le dynasty] relied on the strength of the two regions' soldiers but that the source of its collapse also lay in the arrogant soldiers of the three prefectures. Thus, the Le relied on these troops to establish the dynasty, but in the end, these troops caused their collapse. This [outcome] can clearly be taken as an object lesson regarding previous successes and failures. Thus, if one is skillful in holding the reins, one can use even poor and corrupt people, but if one loses control, they will immediately break away, leading to either success or failure. Thus, one cannot not have a system for supervising soldiers.

[Phan Huy Chu, *LTHCLC*, 8:1a–3a; trans. George Dutton]

DEBATING FRENCH DEMANDS (1862)

The following excerpt from *The Veritable Records of Dai Nam* (1811–) is a memorial presented by court officials to the Tu Duc emperor (r. 1848–1883). In it, the officials describe France's demands and what the Vietnamese response should be. They weigh France's various stipulations for a proposed treaty and assess the impact of accepting

---

41. The two parenthetical comments are in the original text.
42. When the Tay Son armies reached Thang Long in the summer of 1786.

each one. The court officials' general sense is that the Vietnamese ruler should give in to French demands, which they believe will have only a relatively modest impact on Vietnamese sovereignty. The tone of the memorial indicates that this was the thinking of the group known as the "peace faction," which advocated a strategy of appeasing French demands with a view toward reversing them in the long run. This strategy contrasted with that of the "war faction," which argued unsuccessfully for rejecting the French demands, even at the risk of renewed warfare. The emperor's response to this memorial was quite assertive, insisting that many of the clauses were unacceptable and dangerous to Vietnamese pride and security. Ultimately, however, the court was forced to concede to nearly all the French demands, paving the way for France's subsequent annexation of the six southernmost Vietnamese provinces in 1863.

The discussion of peace has been going on for three or four years and still has not been definitively settled. Now [the French] ships have brought us a letter proposing a peace treaty, and although we have not discussed either their demands or their objectives, the main issues are not different from the fourteen demands that the [French] made last year. They are requesting that we give Western ships freedom of transportation and shipping on all the rivers west and south of the citadel of Gia Dinh; they are asking us to pardon all the people taken prisoner while we were fighting one another; they are stipulating that we not erect forts or ramparts or station guard troops on the Bien Hoa and Sai Gon rivers. These three stipulations are not matters of real concern for your officials, and they were considered for inclusion in the earlier treaty. But there still are eleven more stipulations.

One clause grants permission to [French people] to teach and preach [during] public travel. With respect to the two characters—"public travel"—this means in essence that all [these French people] are followers of the Way [Christians], that they be permitted to preach freely, and that any person who wants to follow and study that religion will be permitted to do so freely. In this case, these people could do as they wished, and we would be unable to draw up regulations to stop them. We had thought about this clause earlier. The people of our country who already are followers of the Way would be permitted to gather together freely, and those who wish to abandon the Way and no longer wish to follow it also could not be prevented from doing so.

Another clause states that people from the West who violate the law will be sent to Western officials to be adjudicated; this clause also is reasonable. Likewise, if people of our country who visit the areas where Western people engage in commerce and violate their laws, it would be only fair that they be sent back to our officials to be tried by our laws.

One clause stipulates that Western people should be free to travel anywhere in our country but that they must continue to obey our laws. We have already thought about this clause, too. People from that country [France] already have places where they engage in commerce. If they have any other matters that they need to discuss or have resolved, local officials can address and settle these matters. [French people's] traveling to other places also is not a problem, but we do not want any disorderly free movement.

Another clause stipulates that Western trading vessels be permitted to enter any port they wish and that Western officials may be stationed anywhere they like. We also thought about this clause earlier: our country already has established places for conducting commerce and has made arrangements to enable ships to come and go conveniently to those places. [But] all the other ports should remain closed to them.

Another clause stipulates that we must pay damages, in cash, for the lives of the two or three Western people who were killed. This clause was one that we thought about earlier: we need not be stingy about making this small reparations payment, but the invoice they sent us did not specify the amount of the damages. Thus, we must clarify this oversight so the matter can be rectified and resolved.

Another clause stipulates that we may no longer force the country of Cambodia to pay tribute. This, too, was a clause to which we had previously given some thought: Cambodia is a dependency of our country. Whether or not it sends tribute, the French originally did not have the power to interfere, and so there is really no need to consider this. If the [French] insist on these six clauses, I suggest that we follow what we have decided and reply to them. But if those people have other requests, we also should consider and act on them.

Earlier, those people [the French] asked us to turn over all the provincial citadels and the lands of Gia Dinh and Dinh Tuong, and requested permission to station troops in Thu Dau Mot in Bien Hoa; [they asked] that the capital cities of the two countries station both troops and senior officials there; [and they asserted that] the amount of silver reparations earlier demanded was 4 million *dong*. In addition, Spain requested [permission] to establish offices in the district of Do Son in the province of Hai Duong and at the port in the district of Nghieu Phong in order to collect tax revenues for ten years, after which time they would revert to our country. The Western people have repeatedly made these five demands, asking that we accept them.

The group of stubborn officials cannot again escape the insistent requests to separate the territories of Bien Hoa and Vinh Long and turn them over to the French, in the hopes of waiting for the old peace treaty to be accepted. Now I beg you to consider that in Gia Dinh, at the site of the old citadel, those people have already built a fort where they have stationed their troops. I think that we should temporarily allow them one office at Thu Dau Mot in the province of Bien Hoa, and the neighboring territory outside the citadel of the province of Dinh Tuong in the territorial borders on both sides of the river in the two districts of Tan An and Cuu An—and also [permit them] to live there. The territories in other regions, including the whole province of Vinh Long, should be returned to our country to be administered. Furthermore, the port of the capital city is not a place of commerce but a place where that group has built houses. They already have people there managing things, and all the tasks are being carried out adequately, so there is no need to set up a great *yamen* [government office] to do anything. [But] if they really want this, we should respond by saying that the port of Da Nang is very close to the capital, and their ships still can easily come and go, so they will be permitted to set up one of their offices there. We will ask that the silver indemnity and fine be resolved for us to pay them 1 million to 2 million cash, and no more. Also, the country of Spain, which has been alongside [France] in Gia Dinh for many years now, has strongly requested that they [be permitted] to live on the land at Do Son and to engage in commerce, and has asked to collect taxes for that district's port for ten years, after which time [tax collection rights] will be returned to our country. I recommend that we accept one of these two stipulations.

When the Christians of Bac Ky [the northern region] heard the news that this country [France] was disseminating the religion, they asked the court to honor the earlier concession given to France regarding permission to practice the faith. It is not necessary to discuss all the clauses in this treaty. Again, we earlier thought about and discussed restoring Gia Dinh and Dinh Tuong to our country for supervision and governance, and if they do not listen to us, then we should consider opening an office that follows the customs of Guangdong, which in earlier times were established provisionally and then were restored. If they make any demands about the cost of the redemption purchase, I estimate that 1 million to 2 million cash will be the fixed settlement price. Any subsequent promises will be paid gradually, or this matter can also be completed earlier. If they demand the transfer of all the provinces they have already seized, then we should refuse. While discussing this, we should weigh the pros and cons and debate it in great detail.

[*DNTL* (2004–2007), 7:768–73; trans. George Dutton]

PHILOSOPHY AND RELIGION

GIA LONG EMPEROR

EDICT OUTLINING PROPRIETY AND RITUAL (1804)

After the Tay Son wars, one of the Nguyen rulers' primary objectives was restoring order to the Vietnamese state and its people. At one level, this order was a material one of reestablishing government structures, rebuilding infrastructure, and implementing systematic taxation. At another level, however, this project was a sociocultural one of restoring ritual order in both religious and cultural practices. As we have seen in earlier texts, most notably the Le Code, such ideological intervention by Vietnamese rulers was a long-standing practice, so the Nguyen's project was not new. It was, however, carried out in a particularly forceful style, in large part because of the circumstances under which the dynasty came to power, and the long period of disorder and dislocation that preceded its rule. The following excerpt is from a much longer edict, in which the Gia Long emperor sought to impose order and propriety on a range of ritual practices. Equally important, this excerpt reveals an attempt to impose fiscal restraint on what had become elaborate and extremely expensive ceremonies relating to the spirits. Such state efforts to control expenditures among commoners is another long-standing theme, seen earlier in Trinh Cuong's 1720 guidelines regarding sumptuary practices.[43] Here the new emperor offers a critique of ritual practices, particularly those related to Buddhism and the worship of spirits. His critique also is an indictment of using magic to exploit the gullible. Finally, the edict offers a brief comment on Christianity and its putative effects on its adherents. This decree therefore is a useful glimpse into existing ritual practices as well as the expectations of the state and hints at the long-running tension between popular practice and the state's desire to regulate ritual behavior.

Worshipping Spirits and the Buddha

First of all, we must be concerned with matters relating to the people and only afterward turn to matters of the spirits. The *Classic [of Documents]* notes: "The commonplace ritual offerings to the spirits is what is called a lack of respect." And the *Zuo Commentary* states: "Respect the ghosts and spirits but keep them at a distance."[44] It also says: "Worshipping a spirit that is not one's own is merely an act of flattery." Surely there is a reason for all these comments on matters relating to ghosts and spirits. Recently, many people were flattering the spirits and venerating them at the temples of the city gods; they constructed heavy doors and complex chambers; they erected tall ridge poles, carved beams, and painted pillars; they used sacrificial utensils and guards of honor ornamented with gold and silver draperies and parasols, banners and flags, and embroidered silk gowns; and they offered prayers of supplication in the spring and prayers of gratitude in the fall. Large singing feasts would last for ten days and nights, and smaller ones for eight or nine days and nights. There were dramatic performances, bawdy songs, and countless rewards and prizes. Eating and drinking were extravagant, and expenditures were incalculable. In addition, there were boat races, puppet shows, and miscellaneous amusements. Some selected and took underage boys and young girls while others played chess or gambled with cards. They called this an event for the spirits, but in reality it was about private human desires. People were forced to make contributions, thereby squandering the possessions of their heirs.

Henceforth, if a spirit has virtue or merit, it may receive sacrifices if a separate petition has been made to the district magistrate, who will then examine the situation and permit it if worthy. If the temples are being rebuilt or newly

---

43. See Trinh Cuong, "Edict Regarding Local Customs" (chap. 4).
44. In fact, this quotation is from the *Analects*.

built, they may have only one interior compartment, three central halls, and two secondary gates, which may not be carved or decorated with vermilion drawings. Local temples may not improperly be called palaces, and the ritual objects and honorific banners may not use red lacquer or light-colored gold. Only dyed and scented silk fabrics are permitted for screens, parasols, banners, and flags, and embroidered cloth may not be used. The annual sacrificial rituals that people attend for banquets and singing may last for only one day and night, and prizes and awards may not be excessive. And when metal drums are used in a commemoration to carry out the ritual, after the commemoration has been completed, [they must not be used again]. All other miscellaneous amusements are forbidden.

With respect to worshipping the Buddha, the *Zuo Commentary* states: "Engaging in heterodoxy is extremely harmful." It also states: "When one offends Heaven, there is no recourse to entreaty." Those who worship the Buddha do so to request blessings and rewards. The Buddhist scriptures state: "If it is fated to be, this is the Buddha's doing, but if it is not fated by the Buddha, then it will not come to pass." It also states: "Serving one's parents will not get you to the other side, even though one gives alms to monks every day. It is of no benefit. Being loyal to the ruler, one may reach this place, even though one does not venerate the Buddha. It will not be a hindrance." If so, then there is no need for those with merit to entreat the Buddha for deliverance. [But] what can the Buddha do for those without merit?

We should examine and consider the various ancestors who achieved Buddhahood, like Mu Lian, who, despite this, was unable to help his mother,[45] or those who esteemed Buddhism as [Emperor] Xiaoyan [r. 502–549] did [but] who could not use it to preserve his body.[46] Never mind the disloyal and unfilial people who do not know that their king is the Buddha of the present time, and who have carelessly abandoned their father and mother whom the Buddha brought into being, and pray to a remote and formless Buddha, all to seek some future good fortune, which has not come. How can this be logical?

Recently, someone who venerated the Buddhist scriptures erected a very tall Buddhist pagoda with numerous imposing stories, and he strove to make it as grand and as beautiful as possible. He also cast a bell, sculpted richly decorated statues, and provided meals to the monks. He cleaned their altars, and on the three origination days,[47] he organized Buddhist assemblies at which offerings were made to the Buddha and the monks were fed, and the expenses for all this

---

45. Mu Lian was a devout Buddhist practitioner who journeyed into the lowest levels of the Buddhist hell in order to rescue his mother. This tale sought to reconcile Confucian notions of filial piety with Buddhist belief and doctrinal systems.

46. Xiaoyan, an emperor of the Liang dynasty, was a devoted Buddhist who died at the end of a civil war after a lengthy siege of his palace.

47. The "three origination days" are the fifteenth day of the first, seventh, and tenth lunar months.

were such that not all could be recorded. But in doing all this to obtain good fortune, he merely exploited himself, as well as his heirs. Henceforth, the restoration of any Buddhist temples in disrepair, the new construction of Buddhist temples, as well as the casting of bells and statues and the setting up of altars for religious assemblies, all will be banned. [In addition,] the local village leader must make a list of the full names and places of origin of temple monks who are truly learned and then must submit [this list] to the provincial officials so that they might know their number.

Again, the fates of peoples' lives are fixed: disasters cannot be avoided, and good fortune cannot be actively sought. Praying and confessing faults to solve and eliminate problems are utterly without benefit. In ancient times, this obscene wizardry was among the things that Gao Xin clearly put forth so as to make sacrifices and thus delude the people. Accordingly, the emperor ordered that [these wizards] be killed. All this was done to eliminate delusions and repudiate heresy and to return people's customs to uprightness. Ximen Bao [fifth century B.C.E.] hurled the witch [into the river]. Di Renjie [630–700] destroyed the heterodox temples.[48] There is agreement about what is good. Now the custom of worshipping ghosts has become deeply entrenched, and our people are unable to remain calm and abide by their fate. They frequently ask for amulets and incantations and curry favor with witches and wizards. They set up altars and beat bells and gongs, and they bend with the blowing wind, passing down their established customs and their petty, foolish superstitions. Some people have embraced black magic, feign trustworthiness, act mysteriously, and create confusion for those who listen and hear. They groundlessly rely on amulets when drawing up contracts and violate laws and regulations in order to earn a living. They claim to be able to alter their fate and to revive the dead, and they regard illnesses in families as strange marvelous commodities. Some mediums even go into a trance and claim falsely to speak for a spirit. They urge people to fast to the point of death and prevent doctors from being summoned until recovery is impossible. Furthermore, they use votive figures made of paper and horses made of straw, build gates and burn votive houses, and employ all sorts of superstitious amulets and drugs, even those that cause wives to despise their husbands, and husbands to fall madly in love with their secondary wives. They already have used these arts to disturb the people and, again, knock on doors offering cures and appear in droves to practice deception. This is truly a great harm to the people's lives.

From now on, when people become ill, they must consult only medical doctors to be cured, and they should be careful to protect their health in daily life; they should not believe anything they hear from magicians who pray and offer nonsensical sacrifices at the various doors to [Buddhist] enlightenment. Sorcerers

---

48. Ximen Bao, an official in the Warring States period (Wei dynasty), was known for his clear and appropriate judicial decisions; Di Renjie, an official in the Tang dynasty, was noted for his honesty and uprightness.

and sorceresses also are not permitted to worship and make offerings or to use burning incense to ward off evil spirits or prayers to ward off misfortune. Those who break with the old customs must be severely punished. In addition, "the way of Ye-Su" [Christianity] is a religion from distant lands that has been brought into our country by foreigners. It speaks of a hell full of devils and a heavenly paradise full of spirits, and it seeks to persuade the masses to run about as though they were mad and to convince them of this superstition without their realizing it. Henceforth, all the people in villages and hamlets with Christian churches that are in disrepair must report this information to the provincial officials to request permission to repair them, and the construction of new churches is completely prohibited. Everyone should repent their previous faults and hold carefully to these teachings. If village customs persist in violating the laws of the state and people become aware of this, the village chief must intervene and circulate this information around the prefecture. If the violator's crime is severe, he must perform corvée labor, and if it is minor, he must be beaten with the rod or cane in order to reduce the costs to the people and to teach [him more appropriate behavior].

[DNTL (1961–), 1:645–46; DNTL (2004–2007), 5:583–87; trans. George Dutton, with Joshua Herr]

TRINH HOAI DUC

TEMPLE OF THE GENERAL OF THE SOUTHERN SEAS (1820)

In addition to the practice of Buddhism and the veneration of ancestors, the Vietnamese worshipped a wide range of more local spirits and deities. *Departed Spirits of the Viet Realm* (1329), a collection of cultic tales by Ly Te Xuyen,[49] already made clear the importance of such figures to the popular belief systems, and even though over time, Buddhism and Confucianism became dominant institutionally, the Vietnamese people's belief in spirits remained very strong. The veneration of spirits was typically quite localized, tied to particular places, regionally specific historical figures, or even animals. The following excerpt from Trinh Hoai Duc's *Gia Dinh Citadel Records* describes the veneration of the Whale Spirit, a deity held in high regard by fishermen along the central and southern coasts of Vietnam where whales were often seen. The Whale Spirit was regarded as benevolent, protecting fisherman as they carried out their often perilous profession. Trinh Hoai Duc also looks at the importance of the correct ritual treatment of whales and the benefits that they might bring. This cult of the Whale Spirit continues to thrive among Vietnamese in the same region, as reflected

---

49. See Zeng Gun, "The Spirit Cao Lo" and "The Mountain Spirit," and Zhao Cheng, "An Indigenous King" (all in chap. 1), and Ly Thuong Kiet, "The Southern Land"; "The Spirit of To Lich"; "Lady God of the Earth"; "The Spirit of Phu Dong"; and Ly Te Xuyen, "The Cult of Phung Hung," "The Trung Sisters," and "The Ideal Official" (all in chap. 2).

in regular rituals and the construction or renovation of numerous commemorative temples dedicated to "Sir Fish."

The spirit of the Temple of the General of the Southern Seas is that of a whale. It has a hollow flipper and its head is round and smooth, and at the tip of its head is a hole from which water spouts like rain. It has the lips of an elephant and the tail of a shrimp, and it is more than two or three *truong* [twenty-four to thirty-six feet] in length. It frequently jumps on the surface of the ocean. When fishermen lower their nets to catch fish, they usually call out to this spirit, and then it chases throngs of fish into their nets, and the people are very thankful. In rare instances, this fish finds its way into their nets. When this happens, the fishermen open one side of the net and call to the whale, and it then swims to the opening of the net and escapes back into the sea. When ships are endangered by waves and winds, this fish is often seen coming to support the ship until the waters are calm again. If a ship founders, and water pours into it, this fish will ferry the passengers to the shore; the protection of the Whale Spirit is thus very clear. Only our southern country, from the Linh River down to Ha Tien, has a supernatural spirit of this type; in other seas they do not have anything like this. This is because in the southern regions, the mountains and seas produce sacred vapors, which secretly provide assistance to our people. We have already conferred on [the Whale Spirit] the title Southern Seas Troop General Jade Unicorn Venerated Spirit, which has been recorded in the ritual records. If one of these fish is attacked by another, cruel fish and is wounded and dies, it will float on the surface of the sea. The people along the seacoast then contribute money to purchase a coffin shroud as well as articles for preparing a burial. They choose a man from the clan of fishermen to serve as the chief mourner. He selects a place to bury [the whale], and then the [fishermen] build a temple at that site. In places that have such whale graves, the people enjoy very good fortune; places without such graves still erect temples at which the whales are venerated. These can be found all along the coast.

[Trinh Hoai Duc, *GDTTC*, 510 (31b–32a); trans. George Dutton]

MINH MANG EMPEROR

COMMENTS REGARDING CHRISTIANITY (1839)

Since the earliest years of the Catholic mission in Vietnam, the Vietnamese state was suspicious of both the Christian doctrine and those who preached it. While because of their scientific skills, Jesuits were sometimes tolerated, Vietnamese rulers remained uneasy about the social implications of the Catholic message, which threatened the idealized Confucian hierarchy supported by the state. Catholic missionaries, most notably Bishop Pigneau de Béhaine, supported the Nguyen during their eighteenth-century struggle with the Tay Son, and the first Nguyen emperor acknowledged this debt by tolerating European clerics and their converts. But this tolerance waned under the more orthodox Minh Mang emperor, who suspected Catholics of contributing to political factionalism, both at the court and in the southern Gia Dinh region. Moreover, attempts to deport the missionaries repeatedly failed as they returned in defiance of imperial edicts. This excerpt from *The Veritable Records of Dai Nam* is a discussion that reveals the emperor's views of the religion's impact and his challenge to two officials' claims that their own Christianity was a result of filial adherence to their fathers' and grandfathers' practices. Minh Mang counters their claims with classical references and the observation that blind adherence to one's father's actions, regardless of the inherent qualities of those actions, does not constitute filial piety.

The soldiers Pham Viet Huy and Bui Duc The from Nam Dinh Province came to the capital to make the following appeal: For generations, their grandfathers and fathers had accepted the "Ye-Su Dao" [Christian faith], but last year they trampled on the cross. This was an action forced on them by provincial officials and did not come from their hearts. The soldiers begged permission to remain faithful to this religion, to perfect their actions of filial piety. If they had to die, they said, they would not regret it. This was a case reported by a judicial office.

The emperor considered this very strange and stated: "These men have been lured into this state of illusion by the vicious religion for a long time, and they have not repented. Previously, when this case came up at the provincial level, each official in every ministry said they should be killed. But I could not bear to condemn them hastily according to the laws, and in each case I sought to understand and find evidence of their awakening to the truth. Then the province reported that they had sincerely abandoned the religion, and so we immediately released them and again rewarded them. Now they have continued in their stubborn dimness and have dared to come to the capital to appeal while abandoning their military posts. These men are creating chaos among the people; how can we tolerate their living in this world?"

The emperor ordered the royal guards to take them to the seashore, to cut them in half with a big ax and then to throw them into the sea. He also ordered that Dinh Dat, who had been involved in the same case but who had stayed in the province, be questioned again. [Dinh] Dat also persisted in refusing to abandon the religion, so was beheaded. The governor-general of the province, Trinh Quang Khanh, was punished with a one-level reduction in rank because he had reported [this transgression] only vaguely. In addition, the emperor secretly ordered the organization of investigative units to visit and find out whether the soldiers and people who had followed the false teaching of "Ye-Su" and had already expressed their intention to abandon the religion had in fact turned from evil to uprightness, or whether they had acted reluctantly and not yet truly given it up. The units had to verify whether those people who had not come to the capital of the province but had reported by themselves because they feared the law and had actually come to repent, or whether they still secretly flocked together for religious teaching and study. In the event that their behaviors were still the same as in the past and had not changed, then the units were to report secretly and truthfully and were not to hide or distort reality.

The emperor spoke with the minister of justice, saying: "Christianity came from the West. In the beginning it did not attract more than one or two dull persons, but eventually reached the point of gathering a great many followers, who then plotted rebellion. The former case showed this very clearly.[50] But I think the persons who follow this religion will eventually find that it is false and a great illusion. If you think about the story of the Cross and Jesus Christ, it is surely without foundation. This talk of Heaven and holy water is also nonsense, as is this matter of removing the eyes of corpses with the excuse of praying for their souls. In the name of virginity, they seduce the wives of other men. It is not enough for them to stop at disrupting harmony and harming our customs.

Furthermore, the ignorant and foolish are seduced into wrongdoing, and from time to time groups of disloyal and unfilial people also fall into the religion. They practice and study it for a long time, so that they are already deeply contaminated by it and form noisy groups who follow the evil way. In the end, ordinary villagers cannot escape believing what they hear and pay no attention to these fundamental laws. Previously, we strictly established regulations banning [this religion]; we burned its books, destroyed its residences, and chased people away so that they no longer could gather together. In turn, we promulgated edicts with the desire to make my people turn back to the good and keep their distance from such crimes. Several times we exposed the legal cases regarding Christianity. We killed stubborn [adherents] and released those who repented. Both central and local subjects heard and saw all this together. These Nam Dinh soldiers, Pham Viet Huy and Bui Duc The, willingly rebelled, so our laws can hardly be lenient toward them, and we already have executed them. Even the one phrase they cited, "We do not change what [our] grandfathers and fathers did in order that we might be called pious," is truly despicable, so these men deserved to be killed. It is difficult to believe that the hearts of people could have fallen and been deceived to this extent.

You again must send an edict to the officials in provinces near the capital so they will clearly understand that any soldier or commoner under their jurisdiction who foolishly adopts Christianity as his family religion, but then abandons it by stepping on the cross in a government office, must truly be repentant and cannot secretly violate the law by once again following this vicious religion. All those who have not previously abandoned the religion must now appear at the

---

50. This refers to the Le Van Khoi revolt of 1833, which was supported by Vietnamese Christians. See Minh Mang Emperor, "Edict to the Literati and Commoners of the Six Provinces of Southern Vietnam" (this chap.).

provincial capital to confess the truth, and they will be ordered to step repeat-edly on the cross, and you must carefully observe them. If they act out of real sincerity, then you should immediately release them. But if the family has already been ensnared, so that the vicious thinking cannot be erased, and if anyone defends himself using the sentence "Not changing from the actions of one's grandfather and father is being filial," you should enlighten him regarding the great teaching, which states that of the hundred behaviors, none is greater than being unfilial. But this "being filial" is as follows: "The beginning of filiality is not daring to harm any piece of hair and skin because you received them from your parents, and the end of filiality is to honor your parents by establishing yourself and spreading your name in the world." How can a person state that to be filial is not to change from the actions of one's grandfathers and fathers? Confucius said being filial is not changing the teaching of your parents for three years. Zhu Xi said that if it is a genuine teaching, then you need not change it during your whole life, but if it is a false teaching, then why would you wait three years to change it? Thus, if one's grandfather or father has acted incorrectly, then one's children and grandchildren must change their behavior immediately. What is right is already clear. If you do not ask whether or not the matter is right, would this mean that if your grandfather and father lived by robbery and theft so that it led to their being punished by death, their children and grandchildren should also follow in this path and not change it?

In truth, both the knowledge of good nature and that of instinct are common throughout humankind. Not to regard one's own father as father but, rather, to regard the Westerner as one's father; not to regard one's own grandfather as grandfather but to regard Western religion as one's ancestor; not to know how to pay respect to the bright souls and also not to perform ceremonies for one's an-cestors, how can we call this acting in a filial manner? If your grandfathers or fathers are still alive, and you realize that they are heading in the wrong direc-tion, you should take pains to change them. If your grandfathers and fathers were living in the late Le period, or during the [time of the] false Tay Son court, when education was in decline and governance was neither calm nor prosperous, they could not be shown the grand teachings, despite the regulations banning Christi-anity, and consequently they became badly deceived for their entire lives.

Now the court is at peace, and the laws have been brightly polished. Virtuous people should be praised, and wicked people must be punished. No one under Heaven cannot be made cultivated. They know that their grandfathers and fathers have already died, so why do they not want to avoid the disaster of being com-pletely destroyed by covering up previous misdeeds based on lamented changes by their children and grandchildren? Anyone who is a child and grandchild in a time of great peace must console the souls of his grandfather and father by eradicating deep-rooted bad habits.

[DNTL (1961–), 12:96–98; DNTL (2004–2007), 5:501–3; trans. Choi Byung Wook]

THIEN MU PAGODA (1870S–1900S)

The Unification Records of Dai Nam (1811–) is a comprehensive official gazetteer of the unified Vietnamese realm. Compiled and elaborated by scholars over the nineteenth century, it surveys the major features and personages from each of the provinces. Organized by province—with subheadings for matters from climate and topography to tax receipts, markets, dikes, and bridges—the text is an invaluable description of the Nguyen realm. It preserves a significant amount of local knowledge, albeit refracted through the lens of the central government and its administration. This excerpt is a description of the physical features and history of the Thien Mu pagoda. Among its prominent artifacts was a large bell, long an important feature of Buddhist pagodas, as attested earlier by the commemorative inscription in 1109 of a bell dedicated to the Thien Phuc temple near Hanoi. The Thien Mu pagoda was constructed in the early seventeenth century by the Nguyen progenitor Nguyen Hoang (r. 1558–1613) on a hill outside his new capital at Phu Xuan. It was a significant marker of the Nguyen rulers' interest in Buddhism, but as this excerpt makes clear, the pagoda and its dramatic setting are an admixture of Buddhist beliefs, local spirits, and supernatural events. The reinvigorated Buddhism of the Nguyen realms proved an important spiritual and eventually political force. In the nineteenth century, Confucian-oriented Nguyen rulers actively sought to restrict the power of Buddhist institutions, while in the twentieth century, Buddhists forcefully challenged the pro-Catholic regimes of South Vietnam.

Thien Mu pagoda is situated outside the walls of the capital to the west on a hill in An Ninh village. A Buddhist pagoda has been there from ancient times, and it was rebuilt during the fourteenth year of Gia Long [1815], with the middle becoming the grand hall. Behind this on the left- and right-hand sides are two cooks' houses. Also behind it are the palaces of the Maitreya and Guanyin [Quan Am] buddhas. Behind those palaces on the right-hand side is a building for storing the scriptures, and in front of the Grand Majestic Palace from west to east are the palaces of the Ten Kings.[51] Each has his own palace, and in front of each one is a "home of thunder," and directly in front of these in the middle are ceremonial gates. Above each gate are towers. The one on the left is a bell tower, and the one on the right is a drum tower. Outside the gate and to the left is a hexagonal pavilion for a stele, and on the right is a large hexagonal bell tower, surrounded on four sides by a brick wall in which there are eight gates of varying sizes. In the third year of the Thieu Tri reign [1843], the emperor wrote the poetry [collection] *Twenty Scenic Views of the Divine Capital*, and one of the poems is entitled "Sound of the Thien Mu Bells," which was engraved on a bronze placard. In the fifth year of this reign [1845], a stone pagoda was built directly in front of the ceremonial gates, to the height of five *truong*, three *thuoc*, and two *thon* [sixty-four feet]. It was named the Pagoda of Compassion and Benevolence, but

---

51. The Ten Kings are the rulers of the Buddhist underworld who pass judgment on the dead.

later the name was changed to the Pagoda of the Treasure of Fortuitous Destiny. The tower has seven levels, and each one venerates the Sakyamuni buddha of the golden body. In front of the pagoda is a pavilion for burning incense and praying, on whose top is fixed a wheel of the law, which constantly spins in the breeze. To each side of the pagoda are two stele pavilions; to the front to the left and right of it on three sides stands a railing near a gate made of two stone pillars carved with flowers and that sits close to the bank of the Huong River.

We now move humbly to its history under the present dynasty.

In the *tan suu* year [1601], the forty-fourth year of our Great Ancestor Emperor [Nguyen Hoang], the king's procession came to Ha Khe, and the king saw a hill rising up from the plain like a dragon's head looking backward; the Truong River was flowing in front of it, and Lake Binh lay behind it. It was an extremely beautiful view, and when he took the occasion to ask local people about it, they answered that this hill was very sacred. There is an old story that one night someone encountered an old woman sitting on the hilltop dressed in a red tunic and a green dress, who said: "A true leader should come here and erect a pagoda to collect all the ethereal forces to keep the royal line stable." After saying that, she disappeared. This is why it was called Thien Mu [Heavenly Mother] Mountain. Because of the ethereal forces at the mountaintop, they built the pagoda there, which is the Thien Mu pagoda.

In *at ti* [1665], the seventeenth year of Emperor Thai Tong, the pagoda was renovated.[52]

In *canh dan* [1710], the nineteenth year of Emperor Hien Tong, the large bell was cast.[53]

In *giap ngo* [1714], the twenty-third year, the altar halls were renovated. The eight [*sic*] altar halls, stretching from the entrance to the monastery, are

The Heavenly King's Palace
The Jade Emperor's Palace
The Majestic Treasure Palace
The Hall for Expounding the Dharma
The Tower for Storing Scriptures
The Palace of the Ten Kings
The Hall of Water and Clouds
The Hall of Knowing the Taste
The Palace of Great Grief
The Palace of the Grand Master

---

52. Emperor Thai Tong is the posthumous title given to the Nguyen lord Nguyen Phuc Tan (r. 1648–1687).

53. Emperor Hien Tong is the posthumous title given to the Nguyen lord Nguyen Phuc Chu (r. 1691–1725).

Also behind the pagoda are many monks' cottages and meditation chambers and "brother and master" gardens belonging to the abbot.

In *at mui* [1715], the twenty-fourth year, the king personally engraved a stone that was erected in front of the pagoda. And on the riverbank, a fishing pavilion was erected where the lord often came for pleasure. Later this pavilion was destroyed by fire in a battle, but the remnants are still there. At the beginning of the Gia Long era, Cao Duc Sieu of the Board of Rites could still remember where it had been. Its large bell and inscribed stone have survived.

The *Recent Records of Trieu Chau* says that the pagoda is in Ha Khe village in Huong Tra county, that it lies beneath the peak of the mountain above and rests along the river flowing below. It rises three thousand feet above the vulgar world but is within feet of the pools of Heaven. Once a visitor went for a walk, climbed nearly to the top, and unconsciously his heart became pure and all his vulgar thoughts evaporated. It is truly a place fit for an abbot.

In the sixteenth year of Thanh Thai [1905], many gales caused great devastation. In the nineteenth year [1908], the Palace of Maitreya and the ten palaces and three buildings around it were moved and rebuilt, and the incense prayer pavilion was moved and reconstructed on the foundations of the old Palace of Maitreya.

[*Dai Nam nhat thong chi*, chap. 1, 51a–52b; trans. Catherine Churchman]

PART III

Modern Vietnam

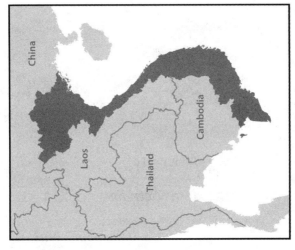

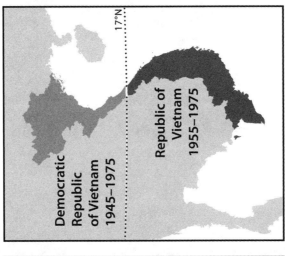

**French Indochina
1884–1945**

Tonkin
Laos
Annam
Cambodia
Cochinchina

**Democratic
Republic
of Vietnam
1945–1975**

17°N

**Republic of
Vietnam
1955–1975**

**Socialist Republic of Vietnam
1976–present**

China
Laos
Thailand
Cambodia

Chapter 6

THE COLONIAL ERA

The modern period in Vietnam's history ushered in a series of new challenges and rapid changes engendered by French colonization and the impact of Western and Asian ideas. After the conquest of the entire country by the French in 1884, the Vietnamese were faced with European occupation and control as well as the question of how they could fit into the modern world. At first, the imperial court and its scholar-gentry allies mounted a series of sporadic, anti-French attacks, none of which succeeded, although they kept alive the flame of revolt. Although most officials switched their allegiance to the French, some Confucian scholars retreated to the countryside, refusing to serve the new rulers. By the start of the twentieth century, new voices and forms of organization had begun to challenge the French. The most notable among them was Phan Boi Chau, a scholar trained in the Confucian classics who rejected French rule on the moral grounds that it would lead to the extinction of the Vietnamese nation and race. His approach reflected a search for modernity based on the ideas of social Darwinism and the model of Japan, a rising power in Asia, while resisting the French through violent means.

The debates about modernity that preoccupied Vietnamese thinkers in the early twentieth century centered on how modern ideas could be brought to bear to "strengthen" the country and defeat the French. Like Phan Boi Chau, who left Vietnam for Japan in 1905, the reform-minded Confucian scholars who organized the Tonkin Free School (Dong Kinh Nghia Thuc) in 1907 forcefully argued that only "modern learning" (as opposed to Confucian learning) and cultural and national revival could save Vietnam. This new approach called for replacing Chinese characters with the romanized script, *quoc ngu*, a modern educational system that encompassed science and technology, modern political institutions, and business activities. Phan Chau Trinh, a founder of this school, was one of the principal proponents of popular rights and political democratization. In general, these modernist scholars sought to "awaken" and invigorate nationalist consciousness and forge a new Vietnamese identity despite French assimilation efforts.

By the 1920s, the ideological and nationalist options available to the Vietnamese in colonial Indochina had expanded while the political and social crisis had shifted and deepened. New forms of political, cultural, and religious activity were attempted in order to break out of the colonial straitjacket and the sense of cultural decline. Independence was still the overriding and ultimate goal among most of the Vietnamese educated class, but would it be achieved through violent or nonviolent means, reform or revolution, or some other form of renewal? Would Vietnam become a monarchy, a republic, or a socialist state? The different currents of thought now included Marxist ideology, democratic nationalism, and neotraditionalist collaborationism. The failure of the uprising by Nguyen Thai Hoc's Nationalist Party (VNQDD) against the French in 1930 seemed to foreclose the option of a non-Marxist nationalist solution. All these new approaches grappled with which aspects of the traditional values to maintain while preserving an imagined "national soul" (except for Marxism). All entailed the formation of new elites and new organizational forms.

French culture, sometimes refracted through the lens of colonialism, inevitably had an impact on the evolution of Vietnamese modernity, even though only a fraction of the Vietnamese people were educated in French schools. The rest were illiterate. New Westernized ideas took shape against the backdrop of the older scholars' reliance on Confucian scholasticism, and by 1919, the Confucian examinations for administrative appointments had been discontinued.

In the 1920s, *quoc ngu*, the romanized writing system, largely replaced Chinese characters, spurring an outpouring of new media such as journals and newspapers and new literary forms such as novels and European-influenced forms of poetry. A new national literature began to take form. The Self-Reliance literary movement of the 1930s enthusiastically embraced Westernization and modernization and advised discarding all the old ways. During this decade, literature was based on new themes of romantic love and personal self-expression (as opposed to familial obligations) while also exploring naturalism and surrealistic forms. At the same time, the cultural arena was crowded with neotraditionalist arguments, and Confucianism continued to influence Vietnamese society, morality, and politics. Buddhism also experienced a revival and a renewal, and in the south, two new religious groups, the Cao Dai, a syncretic movement, and the Hoa Hao, an offshoot of Buddhism, became popular.

By the 1930s, though, Vietnam had largely broken with the past. Economic dislocations engendered by the increasing commercialization and monetization of the economy and its links to global capitalism had profound repercussions in the country. Western individualism was not, however, universally accepted as the model for a new society. Instead, new visions emerged, including collectivistic solutions based on submerging the individual to the society's broader needs. With the approach of World War II, various political parties competed with one another to determine the contours of Vietnam's political and socioeconomic system. The country again faced the prospect of fundamental change as social, political, and international forces converged to grant Vietnam the possibility of political independence.

THE LAND

HOANG DIEU

FAREWELL APOLOGIES TO THE EMPEROR (1882)

The French had completed their occupation of the south by 1867 and were looking for a way to extend their influence to the north, particularly to the strategic area of Hanoi and the Red River. In April 1882, French troops attacked Hanoi and took control of the citadel. Hoang Dieu, commander of the citadel and viceroy of northern Vietnam, failed to defend the city. He thereupon committed suicide to honor his loyalty to the emperor and as a protest against the court's halfhearted efforts to mount an effective resistance. In so doing, Hoang Dieu provided a model of self-sacrifice and devotion to the cause of saving the country. By 1884, the French had annexed the north and the center, creating the colonial dependencies of Tonkin, Annam, and Cochinchina.

I, the undersigned, am convinced that the imperial confidence has appointed me to a position that far surpasses my abilities. I, who am a modest scholar inexperienced in managing frontier areas, was invested with the responsibility of maintaining order and peace in a strategic region where rebellions swarm like flies.

For ten years we have been negotiating, and yet the enemy's intentions remain inscrutable.[1] It will soon be three years since I came, on imperial orders, to administer the region of Hanoi. During this time, I have never dared neglect the training of our troops or the consolidation of our fortifications. Not only have

---

1. Since 1874, when the French first intervened in northern Vietnam.

these measures contributed to the maintenance of peace within these borders, but they also have discouraged evildoers from even initiating their plots. But who would have guessed that birds of prey were poised for flight or that ravenous carnivores were in search of meat?

In the second month of this year, many French battleships sailed toward northern Vietnam, and most of them anchored not far from Hanoi. The population of the citadel became uneasy at their approach.

I ventured to think of Hanoi as an opening to all the regions of northern Vietnam. It certainly is a strategic stronghold. Were this place to fall into enemy hands, the rest of the territory would sooner or later follow.

For this reason, I both sent instructions secretly to the governors of the neighboring provinces to warn them and memorialized the throne to ask for reinforcement. Imperial edicts rebuked me, however, for repeatedly being excessively concerned with military matters or for not knowing the proper way to resist the enemy.

I investigated myself and found that I was not in command of any real power. Nevertheless I could not, with decency, forsake my duties as I am, after all, an important official. Conforming my conduct to that of my predecessors, I maintained an unwavering loyalty to the emperor.

Almost daily, I discussed the situation with my subordinates. Some suggested that we open our citadel to the French so that they might come and go freely. Others proposed that we withdraw our troops in order to allay their suspicion of our planned resistance. I vehemently opposed these counsels and felt that even if I [ended up being] annihilated, I would not comply with such expedients.

While our plans and preparations for defense were still indefinite, the enemies suddenly broke their earlier agreement.

On the seventh day [April 24, 1882] they submitted their ultimatum, and on the following day they unleashed the main force of their troops against the citadel.

> The enemy troops surrounded us, numerous as ants.
> The Western cannon exploded, deafening as thunder.
> In the city, fire spread throughout the houses in every street.
> In the citadel, fear wrung the hearts of the whole population.

Although I had just recovered from an illness, I made every effort to command our troops. We killed more than one hundred enemy soldiers. We succeeded in defending the citadel for longer than half a day.

But what else could we have done?

We were weak while they were strong. In vain, we waited for reinforcements. In vain, we fought for certain strategic points.

What more could we have done when our military officers, terrified by the enemy's advance, scattered in every direction and when our civilian mandarins sought only a means of escape?

My heart hurt me as if it had been cut with a knife. I could not, however, single-handedly hold the citadel.

A military commander of no talent like myself does not deserve to live longer. Responsible for the loss of the citadel and devoid of any hope of recovering it, I feel the death sentence too mild a punishment for my misdeed.

I dare not follow Zao Mo's example and save my life for future revenge.[2]

My only recourse is to imitate Zhang Xun by ending my life in order to honor the great responsibilities entrusted to me.[3]

I can claim neither loyalty nor righteousness, for I have been compelled to make this decision.

I am filled with shame for having allowed the enemy to seize the capital of the North.

Will the scholars of this part of the country forgive me? Bound to the destiny of the citadel, I am determined to walk in the steps of my predecessor, Nguyen Tri Phuong.[4]

Will my sovereign, a thousand *li* [one *li* is approximately one-third mile] away from me, understand my situation?

The only wish I have is that the sun and the moon send their rays to witness my devotion.

> Completed on the eighth day of the fourth month of the
> thirty-fifth year of Tu Duc [April 25, 1882]
> [Adapted from Truong Buu Lam, *Patterns of Vietnamese
> Response to Foreign Intervention*, 108–12]

HAM NGHI EMPEROR

ROYAL EDICT ON RESISTANCE (1885)

Under the Patrenotre Treaty of 1884, the Vietnamese court had ceded control to the French over all of Vietnam. Despite this, the young boy emperor Ham Nghi joined

---

2. Zao Mo, a seventh-century B.C.E. general of Lu, was defeated by the Ji and forced to give up his territory in return for peace. He later reconquered it.

3. General Zhang Xun defended Sui Yang against the son of An Lushan in the mid-eighth century. After Sui Yang's defeat, he was put to death after refusing to pledge allegiance to the victor.

4. Nguyen Tri Phuong, the commander of the Hanoi citadel when French forces seized it in an earlier raid in 1873, committed suicide just before the citadel fell. Nguyen Tri Phuong also was the commander in chief of the Vietnamese army when it was defeated by Franco-Spanish forces near Saigon in 1861.

forces with a royal faction to repel French troops by force when they arrived in Hue, the imperial capital, to set up their government. Upon their defeat, the emperor and his loyalists fled to the mountains, where they continued to mount and plan resistance efforts against the French. The Ham Nghi emperor was finally captured by the French in 1888 and was exiled to Algeria for the rest of his life. The Can Vuong (Save the King) movement, however, persisted until 1895. This edict was the Ham Nghi emperor's call to arms and follows the pattern of previous proclamations that called on the people to help defend the ruler after the emperor had fled the capital, such as Le Duy Mat's call to troops to overturn the Trinh and restore the Le.[5]

The emperor proclaims:

From time immemorial, there have never been more than three alternatives when planning military strategy: to fight, to resist, and to negotiate. We have missed the chance to fight. [If we] resist, we can hardly hope for the necessary strength. [If we] negotiate, we can never meet the enemy's demands. Therefore, we now find ourselves in a thousand difficulties, in ten thousand hardships. Unwillingly, we now resort to expedients. There have been numerous such cases among the famous men of antiquity: King Dai moved to the mountains of Ji;[6] Tang Xuanzong fled to Shu.[7]

Our country has recently experienced much suffering. Although I ascended the throne at a very young age, I have always been greatly concerned with the problem of strengthening and administering our country. But each day, the pressure from the Western envoys becomes increasingly imperious. Recently, they even brought in additional troops and battleships. Their demands were then all the more difficult to satisfy. As usual, we received them cordially. But they were not disposed to accept anything.

The people of the capital were keenly aware of the impending danger. The great ministers of the court tried to construct a policy that would maintain peace in the country and secure respect for the national authority. They were caught in a dilemma: should they bow their heads and take orders from the enemy, sit quietly and let opportunities pass by, or should they scrutinize the enemy's movements in preparation for an appropriate reaction? Now, since we can no longer evade the course of events, we shall have to build on today's gains for a better and brighter tomorrow. Such is, after all, the necessity imposed by circumstances. All those who have shared our anxieties surely appreciate the situation. If they do not, let them join the resistance, grit their teeth, and, with their hair on end, swear the destruction of every last enemy. Who would not be moved by such determina-

---

5. See Le Duy Mat, "Proclamation to Rally Troops" (chap. 4). Also notice the historical reference to "grasping the spears" in note 10.

6. King Dai of the Zhou dynasty (ca. 1100–256 B.C.E.) left his territory, which was under pressure from the barbarians, and fled to the mountains. All his people followed him.

7. This refers to Tang Xuanzong's flight during An Lushan's rebellion.

tion? Will there be no one to make a pillow of his sword,[8] to beat his oars against the bark,[9] to grasp the spears,[10] or to roll the jar?[11]

Moreover, officials of the court should observe only righteousness. Knowing righteousness, they should live and die by it. Gu Yuan[12] and Zhao Zui[13] of the Qin dynasty, Guo Ziyi[14] and Li Guangbi[15] of the Tang dynasty were indeed persons who lived by it in antiquity.

My virtue is like gossamer; now that I am confronted with these changes, I am unable to take the lead. The capital has been lost. The imperial carriage has departed. I am responsible for all this, and I feel an infinite shame. However, since we still are bound by moral obligations, none of you—mandarins, ministers, literati, high, or low—shall abandon me. Those with intelligence shall contribute ideas; those with strength shall lend their force. The rich shall give money to buy military supplies. The peasants and villagers shall not refuse hardship or evade danger. It is right that this should be so.

To uphold the weak, to support the faltering, to confront difficulties, and to reduce danger, none shall spare their efforts. Perhaps with Heaven's assistance, we shall be able to turn chaos into order, danger into peace, and finally retrieve our entire territory. Under these circumstances, the fate of the nation must be the fate of the people. Together we shall work out our destiny and together we shall rest. Is this not the best solution?

On the contrary, should you fear death more than you feel loyalty to your emperor, should your domestic worries override your concern for the affairs of state, should officials flee danger on every occasion and soldiers desert their

---

8. Liuzhu of Qin said: "I rest my head on my sword, awaiting the morning to behead the enemy."

9. Emperor Qin Shihuang di of the Qin dynasty (221–207 B.C.E.) declared as he beat his oars against a bark: "If I fail to pacify these rebels, I shall never cross this river again."

10. The Vietnamese general Tran Quang Khai composed the following poem during the battles against the thirteenth-century Mongol invasion:

> At the port Chuong Duong, I grasped the enemy's spears
> At the pier of Ham Tu, I captured their chief
> We must strive for peace
> Our mountains and rivers shall last forever

11. Diao Gan of Qin strengthened his determination to resist the enemy by rolling a jar to and from his house every day.

12. The identity of Gu Yuan is unknown.

13. In the seventh century B.C.E., Zhao Zui followed Zhong Er, the son of Duke Xian of Qin, into exile among the tribes of the north. On his return, Zhao Zui was rewarded with the post of prime minister.

14. Guo Ziyi (697–781) was a renowned Chinese general. In 763, the Turfans invaded Shanxi and seized the capital. The emperor was forced to flee. Guo Ziyi then collected four thousand demoralized troops and managed to drive out the Turfans so that in 764 the emperor could return to the capital.

15. Li Guangbi cooperated with Guo Ziyi.

ranks to hide; again, should the people withhold righteous assistance to the state in this time of danger, and scholars shun prominent positions for obscurity, would they not then be superfluous in this world? You might wear robes and headdresses, but your attitude would be that of animals. Who can accept such behavior?

The court has always had its tradition of generous rewards and heavy penalties. Act to avoid remorse in the future.

[Adapted from Truong Buu Lam, *Patterns of Vietnamese Response to Foreign Intervention*, 116–20]

PHAN BOI CHAU

THE HISTORY OF THE LOSS OF THE COUNTRY (1905)

Phan Boi Chau, the most important figure in Vietnam's early anticolonial movement against the French, wrote this original and influential text while living in Japan. In it, he warns that the French colonization of Vietnam risks the disappearance of Vietnam as a country and the Vietnamese as a people. The first two parts of the text explain his reasons for the loss of the country and present detailed biographies of the "heroes" who fought for Vietnam's independence in the past. In the third part, "How the French Entrapped Weak, Stupid, Blind Vietnam," translated here from Chinese, Phan Boi Chau shows, as did Nguyen Truong To before him,[16] how the Vietnamese were duped by the French and why they had to understand the extent of the colonizers' perfidious intentions and oppressive rule. In particular, Phan Boi Chau attacks the French system of taxation, which weighed heavily on all Vietnamese. Note that Phan Boi Chau refers to Vietnam as the South and to the Vietnamese as the Southern people.

Alas! Within thirty years, the Vietnamese, after already battling with spear and shield, were faced with disasters of discord like fire and water. After these were finished, there came fights with dagger and sword. These many violent destructions left us with only a last gasp, so how could we defend ourselves against the poisonous meddling of the French? Every day they proceeded to carve us up like fish and meat. Alas! Soon will it not end with no survivors of our own kind in Vietnam? When someone speaks of the poisonous meddling of the French, people fear that he will be overheard [and cause trouble], so they blame people who talk like this. France is a strong and vigorous country, but it picks on and insults small and weak Vietnam. What kind of country does that? The French are supposed to be civilized, and yet they treat the stupid, blind Vietnamese as if they were fish or meat. What kind of laws are they sup-

---

16. See Nguyen Truong To, "A Plan for Making the People Wealthy and the Country Strong" (chap. 5).

posed to have? This is why I speak, although I fear no one will believe me. I rely, however, on what I have seen and heard with my own eyes and ears, and I speak the truth without prejudice or false accusation. It is why I lay the blame on the French. If what I say contains even the tiniest untruth, then Heaven and Earth will not forgive me.

Vietnam has a ruler—how do the French treat him? The Ham Nghi emperor, the former ruler of Vietnam, was a minor on the throne for just one year. Did he commit an immoral act? Did he commit a wicked crime? He was no more than a weak and bookish leader, that is all. When the French attacked the capital, the Ham Nghi emperor fled, but every inch of the ground he trod on was the land of his ancestors, so what business was it of the French? But the French pursued him, captured him, and moved him to an isolated place called the city of Algiers in the south of Africa [*sic*], where they isolated him in a secret chamber, banned him from communication with outsiders, and strictly forbade any Vietnamese from coming or going with any news of him. They took a virtuous and innocent ruler and kept him captive in a foreign land. If the French wish to kill him, they should just kill him, but they keep him alive and take tens of thousands of taels of gold as a fee to provide for him!

(The tax that the French exact from the Southern Country is divided into three parts. Two-thirds go straight to the French, and the Vietnamese can do nothing about this. One-third is for a public fund for the upkeep of the ruler and mandarins and amounts to thirty thousand taels, which is paid to the French every year; this fund is called "Money for the Provision of the Vietnamese King.") How do the people of Vietnam know whether they are actually providing for the emperor? The French just borrow these thirty thousand taels to keep his soul alive, stuck in a life that is unbearable, like death but not truly death.

Such poisonous cruelty this is! The French blatantly take these thirty thousand taels, and no Vietnamese dares do anything about it. The French use this as a pretext to earn themselves the false reputation of being kind and virtuous. Such is the treacherous cunning of the French!

The current ruler of Vietnam is the Thanh Thai emperor. The French have left him only the inner palace to live in and have allowed him to retain only the title of emperor. But the French actually have surrounded the palace gates with French soldiers. Whoever goes in or out is watched and controlled by French soldiers. If the ruler of the land takes so much as a step outside the gate of the capital, he must obey the commands of the French. All governmental proclamations and commands in the country must first be reported to the French, and only with the approval of the French do the Vietnamese dare to carry them out; otherwise, the French just issue their own directives. The Vietnamese act as slaves and do the five bows and three kowtows to them (which is the proper behavior for Vietnamese toward their rulers), answer them respectfully, and follow their orders. Toward the emperor, they put their hands together and bow their heads a bit, but they are not allowed to open their mouths to ask him anything. What is going on? Would it not be better for the French just to get rid of such a ruler and publicly declare themselves emperors of both Great France and Great Viet? Who would dare question this? Wouldn't this be a much cleaner and clearer way of doing things?

The French keep the empty palace building and throne, so when news of their myriad evils and abuses spread throughout the land and is heard in foreign countries, they can say: "These are the wishes of the Vietnamese ruler and his mandarins" and "This is what your Vietnamese ruler and his mandarins have agreed to do." The French think that the Vietnamese do not have eyes or ears or that foreigners do not openly discuss what they are doing. Since the French are not challenged, they believe their deceptions are successful. Who would dare dupe Vietnam so openly? Who would dare to trick foreign countries so openly? But the fact is that they have duped Vietnam and have tricked foreign countries. No one investigates their evil deeds. Now isn't that treacherous cunning on the part of the French?

The French use the word *protect* to deceive the powerful nations of the five continents.[17] When one [imperial] country benefits, other countries can share. This is the convention. But the French cover and conceal their misdeeds. They claim that Vietnam has a ruler here and that they are only guests "protecting" him. How does this benefit Vietnam? A strong guest never represses his host. If we think that powerful countries believe the French, then the French have concealed their misdeeds. Over the past thirty years, not a single trading ship from a strong nation has come to Vietnam; not a single powerful nation has opened a trading post or embassy. I would suggest that the French have not necessarily tricked these powerful nations. There might be another reason that I am just not able to explain yet. The French have bound and bundled up the royal family very tightly and check their names on the royal family tree two or three times a month, taking a roll call. If anyone is missing, the French will pursue him to the utmost, fanning out in every direction and punishing [the escapee] very harshly for his crime. Are the French afraid their secret will leak out? Also, the French have recently reduced the royal family's allowance, so how are they going to live? But if no one goes abroad to accuse them, then things will just continue like this.

Vietnam has mandarins [who serve the court]. How do the French treat these mandarins? Let me tell you. The land of Vietnam was destroyed, and our ruler was lost. This was a painful and hateful affair. When this happened, how could these mandarins, who had enjoyed the royal favor, put up with this quietly? If all Vietnamese were made to bow their heads, listen to, and happily serve the French, what sort of world would this be? The power of the Vietnam-

---

17. The official French terms for Annam and Tonkin were "protectorates," and Cochinchina was called a "colony."

ese is far inferior to that of the French. If we were to fight the French to the death, it would be like a fight between a three-year-old child and Meng Bi, who could pull out the horns of live bulls.[18] How could we not be defeated? When the Vietnamese were defeated, some could not bear to surrender. Some people killed themselves out of anger, and some bowed their heads and begged to be forgiven for their crimes. Those who would not surrender were like Phan Dinh Phung and Pham Doan. If the French had allowed them to escape into the mountain valleys, they would just have rotted away there with the grass and trees. What harm would this do the French? But the French did their utmost to be malicious and captured their wives and families, rounded up their fellow villagers, and dug up their family graves. If they did not submit, that was their own business. But of course, the French took retribution against them, like owls with no sympathy for the sick (as the popular Vietnamese saying goes). How would one dare bear any animosity toward corpses? One should feel pity for the dead. What crimes did they commit to justify the French violently disinterring and chopping them up, hanging them on the city gates, or casting them into fire and water? How could this not make us extremely bitter toward the French?

Those who killed themselves in bitterness and anger, as Nguyen Cao and Ha Van My did, and destroyed themselves without having committed any crime [meant that] their wives and children would live in poverty with no one to rely on, crying over the injustice and sobbing in distress, the sounds rending the heavens and cracking the earth. If the French had stopped there and allowed their blood to seep into the ground, what harm would it have done them? Yet the French instantly became enraged, went off and dug up their bodies and burned them, cut off their heads and put them on display. How can corpses still be rebels when their souls have been destroyed and their bodies decimated? The blackened skeletons underwent all the suffering between Heaven and Earth; the French tried to scowl at them like wolves or clapped their hands in joy. How could this not make people fear and loathe them?

Some people, like Nguyen Thanh, Phan Trong Muu, and Nguyen Quang Cu, bowed their heads and begged for forgiveness. The French did not kill them, as two of them were presented scholars[19] and one a provincial graduate, so the French kept them as an enticement to others to surrender. These individuals are truly craven and foolish fellows! How can someone be considered a great man if he lowers his head in submission in defeat and begs for mercy? These worthless people! It is hateful that [the French] keep them alive and yet do not have not the heart to kill them. From the French point of view, they already have surrendered, so why is it necessary to kill them? Have pity on all those who surrendered outside the north gate of An Hoa and were put to the

---

18. Meng Bi was a warrior of the Warring States period (475–221 B.C.E.), said to be capable of great feats of strength.

19. Called *tien si*.

sword. After killing them, the French forbade their families and relatives from finding their bodies and taking them away for burial, [instead] leaving their blood to flow and their bones to dry, so that travelers would not pass by there anymore. Added to that, the French were extremely devious: at first, a few people came out to give themselves up, and the French spoke to them with sweet words and rewarded them in order to tempt others. This continued until all of them came out, leaving their mountain hideouts in the trees and caves. Then the French marched all of them to An Hoa gate. All the people who gave themselves up at that time received the gift of a sword; making the heroes who had been unwilling to give themselves up pound on the tables and shout "Hurrah!" Because the French had the reputation of killing all those who surrendered, [by not capturing the holdouts], they both satisfied the ambitions of these heroes and strengthened the hearts of those who longed for the old times. How can civilized people carry out these kinds of unspeakable punishments and massacres of innocent people?

You Vietnamese, open your eyes! Do not say that the French can be trusted! Before their hold on the country was secure, the French exhorted the people thousands upon thousands of times to give themselves up, saying that they would be not be charged with any crime. Now, how do you regard the French? Do you still believe the French can be trusted? The French have the most wicked and cruel methods; deep down, they are treacherous and tricky. When they first took Vietnam, they enticed the Vietnamese with extremely sweet words and good rewards and used good positions and big salaries as bait. They used Vietnamese like Nguyen Tan and Hoang Cao Khai (these two are very capable at quelling "banditry"), sending them off like hunting falcons for their various evil works. Those who grasp and gnaw away as they please are immoral good-for-nothing thugs in the land of Viet; they have the faces of monkeys and the innards of swine. In fact, the Viets usually do not regard these people as equals of themselves, but the French have the greatest respect for them, such as those like Vo Doan Nha, an interpreter for the provincial government. Others, like the governors named Loc and Phong, interpret for the French, helping Jie in his wicked work.[20] All the evil things that the French do, they first tell to this servile bunch, commanding them to go east or west as they please. These types run and scurry about without rest while the French sit and enjoy the benefits of it all. The blood and grease they obtain by dividing up the fat and dirtying their fingers accumulates in piles and heaps over the months and years. As soon as the French know how much this is, they blow off the dust to look in the cracks, punishing this one and that one. Then they pick up the whole stinking lot that has been saved up for decades and present it to the officials of the protectorate, so that all the benefits will end up with the French, whereas the bad reputation

---

20. Jie was the last king of the Xia dynasty (which ended around the sixteenth century B.C.E.), whose reign was known for its cruelty and tyranny.

will stick to this bunch of people. The methods of their evil and trickery are truly without compare in either the past or the present.

The land of Vietnam has common folk, let us see how the French deal with them. Common people of Vietnam, please look here. I think that in listening to the things that I have said up to this point, those people who do not pound the table and who cry out in despondency, or entreat Heaven in despair [must] have no eyes or ears or have no heart or blood or are not human. I dare to state categorically that this is not the will of Heaven! This is inhuman! If my compatriots keep listening to this, I fear only that I will suppress their tears and restrain their rage, and therefore I cannot bear to speak. But if I do not speak, then how would my compatriots be able to know such things? Would I then not have committed a crime punishable by death? I shall keep speaking.

Taxes

In the time before the country was lost, what the ruler of the land collected from the common people was called *dung tien* and *to tien*, and besides these there were no other sundry taxes. *Dung tien* was a tax on people, but it ranged from only eight or nine thousand up to twenty or thirty thousand people; that is, a single amount for each household, each amount being only three hundred *dong*. Because taxes were based on households and not on individuals, this was very little. Also, if one's strength was failing, there was a tax exemption. The *to tien* was a tax on fields; if one owned thirty or forty *mau* of land, then one would have to pay a tax on each *mau*. The tax for one *mau* was set at an official bushel of grain. Because the common folk provided this openly and the official did not ask for anything beyond it, this tax was very light. So Vietnam was very lenient toward its common folk. This was an indulgent but peaceful way to govern, but it gradually resulted in habits of indolence and deception and, in fact, was not an effective way to make the country rich or strong. When the French got hold of the country, they gradually began to pay attention to turning such stagnation into prosperity and to relieving the poor. They made the people pay money in order to enlighten them and make things run profitably. How could it be that the common people were not happy about this? Why would they complain about it? The French, however, had no intention of benefiting the people, and all economic interests ended up passing into French control. Now the Vietnamese do not enjoy even so much as a tiny piece of it, and the French use many different methods to collect the people's riches, the people's strength, and the people's fat. The people have to pay from dawn until dusk and then from dusk until dawn. If they continue like this for months and years, the Vietnamese people will have no food to eat and no clothes to wear. They can see various things happen with their own eyes, but since they perceive these things only in fragments, they are unable to talk about them [as a whole]. So allow me to select the most important aspects and explain them [as follows] to my compatriots.

ONE: LAND TAXES

In the beginning, the French ordered a complete assessment of all fields and pastures, with an open disclosure of the total. Deceptively underestimating one's land was not permitted. People who attempted to do so were punished, and their land was confiscated by officials. Anyone who informed on someone else was well rewarded. . . . Taxes on fields were divided into three rates, the top rate being one silver tael for each *mau* [1 *mau* is 3,600 square meters]. Taxes on pasture were the same. The middle and lower grades of land were calculated according to the top rate; the French made a contract with the people that these rates would be permanent. But after assessing this rate for only one year, the French said that the Southern people were leaving too many fields and pastures fallow and that they should raise the taxes to make the Southern people work harder in agriculture. Whenever the French want to do something, they always try to dress it up as an act of kindness to deceive the people, which is why they speak of "protecting Vietnam." Land taxes are like this, too—they increase each year; the lower rate becomes the middle rate, and the middle rate becomes the top rate. Since the top rate cannot be increased, the French just expand the numbers of fields to be taxed at the top rate; for every hundred *mau*, an extra ten *mau* are added, and one extra *mau* for every ten. After a few years, only the top and middle rates remain, minus the lower rate. Village dwellers who could not bear this [burden] begged the French to thoroughly investigate the tax situation, but the French made no effort to look into it. They just ended up giving the land [of the people who could not pay their taxes] to the French Bureau of Agriculture to cultivate and [then] made tax delinquents pay their taxes in the form of a fine to the *thong-li* [tax officers]. Now many people pay taxes on their fields for land occupied by the Bureau of Agriculture, and there really is no way they can complain about it.

TWO: HEAD TAXES

In the beginning, the French said that people must perform corvée labor for the government. If they wished to take time off at the end of the year, they would have to pay a labor tax in addition to their poll tax. The head tax was called "publicly collected money," which meant that every year all able-bodied men had to pay two taels and twenty cents. Added to this was the corvée tax called the "public increase tax," for which all able-bodied men had to pay eighty cents. Now all able-bodied men have to pay three taels. When this tax was first announced, it was only one tael, but with each passing year, it went up. The people of Saigon must pay five, six, or more taels per year. In the provinces of the other two districts [Annam and Tonkin], a man must pay three taels, but if he is in his first year of adulthood, he does not have to pay the full three taels. As the years have gone by, this tax has always increased.

THREE: RESIDENTIAL TAXES

The amount of money varies according to the house and is levied differently in every case. For those houses with surrounding walls and side chambers, the upper rate is ninety to one hundred taels per year, the middle rate is fifty to sixty taels, and the lower rate is twenty to thirty taels. For the front and back of houses, there are hallway and pavilion taxes; for the area outside hallways, there is a courtyard tax; for the area outside courtyards, there are gate and wall taxes; and for the area beyond the gates and walls, there are garden and residential taxes. There are no set rules, however, and the money must be paid on a case-by-case basis, increasing and decreasing in accordance with the rules for houses. It is compulsory to have a record of this tax in French posted outside on every gate. Not having this is considered to be tax evasion and is severely punished and is immediately taken care of. In small villages and the countryside, this tax is lighter.

FOUR: RIVER-CROSSING TAXES

Everywhere there is a place to cross a river or a separation of a few yards of water, there is a tax-collecting station. The responsibility for these stations is in the hands of the Southern people, but the money goes to French officials. Every time a person crosses a large river, he must pay thirty to forty copper cash, and for small rivers, he must pay six or seven copper cash. This causes extreme hardship for poor merchants and peddlers.

FIVE: TAXES ON BIRTH AND DEATH CERTIFICATES

When a boy or girl is born, his or her birth must be reported to the French registrar's office and a reporting tax must be paid; and when a boy or girl dies, the death must be announced to the registrar's office and a tax must be paid for announcing the death. The amount of these taxes depends on differences in wealth and are assessed to prevent the evasion of poll taxes. This [assessment] is carried out in Saigon, but not in other places. The French do not levy taxes all at once but do so gradually, surreptitiously, squeezing out the lifeblood of the people.

SIX: CONTRACT TAXES

The French knew that people made contracts when they borrowed, rented, bought, or sold land and houses. So they came up with the trick of affixing French seals to Vietnamese contracts, and for all such affairs, people must go to the French to pay a tax to buy permission to do so. If they do not use such contracts, they will be accused of breaking the law, and be prevented from further activity.

SEVEN: VARIOUS CEREMONIAL TAXES

To invite monks to perform the winter sacrifice or exorcisms, to change a beam or fix a tile, to conduct a funeral or a celebration or something similar—for all gatherings and parties, whether beating a drum for an hour or playing a flute, regardless of whether someone is rich or poor or of whatever station—they must give thirty to fifty cents to the French official. The tax is calculated according to the size of the ceremony. . . . This tax is assessed for larger houses in the cities and is not yet [assessed] in small villages and the countryside.

EIGHT: TAXES ON BOAT DWELLERS

The tax [on boat dwellers] also is divided into upper, middle, and lower rates, as is the tax on dwellings. . . . But boat dwellers have no land, no houses, no skills in trade or business. They rely on a tiny vessel as their livelihood. If they catch fish in the morning, they have something to eat in the evening. In the old days, the ruler of Vietnam did not levy taxes on these people but required them only to do some corvée labor, for which they received money.

NINE: MERCHANT TAXES

This most burdensome of taxes on inns and shops also is divided into three rates: high, middle, and low, and is based on income from sales. The high rate is around two to three hundred taels per annum, the middle rate is half that, and the low rate is half that again. So a tiny business set up to sell a few things, even those that sell very few things like starch, vegetables, kindling, or betel nuts, must have a tax certificate. Those who do not are [considered to be] tax evaders and are punished severely.

TEN: MARKET TAXES

Markets are divided into three sizes, large, middle, and small. The tax collected for these goes to the French official. For a big market, the tax is seven or eight hundred taels of silver, less for a middle-size market, and even less for a small market. Those who go on foot to sell their wares also must also pay a tax. If you carry a load of wood or a basket of vegetables, you also will have to pay a tax; otherwise you will not be admitted to the market. Woodsmen and country folk and those who rely on their hands and feet to do their business endure great hardship, and on the road home, the only thing heard in their chatter is "How much tax did you have to pay this morning?" and "How much tax did you have to pay this evening?"

ELEVEN: ALCOHOL AND SALT TAXES

At first, the French made the salt makers responsible only for paying a salt-field tax. But later, they saw how much the Vietnamese liked salt, so they began to get greedy and demanded that all salt producers pay a tax on their fields, basing it on the field and pasture tax and doubling its rate. Because the French monopolize the production of salt, they force all the salt-making households to carry out corvée labor and pay them a little for it. Once the salt is prepared, [the salt makers] pay money to sell it to the French. For the exchange of money for salt, they issue a certificate. . . . For one peck of salt, there already were two taxes, the field tax and the certificate of purchase tax. To buy salt one must go to a French company . . . and pay money to buy a certificate of purchase. The first two taxes are to prevent the clandestine production of salt, and this tax applies to only the salt itself. So now, three taxes are imposed on one peck of salt, and only after these three taxes have been paid is the salt allowed to go on the market. But when it goes on the market, the market tax must be paid. So now there are four taxes on salt! How can salt production survive? Is it possible for salt prices not to increase? Previously in this country, one peck of salt cost only fifty or sixty copper cash, but now salt costs four or five taels in silver! Alcohol taxes are the same as salt; those who sell alcohol must also get a certificate of purchase from the French, but this comprises only two taxes.

TWELVE: TEMPLE AND MONASTERY TAXES

The French do not worship gods or the Buddha. They divide temples and monasteries into three grades: large, middle size, and small, [all of which] must pay a tax to French officials. Only with a certificate from the French can they perform worship ceremonies. This costs fifty taels for a large temple, thirty for a middle-size one, and half of that for a small one. So now in Saigon, most temples are empty and can be seen only here and there in a few rich communities. . . .

THIRTEEN: ARTISAN TAXES

Many artisans in Vietnam live in villages devoted to specific crafts. So where they live depends on their craft. For example, Bat Trang makes ceramics, and Phong Lam makes clogs, ironsmiths live in Van Lam, and so on. Besides the head tax, the French have ordered [the people] to pay an artisan tax, which is determined according to the wealth of their profession, and they also have to pay a certification tax. Those who have no certificate are prohibited from doing business and are allowed only to provide corvée labor for the officials. Poor people rely on handicrafts for a living, so how can they bear to clasp their hands together and wait for death? Alas!

FOURTEEN: LOCAL PRODUCT TAXES

There are too many [local product] taxes to enumerate. The mountain areas produce ivory, rhinoceros horn, ornamental stones, and jade; the sea produces tortoiseshell, coral, swallows' nests, pearls and cowries, and so on. The cinnamon of Thanh Quy, the malt sugar of Quang Nam, ironwood and gardenias from Nghe An. . . . All these local products have specific taxes. Local people are not permitted to exploit those products that have been monopolized by the French, and they do not have to pay taxes on them, being obliged to pay only the land tax. In addition to this, calculating these taxes is extremely complex, and it is hateful to have to talk about them. I fear that to do so would make my compatriots run away with their hands over their ears! So for the moment, I shall give only an example of tobacco taxes, and from this you will know the rest.

FIFTEEN: TOBACCO-FIELD TAXES

Everyone who grows tobacco must pay a land tax to the French company, based on the number of fields usually in cultivation; only after this are they permitted to grow [the tobacco]. This is the first tax.

SIXTEEN: FRESH-TOBACCO TAXES

When tobacco leaves are brought in from the fields, they must be cut up into strips and made into catties and bushels within three to five days. The resulting tally of catties and bushels must be presented to the French company and a tax paid on them. This is the second tax. Both these taxes are paid by the growers.

SEVENTEEN: DRIED-TOBACCO TAXES

When a tobacco wholesale company buys tobacco from the grower . . . they cannot transport it elsewhere without paying a tax on the total amount and obtaining a certificate of approval from the French.

EIGHTEEN: TOBACCO-OFFICE TAXES

If a wholesaler wishes to transport tobacco from one province to another . . . he must pay a certificate tax, and only then is he permitted to sell the tobacco.

NINETEEN: PRIVATE-TOBACCO-BUSINESS TAXES

Tobacco merchants who sell a small quantity of tobacco obtained from whole-salers . . . also must obtain a certificate before they sell it. Then when they enter the market with the tobacco on their shoulders or carried in their hands, they have to pay the tax to the manager of the market before they are allowed to sell it there.

Because of the heavy weight borne by the Vietnamese and the utter ruthless-ness [of the French] in acquiring Vietnamese goods, the French plot and devise hundreds of ways and use myriad devices to snatch up and appropriate these goods for themselves. To sum up, the French are able to satisfy their desires, but the Vietnamese have no way to make a living.

[Phan Boi Chau, "Viet Nam vong quoc su," 373–89;
trans. Catherine Churchman]

RESPONSES TO THE FRENCH

PHAN BOI CHAU

A LETTER FROM ABROAD WRITTEN IN BLOOD (1907)

In this call to action, Phan Boi Chau conveys a sense of urgency and national re-sponsibility in his appeal to his compatriots to wake up to the mortal dangers posed by French colonialism while at the same time condemning the behavior of the Viet-namese court and the mandarins. This text is notable for its new ideas about political sovereignty and how the will of the people must be mobilized to evict the Europe-ans. Phan Boi Chau claims that it is the responsibility and duty of the citizens to protect the country's integrity and independence. By the time this letter was written, loyalty to the king had shifted to a concept of popular sovereignty. In his letter, Phan Boi Chau also further develops his ideas about the importance of collective unity and popular heroism. He stresses the need for violent action, contrary to the gradual political and social reform advocated by Phan Chau Trinh,[21] as the most effective route to independence. The excerpt here, the second part of his letter, was translated from Chinese.

As a man of my country writing a letter in blood from abroad, after writing for a day or more, I feel only European fashions and American styles piercing and exciting my heart and mind, and my national spirit seems increasingly dulled, as though there is no Heaven to ask or any earth to seek.

    Mountain mist and the tumult of the seas prick my eyes and stab at my ears.

---

21. See Phan Chau Trinh, "Monarchy and Democracy" (this chap.).

If I were to kill myself in despair of my compatriots' journey toward oblivion, it would be of no benefit.

Overcome by love and emotion, need I repeat my humble loyalties?

Beginning from the time of disasters, insults, and omens of warning, will my words not be used as our frontline force?

Alas! The country has perished! First, let me give here an account of the accumulated misdeeds that have led to this:

One is that the rulers of the land have never known their people.

Another is that the mandarins of the land have never known their people.

Another is that the people of the land have never known their country.

By the hard labor of the muscle of thousands upon thousands of millions, spending the flesh and blood of thousands upon thousands of millions, organizing the rice fields of thousands upon thousands of millions, the country was created.

This land is the people's land, so how can it be owned by that one person?

By relying on good fortune as great as Heaven, expecting as sound a sleep as that of the black dragon, this single person can lie about on his belly above those thousands upon thousands of millions. Being bossy and forceful, acting arbitrarily only according to his personal interest, trampling not just on the grass but on our people too!

Looking back through thousands of years of history until now, searching up and down looking for something that was profitable for the people to rid them of disasters, researching the principles that protect the health to save them from death, I found that, like snow in the summer or stars at dawn, it was distant and unobtainable.

In the palace, the imperial physicians number in the tens of hundreds, but does the ruler show compassion for the diseases and sicknesses that plague the people?

His food tribute is worth millions of taels in gold, but does the ruler have compassion for those of the people who have died from famine and had their families decimated?

Those who are vile and lowly are interested only in following the wishes of the empress, the concubines, and beautiful women. Those who are upstanding and righteous are interested only in satisfying the wishes of the various officials and attendants.

Our people have become widows and widowers; they are starving, are in pain, they lack clothing, their hands are rotted, and their feet scorched. Although they have been abandoned and are in utter distress, that person [the ruler] sees and hears nothing, although he has eyes and ears.

In addition, this single person controls the land and lives of the common folk, so there are myriad evil corruptions whose total amount is difficult to ascertain.

In his mind, this person most likely thinks, "What do these rustics know? They are no more than flesh on corpses that provide labor and taxes and need to be whipped to work like horses." But because this corpse flesh is there, one person gnaws on its fat and becomes glutted on it.

Whatever is left over, he gives to his oversexed, lazy, and stupid relations in the imperial household, or he collects it to feed, like swine, his spoiled and favored eunuchs and musicians.

Whatever may be left after that, this person gives to those who share his surname, their families, and their lackeys and running dogs.

Alas! The lives of thousands upon thousands of millions, the fat of thousands upon thousands of millions, what crimes have they committed to deserve to die pickled and peeled? The blue heavens shed tears for them, and the emerald seas flow backward on their account.

So it has gone on, until the incursions of foreign brigands and the collapse of our home forces. That person donates our people's children to them and sells our people's fields to them, in order to purchase for himself clandestine moments of comfort and pleasure.

When the Western armies first arrived, they took over three provinces for themselves. The next time they took six, and then the whole northern region. The Western armies kept coming and carved up the whole country and all its people.

Carving up our people so that [the ruler] might attain glory and get fat, so that he might be warm and full of food; these are the things he tells himself are the best policies.

Certainly he is unaware that the common people are the cornerstone of a state or that the king should consider his subjects as important as he does Heaven. When he casts away this cornerstone and loses what he should consider as important as Heaven, how can he continue to exist?

The ruler of the land of Japan respects his people as would a respected teacher or strict father, and he loves them with the love of a kindly mother for her child. In educating those without parents, caring for the sick, [providing] hospitals and schools, there is not one affair in which he puts his own interest before that of his people. Even affairs like peacemaking, declaring war, collecting taxes, and recruiting an army all must be decided by a house of representatives of the people.

Foreign countries treat their people like this. If we had taken them as an example, how could our nation ever perish before theirs?

Gradually up until the present day, even the blue heavens have not been able to avoid giving their love mistakenly. When a ruler behaves like ours does, it makes one's teeth hurt to even think of it.

Even so, one or two officials serving the court had great wisdom and heroism, lofty and sturdy as Mount Dizhu;[22] they stood in the middle of the stream and patched up the holes in Heaven with colored stones. They feared a rottenness

---

22. In Shanxi Province in China.

that would easily snap off the branches, and therefore they strengthened the roots of the state.

I would rather commit an offense against one man than commit evil against all the common people.

Even though the branches and leaves have withered, the roots still flourish.

Why do swift winds and terrible frost blast toward them to cover them?

And how can it be that [recognizing] the poisonous fires of his cruel oppression, his officials follow after him and fan him? They are deluded and ignorant, concerned only for their own safety and that of their wives and children. The ruler has hundreds and thousands of greater concubines, as well crowds of lesser concubines and female servants. His imperial family is oversexed, lazy, and stupid. His mandarins have illegitimate children and grandchildren, like herds of beasts. Taking the fish and meat from our people just to flatter and fawn on this one person, whose ulcers they suck and whose shit they taste in their sycophancy, makes their eyes sparkle and their nostrils dilate with joy and makes their hearts puff up and excites their minds.

Outside the palace, in the dwellings of the common folk, there is sickness and pain, and the death of infants. They are like the people of Qin were toward the Viet.

One day, there will be great changes inside the walls and on the mounds, in the altars and houses, like vast oceans transforming into fields of mulberry bushes. Then they will change their expressions and their words. In the morning they will be European, and in the evening, Asian.

Then who will our people allow to treat them like rubbish, and for whom will they allow themselves to be sacrificed?

Anyway, for [the ruler's] own protection and that of his family and their riches, there already are good methods, namely, getting down on his knees and begging for forgiveness.

Apologizing to one family and thanking another.

Then his command will come to an end and his status will be gone.

What shall the people do? What shall the people do?

Ah! Those fools who do nothing more than provide his mouth and belly with the stuff he desires.

Oh, woe! Turning back to observe the events of a thousand years past, through the black mists and bewitched clouds, my heart is in anguish for the millions who still survive, like the remnants of fish or leftover meat.

Those robbers of the people, the mandarins! Are they not already contented in their hearts and gratified in their mouths?

Oh, that ruler and those mandarins! Were the nation to be lost, it would be a blessing, and I would not have the heart to regret its loss.

[The ruler's] role as leader is no more than that of a headman over a village or the manager of a trading company. Were we to be rid of them by their deaths, the village and trading company they oversaw certainly would continue to exist.

[The ruler] is no more than one person in the country, so what difference could his nonexistence have on the nation? This is why I do not blame him.

The imperial mandarins make up only the tiniest percentage of the people in the country, so how could the survival or death of a country depend on them? Anyway, my love is not for these people, so I do not blame them.

Those whom I blame most deeply are my people themselves; my deepest love is for my people, and my deepest blame is on my people.

Will my countrymen awake and be repentant and wish to strengthen themselves? I regard them as if they acted as corpses at a funeral; I pray for them. Allow me to weep bitterly for them as I state my case.

Climbing and gazing northward from Kunlun Mountain, ascending and looking southward from Motian peak to the west of the great sea and to the east of the River of Nine Dragons; if my people did not exist, this place would be no more than a vast forest on a plain or an immense deserted wilderness, no more than the dwelling for wolves, leopards, jackals, and tigers, no more than a place where foxes and badgers make their burrows or where adders and vipers coil. Otherwise, it would be no more than the lair of the people of Linyi, Ailao, and Chenla [Champa, Laos, and Cambodia]. How could a nation exist there? Where would Vietnam have been?

Gradually cutting through the jungle and opening up the wild forests, carving the mountains and making a pattern of the rivers to create this 270,000 square *li* of our land, Vietnam. How wonderful it is! How glorious!

From such humble origins, riding carts in rags, opening up and developing this world; was this not the work of the hands and feet of our millions of ancestors? Did they not drag and transport loads morning and night to block up the mountain streams; was this not accomplished by the blood and sweat of our millions of ancestors? Our ancestors bequeathed this land to us, their descendants, and we, the descendants, inherited this land from them. This country is our family fortune, and our treasured heirloom.

We have such an unparalleled family inheritance and immeasurably valuable fortune, but we gave it up as though it were a paddy field full of stones. We balked at its being too sacred, then we shirked our responsibility for ensuring its existence by giving it to a tiny number of people, the ruler and his mandarins.

I say we should hold the ruler and his mandarins accountable for the encroachment of the bandit enemies. I say punish the ruler and his mandarins for the loss of the towns and cities. They are carefree and dazed by their fame and wealth, bound up in their desire for food, wine, and women. When someone comes kowtowing and asking whether they possess the country or whether the country exists, they are confused and cannot answer.

Alas! My country is no longer the precious heirloom of generations of our people. Our people are no longer the owners and masters of this precious inheritance. What is to be done when we cast off and wastefully discard our duties and rights of ownership? Having shirked the responsibility for the life and death, rise and fall of their entire inheritance to those who were paid to look after it, they not only have ensured that they cannot be the recipients of this inheritance, they now do not even consider this inheritance to be their own property! What a tragedy! A tragedy!

The human beings of all the countries of the five continents tread on the earth and eat its produce, but to be as stupid and weak as those of our land are is an immensely monstrous thing in the universe.

If we pulled the blindfolds from our eyes, we would see the surging waves of the seas and the sudden flashes of storm lightning, and what time would this be? Is it not time for nature to sift out the stupid and wash away the weak?

Taking these 270,000 square *li* of our precious inheritance and giving it to the most stupid and weak of masters to enjoy lavishly and squander, handing it down for a hundred years, this is what bends back the tongue and oppresses the heart, snatching away our people and delivering them to the French. What more can be said? What more?

Oh what a tragedy! The millions of our people, old and young, men and women are all my uncles and aunts, brothers and sisters. It would be unbearable if they were harmed or destroyed. It is unbearable. If I love them and have pity on them, what am I to do?

Our country has been handed down to our people as their inheritance, but our people also have abandoned it. Consequently, our people also must take it back. Our people were stupid in their honesty and yielded to their weakness. That is why things are as they are. But it still is not certain that our people will [be defeated].

Our hearts have been dead for a millennium or more under a barbaric government and its teachings, with our heads bowed to autocrats ruling from within palace walls. A few centuries ago, we were able to destroy the Yuan [Mongol] army and pacify the Wu [Ming] bandits, defeat the Qing armies and extend this great land, coiled in the south and bordered in the north, before wide in front and open behind [*sic*]. Thinking about our race, we are most definitely not a kind of ignorant, squirming, weak animal. The waves of the Bach Dang River brought forth the Tran king, and from the mists of Lam Son valley suddenly arose the first emperor of the Le. Moreover, there was glory and heroic valor in our ancestor the Quang Trung emperor, who once flourished in the region of and beyond the Hai Van gate and Mount Hoanh. Now Heaven has reopened the divine gate, so it is almost time.

My inheritance, my inheritance, return it to its master, let me rub my eyes in anticipation.

Here I shall relate the means by which we should repossess it. In all Heaven and Earth, the superior and matchless plan is as follows:

All the people of the country united in a common will.

This inheritance of who knows what worth is the common possession of tens of millions of people but was abandoned to others by tens of millions of people.

If we now wish to take it back, we must have the strength of the common purpose of tens of millions of people. How can tens of millions be united in strength? By virtue of their common will.

The enemies who occupy our land like coiled serpents are at the very most only fifty thousand in number, whereas even half the number of able-bodied men in our country is, in the most conservative estimate, five hundred thousand. If we were to pit five hundred thousand of our compatriots against fifty thousand of the enemy in a life-or-death struggle, not to speak of the speed of pistols or the effectiveness of cannons; if we were united together to drive them out, a small number would not be able to defeat the large number, and they would clasp their hands together and beg for their lives. If one has only 10 million men and they are united in purpose, so that one person sings and then the multitude sings in harmony, one shouts and then the multitude answers, we will not need our pistols to shoot rapidly and our cannons to be effective.

The enemy requires our labor and our money, but if no one in the whole country gives it to them, what could they do to us? If they have no soldiers, and not one person in the whole country agrees to [become a soldier], what could they do to us? If they threaten us as bandits or sentence us with guns, as a single person I would be in peril. But if a multitude of people come to save me, could they round us up and exterminate the entire population of the country? What could they do to us? We should not declare war, nor carry out banditry. We only should unite our arms and legs, clear our eyes, cultivate our courage, hold on to true principles, and uphold the law. If we approach them to ask for our inheritance, then what could they do to us?

By these numerous methods, we will surely be able to bring death to our enemy, by making them unable to swallow.

But our fellow countrymen are still unable to do this; why? Because they are not united in purpose. The person on the left has not yet said "chalk," and the person on the right has already said "cheese." One lights a fire, and right away another throws water on it! [This is] cruelly robbing their own race for the sake of enjoyment for those of another; trapping their compatriots to barter for the happiness of our enemies. But just as Guo was wiped out, so shall Yu certainly follow.[23] If the beans in the pot burn, then the pot itself will also burn to ashes. If we have no common purpose, how will these disasters ever stop?

Ah! Why do our fellow countrymen know nothing of the joy of flocking together and think nothing of the tragedy of extinction? And where does the

---

23. Guo and Yu were allied states in the Spring and Autumn period (722–481 B.C.E.). The state of Jin wished to conquer them, but together, they were too powerful. So Jin turned them against each other and thus was able to conquer them individually.

cause for this separation of minds lie? Only in stupidity! There is mutual suspicion and no mutual trust, mutual hatred and no mutual love, but only ambition to harm others and none for working together for others. With hearts filled with mutual trust, love, and the desire to cooperate, we can defend ourselves against the insults of foreigners. Will we then lag behind the Japanese in their swift rise to strength? Hearts filled with mutual suspicion, hatred, and harm lead to discord within our family, and this will lead only to the ruination of our country.

And now that our four limbs have failed and only a last gasp remains, the heart is the only small thing left we can rely on.

But we still seek the trail to doom following the ruts of an overturned cart, and in a daze, we do not turn back. Drinking the blood of our former kings, former lords, and forefathers, what hope remains? What hope remains?

Alas! If we treat our country as we should, treat our people as we should, treat our hearts as we should, who will be able to prevent our unity? In a flash, awakening to realization; in anger, rising up with determination, these millions with one mind. Let us begin now!

Let the elder brothers carry the kindling, and the younger brothers light the fire with it; let the elder brothers cut the timber, and the younger ones build fences with it. When the strength of the elders is insufficient, let the younger ones carry on their tasks for them; if the plans of the younger brothers do not reach their goals, then let the elder brothers make plans for them.

The sound of thousands of axes swinging in the forest, the commotion of hundreds of walls being erected for houses; with so many hands making the work light, what undertaking would not be successful?

We shall reconstruct our realm of mountains and rivers and take back this inheritance left to us by our forefathers! The glory of such united purpose will certainly rock the ages and illuminate history!

Let me go into more detail about the means by which such a purpose shall be attained and the requirements for a task like this to be completed.

These are the common purpose of the rich, the common purpose of the nobility, the common purpose of scholars and mandarins, the common will of all in the country who are trained in arms, the common will of the followers of Catholicism, the united purpose of ruffians and of the secret societies, the common will of heroic women, the common will of translators and clerks, the common will of the sons of families who bear a grudge, and the common purpose of those inside and outside the country.

What the stars gather together, when the mountains and seas unite as one, when the heroes whose fame resounds through the heavens and sears across the earth, the paladins will rock the past ages and shake up the present. What era lacks people like this? Why do they stay so deeply hidden and not come forth? We see and hear nothing of them; why do they remain silent? Is it because they have run out of energy or because their power has yet to be unfurled?

Without thousands of taels in gold, who would have gone with Zhang Zifang?[24] Without a granary full of grain, who would have followed the Duke of Zhou?[25] To take advantage of the times, we must wait for heroes, and of those heroes who create more heroes, none occupies a higher place than those who are rich. Certainly some of our countrymen already possess much capital, the richest men in the provinces. They squander a thousand taels to buy a smile and throw away millions on gambling. At times they lose their hard-earned capital for not an ounce of benefit. Certainly something that has been collected for a long time will one day be dispersed, and something that has been stored up in great amounts will one day be lost in large volumes.

If not by sudden disaster from bandits or enemies, these bounties will meet their end in flood or fire. In these days of disaster and desperation, can there be anything better than to unfurl one's treasures and abilities to do good and kind deeds, manifesting one's bodhi heart and extending one's generous hands, when all is said and done? To rear young dragons and send them off to make rain, to sell fine steeds and spur them to pursue the winds. This is one chance in a thousand years to spend small savings and attain great ones. Only those of my brothers who are rich have the means to be the heroes who create heroes. This is what I hope from those with common purpose among the rich.

Those poor folk who wear rough cloth and destitute scholars who live behind wicker doors, how could they not hope for salvation? [Listen to] the sound when they cry mournfully over the present situation. They have low status and enjoy little prestige. In uncultivated eyes, they are of little importance. With their purses empty and their hands bare, how can they explain their chivalrous ambitions? Looking in all four directions with urgency, they seek those who sing the same tune, but there are so few. They can rely only on the great bell- and tripod-owning families,[26] those high households that own carts drawn by four-horse teams, people whose words have power and whose very breath is efficacious.

Gathering together determined men to see this succeed; raising heroes to await this change. Free and independent, raising the future roof for these people and this time. Rewarding virtue and paying back meritorious deeds, answering to the former kings and lords in the underworld. How strong are the sons of our noblemen! How great are the sons of our noblemen! They are truly an outstanding group of young men. This is what I hope from those with common purpose among our nobility.

If one plots against the enemy from outside their noose, the work is easy to do but success is difficult. However, if one plots against the enemy from within

---

24. Also known as Zhang Liang, Zhang Zifang was an adviser to Liu Bang (r. 206–194 B.C.E.), the first emperor of the Han dynasty (206 B.C.E.–220 C.E.).

25. The Duke of Zhou was the regent for the second king of the Zhou dynasty who helped consolidate its rule.

26. This is an allusion to wealthy families.

their noose, success is difficult and the work is especially difficult. The reason that Yi Yin went to Jie was to spy for Tang.[27] The reason that Zhou Bo went into the service of Lu was to plot for the Han.[28]

Finally with the attack at Mingtiao, Xia was overturned, with a cry of "buttons on the right!" The Liu were safe. Truly these were very loyal people. How could these insignificant virtues be allowed to compare with those? Oh! When they were appointed to their official posts, they went down on bended knee to their rivals. In a biased discussion of these things relying only on superficial appearance, it could be said that this is "forgetting one's rivalries and putting up with shame." It also could be called "the root of the slave mentality." But how do we know that among them there were no heroic, talented, or wise people? No one of the caliber of Yi Yin or Zhou Bo? Silently, quietly, go with your heart's desire to secretly arrange your wicked plan; stealthily grasp the key, enter their chambers, suddenly snatch up their halberds, take hold of their spears, and stab them through their shields!

Upending the mountains and overturning the seas, doing wondrous deeds known worldwide.

Raising the rain and lifting the clouds, doing awesome heroic works.

All of you offering prayers with incense for our pursuit while we pursue it, this is what I hope for from our mandarins with a common will.

Those with hardened spears and bent backs, who are the frontline troops for the French, those who kick to the east and punch to the west, obeying the French with their blue and black sashes and their yellow and white hats. Are these people what we would call the trained soldiers of our land? Are they not our great sons of Vietnam? All of you are definitely the great sons of our land, but for ten pieces of silver a month, you give your bodies up to the French and attack and kill the people of our land. Originally grown from the same root, why do we burn so furiously together?[29] But when raising our swords and letting bullets fly, you will become those whom their eyes and mouths cannot bear to see or speak of. The people who run around for the French, though, cannot help it and are mostly compelled to do it. They think of getting a chance to

---

27. Yi Yin was the prime minister for Tang, the founder of the Shang dynasty (ca. 1600– 1100 B.C.E.).

28. After the death of the Han emperor Gaozu (r. 206–194 B.C.E.), his wife, the empress Lu, appointed members of her family, the Lu clan, to many important positions, thereby endangering the rule of the Han imperial family, the Liu. Zhou Bo became a general in the army, and one day announced to the soldiers that they should fasten their clothes on the left if they were loyal to the Lu and on the right if they were loyal to the Liu. They all fastened their clothes on the right, showing their loyalty to the Liu family, and thereafter the rule of the Liu was safe.

29. This is a quotation from the "Seven Step Poem" by Cao Zhi (192–232). He composed it as a retort to his jealous brother, the emperor of Wei, who told him that if he could not compose a poem while walking seven steps, he would be sentenced to death. This line refers to discord between brothers.

show that they have not forgotten their compatriots. One morning there will be a change in the wind, it will be an autumn in which strong men can do great deeds. I know for sure that our trained soldiers will use this time to repay their country. All you gentlemen see the French bossing around your sons and fathers every day, reducing your families and the folk of your villages to pulp through their oppression. This surely makes you harbor the deepest of grudges against them. However, being drilled with the weapons of the French, and going around with them every day makes it very easy for you to vent your anger. You bear the deepest of grudges but also have the easiest means at hand to vent your anger. You gentlemen can do great deeds, make a great name for your-selves, and do a great favor for our compatriots, if you would only turn your spears against [the French] in mutiny. The French treat the several thousands of lives of our compatriots as no more than fish and meat and give out only the ti-niest bit of cash to keep our trained soldiers in their clutches. My brothers, our trained soldiers, how can it be that those white rogues keep you in their clutches? Alas, it now is critical! The situation is urgent! The lives of your brothers in all the land are in your hands, our trained soldiers! All you gentlemen who are trained as soldiers, do not be ridiculed and sworn at by those of another race! Do not be regarded with scorn by those of your own kind in the underworld. This is what I hope from those trained soldiers of our land with a common will.

Since the religion of Jesus came to the South, our countrymen have been suspicious of it, and this has stupidly given rise to suspicion and distrust. But some of them falsely teach the people to submit to the French and make ene-mies of the Southern people. Ah, I wish my fellow countrymen would realize this now! Do we all not tread on Southern soil, enjoy the Southern sky over our heads; who of our ancestors, fathers, mothers, brothers, or wives, is not a person of our Southern land? Suffering disasters and imminent danger, we all seek to push forward without stopping toward our salvation, what is the use of being enemies? What urges them on most are the teachings of the Catholics. The guiding idea of the Catholics is the salvation of the world; they see universal love as a virtue and view abstention from greed and killing as tenets of their beliefs. Seeing the unkind, virtueless, greedy, lewd, and cruel French, they should keep apart from them as ice does from hot charcoals and reject this submission! Even if Catholic believers do actually submit to the French and make enemies of the Southern people, our countrymen should entreat them with tears, use sor-row to make them repent and realize, certainly not by grasping spears pointed toward them, but with nothing other than love. If believers decide on principle not to submit to the French and make enemies of the Southern people—the same race loving those of the same race, and the same race saving those of the same race, advancing along different paths but joining forces to meet adversity—this will surely allow our Southern people to escape from the French hell. This is what I hope from those with common will among the Catholic believers of the land.

Then there are the strong sons of the green woods, the manly fellows of the embroidered sails, with short pistols hidden at their waists and sharp blades concealed in their sleeves. Some call themselves the Association of Heaven and Earth, and some name themselves the Disciples of the Roaming Staves. They kill folk for sport, and no grudge is left unpaid. Their attitude, disdainful of life and daring to die, and their manner of going straight forward as if nothing were in their way make me look up to them and respect them thousands of times over. I salute them a hundred times, a hundred times. But there is something about these gentlemen that I pity, and there is especially something about which I would like to give my advice. Oh you gentlemen! If dogs and sheep were to get what they wished for, jackals and tigers would eat men!

Now is not the time for our valiant to die gloriously. I wish only that you would be able to die meritoriously. Your recent deeds have been based mainly on personal anger or petty mindedness, if not just to scowl angrily at one of your enemies, then to brandish your swords at them in a fit of rage; then if that does not satisfy, you follow it up with murder. Although there really is no harm in this for grudges between bandits, it is harmful to your own people. Groping women's breasts on the street and spilling blood for the sake of pretty maidens, getting involved in drunken fights, doing what you will in broad daylight. These are crude and lowly activities, yet you gentlemen throw away your lives in order to do such things.

The death of a great man can be graded. If one dies like Jing Ke[30] or Nie Zheng,[31] such a death is admirable and enviable; it makes gods weep and ghosts wail. The ways in which you gentlemen have died are horrible and detestable. The bodies are buried and the names disappear. So death is an awful thing, and not to fear death is very difficult. Why do you gentlemen not change your ways? The Westerners have entered our land. They presume to overawe us and do violent deeds, using thousands of ways to collect riches and hundreds of ways to take lives. They should be killed! They should be killed! They most certainly should be killed! In our country, one or two people have lost their minds and forgotten their own race; they assist the evil work of the tigers as their confidants and lead elephants to trample on graves. They should be killed a thousand times over! Ten thousand times! There is nothing as bad as these kinds of people.

If you gentlemen insist on treating your lives lightly and dare to die, why not do so with these sorts of people as targets, for the sake of our honor? Conceal secret letters in your breast, detail the crimes of helping wicked people to do cruel deeds, meet them on the roads, wait for them in hidden chambers, and finish them off with sword and pistol!

---

30. Jing Ke was an assassin who tried and failed to kill the first emperor of the Qin dynasty and was killed by the emperor's guard.

31. Nie Zheng was an assassin from the state of Han during the Warring States period who killed the prime minister of Han and then committed suicide.

If I myself am fortunate and my body is whole, I shall be satisfied with my purpose in life; but if I am not fortunate, then I would certainly be willing to die for the sake of my countrymen. The Southern people would receive good fortune from it, and the French rogues would be in awe of it; all under Heaven would think of its grandness, and the glory of my name would be retold for aeons.

Those who have drunken brawls and grope women's breasts, would you not, my brothers, prefer to distinguish honor from disgrace and right from wrong?

Alas! A rank smell offends my nose, and I lament that the swashbuckling swordsmen lack souls. Anger builds up in my breast, but I still have hope in our staff-wielding heroes and pray to them from afar. Emperor Heaven and Empress Earth, can you look into my heart? The wandering disciples of the secret societies, will you take heed of what I say? This is what I hope from those with common purpose among these gentlemen.

For a long time, the names of the female generals of our country have not been mentioned. Nonetheless, the strange airs of our mountains and rivers have produced extraordinary people. In the time we belonged to the North, the two Trungs were able to found a state by themselves. Bui Nguyen Xuan [Bui Thi Xuan] of the Tay Son also was good at leading armies. Heroes in head scarves can slay those with whiskers and eyebrows; wearers of hairpins and dresses are not ashamed to wear armor. Do not say that there are no shining paladins among them! Let me give some more recent examples of women who have a deep understanding of great virtue and are respectably courageous. Even a few of the red-girdled officials are inferior to them. I have noted the mother of Bac Ho Bich of Hung Nguyen and the mother of the examination graduate of Thanh Thuong. Others use their own wealth to provide for scholars, live a virtuous life and strive for their sons, help their husband make a distinguished name for himself, and follow the customs of the times to move the airs of the mountains and rivers. When pondering the great heroines of our Southern land, what do we lack? How, then, can I worship them respectfully and represent each one of them with pen and paper? At present on the five continents, heroism is burgeoning, and like the great welling up of the incoming tide, there is nowhere that it will not fill. In the war between Japan and Russia, a Japanese dancing girl beguiled a Russian general to get into the Russian mansions; she then stole all the books and maps of their plans and strategies, got away, and presented them to the Japanese generals. All the Russian plans were leaked, and the Japanese gained a great victory. How can we find this kind of female Huang Gai[32] in the bordellos of our country? This is what I hope for from the heroines of our country with a common will.

For a great tree to fall, a swarm of bugs must first go inside and chew it up; for enemies to be captured, people must go among them to spy on them. How will we Southerners manage to go among the French to spy on them? Ah, at

32. Huang Gai was a famous general from the Eastern Han dynasty (25–220).

one time, did not our Southern land know great tricks of defense and clever methods of winning battles? I dare say we certainly did! Now the reason that you serve as translators and clerks and cooks for the white rogues is simply to feed and clothe yourselves; it is not in your mind at all to forget us Southern people. Your parents, brothers, and sisters, and wives all are Southern people, so how can you possibly forget them simply because [the French] feed and clothe you? Even if you were to become the eyes and ears of the French, this would not give you additional food or clothing. On the contrary, it would give you a bad name. But if you were to become the eyes and ears of the Southern people, this would not result in less food or clothing, but it would give you a reputation for doing good deeds. I would ask that you gentlemen write down your creed, which should be "My body is with the French, but my heart is with the Southern people."

What is for your benefit is fortunately also for the people of our country, so please make your utmost effort to work for this. This is what I hope from those with a common will who are translators and workers for Westerners.

Now with the sentiment of Yu Rang on the bridge and Fu Chai outside the courtyard,[33] have you forgotten that your enemy killed your fathers? Have you forgotten that your enemy killed your brothers? Have you forgotten that your enemy insulted your fathers and brothers? This is what is in the minds of the sons of families that have been wronged.

Through discipline, we shall certainly wipe out these grudges.

I wish to tell my brothers that we have the same ambition, the same ambition. This is what I hope from the sons of families that have been wronged.

What I have just said applies to eight or nine of ten of our countrymen.

But there is a weakness in this. In some years, when forces are lined up to compete with one another at a time when Heaven has deemed it suitable, if we still have not adopted civilization from overseas or united our forces with those of strong neighboring lands and still rely on only our tiny selves to lock horns with this huge enemy, then we shall surely achieve nothing more than failure. How can we neglect people outside our borders?

If we use those people outside our borders, we would find that those who travel here and those who live here cannot make plans together and that they do not trust each other. One group would make the road go east while the others would make cart tracks to the west; one group would be masters of the lookout turret while the others take control of the oars. If they are unable to work together successfully, then they certainly will not be able to succeed together.

---

33. Yu Rang was an official for Earl Zhi of Jin (d. 453 B.C.E.). After the state of Jin was split into three states and Earl Zhi had been killed, Yu Rang tried twice to assassinate Viscount Xiang of Zhao, the ringleader of the plot to divide Jin, to avenge his lord. Fu Chai (d. 473 B.C.E.) was the king of the state of Wu. His father had been killed by King Goujian of Yue state, and he employed someone to stand at the entrance to his courtyard to remind him of the insult whenever he went in or out, so that he would not lose his thirst for revenge.

Despite this, the common will of those inside the country and those overseas is still of the utmost importance.

My brothers young and old! My uncles! My parents! There is no mountain we cannot move, no sea we cannot cross! I worry only that our hearts are not resolute. If all of us are resolute in our hearts, there is nothing under Heaven that we cannot accomplish. I wish for my fellow countrymen who have a fixed abode to understand the bitter circumstances of those who are sojourners, and for the sojourners to forgive the difficulties in the hearts of those who have a fixed abode; they must trust each other and not be suspicious; they must work together for success and not for mutual harm; and they must not act rashly and spoil affairs or spend too long waiting and lose the moment; then Westerners and Japanese will truly trust each other. A request for money in the thousands, even though it might come from thousands of miles away but the recipient does not use deception, and the sender has no doubts—this kind of solidarity is of great importance. The people of Japan consider time to be extremely important. [So] in school when a teacher is teaching, even if an important guest arrives he will not receive him, out of fear that it would disrupt the schoolwork. Our own scholars have become all too wasteful with their time, which is a great pity.

If one makes broth by dripping blood into it, then Heaven will take heed of it. If one concentrates one's spirit on a single arrow, it will be able to split metal and stone.

My brothers young and old! My uncles! My parents! What I hope from the people of like mind inside and outside the country is that our fellow countrymen might have a common ambition like this. Then what foundations will we not be able to establish? What structures will we not be able to complete?

If we say that the French will never lose and the Southern people will never become strong, this is just like saying "the sun doesn't shine during the day" or "the moon doesn't shine at night" or "Heaven is not high" or "the ocean is not deep." Even with a sword put to my throat I will not accept it.

Even if I acted as though this were true, I still would not be able not to feel despair for my fellow countrymen.

My countrymen have grown up in a wild barbarous period, have been sunk in a river of immaturity; they are blind and dim and dull and stupid in a place with no government and no moral teachings. With a common purpose, we will certainly be able to protect the country, but a lack of common purpose will lead to the country's destruction. Those who have a common purpose can make slaves of men, and those without it end up as the slaves of men. My countrymen still do not understand the reasons for this.

If the reasons are known, then the people will unite without effort. That is, if our people, the Viet people, are together in the same boat and encounter a great gale, they will quickly be able to save one another. But if the reasons are unknown, then even if one wants to force people to unite, they still will end up disunited, like the chickens in a cage pecking at one another or like fish in a bowl eating one another. Alas for the knowledge of our fellow countrymen! How far away are we really from the chickens in a cage or fish in a bowl? To sordid and lowly notoriety they flock like ducks to water; for as tiny a benefit as the tip of a hair they sacrifice themselves.

They fawn on foreigners as if they were the emperors of Heaven and look upon their compatriots as they would upon thorns and prickles. If one tells them the result to be gained from a common ambition and demand that they achieve this in a short period of time, they will be uncertain whether they can do it. Why are they lacking in joy and full of hate? Why do they not run toward good fortune but just try to avoid disaster? Only out of their own stupidity. When people are stupid, they suspect one another, hate one another, and harm one another. The miasma of mutual suspicion, hate, and harm has already resulted in a terminal illness that they cannot shake.

Speaking again and again of common purpose is almost like whipping a turtle to make it fly or trying to get a lame man to leap about. Oh alas and alack! These adverse billows and mad waves! Who will stand straight as a pillar among them? These black mists and dark vapors! Who will fan them away? The dreams of a visitor who has fled thirty thousand leagues are still cold and miserable, but the soul of a land that has been handed down for a thousand years by our forefathers may yet return.

Does our land have any scholars who have the foresight, and classes of people who are magnanimous as heroes, anyone who will cry out as loudly and with such urgency as I?

Manners and morals and the hearts of men are also the responsibility of ordinary people.

Restoring and protecting, rectifying and rescuing, how can our pens and tongues leave these tasks to others?

In the civilized laws of all nations, there is the right of freedom to publish and debate. My humble wish is for all my great brothers, you renowned people, you scholars with ambition, to hurry to awaken the people to their own fate. Rise up to the task of rescuing them from the flames and saving them from drowning. To one sort of people, explain these reasons, and to other sorts of people, explain other reasons. Let your mouth become a sword to vanquish evil; let your tongue become a mirror in which demons can be reflected.

I conceal no weapons to kill men and will not kill men with my hands. I lay out simply what is right and what is wrong and distinguish what brings disaster from what brings fortune in order to rescue the people of my country. I do nothing that will make me enemies of men; what could my enemies do to me, anyway? My brothers, my brothers, do not keep these things hidden. Today, one person awakes, tomorrow another. Then it will spread out to tens, hundreds, thousands, hundreds of thousands of people, spreading so that not one person in the land does not know of the solidarity of the masses, spreading so that not one person in the land cannot but be in solidarity with the masses.

The ten premises of common will that this humble writer has described will suddenly sweep through the land like wind and move through it like thunder. Then we shall ring our bell of liberty and raise our flag of independence. We shall demand back our inheritance from those robbers who snatched it from us in the past. Will those robbers who snatched it from us dare to take our inheritance again? Will they dare not to offer it back to its owners with both hands in supplication? They won't dare! They won't dare! They most certainly will not dare!

At this time then, let the lanterns of celebration shine resplendently on the earth; let the altars of happy welcome be raised majestically to the heavens; let a tower of remembrance stand loftily, grandly, in the capital of our land of Vietnam![34]

Struggle on my countrymen! Be like Rousseau and Fukuzawa Yukichi[35] and struggle on!

[Phan Boi Chau, "Hai ngoai huyet thu," 414–34;
trans. Catherine Churchman]

TONKIN FREE SCHOOL

A CIVILIZATION OF NEW LEARNING (1904)

"A Civilization of New Learning" lays out a program of reforms by the advocates of new learning at the beginning of the twentieth century. In the wake of the failure of the Can Vuong movement, the Tonkin Free School (Dong Kinh Nghia Thuc) advocated a "new learning" based on Western educational models in order to compete successfully with the West. Although the school operated for only nine months in 1907 before it was closed by the French, it generated a large number of texts that continued to circulate and have a long-lasting influence. Among the most prized was the text presented here, originally written in Chinese, which proposed fundamental linguistic, social, economic, and political innovations and which has been translated and excerpted from the romanized Vietnamese version. In the 1870s, Nguyen Truong To had begun to make the same arguments,[36] but to a completely unreceptive audience. Much had changed in the intervening years.

---

34. This may refer to the centuries-old Bao Thien Thap (tower), destroyed by the French two decades earlier.

35. Fukuzawa Yukichi (1835–1901) was a Japanese political theorist whose ideas greatly influenced the modernization of Japan after the Meiji Restoration in 1868.

36. See Nguyen Truong To, "A Plan for Making the People Wealthy and the Country Strong" (chap. 5).

We believe that *civilization* is a fine word, one that seems to connote a glittering facade of wealth. In truth, however, it consists of benefits that cannot be acquired in a short period of time. If we wish to acquire civilization, we must have a strong intellectual vision and a program of action. What do these consist of? They entail improving the intellectual level of the people. Some of the world's countries are still quite backward; others are partly civilized; and only a few have become civilized. Civilization depends on the degree of development of the people's knowledge that each country has acquired. A Western scholar once said: "Civilization does not come from [a country's] values alone, but also from difficult challenges." What did he mean by values? Values are ideology and intellectual accomplishment. What kind of challenges? Competition. The more intellectual endeavor there is, the more competition there will be. More competition brings about more intellectual accomplishment and intensive growth in the sciences, such as acoustics, optics, gravity, electricity, mineralogy, hydrology and hydrography, chemistry, geography, astronomy, mathematics, and engineering. This leads civilization to new heights. Civilization and the level of the people's knowledge are mutually interdependent. In order to raise the people's knowledge, one first of all must know where the gaps are and begin to address them. Otherwise, one can only sadly look out at an immense sea.

. . . In ancient times, Asia was the source of civilization. Our country of Dai Nam [Vietnam], located between the tropical zone and the temperate zone, with fertile land, a moderate climate, plenty of rice, silk worms, and forestry products, and a seacoast longer than most, was also a civilized country. . . . What is the current situation? We no longer have valuable forestry products and other resources. We no longer control hundreds of goods and benefits of our country, such as cloth, crepe, velvet, wool, silk, shoes, sandals, handkerchiefs, spectacles, umbrellas, gasoline, pottery, crystal glass, clocks and watches, thermometers, welding devices, telephone apparatuses, microscopes, camera glass, writing paper and pens, China ink, needles, thread, buttons, dyes, soap, perfume, watches, milk cakes, sweets and candied fruit, medicines, cigarettes, tea, and brandy, all of which must be imported from either France or China. Just look at the annual import and export figures and try to recover all the money spent on such items. What a pity indeed!

In today's world, agriculture is controlled by agencies and associations and involves competition. But we still do things in the old way. Do we use tractors and electricity for improving agricultural production, and new methods for dealing with drought and insects? Trade [in other countries] is controlled by the Trade Ministry and involves competition. But we still do things in the old way. Do we have merchant ships, big companies set up by the government, and people's shares for promoting trade? Industry [in other countries] is developed with companies and workshops and involves technological competition. But we still do things in the old way. Do we have talented persons like Watt and Edison who continually invent things? The lack of talent in this country is truly frightening.

Many people in our country indulge in musical entertainment, gambling, chess, poetry contests, horoscopes, geomancy, and fortune-telling, all of which is useless. People with some qualifications put on airs and cling to old-fashioned theories and do not care to learn about new civilizations. Other persons only care about rank and promotions to the exclusion of everything else. One dignitary even told his younger colleagues, "When you become a mandarin, take care to refrain from reading new books and journals." Not reading new books and journals is bad enough. But it is even more painful to see people deprived of human dignity trying to conceal or ignore new books and journals, thereby further enhancing their condition of slavery.

For thousands of years, [Dai Nam's] civilization was *static* in character and lacked the *dynamism* that characterized other countries. We should feel sad and grieved. In order to be civilized, improving the people's knowledge must be the first principle. Yellow-skinned people are just as able as white people. But without seeing how things work, we cannot imitate [others] and make progress; without capital and money, we cannot go into business. Therefore, if someone does not show us the way, we cannot forge ahead. . . .

Thus, having craned our necks and looked all around and thought about the matter deeply, we see six reforms as part of a program of action to develop the people's minds and knowledge in the midst of countless difficulties.

1. Use our country's writing system: . . . Not long ago, a Portuguese priest developed the *quoc ngu* alphabet, which has twenty-six European letters, six tones, and eleven vowel sounds, is spelled phonetically, and is simple and quick. Everyone should learn *quoc ngu*, which can be easily mastered in a few months by men, women, and children alike. One can use *quoc ngu* to record the past and use it in the present to write letters and messages. Learning *quoc ngu* is the first step in developing our wisdom and our minds.

2. Reform our system of textbooks: Our country has many books . . . which provide information and knowledge about geography, customs, regulations, and rules to be applied and followed by successive generations. Yet as a rule, most of our students in the past neglected our country's own writings and read Chinese books. . . . Chinese books refer only to what happened in China, which is not at all relevant to Vietnam. . . . If this is what our classics and history books are like, what are the rest like?

Human beings live, at most, one hundred years and need to undertake many tasks and cannot devote all their strength and energy to digest a voluminous collection of ancient books! . . . Thus, reforming our system of textbooks is a necessity. To this end, it is essential to create an editorial committee to select the books to be read at the appropriate level of education. . . . The main books selected and recompiled should be Southern [Vietnamese] history books. Other books should focus on the rise and fall of regimes, the reasons for success and failure of great events, and the principles concerning the establishment of dynasties and regimes. Chinese history should be read to grasp only its general outlines. . . . Western history books . . . should be recompiled so that students can absorb the essential points. . . .

3. Reform the examination system: Because today's knowledge is wide and deep, how can we possibly use literary composition and rote learning to test the depth of a student's knowledge? Therefore, reform of the examination system must accompany reform of the textbooks. Otherwise, it will be a halfway reform. Does interpreting passages in ancient Chinese classics, writing essays, poetry, imperial orders, memos to the emperors, and methods and rules for writing poetry and prose have any real utility for practical work? Do the old Confucian scholars know about the five continents of the world, about the history of the world, including the current century?. . .

Although we are not yet able to follow Europe's specialized examination system, we can temporarily use dissertations and prose compositions to [create] specific questions as examination methods. . . . On the basis of [the Chinese classics] and Southern [Vietnamese], Chinese, and European history books, we should work out questions to which candidates can give free-form responses. Examination subjects should also include mathematical problems and *quoc ngu* prose compositions. All this will help candidates tackle practical questions relevant to their real work. This will be acceptable [for now].

4. Encourage and promote gifted students: . . . When the textbooks have been corrected and the examination system reformed, we can expect good performance from thousands and thousands of graduates and current mandarin officials. . . . The National School [in Hue][37] is supposed to be an educational and training institution, yet its current curricular emphasis on contemporary literature is unrelated to present practical realities. It has been in existence for eight to nine years now and has produced good graduates, but no one has employed them. If they finish their studies but are not employed, who will follow in their path? Mandarins should be instructed to appoint graduates to various ministries and departments. If circulars are issued, the graduates should be asked to translate them [into *quoc ngu*]. . . . Those who cannot study French should be sent to a new training institute to learn about texts like *Public Law, Western History, Administrative Rules and Regulations, Collected Imperial Statutes, Maps, Mathematics,* and so on, kept in that institute. . . . They should take annual examinations, and graduates should be appointed to available positions. In this way, in a few years, the older generation will start to change and join the new class of graduates.

---

37. Established in 1896 to provide Western-style education for the children of the political elite, the National Academy was the successor to the Quoc Tu Giam, which previously had prepared scholars for the traditional civil service examinations and future careers as government officials.

5. Promote industry: . . . In the West, if someone invents and produces new goods, they are copied and improved by others, no matter how much time and effort it takes to learn how to do so. See how beneficial learning from others can be! If only a few people have the authority or exclusive right to use high-quality goods, how can they give orders to people below [to copy the models]? If we know someone who makes something better than we do and we do not try to improve it, how can our country possibly progress? Instead of restricting spending on foreign goods, why do we not allow more of our own goods to be produced and consumed?

Our country has only one well-known product: mother-of-pearl inlays. Although other goods, like conical hats made of feathers and pineapple leaves, rattan chairs, mats with flower decorations, ceramics, crepe, cloth, and silk are produced by both China and our country, the quality of our goods is inferior to that of Chinese goods. The reason is that we have not given enough attention to developing our industry. As reported in the newspaper, Tonkin has recently acquired a new method of raising silkworms, and an agriculture department and a vocational school have been established in Hanoi. These are good educational institutions. Our people should devote their time to studying these subjects in order to work more efficiently. But the imperial court has ignored these two institutions, and scholars hold them in contempt. As a result, students of the vocational school are regarded as coolies, and students of agriculture are seen as tree planters. This approach betrays our complete ignorance of industrial development.

Industry is very important to our country. If we cannot overtake others, we will lag behind. The worst will be if we lavishly spend our money in foreign countries by importing foreign goods. What we need are good teachers, good models, skilled and intelligent students; let the imperial court train them. Notice should be given to the whole country that whoever learns a new model and produces a new product will be given a financial reward, certificate of merit, or patent, as is done in European countries. Persons who perform well in the natural sciences, meteorology, and chemistry should be given greater honors than [are given to] the graduates of the imperial civil examinations, so that they will work and compete hard in order to surpass others. [If this is done], there will be no reason for talented individuals not to step forward.

6. Develop the press: Most countries have daily newspapers, weekly papers, and biweekly and monthly journals. These papers provide information and commentary on various subjects: the news, political issues, current events, and advertisements. Various sectors in the country—businessmen, legislators and lawyers, scientists, medical practitioners, farmers, workers—have their own papers. France has more than 1,230 newspapers and journals, Germany more than 2,350, Great Britain more than 2,180, Russia more than 430, the United States more than 14,150, and each Japanese province has its own paper; in recent times

China also has had many papers. The press has a big impact on the development of the people's knowledge. But Saigon and Haiphong have only French newspapers that are read by few inhabitants, and we have only one daily newspaper, which is in Chinese. . . .

In our opinion, our capital city should establish a newspaper, with a senior mandarin as the editor in chief and a staff composed of scholars. Half the newspaper should be in *quoc ngu* and half in Chinese characters. Its content should include new ideas; new trade [ideas] and new methods from Europe and America; items from Vietnamese books, lives, and personalities in history and today, which can serve as models; and new techniques developed by our industrialists that can be useful to our country. Newspapers should be sold at a low price and should be free to both senior and junior mandarins and to various communes and villages. Individuals who subscribe to papers should be encouraged by rewards. . . . Sales should cover operating expenses, but what is most important is breaking through the barriers of nonsense and obscurity [and reaching all the sections of the population].

It takes years to learn a foreign language, and [even then,] one still does not know it perfectly, but [it takes] less than six months to learn our own writing system. Therefore, it is completely obvious that there is no excuse not to study our own language. If you study an ancient literature and its various forms of expression, which you learn by heart without giving much attention to the content, in the end you will learn something about mere formalistic literature. But if you focus on what is clear and essential [in *quoc ngu*], you will gain real knowledge. Thus, it is essential to reform our system of textbooks and the examination system and to promote and encourage gifted students. This could not be more apparent.

If we are contemptuous of industry, our gold, silver, wood, and quarries will become the raw materials used by foreigners; if industry is encouraged, our water, fire, wind, and electricity will serve the daily needs of our people. Therefore, developing industry is a basic necessity. There is no use in shutting yourself up in your own village. Instead, you should allow your mind to venture into the outside world and take a close look. There is no point in reading ancient texts over and over; instead, you should read current newspapers, which give everyone new and wonderful knowledge. Establishing newspapers and journals is obviously essential.

Some people say that as a country, our native Southern land has had clearly marked borders and old cultural traditions. We have the six ways of writing Chinese characters, so why do we need a new writing system? We have many books, so why do we need new ones? Our examination system is able to select officials, so why do we need new methods? Should we really drop our thousand-year-old cultural traditions and imitate the new ones, and how could we do this, anyway?

Regrettably, if we follow this reasoning, there will be no end to the darkness that will fall on the minds of our people, and there will be no way for our country to progress. . . . If the "closed door" does not give way to "electric wire and engineering," the reasons for our predicament and the ways to solve it, as just mentioned, will never get far in the minds of our philosophers and statesmen. If something goes wrong, they will try to fix it, but they will inevitably gloss over the situation, all the while claiming that our civilization is adequate. The trouble is that you cannot varnish over the predicament in this way. . . . Liang Qichao, [the Chinese reformer], said that if the house is too old because people have lived in it for more than a thousand years, it has to be dismantled and rebuilt so that people can live in it again. If that is the case, there is no other way. Are you familiar with Japan? For the last thirty years or so, Japan has incorporated European thought and civilization and has achieved its goals. What about Siam? Thirty years ago, Siam [Thailand] came into contact with Europe and sent its students to Europe, and now its political system has changed and become quite adequate. What about China? An ancient country, yet both spurred from inside and outside, the Chinese have woken up and realized that European methods are well worth following. . . . The Chinese are now incorporating modern ideas into their ancient classical system.

Alas, we are asleep while the rest of the world is fully awake, and we are stationary while others have crossed the river. Accordingly, how can we gain access to the next level of civilization? As civilization continues to change, progress itself is always moving forward. What in the past was a civilized society is now only a *half-civilized* one. What previously was a *partly civilized* society is now a *barbaric* one. . . .

As a result of their intellectual accomplishments and the economic means acquired over the past several hundred years, Europeans are now civilized and have embarked on continuous expansion into Asia. . . . If we continue to have singing parties while contemplating lakes and mountains without being concerned about [the plight of] our country, what will happen to our 25 million fellow compatriots? How will posterity judge us?

[Adapted from Dong Kinh Nghia Thuc, "Van minh tan hoc sinh,"
208–11, 215–27; trans. Jayne Werner and Luu Doan Huynh]

PHAN CHAU TRINH

MONARCHY AND DEMOCRACY (1925)

Phan Chau Trinh, a founder of the Tonkin Free School, was a forceful proponent of reform and democratization. From early on, in contrast to Phan Boi Chau, he denounced any efforts to restore or reform the monarchy. Although Phan Chau Trinh urged his fellow modernizers to pursue popular rights and a nonviolent path to political independence, he retained the imprint of Confucian ideas in the mold of Mencius by identifying with the people. In this final passage from a speech given in 1925, Phan Chau Trinh sums up his ideas. Only when the people exercise their popular rights, he argues, will they truly learn to love their country and achieve self-determination.

Monarchy or Government of Men?

To make a long story short, *quan tri* [monarchy, autocracy] is *nhan tri* [government by men]. Autocratic countries have laws, but these laws are deliberately made by the king, and the people are completely unaware of anything. If a country is fortunate enough to have a wise and heroic king, one who understands the relationship between the people and their country and is able to punish corrupt officials so that people can live in peace and be content with their lives, that country will enjoy prosperity and peace as long as that king is on the throne.

But if the king is a despot, who lives with concubines and eunuchs, knows nothing of national affairs, and leaves his country's governance to his deceitful ministers, his country will certainly collapse because the king, its ruler, is so negligent. Confucius thus said: "The government of King Wen and King Wu is displayed in the records. . . . If there are men, the government will flourish; but if there are no men, the government will decay and die." Xunzi, in contrast, said: *You zhi ren, wu zhi fa*, literally, "There are men who are able, but there are no laws that are able"[38] [implying that "there are men who are capable of governing their country but there are no laws that, by themselves, could govern the country"]. Mencius, encompassing the views of Confucius and Xunzi, said: "Virtue alone is not sufficient for the exercise of government, [and] laws alone cannot put themselves into practice."[39]

For thousands of years, able kings and generals have done their best to prevent monarchy from being *nhan tri*, but without any success. This is because the laws were made by kings, and the laws also were abolished by them. These kings concerned themselves with modifying *nhan tri* before the Song and the Tang dynasties, because after that monarchies became extremely autocratic. The Hongwu emperor [1368–1398] of the Ming dynasty created a law against "having talents but not allowing the king to use them" in order to put everyone under tyrannical rule by not allowing anyone to retire out of frustration. The Qianlong emperor [1736–1795] added a law against "wheedling the king," to punish those who had talents but forced the king to beg for their services. In

---

38. Xunzi, "Jundao" (The Way of the Sovereign), in *Kadokawa daijiten* (*Kadokawa Dictionary*), ed. Ozaki Yujirō et al. (Tokyo: Kadokawa shoten, 1992), 1003. [All notes and bracketed comments in this selection are the translator's]

39. *Mencius*, book 7 (Li Lou, part I), in *Han-Ying sishu* (*The Four Books in Chinese and in English*), trans. James Legge and annotated Luo Zhiye (Hunan: Hunan chubanshe, 1992), 388–89.

ancient times, the kings looked for talented people, but those in later times just lay back, making no attempt at searching. Even so, they arrested those who had talents yet did not come forth.

I have spoken about the history and philosophy of monarchy as *nhan tri*. I would like to add a few concrete and easily recognizable illustrations. *Nhan tri* is a form of government that may be liberal or harsh, depending entirely on the joyful or sorrowful, loving or unloving, mood of the king, and it is a form of government in which the laws exist for nothing.

For example, Mr. Gia Long [r. 1802–1820] adopted the law enacted during the time of the Qianlong emperor [of the Qing dynasty] to govern the Vietnamese. This law stipulated that "without acquiring military merits, one cannot be given the rank of marquis." Nguyen Van Thanh [1757–1817] was appointed to the rank of marquis and was even promoted to military secretary because Mr. Gia Long was fair in his assessment of the military achievements that Nguyen Van Thanh had accumulated since his youth. Afterward, however, when Mr. Thanh's son composed a poem for pleasure, quite an innocent one, Mr. Gia Long ordered the execution of his three generations [Nguyen Van Thanh, his sons, and his father]. In other words, because he was so infuriated he ordered the execution, and this had nothing to do with the law!

I would like to tell you another story about Mr. Tu Duc [r. 1848–1883].[40] In the twenty-fifth year of the Tu Duc era [1873], people in the Trung Ky region nearly starved. After the government had provided a small measure of relief, officials requested that a portion of the tax collected in the provinces, prefectures, and districts be kept in the village granaries in anticipation of future food shortages. At that time, Mr. Tu Duc told the people that they could pay in money or rice, and in return, they would receive the titles of *ba ho*,[41] eighth rank, or ninth rank. But the people were starving, how could they have money or rice to be collected? Mr. Tu Duc then issued a decree ordering his officials to allow them to pay on credit: with an initial installment of 300 piastres (of the 1,000 piastres required), they would receive a certificate, and when they paid the balance, the official title would be granted. The decree mentioned specifically that the money collected in each village was to be kept there. The following year another decree appeared ordering that all the money that had been paid or was still due on credit should be transferred to the provinces to be used as funds to stave off rebellions. Orders flowed down from provinces to prefectures and districts and then from prefectures and districts to villages. The people responded, saying that the king had allowed them to pay on credit, rather than requiring immediate payment and because the people had had a bad harvest that year,

---

40. Phan Chau Trinh purposely addressed the Tu Duc emperor as "Mr." to demonstrate his lack of respect for him.

41. Literally, "one hundred households." The original Chinese term was used in Vietnam to refer to persons of great wealth.

they simply did not have the money to pay—whatever disciplinary measures might be taken. Provincial officials reported [this news] to the ministry, and the ministry then reported to the king. The king decided that all the people should be punished.

Vietnamese law, however, has no clause dealing with transactions of money between the people and the government. The government officials thus could not find a legal basis on which to charge the people. They reported to the king. The king said that the law to be applied was *thuong thu bat di that*, that is, the clause concerned "an official who makes a political report to the king untruthfully." The officials at the ministry level then brought charges against the officials at the provincial level [the very people who had received the titles for paying their taxes in full]. Some punishments were six years, some were eight years, and some were twelve years of imprisonment. In the midst of famine and with their family members scattered, these people had thought it would cheer them up if they could make the payment and earn a low-ranking title (eighth or ninth rank), but to their unforeseen dismay, they were put into prison instead. Their families and their clans were heartbroken. Fortunately, when this case reached Quang Ngai Province, the provincial judge was well versed in legal matters and took seriously the concerns of the people and those regarding national affairs. His name was Nguyen Thong, pen name Ky Xuyen [a native of Ben Tre, in Vinh Long Province, he had escaped to Phan Thiet following the loss of the six provinces (Nam Ky)].[42] This man methodically demolished the charges, sentence by sentence, against the low-ranking officials. He wrote to the ministry, saying: "In this case, it was the king and officials who lied to the people—the people did not lie to anyone. It is completely out of place to apply the law *thuong thu bat di that*." Mr. Tu Duc realized that it was his fault, but he was ashamed of himself, so he got somebody to sue Mr. Nguyen Thong by bringing a serious charge against him and had him deposed [removed from office]. But the people in Quang Ngai and elsewhere did all they could to support Mr. Nguyen Thong, so damage was limited to his expulsion.

These are only a few examples; if I were to talk about Chinese and Vietnamese histories, I could go on and on for days.

A Brief Account of Democracy

In the present world, in the countries that have, more or less, adopted European civilization or are exposed to liberalism and freedom of expression, everyone understands the meaning of democracy. Although several countries in Europe

---

42. Nguyen Thong (1827–1884) was a native of Gia Dinh (present-day Long An Province). After the outbreak of the French military campaign against Vietnam in 1859, Nguyen Thong helped defend Nam Ky. After Nam Ky was lost, Nguyen Thong "took refuge" in Trung Ky (in central Vietnam), where he served as the provincial governor of Quang Ngai from 1868 to 1871.

have monarchs, in every country, the upper and lower houses have a democratic party. In Vietnam, however, the French have dominated the six provinces
[Nam Ky] for sixty years and the term *république* is continually bandied about,
yet no one investigates its meaning and compares it with the meaning of monarchy. This is the situation in the learned circle, and it appears to me that this
group prefers a monarchy. The people in rural areas know nothing about democracy; they worship the king in their heads as if he were a deity or a sage. Not
only do they not dare think about the question of "whether or not we should
have a king," but they act as if a person raising this question would be struck by
a thunderbolt, buried under rocks, trampled by elephants, and torn apart by
horses.

Upon hearing the name of a king, whoever he is, people are jubilant and
ecstatic, placing their hope and expectation in him. So silly was the recent case
of Phan Xich Long.[43] The poison of autocracy has therefore entered deeply into
the minds of our people, and their intellectual level is very low. The people understand if someone tells them, "You must be loyal to this person, or respect that
person," but if anyone mentions the name of Vietnam and tells them, "That is
your motherland, you must love it," they do not understand because they cannot
touch it with their hands or see it with their eyes. How is it possible for them to
love it? They can love only a house, a garden, and some acres of land—things
they can see with their eyes.

I have noticed in the last few years that whenever journalists and public
speakers open their mouths, they mention the 20 million people of our country.
The tone is a mixture of pride, boastfulness, and expectation. In my opinion,
these 20 million people know only their family and do not know their country.
For example, if a family's sons have died and there is no heir, or a family has a
lot of land and rice fields but is being sued, or a family has children who are
addicted to gambling, or whatever—people consider these things the most important and gather to gossip. But if one talks about "the loss of national independence," not a single soul cares. How deplorable if the attitude of a people
toward their country is so indifferent and disinterested! Considering the state of
the people, some of you might be surprised at the suggestion to abolish monarchy and create a republic. In my view, since the poison of autocracy has fatally
injured the patriotism of our people, there is no better way to make them aware
of the fact that Vietnam is indeed their country than to throw away those lackeys,
and only after that is done will they be able to find out to whom this country
belongs. One day our intelligent people will find that, in this land, handed
down to them over thousands of years, much still remains of their interests,
much is still to be found of their rights. They will realize that those who have

---

43. In 1913, Phan Xích Long (Phan, "the Red Dragon") declared that he was the "crown
prince" of the Ham Nghi emperor and led an uprising in Saigon against the colonial government. He was soon arrested and imprisoned.

been called kings and officials since the olden days are, after all, just their representatives acting on their behalf, and if they cannot do a good job, there is nothing wrong with chasing them away.

When the people begin to see things in that light, they will know how to love their country. Only when they know how to love their country may they hope for their freedom and independence; otherwise, they will remain slaves from generation to generation.

Why It Is Called Democracy

To the people in Europe, there is no need to explain "why it is called democracy," but in our country, this is not so. I will therefore provide a brief explanation so that you will have a general understanding. . . .

The author follows with a brief account of the origin of popular assemblies in Greece and Rome and the emergence of Parliament in England.

A Brief Description of Democracy

At present, all nations in Europe practice democracy, with the exception of those countries whose peoples still are ignorant.

Let me describe for you the political structure of France. The Lower House, that is, the Chamber of Deputies or the National Assembly, is the most important house. The number of seats is approximately six hundred. Citizens twenty-one years old and older have the right to vote. Those over age twenty-five have the right to become candidates in the election. If elected, one becomes a deputy in the Lower House. France's fortune is decided by this house, which has legislative power. In addition, there is the Senate. The senators are not elected by the people, but indirectly by a *collège électoral* consisting of municipal councillors in each *département*, the administrative units into which France is divided. The Senate looks after fiscal matters. The president is elected by the two houses. The candidates for the presidency are members from these two houses, and the candidate who receives the most votes is elected. Once the president has been elected, he has to take an oath in front of the two houses, stating: "On the basis of our democratic constitution, I vow not to betray our people and not to be partisan; if I am guilty of breaking these promises, I will be subject to impeachment."[44] Because of their violations against the constitution, French presidents [Patrice de] MacMahon and, more recently, [Alexandre] Millerand were removed from office.

---

44. The source of the quote is unknown.

The government also is formed from members sitting in the two houses. The party that occupies the largest number of seats is allowed to form a cabinet. The current cabinet has a few dozen ministries, but their ministers are not dysfunctional and haughty like the ministers in our country. Each of them has specific responsibilities. If they do not meet the expectations of the people, they will be criticized. Because there are two political parties in the National Assembly, one left wing and one right wing, if the left-wing party holds the majority of the seats, the right-wing party will be the watchdog and be ready to level criticisms; therefore, it is difficult to do anything outrageous.

Everyone in the country must observe the constitution. The power of the government also is stipulated in the constitution, and therefore it has little room for negligence and autocracy. In addition, according to the law, anyone who violates the constitution is treated the same—from the president to a common person in the countryside.

The government officers have only administrative power; judicial power is entrusted to judges with the required training and qualifications. The judges specialize in making judgments in the courts. In making their decisions, they have independent power and rely on the letter of the law, fairness, and their conscience. They deal with government officials and private citizens in exactly the same manner. The judges belong to a separate department, the Department of Justice. The judicial power, the administrative power of the government, and the legislative power of the parliament are separate, not controlled by a single person.

The preceding is just a brief outline; to have a thorough understanding of democracy, one must be more specific.

Seen in this light, democracy is a government of laws. The rights and duties of everyone in the country are well described by the laws—like a road on which lines have been drawn clearly, so that you can walk freely, there is nothing to stop you, and you may go on as far as you like, as long as you do not violate the rights of others. This is because before the laws, everyone is equal, regardless of whether they are officials or common people.

Comparing the two concepts of monarchy and democracy, we see that democracy is far better than monarchy. To govern a country solely on the basis of the personal opinions of one individual or of an imperial court is to treat the people of that country as if they were a herd of goats—their prosperity and joy, or their poverty and misery, are entirely in the hands of the herder. In contrast, in a democracy the people create their own constitution and select officials who must look after their nation's business in accordance with the will of the people. Even when there are no excellent talents among the government officials, the people do not have to submit themselves to becoming servants for a family or a clan [as has happened under monarchies].

History has proved that wise people who follow the path of self-strengthening and self-reliance to search for their common interests become happier each day. In contrast, ignorant people who remain idle without doing anything—only wait for help from Heaven or favors from government officials, and entrust their rights to the hands of a single person or government—suffer all sorts of hardships.

My compatriots! Now that you have seen the reasons, you should take part in tackling our national affairs; without doing so, we will not be able to raise our heads.

[Adapted from Phan Chau Trinh,
Phan Chau Trinh and His Political Writings, 125–39]

NGUYEN AN NINH

THE IDEAL OF ANNAMESE YOUTH (1923)

Nguyen An Ninh (1900–1943) was the first of the Vietnamese elite's French-educated youth to engage in modern politics, which followed his return from Paris, where he had obtained a degree in law from the Sorbonne in 1922. Nguyen An Ninh started the journal *La cloche fêlée* (*The Flawed Bell*), which ran from 1923 to 1926 in Saigon and was influential in the publication of other important newspapers. He also introduced new methods of mass engagement, such as organizing popular meetings, distributing tracts, and politicizing legal cases. He advocated the creation of a powerful national culture to elevate the Vietnamese from their colonial servitude, and he decried both low- and high-level Vietnamese officials who allowed themselves to be co-opted into the French colonial administration. Nguyen An Ninh's speech, given in October 1923 and published in French in *La cloche fêlée* in January 1924, is remembered for its call to action directed to a generation of Vietnamese youth. Although Nguyen An Ninh agreed with Pham Quynh that both Western and Eastern ideas should shape Vietnamese culture,[45] his emphasis was less on discipline and loyalty than new ideals and passions and a life of action. Note that Nguyen An Ninh uses the colonial French names Annam and Annamese for Vietnam and Vietnamese.

As I have said before, "It is not in Indochina that an Annamese youth, trained for the bureaucracy, will find the feeblest idea of the French culture." Even of those favored by heredity and circumstance, precious few are capable of the efforts necessary to equal the cultivated minds of Europe. And in these times, all Asian minds must be nourished by two cultures, one occidental and one oriental. . . . I will soon speak to you of the social obligation that rests on the most intelligent and strongest among us. Here I want to discuss further the necessity of an intellectual culture for our race. . . .

---

45. See Pham Quynh, "Intellectual and Moral Reform" and "*Kim Van Kieu* and the National Language" (both in this chap.).

Many people owe to their culture the duration of their name, their influence in the world, and the messianic role that they play in the world. No people dominated by a foreign culture can know true independence if it does not possess an independent culture. A people's culture is its soul. Just as a man of elevated soul knows the superior joys of existence, so a people of high culture knows the privileges denied to those less cultivated. . . .

Let us take as an example a culture to whose influence we still are subject: the Chinese culture. Vanquished constantly by brute force, conquered by barbarian neighbors, China owes her continued existence to her culture. Moreover, the social changes that should have reduced her to servitude and eventual destruction in fact extended her boundaries and steadily increased her influence. The dominators, having conquered, were, in turn, conquered by the Chinese culture, abandoning the customs and literature, and even the language, of their own country. Thus China was frequently dominated, but every time she regained her liberty, she found her empire enlarged, thanks to the addition of new realms.

It is not very difficult to demonstrate our race's need for a culture. The predicament is finding a solid intellectual heritage that can serve as the foundation on which to build our dreams. If we take stock of the purely literary and artistic achievements that have been produced here, the intellectual legacy of our ancestors would certainly be meager alongside the heritages of other peoples. This is the first great discouragement that our enthusiasms encounter. The sum of literary achievement bequeathed to us is sparse, and in general it gives off a strong scent of decadence, sickness, and lassitude—the foretaste of an impending agony. This is not the kind of heritage that will help us add more vigor and life to our race's struggle for a place in the world.

Wasn't the so-called elite fashioned by Chinese books obliged to cling to Confucian ideas like castaways to a wreck? Even in comparison with India, Annam looks like a pygmy standing next to a giant when one considers India's glorious past. And today when India and Japan are producing thinkers and artists whose talent and genius shine forth as brightly as those of Europe, Annam is but an infant that does not yet even have the notion or power to grope toward a better destiny and genuine deliverance. There are those who dare speak of political autonomy and of liberty, but [only] in the hollowest speeches and in the most foolish demands, which only squander further the strength of our race. What liberty is being demanded? Liberty to do what? Does a child who is not yet sure of his steps need the whole earth to learn to walk? Liberty is not something that can be transmitted, given, or sold. It is a possibility for all. Those who are born free are free, even in servitude, just as those who are born slaves remain slaves, even those that ascend the throne. Finally today, a handful of enlightened minds are thinking of preparing a solid foundation for the future of our country. Everyone else is speaking of politics as if it were from there and from there alone that the grand promise so eagerly awaited can come—as if the vital problem of our race were a political problem and not a social problem. No, no! When ignorance extends this far, the silence of enlightened individuals can be called a crime. The vital problem of our race is a social problem; in fact, it is not even yet a social problem; it is the problem of a common ideal that could provide the seed from which the tree of a better future could emerge. These words of Tagore, speaking of India, must be meditated on by those who are contemplating firm creative action: "My spirit," he said, speaking of an earlier time, "refused to allow itself to be seduced by the banal intoxication of the political movements of that time, empty as they were, it seemed to me, of all force proceeding from real national consciousness and completely ignorant of the country and indifferent at heart to any real service to the motherland." . . .

"For the grand idealists among Indian youth," continues Ananda Coomaraswami, "nationalism is not enough. . . . The only real importance of India to the world will derive from the great men whom she will offer to all humanity: A grand philosopher, a poet, a painter, a scholar, or a singer will count more on the day of judgment than will all the concessions extracted by all the congresses in a hundred years."

Isn't the tone of these sentences strangely new to your ears? How distant and, as yet, inconceivable to you this dream is. I would like these quotations to demonstrate how the young India stands next to the young Annam. I know it is too early to summon the arrival of the great men for our country. To speak of great men to human beings without energy or will, to people discouraged by the least effort—as though life itself were not a struggle—to speak of great men to a people who fear effort and seek only indolence and the absence of responsibility may indeed seem laughable. But really, why shouldn't we talk about great men, since we need great men, a flourishing of great men, those personalities who can give status to their own people. Despite the oppression of the English, India has its philosophers and poets, its intellectuals, and its leaders who guide the actions of the masses. And more than India, we need men who understand the soul of our race, its needs, and what is best suited to it. We need men who can guide the steps of the people and illuminate their path. We need artists, poets, painters, musicians, and thinkers to enrich our intellectual inheritance. Thus, not only must we speak constantly of the need for great men, but we also must wish for their arrival. More than that, we must call with all the force of our lungs—in the marshes and mountains and in all places where the existence of a supernatural power reverberates and where the voice of man carries to the invisible infinities of space—with all the force of our lungs, we must call for the arrival of these great men. Perhaps then, from our sincere and ardent calls, will come the power that begets geniuses, those exceptional beings. May the waiting for those great men become for us like a religion; may our lips always murmur, as in prayer, the expectation of these great men. Let us call out, pray, and implore. May Annam, *all Annam*, in anguish and impatience, call and wait—

then, I assure you, in a very short time, the echo of our voices will respond to our calls and our wait will not be in vain.

Below these superhuman dreams are more human ambitions, still too high for the majority but far from unattainable for those with energy. To possess the power of a king with all the force of a nation at his disposal, to be a financier whose coffers balance the destiny of an entire people, aren't these the ambitions that make life worth living? I speak of ambitions still too remote for you. Because the ambition of today's youth is to be a Bui Quang Chieu, a Nguyen Phan Long, a doctor like our Drs. Thinh and Don, or an engineer like M. Lang.[46] Look at them, observe these ambitious young people who stroll amid the baskets of itinerant merchants and sniff at passing women; look at them for a moment, these youths with the strut of a duck and all dressed up in European clothing, and you cannot help but laugh. . . . To be a doctor like Thinh or an engineer like Lang takes the intelligence and tenacity of a Thinh or a Lang. . . . And of what effort is this youth actually capable? We are not prohibited from sketching out our ambitions or from having ambitions and dreams. It even is necessary to dream, since from human dreams innumerable and powerful realities have emerged; but one must dream only in order to act. Dream, dream, but act too. Life is action. To say action is to say effort. To say effort is to say obstacles. And they are many, the obstacles to our ambitions, the greatest of them being ourselves. We lack the breath that sustains those dreams, [and] above all, we lack the will to succeed. . . .

People speak of ingratitude, immorality, anarchy; but do not listen to these reactionaries, these poisoners. Are they worthy of our gratitude, those who count their "good deeds"? Trammeling life, killing the energy of others, isn't this an act of immorality, more than immoral, of barbarism? They speak of anarchy—but what are they calling anarchy? What are they calling order? What is their order if not forceful constraint, barbarism, and anarchy? But let us not make too much of this, and recall that vigor always creates a little trouble around itself. The law of life demands amorality. After all, upon reflection, for the continuance and progress of human society, isn't anarchy necessary for unity, just as unity is a consequence of anarchy? . . . They speak to us about the perfection of the organization inherited from our forefathers, the doctrines of the ancient sages. But man lives with the present, and forgetting is the only virtue that sustains his will to live. . . . Those feeble voices that recall for us the advice of the ancient sages are nothing more than distant echoes that arrive only to die at our ears. The current generation needs new ideals, *their ideals*; a new activity, *their activity*; new

---

46. Bui Quang Chieu was the leader of the moderate Constitutionalist Party, and Nguyen Phan Long was one of his associates. Drs. Nguyen Van Thinh and Tran Van Don were prominent in Saigon political circles, and Luu Van Lang was celebrated as a product of the French education system.

passions, *their passions*. Under these conditions—under these conditions alone—will the realization of a better future be possible. Life, not just life in Annam, but all life, demands to be eternally new.

The task that is incumbent on the present generation is heavy. This period of our history renders that task doubly heavy. Every man has the right to think only of his well-being and his own life. Today, in order to achieve this well-being and not be considered suspect or be mistreated, men have to sell themselves. Under these conditions, how can they assume a role that demands, above all, the absence of constraints weighing on them, a role that demands the awareness of a mission and the obligation to constantly live up to that mission? Birth has placed us in a country where everything is to be created, and at a time when all intelligent initiatives are viewed with great suspicion. Here, two forces are present, two lives: one is weak and seeks its place in the sun; the other is strong and grasping, and sucks and exhausts on behalf of a distant body. And it is weakness that calls for our aid. Our birth and intelligence impose on us a mission. And who better than us to take on this mission? The blood that runs in our veins can alone reveal the needs of our race. Even France's goodwill cannot prevent her from fumbling and wasting her efforts. In this work, France can do only one thing: help us. And it is her duty to assist us, since *protectorate* means *tutelage*, but *tutelage* does not mean being kept a minor forever. Since this work is to be created, today's youth must turn their eyes to the future in order to make the creation as quickly as possible. They must have one foot in the present and the other in the near future that, for them, must be the true present. They must be at once inside and outside the present; present in order to be in touch with the aspirations of the race, and outside it because its main preoccupation is not in the present. They must accept certain facts and certain states as inevitable and, having mastered these social laws, create a new order to oppose this order, a force to oppose this other force, so as to reestablish an equilibrium. For when two forces are present, as long as disequilibrium endures, strife will as well. And in all strife, there is injustice, since there are conquerors and the conquered, and the latter are not always happy.

We should think only of creation, of creation above all else, and of being creative spirits. But those who would create must be mature enough to impregnate and give birth. What we need is not servile imitation that, far from liberating us, will attach us more closely to those things we imitate. What we need is personal creations that spring from our very blood or works that derive from an actual change within ourselves. People have often spoken of the educational and civilizing role of France as represented by the present caste of leaders. They have paid servile homage to the "bringers of light," to the "makers of miracles in Asia," as if the louts sent by the Ministry of Colonies and not by France's intellectuals could quickly mold—as if from dough—the soul of a perfectly functioning race. People have spoken of the French miracle in Asia. . . . But what is that miracle? It is indeed a miracle to have, in such a short time, reduced into the thickest ignorance an intellectual level that was already much diminished; it is indeed miraculous to plunge a people with democratic ideals into the most complete servitude. Who could argue that this is not a miracle, a social miracle? The sudden achievement of a state that people have been pursuing for thousands of years, because aren't ignorance and nonaction the two first conditions of happiness? . . . Those who officially represent France in Indochina can speak only of the expensive construction of railways, of ruinous enterprises to set underwater cables, of maintaining its formidable army of functionaries, of annual national borrowing; in short, of the exaggerated *exploitation* of Indochina understood in both senses as use and abuse. Her role must be, above all, economic, that is to say, devouring. But when it comes to more delicate questions like education and intellectual development, France ought to exercise greater circumspection. She can do nothing but offer us her intellectual heritage as a contribution to the nourishment of our researchers and creative thinkers. Assimilation demands liberty of choice, an absolute liberty. Any constraint leads to indigestion, and indigestion can be fatal.

One thing I mention in passing, and on which no authority can contradict me, since I carry within myself the proof of my proposition, is that on the contrary, thirsty men who run quickly in search of what they need and those who stumble forward to arrive at an awareness of themselves at an encounter inside their deepest self with the soul of their race—those individuals have thus far never been able to receive the least outside encouragement.

I say this to prove to today's youth that in all things they can count on no one but themselves to rise to the level where man, conscious of his own strength, also begins to be conscious of his dignity. It is to show them that their struggle, which has hardly been encouraged by the achievement of knowledge or the desire for human pride and dignity, also encounters multiple unforeseen discouragements thrown up often by powerful forces. On the road they must travel, active young people who desire self-affirmation will find themselves in the presence of talents proclaimed with trumpet calls, and false gods elevated amid a simulated glory. Believing in appearances, the population disregards those talents that are nobly and laboriously acquired. The road that leads to deliverance of the individual is rough. And in this country more than anywhere else, free, elevated, proud, and noble spirits must endure a long torment. And why is that? What is the cause? Ignorance. It is the dull and heavy ignorance of the masses. It is the gilded ignorance, the hollow knowledge of today's self-proclaimed elite. The masses, just as much as the so-called modern elite, fashioned by the school of this "democracy of bad taste" that is so rampant throughout all of Europe, do not know how to tell the true from the false. These sad observations are not designed to paralyze goodwill and enthusiasm. They are meant to serve as a demarcation between those energies that are determined, cautious, self-reflective, laborious, and directed toward their goal, and those energies that are sonorous but hollow. The latter should change course before the sign listing the obstacles, because otherwise their disillusionment and bitterness will later be sung in famous verses like the glorious actions of the failed heroes of antiquity.

For one's personality to affirm itself, the first condition must exist. And to exist requires struggle, contraction, and wariness. I know that today's youth cannot conceive of any struggle outside politics. Moreover, what they call political life is nothing like the noisy politics of the European nations; it is the daily chattering, high sounding and hollow, displayed in the newspapers of Indochina. Ah! If young people today could only glimpse what goes on under this crust of high-sounding and hollow quotidian gossip. They would be outraged and no longer insist on pursuing what they call politics, for it impairs and sullies the energies of this country, which already is almost without life or strength. I know, and it is sad to know it, that today's youth pay exclusive attention to what they call politics—to the point that for them, to be under suspicion, to be spied on by informers, is a mark of glory and cause for bragging. I know youths, groping to find their way who, when they encounter one of the innumerable stumbling blocks erected by the government, use up all their energy opposing this enormous rock instead of going around it. And these youths call that the life of struggle. No, what you call the life of struggle is nothing but a waste of your strength against a shadow. What can be gained from such a struggle besides the utter fatigue that puts us in a state of constant inferiority and at the mercy of those who control this chimera? It is against your environment that you must struggle; against your family that paralyzes your efforts; against the vulgar society that weighs on you; against the narrow prejudices and snares that lurk around your actions; against ideals that lack vigor and nobility, that are humiliatingly base and further reduce the status of our race with every passing day. Here is where the struggle must take place, and it is much more weighty, ten thousand times weightier, than the other pretend struggle. Only this true struggle can give you real victory. The greatest idealists have always counseled those who would be their disciples to flee "their father's house." We, too, must flee the "house of our father." We must escape from our family, escape our society, distance ourselves from our country. We must have a life of struggle that awakens the little vigor that is left to us; we must have a society that reveals our true worth. We need an environment that elevates our intelligence and our soul. We need a summit where, in solitude, we can sense all our strength and take possession of our soul and, with a glance that can encompass all of life and love, understand the world and our harmony with it. And then we will leave the summit that we have reached and that will have been for us a temporary place of exile, to return to a society where we can make maximum use of our creative strength. In other words, we Annamese who will have arrived at the consciousness of our own worth, of the highest possible worth of the individual and of the laws that govern the world, we will return to Annam, where the accident of birth has placed us in a position to understand better than others the needs of the race from which we are born, and where, as a result, our fertile and creative strengths will not be too wasted.

Today's youth must especially avoid all talk of fatherland and patriotism. They must concentrate all their strength on seeking themselves. The day that they find themselves, the words *fatherland* and *patriotism* will have taken on a larger, more elevated and noble meaning; and they will be embarrassed to have confused, through their ignorance, the names fatherland and patriotism with ideas that were less noble and even mean. The day that the youth of Annam pay no regard to diplomas, social prejudices, the embroidered uniforms of valets, the imposing pomp of false gods, or the consideration enjoyed by false talents and ineptitudes; the day when the youth of Annam refuse to give the least credit to appearances and lies and instead march with heads high down the road cleared by their self-consciousness—on that day we will be able to closely examine all the beautiful dreams, on that day we will be able to joyfully resolve the problem of a culture for our race—then will the motto of our temples be restored: "Honor only those men whose genius or talent raised the rank of our people in the world and those who contributed to the improvement of the conditions of our race."

[Nguyen An Ninh, "L'idéal de la jeunesse annamite"; trans. Judith Henchy]

PHAM QUYNH

INTELLECTUAL AND MORAL REFORM (1930)

No other figure exercised as much influence in espousing neotraditionalist ideas in early-twentieth-century Vietnam as Pham Quynh, a noted essayist and public intellectual. With his pro-French review *Southern Ethos* (*Nam Phong* [1917–1934]), Pham Quynh launched a cultural and literary revival in Vietnam that introduced the new Vietnamese elite to modern French ideas while helping offset the decline in Confucian learning. In the realm of politics, Pham Quynh's legacy was ultimately less successful. He advocated a conservative nationalist agenda, with a Vietnamese government led by an elite educated in both French and Vietnamese schools, which would continue to rely on French colonial tutelage and only gradually acquire political sovereignty. In the following essay, originally published in French in *Southern Ethos* in 1930, Pham Quynh suggested that the new Vietnamese elite be disciplined and of high moral fiber, and he espoused a blend of both traditional and modern ideas. He suggests that Japan's experience of training "good sons, good citizens, and good soldiers" could well serve as a model for Vietnamese intellectual reform.

I spoke in a previous article of the necessity of a true "intellectual and moral reform" that must be undertaken in this country, and I said that this reform must be, above all, the work of the Annamese elite, which must become conscious of itself and its duties and responsibilities.

Today I would like to give this opinion the development it requires, reserving for later an examination of the other necessary political and administrative reforms, because it is beginning to be of interest at high levels, and official commissions will soon be working in this direction.

Moreover, all these reforms are of a piece, and the moral and political perspectives are not far from one another and sometimes even seem to blend into one. One cannot conceive of the intellectual and moral reform of an entire people without the existence of a national government that would have in the area of education all the necessary powers for making and sustaining new initiatives. This government may be directed, controlled, and counseled in all branches of political and economic activity, but its total, concerted action is indispensable to the education of the people. No foreign authority, no matter how eminently well intended and tutelary, can take its place in this earliest essential stage of the project and not risk falling into inextricable difficulties and ending in certain failure. Perhaps an elite can receive a foreign culture as a useful complement to its national education, but the masses can be trained only by a national education, which can be provided only by a national government. Of course, this government must have the powers necessary to devote itself usefully to this project. And this is precisely the question we must ask. But we will not pursue it for the moment, our purpose here being simply to show that intellectual and moral reform is in fact closely linked to political reform.

No people can live and prosper without being able to keep to a certain moral and national discipline that is in harmony with both the hereditary tendencies of the race and the requirements for a healthy evolution. This discipline cannot simply be self-imposed. It must be recognized as necessary and accepted by the elite of the nation, who must set the example for the masses and who are ultimately responsible for their education. Therefore the elite first must impose this discipline on itself before imposing it on the people. The elite must choose between traditional and modern ideas, thereby forging the synthesis that would be most appropriate for favoring the development of a "national life" and one truly worthy of this name. This selection process is not carried out without sacrifices. The libertarian and individualistic theories that come from the West are certainly not without attractions, and these attractions are often irresistible to the minds of those who have barely escaped the rigors of a patriarchal organization over which absolutism reigns triumphant. [These theories] are not, however, without dangers, and therefore, it is best to incorporate them cautiously. They can give a positive character to old traditional ideas that tend to discount individuals a bit too much by inscribing them completely within the family unit or the community and in this way hinder often the full development of the personality. But [if they] act alone, without the solid base of good traditional training, these theories may cause dissolution and destruction. The delicate matter of the dosage must be respected, as it requires much foresight and tact and can be the work only of an elite truly conscious of its role as initiator and guide.

The basic elements of this elite exist. There remains the task of uniting them and giving them a common inspiration. There is absolutely no doubt that the only idea capable of achieving this union or spiritual unity is the national idea. One cannot deny that this idea exists in this country; the fact is that it is spreading, developing, and intensifying every day. Nothing is served by opposing or stopping it. One is better off using and directing it—making it the foundation of the education of the masses as well as of the elite. If one knows how to accommodate it, it can prove to be a great force capable of reconciling all.

Therefore, the formation of a "conscious and organized" elite (to borrow a well-known formula) that knows how to impose on itself a strong national and moral discipline—along with an education by this elite of the popular masses centered on the same beneficial and necessary discipline—is, in our view, the necessary work of intellectual and moral reform to be undertaken in this country.

The example of Japan shows us that this work is possible and can be achieved. If this country managed in so little time to accomplish a formidable evolution that provokes the astonishment and admiration of the world, it is thanks to the presence of a far-sighted elite infused with a national idea at the beginning of the Meiji period; an elite that, conscious of its role, took up with ardor the task of educating the people and creating a public spirit whose force and vitality have been felt on numerous occasions.

Served by a national dynasty that participates in the same ideal as the elite of the nation, Japan succeeded in completely transforming the mentality of its people, namely, by destroying the clan spirit that divided it and inculcating the worship of honor and the homeland as symbolized in the person of the emperor—in other words, by making it a most coherent and disciplined people and one that was highly compliant with the suggestions of its elite and the most capable, under the latter's direction, of accomplishing grand projects for the glory of the entire nation.

What, then, is the secret of this marvelous transformation?

It is in a national education that, on the one hand, succeeded in forging a harmonious synthesis of the ideals of the Occident and the Orient and of the ancient moral tradition and the modern scientific culture, and, on the other hand, is inspired and animated by a single idea that dominates and absorbs all: a love for the homeland and the race for which the living symbol is the emperor.

This education, undertaken with both ardor and tenacity by men whose sole concern was the grandeur of the country, managed to galvanize the entire nation and to create the public spirit of which we spoke earlier, a spirit whose vigorous exercise contributed greatly to the glorious victory of Japan over czarist Russia.

A reading of [Japan's] famous Imperial Rescript on Education promulgated on October 30, 1890, is particularly edifying. This document, which hangs publicly in every school and is read aloud on every holiday, can rightly be called a veritable catechism of the religion of the state, in other words, of patriotism.

The mikado [emperor] puts forward here before his people the essential principles of national education: . . .

> Be respectful to your parents, affectionate to your brothers and sisters, united in your conjugal ties, and faithful to your friends; let your conduct be courteous and frugal, and your caring attention extend to all! Apply yourselves to your studies, and carry out your respective occupations; cultivate your intellectual faculties, and develop your moral feelings; [and] contribute to the public good and watch over the general interests of society. Obey the constitution and the laws of our empire; and if the occasion presents itself, devote yourself courageously to your homeland. In this way, you will give us your precious help in developing and maintaining the honor and prosperity of our empire, which is as old as the sky and the earth. . . .

This rescript was the object of commentary in a 1891 ministerial circular in which teachers received the following instructions: "Because forming a character that is inclined toward virtue is the supreme goal of education, it is necessary that in all our teaching, we privilege those subjects that lend themselves to moral and patriotic applications."

Moral and patriotic—this is the essential, fundamental character of Japanese education. And in it lies the secret of the astonishing transformation that, in just a few years, allowed a feudal people to become a great nation—one that was able to appropriate the most rational methods of modern organization while preserving the traditional virtues of the race. For this national education is itself organized scientifically. . . .

This decidedly moral and national education has been completely successful, for it can be said that it truly shaped the modern Japanese spirit. That spirit has not fabricated a series of good little parrots capable of long, mechanical, and sometimes uncomprehending recitations of foreign words and who, once they have acquired the rudiments of that language, rush to exploit their meager knowledge by soliciting the outsized administration for jobs and subaltern positions with no future and no dignity. On the contrary, it has trained "good sons, good citizens, and good soldiers blindly devoted to the emperor and the homeland," and this is certainly the secret behind the force and prosperity of the Japanese.

Japan has, it is true, undergone several crises over the course of its moral and intellectual evolution. The West's most harmful theories caused much damage there, as they did everywhere else. But this damage was contained, we could say, thanks in part to a deeply moral and patriotic system of education that this country owes to the enlightened vision and wisdom of a singularly well-informed national elite, which from 1875 to 1900 worked to consolidate the nation's moral cornerstones. Of equal importance was the vigilance of a national government that always considered its first duty to be the education of the people and never neglected to take the necessary steps to cleanse and preserve its moral health. Didn't it forbid, if I'm not mistaken, the translation of *La dame aux camélias* and certain works by [Émile] Zola?

What the Japanese were able to do, we can do too—helped by France, which, we are certain, will prove itself generous and skillful enough to encourage the blossoming and growth of a good, conscious, and enlightened Annamese patriotism, which would be the most powerful antidote against the propagation of the most harmful theories imported from abroad.

[Pham Quynh, "Réforme intellectuelle et morale," 36–38;
trans. C. Jon Delogu]

NGUYEN THAI HOC

LETTER ADDRESSED TO THE FRENCH CHAMBRE DES DÉPUTÉS (1930)

Nguyen Thai Hoc (1902–1930), who founded the Vietnam Nationalist Party in 1927, advocated seizing power from the French through violent means. In 1930, his party staged an abortive uprising in Yen Bai that was brutally repressed by the French and resulted in the party's virtual destruction. Nguyen Thai Hoc became a revolutionary martyr for his implacable defiance of the French colonial authorities. In this letter, written on the eve of his execution, Nguyen Thai Hoc assailed the French for their callous treatment of the Vietnamese people and their refusal to countenance political reform. The letter, translated from Vietnamese, is addressed to the lower house of the French National Assembly.

Yen Bai, March 1930

Messieurs Députés,

I, the undersigned, Nguyen Thai Hoc, a twenty-eight-year-old Vietnamese, chairman and founding member of the Vietnam Nationalist Party [Viet Nam Quoc Dan Dang], have been arrested and am being detained in the Yen Bai provincial jail, in the northern part of Indochina. I have the honor to present the following views:

It is a matter of truth that all citizens have the right to aspire to the independence of their fatherland. In the name of humanity, every citizen has the duty to provide relief and assistance to his endangered fellow countrymen.

As I see it, my fatherland has been conquered by the French for more than sixty years. Under your tyrannical rule, my compatriots have had to bear countless sufferings; my nation will be completely and gradually destroyed in accordance with the law of natural selection. Therefore, in line with my duty and in the interest of my fellow countrymen, I am compelled to do my best to defend my fatherland, which has been seized by foreigners, and [to save] my nation, which has been endangered.

At first, I tried to work closely with the French in Indochina in the interests of my compatriots, my fatherland, and [my] nation, in particular to develop education and the economy. For economic purposes, in 1925, I sent a letter to Mr. Varenne, the governor-general of Indochina, in which I requested the protection of indigenous industry and trade; in particular, the establishment of a technical college in the north. In 1926 I sent another letter to the governor-general about a project designed to make the life of impoverished people more bearable. In 1927, I again sent a letter to the *résident supérieur* of Tonkin, seeking permission for the publication of a weekly journal, whose aim would be to defend and encourage indigenous industry and trade. In the educational field, I sent a letter to the governor-general in 1925, requesting (1) permission to open schools to provide free education to the people, particularly workers and peasants, and (2) permission to open public libraries in villages and industrialized towns.

But my letters went unanswered, my project was not implemented, my requests were not approved, and my newspaper articles were subjected to censorship and discarded. These rejections show clearly that the French are not well disposed toward my fatherland, my fellow countrymen, and my nation, so the only alternative is to drive them out of my country. Therefore, in 1927, I started to organize a revolutionary party named the Vietnam Nationalist Party. The party's objective is to overthrow the oppressive rule of the French and establish a government of the Republic of Vietnam composed of persons genuinely dedicated to the welfare of the people. This was an underground organization that was discovered in February 1929 with the subsequent arrest and condemnation of fifty-two party members to prison terms ranging from two to twenty years. Despite the numerous arrests and arbitrary trials, my party was not completely destroyed. Under my leadership, it continued to try to achieve its goals. A revolutionary upsurge broke out in northern Vietnam, particularly in Yen Bai, resulting in the death of some [French] military officers. It was alleged that this movement was organized and led by my party and that as chairman of the party I had ordered the attack. In fact, I never gave such an order. I provided evidence to the Yen Bai tribunal to this effect. Many members of my party who knew nothing about the recent revolutionary upsurge also were arrested and were charged with participating in [the upsurge]. The government of French Indochina burned and destroyed their houses, and its troops confiscated their paddies and rice, distributing them among themselves. Not only were the members of my party the target of unjust measures—the word *ruthless* would be more accurate—but the majority of rural compatriots were treated like buffalo and horses, persecuted. At present, in Kien An, Hai Phong, Bac Ninh, Son Tay, Phu Tho, and Yen Bai, tens of thousands of innocent men, women, old folk, and children have been killed or have died of starvation or cold because the government of French Indochina has burned and destroyed their houses. Therefore, I earnestly request that you investigate and clarify that these unjust measures will lead to the complete destruction of my nation and to the degradation of human values.

I have the honor to inform you that I bear full responsibility for all political upheavals that have taken place in my country since I assumed the leadership [of the Nationalist Party] in 1927. Therefore, executing me will be sufficient. May I ask you to refrain from persecuting the other persons who are detained in your jails, because I am the only culprit and the others are innocent. Among them are a number of party members, but they are innocent. They joined the party because of my exhortations about their duties as citizens of their country and about the sufferings and ignominy of the people who have lost their country. The others are non-party members who have been arrested because of false charges brought against them by the enemy, informers, or spies or by false accusations made by their friends under the duress of torture by the intelligence service, who had to make such accusations to avoid continued torture. May I reiterate my request: please execute me alone. If that is not enough, you can execute all the members of my family. But please release the afore-mentioned innocent persons.

In conclusion, I wish to tell you that if the French wish to stay in Indochina and remain free from attacks by the revolutionary movement, they must abandon their current ruthless and barbaric political agenda; they must behave like real friends of the Vietnamese and refrain from acting like ruthless and oppressive bosses. They must try to reduce the spiritual and physical sufferings and hardships of the Vietnamese by allowing them to enjoy elementary human rights such as the freedom of movement, the freedom to be educated, the right of assembly, and the freedom of the press. They must curb corruption and the debased lifestyle among Vietnamese officials [who work for the French], provide education to the people, and help develop indigenous industries and trade, free from harsh and wicked obstacles.

Please accept, Messrs Députés, the assurance of my highest consideration.

Nguyen Thai Hoc, the Revolutionary
[Nguyen Thai Hoc, "Thu gui Ha Nghi Vien Phap," 813–15;
trans. Jayne Werner]

HO CHI MINH

THE REVOLUTIONARY'S CODE OF CONDUCT (1926)

Ho Chi Minh's (1890–1969) view of what made a good Communist was based on his belief that human beings could always be trained and educated to improve their character. But Communist cadres had to follow a strict moral code, for morality and good character were the essence of an effective revolutionary. Without morality, Communists would fail to persuade the people to follow party policies. In *The Road to Revolution*, Ho Chi Minh's training manual for young Vietnamese revolutionaries in Hong Kong, he enumerates a revolutionary's virtues. This excerpt is the preface to the manual. This and the following text are lists of exemplary behavior similar in form, if not in entirely in content, to Confucian precepts, such as Minh Mang's "Ten Moral Precepts."[47]

For oneself:

> Be industrious and thrifty.
> Cooperate with others, and do not be individualistic.
> Resolutely correct your mistakes.
> Take care not to be too timid.
> Often ask questions.
> Be patient and endure difficulties.
> Inquire about and investigate matters frequently.
> Be public-spirited and not concerned with private matters.
> Do not seek fame or be arrogant.
> If you say it, do it.
> Be steadfast and protect the doctrine.
> Be prepared to sacrifice.
> Do not yearn for material things.
> Maintain secrecy.

Toward others, one must:

> Be tolerant.
> Strictly follow organizational rules.
> Go to great lengths to be kind.
> Be watchful but not reckless.
> Observe other people closely [as exemplary models].

---

47. See Minh Mang Emperor, "Ten Moral Precepts" (chap. 5).

In work, one must:

> Examine the situation carefully.
> Be decisive.
> Be brave.
> Follow orders.

[Ho Chi Minh, "Tu cach mot nguoi cach menh," 231; trans.
Lauren Meeker and Jayne Werner]

HO CHI MINH

REVOLUTIONARY CHARACTER AND MORALITY (1947)

Ho Chi Minh further elaborated the meaning of revolutionary morality in the pamphlet *Reforming the Way We Work*, which was distributed to Communist Party members in the early years of the Viet Minh war against the French (1946–1954). Ho Chi Minh's list of revolutionary virtues permeates the essay excepted here. But he also admonishes party members that besides paying strict attention to self-discipline, they must reform their personal faults and mistakes, which inflict untold damage on the Communist cause. He goes on to describe the endurance, sacrifices, inner strength, and collective spirit required for the Communist cause to achieve victory.

The [Communist] Party should not conceal its mistakes or be afraid of criticism. It needs to admit its mistakes and correct them in order to make progress and educate its cadres and members. The party should select its most faithful and enthusiastic members to become leading cadres and must always expel corrupt and depraved elements from its ranks. The party should enforce strict discipline from the top down, which means unity in thought and action and unswerving loyalty in carrying out one's duties and work. The party must always check to see how its resolutions and instructions are being implemented; otherwise, they will remain empty rhetoric and, moreover, will undermine the confidence of the people. To ensure the party's success, these points must be observed; not a single point should be overlooked.

Duties of Party Cadres and Members

UPHOLD THE INTERESTS OF THE PARTY

The only interests of the party are those of the nation and the fatherland. Therefore, the party must try to organize the people in order to liberate them and improve their living, cultural, and political conditions. The liberation of the people means the liberation of the party. Each party member must understand that private interests must be completely subordinated to party interests, group interests to collective interests, and temporary interests to long-term interests. Party interests must be put above everything else because they are the interests of the nation and the fatherland. . . .

Party members and cadres must never hesitate to sacrifice their own interests and, if need be, their own lives. This is what it means to be a party member. If party interests contradict those of the individual, the latter must absolutely give way to the former. Every party cadre and member must clearly understand this. It is because of this principle that our party has many martyrs who have gloriously laid down their lives for the party, the nation, and the fatherland and whose reputations will last forever. These martyrs set a heroic example for all party members and cadres to follow.

There are times when personal interests coincide with those of the party. Examples include party members and cadres who carefully maintain their health in order to carry out their work, and those who eagerly study to raise their educational level. The people trust, admire, and love party members and cadres who are industrious and thrifty, have integrity, and are upright in character. The party wishes its members and cadres to be like this. But other traits, such as seeking status and wealth, becoming a hero, and being arrogant, are contrary to the interests of the party.

REVOLUTIONARY MORALITY

It is not difficult for a party cadre or member to become a real revolutionary. It depends on one's heart. If one's sole interest is the party, the fatherland, and one's compatriots, one will be selfless and serve the greater public good. In doing so, one's personal faults will decline, and one's good qualities will increase. In short, revolutionary morality consists of five things: benevolence, a sense of duty, knowledge, courage, and integrity.

Benevolence means genuine affection for and complete devotion to one's comrades and fellow countrymen. Benevolence leads us to resolutely oppose people and actions that are harmful to the party and the masses. A benevolent person is the first to endure hardship and the last to enjoy happiness. He or she does not covet wealth or honor and is not afraid to fight people in power. Benevolent people fear nothing and will always succeed in doing the right thing.

Having a sense of duty means being straightforward, upright, not being egoistical, doing nothing unjust, and having nothing to hide from the party. It means having no personal interests in conflict with the party. Someone with a sense of duty devotes himself or herself completely to any task assigned by the party, large or small, and carries it out conscientiously. Duty requires that when one recognizes when something is right, he or she speaks out honestly to that effect. It also means taking criticism from others, and bearing in mind everyone's interests when criticizing others.

Knowledge: If one's mind is clouded by egotism, one cannot have a clear and judicious mind and find the right way to do things. A knowledgeable person is a good judge of other human beings and can weigh the pros and cons of an issue, thereby determining which actions are beneficial or harmful to the party and which should be avoided. He or she [can] recommend people for party membership; and is on guard against evil persons.

Courage: A courageous person boldly carries out what is right, is unafraid to correct mistakes, undertakes difficult assignments, and endures hardship. Courage means resisting the temptations of fame and wealth. If necessary, it means sacrificing one's life for the party and the fatherland, without qualms.

Integrity means not coveting status or wealth, happiness, or flattery. Persons of integrity are levelheaded and straightforward and never become corrupt; they are eager to learn, work, and improve themselves.

These are *revolutionary ethics*, which are different from the old, conservative ethics. Revolutionary morality does not aim at increasing individual prestige but serves only the interests of the party, the nation, and mankind. A river cut off from its source will dry up. A tree severed from its roots will wither. A revolutionary lacking morality cannot lead the people, no matter how talented he or she may be. Liberating the nation and humanity is a great task. But if we ourselves are immoral, rootless, and corrupt, what can we accomplish?

OBSERVING DISCIPLINE

The party's interests are only those of the nation; party members' interests are only those of the party. Therefore, the success of the nation depends on the development and success of the party and its members. Only when the party is victorious can party members enjoy victory. Consequently, party members must always place party interests above their own interests. No one is forced to join the party and become a vanguard fighter. People volunteer to join the party to become the vanguard and do so out of enthusiasm. As such, all party members must do their utmost to be worthy representatives of the nation.

Cadres and leaders, in particular, must be worthy of the confidence of the party and the nation and must set an example for all party members and the masses. It is in the interest of the nation that the party encourages and praises its members for their merits and talent, helps them learn and work. Whenever necessary, the party must help its members improve their living conditions and take care of them in case of illness, thereby motivating them to work with enthusiasm and joy. All party cadres and members must fully serve the interests of the party and have no private aims or seek favors from the party. They should not complain if they feel that party has not helped them or praised them.

Party cadres and members must always strive to do their best work and study hard to improve their cultural, intellectual, and political knowledge. They must always observe discipline and remain worthy of their status as party cadres and members. . . .

MISTAKES AND SHORTCOMINGS

Some people in our party are selfish, uneducated, and lack impartiality; as a result, they are afflicted by individualism. Individualism is very damaging and leads to dangerous traits like the following:

Greed: Greedy people put their own interests above the party's and the nation's. They use public resources to serve their private aims, relying on party authority to do so. They like to live in luxury and indulge in lavish spending. Where does their money come from? From the party and their fellow countrymen. Greedy people engage in black market activities and smuggling, without considering how this behavior damages the prestige of the party and their own reputations.

Laziness: Lazy people think they are good at everything and know everything. They are lazy when learning and thinking. They prefer easy work assignments, pass the buck when given difficult tasks, and try to avoid dangerous tasks.

Arrogance: Arrogant people have an elevated opinion of themselves, put on airs, seek power, and like to be flattered and give orders. If they do something well, they always brag about it and flaunt their merits. They refuse to learn from the masses and avoid criticism. They always want to instruct others.

Vanity: Vain people think they are terrific, great heroes. Their ambition leads them to perform unnecessary tasks. When they are criticized or attacked, their morale is shaken. They enjoy being promoted but cannot bear being demoted. Their only concern is to enjoy life and to avoid hardship. They are eager to be a chairman or committee member but avoid effective work.

Lack of discipline: Individualistic people put their own interests first in both thought and behavior, and disregard the guiding role of the party. They criticize comrades they do not like and promote cadres as a personal favor.

Narrow-mindedness: Narrow-minded people do not promote party members on the basis of merit because they are afraid such people will overtake them. They look down on people outside the party, considering them to be un-revolutionary and less capable. As a result, they fail to make contacts and alliances with people of good character and talent outside the party, making them angry and isolating themselves.

Parochialism: Although parochialism is not as bad [as narrow-mindedness], it also causes a great deal of damage. Parochial people are concerned only with their own group's performance, not that of other groups. They are shortsighted and lack an overall perspective, failing to understand that minor interests must be subordinated to the general interest, partial interests to the whole.

Commandism: [Would-be commanders] think they are brilliant and heroic and should be promoted to the top after a few successful battles or achievements. Of course, our party wishes to have many heroes and leaders who enjoy the confidence, admiration, and love of the people. Heroes and brilliant leaders are extremely valuable to the party and the nation. But such people emerge in the process of struggle, having been tempered by experience and education and promoted on the basis of the confidence of the masses and other party members. Someone does not become a top leader or a hero out of sheer personal desire.

From earlier times until now, the masses have never given their confidence and love to arrogant people or to self-styled leaders and heroes. Heroes have played only a minor role in the world's major accomplishments. If each of us tries to fulfill the tasks given to us, knowing that we have done our work well, that will be enough for us to make progress. . . .

[Some party members] refrain from accepting self-criticism because they think their prestige and pride will be damaged. In sum, they believe that if we criticize our own faults, as well as those of our own comrades, our party, and government, the enemy will take advantage of this to attack us. This is wrong. Faults and mistakes are like a disease, and criticism is like taking medicine. Fear of criticism is like being ill but trying to conceal your illness and refusing to take your medicine. As a result, you will get worse, get weaker, and die. . . .

If you refrain from criticizing party members, they will sink further and further into error, and the party will suffer. This is like seeing a sick comrade and refusing to give him medicine. Refraining from self-criticism allows faults and mistakes to accumulate. It is like poisoning yourself. A party that hides its mistakes is a damaged party. A party that has the courage to admit its mistakes, to clearly identify them and the reasons for them, and to try its hardest to correct them is a progressive party, a genuine party, a courageous party that can make steady progress. The party must be able to identify its mistakes and its shortcomings, to educate its members and the masses. Fear of criticism is like a cat chasing its own tail. This is arrogance and bureaucratism. Criticism, however, does not mean attacking, slandering, and insulting others.

REASONS BEHIND MISTAKES AND SHORTCOMINGS

Why are there so many shortcomings, and where do they come from? We are a big party, which comprises people from all social strata. The party attracts people with remarkable abilities, including those with unswerving loyalty and steely determination. But it also is affected by bad habits, poor character, and other personal failings from the society at large. This should not alarm us. We are familiar with these faults and can find a way to correct them. Every party cadre and member should honestly examine himself as well as his comrades and sincerely try to help one another correct their mistakes. The best and most effective way is to engage in *criticism and self-criticism*. Treading on stones eventually wears them down. Whetting sharpens iron. Thanks to our corrective efforts, faults can be reduced and behavior will improve. As time goes by, cadres and members will become genuine revolutionaries, and the party will develop further. [I] hope all of us will effectively improve ourselves.

Our party is a very progressive organization with many glorious achievements to its credit and includes very capable and ethical people. The most enthusiastic, patriotic, intelligent, steadfast, and courageous people in society belong to our party. As a result, we will certainly achieve success and victory. But not all our members exemplify good behavior, and not all that we do is good. Our party still has a number of second-rate members and has taken actions that are less than justified. A family with a stupid son-in-law or a dull daughter-in-law cannot prevent them from having contact with all the relatives. Similarly, even if our party wishes to hide its second-rate members and cover up its unjustified actions, this cannot be done. The masses are in constant contact with our party; many of them support the party's program and work with us. Consequently, they see good party members and good actions but also bad behavior and bad actions. . . .

While carrying out the task of national liberation, our party must educate its cadres and members and persuade bad elements to correct their bad behavior. Mistakes and failures need to be corrected in order to make the party stronger and safer. . . .

In sum, when carrying out their work, struggle, and training activities, party cadres and members must constantly examine their behavior, review their work and that of their comrades, and *always use* criticism and self-criticism in a skillful manner. They should never leave things just as they are. If we work in this way, mistakes will certainly decline, behavior will improve, and our party will certainly achieve victory. . . .

[Ho Chi Minh, *Sua doi loi lam viec*, 250–56, 260–63, 265; trans. Jayne Werner]

SOCIETY AND CULTURE

PHAM QUYNH

KIM VAN KIEU AND THE NATIONAL LANGUAGE (1924)

In the 1920s, the supporters and opponents of French rule used Nguyen Du's literary masterpiece *The Tale of Kieu* (*Kim Van Kieu*) to conduct an intense debate about how and whether Vietnamese culture would survive under colonial rule. Pham Quynh, the pro-French literary and political figure mentioned earlier, famously argued in 1924 that as long as *The Tale of Kieu* survived, the Vietnamese language would survive and, by implication, Vietnamese "culture" and the sense of Vietnam the country would survive; hence, French influence could not and would not erase either one. Opponents of colonial rule contemptuously dismissed these claims for *The Tale of Kieu* and Pham Quynh's argument. Pham Quynh's view, however, has stood the test of time and is now generally accepted by Vietnamese of all political persuasions. This text was translated from French.

Today, the tenth day of the eighth month, is the anniversary of the death of the great Annamese poet Nguyen Du, the immortal author of *Kim Van Kieu.*

The literary committee of the AFIMA [Association for Annamese Intellectual and Moral Development] has chosen to make this the occasion for a solemn homage to the memory of this brilliant man of letters who, more than one hundred years ago, bequeathed to his country and language an incomparable masterpiece.

In the course of our long history, many celebrated writers, famous poets, and learned humanists have been the focus of circles of fervent admirers from generation to generation. But all these authors wrote in Chinese characters, the Latin of our forebears and the only honorable language for centuries of scholarly culture.

Nguyen Du was the first to think of applying his inspired genius to his national language and to devote all his talent, heart, and soul to the realization of a perfect work of art. This work has resisted the test of time. It shines every day with greater purity and brilliance. It stands now as the most beautiful jewel of our language, a language that some consider poor and imperfect but that could not have more riches, suppleness, charm, harmony, and subtlety for painting the most delicate feelings of the human soul.

This poet is therefore the guide and master for all of us who are working today under the kind influence of Western culture to restore and renovate the national language and to guarantee its rightful place in the literary and artistic education of our compatriots.

Ladies and Gentlemen, you certainly have heard of *Kim Van Kieu,* and you are familiar with the name of its author, especially since the attempt by an Indochinese poet to translate the immortal poem into French verse and a local company's project to adapt it for the cinema.

Kieu is a novel in verse of some 3,260 lines that alternate between six and eight syllables each, a form particular to Annamese prosody. Its subject was adapted from a popular Chinese novel in a way similar to how Corneille's *Le Cid,* for example, borrowed from the Spanish drama of Guilhem de Castro. In other words, the author was able to add features to his work that were absent from the original and that transform a mostly ordinary tale into a poetic masterpiece of rare quality. It is the story of a young woman blessed with all the gifts of mind and body, a woman of an elite nature, who, in an agonizing choice between love and filial piety, deliberately chooses the more difficult path. She sells herself to save her father and, from that day onward, goes from misery to misery, eventually sinking to the most abject depths, but like the lotus in the song, she conserves within that abject state the pure scent of her original nobility.

Some say this romantic tale of a young Chinese woman is a novel about the life of Nguyen Du himself. Of course he was not, like his heroine, "a victim of fate" but instead a mandarin poet selected by the great Gia Long [emperor], as prefect of Thuong Tin, promoted regularly up to the office of the vice-minister of rites, and sent on two occasions as ambassador to the Beijing court (the last time shortly before his death). But in order to write [these] verses, some of which, like those of Musset, are pure lamentations, this high dignitary, this perfect man of letters, must have experienced great suffering. And in fact, he did suffer, though not in his sentimental life like his romantic French counterpart, but in his public life. From an ancient family from Ha Tinh that had remained loyal to the Le dynasty, circumstances nevertheless obliged him to serve new masters, the Nguyen. Despite the latter's generous policy toward the fallen dynasty's former subjects, [Nguyen Du] accepted the new regime only reluctantly, and his conscience as a man and scholar was troubled. This was the drama of a life that could have been happy and glorious but instead was marred by a secret bitterness.

Despite its dry administrative tone, the biographical notice devoted to him in the annals of the current dynasty offers the reader a portrait of the poet's character that conveys a sense of his internal suffering.

"Nguyen Du," it says, "seemed outwardly to be a sweet, reserved man, but he had a proud and independent temperament. Each time he appeared before the emperor, he remained silent. His Majesty would often reprimand him and say, 'When choosing its collaborators, the government tries to select knowledgeable and capable men, without distinguishing between those from the north and those from the south. I have had occasion to get to know and understand you, and you now occupy the rank of vice-minister. You must speak and express your views in the councils. Why[, then,] do you wrap yourself in silence and never answer with more than a yes or no?'

"Nguyen Du was well versed in poetry and especially excelled in poetry composed in the national language. He brought back from his embassy in China a volume of verse entitled *Collected Poems from a Journey to the North* [*Bac hanh thi tap*] and was the author of a history of Thuy Kieu that became very popular. Having descended from a great family that had served the Le for generations, he did not want to accept any post during the Tay Son revolution and instead retired to the mountainous region of his childhood, giving himself over to the pleasures of wandering and hunting amid the ninety-nine summits of the Hong Linh. Called on later by His Majesty's government to fulfill public functions that he could not refuse, he was forced to enter the mandarin caste. But he often had problems with his superiors that caused him considerable internal suffering such that he always appeared unhappy. After falling seriously ill, he refused to take care of himself and rejected all medicines. One day his friends found him cold in bed. He had expressed no instructions or final wishes before dying."

Thus died a man who lacked not genius, glory, or anything else but who, because of his especially great and loyal sympathy for an unhappy dynasty and a fallen regime, failed to profit from the fruits of his genius and glory.

He wished to symbolize the pathos of this life through the features of a young unhappy noble woman—a woman unhappy precisely because of the nobility of her soul and the great extent of her sacrifice.

Thus, besides its literary merits, *Kim Van Kieu* has psychological value as a testimony to the personality of its author, who adds to the beauty of this work, which is at once a pure masterpiece of a national literature and a precious document of one man's sincerely touching humanity.

When I call it a pure masterpiece, I hardly think of this as an exaggeration. Indeed, the more one studies *Kieu*, the more one feels its perfection, the full and harmonious perfection of a work of art that completely achieves an ideal of beauty that corresponds not to a particular aesthetic but to the very pattern and rhythm of universal art. Unlike Chinese texts that can be complicated and over-wrought or Indian texts that very often are only compilations or "mosaics," as one eminent French Sinologist calls them, *Kieu* was conceived and composed according to a general plan whose every part, down to the smallest detail, accords with the whole. It is an orderly ensemble that is as faultless in its lines and proportions as a beautiful antique censer. And what finish in the execution! Every verse is struck like a medal, cut like a precious jade, carved like a fine sculpture. The degree of simplicity and harmony covering the whole and the amount of art and perfection in each detail are amazing. Because of this sense of proportion and the high art of its composition, one can say that *Kieu* is a "classic" work in the same way that European critics use this term when speaking of a tragedy by Racine or a funeral oration by Bossuet.

[*Kieu*] is classic in form and romantic in its inspiration, although its romantic side is strongly tempered by a lucid reason that I would call Latin if it were not Confucian. Moreover, what elegance there is in the expression of the most violent feelings, and what restraint, even at its most exalted! There is none of the disheveled lyricism of a Tagore, for example, or the decadent mannerism of Chinese poets. Instead, one finds a sense of measure and the supreme distinction and fullness of proportions that characterize those works inspired by the purest vein of French taste.

That this poem, the product of an Annamese mind as yet unaffected by any foreign influence other than Chinese, should have so many features in common

with the greatest productions of the French spirit is not the least originally striking thing about it.

What can one say except that two peoples separated by the entire expanse
of Europe and Asia share a certain conception of literature and art or, rather,
that between the spirit of the French and the Annamese are certain natural
affinities that would be interesting and even desirable to cultivate, given the
rapprochement that is eagerly desired on both sides and that must be achieved
by the elite of these two peoples through the intimate communication of art
and poetry?

It is with this wish that I conclude, Ladies and Gentlemen, and invite you to
join us in paying homage this evening to our greatest poet.

[Pham Quynh, "Bai dien thuyet bang Phap van
cua ong Pham Quynh," 94–96; trans. C. Jon Delogu]

HOANG DAO

MODERNIZE COMPLETELY AND
WITHOUT HESITATION (1936)

Hoang Dao (1906–1948) was the chief theoretician of the Self-Reliance Literary
Group, headed by his brother Nhat Linh. This pioneering and influential group, writing in the 1930s, advocated a new literary style based on Western themes and genres
such as novels and romantic poetry, written in the national language. They selected
the name of their group in opposition to Pham Quynh and his colleagues, who were,
by implication, tainted by their reliance on French financial and political support. The
writers of this school were enamored with French literature and individualistic values
while they also expressed concern for social conditions and an intense desire to "modernize" social customs and values. The following text is an excerpt from the group's
manifesto, *Ten Fundamental Concepts*, which advocates the wholesale adoption of "the
new," since, in their view, Western culture and Eastern culture could not merge.

Along with the other countries in the Far East, more than fifty years ago Vietnam was suddenly awakened from a deep sleep of a thousand years. Although it
was not like that of the princess of a certain fairy tale, who was awakened peacefully to find herself in resplendent surroundings and being greeted with the
affection of a loving prince, it was better than continuing in an endless sleep.

That was the old way of life. As with all dreams, at the moment of waking,
one tends to recall fleetingly the idyllic aspects of the past. It was a life of ease
and simplicity: the men would recite poetry and study literature for the examination, and the women would weave and pound rice to await the arrival of the
mid-August moon when they would raise their voices in love songs under the
full moon.

In reality, it was not as beautiful as all that. Constrained by complicated rituals and customs that often were absurd, the people lived a confused and troubled life. Inside the family, it was a life of repressed sorrows for the daughters-in-law and the young; outside, in society, it was a life of hardships for the peasants, who occupied the lowest level of a very rigid social hierarchy.

The number of people who do not perceive the truth is often very large. Survivors of that period, they have continued to cling to their illusions because they feel lost and bewildered in a period that they do not comprehend. Along with these people, the old way of life and the old culture would be eliminated.

The ancient culture has survived only in the common customs, which themselves are fast disappearing, and in the minds of those who advocate the "Middle Way." This faction is still thriving in our country and still has much influence. [Its members] advocate the synthesis of the ancient and the modern cultures. Their arguments sound very profound at first hearing. What could be better than to take what is good in Chinese culture as the basis and to enhance it by absorbing what is best in French culture? In this way, before long, our culture will become the best of all the countries in the world!

Such thinking is only fantasy. The two cultures, like two streams flowing down a mountain, one toward the east and the other toward the west, can never merge. Western culture is dynamic; its essence lies in constant change, and at no time does it remain at a standstill. Eastern culture, however, emphasizes tranquillity and always is static.

In all practicality, the idea of striking a happy medium has failed completely. In wanting to pick and choose, the people have become hesitant, timid, and without any guiding principles as to what to retain or what to discard. For example, they want to adopt Western individualism because they rightly think that an individual has to develop his talents before he can rapidly achieve progress. Strangely enough, they also want to maintain the system of the "big family" whose essential principle is obedience. So the people become indecisive, like the ass of Buridan[48] standing between a bowl of water and a fistful of grass, not knowing whether to drink or to eat, or like a man lying between his first and second wife, not knowing which direction to face. Such hesitation cannot lead to any result.

In worrying about moving forward or backward, the people are left fixed to a single spot. They are, like a horse, kicking the ground looking very enthusiastic but unable to move a single step.

In face of the failure of the "Middle Way," there is nothing else to do except to modernize decisively.

---

48. This refers to Aristotle's paradox of a jackass placed between two stacks of hay that will starve to death due to indecision.

To Modernize Is to Westernize

Westernization does not mean to dress ourselves in Parisian fashions, to dance the latest steps, to have our noses straightened or our eyes made blue. To Westernize is to seek out the essence of Western culture and apply it to our lives. When transplanted to our soil, Western culture will naturally be transformed. What is compatible with our Vietnamese character will remain and flourish, but what is not suitable will naturally be eliminated. We should not worry about becoming half Frenchmen who speak pidgin French. For a thousand years, our people were dominated by Chinese culture, but we still maintained our individual characteristics and did not become Chinese. So, now when we introduce Western culture into our daily life, our noses will not become straight, and we will not lose our Vietnamese soul.

The conservatives often consider the slightest change toward Westernization as something evil. When women dress in white or part their hair on one side, they are accused of undermining morality. Those who advocate individualism are accused of liberating their vulgar desires. We, the young, must ignore those conservatives and continue along the path of progress without hesitation, without losing heart. The future will bring us its precious rewards.

Quite naturally at the moment when we are rushing toward Westernization, some people will inevitably go astray. Indeed, many people, misunderstanding Western culture, will perceive the world as a place to enjoy temporary thrills. But such occurrences cannot be used as arguments against Westernization. Even a knife sometimes cuts the hand, but does anyone ever say that a knife is a useless object?

So, boldly and enthusiastically, we should forge ahead toward the new, wide, and bright path of Western civilization.

Progress

Without further doubt, our people, our country must be completely modernized.

We have been in contact with the West for half a century, and yet we still have to make this appeal. It is already very late—very, very late!

We must endeavor with all our energy and fervor to make up for lost time, to compensate for the sluggishness of the past.

Without fear of criticism, we must boldly resolve to Westernize, starting this very day.

We need two revolutions. First a revolution inside ourselves. Before doing anything, we should examine whether in our action and thought still lingers any trace of conservatism that we should discard.

There also must be a revolution in the family and society. Anything compatible with the new way of thinking should be accepted as a matter of course, but we must also explain our actions and set persuasive examples for those around us. Anyone who wishes to modernize must advocate Westernization.

We should not let obstacles discourage us. We must constantly believe that there are, behind us, people who share our belief and give us their support and encouragement.

Those of you who sincerely wish to help our country, to help our people live a new life worth living. . . . Arise!

[Hoang Dao, "Theo moi hoan toan theo moi khong chut do du";
trans. Ng Shui-meng and Huynh Sanh Thong]

NEW POETRY

Nowhere was French literary influence more profound than on the New Poetry movement of the 1930s, which marked a decisive break with the "former" Tang prosodic rules by focusing instead on the rich tonal and melodic rhythms of the national language in new forms of versification and modes of expression. Associated with the Self-Reliance Literary Group, the New Poets challenged many of society's most cherished conventions, unabashedly exploring the passions of love, the indulgence of the senses, the search for individual self-expression, and the emotions of melancholy, despair, and alienation. Above all, New Poetry explored the mind of the poet and his or her personal feelings and preoccupations, celebrating the individual's personal quest. Xuan Dieu's "Courtesan" (1940) exemplifies the intense romantic yearnings of the New Poets in a poem famous for both its depiction of loneliness and its romantic metaphors. The rhythms and alliterations in "The Sounds of Autumn" (1939) by Luu Trong Lu reinforce the sense of melancholy, apprehension, and foreboding. "The Mighty River" (1940) by Huy Can uses the powerful metaphors of river, water, and currents to hint at the different paths that human destiny can take in modern times.

In "This Is Vi Gia Village" (1939), Han Mac Tu creatively uses double narration, both male and female voices, and juxtaposes time and space to achieve a surrealistic and ambiguous effect. The female narrator in the first stanza is in a dreamlike state, imagining her lover and beckoning him back to her hamlet. Or is it a male voice talking to himself? His voice (and possibly her voice, too) responds in the second stanza, in a questioning but forlorn tone. In the third stanza, the male voice is not sure of her love, as he imagines her walking away in the distance. Although not a part of the New Poetry movement, To Huu, who became the "official" revolutionary poet of the Democratic Republic of Vietnam, was first known for his prison poems, which themselves were a type of literary genre in colonial Vietnam. "Prison Thoughts" was composed in 1939 when To Huu was confined by the colonial authorities in a jail in central Vietnam.

XUAN DIEU

COURTESAN

Sit with me a little while longer
Why hurry, dear, the moon is so bright
Full moon tonight, the sky a banquet of light
If you leave, it will kill my heart

Please stay, a pillow for your head
Here's my arm to nurse an intoxicated dream
Here's your drink and here is my soul
Which I place at my prince's feet

Don't tread on my soul!
From afar the moon
Stately rises to the peak of the sky
Wind follows moon, blowing in from the sea
Grief follows wind, spreading shivering ripples

The heart of a courtesan, an ocean of sadness
Don't let me face my heart by myself
These loving arms, take them as your reef
And my lush hair your hammock

Help my soul ride the endless waves
Like a boat drifting in aimlessness
My body must not get in your way
And my hair must not shackle your love

I'm afraid. Icy winds fill all paths
Full moon sky, cold cuts to the bone
A woman's beauty: the landing under an old tree
Passing lover: a boat, loosely tied, floats by

Sensual love gains a bitter hint of passing fun
The lover now thinks of other horizons
The courtesan's voice breaks into tears
Unhook the twining arms, listen to the wind and the water

Cockcrows desolate. Ivory moon bitter cold.
Eyes blurred with tears, the courtesan sees the flowing river

Her lover is gone
Yesterday's lover is gone

[Xuan Dieu, "Loi ky nu," in Tuyen tap Xuan Dieu, 108–9;
trans. Ton That Quynh Du]

LUU TRONG LU

THE SOUNDS OF AUTUMN

Don't you hear
   the sounds of autumn
In soft moonlight
   the stifled sobs

Don't you hear
   the stirring desires
The image of
   an absent soldier
In the heart of
   a lonely woman

Don't you hear
   the forest in autumn
The falling leaves
   rustle
A golden deer
   startled
As it steps onto
   dry golden leaves

[Luu Trong Lu, "Tieng thu," in Tieng thu, 25;
trans. Ton That Quynh Du]

HUY CAN

THE MIGHTY RIVER

On the mighty river, ripples spread like endless grief
A boat glides by, its oars folded, parallel lines in its wake
Drifting boats, swirling water, sadness grows a hundred fold
Floating driftwood, caught where the currents cross

An islet, tufts of trees shiver in the lonely breeze
Late-market sounds float above a distant village

The sun bears down, the sky lifts to dizzying heights
The river is long, the sky spreads, a desolate wharf

Where to, drifting rafts of hyacinth?
The river is vast, here no ferries cross
No bridge to spur a sense of togetherness
The green bank quietly meets the golden sand

High above, mountains of silver clouds push upwards
Small birds spin, faint wings catching the falling sun
Thoughts of homeland stir like the changing tide
How I miss home, with its tendrils of evening smoke

> [Huy Can, "Trang giang," in *Tuyen tap Huy Can*, 113–14;
> trans. Ton That Quynh Du]

HAN MAC TU

THIS IS VI GIA VILLAGE

Why do you not return to visit Vi Gia village?
To see the sunlight newly risen on the areca palms
Whose glittering garden, green as jade
Bamboo leaves slant across a lucid face

Winds follow winds' path, clouds clouds' way
The melancholy current, trembling corn flowers
Whose boat is moored on the moon river
Will it carry the moon back in time tonight?

Dreaming of a distant traveler, distant traveler
Your dress is so white, indistinguishable
Here fog and smoke blur the human image
Who can tell whose love is true?

> [Han Mac Tu, "Day thon Vi Gia,"
> in *Tho Han Mac Tu*, 74; trans. Kim N. B. Ninh]

TO HUU

PRISON THOUGHTS

How lonely it can be in jail!
Ears open wide and heart athrob,

I listen—with that vibrant life,
how happy they must be out there!
It's dark in here—faint rays of sunset light
can hardly infiltrate through window bars.
It's cold within four dismal whitewashed walls
and on a wooden floor with dirt-gray planks . . .

How lonely it can be in jail!
Ears open wide and heart athrob,
I listen—with that vibrant life,
how happy they must be out there!
I hear birds sing of flood tide on the wind,
a bat flaps wings, aflutter in the dusk,
a horse with tinkling bells stops by the well,
some wooden clogs walk home down that long road . . .
Oh, why today do such familiar sounds
seem pregnant with the sap of life itself?

The wind is lashing at the trees, the leaves—
I hear creation's power quite unleashed.
I fancy all the world on the outside
is throbbing under heaven's vault with joy,
is sucking honey from the flower of life,
is breathing freedom's scent forever now.

Oh, sheer delusions of a fuddled mind!
Can I forget dire woes are rife out there?
The world's a prison, dooming countless souls
to grief and torment in abysmal pits.
Confined, with rancor in my heart, I'm one
of the victims in the millions on this earth.
I'm just a little fledgling who's cooped up
in this small cage within a larger cage.
To answer freedom's call and change the world,
I'm one among a host of fighting men
who still walk tall along a blood-stained road,
too proud to ever backtrack or retreat.

For now I'm being held far from the flag—
the fighting spirit animates me still.
Who says Dak Pao, Lao Bao, Poulo Condore
are exile hells and valleys of despair?

I'll smile a true believer's smile and keep
my soul immaculate amidst the filth.
I'm not yet dead—that means my hate still lives.
That means the age-old shame is not yet cleansed.
That means I'll have to struggle on until
we have wiped out the breeds of snakes and wolves.

Far off, upon the wind, a whistle shrieks.

[Huynh Sanh Thong, *Anthology of Vietnamese Poems*, 159–61]

TRAN TRONG KIM

CONFUCIANISM (1932)

Tran Trong Kim (1882–1953), an intellectual, educator, and prime minister of the Japanese-controlled empire of Vietnam from March to August 1945, published an influential book-length history of Confucianism in 1932. Tran Trong Kim regarded Confucianism as the "national essence" of Vietnam, responsible for its past glories and achievements. In his view, Confucianism had to be rehabilitated because it provided a path (*dao*) superior to Western reason, although he did not reject Western science and education. In contrast to Western modes of thinking, Confucianism enabled educated individuals to make intuitive judgments based on a consideration of the whole problem in the context of an ethical evaluation. This argument was in line with Tran Trong Kim's claim that Confucianism was based on "intuition" (which he compared with the thought of the French philosopher Henri Bergson), which was superior to reason. In addition, he argued, Confucianism was more consistent with Vietnam's core values and provided stability, continuity, and gradual change. As did the Quang Trung emperor in 1788 and the Minh Mang emperor in 1834,[49] Tran Trong Kim posits an explicit link between social rectitude and a strong state. Along with Pham Quynh, Tran Trong Kim views the education and cultivation of an elite to be essential to national progress.

An old and beautiful house, neglected for many years, collapsed during a storm. The residents are dumbfounded and do not know what to do. Even if they wish to rebuild it, they have neither the human nor material resources to do so. As the times have changed, people in our country are eager to abandon the old and adopt the new, so they no longer think about the old house. Yet by itself, the house is a priceless object and should not be allowed to disappear without trying to preserve it as an historical relic. Let us therefore redesign the house

---

49. See Quang Trung Emperor, "Edict on Ascending the Throne" (chap. 4), and Minh Mang Emperor, "Ten Moral Precepts" (chap. 5).

so that posterity will know how beautiful it was and how it fell into ruin. This analogy applies to the present cultural situation of Confucianism [in our country]. . . .

2

In the past, Vietnam followed Confucianism, which it regarded as the sole correct path. Ethics, customs, politics, and everything else took Confucianism as their core principle. In the past and at present, Confucian scholars have given undue importance to form and caused the spirit of Confucianism to go far astray. Furthermore, in learning, our people focused on formalistic literary techniques and rote learning to pass the examinations in order to become mandarins. As a result, Confucianism increasingly deteriorated; although it was renowned, it lacked real substance.

If a country's intellectual elite has poor judgment and spirit, how can its people make progress? People used to follow the fixed framework left by their forebears. Right and wrong were judged according to this framework. As a result, criticism, judgment, and prediction were circumscribed, and people were not familiar with other doctrines with which to compare their own in order to determine which was better. As a result, we became like snails and shellfish that retreat contentedly into their hard shells and never change. As a rule, things that do not change are bound to deteriorate. When the times change and a new doctrine or new forces suddenly emerge and invade, and if the new forces are stronger and more dynamic, how can we stand firm against them? When this happened to us, people suddenly woke up from a deep slumber, were dumbfounded, and did not know how to respond. At first, we tried to offer resistance, and then found that the more we resisted, the more we were reduced to powerlessness. We stopped resisting, although reluctantly. Gradually we realized that other peoples were strong and prosperous, whereas we had become increasingly weak, and that those who gave up the old and adopted the new had become prosperous and strong. Then we started to imitate others and to change everything. Many people had a vested interest in rejecting change and tried to stay in their shell and old skin to preserve their high positions. Uneducated people in the countryside also did not favor change. But people with education clamored for reforms in our country, convinced that our society was in decline and the old culture was worthless. They believed that the most advisable course was to abandon everything and begin modernizing. This is what is behind the movement that proposes to abandon the old and adopt the new. It has gathered strength over time, so much so that after several decades, our cultural spirit has been greatly eroded. Even families that abide by the old rituals and refuse to adopt the new learning are now criticizing the old learning more harshly than ordinary people do. . . .

At present, with the growth of the movement for new learning, everyone is competing with one another in intelligence and skills for the sake of their own interests and gain. They are hardly concerned with morality, benevolence, and righteousness. . . . We have seen that intellectuals in our country have been eager to drop the old and adopt the new. Young people advocate the new learning, partly because they have seen how their elders castigate the old learning and partly because they lack a good grasp of the spirit of the old learning and feel uneasy about its constraints. Consequently, they hold the old learning in great contempt and regard it as anachronistic and out of step with the present. Furthermore, young people are moved by enthusiasm and like freedom and equality, and so on. They find they can learn more with the new learning than the old learning. It does not occur to them that there is still something worthwhile in the old learning. Upon graduation, the young have been given social positions that somehow endow them with respect from the people. Some parents try to have their children obtain the new learning in order to advance their careers. Of course, earning one's living is understandable, but this is another reason for the rapid loss of our old culture.

Everyone regards the strict hierarchy imposed by Confucianism as a fatal defect in the old culture that should be quickly removed. Confucianism holds that people in authority have the right to require their subordinates to respect and obey them. If those in authority are noted for their talent and ethics, people will abide by hierarchical rules without complaint. When such persons fail to elicit admiration from the people, the harder they try to maintain their position, the more people will resent them and find such efforts unjustified. At present, when differences between the old and the new are still unclear, many suspect that the old order hinders progress and should be abolished and that new learning should be adopted to help improve the situation. This is another reason behind the increasing desire for change. In my modest view, this is what has caused the rapid erosion of our old culture.

After careful consideration, one can see that abandoning the old and adopting the new, as we have been doing, has an undeniable urgency. But the problem is that our people are thoughtless and have not given careful consideration to the issues, thereby hastily destroying everything. As a result, although we have been unable to eliminate everything that is bad, we have in effect destroyed the very quintessence of our culture, which has been instrumental in maintaining the stability of our society for several thousand years. If we want to get rid of something old and rotten, we need to replace it with something better and more beautiful. At present, we lack what is new, and yet we have hurriedly abandoned the old. As a result, everything has disintegrated, and we do not have any substitutes. This is the current situation in our country. We are like a ship that has lost its compass and lacks direction in an immense sea. As a result, the ship keeps drifting; it will be knocked around by large waves, run up against rocks, and be completely destroyed. We must assess this situation and find a remedy to alleviate the problem. . . .

Confucian culture mainly follows the way of Heaven and is designed to maintain the richness of feelings, and abides by ethics, benevolence and righteousness, simple heartedness, and simplicity. As a result, our people like to preserve the old and enjoy quietness and peace in life. This culture is in keeping with the mental disposition of a people engaged in agriculture, as has been the case of our country. Western culture involves action based mainly on human desires. It attaches importance to the development of the human intellect. It uses reason to assess everything, to conquer nature, and to build a life marked by strength and prosperity. Therefore, science is very developed; people are fond of clever tricks and highly appreciate intelligent and clever persons; and everyone is very active. Western culture is quite in keeping with nations engaged in industry and trading. In Confucian culture, human life is not as radiant and glittering, but people enjoy happiness in life. Western culture gives people a magnificent life, with the full development of intellectual potential, and everything is arranged in good and stable order. But it also gives rise to increasing needs, stronger competition, and complicated living conditions. People seldom have a relaxed and serene life.

These two cultures are opposed to each other. Each has its strong points and weaknesses. In the past, our people focused only on maintaining morality and neglected intellectual and scientific progress, and therefore in the long run, the spirit deteriorated to such an extent that we could not avoid our weaknesses and our strengths eroded. In the meantime, other countries made headway in the intellectual field, and their strengths kept increasing, although they had their own weaknesses. . . .

Confucianism is a systematic and methodical doctrine. As a system, Confucianism holds that "the universe is a whole," and in methodology, it uses arguments along with evidence, taking as its foundation the way of Heaven and cyclical evolution. We need to understand, however, that our country's learning was characterized by the use of intuition. In doctrinal thinking and method, we use intuition to look at the entirety of something in order to grasp its nature. If we use reason to assess and judge each component of an entity, we usually cannot see anything. For example, if we use intuition to look at a Chinese painting, we can see many wonderful aspects, but if we use reason to assess the same painting, we will see nothing remarkable. This is because Chinese paintings generally try to bring out the spiritual qualities of beauty and skill and are not concerned with external form and appearance. At times, form and appearance are not rendered accurately, but the spirit of the composition is expressed in a very sophisticated manner.

This also applies to education. The Chinese usually think intuitively and sum up their ideas in a few short sentences. Therefore, one should try to capture the ideas that lie outside the words written in the text; only by doing so can one understand their full meaning. The monosyllabic character of the Chinese language and pictographic character of the Chinese writing system make it difficult to compose academic works that clearly connect thoughts and the full expression of ideas. The saying *bat di tu hai y* [focusing solely on the words risks missing the meaning of the ideas] means that when reading a text, one should try to fully grasp its ideas in order to understand clearly the author's thinking, instead of merely sticking to the written words and thereby missing the author's point. Western learning is not like that; it strictly uses reason and makes deductions and inferences, proceeding continuously from one point to another. Its method of writing is lucid, thanks to a sophisticated style; closely linked words and ideas clearly express the connections between ideas. People trained in Western learning sometimes claim that Chinese doctrines have no method, because when they read a text they do not realize that Chinese learning mainly involves thinking about how to capture the main idea, rather than using reason to make deductions. Hence, written words do not mean everything. Chinese thinking does involve a method, but the method lies in the general spirit, not in the form of each component analyzed individually, as with Western texts. In order to find the Confucian method, it is necessary to take an intuitive approach to capture the ideas and ponder them. Then one can clearly see the connection among various components of thought which, in external appearance and form, may seem quite loose and incoherent but, in spirit, form a consistent entity from beginning to end. . . .

Confucianism studies evolution and change in accordance with the *Yijing* classic, uses dotted lines and solid lines to show one's evolution in accordance with the way of Heaven, and uses the numbers associated with one's birth date (year, month, day, hour) to calculate and predict the fate of the world on earth; this is like Pythagorean arithmetic. But it is a bit different: Confucianism holds that the universe is created by Heaven and that each living being freely acts in accordance with the way of Heaven. After the death of a living being, the special character of its spirit will be preserved and will continue to evolve, fully integrating with the universal whole, as maintained by the Western theory of pantheism.

Confucian learning has two sides, the metaphysical and the practical for popular dissemination. The metaphysical side usually involves intuitive learning, which deals with the Creator's mystical path. This side is reserved for qualified people who can go deep into the essence of the doctrine. The practical side deals with the philosophy of life and is taught to everyone. . . .

In short, the three essential elements of Confucianism are that in belief, it follows the concept of the relationship between Heaven and human beings; in practical action, it attaches great importance to pragmatism; and in intellectual terms, it uses intuition to perceive and understand all creatures and the universe. . . .

Confucianism is clearly aware of the way of Heaven and the necessity of honesty in morality because of a certain natural aptitude given by Heaven. This is psychological awareness, or what today we call intuition, which is the ability to perceive very quickly and clearly the spirit of the whole. Using an intuitive approach to life means to use the eye spirit to look deeply into and scrutinize the spirit of all creatures. In so doing, one will not make mistakes. To this end, one should do away with one's personal concerns and desires and then focus in a clear-sighted way on the spirit of the living entity in question. In this way, one can clearly see its true face and identity. Confucianism's use of intuition in learning is similar, to some extent, to the philosophy of Henri Bergson, a famous French philosopher, who advocated the use of intuition to assess the truth. In formal logic, Western learning is sophisticated and more in keeping with the scientific method, but in spirit, the two doctrines are not far apart. The more carefully we examine Henri Bergson's philosophy, the more clearly we will see the remarkable and elevated spirit of Confucianism. . . .

By looking at the universe and assessing past and present, Confucius grasped the way of Heaven and Earth. He wanted human beings to act in accordance with the Way so that human affairs would be in agreement with the way of Heaven and in harmony with the universe. Confucius believed that when human beings are born, they already have absorbed the spirit of Heaven and Earth, and therefore there is an empathetic relationship between humans and Heaven and Earth. This empathetic relationship has always existed, but when human beings allow their personal desires to become strong and use only reason to assess what is good and bad for themselves, their spirit is disrupted, their intuition is corrupted, and they are no longer aware of the empathetic relationship. If, in contrast, humans know how to suppress their personal desires, maintain a moderate attitude, and make sure that their spirit and intuition are fully in harmony, their intuition will develop further, so that they can see down to the bottom of things, no matter how deep or mysterious.

Maintaining a moderate, temperate, and obliging attitude means maintaining the middle course [and avoiding extremes]. If humans adopt the middle course, behave according to the Way of Heaven, and nurture their feelings, they will acquire benevolence. If, by means of self-cultivation, a person acquires benevolence, he will have a lively spirit, be able to distinguish right from wrong, and will always act in accordance with the law of change of Heaven and Earth. If *benevolence* is combined with *honesty*, this person will become a sage. Honesty is in keeping with the natural path of Heaven and Earth. An honest person is someone who has become pure, akin to the initial nature given to him by Heaven. Such a person comprehends the nature of all creatures and is capable of contributing to the creation and raising of humans by Heaven and Earth. He is on an equal footing with Heaven and Earth and is therefore considered to be a sage. This is the essence of Confucianism. All other notions, such as filial piety, righteousness, rites, wisdom, loyalty to the emperor, and trust, derive from this.

According to Confucius, all creatures in the universe evolve indefinitely, without interruption, in a moderate and relative manner. Because the way of Heaven is not fixed, there is nothing certain in human affairs. Therefore, we must act according to circumstances. Provided that we always maintain a moderate, temperate, and obliging stance, our acts will always be righteous and just. In any action, let us try to maintain the middle course, be moderate, refrain from excess, and refrain from falling short of standards. The middle course is the most correct. With this principle as the basis, Confucius worked out a *humanist philosophy*, that is, an ethical code, which is mild, gentle, provides serenity and happiness to humans, and frees them from fear and sadness. . . .

We need to know that the main tenet of Confucianism is benevolence. Benevolence is quiet, sensitive, and receptive to any thing and any occurrence and leads to levelheaded action in keeping with the Way of Heaven. A benevolent person usually has well-developed intuition. He can clearly see things at a glance and quickly perceive the subtle significance and the general nature of things, without having to take time to explore the situation. A non-benevolent person has poor intuition, cannot immediately comprehend things, and therefore must use reason in order to assess private interests and gain. . . .

. . . Human reason, however lucid it may be, has its limits and cannot acquire rapid and deep knowledge like intuition. With natural intuition, we can immediately understand certain issues, but using reason, it takes a long time to think over a matter, without being able to reach a conclusion. Judicious and profound knowledge results from intuition and not from reason. After acquiring knowledge about something, however, it is necessary to use reason as a check, to obtain clear knowledge about what intuition has revealed. We should not trust reason too much because it may cause us to waver from adopting the middle course. This means that reason is not in keeping with the natural path of Heaven and Earth. The excessive use of reason will make some people extremely devious, causing human life to experience tragic struggle. This is harmful to happiness in life.

. . . [B]enevolence cannot be practiced on a universal basis by the majority of the population. Only a small number of specially trained persons can engage in self-cultivation and acquire benevolence. . . . [In addition], only the intellectual elite—not the common people—can use [intuition] efficiently. Intuition relies only on the light of the spirit, but if the user lacks a righteous heart and honesty, the strength of customs and other forces may prevent this ray of light from focusing on the truth. Therefore, it is necessary to use reason to ascertain what one knows in order to be assured about the accuracy of one's knowledge. Nowadays, people still use intuition as a valuable and useful tool of learning, but for the sake of clarity and certainty, they also need to use reason to conduct experiments or analyze what is already known. Reason is useful if one does not allow it to become the slave of one's personal desires. This view does not run counter to Confucianism, which advocates change, depending on the situation, while maintaining the middle course. Therefore, at present, we must use both intuition and reason. Intuition is used to acquire knowledge, and reason to monitor it. To be really scientific, current scientific methods must combine both intuition and reason.

Given the current need for scientific progress, we cannot return to the old way of living. But the spirit of Confucianism is good and has deep roots in the minds of our people. If we hastily throw away this spirit instead of thoroughly grasping it, the future of our society will be jeopardized. We should try to maintain the old morality while participating in modern life, so that *heart* and *mind* can progress in harmony with each other. In this way, perhaps more light can be shed on the path of the sages and saints, and people's minds will not remain hazy, like someone walking in the dark. Confucianism values righteousness in one's heart and self-cultivation. But let us also regard the natural sciences as our main subject of learning. Combining Confucianism with modern science does not contradict the principles of Confucius and Mencius, who advocated change appropriate to the times. Provided that we continue to maintain benevolence and righteousness, change will help strengthen our harmonious ties with Confucianism that much more. . . .

3

In education, Confucianism holds that honesty is a natural quality that Heaven has given to all good-hearted people. Thus, from the time they are born, human beings are endowed with four properties: love for one's fellow man, the desire for self-cultivation, the tendency to compromise, and the ability to distinguish between right from wrong, all of which are the basis of benevolence, righteousness, rites, and wisdom. People indulge in evil acts because they allow private desires to infringe on these four elements; education is designed to nurture the four good properties while restraining evil tendencies. The person who practices benevolence, righteousness, rites, and wisdom is a superior man endowed with noble qualities.

The superior man is upright and righteous, clearly knows the way of Heaven and Earth, and acts in accordance with the way of human beings. Confucianism regards the superior man as the symbol of the ideal man. In order to become a superior man, one must, first of all, start by obtaining a good education in morality to nurture one's heart and mind. After that, the six arts will provide intellectual training to be used in life. How one lives one's life is more important than being involved in state affairs and politics.

A society inevitably has laws and discipline, rules of social engagement and hierarchy, and moral principles and ethics in order to maintain and strengthen the state. [A society] must have a king and mandarin officials to govern the population. If the king behaves like a king, the subjects will behave like subjects, the father like a father, the son like a son, the elder brother like an elder brother, and the younger brother like a younger brother, and husband and wife accordingly. Then the country will be stable. Otherwise, the country will experience disorder and disturbances. Therefore, Confucianism believes that politics must accompany education. If a subject is properly educated, he will be aware of his duties and interests and will respect righteousness, rites, and hierarchy. Thanks to education, the king and his mandarin officials will be fully aware of their responsibilities and will refrain from arbitrary and cruel behavior.

Confucianism pays attention to the king and the mandarin officials because the country's prosperity or decline depends on them. If these people are not duly trained to behave with benevolence, righteousness, rites, and wisdom, they will become thieves and bandits who use ruses and tricks to harm the country. The country belongs to everyone, not to a few, and if these thieves and bandits use the country as their own property, without regard for the ill effects on or benefits for the country, they can be discarded as wayward elements. Thus, the king's legitimate authority lies in exercising the Mandate of Heaven and ensuring the happiness of the common people. If and when the king no longer effectively carries out his duty, the Mandate of Heaven will be terminated. The power used to enforce his authority will be only the power of thieves and bandits. Therefore, Confucianism holds that it is justified for benevolent persons to punish bad rulers in order to save the people. Accordingly, Mencius said: "The people are of supreme importance; the altars to the gods of earth and grain come next; [and] last comes the ruler."

The mandarin's duty is to help the king govern the country; he must fully grasp this principle and persuade the king to act in accordance with this principle and follow the right path. A person who is not properly educated cannot steadfastly abide by this principle. All this shows that for Confucianism, education and politics are closely related.

Education takes morality as the root of Confucianism, with the education of intellectuals as the priority. If the roots are firm, the top will flourish. Thanks to moral education, people are imbued with morality and righteousness and suppress evil thinking. A duly educated person is usually bound by ethical considerations. Therefore even if evil thinking emerges, it will not be able to grow and prevail. Thus, the merit of Confucianism is that even if people cannot fully practice the teachings of the sages, their teachings will have created a healthy environment for society.

Some people say that Confucian morality was appropriate in the past when life was simple and people were simple-hearted. At present, human intellect has developed further and the situation has changed, including in politics and education. Is Confucian learning of any use to the country any more? Such a question betrays a failure to ponder the meaning of Confucianism. Life circumstances may have changed, but human society remains the same. It still is necessary to organize society in a way that is in keeping with morality. If the current society is governed by ethical people, isn't this better than being ruled by greedy, unscrupulous, and devious individuals? It is true that at present when science is developed and life is no longer as simple as in the past, we must inevitably pay attention to intellectual education. But should we abandon moral education? An intellectually talented person who lacks a conscience and a staunch and kind heart will end up as an egoistic and cruel individual, no matter which era he lives in. Under such conditions, how can we possibly distinguish between good and bad people! Confucianism did not pay any attention to business and enterprises and physical amenities because in the past, our East Asian societies did not have such needs. But thanks to Confucian education, there have been many persons with benevolence, righteousness, moral integrity, and lofty human dignity who selflessly labored and fought for their countries. Aren't these persons better than present-day devious and hypocritical elements who are interested only in their personal gain at the expense of everything else? Focusing solely on intellectual education produces people who are unable to follow the way to train people to be good human beings. When members of a society are very clever in all respects but are not governed by morality, they will be like a group of wild beasts ready to devour one another for the sake of their personal interests. Can such a life be called human?

Our moral education has been developed by Confucianism for several thousand years now and has proved effective and satisfactory. Therefore, let us preserve it as our own heritage. In addition, we should develop intellectual education, a field in which we still are weak, in order to enrich further our existing heritage. In this way, both ethical and intellectual education will be in harmony and will ensure progress. In this way, our learning will have a [solid] foundation, and whatever changes are made will involve fewer mistakes.

It is not our intention to trouble educated persons with our modest knowledge of Confucianism. Rather, we wish to spur the thinking of our scholars to carefully reexamine the heritage that our country already has. They should evaluate its positive and negative aspects, clearly assessing its merits and demerits in order to determine what should be kept and what should be abandoned. They should refrain from hastily judging that everything new is good and everything old is bad. Even European intellectuals today recognize that ancient learning is erudite and more in keeping with the truth than today's shallow learning. Indeed, we have in Confucianism a solid and viable tradition. It would be stupid to neglect it. If we behave stupidly here, how can we compete with other countries in other matters?

By advocating the preservation of Confucianism, we are not talking about preserving the anachronistic learning of decadent and delinquent Confucian scholars. Their minds were dark, they saw nothing, they heard nothing, and [they] knew nothing about world developments. In times of peace, they indulged in self-congratulation over their own poems and regarded themselves as gods, trying to persuade humble men and women that they were great scholars. But when confronted with danger and change, they caved in thoughtlessly and joined hands with others in criticizing Confucianism. They studied Confucianism without having a good grasp of its spirit, without knowing the Confucian teachings on integrity and righteousness, because they were interested in literature only for form's sake to succeed in the examinations and gain social position. Far from recovering their consciousness and correcting their own mistakes, these decadent scholars even attacked and denigrated Confucianism, without realizing that students of Confucianism must grasp its spirit and its meaning and adapt to changing situations.

Constant change is necessary, but there must be a foundation so that change is meaningful. In learning Confucianism, we must grasp its robust spirit and try to advance our thinking to the utmost, to evolve along with the universe, and to create a human life that is strong enough to be in harmony with all creatures. We must seek to change with the times without forgetting our ancient roots. Then we will be able to become a group of individuals endowed with the highest level of dignity, benevolence, and strength, to live and compete with other peoples for the common cause of humanity.

In short, I submit that our people today should study in accordance with the times: they should learn trades, economics, military science, mathematics, physics, chemistry, and other branches of learning, just as people in other countries do. At the same time, we should use Confucianism as the basis for moral education. We should grasp its spirit and remain, above all, individuals of high integrity and dignity, worthy of the statement that human beings are more intelligent than other living beings. If our learning and behavior are governed by this guiding principle, then the potential of our education will be assured in the future.

> [Tran Trong Kim, *Nho giao*, i, ix–x, xii–xiii, xv–xvii,
> xix–xx, xxii–xxvi, 387–92; trans. Luu Doan Huynh,
> Jayne Werner, and John Whitmore]

DAO DUY ANH

VIETNAM IN THE MODERN AGE (1938)

In his influential *An Outline of Vietnamese Culture*, Dao Duy Anh (1904–1988) surveyed Vietnamese civilization and culture to assess historic influences and the new directions that Vietnam was taking. In contrast to Tran Trong Kim, Dao Duy Anh viewed Confucianism as only one element in the development of Vietnamese civilization and culture, which he believed was influenced also by economic, geographical, and social factors. His other main concern, as he explains in this excerpt, was how the changes introduced by the French would affect Vietnamese life and culture. To Dao Duy Anh, Westernization would inevitably have a large impact on Vietnamese society and culture.

What will be the impact of this phenomenon of Westernization? In other words, how will the drama of the transition from ancient times to the modern era [in our country] end? As yet, there can be no definitive answer. Here, we wish to consider only a few general views that may be classified according to three main tendencies.

According to the first, ever since our country came into contact with the culture of the West, we have been aware that the reason why Europe and America have been rich and powerful enough to manage the world is that their material culture is one of national wealth and military power. In the East, Japan learned how to imitate their material culture and, in only half a century, became a powerful country. But Japan imitated Western science and technology only while keeping the spirit of Eastern culture. Therefore the materialism of Western culture could not destroy the structure of its society. Our country has been under French control for a little less than half a century and has made some material progress, but at the same time a portion of our youth, passionately interested in new doctrines and no longer holding to the old teachings, have displayed rebellious attitudes toward their families and society. If we wish our country to achieve both material and spiritual power, we must retain the old culture as the *substance* and adopt the new culture as the *practice*, meaning that we must harmonize the essence of Eastern culture with the scientific and technical strengths of Western culture.

Some people will respond immediately that such harmonization is an illusion. We cannot separate the spiritual and material aspects of a nation's culture; they are too closely connected. Our country is weak not only because of its political and economic situation but primarily because of the spirit of the old culture, whose outdated teachings and ideas have strangled and oppressed our people. Our country not only should adopt the science and technology of the West but also should accept its ideas and teachings, because Western culture has a spirit of nobility and strength that stems from the ideals of fraternity, equality, and liberty, as well as the scientific spirit, which cannot be separated from its [political] system and its science and technology.

The third group acknowledges that our culture is corrupt and on the verge of disintegration, unable to resist the competition from Western culture, on both the material and spiritual fronts. Therefore we should not regret this, for there is no way to [go back to the old ways]. But we also should understand what the values of Western society are before we enthusiastically adopt them, as some wish to do. Europeans themselves are skeptical nowadays about a culture of wealth and power that only brings people into terrible conflict—class conflict within and international war without. For every step of progress made, the crueler are the weapons produced for these conflicts. In our country particularly, the influence of Western culture (especially in the social and economic spheres) has created complications in social problems. From this point of view, the path that Europe follows is not a suitable one for us. But these difficulties are not peculiar to our nation, as they are common to most of the people in the world. If we consider the current situation of nations and international conditions, we will see that the world is in a period of grave crisis. In this sad and dangerous situation, only the creation of a completely new culture can save the world. . . .

These three tendencies reflect the attitudes of three groups [in Vietnam]. [They include those who advocate the] harmonization of East and West, complete Europeanization, or fundamental revolution. We now shall attempt to examine the social repercussions of these ideas. Our current society is the product of the impact of Western cultural influences on the foundations of the old society. These influences have given rise to many changes in every sphere of life. We shall mention only a few here.

In ancient times, people were classified in society according to their function. There were four social classes: *si, nong, cong, co*—intellectuals, farmers, artisans, and traders. The *co* [*thuong nhan* (merchants)] were the least respected; in comparison with the *si* [officials and scholars], the other three classes were commoners. The *si* were the privileged and propertied class, so we may say that in the old society there were only two classes, the aristocracy and the common people, with no middle class, as [there is] in the modern societies of the West. The aristocracy was not, however, a stable class because the examination system opened the door to every man, whether he was the son of an official or an ordinary man, to study and pass the examinations and thus be promoted into the first rank.[50] In addition, the family system created a close bond among the four social classes because sometimes one household had members in all four. The situation today is entirely different, especially in the large cities like Saigon and Hanoi, where a new class has emerged, which consists of wealthy people, such as high-ranking officials, landowners, big businessmen, contractors, merchants, doctors, lawyers, and engineers. The new way of life forces these people to acquire some education. Before their children go out into the world, they have completed high school or college or have graduated from a business or professional school, and they usually occupy positions that are advantageous and very profitable. Together, these wealthy families form the new middle class. They are influential in political circles, and the [colonial] government seems to rely on them to rule the country.

This middle class originally came from the countryside, but gradually they left their native regions to settle in the cities, which are the centers of their activity. They no longer adhere to the old teachings and customs of their ancestors. A large number of young people from the middle class are educated in the new style and are imbued with Western ideas of freedom and individualism. They thus are strongly critical of the old values and live in accordance with the new spiritual and material conditions. They have learned to like multistory European-style houses, with bathrooms, electric lighting and electric fans, spring mattresses, and big armchairs. The arrangement of the house is completely in

---

50. Except for sons of theater people (singers on the margins of society) and prostitutes, who were not permitted to take the examinations [note in the original text].

the modern style. When they go out, they often drive automobiles. In social relationships, their conduct imitates Western styles of behavior. The old conventions of the strict separation of the sexes and the young and old is meaningless to them. Young married couples usually live by themselves [not with their parents]. They entertain their friends in restaurants. They go to work during the day and at night to the movies or to parties. In the old days, women and girls had to stay at home, and young men and women had to maintain the rule of *thu thu bat than* [no intimacy], but these days crowds of young men and women go out together freely and embrace each other when dancing. Women and girls ride bicycles, drive cars, and wear bathing suits at the beach, all of which is normal. Nearly all middle-class men dress in the Western style, while women and girls have abandoned their former clothing style for "modern" fashions. The [new-]style *ao dai* [designed] by Lemur and high-heeled sandals are popular because they emphasize the natural shape of the body and make the wearer appear graceful and slender. Some women wear short-sleeved shirts with an open collar.

Marriage is becoming more and more a matter of personal choice. Young professional men usually choose their bride first and then ask for parental approval. If the young man does not have sufficient means, he nevertheless asks his parents' permission to marry the girl of his choice. Although the parents may still attach importance to the idea of "a marriage between parties of equal rank," they are not likely to force him to marry according to their wishes. The young people who marry independently are usually far from their family home, so the wife does not have to fulfill the duties of a daughter-in-law, but she still is subject to the authority of her husband. If she works, her husband's authority is somewhat diminished. The trend among young middle-class people toward independence in matters of love and social relations is further influenced by romantic films and romance novels that are lurid and often harmful.

It is evident, therefore, that in the cities, the middle class now pursues a way of life that is much more independent and luxurious than that of the former agricultural society. They devote themselves to acquiring all the useful elements of Western culture. The more comfortable their living conditions, the more ardent their passion for that culture will become. But we must recognize that this middle class is still inexperienced and is neither as large nor as stable as the European and American middle classes.

In contrast to this middle class, there has arisen a working class in the cities and industrial centers. More and more workers are being employed in the factories of Haiphong, Nam Dinh, Hanoi, Cholon, Saigon, and Vinh and in the mines and rubber plantations. These workers and coolies have crowded in from the countryside, and the products of these factories as well as those of foreign industry are sold everywhere. The new industry therefore influences not only the lives of the workers but also the psychology and customs of the entire population.

In earlier times, the wealth of the people resided in their fields and the local trades and crafts. These days most of it has been diverted to the cities, where it is expended in workshops, stores, and rented housing. As a result, the countryside has steadily become poorer, and in many places, only a few men in an entire district can be described as "well-off." The poor inhabitants of the countryside are constantly threatened with natural disasters such as floods, droughts, and crop failure. Many of them consequently leave their villages for the city to find work, where they undergo further hardships. In the old days, the family lived together in the countryside, where relatives helped one another in times of misfortune, old age, or illness. Now they live crowded around the workshops, isolated in an area of bitter competition. If they are well, they can look for work, but if they fall ill or are crippled, they have no one to depend on for help. Even though a peasant works hard all day, he is out in the fresh air. He may have only rice and vegetables to eat, but his food is fresh and nutritious. Factory workers and mine coolies work in stagnant air and live in crowded, stuffy apartments or shacks. Their food is processed rice, stale vegetables, and dry fish. (Coolies on the rubber plantations work outdoors, but their diet and housing are similar to those of factory workers.) Such living conditions are harmful not only to the health of the worker but also to his moral life. The slums of the large cities are centers of disease and hotbeds of crime and prostitution.

Since 1937, there has been a small amount of social legislation in French Indochina, and working conditions have improved. Although workers do not have the right to organize unions to defend their interests, they may form associations for mutual assistance in times of misfortune. The strike is a weapon generally used by labor in dealing with capitalists, and although it is not yet legal, workers need to use it now and then to demand reforms in their working conditions.

The middle class and working class are direct products of the new culture. Let us now consider peasants, who have always been the majority in the country (more than 90 percent of the population). How has Europeanization affected their living conditions? Life in the countryside has not changed as much as it has in the city, but peasants who used to plant rice for their food, weave material for their clothing, and grow bamboo to build their houses must now sell their rice to buy other necessities of life sold by merchants from the city. Articles that were considered extraordinary fifteen or twenty years ago, such as bicycles, flashlights, and thermos bottles, are now used by some country people. Soap, matches, and cigarettes are in use almost everywhere. People have learned to travel by automobile, train, or ship. The sedan chairs, palanquins, and horses that served for transportation in the past have become rare or have disappeared altogether. Farming, especially in Nam Viet [that is, the South], employs new methods tested by the Department of Agriculture. Sericulture uses improved species distributed by this agency. Weavers buy factory-spun thread and, in some places, use only artificial silk. In many of the upland rice fields, where droughts were frequent, there now are state-operated irrigation projects, and the harvest has been doubled. Increasing numbers of peasants conduct business with the Agricultural Bank. In a few regions the government has established agricultural co-operatives to help the peasants sell their products. A number of young farm people who have returned to their villages from studying or working in the city have urged reform of communal customs, and some places have abandoned village festivals, ritual banquets, and social-rank competitions. In the villages, the study of *quoc ngu* [national script] has replaced the study of Chinese characters, and a few villages have schools to teach writing and general subjects to children who are too young to work in the fields.

All this seems to indicate that generally the attitude of the peasants and the Vietnamese people toward Western culture has definitely changed since the time they first came in contact with it.

Rural people no longer regard the French as a race to be feared or consider the products they produce as magical or ludicrous. Intellectuals no longer view European ideas and customs as ridiculous or corrupt. From now on, the Euro-peanization of our society will deepen. We cannot foresee how far it will go or what difficulties will arise. But one thing we can be sure of is that in the new global culture of the future—in which our country's culture will have a part—it will be impossible to say whether East or West will play the greater role and whether discrimination and distrust between East and West will be completely eliminated.

[Dao Duy Anh, *Viet Nam van hoa su cuong*, 332–40; trans. Jayne Werner]

RELIGION

CAO DAI

THE NEW CODE AND THREE SPIRIT MESSAGES

The Cao Dai (Great Way of the Third Period of Salvation) religious sect was founded in 1926 in colonial Cochinchina with the aim of "combining" and unifying the world's religious teachings. Its basic tenets reflected the "three-religions" tradition in Vietnam, the belief that Confucianism, Daoism, and Buddhism come from the same root, and also the popular practice of intermingling these religions. Twentieth-century elements of Christianity and spiritualism were incorporated into Caodaism as well. Among the many deities worshiped by the Cao Dai, the highest was the Jade Emperor, an immortal also known as Cao Dai Tien Ong Dai Bo Tat Ma Ha (Immortal Bodhisattva-Mahasatva who resides in the highest tower [in Heaven]). Spirit messages from the Jade Emperor conveyed the early religious tenets of the Cao Dai, which included the New Code and two collections of spirit writings. Spirit sessions conducted by Cao Dai mediums interpreted oracles transmitted from the spirits, saints, and other deities though mediums' writings on sand or paper. The Cao Dai believed that the Creator had chosen Vietnam as the site for the third and final attempt to save humankind from its transgressions, the two previous occasions ("eras") having failed. In Cao

Dai eschatology, the Third Period of Salvation incorporates the entire corpus of the world's religious teachings; if humankind refuses to heed these teachings, the Gates of Heaven will be closed forever. The first text is from the Cao Dai's New Code (1926), which includes the canonical laws regulating all aspects of Cao Dai religious practice. The excerpt presented here is from the preface of the New Code outlining the religion's goals. The next three texts are spirit messages from the Jade Emperor transmitted during the autumn of 1926 and the spring of 1927 as the movement was beginning to take shape. The first spirit message explains how to reach salvation by living a moral life and following the religion. The second spirit message describes the cycle of reincarnation and why humans cannot escape this cycle, as well as how to overcome the obstacles in one's path and reach the Diamond Palace, or nirvana. The third spirit message underlines one of the main characteristics of Caodaism—that enlightenment comes from Cao Dai missionaries' propagation of the faith. This message also explains the correct, but different, standards of behavior between men and women.

The New Code

All human beings must recognize what is over their heads. The infinite space over our heads is Heaven. The Supreme Being who rules in this space is the Creator, the Celestial Jade Emperor and the Supreme Chief of all the Universe and the Cosmos. This Creator has come today under the name of Cao Dai Tien Ong Dai Bo Tat Ma Hat Tat to found in our Vietnam, through a supernatural and a mysterious communication with the Immortals, a pure religion of high moral and philosophical value to save humanity from the rigors of karmic law.

This religion calls itself the Great Path/Way [Dao] or the Great Religion of the Third Salvation [Amnesty]. In his great love and mercy, the Celestial Jade Emperor calls himself Master and calls us his Disciples. Consequently, we must bring all our respectful adoration to the Creator and all our faith to the religion of his mysterious and miraculous Way.

The aim of the Great Religion consists of embracing and synchronizing the doctrines of the three major religious teachings [of the East]: Confucianism, Buddhism, and Daoism, and harmonizing them into one. This is why in Caodaism, we must observe the basic principles of the Three Religions to improve and purify ourselves by strictly following the three duties and the five cardinal virtues [of Confucianism],[51] the three obligations and the five prohibitions [of Buddhism],[52] as well as the union of the three jewels and the five elements

---

51. The three duties are between king and subject, father and children, and husband and wife. The five cardinal virtues are love or brotherhood, justice or faithfulness, good behavior or politeness, wisdom, and loyalty.

52. The three obligations are to the Buddha, to his law, and to his community. The five prohibitions are do not kill, do not steal, do not commit lewd acts, do not abuse the use of alcohol or live a high life, and do not tell lies.

[of Daoism].[53] Whoever is able to fulfill these three religious teachings will reach the level of the Genie-Spirits, the Saints, the Immortals, and the Buddhas.

[Dai Dao Tam Ky Pho Do, *Tan Luat*, 1; trans. Jayne Werner]

Spirit Message 1

Monday, December 6, 1926 (second day, eleventh month, lunar year *binh dan*)

Greetings to all disciples, beloved daughters, and believers,

Listen.

I, out of great love and mercy, have founded the Third Amnesty of the Great Way based on love of life, with the purpose of elevating the predestined spirits to higher levels, thereby avoiding reincarnation and bringing the virtuous to a more precious and peaceful domain free of struggle compared with this poor, vile earthly world.

Alas! Many people partake in worldly happiness while ignoring that a moral path would lead them to escape this life. They argue and criticize the Way and Heaven, thinking that they are now in higher secular positions than other people [are], without knowing that only punishment awaits them in hell without the prospect of any pardon.

Whoever is blessed will be in a higher world; whoever is unfortunate will remain confused. Knowing is unknowing. The celestial laws have determined so. In the end, the more meritorious your life, the better world free of struggle you shall have.

It is a rare privilege to be living in the days of the founding of the Religion. It is even rarer to find precious stones in the deep, dark forest after confronting difficulties and hardships in life. It all depends on your state of mind: if you believe the path will be difficult, it will be so. But do not confuse the path of religious virtue with an indecisive mind; otherwise you will regret it.

The Jade Emperor written as Cao Dai
Teaching Religion to the Southern Country[54]
[Cao Dai, "Ngoc-Hoang Thuong De viet Cao Dai giao dao Nam Phuong,"
in Dai Dao Tam Ky Pho Do, *Thanh Ngon Hiep Tuyen*, 1:69–70;
trans. Jayne Werner and Jeremy Jammes]

---

53. The three jewels are matter, spirit, and soul. The five elements are metal, air, water, fire, and earth.

54. Spirit messages were transmitted in séances conducted by mediums who wrote down the messages in trays of sand or on paper. Hence the author of a divine message identified himself or herself by means of a written symbol.

Spirit Message 2

Sunday, December 19, 1926 (fifteenth day, twelfth month, lunar year *binh dan*)

Listen, children:

Two things that you have not yet learned are the most precious qualities of religion and religious experience. They are improving your consciousness and the capacity of your heart.

Children, you were born here on this earth: you live and suffer here, and you also will die here. Let me ask you: do you know what happens after you die? Where you will go?

None of you understands this miraculous mechanism. I will now teach it to you.

For many thousands of years, all beings have been transformed through the cycle of reincarnation from minerals to plants to animals, finally reaching the stage of human beings. Human beings are themselves divided into different classes on this earth. For example, the class of "emperor" as we understand it on this planet [the sixty-eighth planet] does not even reach the lowest level in the next planet, the sixty-seventh.[55] On the sixty-seventh planet, human beings also are placed into different classes. The value of the planets increases as their assigned number decreases, from the three thousandth world to the first. When you pass through the three thousand worlds, you next go through the seventy-two earths, then the four great ethereal continents, and finally the thirty-six celestial kingdoms. Once there, human beings will be reincarnated one more time if they persevere in cultivating themselves. Then they will reach the pinnacle, the Bach Ngoc Kinh [White Jade Palace]. In Buddhism, this place is called nirvana.

Children, you can now understand that all these social categorizations are not really the point. This life has a Celestial rank [a high rank given by Heaven]. It is exactly the same for the class of demons. They have used devious methods to insinuate themselves into the Celestial Palace where they have organized their own hierarchy with corresponding positions for the sole purpose of punishing and harming you. I gave them the great privilege of trying to seduce and tempt you into becoming their servants. I have always told you that if the two sides [of suffering and virtue] are not balanced, there will not be justice. The law of spiritual justice demands this [that is, a life beset by temptations]. Nevertheless, I often have lost many of my disciples to the demons.

---

55. The earth is the sixty-eighth out of seventy-two worlds. According Caodaism, the current sixty-eighth Blue Planet is part of the third and last cycle before the end of the world.

I have clearly shown you the different paths between good and evil. I have also shown you the direction to follow so you do not become lost. Children, you are aware that the demons have been reincarnated up in the three thousand worlds, so why would you think there are no demons down among the seventy-two earths? Unfortunately, these demons are innumerable and dispersed everywhere: they are the makers of your illusions and temptations.[56]

This is why I have warned you: I have placed many ferocious beasts among you and ordered them to devour you. But I also have given each of you the armor to protect yourself. This armor is your virtue, which is invisible to these beasts. Thus, your virtue is the method capable of exterminating the demons and leading you to return to me. Those who are not religious will become slaves of the demons. As I have said, your virtue is like an endless ladder that will help you reach the highest position, my level. I can also lower myself so you can go higher.

Children, I advise you again: if you are not religious, fulfilling your duty honestly and justly, when your soul leaves your body and reaches the next level, how long will it be before you come back to me? Anyone can return to me after only one lifetime if they spend that life in religious practice. This is an enormous privilege I have given you, to save all human beings. Alas! Unfortunately, I have never had the pleasure of seeing anyone who has accomplished this.

Therefore, I repeat: You should admire and respect my religion.

The Jade Emperor written as Cao Dai
Teaching Religion to the Southern Country

[Cao Dai, "Ngoc-Hoang Thuong De viet Cao Dai giao dao Nam Phuong,"
in Dai Dao Tam Ky Pho Do, *Thanh Ngon Hiep Tuyen*, 1:74–76;
trans. Jayne Werner and Jeremy Jammes]

Spirit Message 3

March 5, 1927

Great Altar at Cau Kho

Children, many of you may think that in order to practice a religion, you have to be completely detached from secular activities, yearning day and night for a secluded place for religious self-improvement. I am telling you now that if you have not paid all your karmic debt and have not accrued enough merit, you cannot become enlightened. In order to be enlightened,

---

56. Thus Cao Dai, or the Jade Emperor, grants demons the ability to hinder humans' self-cultivation, divert them from the Great Way, and prevent them from achieving nirvana.

you must first accrue merit by bringing salvation to all wandering souls. If you cannot do it in this way, then you may then find other ways, such as self-cultivation, that also can lead to the elevated position of enlightenment. Children, you have to understand my Holy Will in order to cultivate your mind and determine your goals. For any path you choose to take, you will need a spiritual guiding light to see the path clearly with confidence, whether you are a king, a teacher, an artisanal worker, or a Daoist priest. No profession is useless, only people who act unprofessionally.

Dear, beloved women! Daughters, you often look up to people who are higher in status and richer than you are and think that you are unfortunate, whereas you look down on and despise those who are lower and poorer than you are. This is not religious at all! I tell you to open your hearts and love humanity. This would please me. You need to cultivate virtue. Be modest to superiors and generous toward inferiors. Obey this, my daughters!

Men disciples and new disciples, listen, my sons. Under the justice of the Celestial Way, you endure suffering. It is because you do not know how to cultivate the noble mind that I have given you. Your minds still are narrow, which is why you do not make progress and the path becomes increasingly difficult. From now on, sons, you must take heed to adhere to the path of Orthodoxy [the Cao Dai religion], and guide one another to avoid the path of difficulties and sorrows. Sons, do not lose your [moral fiber] because of a desire for personal profit; this would only squander the priceless spiritual light that I have bestowed upon you. Sons, heed Me!

The Celestial Jade Emperor written as Cao Dai
Teaching Religion to the Southern Country
[Cao Dai, "Ngoc-Hoang Thuong De viet Cao Dai giao dao Nam Phuong,"
in Dai Dao Tam Ky Pho Do, *Thanh Ngon Hiep Tuyen*, 1:101–2;
trans. Jayne Werner and Jeremy Jammes]

TRI HAI

WHY WE MUST REVIVE BUDDHISM (1938)

In the 1920s and 1930s, Buddhism underwent a revival as a result of the perception that it was ill equipped to provide the spiritual and philosophical foundation for national progress. The major form of Buddhism practiced in Vietnam is Mahayana Buddhism, as distinct from Theravada Buddhism. Reform-minded Buddhists in the Mahayana tradition promoted stricter standards for monks and nuns, changes in monastic life, translations of sutras and texts from Chinese into the national script, the development of lay instruction as a way to encourage the popularization of Buddhist principles, and educational, charity, and publication initiatives. The Buddhist revival was particularly strong in southern Vietnam, although it also spread to pagodas in the central and northern regions. The monk Tri Hai, a leader of the revival in the north, called for enlightenment through Buddhism as a way to lift Vietnam's populace from ignorance and dependence on others, as he explained in this February 20, 1938, article in the Vietnamese Buddhist review *Torch of Wisdom* (*Duoc Tue*). He advocated pagoda schools to compensate for the dearth of village schools, as well as social programs to cater to the population, which was, in his view, impoverished both materially and spiritually.

Many people have not read the Buddhist sutras and do not understand the teachings of Buddhism. They believe that the pagodas have too many rituals and that Buddhism involves superstition. They also claim that Buddhism acts against people's desires by forbidding them to eat meat, drink alcohol, smoke opium, have love affairs, and spend big sums on luxurious items and entertainment; that Buddhism is a life-averting and negative religion, is uncivilized and backward, and is even a hindrance to human progress. They claim that Buddhism lulls people to sleep. Alas! How can people with such narrow minds criticize a compassionate religion that has prevailed in the world in both the past and the present and has so many followers? What they do not know is that Buddhism is a positive religion that loves life and is not averse to it. The teachings of Buddhism have an abundance of the spirit of compassion and wisdom, equality, and universal love, courageously progressing in the good and eliminating the evil, enduring disgrace and insults and joyfully letting go, enlightening oneself while enlightening others, benefiting oneself while benefiting others, completely enlightening the world's people that they must love and help one another, giving up one's life for righteousness, and even sacrificing life and property, all of which must be considered [a part of] "impermanence."

Buddhism also teaches that the human body is ephemeral and will disintegrate in a few decades, and therefore when human beings are still healthy, they should perform good and useful deeds for people, society and sentient beings. All the buddhas, bodhisattvas, sages, and worthies also relied on their human bodies to accomplish their mission. Therefore, human beings must cultivate themselves and not allow their bodies to be wasted. To this end, they must do away with excessive desires for position, fame, and wealth, which are like drops of honey on a sharp blade that cuts the tongue of whoever licks it. The Lord Buddha warned people against excessive greed and advised them to focus on fidelity, filial piety, righteousness, and ethical behavior to attain ever-lasting spiritual pleasure. The Buddha taught that overindulgence in sexual pleasure is like drinking poison to relieve one's thirst: a liquid that at first makes you feel less thirsty but afterward enters the body and gives you innumerable terrible illnesses. When intoxicated, you cannot comprehend the dangers at hand, and you tend to think that you are doing the right thing. The Buddha and other sages were well aware of such evils, and out of extreme pity for human beings, they composed sermons and teachings to awaken people [to their follies]. So Buddhism definitely does not tell people to put aside progress or lull people to sleep. Regrettably, few people are able to grasp and abide by the correct teachings of the Lord Buddha, and therefore few of them enjoy the benefits of Buddhism, like people who are unable to eat good food to which they have access and therefore cannot appreciate its delights.

It is wrong to regard ritual as a troublesome thing and as superstition. Because we live in the world, polite and courteous behavior shows that someone is honest and good. Courtesy entails certain rites that should not be construed as superstitious. When we perform rituals in honor of Confucius or at the Hung kings' temple,[57] or offer wreaths on the death anniversaries of meritorious mandarins and heroes and righteous persons, this is not superstition. The same applies to the Lord Buddha, whose teachings guide people to understand self-cultivation, mutual affection and respect, sinfulness and blessedness, the law of cause and effect, samsara, and the karmic rewards of good and evil. If the world correctly abides by the Lord Buddha's teachings, everyone will attain peace. If humankind closely abides by his teachings, all will enjoy happiness and serenity of mind. For these reasons, people respect the Lord Buddha and worship him. But he does not require this. He was a king with immense power and wealth, and yet he gave it all up, left home to retreat [from daily life], and undertook self-cultivation and practice in order to find the genuinely right path and, subsequently, to educate human beings. The Lord Buddha does not require worship from humans. In performing rituals in his honor, people are inspired by his wise example and try to follow it in order to escape desire and suffering and to achieve liberation. He said that all sentient beings have enough virtue and wisdom to cultivate and ultimately become a buddha. It is regrettable that sentient beings are not willing to follow the Buddha's teachings. But all this shows how egalitarian Buddhism is.

About our people now, let us mention the extent to which morality, customs, manners, and mores have deteriorated and human hearts have gone astray; the suffering to which people have been subjected; the murder of fathers by their children and the murder of husbands by their wives; and the great amount of chaos. How many persons have no food, no clothing, and no employment and have put up with so much suffering in their precarious lives? These people are like trees without roots, like duckweed floating about aimlessly, not knowing which direction to take. As for spiritual suffering, in any village today, how many children do not attend school and just play in the mud? They will become foolish and stupid and will be bullied, with others riding on their necks and becoming their slaves forever. They will be ignorant of moral principles. If this happens in a particular village, it will affect the district, the county, the province, and the region. How many children have no place to learn, with no

57. See "A Vietnamese Antiquity" and "The Literati's New Worldview" (both in chap. 2).

one to teach them? How can the nation ever make progress? Thus, spiritual suffering is even greater than material suffering.

While the government has done much in the area of education, [the existing] schools and teachers cannot meet the needs of a growing population. Each village has about three hundred to four hundred children, while its school can accommodate, at most, fifty to seventy or one hundred children. Therefore, how can we offer universal education? To fill the gap, we need to revive Buddhism and impart the teachings of the Buddha to enlighten the population. To this end, our association has set up a research committee on the Buddha's teachings, to translate them into Vietnamese and publish them as books and in *Duoc Tue* [*Torch of Wisdom*] journal so that Buddhist followers can understand the Buddha's teachings and the Way and follow it.

The lecture committee has decided that on every first and fifteenth of each lunar month, the pagodas will teach the Buddhist sutras to the public so that Buddhist followers may properly understand the teachings of their own religion. Our association has set up a sutra recitation and prayer committee for people who are sick or injured and will hold prayer sessions to help them heal. For those facing death and for the departed, we will hold prayer sessions to ensure a safe journey to Heaven/rebirth for their souls. We have established a Buddhist school for training monks and nuns so many talented people will have knowledge of the Buddhist sutras and monastic rules and can go out and propagate the dharma with benefit for all sentient beings. Our association also should do charity work. In case of calamities and emergencies, our association should think of ways to provide relief. If a pagoda is destroyed or damaged, the association will, depending on its financial circumstances, help with renovation or repairs. When villagers wish to open a school to teach children the Buddhist sutras and teachings, the association will provide them with well-trained monks and nuns as teachers. The Committee on Children's Education will help children thoroughly learn the rituals, recitations, and Buddhist teachings, so that they will become filial children and be a help to their families and will do good things for society; truly this is very precious.

All pagodas should have a library to make available to the people sutras, books, and journals about Buddhism. Each pagoda is a public space, must be repaired, look dignified and splendid and have flower gardens where people can enjoy the scenery and worship. In this way, each pagoda will be a place of worship, a school to teach the sutras to Buddhists, a library, and a public park for the whole village. Is this not [the way] to be civilized?

At present, the objective of our association is to make as many people as possible understand and abide by the principles of Buddhism. To this end, the branches of our association and its members should strengthen their religious devotion, encourage more people to join the association and to read our books and journals, and should provide financial assistance to the Buddhist schools, making further study possible so that many people can propagate Buddhism to benefit all sentient beings. In this way, everyone will return to the right path and enjoy peace and happiness together. We thus will earn immeasurable merit.

[Tri Hai, "Vi sao ma phai chan hung Phat Giao," 8–12; trans. Elise DeVido]

HUYNH PHU SO

THE WAY TO PRACTICE RELIGION AND RULES
FOR EVERYDAY LIFE (1945)

The Hoa Hao (Peace and Harmony) was a new Buddhist movement founded in 1939 by the charismatic Huynh Phu So in the western Mekong Delta. The religion grew out of a century-old tradition of Buddhist millenarianism as well as the 1930s Buddhist revival movement, and it also was based on religious practices prevalent among the southern peasantry. In the 1940s, Huynh Phu So systematized Hoa Hao precepts, emphasizing home worship and simple Buddhist rituals. In addition to the principles of self-cultivation, filial piety, and the "Four Gratitudes," Huynh Phu So stressed the Buddhist dharma, the Three Treasures, and the Eight Noble Truths. The Hoa Hao eschewed an elaborate *sangha* (there are no Hoa Hao temples) and an elaborate Buddhist ritual statuary. This text, written in 1945, is an excerpt from "The Way to Practice Religion and Rules for Everyday Life," which also demonstrates Huynh Phu So's strong emphasis on national affairs and concerns for the world at large.

Fundamental Precepts Hoa Hao Buddhists Should Know

There always have been two categories of Buddhists, those who leave their families and become monks and those who practice Buddhism at home. Monks and nuns who have left home, their native villages, and their friends live permanently in a Buddhist temple or in the mountains and spend the rest of their lives praying, taking care of temples, cultivating virtue, and purifying their minds in order to explain and help people understand and practice Buddhism are not interested in temporal matters. [Rather,] their family and home are their world, and their relatives are all of humanity. Monks devote themselves to their religion in order to become buddhas and free themselves from the cycle of reincarnation.

Those who practice Buddhism at home are all of us—men and women believers who cannot leave their homes to become monks or nuns because they feel bound to their country, their families, and their fellow countrymen. These are people who cannot become monks or nuns. They are eager, however, to acclaim and praise the ideals of mercy, compassion, and the universal concord of Buddhism and the law of cause and effect [karma] as preached by the Buddha.

Therefore they worship Buddha at home, take vows to take refuge in the religion, observe a number of abstinences, read books of prayers to improve themselves, and assist the monks. In so doing, they gradually achieve release from their attachments. These persons study Buddhism in order to gradually reach deliverance.

From the preceding, we can see that in our religion, we belong to the group of people who practice Buddhism at home and study Buddhism in order to improve ourselves.

The Four Debts of Gratitude

We read in an ancient book the following: "In thousands of Buddhist prayer books, filial piety and righteousness are always taught first." Now that we have taken refuge in Buddhism and practice it at home, let us do our best to obey our master in observing filial piety.

Our Buddha master of Tay An [Western Peace] used to advise us that in order to observe filial piety, we must strive to comply with four debts of gratitude.

1. Be thankful to our ancestors and parents.
2. Be thankful to our country.
3. Be thankful to the Three Treasures [Buddha, the Buddhist law, and the *sangha*].
4. Be thankful to our compatriots and to humanity (for monks, gratitude to donors).

GRATITUDE TO OUR ANCESTORS AND OUR PARENTS

We are born with a body to be active from childhood to adulthood and [our parents nurture] us in wisdom and knowledge. Do we realize how much our parents have sacrificed for all these years? [Remember that] our ancestors gave birth to our parents and that we should be grateful to our ancestors as [much as] we are grateful to our parents.

To show our gratitude to our parents, we must learn from the good things they have taught us and must not cause them any trouble. If our parents did anything wrong or acted against ethical principles, we should do our best to advise and prevent them from doing so. We also should support them and keep them from hunger and illness. To please our parents, we should strive to achieve harmony among our brothers and sisters and to bring happiness to our family. We pray for our parents to enjoy happiness and a long life. When they die, we pray for their souls to be freed from suffering in the land of the Buddhist kingdom.

To show our gratitude to our ancestors, let us not do anything wicked or that would bring shame to our family name. If our ancestors did anything wrong, or left a legacy of suffering to their descendants, we should dedicate ourselves to acting in accordance with moral principles in order to restore our honor.

GRATITUDE TO OUR COUNTRY

Our ancestors and our parents gave birth to us, but we owe our living to our country and our native land. Because we enjoy the fruits of our land, it is our duty to defend our country if we want our life to be sustained and our race to survive. Let us help safeguard our country, making it strong and prosperous. Let us try to liberate our country from foreign domination. We are safe only when our nation is strong and wealthy.

Let us try our best to dedicate ourselves to our country in accordance with our strength and ability. If we lack the talent to assume important responsibilities or the opportunity to help our country, we must try to avoid doing erroneous things that may damage it. We must not help the enemy in harming our native land.

This is how we show our gratitude to our country.

GRATITUDE TO THE THREE TREASURES

What are the Three Treasures? They are the Buddha, the teachings of Buddhism, and the *sangha*. People are born and brought up thanks to their ancestors and parents. They owe their existence to their country; this is the physical aspect of life. To open their minds in their spiritual life, people need the help of the Buddha, the teachings of Buddhism, and the monks. The Buddha is the most flawless and perfect creature who is infinitely compassionate and determined to save living creatures from misfortune and suffering. That is why he bequeathed his teachings to the monks to disseminate them throughout the world. Monks are none other than Buddha's great disciples. The Buddha always guides and saves human beings from bewilderment and suffering, so we must respect him and believe and have confidence in his work in saving the world, [by] complying with his teachings as conveyed by the monks. Our ancestors knew the miraculous and deep love of the Buddha for human beings. They respected and venerated the Buddha, acted in compliance with his teachings, and cultivated and strengthened our religion in order to expand it, thus building a foundation of peerless and unparalleled virtue bequeathed to posterity.

It therefore is our duty to follow our ancestors' highest virtues, to have a clear mind in order to reach the path of release from suffering, and to help those who fall into misfortune. In particular, we must continue to cultivate compassion and fraternity everywhere among humanity. Only then will we not be ungrateful to the magnificent work left by the Buddha and our ancestors and not be remiss in our obligations to future generations.

GRATITUDE TO OUR FELLOW COUNTRYMEN AND HUMANITY

From the day we are born, we are dependent on those around us, and as we grow up, this dependence increases. We need other people to produce the rice that feeds us, the clothes that keep us warm, and the houses that shelter us from storms. We share happy times and misfortunes with them. We and they have the same skin color and speak the same language. Together we form a nation. Who are these people? They are those we call our fellow countrymen. We and our compatriots come from the same race, have the same illustrious and heroic history, help one another in distress, and have the common task of building a bright future for our country. We have a close relationship with our compatriots, are indivisible, and cannot be detached from one another. We would never be where we are without them. Therefore, we must do our best to help them and show them gratitude in some way for the assistance we have received from them.

Besides our compatriots, there are other peoples in the world, those who work hard to supply us with what we need. They consist of the human race and the people who live with us on this earth. What would become of us if there were no other human beings? Would we have enough materials for our needs? Would we be able to be self-sufficient? In brief, would we be able to cope with natural disasters, illness, and dangers and maintain our present standard of living all by ourselves? Definitely not. Therefore we need humankind, that is, other people, and we must be grateful to them. We need to think of them in the same way as we do of ourselves and our own kind.

Moreover, Buddha's mercy and compassion are very wide and deep. They are boundless without discriminating on the basis of race, color, or social status and are bestowed on all living creatures, because there is only one humanity.

There is, therefore, no valid reason for us to harm other people for our own sake alone or for that of our fellow countrymen. On the contrary, we should have a spirit of concord and indulgence toward them and make it our duty to help them in case of distress.

Monks and nuns who have taken refuge in Buddhism should, in addition to their gratitude, as stated earlier, be directly thankful to their donors who supply them with their daily needs. They depend on donors for the rice, clothes, and medicine that they need to live. Finally, they are entirely dependent on the kindness of people for their life. They are deeply indebted to everyone. They should, therefore, guide humankind in the search for truth in order to show their gratitude for the favors received.

How a Hoa Hao Buddhist Worships and Conducts Celebrations

WORSHIP

Up until now, too many statues have been displayed in pagodas and temples. Although some of these statues were created to worship the Buddha, others have been abused for financial gain. We should not create more of them. We do not wish to cast aspersions on how worship is conducted in temples and pagodas. We must respect the way that worship in pagodas is conducted by the monks. But for those who practice their religion at home, there is no need to create more images; let our worship be simple, and let our faith come directly from our hearts instead of aiming at ostentatious presentation. Until now, we have always worshipped the relics left by our master Buddha of Tay An. But recently, many people believed that the red color we used to use for worship had been appropriated by those who worked against the rules and the ideals of the Buddha. This is why we adopted brown as our color. Furthermore, monks use brown to symbolize taking the holy orders. Since brown is the combination of all the other colors, it symbolizes the harmony of humankind without distinction to race or individual. That is why we use brown where we worship to represent Buddha's sublimity.

If one's house is narrow, all one needs is an incense burner on an altar to worship Heaven, because religious observance primarily consists of improving oneself rather than overt acts of worship. People who have Buddhist statues in their homes can keep them. But they should not use paper images, and should burn them. People who live with other individuals in the same house who have not taken the vows, who belong to a different religion, or whose house is too small for worship, can, when praying to the Buddha, pray in a low voice.

When praying and presenting offerings to the Buddha, only fresh water, flowers, and incense sticks are required. Fresh water represents cleanliness, flowers represent purity, and incense is used to freshen the air. These offerings are sufficient. One can use any offerings to pray to one's ancestors.

Besides praying to the Buddha and worshipping our ancestors, grandparents, parents, and our country's heroes, we should not worship any spirits with whose origins we are unfamiliar.

RELIGIOUS CEREMONIES

One prostrates oneself only before the Buddha, one's ancestors, grandparents (while still alive), and parents (also while still alive), and national heroes. Let us stop prostrating before those who are living. Even to our master, we only bow.

We must think very carefully about our actions in our religion and in society and not do crazy and absurd things. First, we should not take advantage by relying on the powerful. Second, we should not rely on the help of saints and spirits. Third, we should not count on the support of our master. We must always remember the Buddha's law of cause and effect. If the cause is well intentioned, the effect will be beneficial as well. Those who act in a crazy manner without thinking carefully will end up failing, encountering difficulties, and suffering. Afterward, they will blame powerful people for not having saved them or reproach our master and the Buddha for not having blessed them. Such erroneous thinking is pitiful.

Let us all use our intelligence to understand our religion's principles and our master's teachings and not blindly follow precepts that we have not thought about carefully. Only by doing so will we be able to progress on the path of religious virtue.

We hope that these explanations of our fundamental precepts will be carefully pondered by all our followers and acted on in order to eliminate crazy superstitions held by a small number of people in our religion, so that the spirit of virtue and peace of Buddhism can be rapidly expanded.

FUNERALS

When our grandparents or parents die, we maintain the ancient mourning customs with some modifications, as follows:

Now that we have taken refuge in religion, prayers for the release of the dead person's soul from suffering in the next world must come from our sincere praying and from that of our coreligionists. We should not send for sorcerers to offer flowers and burn votive paper because this is a waste of money. We must realize that the body is destructible, and it should be buried discreetly without letting it decompose, which is harmful to the living.

Filial piety should be shown during the deceased's lifetime and should spring from the religious life one leads and from sincerity in prayers and not from calling in an outside person to lead the prayers. All one has to do is to set up an altar in the middle of the house or in the open air for prayers and to bury the dead discreetly.

To venerate grandparents and parents, we can offer anything that we have on hand on death anniversary days, as is customary. One is free to invite guests for the meals on these occasions. Everything should be done simply, conveniently, and in a way that does not waste money.

HOW TO PRAY FOR THE DEAD

One stands before the Buddha's altar and prays: "Hail our Master Buddha Sakyamuni" (three times) and "Hail Amida Buddha" (three times). Then one prays: "Buddha, Master Buddha, I now sincerely pray for (name of the deceased) who, thanks to Merciful Buddha, has saved the soul of (name of the deceased) from the path of error and has been able to go to Paradise."

At home as well as during the funeral, we should walk in procession and pray: "Hail the Buddhist Paradise of Tay-Phuong [of the West], Hail the multitude of Buddhas most merciful, lead the soul of the dead, Amida Buddha." (If the deceased is a monk, the last sentence will be: Lead the religious official, Amida Buddha.)

Note: The bereaved family should not cry but pray quietly for the deceased, because crying will hinder the release of the dead person's soul from suffering in the next world.

MARRIAGE

The duty of parents is to choose a suitable spouse for their children by carefully observing the characters of the boy and girl. They should not force their children to accept a match if it would cause them to be miserable later, but they should also not give them too much freedom to choose whom they wish, as their lack of experience may lead them to become spoiled and bad persons. The custom of asking for expensive marriage gifts from the bridegroom's family should be abandoned. The parents of the two parties should not cause each other difficulties. In addition, big banquets and pretentious celebrations should not be held because the costs will only impoverish us.

[Adapted from Giao-Hoi Phat-Giao Hoa Hao,
Tieu-su va giao-ly cua Duc Huynh Gao-Chu, 59–65, 79–83;
trans. Jayne Werner]

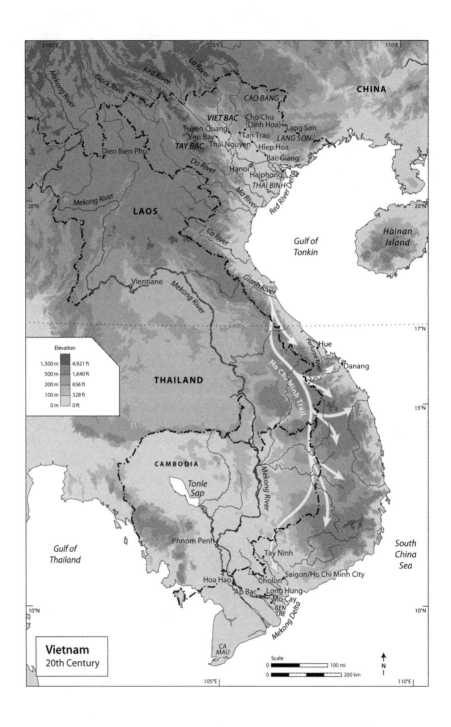

105°E

Mekong River

Black River

Red River

Lo River

CAO BANG

CHINA

VIET BAC

Cho Chu
(Dinh Hoa)

Tuyen Quang
Yen Bay
TAY BAC
Thai Nguyen

Tan Trao
Hiep Hoa

Lang Son
LANG SON

Dien Bien Phu

Da River

Bac Giang

Hanoi

Haiphong

THAI BINH

Ma River

Red River Delta

20°N

Mekong River

LAOS

Ca River

Gulf of
Tonkin

Hainan
Island

20°N

Vientiane

Mekong River

Gianh River

17°N

Elevation	
1,500 m	4,921 ft
500 m	1,640 ft
200 m	656 ft
100 m	328 ft
0 m	0 ft

THAILAND

Hue

Danang

Perfume River

Ho Chi Minh Trail

15°N

CAMBODIA

Tonle
Sap

Mekong River

South
China
Sea

Gulf of
Thailand

Phnom Penh

Tay Ninh

Saigon/Ho Chi Minh City

Hoa Hao

Cholon

Ap Bac

Long Hung
Mo Cay
BEN
TRE

10°N

CA
MAU

Mekong Delta

10°N

Vietnam
20th Century

Scale
0 ____ 100 mi
0 ____ 200 km

N

105°E

110°E

Chapter 7

THE INDEPENDENCE ERA

Following World War II, events both inside and outside Vietnam had a decisive impact on which road the country would take toward independence and sovereignty. In 1940, the Japanese army occupied Indochina and forced the French to rule the colony with them until 1945. But the fascist alliance between Vichy France and the Japanese army gave the Indochinese Communist Party, led by Ho Chi Minh, the opportunity to organize an underground movement, the Viet Minh League for the Independence of Vietnam, to fight both the Japanese and the French. The Viet Minh and the Communist Party captured the mantle of nationalism for their anticolonial struggle, and in the August Revolution of 1945, they established the Democratic Republic of Vietnam. As a result, Marxism-Leninism emerged as the prevailing paradigm both for waging war against two Western powers and for Vietnam's political-economic system. In 1954, the Viet Minh emerged victorious against French colonialism at Dien Bien Phu, thereby solidifying the state of the Democratic Republic of Vietnam. But another system emerged to compete with the Communist version: a southern republic initially established in 1955 under Ngo Dinh Diem, who fostered a philosophy of personalism that was based on both the ideas of the conservative French Catholic thinker Emmanuel Mounier and Confucian precepts and that was adamantly anti-Communist and strongly supported by the Western powers.

The Indochinese Communist Party was dominated culturally by the ideas of Truong Chinh, who announced the party's cultural policy in 1943, arguing against art for art's sake, in reaction to the freewheeling literary flights of fancy and personal liberation in the 1930s, and instead for art in the service of society and politics. For military purposes, Vo Nguyen Giap adapted historical East Asian and Vietnamese precepts to modern military strategies and tactics, which he used during the wars against both the French (1945–1954) and the United States (1960–1975), including taking advantage of local conditions and strengths against a militarily superior enemy. The Tet Offensive (1968), the climax of the war against the Americans, also harked back to premodern Vietnamese military strategies, while the Communists also demonstrated their ability to adapt to new American battlefield tactics and their relentless aerial bombardments.

Vietnamese Communism has never been monolithic. As early as 1956, an influential group of critics in the army and the party maintained that intellectual freedom would strengthen the party rather than weaken it. Moreover, these voices supported a brief flowering of artistic and literary expression in the humanities and letters movement in 1956, when writers were permitted to publish without party censorship. Their wings were quickly clipped, however, and it was not until after 1986 that this mode of thinking was allowed to return to public discussion. In the south, under the republican regimes, literary expression was freer but marked by a sense of existential doom. Although most northern poets and novelists adhered to the party's cultural line, a fresh poetic voice occasionally was able to capture the wistfulness and sadness of a young soldier about to go to war.

Both the north and the south sought ways to cope with social conflicts and achieve social integration. In the north, the Communists pushed for the equality of women as well as for ethnic diversity within one nation. In the more culturally heterogeneous south, the large and economically powerful Chinese community was forced to adopt Vietnamese citizenship under Ngo Dinh Diem in his attempt to integrate them into the collectivity. By 1954, about 500,000 Catholics had moved south, providing the political base for Ngo Dinh Diem's regime. Buddhism as a social force emerged in southern Vietnam in partial response to the regime's religious policies but also to the political crisis that enveloped the regime in the early 1960s. Some elements in the Catholic community added their voices of discontent as well. The new governments of both the north and the south recognized the need to institute new land regimes, just as the Le (fifteenth century) and the Nguyen (nineteenth century) dynasties had before them. The north instituted land reform in 1955 in order to eliminate the landlord class and distribute land to peasant farms (all of which were collectivized shortly thereafter). The south, confronted with absentee landlordism, eventually enacted its own land reform program in 1970, when the war was almost over. By that time, however, the Communist National Liberation Front (NLF) in the south already had redistributed land to the peasants in the areas under its control.

Following the end of the American war in 1975, with the victory of the Communists and the reunification of Vietnam in 1976, the north tried, unsuccessfully, to impose its system of collectivized agriculture and central planning on the south. But the south had fundamentally changed, and now its peasantry preferred owning their farms and marketing their own goods. In fact, the south became the economic model and engine for the reforms enacted in 1986 to lift Vietnam out of its economic crisis. These reforms transformed the command-economy system into a market-based system and are known as Doi Moi (Renovation). This new period in Vietnam's history adopted and amplified several trends that had emerged earlier. Economically, Vietnam accepted the market economy as the basis of its system, encouraging local capitalists, just as the Tonkin Free School had urged in the early twentieth century.[1] Another land reform was instituted in 1988, this time a return to individual- and peasant-based ownership, as had existed before agricultural collectivization. But the attendant problems of village "bullies," which had plagued peasants in Vietnam's dynastic past, resurfaced when taxes and fees were piled onto the peasant proprietors who had just gained title to their land after decollectivization.

In foreign policy, Vietnam moved away from its exclusive identification and reliance on the Communist bloc to an open-trade policy with the capitalist world's economy, as it had done during colonial times. Some writers even openly questioned the horrendous losses of two wars and, by implication, whether the sacrifices had been worth it.

Culturally, literary expression in Vietnam became freer, and the ghosts of 1956 resurfaced as it once again became possible, to some degree, to challenge the political and cultural orthodoxy. The reputations of the free spirits and romanticists of the 1930s were reexamined and judged to be part of the national patrimony. Even the works of some of the southern republic's poets and novelists began to appear under the imprint of state-controlled publishing houses.

Confucianism, too, was reexamined as part of the "Asian values" debate and was found to offer useful counsel for moral, educational, and economic development purposes. At the same time, Vietnam under Doi Moi underwent a notable revival of religious practice, as Marxism-Leninism no longer provided the ideological framework for everyday life. Buddhism, as well as the Cao Dai and the Hoa Hao, Catholicism and Protestantism, and especially folk religious practices all have experienced a resurgence of believers flocking to the many shrines, pagodas, temples, and churches dotting the landscape of modern Vietnam. The diversity of beliefs and mingling of ethnicities that had been characteristic of most of Vietnam's history seemed to be reappearing.

During the twentieth century, Vietnam underwent a series of astonishing transformations while finding its way into the modern age. By the early twenty-first century, Vietnam was catching up economically with its more prosperous neighbors. Independent statehood, the most pressing concern of the early modernist scholars, had been resolved. But other issues—such as the most appropriate economic system, democratic rights versus state control, the rights of the

---

1. See Tonkin Free School, "A Civilization of New Learning" (chap. 6).

individual versus those of the community, and Western culture versus Eastern values—continued to stir heated debates. The very boundaries of "Vietnam," however, had expanded, with the Vietnamese communities residing abroad (up to 4 million in Europe and the United States) actively engaging with their former homeland in economic and financial affairs, cultural, social, and religious activities, and even political discourse.

THE LAND

HOANG CAM

ON THE OTHER SIDE OF THE DUONG RIVER (1948)

In this haunting and elegiac poem, the poet Hoang Cam evokes the toll of warfare on the land and people of Vietnam. Written at the start of the first resistance war, "On the Other Side of the Duong River" came to symbolize for many Vietnamese what was at stake in their struggle for independence from the French. Hoang Cam (1922–2010) said that the words came to him in the middle of the night, the searing images flooding his mind as he struggled to write them down. The Duong River flows northwest of the Red River, and an expanse of villages along its banks was the site of a scorched earth policy by French troops searching for Viet Minh guerrillas. Hoang Cam's village was among those destroyed.

> My love, no need to be so sad
> Long ago it was smooth with white sand
> I will take you to the Duong River
>
>   A gleaming stream
> Leaning along the length of the resistance
>   The Duong River flows
>
> Green, green cane fields and banks of mulberry
> Corn and sweet potatoes shimmering emerald
> Such longing standing on this side of the river
> As painful as losing a hand
>
> On the other side of the Duong River
> Our country fragrant with rice
> The freshly drawn pigs and chickens of Dong Ho paintings[2]

---

2. Often depicting animals in scenes of daily life, Dong Ho paintings—that is, woodcuts from Dong Ho village in Bac Ninh Province—were very popular, particularly as decorations for homes during Tet, the Vietnamese lunar New Year.

The colors of our nation glowing on *diep* paper
Our country, from that horrifying day
When the enemy arrived in fiery brutality
      Our fields were scorched
      Our homes were burned
      A group of rabid dogs,
      Blood red tongues dragging

Down the deep lanes and to the end of the wild banks
The family of pigs
Is separated
The mice wedding was in the midst of the joyful celebration[3]
      Now all scattered to where?

      To whoever is going to the other side of the Duong River
      Let me send along a piece of black silk
      For hundreds of years
          the dream of peace is fleeting
      Festivals and celebrations
      On the Thien Thai Mountain
      In the But Thap temple
      In the middle of the Lang Tai District
      To whom do I send this silk?

The pagoda bells toll faintly but where are you
The young girls with lips stained with betel juice
The white-haired old men
The children rustling in their brown pants
Where have they gone? Where are they now?

To whoever is going to the other side of the Duong River
Please remember the lotus faces
The young market women with their black-lacquered teeth
Smiles as bright as a sunny autumn
The jostling crowd at the Ho market, the Sui market
At Bai Tram, people were like threads weaving, blocking all paths
The women spinners
Selling their colored silks
And those artisan fabric dyers
Who came from Dong Tinh, Hue Cau
Where have they gone? Where are they now?

----

3. *The Mice Wedding* is probably the best-known Dong Ho painting.

On the other side of the Duong River
A wizened old woman carried her wares for sale
A few pieces of dried betel nut
A few jars of pink dyes
A few sheaves of paper damped with morning dew
Suddenly the devils with blue eyes glaring
Raised their boots crushing the flimsy stalls
Speaking in foreign tongues they robbed and looted
Dispersing the poor market session
Banyan leaves falling before the hut
Slivers of blood staining the wintry evening
Not yet having sold anything even worth a piaster
The old woman once again picked up her wares
Uneven steps alongside the bamboo hedge
A white crane flies swiftly
Skimming across the Duong River, where to?
The old mother, hungry and sad
Slippery road, cold rain, a head full of gray hair

On the other side of the Duong River
We have young children
Fighting each other daily for a bowl of corn soup
Huddling together at night under the bed to evade bullets
Surrounding themselves with winnowing baskets
As if a warm nest
In the sleep of the innocents, gunfire sounds like lightning
Incoherent dreams
Awake with a start
The specter of the enemy torments the lips of the young

Our rage will not subside
This land will note their crimes

Night falls upon the Duong River
—Child, who are you? Where do you come from?

A flimsy bamboo screen slightly opens
—Do come into these four walls, my child
The flickering light shows a mother's love
Her face brightens like a rising moon
In grief, her white hair is whispering instead
Stories that never could be told

The night sinks deeper than the Duong River
Our soldiers have returned from across the river
You, my son, are on the move
The enemy camp trembles in the morning fog
Knives are flashing in the middle of the market
Clubs are rounded up at the end of the village
The ripening golden field, enemy losing spirit

> They can't eat
> They can't sleep
> They can't stand firm
> They are losing their minds

Turning restlessly as if on fire
Yet our fields are still overflowing
With the lovely light of the spring
The wind carries near voices singing
Farmers fight, soldiers till the fields
A grandmother sings her grandchild a lullaby in the afternoon
The summer sun burns, the hammock swings sadly
". . . Your father died in battle long ago
The older you grow, the deeper the hatred for the enemy"
Once, the sound of you cutting the grass
The cold wind blew, the misty rain fell
"My body is tainted by the enemy
My anger is forever and of one with this land . . ."

My love, stop your singing! My soul aches
Mother, stop your crying! My heart is in sorrow
The field is perfectly still
Let me go kill the enemy
Take revenge by their blood
Take their guns firmly in my hands
Each night is a festival
Birds sing and flowers smile in my heart

> Because the sun will soon rise
> The horizon is already glowing
> The Duong River keeps flowing
> Let it take straight out to sea
> All the shattered enemy posts
> All the tears

All the sweat
All the shadows
All life's sorrows

When I make it to the other side of the Duong River
I will look for you again, my love
In a carmine chemise
With a pink silk sash
You are going on a national pilgrimage
Your enchanting smile will brighten the youthful hearts of thousands

[Hoang Cam, *Ben kia song Duong*, 29–34; trans. Kim N. B. Ninh]

HO CHI MINH

APPEAL TO THE NATION (1966)

Under intense military pressure from the United States, Ho Chi Minh (1890–1969) used a historic formula in his appeal to the nation to stand firm and resist foreign aggression. Dated July 17, 1966, at the height of the U.S. escalation of the war, this appeal was issued when the United States was carpet bombing North Vietnam and had sent 400,000 troops to South Vietnam. President Lyndon B. Johnson had announced his intention to do whatever was necessary to bring North Vietnam to its knees. In this appeal, Ho Chi Minh insists that he and his fellow compatriots will achieve final victory, no matter what the cost, because "nothing is more precious than independence and freedom."

Compatriots and fighters throughout the country!

The barbarous U.S. imperialists have unleashed a war of aggression in an attempt to conquer our country, but they are sustaining big defeats. They have rushed an expeditionary corps of about 300,000 men into the southern part of our country. They have fostered a puppet administration and a mercenary army as instruments of their aggressive policy. They have resorted to extremely savage means of warfare—toxic chemicals, napalm bombs, and a "burn all, kill all, destroy all" policy. By committing such crimes, they hope to subdue our southern compatriots.

But under the resolute and firm leadership of the National Front for the Liberation of South Vietnam, the South Vietnamese armed forces and people, closely united and fighting heroically, have scored splendid victories and are determined to struggle until [they have achieved] complete victory in order to liberate the south, defend the north, and proceed toward national reunification.

The U.S. aggressors have brazenly launched air attacks on the north of our country in an attempt to get out of the quagmire in the south and to compel us to "negotiate" with them on their terms.

But North Vietnam will not falter. Our army and people have redoubled their efforts in emulation [campaigns] to produce [goods and materials] and to fight heroically. So far, we have downed more than 1,200 enemy aircraft. We are determined to defeat the enemy's war of destruction and, at the same time, to extend all-out support to our kinfolk in the south.

Of late, the frenzied U.S. aggressors have taken a very serious step in the escalation of the war by launching air attacks on the suburbs of Hanoi and Haiphong. That was an act of desperation comparable to the death throes of a mortally wounded wild beast.

Johnson and his clique should realize this: they may bring in 500,000 troops, a million, or even more troops to step up their war of aggression in South Vietnam. They may use thousands of aircraft for intensified attacks against North Vietnam. But never will they be able to break the iron will of the heroic Vietnamese people in their determination to fight for national salvation against U.S. aggression. The more truculent they grow, the more serious their crimes will become. The war may last ten, twenty years, or more. Hanoi, Haiphong, and other cities and enterprises may be destroyed, but the Vietnamese people will not be intimidated! *Nothing is more precious than independence and freedom.* Once victory is won, our people will rebuild their country and make it even more prosperous and beautiful.

It is common knowledge that each time they are about to step up their criminal war, the U.S. aggressors always resort to a "peace talks" swindle in an attempt to fool world opinion and blame Vietnam for its unwillingness to enter into "peace negotiations"!

President Johnson: answer these questions publicly before the American people and the peoples of the world. Who sabotaged the Geneva Agreements, which guarantee the sovereignty, independence, unity, and territorial integrity of Vietnam? Have Vietnamese troops invaded the United States and massacred Americans? Isn't it the U.S. government that has sent U.S. troops to invade Vietnam and massacre the Vietnamese people?

Let the United States end its war of aggression in Vietnam and withdraw from this country all American and satellite troops, and peace will be restored immediately. The stand taken by Vietnam is clear: it is the four points of the Government of the Democratic Republic of Vietnam and the five points of the National Front for the Liberation of South Vietnam.[4] There is no other alternative.

---

4. The Four-Point Position of the Democratic Republic of Vietnam:

1. Recognition of the fundamental national rights of the Vietnamese people: peace, independence, sovereignty, unity, and territorial integrity. According to the Geneva Agreements, the United States must withdraw from South Vietnam and all its troops, military personnel, and weapons of all kinds; dismantle all U.S. military bases there; and cancel its "military alliance" with Saigon. It must end its policy of intervention and aggression in South Vietnam. According to the Geneva Agreements, the U.S. government must end

The Vietnamese people cherish peace, genuine peace, peace in independence and freedom, not sham peace, not "American" peace.

To safeguard the independence of our fatherland, to fulfill our duties to all peoples struggling against U.S. imperialism, our people and army, united as one and not fearful of sacrifices and hardships, will resolutely fight on until they gain complete victory. In the past, we defeated the Japanese fascists and the French colonialists in much more difficult circumstances. Now that conditions at home and abroad are more favorable, our people's struggle against U.S. aggression, for national salvation, will all the more certainly end in complete victory.

Dear compatriots and fighters, our cause is just; our people are united from north to south; we have a tradition of undaunted struggle, and great sympathy and support of the fraternal socialist countries and progressive peoples all over the world. We shall win! At this new juncture, we are one in our determination to endure all hardships and sacrifices and to accomplish the glorious historic task of our people: to defeat the U.S. aggressors.

On behalf of the Vietnamese people, I take this opportunity to express [my] heartfelt thanks to the peoples of the socialist countries and progressive peoples in the world, including the American people, for their heartfelt support and as-

---

its war acts against the north and definitively end all encroachments on the territory and sovereignty of the Democratic Republic of Vietnam.

2. Pending the peaceful reunification of Vietnam while Vietnam is still temporarily divided into two zones, the military provisions of the 1954 Geneva Agreements on Vietnam must be strictly respected: The two zones must refrain from joining any military alliance with foreign countries and there must be no foreign military bases, troops, or military personnel on their respective territories.

3. The affairs of South Vietnam are to be settled by the South Vietnamese people themselves in accordance with the program of the South Vietnam National Front for Liberation, without any foreign interference.

4. The peaceful reunification of Vietnam is to be settled by the Vietnamese people in both zones, without any foreign interference.

The Five-Point Position of the National Front for the Liberation of South Vietnam:

1. The U.S. imperialists are the saboteurs of the Geneva Agreements, are the most brazen warmongers and aggressors, and are the sworn enemy of the Vietnamese people.

2. The heroic South Vietnamese are resolved to drive out the U.S. imperialists in order to liberate South Vietnam; build an independent, democratic, peaceful, and neutral South Vietnam; and ultimately achieve national reunification.

3. The valiant South Vietnamese people and the South Vietnam Liberation Army are resolved to fulfill their sacred duty, which is to drive out the U.S. imperialists so as to liberate the south and defend the north.

4. The South Vietnamese people profess their profound gratitude to the peace- and justice-loving people all over the world for their wholehearted support and declare their readiness to receive all assistance, including weapons and all other war matériel, from their friends in the five continents.

5. Let our entire people unite, take up arms, continue to march forward heroically, and be resolved to fight and defeat the U.S. aggressors and Vietnamese traitors [note in the original text].

sistance. In the face of the U.S. imperialists' new criminal schemes, I am firmly confident that the peoples and governments of the fraternal socialist countries and the peace-loving and justice-loving countries in the world will support and help the Vietnamese people still more vigorously until [they achieve] total victory in their struggle against U.S. aggression, for national salvation.

The Vietnamese people will surely win!

The U.S. aggressors will surely be defeated!

Long live a peaceful, reunified, independent, democratic, and prosperous Vietnam!

Compatriots and fighters throughout the country, march valiantly forward!

[Ho Chi Minh, "Appeal to Compatriots and Fighters
Throughout the Country," 307–10]

FOREIGN CONFLICTS

VO NGUYEN GIAP

THE WAR OF LIBERATION (1955 AND 1959)

During Vietnam's first resistance war against the French (1945–1954), General Vo Nguyen Giap (b. 1911) drew on historical East Asian military precepts, including those of the eighteenth-century Tay Son, in order to overcome an enemy that was superior in arms and had international support. First among these principles was to rely on guerrilla warfare, including mobilizing the masses and preparing for a protracted struggle. Second was to assess and use to advantage the political dimensions of a confrontation against foreign forces, combining politics with military factors. To Vo Nguyen Giap, the Viet Minh were fighting a war of national liberation and for social justice against imperialism and the French-supported Vietnamese landlords who denied the landless peasantry the means to live on. Third, Vietnamese military planners outlined the strategic stages at the beginning of the French war from a defensive posture, to equilibrium or stalemate, and then to a counteroffensive when the Viet Minh would be able to seize the strategic initiative. By 1950, with help from the Chinese Communists, who had succeeded in their own revolution in 1949, General Vo Nguyen Giap and his Viet Minh troops had moved beyond the guerrilla stage to become a regular army. In 1954, they defeated the French at the historic battle of Dien Bien Phu. Giap's retrospective analysis of the French war comes from two articles, the first written in 1955 and the second in 1959.

From the military point of view, the Vietnamese people's war of liberation proved that *an insufficiently equipped people's army, but an army fighting for a just cause, can, with appropriate strategy and tactics, combine the conditions needed to conquer a modern army of aggressive imperialism.*

The enemy of the Vietnamese nation was aggressive imperialists, who had to be overthrown. But the latter, having long since joined up with the feudal landlords, the anti-imperialist struggle could definitely not be separated from antifeudal action. . . . [I]n a backward colonial country like ours where the peasants make up the majority of the population, a people's war is essentially *a peasants' war under the leadership of the working class.* Consequently, a general mobilization of the whole people is neither more nor less than the mobilization of the rural masses. The problem of land is of decisive importance. Based on a thorough analysis, the Vietnamese people's war of liberation was essentially a people's national democratic revolution carried out under armed force, and it had a twofold fundamental task: the overthrow of imperialism and the defeat of the feudal landlord class, with the anti-imperialist struggle as the primary task.

A backward colonial country that had just emerged to proclaim its independence and install the people's power, Vietnam had only recently acquired armed forces; these forces were equipped with very mediocre arms and had no combat experience. In contrast, its enemy was an imperialist power that had retained a fairly considerable economic and military potential despite the recent German occupation and, furthermore, benefited from the active support of the United States. The balance of forces decidedly showed up our weaknesses against the enemy's power. The Vietnamese people's war of liberation therefore had to be a hard and protracted war in order to succeed in creating the conditions for victory. All the conceptions born of impatience and aimed at obtaining speedy victory could only be gross errors. It was necessary to grasp firmly the strategy of a long-term resistance. To encourage the will to be self-supporting in order to maintain and gradually augment our forces while nibbling at and progressively destroying those of the enemy, it was necessary to accumulate thousands of small victories to turn them into a great success, thus gradually altering the balance of forces in transforming our weakness into power and achieving final victory.

At an early stage, our party was able to discern the characteristics of this war: a people's war and a protracted war, and it was by proceeding from these premises that, during the hostilities and in particularly difficult conditions, the party solved all the problems of the resistance. This judicious leadership by the party brought us to victory. . . .

[A protracted war] generally entails several phases: in principle, starting from a stage of contention, it goes through a period of equilibrium before arriving at a general counteroffensive. In effect, the way in which [a protracted war] is carried out can be subtle or complex, depending on the particular conditions obtaining on both sides during the course of operations. Only a long-term war could enable us to make maximum use of our political trump cards, to overcome our material handicaps, and to transform our weaknesses into strengths. To maintain and increase our forces was the principle to which we adhered, contenting ourselves with attacking when success was certain, refusing to give battle when likely to incur losses or to engage in hazardous actions. We had to apply the slogan "build up our strength during the actual course of fighting."

The forms of fighting had to be adapted completely in order to raise the fighting spirit to the maximum and rely on the heroism of our troops to overcome the enemy's material superiority. In the main, especially at the outset of the war, we had recourse to guerrilla fighting. In the Vietnamese theater of operations, this method brought great victories. It could be used in the mountains as well as in the delta; it could be waged with good or mediocre material and even without arms; and it enabled us eventually to equip ourselves at the cost of the enemy. Wherever the [French] Expeditionary Corps came, the entire population took part in the fighting; every commune had its fortified village, and every district had its regional troops fighting under the command of the local branches of the party and the people's administration, in liaison with the regular forces in order to wear down and annihilate the enemy forces.

Thereafter, with the development of our forces, guerrilla warfare changed into mobile warfare—a form of mobile warfare still strongly characterized by guerrilla warfare—which later became the essential form of operations on the main front, the northern front. While developing guerrilla warfare and emphasizing mobile warfare, our people's army steadily grew and passed from the stage of combat involving a section or company to fairly large-scale campaigns bringing several divisions into action. Gradually, its equipment improved, mainly by the seizure of arms from the enemy—the matériel of the French and American imperialists. . . .

In building rural bases and reinforcing the rear lines to encourage the resistance, the party's agrarian policy played a determining role, in which lay the antifeudal task of the revolution. In a colony where the national question is essentially the peasant question, the consolidation of the resistance forces was possible only by resolving the agrarian problem.

The August Revolution overthrew the feudal state. The reduction of land rents and interest rates as decreed by people's power gave the peasants their first material advantages. Land monopolized by the imperialists and the traitors was confiscated and shared. Communist land and rice fields were more equitably distributed. Beginning in 1953, because they deemed it necessary to complete [these] antifeudal tasks, the party decided to undertake agrarian reform even during the war of resistance. Despite the errors that marred its achievement, this was the correct and successive action to take. It resulted in real material advantages for the peasants and brought to the army and the people new enthusiasm for the war of resistance. . . .

The Vietnamese peoples' war of liberation revealed the importance of building resistance bases in the countryside and [the importance of] close and indissoluble relationships between the anti-imperialist revolution and the antifeudal revolution. . . .

Guerrilla war is the war of the broad masses of an economically backward country against a powerfully equipped and well-trained army of aggression. Is the enemy strong? One avoids him. Is he weak? One attacks him. To his modern armament, one opposes a boundless heroism to vanquish by either harassing or combining military operations with political and economic action; there is no fixed line of demarcation, the front being wherever the enemy is found.

In order to destroy his manpower, troops are concentrated to realize an overwhelming superiority over the enemy where he is sufficiently exposed, [using] initiative, flexibility, rapidity, surprise, sudden attack, and retreat. As long as the strategic balance of forces remains disadvantageous, [we must] resolutely muster our troops to obtain absolute superiority in combat in a given place and at a given time, to exhaust the enemy forces little by little by small victories and, at the same time, to maintain and increase ours. In these concrete conditions, it is absolutely necessary not to lose sight of the main objective of the fighting, that is, the destruction of the enemy's manpower. Therefore, losses must be avoided even at the cost of losing ground, in order to recover, later on, the occupied territories and completely liberate the country.

In the war of liberation in Vietnam, guerrilla activities spread to all the regions temporarily occupied by the enemy. Each inhabitant was a soldier, each village a fortress, each party cell and each village administrative committee a staff. The people as a whole took part in the armed struggle, fighting in small groups according to the principles of guerrilla warfare, but always in pursuit of the one and same line, and the same instructions, those of the Central Committee of the party and the government.

At variance with numerous other countries that have waged revolutionary wars, in the first years of its struggle, Vietnam did not and could not engage in pitched battles. It had to be content with guerrilla warfare. At the cost of thousands of difficulties and countless sacrifices, this guerrilla war progressively developed into a form of mobile war that daily increased in scale. While retaining certain characteristics of a guerrilla war, it involved regular campaigns with greater attacks on fortified positions. Starting from small operations with the strength of a platoon or a company to annihilate a few men or a group of enemy soldiers, our army later graduated to more important combats with a battalion or regiment to cut into pieces one or several enemy companies, finally reaching greater campaigns that brought into play many regiments, and then many divisions, ending at Dien Bien Phu where the French Expeditionary Corps lost sixteen thousand men from its crack units. It was this process of development that enabled our army to move forward steadily on the road to victory. . . .

If the enemy attacked the regions where our troops were stationed, we would give battle. Should he ferret about in the large zones where there were no regular formations, the people would stay his advance with rudimentary weapons: sticks, spears, scimitars, bows, flintlocks. From the first days, there appeared three types of armed forces: paramilitary organizations or guerrilla units, regional troops, and regular units. In their organization, these formations were the expression of the general mobilization of the people in arms. They cooperated closely with one another to annihilate the enemy.

Peasants, workers, and intellectuals crowded into the ranks of the revolution's armed forces. From the first moment, leading cadres of the party and the state apparatus became officers. The greatest problem to be solved was equipment. Nowhere in Vietnam was there a factory manufacturing war matériel. For nearly a century, the possession and use of arms were strictly forbidden by the colonial administration. Importation was impossible, as our neighboring countries were hostile to the Democratic Republic of Vietnam. The source of supply could only be the battlefront: take the matériel from the enemy and turn it against him. While carrying on the aggression against Vietnam, the French Expeditionary Corps fulfilled another task: it became, unwittingly, the supplier of the Vietnam People's Army with French, even U.S., arms. Despite their enormous efforts, the arms factories set up later with makeshift means were far from being able to meet all our needs. A great part of our military materials came from war booty.

As I have stressed, the Vietnam People's Army at first could bring into combat only small units like platoons or companies. The regular forces were, at any given time, compelled to split up into companies operating separately to promote the extension of guerrilla activities, while the mobile battalions were maintained for more important actions. After each victorious combat, the people's armed forces marked a new step forward.

Tempered in combat and stimulated by victories, the guerrilla formations created the conditions for the regional troops to grow. And in turn, the latter promoted the development of the regular forces. By following this heroic path bristling with difficulties, our People's Army grew for nine successive years [1945–1954], determined to win at all costs. It became an army of hundreds of thousands strong, forming regiments and divisions and progressively standardizing its organization and equipment. This force, ever more politically conscious and better trained militarily, succeeded in fighting and defeating the 500,000 men of the French Expeditionary Corps, who were equipped and supplied by the United States. . . .

Our army is a *people's army* because it defends the fundamental interests of the people, especially those of the toilers, workers, and peasants. The great majority [of the army] is made up of selected fighters of peasant and worker origin, and intellectuals faithful to the cause of the revolution. It is *the true army of the people, of toilers, the army of workers and peasants, led by the party of the working class.* Throughout the war of national liberation, its aims of struggle were the very ones followed by the party and people: independence of the nation and land for the tillers. Since the return of peace, its mission as a tool of proletarian dictatorship is to defend the socialist revolution and socialist building in the north, to support the political struggle for the peaceful reunification of the country, and to contribute to the strengthening of peace in Indochina and Southeast Asia.

In the first of the ten points of his Oath of Honor, the fighter of the Vietnam People's Army swears "to sacrifice himself unreservedly for the fatherland; to fight for the cause of national independence, democracy, and socialism under the leadership of the Vietnam Workers' Party and of the government of the Democratic Republic; to build a peaceful, reunified, independent, democratic, and prosperous Vietnam; and to contribute to the strengthening of peace in Southeast Asia and the world."

This is precisely what makes the Vietnam People's Army a true child of the people. In return, the people give it unsparing affection and support. Therein lies the inexhaustible source of its power. . . .

The Vietnam People's Army was created by the party, which ceaselessly trains and educates it. It has always been and will always be under the *leadership of the party* which, alone, has made it into a revolutionary army, a true people's army. Since its creation and during its development, this leadership by the party has been made concrete in its organization. The army has always had its political commissars. In the units, the military and political chiefs assume their responsibilities under the leadership of the party committee at the corresponding echelon.

The People's Army is the instrument of the party and of the revolutionary state for the accomplishment, in armed form, of the tasks of the revolution. Profound awareness of the aims of the party, boundless loyalty to the cause of the nation and the working class, and a spirit of unreserved sacrifice are fundamental questions for the army, and questions of principle. Therefore, the political work in its ranks is of the first importance. *It is the soul of the army.* In instilling Marxist-Leninist ideology into the army, it aims at raising the army's political consciousness and ideological level, at strengthening the class position of its cadres and soldiers. During the liberation war, this work suffused the army with the policy of protracted resistance and the imperative necessity for the people and army to rely on their own strength to overcome difficulties. It instilled into the army the profound significance of mass mobilization in order to reduce rents and to [fundamentally] reform agriculture, which had a decisive effect on the troops' morale. In the new stage entered since the restoration of peace, political work centers on the line of [the political position] socialist revolution in the north and the struggle for the reunification of the country. . . .

The Vietnam People's Army is always concerned about establishing and maintaining *good relations between officers and men as well as among the officers themselves.* Originating from the working strata, officers and men also serve the people's interests and unstintingly devote themselves to the cause of the nation and the working class. Of course, each of them has particular responsibilities. But their comradeship is based on political equality and fraternity of class. The officer likes his men; he not only must guide them in their work and studies but also must take an interest in their life and consider their desires and initiatives. The soldier must respect his superiors and correctly carry out all their orders. An officer of the People's Army must set a good example from all points of view: to show himself to be resolute and brave, to ensure discipline and internal democracy, and to know how to achieve perfect unity among his men. He must behave like a chief, a leader, vis-à-vis the masses in his unit. The basis of these relations between soldiers and officers, like those between officers or between soldiers, is solidarity in the fight and the mutual affection of brother-in-arms, love at the same time pure and sublime, tested and forged in the battle, in the struggle for the defense of the fatherland and the people.

The Vietnam People's Army practices strict discipline, similar to a wide internal democracy. According to the second item of its Oath of Honor, "The fighter must rigorously carry out the orders of his superiors and throw himself body and soul into the immediate and strict fulfillment of the tasks entrusted to him." Could we say that guerrilla warfare does not require severe discipline? Of course not. It is true that it asks the commander and leader to allow each unit or each region a certain margin of initiative in order to undertake every positive action that it might think would be opportune. But a centralized leadership and a unified command at a given degree always have proved necessary. He who speaks of the army speaks of strict discipline.

Such discipline does not contradict the internal democracy of our troops. In cells, in executive committees of the party at various levels, as well as in plenary meetings of the fighting units, the application of principles of democratic centralism is the rule. The facts have proved that the more democracy is respected within the units, the more unified they will be, the more disciplined they will be, and the more orders will be carried out. The combativeness of the army thereby will be all the greater. . . .

> [Adapted and reformatted from Vo Nguyen Giap, "War of Liberation,"
> 95, 92–96, and "People's War," 105–6, 108–13]

TRAN VAN TRA

TET, THE YEAR OF THE MONKEY, 1968 (1988)

In his review of the Tet Offensive of 1968, written twenty years after the military action, General Tran Van Tra (1918–1996) claimed that the Communist side had won a strategic victory over the U.S. and ARVN (Army of the Republic of Vietnam) forces, which created a turning point in the war leading to the Communist victory in 1975. Although the Communist forces incurred enormous losses and failed to drive out the United States, Tran Van Tra argued that the Tet Offensive had shaken the "aggressive will [of the United States] to its foundation" and thus had been as much a military as a psychological success. As in Vo Nguyen Giap's writings, Tran Van Tra based his analysis on the political and military balance of forces and the intangible factors of "morale" and "will" when weaker forces confront far stronger forces on the battlefield. The Communist strategy during the American war, however, included an important urban component that would prove decisive during Tet in 1968 and the final campaign in 1975. Tran Van Tra was the commander of the People's Liberation Armed Forces of

South Vietnam from 1963 to 1975 and the deputy commander of the Ho Chi Minh Campaign, which culminated in the Communist victory in the south in 1975. General Tran Van Tra's text recalls Nguyen Huu Chinh's advice to the Tay Son leader, Nguyen Hue, that according to the principles of warfare, timing is the most important factor; the second is position; and the third is opportunity.

A great success of Tet Mau Than,[5] which many viewed as a miracle, was that the secrecy of our goal and actions was maintained until the very baptism by fire; this greatly surprised the enemy. A book on military history published by the general staff of the puppet army with the endorsement of its chief, General Cao Van Vien, conceded, "An obvious fact was that the plan for the general offensive/general uprising had been kept secret until the attack broke out throughout the country."[6] So we and the enemy agreed on that score. The fact is that in war, secrecy and surprise are guarantees for victories, strategic, tactical, and operational alike. It is important, however, to understand these factors. Many will see secrecy as merely a requirement for the timing of an attack. That is not incorrect. But this was only one of the secrets of Tet Mau Than. In fact, if the timing of an attack is the only secret in a military campaign, its usefulness will soon be exhausted.

The most important secret was our method of attack, strategically, tactically, and operationally. This factor made Tet Mau Than famous around the world and caught the enemy completely off guard, making both the Pentagon and the White House unable to anticipate our next moves. Suddenly, within twenty-four hours, all the most secure areas in the enemy's rear—including cities, provincial capitals, and towns, which before the lunar New Year's Eve still appeared a world away from the war—came under simultaneous attack. The most important points—from the office of the general staff of the puppet army to the headquarters of the Capital City Military Zone, from the puppet regime's presidential palace to the U.S. embassy compound—all fell under fierce assault. An AFP [Agence-France Presse] dispatch on February 3 reported, "This is probably the largest battle in the war. The whole of Vietnam is under fire, from Khe Sanh to Ca Mau."[7]

The war positions of both sides were reversed: in no time, the rear was turned into the front, and the latter into the former. Crack units, which had been sent to the "enemy's base areas" to "search and destroy," all were immediately recalled to "their own strongholds" to rescue the nerve center, to try to check and counter-

5. Tet Mau Than is the name used in Vietnamese military writings for the Tet Offensive. It refers to the lunar New Year, which in 1968 was the year of the monkey. In military terms, however, Tet Mau Than refers to the entire campaign of the general offensive and general uprising that began at the start of the lunar new year and lasted throughout 1968. This excerpt is part of a longer article that explains the timing and rationale for the Tet Offensive in light of the Vietnamese military planners' assessment of the war from 1960 to 1967 and U.S. strategic options in 1967.

6. Quoted in documents of the puppet army's general staff [note in the original text].

7. Agence-France Presse, *Vietnam: L'heure decisive. L' offensive du Tet (février 1968)* (Paris: Laffont, 1968), 91 [note in the original text].

attack the enemy, and then to "clear and hold" until the very day they were forced to pull out of the war. An Agence-France Presse dispatch pointed out, "U.S. power has lost its prestige. The mightiest army in the world has been driven onto the defensive over the whole territory. At times, it has been overwhelmed."[8]

This obviously was the result of our unique fighting method in the revolutionary war. It combined armed uprisings, that is, attacks from within, with military assaults from without and simultaneous uprisings in all places. It also combined attacks of all forms, by units of all types and sizes, by either individuals or small or large army units that were joined together with different means of organization and provided with different levels of equipment. It was also the result of diverse efforts to integrate the actions of the revolutionary masses—in both the urban and rural areas—with the activities of the armed forces in combined offensives and uprisings. Some observers assert that in our 1968 campaign, there was only a general offensive and not an uprising. This is a denial of the truth and is wrong. In fact, we had planned and made every effort to carry out a general offensive/general uprising. But our general offensive was not up to the level that would enable a general uprising to take place. And without this indispensable condition during wartime, an uprising could not materialize. However, this does not mean that there were no uprisings in various places and at various times. It was impossible to stage the types of attacks we carried out during the 1968 campaign without mass uprisings. Our method of attack was truly unique for any war, past and present. Our strength was born of a combined military and political effort, both at home and abroad.

Besides the timing and method of attack, the large scale, high intensity, and strength of our attacks were another surprise. They took place throughout the south. Extremely savage battles were fought for more than half a year. This was beyond the enemy's expectations. It had never anticipated such strong determination, persistence, resourcefulness, and strength from an enemy that it tended to dismiss. In his review of the combat year of 1967, which was made public on January 27, 1968, U.S. Field Commander General William Westmoreland said, "Interdiction of the enemy's logistics train in Laos and North Vietnam by our indispensable air efforts has imposed significant difficulties on him. In many areas the enemy has been driven away from the population centers; in others, he has been compelled to disperse and evade contact, thus nullifying much of his potential. . . . Enemy bases, with sparse exception, are no longer safe havens."[9] The general staff of the puppet army also commented, "Strategists and tacticians say that the Viet Cong can stage large attacks only from starting bases in border areas. But such attacks will meet with failure. Regarding the hinterland, military

8. Ibid [note in the original text].

9. Quoted in *The Pentagon Papers: The Defense Department History of United States Decision-making on Vietnam*, ed. Senator Mike Gravel (Boston: Beacon Press, 1971), 4:538 [note in the original text].

experts estimate that the enemy can launch attacks only with the engagement of battalion-sized units to attract attention. But even so, the attacks will not last long if the enemy does not want to be destroyed."[10]

As Tet Mau Than was unfolding, however, the attacks "took the U.S. command and the U.S. public by surprise, and their strength, length, and intensity prolonged this shock." And "for the President, the shock and disappointment were especially serious."[11] In its book *Vietnam—The Decisive Hour*, the AFP commented, "The American General John Chaisson of the U.S. Command [under Westmoreland] said that the Viet Cong offensive on Tuesday was a 'big surprise' for the U.S. command. 'Our intelligence services did not inform us that the offensive would be as widespread and as massive as it was. . . . The most serious mistake of our intelligence services, without doubt, was that they did not believe that the Viet Cong could mobilize such a large number of personnel and unleash such fierce attacks in such close coordination and high intensity.'"[12] For the two years before Tet Mau Than, the United States always said that "the enemy's morale had been shaken."[13] Such confidence was belied by the secrecy and surprise of Tet Mau Than. This was impossible for the enemy to understand. And even when events had completely unfolded, their surprise continued.

Tet Mau Than was a period of extremely intense fighting in both the cities and their outlying areas. The repeated and sustained attacks and counterattacks caused more losses to both sides than in any previous period of the war. According to enemy statistics, which were presumably lower than the actual figures, in February and March alone, U.S. forces suffered 24,013 casualties[14] and lost 552 aircraft and a large number of warehouses and war matériel. The puppet army had been weakened by casualties and desertions during the attacks, according to a report by Westmoreland. We also sustained the biggest losses in our military and political forces, especially high-ranking and local cadres who, as demonstrated throughout our war and revolution, were always those who marched ahead of the masses at the most critical times and in the most dangerous places. These losses, both in troop strength and matériel, caused us untold difficulties in coping with the enemy's frenzied counterattacks and rapid pacification activities in 1969/1970 when the Vietnamization policy was put in place. In fact, we had great trouble resupplying our forces in time, whereas the U.S. and Saigon reinforcements were huge and swift. The enemy took advantage of this period to mount continuous attacks, pushing us away from the cities and driving our regular

---

10. Quoted in *L'offensive générale des Viet Cong au Tet Mau Than 1968* [note in the original text].

11. *Pentagon Papers*, 4:539.

12. Agence-France Presse, *Vietnam*, 87, 91–92 [note in the original text].

13. Ibid., 92.

14. American figures are considerably lower. James S. Olson puts U.S. casualties at 1,100 and ARVN casualties at 2,300 during the Tet Offensive, in *Dictionary of the Vietnam War* (Westport, Conn.: Greenwood Press, 1988), 442.

army to the border areas. We also lost control of many rural areas, where our bases in the villages were severely disrupted. With this momentum, the enemy thought that it could push on and destroy us completely by widening the war to Laos to cut off the Truong Son trail [Ho Chi Minh Trail] at Route 9 in southern Laos, overthrowing [Prince Norodom] Sihanouk to expand the war to Cambodia to seal off our transit route from the Sihanoukville port and, at the same time, dragging the peace talks in Paris to a dead end. It was thus an extremely difficult situation in which we seemed to be on the decline. Not a few people, who judged things by their appearances, jumped to the conclusion that Tet Mau Than had been a failure. Even a number of cadres of various ranks, who were faced with the enemy's intense counterattacks and its pacification operations and Phoenix program[15] on the battlefield after Tet Mau Than, were not aware of the extent of our victory and doubted the explanations from the higher command. Only in times like these could we see clearly the firmness and consistency of our leaders at all levels and how they helped change the course of each battle and the whole war. However, even when the revolutionary forces had regained their strength and moved forward in 1971/1972, to the signing of the Paris Agreement, and even after our total victory in 1975, some people still harbored naïve thoughts that

- We failed militarily but won politically during the 1968 general offensive/ general uprising.
- The U.S. puppet forces won militarily but were defeated psychologically, and that led to their political defeat.

Some people even believed the American hawks' smug arguments that we had won in Washington but not on the battlefield. This meant that Washington was forced to withdraw because of its internal conflicts and psychological panic and not because of an impossible Vietnamese victory over an overwhelmingly rich and strong United States. What an example of blind xenophobia! How could one accept the argument that we were crushed on the battlefield, beaten to rags and tatters, and then all of a sudden handed a psychological and political victory by an enemy—the chieftain of all imperialist forces—which was paralyzed by its own frustration and internal splits and which graciously bestowed this glorious victory on us? In fact, there is never an easy "political" victory won by the grace of Heaven or through an enemy's mercy without first having to shed blood and scatter bones on the battlefield, especially in a big war like ours.

Let us take a closer look at the enemy in order to understand ourselves better. On February 12, General Westmoreland, a man of constant optimism who always fed the U.S. president rosy reports about the war, hastily reported to the Joint Chiefs of Staff and the secretary of defense that "as of February 11, 1968,

---

15. The Phoenix program was a CIA effort, in operation from 1968 to 1972, to destroy the civilian infrastructure of the National Liberation Front.

Military Assistance Command, Vietnam (MACV) reports that attacks have taken place on 34 provincial capitals, 64 district towns and the autonomous cities."[16] General Westmoreland also said that the enemy was able to accomplish that while "committing only 20 to 25 percent of his North Vietnamese forces . . . as gap fillers where Viet Cong strength was apparently not adequate to carry out his initial thrust on the cities and towns."[17] The United States shifted its strategy from "search and destroy" to "clear and hold," from escalating the war to deescalating it, from halting the air war over the North to sitting down at the peace talks. This was not the result of psychological or political pressure, or due to moments of frustration on the part of experienced and seasoned U.S. leaders. By the end of February, back from Saigon where he was sent on an inspection of the battle-field and discussions with Westmoreland, General Earle Wheeler, chairman of the Joint Chiefs of Staff, reported his findings to the president and proposed that the war be widened with an additional 206,756 troops, to be sent during the last six months of 1968. This would bring the strength of the U.S. force in Vietnam to its peak of 731,756 troops. The president asked Clark Clifford, his new secretary of defense, to form a group of senior advisers to study U.S. policy. This group became embroiled in intense debates with the military. The Pentagon study showed that the debates were intense and lasted for three weeks. The memorandum prepared by the Clifford group proposed to do "'a little bit more of the same' to stabilize the military situation, plus a level of mobilization in order to be prepared to meet any further deterioration in the ground situation."[18] President Johnson, however, was forced to seek a new strategy and a new road to peace.

In their reports of the events in February and March 1968, Pentagon analysts concluded that the Tet General Offensive had finally forced President Johnson to accept the advice of his civilian advisers and the intelligence community that he had persisted too long in "seeking a military victory." The analysts wrote,

> In March of 1968, the choice had become clear-cut. The price for military victory had increased vastly and there was no assurance that it will not grow again in the future. There were also strong indications that large and grow-ing elements of the American public had begun to believe that the costs had already reached unacceptable levels and would strongly protest a large increase in that cost.

The political reality that faced President Johnson was that "more of the same" in South Vietnam, with an increased commitment of American lives and money and its consequent impact on the country, accompanied by no guarantee of military victory in the near future, had become unacceptable to these elements of

---

16. *Pentagon Papers*, 4:539 [note in the original text].

17. Ibid., 585.

18. Ibid., 603.

the American public. The optimistic military reports of the progress in the war no longer rang true after the shock of the Tet offensive. Thus the president's decision to seek a new strategy and a new road to peace. . . .[19]

The change in U.S. strategy in South Vietnam, the halt in its air war against the north, and its agreement to sit down for peace talks were in fact decided in March 1968, that is, after the first phase of Tet Mau Than. But only after a period of fierce combat on the battlefield, after the second phase of our assaults on Saigon and the third phase of our attacks in the countryside and not until November did the United States declare a complete halt to the air war and accept the National Liberation Front as a party to the peace talks in Paris. This is quite understandable. In any war—especially one as big as the one in Vietnam— the outcome of the fighting on the battlefield is the decisive factor for all developments on the political and diplomatic fronts. Military success determines the extent of political success. One never suffers a military defeat yet wins political victory, nor are diplomatic skills at peace talks independent from the fighting on the battlefield. The end of 1968 and the beginning of 1969 saw the start of the peace talks in Paris, but from 1969 through 1970, the enemy thought that it would win on the battlefield and therefore dragged on the talks, ultimately bringing them to a dead end. But in 1971, the situation on the battlefield again turned in our favor, and in 1972 the U.S. puppet forces suffered heavy defeats in the south. Then the United States lost the battle of "Dien Bien Phu in the air"[20] over Hanoi and Haiphong. Only then were they forced to sign the Paris Agreement. The agreement provided for a cease-fire and the establishment of a tripartite coalition government. But since the enemy still harbored the stubborn illusion that its "Vietnamization of the war" could succeed, it continued the war in an attempt to scrap the agreement so that Nguyen Van Thieu could rule the south under U.S. control. Therefore, we were compelled to mount the Ho Chi Minh campaign—the spring 1975 general offensive/general uprising—in order to achieve total victory.

To evaluate any period of history or an enormous event like Tet Mau Than, it is very important that our assessment be based on its concrete and clear-cut results. We cannot be superficial or let ourselves be misled by prejudices.

The general offensive and uprising of Tet Mau Than—as it was then called, although the general uprising was not a success—matched the conditions at the time. Even though the general uprising did not take place and power was not turned over to the people, Tet Mau Than was still a great victory, creating the most important strategic turning point of the war, eventually leading us to total victory.

Tet Mau Than in fact shook the enemy's aggressive will to its foundation and put an end to the U.S. dream of achieving "victory" by escalating the war; it

---

19. Ibid.
20. This refers to the "Christmas Bombings" of December 18–29, 1972.

awakened the United States to the fact that might, resources, and money have their limits; and it highlighted the conclusion that the United States was not strong enough to force another nation—even a smaller and weaker one—to kneel down and surrender that nation's desire for independence and freedom.

It also forced the United States to take other actions; shift its strategy from an offensive "search and destroy" to a defensive "clear and hold"; gradually deescalate the war; adopt the "Vietnamization of the war"; cut back its commitment and gradually bring its troops home to consolidate the U.S. military might that had declined to a dangerously low level; prop up its severely weakened economy; and heal the seriously polarized American body politic.

The United States was forced to drop its conquering club and sit down for peace talks, not only with the socialist north, now a feared and respected opponent, but also with the National Liberation Front as one of the four sides in the negotiations, since the latter had proved itself a force of real power on behalf of the people of southern Vietnam and a negotiator of real value. The United States also had to halt completely and unconditionally the air war over the north in order for the talks to begin.

Tet Mau Than "shifted our revolutionary war onto a new stage, that of decisive victory." Earlier, Uncle Ho and the Political Bureau of the Party Central Committee had decided that since we were not able to defeat both the United States and the puppet forces at the same time, we first had to drive out the United States and then do away with the puppets to complete our victory. "Knowing both oneself and others" is a trait of the wise and the brave. Tet Mau Than forced the United States to deescalate and gradually extract itself from the war through the "Vietnamization" process. This created favorable conditions for our successes in the spring of 1975 that eventually led us to total victory in the historic Ho Chi Minh campaign. Therefore, it is no exaggeration to say that had it not been for Tet Mau Than, "April 30" would not have occurred. In fact, Tet Mau Than opened a new strategic stage, which concluded on April 30, 1975.

The reason for staging the general offensive/general uprising to transfer all power into the hands of the people in 1968, at a time when the United States maintained a half million troops and even had plans to further escalate the war to seek victory, clearly was not in line with Uncle Ho's correct and astute strategic guidance, which was "First, drive out the U.S., then topple the puppets." We were not able to carry out both segments of the general offensive/general uprising simultaneously. Our inability was determined by the reality of the balance of forces at the time. But we did stage a campaign with victories that forced the United States to pull out, beginning in 1969, and paved the way for the puppet regime's fall in 1975. In other words, even though we had set too lofty and unrealistic a goal, in response to the Party Political Bureau's appeal, our armed forces and people made extraordinary efforts, endured all kinds of hardship and sacrifice, courageously overcoming all trials and difficulties, and, as a result, won a decisive victory that created a strategic turning point and paved the way for the next stage of the war: total victory. In that way, our people and armed forces were following the guiding line of Uncle Ho and our party. It was they, the masses, who made history.

Based on the preceding analysis of Tet Mau Than, we now can conclude that the offensive was a tremendous victory, that it ushered us into a decisive phase of our road to victory in the extremely fierce thirty-year war of our heroic people. But we paid a high price. Tens of thousands of our best cadres and combatants laid down their lives, as did tens of thousands of our fellow countrymen and compatriots in towns and villages. Without such sacrifices, however, would such a glorious victory have been possible? The blood shed by our fallen heroes, both combatants and civilians, during Tet Mau Than was of absolute value and worthy of the magnitude of the victory and will forever be held in gratitude by their children for generations to come. Their sacrifice was valuable not only to Tet Mau Than itself but also to the entire final stage of the war. It played a decisive role in our total victory on April 30. Whereas in 1968 we fought to drive out the United States, that is, the main enemy, in 1975 we pushed on with the Ho Chi Minh campaign and toppled the now-abandoned puppet regime, the other enemy. Tet Mau Than therefore gave us the key to total victory in the war. The Simultaneous Uprisings in Spring 1960, the "Drive America Out" Campaign in Spring 1968, and the "Total Victory" Campaign in Spring 1975 were the three strategic milestones of the war and the three most beautiful springs in the twenty-one years of the Vietnamese people's heroic, fierce, and gloriously triumphant struggle against the United States. They were beacons for national salvation under the leadership of the vanguard party of the working class.

There is another major question about Tet Mau Than that I wish to raise only as a topic of discussion in this essay and it calls for further in-depth research before it can be fully understood. The question is, Why didn't victory come to those who had the overwhelming force in battle, and what was the secret of our success and victory?

At that time, our infantry in all the south was less than 300,000 strong, while the U.S., puppet, and allied forces numbered more than 1.2 million. The ratio was nearly one to five. On top of that, our infantry was supported by just a few lightly armed units, such as engineering, artillery, signal, and transport. Meanwhile, the enemy was backed by a wide variety of armament, had absolute superiority in firepower and mobility and in tanks and other armored vehicles, and wielded total control of the air, sea, inland waterways, land routes, and dense population centers. That is not to mention U.S. forces in the Seventh Fleet and at bases in Japan, as well as contingents from the Philippines and Thailand, which also participated in the war. Nonetheless, we still held the initiative on the battle-field, both strategically and tactically. We also held the initiative in opening attacks while the U.S. puppet forces counterattacked only on the defensive. The attackers were numerically weaker, but their will overwhelmed the morale of the numerically superior defenders. The fact that we won and the enemy lost was due to the genius of our military leadership, the superiority of our revolutionary military art, and the combined result of all our splendidly victorious engagements throughout the battle zone, including encounters in which whole units laid down their lives. Certain people must have seen those battles as defeats and could see only the dark side of death. But in our eyes, these fallen heroes had won. They gave their lives so that life could go on, and it was precisely for that reason that they plunged forward at the enemy with all their hearts and minds. Some units went into battle from which not a single soldier returned. They can be compared with those patriotic soldiers who used their own bodies to seal up the enemy's firing holes so that their comrades could move forward, who charged into the enemy lines, setting off grenades in their hands, who carried bombs and charged at enemy tanks. They were just like those Soviet pilots who flew their planes into the enemy's during their great war of national defense in World War II. The only difference, if there was any, was between individual heroism, on the one hand, and collective heroism, on the other. If we look at things from the perspective of a typical conventional war, in which the balance of forces between the two sides decides victory or defeat, we will be left without an answer to this question. Or else we would think it was all a miracle. The general offensive/general uprising of Tet Mau Than was an outstanding example of a revolutionary war combined with armed insurrection. It followed the rule of offensive-cum-uprising and uprising-cum-offensive. It was brought about by the combination of military and political struggle, a merging of proselytization, armed force, and the forces of the revolutionary masses, as well as the progressive people around the world—including those in the enemy countries. The military units in this type of revolutionary war were in fact a strong organization of the revolutionary masses and were only one of the forces of the revolutionary masses. The party-led revolutionary masses also had other forces at their disposal, such as the village militia, the political struggle units (including the long-haired army and the popular forces for multifaceted struggle in urban areas),[21] the proselytization of enemy troops, and those engaged in espionage and sabotage activities within the enemy's ranks. So, it is incorrect to assess the balance of forces based on only the alignment of military forces. Ours was a just war against foreign aggression and a traitorous puppet regime, against brutality and injustice, for national independence and freedom, and for human dignity. The war was thus in tune with the conscience of our time. Our aggregate forces were therefore stronger than those of the enemy, and the difference could hardly

21. The "long-haired army" refers to the female cadres and supporters of the National Liberation Front who lived in areas controlled by Saigon and who organized demonstrations and other propaganda work against the Saigon regime and the U.S. military. The "popular forces for multifaceted struggle" were the patriotic masses mobilized to wage many forms of resistance (legal, semilegal, illegal) against the enemy and in many fields of activity (political, military, economic, and cultural). The long-haired army was part of the popular forces for multifaceted struggle in the cities and countryside.

be determined by arithmetic calculation. Those who would refute the importance of mass uprisings and insurrections would find themselves thinking according to stereotypes, which is alien to our revolution and to warfare. Lenin, the brilliant leader of the world revolutionary movement, once said,

> There are no miracles in nature or history, but every abrupt turn in history, and this applies to every revolution, presents such a wealth of content, unfolds such unexpected and specific forms of struggle and alignment of forces of the contestants, that to the lay mind there is much that must appear miraculous.[22]

Tet Mau Than was exactly like that.

[Adapted from Tran Van Tra, "Tet," 54–65]

POLITICAL TRANSITIONS AND POLITICS

HO CHI MINH

DECLARATION OF INDEPENDENCE (1945)

Ho Chi Minh is possibly more closely identified with this text than with any other. Written in August 1945 during the tumultuous "revolutionary" uprisings that led to the seizure of power by the Viet Minh Communists, Ho Chi Minh read this declaration on September 2, 1945, when he proclaimed the independence of Vietnam from the Japanese and the French. Ho Chi Minh's public appearance before an immense crowd in Ba Dinh Square in Hanoi was the first he made after years abroad and on the run from French authorities. Previously known as Nguyen Ai Quoc (Nguyen the Patriot), he henceforth publicly adopted the name Ho Chi Minh (Minh [bright/intent or will]), which was the name he used as the first president of the Democratic Republic of Vietnam. While organizing the Viet Minh movement in the mountainous region north of Hanoi, Ho Chi Minh had helped American Office of Strategic Services (OSS; precursor of the CIA) agents searching for downed U.S. pilots. A member of the mission gave him a copy of the Declaration of Independence, together with the French Declaration of the Rights of Man, on which he modeled this text. As with other texts and ideas borrowed from outsiders by Vietnamese rulers, Ho Chi Minh's text reflects an openness to external influences and contacts.

"All men are created equal. They are endowed by their Creator with certain inalienable rights; among these are Life, Liberty, and the Pursuit of Happiness."

---

22. V. I. Lenin, "Letters from Afar, First Letter: The First Stage of the First Revolution," in *Collected Works*, ed. and trans. M. S. Levine, Joel Fineberg, et al. (Moscow: Progress Publishers, 1981), 23:297.

This immortal statement was made in the Declaration of Independence of the United States of America in 1776. In a broader sense, this means that all the people on earth are equal from birth, all the people have a right to live and to be happy and free.

The Declaration of the Rights of Man and of the Citizen made in 1791 during the French Revolution also states: "All men are born free and with equal rights, and must always remain free and have equal rights."

These are undeniable truths.

Nevertheless, for more than eighty years, the French imperialists, abusing the standard of liberty, equality, and fraternity, have violated our fatherland and oppressed our fellow citizens. They have acted contrary to the ideals of humanity and justice.

In the field of politics, they have deprived our people of every democratic liberty.

They have enforced inhuman laws; they have set up three different political regimes in the north, the center, and the south of Vietnam in order to wreck our national unity and prevent our people from being united.

They have built more prisons than schools. They have mercilessly massacred our patriots; they have drowned our uprisings in rivers of blood.

They have fettered public opinion; they have practiced obscurantism against our people.

To weaken our race, they have forced us to use opium and alcohol.

In the field of economics, they have sucked us dry, driven our people to destitution, and devastated our land.

They have robbed us of our rice fields, our mines, our forests, and our natural resources. They have monopolized the issuing of banknotes as well as the export trade.

They have invented numerous unjustifiable taxes and reduced our people, especially our peasantry, to a state of extreme poverty.

They have made it impossible for our national bourgeoisie to prosper; they have mercilessly exploited our workers.

In the autumn of 1940, when the Japanese fascists invaded Indochina to establish new bases in their fight against the Allies, the French imperialists went down on bended knee and handed over our country to them.

Thus, from that date on, our people were subjected to the double yoke of the French and the Japanese. Their sufferings and miseries increased. The result was that from the end of last year to the beginning of this year [1945], from Quang Tri Province to the north of Vietnam, more than 2 million of our fellow citizens died from starvation.

On March 9 of this year, the French troops were disarmed by the Japanese. The French colonialists either fled or surrendered, showing not only that they were incapable of "protecting" us but also that in the span of five years, they had twice sold our country to the Japanese.

On several occasions before March 9, the Viet Minh League urged the French to ally with it against the Japanese. Instead of agreeing to this proposal, the French colonialists intensified their terrorist activities against the Viet Minh. After their defeat and before fleeing, they massacred a great number of our political prisoners detained at Yen Bay and Cao Bang.

Despite all this, our compatriots have always shown a tolerant and humane attitude toward the French. Even after the Japanese action of March 1945, the Viet Minh League helped many Frenchmen cross the frontier, rescued others from Japanese jails, and protected French lives and property.

In fact, from the autumn of 1940, our country had ceased to be a French colony and had become a Japanese possession.

After the Japanese had surrendered to the Allies, our entire people rose to regain our national sovereignty and to found the Democratic Republic of Vietnam.

The truth is that we have wrested our independence from the Japanese and not from the French.

The French have fled, the Japanese have capitulated, the Bao Dai emperor has abdicated. Our people have broken the chains that for nearly a century had fettered them and have won independence for Vietnam. At the same time, our people have overthrown the centuries-old monarchic regime and established a democratic republican regime.

We, the Provisional Government of the new Vietnam, representing all the Vietnamese people, hereby declare that from now on we will break off all relations of a colonial character with France; we will cancel all the treaties signed by France on behalf of Vietnam; and we will abolish all privileges held by the French in our country.

The entire Vietnamese nation is of one mind in our determination to fight all the wicked schemes by the French colonialists to reconquer our country.

We are convinced that the Allies, which at the Tehran and San Francisco conferences[23] upheld the principle of equality among nations, cannot fail to recognize the right of the Vietnamese people to independence.

A people who have courageously opposed French enslavement for more than eighty years, a people who have resolutely sided with the Allies against the fascists during these last years, such a people must be free, such a people must be independent.

For these reasons, we, the Provisional Government of the Democratic Republic of Vietnam, solemnly make this declaration to the world:

Vietnam has the right to enjoy freedom and independence—and in fact has become a free and independent country. The entire Vietnamese nation

---

23. At the Tehran Conference in late 1943, President Franklin Roosevelt, British Prime Minister Winston Churchill, and Soviet Premier Joseph Stalin agreed to form the United Nations. Then, at the San Francisco Conference in 1945, representatives from fifty nations adopted the United Nations Charter.

and people are determined to mobilize all their physical and mental strength, to sacrifice their lives and property in order to safeguard their freedom and independence.

[Adapted from Ho Chi Minh, "Declaration of Independence," 53–56]

NGO DINH DIEM

ON THE PROMULGATION OF THE CONSTITUTION (1956)

Ngo Dinh Diem (1901–1963), president of the Republic of Vietnam from 1956 to 1963, was a proponent of a strong nationalist government marked by Confucian and Catholic elements. Like Pham Quynh,[24] Ngo Dinh Diem advocated the creation of an educated elite imbued with a high sense of discipline and civic responsibility. Ngo Dinh Diem and his brother Ngo Dinh Nhu created the philosophy of Personalism as the regime's official ideology, combining elements of Emmanuel Mounier's Catholic modernism, Neo-Confucianism, and liberal democracy. Relying on the support of northern Catholics who had fled to the south following the 1954 Geneva Agreements, as well as the economic, diplomatic, and military assistance of the United States, Ngo Dinh Diem and Ngo Dinh Nhu inaugurated the Republic of Vietnam in 1955. After his election as the republic's first president, Ngo Dinh Diem expounded the tenets of Personalism in the following address given on October 26, 1956.

My dear compatriots,

On this solemn occasion when in fellowship we worship our heroes with the joy of a great hope, we celebrate the anniversary of the Proclamation of the Republic and the Promulgation of the Constitution. I should like to invite you to look back on the past in order to measure the road covered and thus to prepare the way for the future. For the democracy that we want to build must be a heroic and continuous effort and not a closed and impassive system.

By virtue of the mandate that the nation has vested in me with the referendum of October 23, 1955, I was given the mission to assume the functions of the chief of state and to organize a democratic regime.[25] As soon as the results of the referendum were known, I proclaimed the republic in the declaration of October 26, 1955, and took the title of president. Organized according to the provisions of the ordinance of February 23, 1956, the general elections of March 4, 1956, designated the deputies to the National Constituent Assembly.

After six months of intensive work, the National Assembly put together the constitution that I have just had the high honor to promulgate.

24. See Pham Quynh, "Intellectual and Moral Reform" and "*Kim Van Kieu* and the National Language" (both in chap. 6)

25. By all accounts, this referendum was rigged; Ngo Dinh Diem received 98 percent of the votes.

While other Asian countries needed several years to organize a republican regime, Vietnam, in a much more critical situation, took only one year to lay the foundations for democratic institutions. The pace with which we have organized democracy in our country demonstrates at the same time the determination of our people and the heroic character of our destiny. It also indicates what is left to us to achieve in order to perfect the historical mission that has devolved upon our generation.

The text of the constitution does not create democracy. Democracy develops only when the spirit and the will of the people enjoy favorable conditions. Democracy as a moral regime develops only if the viewpoint of collective interest is constantly expanding in the people and in the government.

In the past century, the political situation in our country has contradicted common sense and has led to a decline in the spirit of justice. Now we must reestablish a spirit of loving the public good, respecting and honoring the nation, and [practicing] the virtue of honesty in official dealings[.] We must forge again a spirit of sacrifice [and] mental discipline, a spirit of responsibility and decency in social relations, [in order to] foster respect for one's fellow man and respect for oneself.

Put differently, we must uphold the traditional principles of *thanh* and *tin*. *Thanh* is sincerity with regard to both wisdom and virtue; it is the acceptance of all our duties with regards to the Creator, with regard to the fatherland, with regard to one's fellow man, and with regard to oneself. *Tin* is the courage and honesty to carry out our duties without shrinking from them, even though we may encounter difficulties. Every person must accept his duties with respect to everyone else and must carry out those duties. [This] will create in our society feelings of trust and confidence, which are the necessary conditions in which democracy can sprout and flourish.

In fact, if the sense of civic duty derives its supreme justification from the ethical principles of the respect for the human person and for the common good, it nonetheless thrives only in a political, administrative, and economic climate that is alive and congenial. In addition to the institutions that allow him to take part in the direction of public affairs and draw the attention of his leaders to his legitimate grievances, the citizen must be able to rely on just laws, on an equitable apportionment of social duties, on a courteous and effective administration, and on the impartiality of the courts.

Even in a healthy environment, the sense of civic responsibility must be nourished further by a careful education in which the molding of character, the sense of personal responsibility and discipline, honesty and devotion to work and to public service must be the constant object, in the school as in the family, in political and social organizations, as at all echelons of the legislative, executive, and judicial branches of government.

My dear compatriots, democracy exists only where a concrete democratic experience exists. In short, democratic life is the putting into practice, by all citizens and all the custodians of public power, the most perfect loyalty and a mutual confidence that is thus total and justified.

It is in this sense that we should endeavor to complete the laws and to apply the constitution.

It is in this sense that we will work effectively for the unification of the country. For it is only with a regime that elevates loyalty and confidence as supreme civic values that we will [be able to] unify our ravaged fatherland.

It is in this sense that a moment ago I took the oath before the Almighty and before the people.

For therein is the import of the human person, the true meaning of progress.

May the Almighty forever protect Vietnam!

[Ngo Dinh Diem, *Major Policy Speeches*, 18–20; Miller, "Grand Designs," 225]

NGUYEN THI DINH

NO OTHER ROAD TO TAKE (1965)

In her memoir, *No Other Road to Take*, Nguyen Thi Dinh (1920–1992) relates the events that led to the resumption of fighting in southern Vietnam and then to the official founding of the National Front for the Liberation of South Vietnam on December 20, 1960. As a former Viet Minh leader in the south, she and other cadres were under orders from the Vietnam Workers' Party in Hanoi to abide by the provisions of the 1954 Geneva Agreements—that is, to not take up arms against the U.S.-supported regime of Ngo Dinh Diem. However, after coming to power in 1954, Ngo Dinh Diem initiated a fierce repression of all Communist forces left in the south. By 1958, most of these cadres had been killed, with the rest forced into hiding. In 1959, the party changed its policy, permitting armed activities in combination with political struggle. In the following excerpt, Nguyen Thi Dinh describes leaving a regional meeting that signaled this change. When she returned home to contact her local provincial comrades to launch the first uprising against the Dinh Thuy post in Ben Tre Province, they complained about the lack of arms and worried that the capture of one of their comrades would expose their plans. The insurrection against the Ngo Dinh Diem regime, however, proved to be a success, in effect helping launch the new revolution in the south. Organized "uprisings" in Ben Tre Province entailed new forms of political action: political demonstrations, combined political-military operations, and face-to-face struggles by masses of women ("the long-haired army") who marched on Ngo Dinh Diem's military posts to persuade his troops not to open fire on their fellow compatriots. In 1965, Nguyen Thi Dinh was named deputy commander of the Peoples' Liberation Armed Forces (the armed forces of the National Liberation Front), a position she held until 1975 when Saigon fell to the Communists.

January 17, 1960 [first day of the insurrection], was a day full of hope and worry for the patriotic people in Ben Tre Province. I waited for the attack on the canton militia unit, composed of two squads stationed in Dinh Thuy village. The comrades had decided to attack while the militiamen were sleeping and off guard. At the appointed time, a hard-core youth who knew the militia commander entered in a panic looking for him in regard to an urgent matter. This fellow was still awake while his troops were sound asleep. Our forces, disguised as ordinary merchants, lay in ambush around the communal house. Being suspicious by nature, the commander pulled out his Sten pistol and came to the door of the communal house. His arms akimbo, he tilted his bearded chin and asked haughtily:

—What's the matter?

Our comrade obsequiously bent down to whisper in his ear, as though to transmit something important, then suddenly raised his arm and hit him hard on the nape of the neck. He collapsed right away. Our forces poured in and called on the troops to surrender. A number of them bolted and fled in disorder, while the rest surrendered. We captured enough weapons to equip about a squad of men. The Dinh Thuy post was only about one kilometer [almost two-thirds of a mile] from here. Hai Thu was afraid that the soldiers belonging to the unit of the canton militia commander would go to warn the post, which would then take precautions, so he ordered the immediate capture of the post at 3:00 P.M. Some of the soldiers in this post were sympathizers, and before the news [of the attack on the militia unit] reached the post, our infiltrators rose up and burned it down. The flames billowed high in the sky. The brothers brought back about ten more rifles.

We let a number of soldiers flee to Mo Cay district town to report that Viet Cong troops had come to take the Dinh Thuy post and were on their way to Mo Cay in large numbers. As we had suspected, the enemy in Mo Cay just fired a few artillery rounds and stayed put in their post, not daring to send out reinforcements. Our first attack was successful, and we seized a large number of weapons. We were greatly encouraged and were even more determined to smash the viselike grip of the enemy. I talked with comrade Hai Thuy about sending two rifles each to Thanh Phu and Minh Tan districts to use as "capital" and to relay the news of victory in Mo Cay to the comrades so they could follow suit. The rest of the weapons were handed over to Hai Thuy and Ba Dao to replace the wooden rifles. . . .[26]

The forces encircling the posts had been ordered to burn down any posts they captured. The people immediately tore up the flags and burned the plaques bearing their house numbers and their family registers.[27] On the roads, the villagers cut down trees to erect barriers and block the movement of the enemy. On both banks of the river where communication trenches and barbed wire crisscrossed in a tangled maze, boats stopped to listen to our propaganda. All the

---

26. Because they lacked arms, the insurgents made dummy rifles out of wood.

27. These were administrative devices used by the government of Ngo Dinh Diem to ensure better control of the population.

posts were surrounded by the people who made appeals to the soldiers through bullhorns. Once in a while, "a heavy gun" exploded.[28] It was a night of terrifying thunder and lightning striking the enemy on the heads. Attacked by surprise, they were scared out of their wits and stayed put in the posts. Occasionally, explosive charges [could be heard], sounding like mortars or grenade launchers. The people who had the most difficult task that night were the units in charge of eliminating tyrannical local officials and agents—the core of the machinery of control in the hamlets and villages. Each member had to disguise himself with a mask and change his clothing in order to prevent the enemy from recognizing him. Only a few comrades appeared publicly to mobilize the people and act as their representatives to condemn this group [for example, the officials and agents]. At 5:00 A.M., we sent for the comrade in charge of eliminating tyrants in the closest village to review the results. Carrying a machete, he came to report:

—Everything's been done. All the local officials and agents dropped their customary arrogance and became humble. When we rushed in and shouted to them, only one reactionary fled; the rest surrendered right away. They all were shaking and trembling.

As the situation evolved in our favor, the leadership of the committee of the concerted uprising immediately that night drafted a military order, which was then posted everywhere in the areas under the temporary control of the enemy to heighten the prestige of the revolution. The contents of the military order included the following:

—All soldiers, no matter how serious their crimes were, if they repent and rejoin the ranks of the people with their weapons, will be forgiven.

—Village and hamlet officials, heads of interfamily groups, security policemen, and informers who resign and surrender to the people will be forgiven by the people.

—Landlords who relied on the power of the enemy to seize the land of the peasants and increase their rents should return to the peasants what they took. . . . During the night of January 18 and the early morning of January 19[, 1960], the villages held a rally to display the strength and ardor of the people. The villagers felt very satisfied, especially when the policemen, tyrants, officials, spies, and landlords with blood debts were led out to be executed in front of the people. Every one of them was guilty of countless crimes and deserved the death sentence. In accordance with the lenient policy of the revolution, however, only the gang leaders—the most cruel and treacherous of them all—were executed. The others, those who had blood debts but confessed their crimes and acknowledged their guilt, were given only a suspended death sentence. They were ordered to move to the district and province towns to live in repentance, and if any of them committed new crimes, they would be executed.

---

28. The "heavy gun" was actually sections of bamboo filled with acetylene.

That whole week, the enemy remained in their positions. They trembled before the power and prestige of the revolution. Because we had eliminated their machinery of control in the villages—their eyes and arms—they had no way of knowing what the real situation was. Two days after the Dinh Thuy and Binh Khanh posts fell, the enemy abandoned Phuoc Hiep post and fled. These three villages were completely liberated. On January 19, Mo Cay District dispatched a column of troops to Dinh Thuy post to check the situation. Forewarned, comrade Hai Thuy organized a "trick" ambush—complete with crisscrossing communication trenches, foxholes, mortars, and submachine gun and machine gun emplacements—and positioned a cell to fire on the landing crafts. When the clash began, the moment we opened fire the soldiers fled toward Mo Cay and then sent reconnaissance agents back to check. Seeing the grandiose defense network, they became frightened and reported to their superiors:

—It's true that large units are involved. It's true that liberation forces from the north [North Vietnam] have arrived!

Emboldened, the villagers stepped up their efforts to eliminate village officials and tyrants, surrounded the posts, called on the soldiers to surrender, and seized weapons. In some places, whenever the soldiers manning the posts wanted to go to the latrine or fetch fresh water, they had to ask permission from the guerrillas. Otherwise if they took the liberty of doing so without asking, they would be shot at by the guerrillas—this was the same tactic of sniping that had been employed at Dien Bien Phu. A week after the concerted uprising began, we reviewed the results and found that we had captured about ten posts and that the apparatus of control that the enemy had spent six years consolidating had either been shaken to the foundations or had disintegrated. The enemy, however, remained completely ignorant of our strength, as though they were deaf and blind. . . .

As a result of these actions, the guerrillas captured about one hundred weapons and resolved to continue more operations to seize weapons. The first platoon of liberation fighters was formed in Mo Cay District. The enemy sent in thirteen thousand troops from Saigon, Tra Vinh, and Ben Tre province towns, focusing their attack on Phuoc Hiep, Binh Khanh, and Dinh Thuy villages starting February 24. But Diem's government apparatus in Ben Tre Province had been broken.

The "sky horse" rifle appeared for the first time in this battle. This was an invention by a guerrilla who created it based on the principle of explosives used in producing land mines. The barrel of the rifle consisted of a long steel pipe. The rifle had legs like a mortar and was detonated when a wire was pulled, as in land mines. The charge consisted of explosives mixed with steel pellets and glass shards dipped in urine and snake poison. The firing range was ten meters [almost thirty-three feet], and anyone who was hit—even if it was just a scratch on the skin—would die right away. The masses spread the rumor that this was a new weapon, and whenever they heard the "sky horse" mentioned, the enemy soldiers fled in chaos.

While the enemy was concentrating their forces to surround us, the leadership committee had each area spread the news that we were about to attack Mo Cay district town and Ben Tre province town. At the same time, we had the people prepare sampans and get ready to supply rice to large units. As expected, the enemy heard the news the next day. They gave up the operation and withdrew their forces in a panic to defend these towns. In this operation, seeing that our losses had been insignificant while the enemy had lost more than one hundred men, the people felt very optimistic. The women used this situation to work on the soldiers, and a large number of them deserted. Small children picked up and delivered to us thousands of cartridges belonging to the enemy. But the reactionary enemy left behind a force to occupy Phuoc Hiep in the hope of intimidating the people and gradually encroaching on our territory and then taking it back. Most of these troops were Catholics, and they were extremely brutal and reactionary. Within ten days, they had arrested twenty youths, executed them, and buried them around the post. They conscripted the villagers to do forced labor, building the road from Phuoc Hiep to Binh Khanh, and brutally terrorized the people.

The villagers' excitement cooled noticeably. The comrades in the village pleaded with us to send armed units to destroy the post. We also wanted badly to destroy this gang and relieve our anger, but our armed forces still were weak. So we discussed ways to stop the enemy's killing while still maintaining the initiative and the legal status of the masses. Everyone unanimously agreed that we should immediately organize a large group of women who would push their way into Mo Cay district town to denounce the crimes of the soldiers in Phuoc Hiep.

The first time, more than five thousand women—including old women, young girls, and children—from the villages of Phuoc Hiep, Binh Khanh, Dinh Thuy, Da Phuoc Hoi, An Dinh, and Thanh Thoi, formed a huge force, wearing mourning bands and ragged clothes and carrying their children, and surged into Mo Cay district town. They demanded an end to the terrorism and compensation for the deaths caused by the soldiers, and punishment of the brutes in Phuoc Hiep village. The district chief was scared out of his mind and shouted to the soldiers to shut the gates tightly and not to allow anyone to enter. The people stayed in front of the district headquarters, defecating and urinating on the spot, and refused to go home. Among the women was an eighteen-year-old girl who had been blind since childhood but was very enthusiastic about struggling against the enemy. A policeman teased her:

—This blind girl can't see anything, and what does she feel she can accomplish by joining the struggle?

She retorted right away:

—I'm blind, but I know enough to follow the path of light, and this is much better than you people who can see but are following a blind road.

The policeman did not know what to say. The women praised her:

—She's blind but she's enlightened.

The girl also was a good singer. During the struggle she sang guerrilla songs, which left the soldiers reflective and less arrogant. The tug-of-war lasted for five days and five nights, and each day the group was reinforced with more women coming to lend a hand, and the struggle became more inflamed. In the end, the district chief had to open the gate and come out to accept the demands of the people, agreeing to withdraw all the soldiers from Phuoc Hiep village. At the height of the "concerted uprising" in Ben Tre Province, the successful struggle of the women in Mo Cay District on March 15, 1960, initiated a new form of struggle by the masses that proved to be very effective. The Americans and Ngo Dinh Diem were very afraid of this powerful force [constituted by the women] and gave it a special name: the long-haired troops. . . .

At the beginning of April 1960, we held a meeting for a preliminary review of the success of the concerted uprising in the districts of Minh island and to learn from it for the uprising scheduled to take place all over Ben Tre Province. Our experiences were very helpful, but our understanding was minimal, so we failed to learn from the best experiences of the masses. Later, higher officials reviewed our experiences and[, from them,] devised the policy of attacking the enemy on "two legs" and with "three prongs."[29] I was very pleased with this policy and proceeded to apply it to mobilize the movement and spread it to every area.

During the conference, the collective [leadership] gave me a key role in the leadership committee of Ben Tre Province. I was very encouraged by the new responsibility but was worried that my limited capacity would prevent me from completing my mission. At first, I declined the responsibility, but the collective [leadership] passed a resolution [that] forced me to go along. The comrades told me:

—The women's movement is very strong now, and they have the capacity to attack the enemy on all three fronts. You deserve to represent them. Don't be timid in your work; the collective [leadership] will help you and things will go smoothly.

In the ensuing phase of the "concerted uprising," which erupted in the few remaining districts, I was assigned the task of keeping close track of and guiding Giong Trom District, the focal point of the province. We held an all-night meeting, and as morning dawned, I immediately had to leave to attend a meeting of district and village cadres. The key leaders of Giong Trom District, such as comrades Be and Khac, were very eager to surpass Mo Cay District. But on this occasion, Giong Trom District did not enjoy the element of surprise. Although the enemy had taken precautionary measures, we attacked using a trick and were better at it than before. The task of proselytizing enemy soldiers proceeded apace. The political struggles in Giong Trom District taught us a new lesson: to

---

29. The "two legs" were military action and political action. The "three prongs" were *chinh tri* (political action), *quan su* (military action), and *binh van* (proselytization of enemy soldiers).

achieve results, women should attack the enemy with pointed arguments while the liberation troops attacked them with weapons. The force taking part in the [political] struggle in Giong Trom District was twice as large as the one participating in the earlier struggle in Mo Cay District. For the first time, we hoisted a vast array of banners and slogans, including those demanding the resignation of Ngo Dinh Diem and the dissolution of the puppet "National Assembly."

Just a few days after the uprising started, six villages in Giong Trom District were liberated, and one hundred weapons were seized. In each village, from one hundred to three hundred people joined the group taking part in the face-to-face political struggle against the enemy. Within a short time, the wave of "concerted uprisings" spread from Minh island to Bao island and broke out all over Ben Tre Province. Vigorous movements developed in each and every province in the south. The majority of villages passed into the hands of the masses, who became masters [of the countryside].

The people of Ben Tre Province who had endured untold miseries during the past six years could now laugh, sing, and live. A new spirit was burning all over the countryside. The political forces held animated discussions about the struggle. Carpenters and blacksmiths raced to produce knives and machetes to kill the enemy. The workshops improved the sky horse rifles, making them more lethal, and produced a batch of new weapons called *mut nhet* [rudimentary muzzle-loaded rifles]. At this time, the armed forces of the province were more than one company in strength, and each district had from one to two squads. Each village had from one to three rifles, but the majority of these were French rifles. Young girls stayed up many nights to sew "main force" green uniforms for the troops. An information office was set up in each hamlet in Giong Trom, Mo Cay, and Chau Thanh districts. On each side of the road, slogans were drawn on tree trunks and caught everyone's eyes. On some days, people from the province towns came by the hundreds to visit the liberated areas.

After the gigantic political force of fifteen thousand arrived at Ben Tre province town, Ben Tre Province's Committee of the National Front for the Liberation of South Vietnam was officially presented to the people. The creation of the Front was of vital significance, for its aim was to consolidate the people's right to be masters of the countryside. While the high point of the concerted uprising was like a tidal wave sweeping away everything in its path, the people became more insistent in their demand that the revolution set up an official organization to represent the strength, unity, and fighting force of the people, which would continue to lead them forward toward new successes in the resistance to save the country and oppose the American imperialist invaders and their henchmen—Ngo Dinh Diem and the gang of traitors. This was why the "National Front for the Liberation of South Vietnam"—the sole organization leading the resistance by the entire population of the South—was created in a timely manner and presented to the people on December 20, 1960.

Aware of this spirit, we made urgent preparations in order to present Ben Tre Province's Liberation Front Committee to the people on December 26, 1960, that is, six days after the birth of the National Front for the Liberation of South Vietnam. We decided to make it a big occasion by holding a conference that would be attended by representatives of every level of the population in order to establish a provincial Liberation Front Committee and by organizing a ceremony for about ten thousand people representing the countryside, the urban areas, all the religious groups, and the families of soldiers. We selected My Chanh, less than five kilometers [a little more than three miles] from Ba Tri district town, as the site for the presentation ceremony. The population here was large, and the village was located in a favorable strategic terrain and had a big market, the Ben Bao market.

At dusk on December 26, the rally began. We had electric lights and microphones that had been sent by workers in the province town as their contribution to the rally. Seeing the flag raised, which brightened up a whole section of the sky, we all felt very moved. So much blood shed by the comrades and people had dyed this glorious and eternal flag.

The Liberation Front Committee was made up of fifteen people who represented every social stratum, religious group, and political party. The committee solemnly appeared in front of the people, and each member gave a speech. Mr. Ngoi, the representative of the Cao Dai Tien Thien sect; Mr. Ho Hao Nghia, representing university and high school students; Mr. Ngoi, representing the national bourgeoisie; Mrs. Muoi Quoi, representing the women; and brother Ba, representing the peasants all condemned the crimes of the enemy, expressed their gratitude to and their confidence in the revolution, and pledged to unite and fight to the end to overthrow the Americans and Diem.

I had the honor of representing the People's Revolutionary Party[30] and the Front, and on their behalf I made promises and pledges and called on the people to push the fight forward. . . .

I looked at the large popular force and was overjoyed. The armed units had expanded rapidly. Ben Tre Province now had close to a battalion of adequately armed troops. This was a real battalion, not a "fake" one. As for the strong and large "long-haired" force, I did not even know how many battalions of them there were. From now on, on the road of resisting the Americans and their lackeys, our people would stand firm on the two powerful legs of military and political strength to fight and achieve victory. There was no other road to take.

In the face of this enormous and imposing force of the people, I felt very small, but I was full of self-confidence, like a small tree standing in a vast and ancient forest. In struggling against the enemy, I had come to understand that

---

30. The People's Revolutionary Party was the southern branch of the Vietnam Workers' Party.

we had to have the strength of the whole forest in order to be able to withstand the force of the strong winds and storms. As I thought about the protection and support of the people, about the enormous efforts that the revolution had expended in educating and nurturing me, about the countless comrades and beloved people—some of whom I had mentioned but all of whose names I could never enumerate—I felt more closely bound, more so than ever before, to the road I had taken and had pledged to follow until my last days. This was the road for which I would sacrifice everything for the future of the revolution and for the interests of the masses. For me there was no other road to take.

[Adapted from Nguyen Thi Dinh, *No Other Road to Take*, 96–101, 103–7]

TRUONG CHINH

COMPLETING NATIONAL REUNIFICATION (1975)

As one of the three most senior party leaders and a former secretary-general of the Communist Party, Truong Chinh (1907–1988) presented the political report to the Conference on National Reunification, which was held in Saigon (Ho Chi Minh City) on November 14, 1975. The purpose of the conference was to prepare for the political reunification of the north and the south following the collapse of the Republic of Vietnam on April 30, 1975, and the military takeover of the south by Communist forces. By 1976, Hanoi had decided to rapidly reunify the two halves of Vietnam politically and administratively in order to centralize control of the south, although many southern Communists preferred a slower approach. Truong Chinh's plans for imposing socialist construction on the south, however, proved to be a failure and resulted in an economic crisis, which eventually led to the adoption of market economic reforms in the 1980s.

The victorious spring drive of generalized offensives and uprisings of our people and army as a whole has ushered in a new period in which the strategic task of our revolution is national reunification and the transformation of our country, rapidly, vigorously, and steadily, into socialism.

After South Vietnam's liberation and the recovery of full national independence, one of the most urgent requirements of our people is to complete national reunification. Over the past forty-five years, our people have never ceased fighting with determination and have foiled all divisive maneuvers and tricks of the aggressive colonialists and their henchmen. During the first days of the resistance, when the French colonialists schemed to sever Nam Bo [the south] from Vietnam, the party led our people to promptly expose the attempt and resolutely to resist it. When the French tried to take over the highlands and set up the so-called Tay Ky [Western Region] state there, the party immediately denounced the move. It was then that President Ho Chi Minh, the great leader of the working class and the nation, trenchantly stated: "Our compatriots in Nam Bo are citizens of Vietnam. Rivers may dry up, mountains may erode, but this truth will never change." In 1960, at the party's Third National Congress, President Ho Chi Minh affirmed: "Our nation is one, our country is one. Our people will certainly overcome all difficulties and achieve our aim: the country reunified, north and south brought together again." This idea, feeling, and determination of 45 million Vietnamese have cemented them into one monolithic bloc resolved to frustrate all the dark plots of the enemy.

As in the past, however, during the confrontation with the French aggressors and their flunkies, when not all the country was yet liberated, we upheld the banner of national reunification to assemble the entire people from all parts of the country to rally all their forces to struggle for national independence and for people's democracy. Today, with the north having been liberated many years ago and having embarked on socialist construction, the cause of national reunification similarly rests on national independence and socialism, which is a higher basis representing a new step forward in that very cause.

Why must national reunification be based on independence?

Because our people, who were strongly against "reunification" under French colonial rule and that of their feudal agents, were also firmly opposed to "reunification" under the neocolonialist regime of U.S. imperialism and the pro-U.S. comprador capitalists, landlords, and feudalists. To us, real reunification can be achieved only with real independence, and only when complete independence is realized can full national reunification be achieved.

Why must national reunification be based on socialism?

Because socialism means freedom and happiness for the people. The socialist order is one that knows no exploitation of man by man: from each according to his ability, to each according to his work. A socialist society is a society with a prosperous economy; a developed culture, science, and technology; a society in which national defense is consolidated; the people's right to mastership is assured; [and] where there is equality among nationalities and between men and women, and freedom of [religious] belief. It meets the aspirations and supreme interests of the working people, both manual workers and intellectuals, and of all progressive forces. It represents the inevitable trend of human society.

But establishing socialism is not an easy task. It requires industriousness and creativity, a high level of technical ability, discipline and productivity, persistence, [and] a readiness to cope with all difficulties and to endure all hardships from the outset, for the sake of future prosperity and happiness. This attitude is all the more necessary because our country is still poor and backward and has been badly devastated by war.

Socialist revolution includes socialist transformation and socialist construction. The central task of socialist construction is socialist industrialization. These tasks are very new and complicated for us. But if we try hard to learn while we work and are resolved to overcome all difficulties and persist in our efforts, our success is certain.

We are resolved to mobilize our power and wealth and the talents of our people to build a socialist Vietnam with a modern industry, a modern agriculture, a strong national defense, advanced culture and science, and a civilized and happy life.

At present, the north is becoming socialist. Only when both north and south have embarked on the road to socialism can our national reunification have a practical and solid foundation. Naturally, to carry out the socialist revolution successfully and build socialism in the south, we must take its specific situation into consideration.

The basis on which to achieve national reunification is a matter of principle. Our people fought the imperialist aggressors and their lackeys, winning back independence and unity in order to build a new Vietnam and ensure for all Vietnamese a civilized and comfortable life. Independence and national reunification are indispensable [conditions]. But once independence and national reunification have been achieved, this problem emerges: what road will our country follow so that our people can experience real freedom and happiness and our country can enjoy real prosperity, wealth, and strength? These are the fond aspirations of our people and also firm guarantees to safeguard and consolidate our independence and national unity.

The party did not wait until half or all our country was liberated to consider the problem of shaping the nation's future. Right at the beginning when our country was founded, we defined in final and unequivocal terms the ultimate goal of our revolution. If we follow the right path to our goal, the revolution will be successful. This vital issue is directly related to the destiny and future of our country and our people, to every social sector and every family among us, both today and for future generations in the thousands of years to come.

Under the current historical conditions, after having regained independence, our country is at a crossroads: we can take either the path of transition to socialism or the path of capitalist development. The second path will likely be soaked with the blood and tears of millions of toiling people because it is the path of ruthless oppression and exploitation and is characterized by the most abominable social evils such as can seen every day in the United States or in any other capitalist country, including southern Vietnam in the past. Most assuredly, we will not follow this dark and painful path. The bright path is none other than the road to socialism, the only road that will lead our land to prosperity and our entire people to happiness while securing national independence and unity forever. Moreover, only socialism can eliminate all forms of oppression and exploitation and all the sources of class difference. Only socialism can bring about perfect unity in our country's political, economic, cultural, and social life and strengthen our people's political and moral unity.

From another perspective, southern Vietnam has completed its people's national and democratic revolution. At present, it is completely liberated; should the south continue as such for a period of time before embarking on the path of socialist revolution and socialist construction? I think not. The great spring victory [of 1975] has put a victorious end to this phase of the people's national and democratic revolution in southern Vietnam and opened up the way for the south to enter a new phase of revolution with a new strategic task, that of socialist revolution.

Now that the U.S. neocolonialist regime has collapsed, southern Vietnam must not halt its journey but must immediately embark on the road to socialist revolution; more concretely, it must begin a step-by-step socialist transformation of its national economy and build the first foundations of socialism. At the same time, the south must complete the remaining tasks of the people's national democratic revolution: putting in place the people's revolutionary administration and helping the population exercise their right to determine their own destiny, repressing reactionary forces and helping former members of the puppet administration and army to undergo reeducation to become useful members of society, abolishing the feudal system of landownership, and putting into practice the "land to the tiller" slogan wherever the land problem still exists in society.

This is the spirit and substance of the Leninist theory of "permanent revolution."[31] Applying this theory to the conditions of Vietnam, the Vietnam Workers' Party assumes that the Vietnamese working class and people must wage two revolutions at the same time: the people's national democratic revolution and the socialist revolution. From the people's national democratic revolution, they must go directly to socialist revolution, bypassing the stage of capitalist development.

To sum up, now that the resistance against U.S. aggression and for national salvation has won total victory and our country has recovered independence, Vietnam has been effectively reunited. But the reunification remains incomplete, and our present task is to finish it. Following our total triumph over U.S. aggression, the two zones [the north and the south] will change their two strategic tasks—from socialist revolution and socialist construction in the north and the people's national democratic revolution in the south—to a common strategic task: socialist revolution and socialist construction.

[Adapted from Truong Chinh, "Political Report to the Conference on National Reunification," 799–805]

---

31. According to the theory of "permanent revolution," the bourgeois democratic revolution would lead directly to the socialist revolution.

TRAN DO

LETTER TO THE COMMUNIST PARTY URGING
DEMOCRATIC REFORM (1998)

General Tran Do (1924–2002) fought at the battle of Dien Bien Phu and was the second-highest-ranking commander of Communist forces in southern Vietnam during the American war. He also assumed important cultural and ideological posts in the 1980s, including director of the Central Committee's Department of Culture and the Arts. With the advent of Doi Moi (Renovation), Tran Do advocated a greater role for intellectuals and greater openness in the party. Although he believed that the party should continue its leading role, he stated that it should share power and become more accountable, abandoning what he called the "unity of the party and the government," or one-party rule. Tran Do sent this letter, written in early 1998, to the Communist Party, the prime minister's office, and the National Assembly to argue his case. Tran Do's petition contains echoes of earlier court memorials identifying problems and recommending reforms.[32] In his letter, Tran Do argues forcefully for democratizing the Communist Party and implementing democratic reforms in the government and throughout Vietnamese society. In the addendum to his letter, Tran Do proposes creating a free press to monitor the party and government and holding democratic elections by letting anyone stand for election, with nominations to be screened by both party and nonparty organizations. In the preface, he says, "These are drops of blood wrung out of the heart of a person, who, for the last several decades, has had a great desire to express his thoughts and to discuss [matters pertaining to] the nation and the party." Tran Do's views, however, put him at odds with the party leadership and led to his expulsion in 1999.

The State of the Nation and the Role of the Communist Party

FACING THE TRUTH ONCE AGAIN

Not long ago, the mass media described the state of the nation as "on the road to great victories," as "having already climbed out of the social and economic crisis," as "blossoming," "encouraging," "very exciting," "promising," and so on, and in the midst of "transformation to a new phase of development in the process of modernization and industrialization." But in recent days, one also heard, in the same media, that the economic expansion has "slowed down," that life in many areas, especially in the countryside, has faced many difficulties, that social evils, notably corruption, are increasing, and so on. The unrest in Thai Binh and

---

32. See, for example, Bui Si Tiem, "Ten Items for Reform"; Nguyen Cu Trinh, "Memorial Describing the Economic Crisis in the Nguyen Realm"; and Nguyen Thiep, "Memorial Regarding the Economic Crisis in Nghe An" (all in chap. 4).

other places has been mentioned very cautiously but enough for us to realize the country is facing new disturbances. The few newspapers that wanted to report the real situation were criticized or banned.

The truth is that these articles told only a small part of what has been happening. Concern in public opinion is emerging: What is going on? Is the country advancing or coming to a halt? Is the good side or the bad side in control?

There is definitely a problem, a fundamental problem. But how do we evaluate the situation correctly? History has taught us many lessons in this respect. Correct evaluation leads to a correct course of action; conversely, incorrect evaluation leads to inevitable blunders. Only by following this principle can we correctly analyze the current state of the nation.

What is the current state of the nation? In truth, after ten years of reform, there have been a number of positive changes and achievements in the country. . . . In the economic realm alone, who would not be happy to hear that owing to our "open door" policy, foreign investors and international financial organizations have poured billions of dollars into our country to help us build our infrastructure, [to form] joint ventures, and so on. Our country has risen from a food-importing country to one exporting 2 million to 3 million tons of rice per year. Living conditions have generally improved for a considerable portion of the population, and so on.

Along with these achievements, however, we need to acknowledge that we should have analyzed the negative effects of reform from the beginning, that is, both the actual and potential contradictions and the major threats to our stability and development. These are now becoming critical problems for the nation.

A few simple questions will suffice to depict the situation:

Why does "the state-owned economic sector taking the leading role" continue to be emphasized, even though this is the least effective sector and the worst "den" of corruption?

Why are we unable to mobilize domestic capital (projected to equal funds borrowed from outside countries) to raise the total GDP to $40 billion to $50 billion, so that the per capita GDP will reach $400 by the year 2000?

What has caused foreign investors to become more hesitant to invest in our country, and some foreign firms are even withdrawing their capital?

Why are we unable to control corruption effectively, but instead, it continues to grow freely, aggressively, and defiantly today?

Why are the people, despite better living conditions, not concerned about and interested in contributing their efforts and wealth to building the country in line with the party's constant appeals? In some areas, why do people even oppose the party's functions and stand up and fight (because they have no other option) to defend their interests?

Why are the reform and open-door policies leading to such deep social divisions and to such bold and illegal get-rich schemes on the part of a small group composed mainly of officeholding cadres and party members? We need to fully evaluate the significance of the ongoing unrest in Thai Binh. This may be the first time that tens of thousands of peasants have joined in the struggle against the "new village bullies" with such scope and intensity. From my personal experience, the peasants of Thai Binh have long been a solid social base for the party in the revolutionary struggle, the anticolonial resistance, and the buildup of the nation. For self-protection, these very peasants are now turning their backs on local party functions (and the party itself). I could never have imagined such an eventuality. I am afraid that the unrest in Thai Binh is an early warning sign of a much more dangerous condition facing the party if it refuses to learn the proper (and painful) lessons from this situation.

With a giant machinery to run the country, why are the campaigns against corruption, smuggling, and social evils almost totally ineffective? . . .

What are the causes [of the present crisis]?

The author claims that the country is drifting aimlessly, and social vices such as drug trafficking and corruption are increasing, as is the gap between the rich and the poor. Honest and constructive debates about this situation need to be aired openly in the press, without any restrictions.

I do not claim to have a complete answer to this matter, but would like to offer a number of ideas:

1. Our country's goals are "economic development, a prosperous people and strong nation, a just and civilized society" while we continue to emphasize "our determination to follow the socialist path." Therein lies an irreconcilable contradiction. In both theory and practice, the market economy—which we must adopt in order to develop the economy—cannot coexist with the socialist path. Eventually, one or the other must be eliminated; otherwise, economic chaos will result, in which neither is recognizable.

We have to choose [between the socialist path and the free-market economy] in order to provide the necessary conditions to develop the economy (although this is a tough choice for socialist-oriented people). This must be a real choice and not the ambiguous "market economy with a socialist path." One or the other, but not both. Are we going to choose the economic development of the country or the socialist path? The choice between the nation's economic development and the socialist direction is not that difficult if *one accepts that the highest priority is the country's interests, not the party's interests.* In other words, economic development requires that the party abandon its ideology, which it has imposed on the entire society. So long as we prolong the current mixture of the two, the country will not be able to develop normally. All we will have is chaos, which creates loopholes for some people to take advantage of, but does not benefit the vast majority of the people.

2. Economic development, especially in today's changing environment, requires an appropriate strategy supported by the majority of the population. So far, we have not come up with such a strategy. Although the party has announced the strategy of "economic development, industrialization, and modernization," this is vague, not a concrete and feasible plan to benefit the whole population. . . .

Today, we almost always commit to just one measure for each problem, and that measure is called supreme just because it is the party's measure. Nobody is allowed to propose another. Nobody is allowed to debate the announced measure freely. I am speaking of the general strategy, not strategies for specific regions or areas. I believe our people, particularly our corps of intellectuals inside and outside the country, have many good ideas. If they are allowed to express those ideas, compare and debate them freely, they can break the current mental blockage and find an appropriate way out for the country. In other words, restrictions on intellectuals, the yoke of supremacy over people's minds, and the labeling of opinions other than the official one as "rebellion" are among *the most important causes of the current stalemate of the national development strategy.*

3. In regard to [the right to hold] power, in all official documents, national political power is expressed as a function "of the people, by the people, and for the people," with the additional notion that "the people know, the people discuss, the people do, and the people inspect." But in reality there is no such thing. The party decides everything—or rather, party members in top positions do. . . . The party hierarchy, from the top down, has absolute authority and is under no legal jurisdiction. As a result, we have "party rule" in a totalitarian regime. The constitution stipulates the party's exclusive leadership but does not mention the party's responsibility to the people. If the party acts correctly, the people will benefit; if it errs, the people will suffer. The record of the last several decades shows that the party has not always been right. This is because the party *holds absolute power without any institution or group to monitor its behavior.* This is the source of abuses of power and corruption, which internal campaigns cannot stop. . . .

In my opinion, *the current economic reform demands vigorous political reform.* Without political reform, economic reform will result in an impasse, and the country will retain an obsolete, party-ruled regime. The party's leadership and prestige will weaken and be critically compromised. The concentration of power in the hands of the party's leading organs is causing the party to deteriorate and party members to become a new ruling class in society, working for their own interests and against the people's interests. We can assert that many party members who hold power have become "new capitalists," guarding their authority, using power to accumulate private wealth, and causing ever more severe social tensions (such as in the situation in Thai Binh Province).

4. The last but most important factor is the party itself. In our society and regime, the party leads, directs, and decides all matters. Every success or failure, therefore, can be attributed to the party. Indeed, many difficulties in developing

the economy and society originate from outside (the world, the region) and from our country's historical and cultural situation. By virtue of its leadership position, the party is responsible for analyzing the situation and coming up with an appropriate position. In many cases, the party has not been able to do that. Unable to master developments, the party has simply followed the situation passively.

Currently, the following points pertain to "the leading role of the party."

The author suggests that many other schools of thought can be applied to the specific conditions of the country besides Marxism-Leninism. The party's monopoly of power completely stifles any democratic tendencies. Many party bosses have become an obstacle to the nation's advancement in all spheres, including the economic sphere.

What is to be done?

What needs to be done to lead the country out of the current crisis so we can continue to develop steadily and rapidly? How can we achieve both an open society in which people can participate in national development while enhancing the leadership of the party? More precisely, how should the party change its leadership to successfully carry out social development and ensure people's acceptance of its role?

The answers to these questions are not simple and seem unknown even to leaders at the highest level. It is, therefore, a matter of life and death to *mobilize the intellectual power of the entire people.*

Various party documents refer to *the need to reform the party's method of leadership.* I think this reform should include the abandonment of the party's absolute and total control. The party should retain only the role of *political leadership and let the National Assembly, the government, and the Fatherland Front have their own responsibilities and independent authority.*

Everyone knows that the people's collective intellectual power can be developed only in a democratic regime. Without such a regime, we cannot keep intellectual power alive, much less develop it. I emphasize the words *democratic regime*, in which democratic rights are fully institutionalized on the basis of law and everyone upholds them. All the talk about people's "democratic awareness" and "democratic ownership" is meaningless without a solid democratic regime.

I would like to stress that *to escape the current grave condition and to ensure a bright future for the country, the most fundamental, critical, and deciding factor is true democracy, a real democratic process to give people real power to carry out their privileges and responsibilities.*

To do that, first we must change our perception of democracy, at least in the following ways:

1. In defining democracy, we should not mechanically divide the concept into "capitalist democracy" and "proletarian democracy" and insist that these two

are mutually incompatible. We should acknowledge that the developed countries, which we customarily call the "Western capitalist" countries, have had much success in building and refining their democracies, despite many shortcomings. We should learn from them. Of course, we will not imitate everything they do; but not everything they do is reactionary, decadent, and deceitful, either. Democracy in these countries was not guaranteed, having been the fruit of the struggle of all levels of the population for several centuries. We have never implemented the rights to freedom and democracy, human rights, a law-abiding government, and so forth and do not even know how to go about doing so. We need [to learn] and accept that *humanity today has a number of common democratic values*, which we must uphold to ensure the power of the people and the benefits that come with this responsibility. We must remember to learn from Ho Chi Minh. President Ho Chi Minh respected the democratic values of mankind and took the two most important sentences on democracy and human rights from the declarations of the American and the French revolutions in the eighteenth century for the opening sentences of the Declaration of Independence of the Democratic Republic of Vietnam. We must continue to think like Uncle Ho on the implementation of democracy in our country. (I can assert that during the first days of the revolution, had we not emphasized the goal of democracy, we would not have gathered the support of the entire people as we did. Should we just talk about democracy instead of implementing it as we promised?)

2. We often proudly claim that "our regime's democracy is many times better than capitalist democracy." Let us make that a clear reality. Let us end the current situation in which people continue to feel more restricted and less comfortable than [their counterparts] in capitalist societies. Many of our leading cadres who have returned from visiting capitalist countries abroad have observed that people's lives in those countries are more open, free, and law-abiding. Everyone there is protected by the law. Their rights to freedom and democracy are not encroached on. Meanwhile in our country, we lack a system of laws, and the laws we do have are not enforced fairly. Many individuals charged with the responsibility of upholding the law have seriously violated it themselves. (In recent years, ever greater numbers of cadres of the Public Security branch, the Inspectorate branch, and even the court system have faced the court as defendants.) . . . We must immediately correct the mistaken view that democracy will bring disorder and chaos. Only the opposite is correct: the absence of democracy is the cause of disorder and chaos. *Democracy with clear and just laws guarantees stability and societal development.* The full implementation of democracy will take away the democratic and human rights flags from the hands of our adversaries. Instead, these flags will belong to us.

3. During the decades of war, people were willing to accept orders from higher-ups in the spirit of "all for victory." People voluntarily restricted and even sacrificed their rights to freedom and democracy. This debt we owe to the people is overdue. We must now repay them fairly in this era of peace and nation building.

The regime that people sacrificed to protect must now carry out the motto "of the people, by the people, and for the people." We cannot let this regime become "of a small group, by a small group, and for a small group." If we fail to do that, people will no longer consider this regime to be theirs.

4. Recently, some people suggested that we improve the economy first and talk about democracy later. Reality demands the opposite. Given a poor and backward nation like ours, to build the country we must mobilize all our domestic strength. [But] we cannot mobilize such strength when people do not even have minimal democratic rights. People must have the right to know and decide what they need to contribute, how much, how efficiently their contribution is used, and what the results are. In the end, external funds must be monitored in a democratic context. What are they being spent on; are they appropriate or not? We cannot allow society to be entirely controlled by a few individuals. The current intractable problem of corruption comes directly from that domination. . . .

Indeed, democracy cannot be built in one day. It takes decades, even centuries, to establish a solid democracy. But that should not be the excuse to postpone building a democracy and implementing democratic practices.

Our country is in desperate need of democratization. I am not saying that democracy is a panacea. Many other factors will be needed to bring the country out of poverty and backwardness and on the road to development. *But democratization is a first and necessary condition to ensure the success of national development.* As long as people lack freedom of thought, freedom of expression, freedom of the press, freedom of association, and other fundamental freedoms of a democracy, all the talk about national development and modernization is useless.

[Tran Do, "Thu cua Tran Do gui Dang," 1–13; trans. Jayne Werner]

ECONOMICS

HO CHI MINH

ON THE BASIC COMPLETION OF LAND REFORM IN THE NORTH (1956)

Land reform in both North Vietnam and South Vietnam reflected the historical concerns of the Vietnamese state to regulate the rural land regime for economic, social, political, and ideological reasons.[33] The Agrarian Reform Law of the Democratic Republic of Vietnam, passed in December 1953, led to the expropriation of large estates held by landlords as well as the rice fields of "middle peasants," often consisting of no more than a few hectares. Land reform teams came into northern

---

33. See, for instance, Le Code, "Public and Private Lands" and "Private Property" (both in chap. 3).

villages to transfer land titles to poor and landless peasants. These teams were composed of cadres from outside the villages and typically used quotas to fulfill expropriation targets. Their highly politicized campaigns relied on class struggle, ideological fervor, and often violence against selected "enemies of the people." Thousands of people were killed or jailed, including members of Viet Minh families. A peasant revolt in Nghe An in the fall of 1956 indicated the seriousness of the ensuing backlash. The following appeal by Ho Chi Minh was the first indication that the Vietnam Workers' Party had decided to launch a "rectification campaign" to correct the errors of the land reform campaign. It was published in *Nhan Dan*, the party's official newspaper, on August 18, 1956. The party's Central Committee had met in July 1956 and decided to replace Truong Chinh, the party's secretary-general and one of the chief proponents of the land reform, with Ho Chi Minh. In his appeal, Ho Chi Minh does not admit that the land reform itself was a mistake, only that its errors had to be corrected. Moreover, as an elder statesman, Ho Chi Minh framed this statement in terms of highly patriotic language, the overriding need for unity in the wake of the social rifts caused by the land reform, and the ultimate goal of uniting north and south.

Two years have passed since the victorious end of the resistance. The northern part of our country has been completely liberated from the colonialists' shackles; now the peasants in the north also have been freed from the yoke of the feudal landlords.

Nearly 10 million peasant compatriots have received land, and tens of thousands of new cadres have been trained in the countryside. Changes have been made in the organization of the party, its administration, and the peasants' associations in the communes.

This great victory opens the way for our peasant compatriots to build a life with sufficient food and clothing and brings a valuable contribution to economic rehabilitation and development and to the consolidation of the north into a solid base for the struggle to reunify our country.

The victory has been secured thanks to the correct policy of our party and government, the united struggle of the laboring peasants, the active support of the army and the people, and the cadres' sacrifices and efforts.

On this occasion, on behalf of the party and government, I affectionately congratulate our peasant compatriots on their victory; congratulate the land reform cadres and the communal cadres and activists who have undergone hardships, overcome difficulties, and perseveringly struggled; [and] congratulate the people and the army who have actively contributed to the common victory.

Land reform is a class struggle against the feudalists; an earthshaking, fierce, and hard revolution. Moreover, the enemy has frantically carried out sabotage work. A number of our cadres have not thoroughly grasped the land reform policy or correctly followed the mass line. The leadership of the party's Central Committee and of the government has sometimes been lacking in concreteness, and control and encouragement have been disregarded. All this has caused us to commit errors and shortcomings in carrying out land reform: in realizing the unity of the countryside, in fighting the enemy, in making organizational changes, in applying the policy of agricultural taxes, and so on.

The Party Central Committee and the government have rigorously reviewed these errors and shortcomings and have drawn up plans to resolutely correct them with a view to uniting the cadres and the people, stabilizing the countryside, and promoting production.

We must correct shortcomings such as not relying fully on the poor and landless peasants, not uniting closely with the middle peasants, and not establishing a real alliance with the rich peasants.

The status of those who have been wrongly classified as landlords or as rich peasants should be reviewed.

Party membership, rights, and honor should be restored to party members, cadres, and others who have been wrongly convicted.

We should abide by the eight-point regulation when dealing with landlords and pay attention to those who took part in the resistance and supported the revolution or those whose children are enrolled in the army or are working as cadres.

Wherever land area and production output have been erroneously estimated, a readjustment is required.

The correction of errors should be resolute and planned. What can be corrected immediately should be done without delay. What cannot be corrected forthwith should be done in combination with the checking-up operation. We must advance the achievements we already have made and, at the same time, resolve to right the wrongs committed.

At present, *the people* have become masters of the countryside; therefore they should be closely united, enthusiastically engage in production, develop and consolidate the mutual aid teams, and so on, in order to become wealthier day after day and to contribute to the enrichment of our people and the strengthening of our country.

Cadres should endeavor to study culture and politics, set an example in work and production, and, in a practical way, take care of the people's living conditions.

The people should frankly criticize and help the cadres in their work.

Cadres at zonal and provincial levels should give practical assistance to cadres of districts and communes so that their work and production may have good results.

Unity is our invincible force. In order to consolidate the north into a solid base for the struggle to reunify our country, our entire people should be closely and widely united in the worker-peasant alliance in the Vietnam Fatherland Front. It is all the more necessary for *veteran and new cadres* of the party and government to assume an identity of ideas, to be united and single-minded, and to emulate one another in serving the people.

All the cadres and people should closely unite around the party and government and try to emulate one another in making our democratic countryside happier and more prosperous.

> [Ho Chi Minh, "Thu cua Ho Chu Tich gui dong bao nong
> thon va can bo nhan dip cai cach ruong dat o mien bac can ban
> thanh cong"; trans. Jayne Werner]

REPUBLIC OF VIETNAM

LAW ON LAND TO THE TILLER (1970)

The southern republican regimes tried different approaches to land reform, under pressure from both Viet Minh revolutionaries who were taxing landlords and distributing the fields of landlords who had fled to the cities and the Americans who were seeking a more stable regime. Ngo Dinh Diem indemnified landlords who relinquished their fields for small-holder distribution, but his reforms stalled. Nguyen Van Thieu's Land to the Tiller Program (March 26, 1970) was more successful. Nguyen Van Thieu's new land law recognized the Communist land reform and gave priority to current tillers, unlike Ngo Dinh Diem's reform. The Land to the Tiller Program gave peasants up to three hectares (about 7.5 acres) of land both free and with permanent title, with the objective of creating a small, independent, peasant, landholding class. By the time this program was initiated in 1970, southern peasants had access to credit, modern fertilizers and seeds, and pumps. Even so, despite these gains, many peasants continued to waver in their loyalty to the Nguyen Van Thieu government because the program was begun late in the war, after large-scale urbanization had already taken place, and military mobilization had depleted much of the rural labor force.

Chapter I: Objective Measures to Be Applied

ARTICLE 1

The Land-to-the-Tiller Policy set forth by this law is aimed at

- Giving ownership to farmers by making them actually cultivating landowners and allowing them to receive all the benefits from their labor.
- Providing equal opportunity for advancement to all farmers.

ARTICLE 2

In order to achieve the preceding objectives, the following measures shall be applied:

1. Expropriate with fair compensation those lands not directly cultivated by landowners, for distribution to farmers, free of charge.
2. Eliminate tenancy and land speculation by middlemen.
3. Distribute communal rice land.

Chapter II: Scope of Application

ARTICLE 3

This law [regarding the scope of application] applies to rice land and secondary cropland belonging to private persons or legal entities, under public or private jurisdiction.

ARTICLE 4

Lands recorded in the Land Register under the name of one owner will be considered as a single property unit. Any transfer not registered before the promulgation date of the law will be null and void. Lands registered separately under the names of a man and his wife shall be considered as a single private property unit, except under the separate property system in the case of marriage.

ARTICLE 5

This law does not apply to the following categories of land:

1. Land, not exceeding fifteen hectares [about 37.5 acres], currently directly cultivated by landowners or their spouses or parents or children or legal heirs. Landowners directly cultivating their land have the right to hire laborers to farm.
2. Ancestral worship land [*huong hoa, hau dien,* and *ky dien*] and cemetery land not exceeding five hectares [about 12.5 acres] for each family.
3. Land currently owned by religious organizations.
4. Industrial cropland and orchard land (excluding crops with a life of less than one year).
5. Industrial building sites.
6. Salt fields, lakes and ponds, and pasture land on livestock farms.
7. Land designated on maps for urban planning, residential areas, and gravesites.
8. Land in experimental centers and agricultural demonstration projects.
9. Land specifically reserved in Montagnard *buons* [villages] and hamlets in accordance with Decree-Laws 003/67 and 034/67 dated August 29, 1967.

10. Land [set aside] for the public.
11. Land that has never been planted in rice and is cleared after promulgation of this law. . . .

Chapter III: Landlord Compensation

ARTICLE 7

Landlords having land expropriated will be compensated quickly and fairly.

The rate of compensation will be determined by a special committee, which shall be established by a decree.

ARTICLE 8

The rate of compensation shall be equivalent to two and one-half times the annual paddy yield of the land. Annual yield means the average yield during the past five years.

ARTICLE 9

Landlords shall be compensated according to the following standards:

- Twenty percent of the value of the expropriated land shall be paid immediately in cash.
- The remainder shall be paid in bonds guaranteed by the government over eight years at 10 percent interest.

If landownership and usufruct right belong to two different persons, the compensation to each should be determined by the special committee just mentioned.

ARTICLE 10

Bonds may be pledged, transferred, and used to pay hypothecs [a type of non-possessory remortgage] and land taxes or to buy shares in private or national enterprises.

ARTICLE 11

Rights of privileged creditors, pledgers, hypothecators, or heirs will become the creditors' right with respect to the amount of compensation to landlords based on the legal status of the land in the Land Register.

Chapter IV: Beneficiaries

ARTICLE 12

Land for distribution will be distributed free of charge to each farm family with a maximum area of

- Three hectares [about 7.5 acres] in southern Vietnam.
- One hectare [about 2.5 acres] in central Vietnam.

A farm family is composed of parents, spouses, and children living together in a house and listed on the family register.

ARTICLE 13

Land for distribution shall be distributed in the following order of priority:

1. Present tillers, those people cultivating land belonging to another person.
2. Parents, spouse, or children of war dead who will cultivate the land, if they have submitted an application.
3. Soldiers, civil servants, and cadres when discharged or retired who will cultivate the land, if they have submitted an application.
4. Soldiers, civil servants, and cadres who had to abandon cultivation because of the war, if they have submitted an application in order for their families to cultivate the land.
5. Farm laborers who will cultivate the land, if they have submitted an application.

In any case, land distributed and added to the land already owned cannot exceed the area fixed in article 12.

ARTICLE 14

Persons receiving land are exempted from registration taxes, stamp taxes, land administration fees, and all other fees relating to the transfer of land and are exempted from any tax related to the distributed land in the first year.

ARTICLE 15

Persons receiving distributed land must cultivate the land themselves.

For a period of fifteen years starting from the date he becomes owner, the person receiving land distributed under this law cannot transfer ownership or agree to establish real right on the land received except in case of prior official authorization. A person (or his spouse) who has sold distributed land will not be given land a second time.

ARTICLE 16

Any farmer who has received expropriated land under ordinance 57 or formerly French-owned land and has not completed purchase payments to the government will be exempted from payment of the balance due. Persons who have paid more than 50 percent of the purchase price will not be subject to article 15, paragraph 2, of this law.

Chapter V: Punitive Measures

ARTICLE 17

Any person acting to prevent implementation of this law will be sentenced from six months to three years imprisonment or fined from VN$20,000 to VN$200,000 or both.

ARTICLE 18

Any landlord as determined in article 5, paragraph 1, who refuses to directly cultivate his land shall have his entire property expropriated without compensation.

ARTICLE 19

Any farmer violating article 15 by not directly cultivating the land will be expropriated without compensation. The land shall be redistributed to other farmers under the provisions of this law.

ARTICLE 20

Any lawsuit that results during the implementation of this law will be under the jurisdiction of the Land Court, which is composed of professional judges.

Any violation of provisions regarding penal law will be under jurisdiction of the Civil Court.

[Callison, *Land-to-the-Tiller in the Mekong Delta*, 347–51]

SOCIALIST REPUBLIC OF VIETNAM

RESOLUTION OF THE SIXTH PARTY CONGRESS (1986)

Passed in December 1986, this historic resolution ushered in Vietnam's era of Doi Moi (Renovation). In doing so, it transformed Vietnam's economic system from a centrally controlled command economy to one based on market principles and the profit motive. Faced with a profound economic crisis, the Vietnamese government was forced to turn to material incentives in production, bring inflation under control, change the two-price system into a one-price system, and abolish other barriers to economic efficiency. In the pre-1986 socialist command economy, one set of prices was determined by the central government according to procurement and consumption considerations, and the other, by supply and demand (the so-called black market). The first set of prices was based on the value of the *dong*; the other, on international exchange rates. Vietnam also turned to light industry instead of heavy industry to support an export-driven growth strategy, opened its economy to international trade and foreign investment, and, in 1988, started to dismantle agricultural cooperatives, returning land to individual peasant proprietors (known as Resolution 10). The Sixth Congress Resolution also paved the way for the decentralization of economic and political power, shifting power to local people's committees.

The Sixth Congress of the Communist Party of Vietnam notes that the past five years were a path beset with trials for our party and people. The revolution in our country took place in the context of fundamental international and domestic advantages, but it was fraught with difficulties and complexities. While implementing the tasks and objectives set by the party's Fifth Congress [March 27–31, 1982], our people have made tremendous efforts, overcome difficulties and obstacles, recorded *important achievements* in socialist construction, and won *great victories* in the fight for the defense of the homeland and the fulfillment of their international duty. Many fairly good production and business establishments and excellent units emerged. . . .

While affirming the successes already recorded, we are fully aware that our socioeconomic situation is faced with tremendous difficulties: a slow increase in production, low production and investment inefficiencies; many disturbances in the distribution and circulation of products; delays in adjusting major imbalances in the economy; the slow strengthening of socialist relations of production; difficulties in the working people's life; [and] negative manifestations in many localities, especially in some places where they are very serious.

In general, we *have not yet fulfilled the overall target set by the Fifth Party Congress, namely, generally stabilizing the socioeconomic situation and the people's livelihood.* The congress has not underestimated the objective difficulties; it has severely pointed out that the subjective causes of the preceding situation are the mistakes and shortcomings in the leadership and management of the party and state.

We have made mistakes in assessing the concrete situation in the country and defining the objectives and the initial stage of socialist construction. From 1976 to 1980, we in fact promoted industrialization even before the necessary premises for it were in place; we displayed both hastiness and a careless approach in socialist transformation; [and] we were slow in renewing the already outdated mechanism of economic management. Between 1981 and 1985, we did not correctly implement the judicious conclusions of our Fifth Party Congress on making concrete the economic line in the first stage; we were not sufficiently resolved to do away with the manifestations of wishful thinking, hastiness, conservatism, and sluggishness in laying out the economic structure in [our] socialist transformation and economic management. Moreover, we made new and serious mistakes in the distribution and circulation of products. We slackened proletarian dictatorship in social and economic management, in the ideological and cultural struggle, and in the fight against the enemy's wicked schemes and acts of sabotage.

These were serious mistakes in *major undertakings and policies*, in *strategic guidance*, and in the *organization for implementation*. The main ideological trends leading to these mistakes, especially mistakes in the economic policy, are wishful thinking and voluntarism, simplistic thinking and action, hastiness, carelessness in economic and social management, and failure to strictly observe the party's line and principles. These were manifestations of both "left" and "right" deviations of *petty bourgeois ideology.*

The mistakes and shortcomings in the economic and social fields originated in shortcomings in the *party's ideological, organizational, and cadre work.* Ideology lags in theoretical perception, and the application of the laws of the transition to socialism in our country is weak. In organization, the greatest shortcoming is the lack of programming and the slow renewal of cadres; the principle of democratic centralism has been violated in party life; the style of leadership and work are fraught with bureaucratism; the apparatus is too big, overlaps, and is ineffective; [and] the education and management of cadres and party members are inadequate.

From the practice of past years, our party has drawn valuable lessons of experience, particularly the following: First, in all its activities, the party must implement the idea "to rely on the people as the root" and to promote the working people's right to collective mastery. Second, the party must always proceed from reality, observe, and act on objective laws. Third, we should know how to combine the forces of the nation and those of the times in the new condition. Fourth, we should take care to build up the party to the level of a party in power, leading the people in the socialist revolution. . . .

On the task of building socialism, [the Sixth Party] Congress asserts: *The overall task and overall objective of the remaining years of the first stage are to stabilize the socioeconomic situation in every respect [and] to continue to build the necessary premises for accelerated socialist industrialization in the subsequent stage.* The stabilization of the socioeconomic situation implies stabilization and the development of production, the stabilization of distribution and circulation of products, the stabilization and gradual improvement of the material and cultural life of the people, the enhancement of the effectiveness of organization and management, the establishment of order and discipline, and the achievement of social justice.

The concrete objectives are to produce enough for consumption and accumulation, to create a rational economic structure to develop production, to take a step further in building and strengthening the new relations of production, to bring about changes to improve social life, and to satisfy the needs of strengthening national defense and security. . . .

The congress entrusts the Central Committee [Sixth Congress] with guiding the implementation of the tasks set out in the political report. The following tasks shall be emphasized:

1. To elaborate and organize the implementation of the three programs for grain and foodstuffs, consumer goods, and exports so as to achieve the following targets by the end of the first stage:

• To meet the needs of society in food grains and to have some reserves and to stabilize essential needed foodstuffs. The level of consumption of grain and foodstuffs should be high enough to ensure the reproduction of the workforce.
• To satisfy the demands in staple consumer goods. . . .

These three programs will guide the streamlining of the national economy into a proper structure, first, the rearrangement of the production structure and major adjustments in the investment structure to effectively use the labor potential, land, and currently available material and technical bases.

We need to ensure that agriculture, as well as forestry and fishery, is at the forefront and is given priority in the provision of investment, energy, materials, and working skills, first in the key areas, so as to achieve high economic efficiency. We should strive to develop light industry, small industry, and handicrafts so as to meet the needs for common consumer goods and processed agricultural, forestry, and marine products; and to rapidly increase the quantity of subcontracted goods for export and other export items. We should continue to build a number of heavy-industry establishments and substructures, first for the energy industry, communications, and transport, in accordance with the real conditions [in the country] to serve the practical objectives in economic life and national defense in the first stage and prepare the foundation for promoting industrialization in the next stage. Service activities in production, circulation, daily life, and tourism should be expanded. . . .

We should broaden and heighten the effectiveness of external economic relations, promote exports to meet the needs for imports, widen our participation in the international division of labor, first and mainly by promoting the all-sided relations in the division of labor and cooperation with the Soviet Union, Laos, and Kampuchea and with other member countries of the Council for Mutual Economic Assistance [CMEA]. We should take the initiative in cooperating with the fraternal countries in charting and implementing the CMEA program for assistance to Vietnam, and the CMEA General Program for Scientific and Technical Progress until the year 2000. We should actively develop economic and scientific-technical cooperation with other countries, international organizations, and private organizations abroad on the principle of equality and mutual benefit. We should seriously observe our commitments in external economic relations.

2. We should continue to carry out the task of socialist transformation, in proper steps, making the relations of production conform to the character and level of the productive forces and promoting the development of the productive forces. We should strengthen the socialist economy according to all three aspects—the system of ownership, the management system, and the distribution system—enabling the state-run economy to exercise its leading role and, together with the collective economy, to hold a decisive place in the national economy and to control the other economic sectors. The development of the household economy should be encouraged. We should use the active capabilities of small-scale commodity production while mobilizing and organizing individual producers into different forms of collective production to enhance the effectiveness of their production and business; arrange, transform, and use small traders; and help transfer those not necessary to the production and service sectors' circulation. We should use the private capitalist economy [small capitalists] in some branches while transforming them step-by-step through various forms of state capitalism; abolish private capitalist trade; [and] expand many forms of association among different economic sectors on the principle of mutual benefit and equality before the law.

3. The economic management mechanism should be renewed with a view to creating a driving force that will make economic units and the working masses eagerly develop production and enhance productivity, quality, and economic effectiveness. We should resolutely do away with the bureaucratic centralized mechanism based on state subsidies, establish a balanced planning mechanism in accordance with socialist cost-accounting and business transactions in strict observance of the principle of democratic centralism. The new mechanism shall make planning its centerpiece, along with the correct use of commodity/currency relations and economic measures as the main form of control, combined with administrative and educational measures. It shall divide managerial power according to the principle of democratic centralism and establish order and discipline in all economic activities. . . .

We should make full and appropriate use of economic levers in economic planning and management, based on the harmonious combination of the interests of the entire society, the collectives, and individual producers. The income of the collective and of individual producers depends on the results of their labor and the economic efficiency of their activities. Policies and regulations regarding the control of materials, labor, consumption of products, pricing, finance, credit, wages, and the like are to steer economic activities to implement the objectives of the country's economic plan and create the conditions and raise the demand for all economic units to undertake accurate cost-accounting methods and business transactions and for all organizations and people to practice thrift in production and consumption.

The division of managerial responsibilities must be based on the principles of democratic centralism. Efforts should be made to overcome manifestations of bureaucratic centralism [and] the lack of discipline, regionalism, and selfishness. The right to autonomy in production, business transactions, and the finances of grassroots' economic establishments and the production collectives' right to mastery must be ensured. Management bodies from the center down to urban wards and villages should correctly perform their financial and economic management functions and should not interfere in the production and business undertakings of local units. The efficiency of centrally run, unified, and concentrated management should be ensured in spheres of national importance. At the same time, efforts should be made to ensure the initiative of local authorities at various levels in the economic and social management based on territory.

4. Resolutely resolve urgent problems relating to distribution and the circulation of products with the following major measures:

- Productive capacities must be released. Efforts should be focused on ensuring the supply of raw materials and the renovation of concrete policies aimed at strongly stimulating the production of essential goods and items that create major sources of revenue for the state budget.
- The state should closely control raw materials and goods produced or imported by state-run economic establishments, issue rational pricing policies and judicious modes of purchase and sale in order to have a firm hold on commodities and money. Socialist trade must be shifted to a commercial basis with a higher quality of service aimed at taking control of the market. The central authorities should work out a decentralized and practical system of price-fixing and price controls [and] ensure the normal operation of production establishments and the initiative of socialist trade in buying and selling.
- To rapidly increase the volume of goods in circulation, we should expand the flow of goods, and remove restrictions, and split up the market according to administrative territories. We should promptly identify and severely punish speculators and traffickers.

- We must markedly reduce the budget deficit by creating sources of revenue and increasing turnover in conformity with our policies. Efforts should be made to cut back on expenditures, cancel or postpone spending on what is not urgently needed, [and] gradually reduce and eventually end the issuing of banknotes for budget expenditures. We should enforce the control of money in circulation, draw in excess cash kept by the public, and quickly turn around funds. At the same time, we should expand modes of clearance without using cash for production and business transactions.

These measures should be taken in equal measure to redress step-by-step the balance between the volume of goods and money in circulation, with a view to solving the pivotal issue, namely, gradually reducing and then ending inflation. On this basis, we will lower the tempo of price increases, stabilize prices and the purchasing power of money, reduce difficulties, and gradually stabilize the working people's livelihood, first for wage and salary earners. . . .

Increase the Effectiveness of State Management

We should uphold the position and role of the National Assembly and the People's Council at all levels; create the conditions for popularly elected bodies to correctly discharge their functions, their duties, and their rights as stipulated in the constitution; [and] strengthen socialist legality and the management of society by law. The duties, rights, and obligations of the state organs should be clearly defined for each level, based on the principle of democratic centralism, distinguishing between the function of administrative-economic management and that of production-business management and combining management by branches with that by localities and regions. We must streamline the state's managerial apparatus to enable it to institutionalize the party's lines [political positions] and undertakings into laws and specific policies, build and organize the implementation of the state's plans, effectively manage and direct social and economic activities, [and] maintain law, discipline, and social order and security.

[Adapted from Socialist Republic of Vietnam,
Sixth National Congress, 182, 184–96]

VO VAN KIET

THE CRISIS IN FOOD, PRICES, AND MONEY (1988)

Despite the adoption of the Sixth Party Congress reforms in 1986, Vietnam was faced with serious food shortages in 1987/1988. Vo Van Kiet, a chief proponent of economic reform who was prime minister from 1991 to 1997, attributed the crisis to the government's inability to control food prices, as well as to hoarding and speculation. He also blamed hyperinflation, the hasty 1984 currency devaluation, bad banking practices, and the two-price system, which was still in effect. In acknowledging widespread food short-ages and the failure of the government's economic polices, Vo Van Kiet laid the blame squarely on the country's Communist leaders. The two-price policy continued to hinder the production of adequate food supplies. Essential commodities were rationed at low prices, but the supply rarely met the demand, in part because producers were obliged to sell at state prices. For its part, the government was unable to deliver production inputs at contract prices, so it had to buy them at higher prices, necessitating the printing of more money, which fueled inflation. In this June 28, 1988, report to the National Assembly, published in the party newspaper *Nhan Dan*, Vo Van Kiet suggested that immediate measures had to be taken to bring the situation under control. Under Vo Van Kiet's lead-ership, Vietnam would move away from its Soviet-style command economy to a market-based system. This text's attributing the state's responsibility for addressing food shortages and hunger as well as currency and pricing problems is reminiscent of Le Thai To's edict on currency (1430) and Ngo The Lan's memorial to the Nguyen ruler of 1771.[34]

Since early this year, our country's northern provinces have been experiencing a very serious grain shortage, in both the state sector and the countryside, which has developed into a social problem that adversely affects the people's livelihood and many areas of the economy. The shortages of grain sources in the northern provinces' state sector became very serious in January and February 1988. The state grain supply available for distribution in the northern provinces in January accounted for only a quarter of the minimum needed in the key areas and only one-sixth of the normal monthly demand. This situation sharply pushed up each day the price of rice in the northern provinces. The price of rice on the market far exceeded that used by the state for wage computation purposes and raised the prices of other commodities, creating extremely grave difficulties for wage earners, especially those with low incomes, such as workers and employees in the mining and border regions.

Immediately after becoming aware of serious hunger in the countryside, the Standing Committee of the Council of Ministers delegated specific responsibility to the central administration and provincial people's committees from Binh Tri Thien Province northward to focus their leadership on hunger alleviation mea-sures. The council sent several official delegations to the local areas to assess the situation and help the provinces direct hunger alleviation efforts, and distribute paddy from the state warehouses for immediate assistance to compatriots of areas in dire need.[35] The Standing Committee of the Council of Ministers directed

34. See Le Thai To and Nguyen Trai, "Edict on Currency" (chap. 3), and Ngo The Lan, "Memorial on Currency Crisis" (chap. 4).

35. Paddy, used for storage and transport to reduce spoilage, is unhusked rice. The word *state* in this article includes the government, National Assembly, and judiciary but does not include the Communist Party. In Vietnam, the state or government runs the economy, the administra-tion, and foreign affairs.

the immediate mobilization and transport of food from southern to northern Vietnam and arranged for additional food imports. *So far, the south has supplied the north with 260,000 metric tons of rice, twice as much as last year.* Provinces that have made significant efforts in this mobilization include Tien Giang, Cuu Long, and An Giang. Ho Chi Minh City strove to meet its own food needs, thereby reducing the amount of rice received from the central government, so that more rice could be reserved for the north.

The government diverted a portion of the existing food resources and granted additional budget allocations to help the localities alleviate hunger and provided more vegetable seeds and fertilizer to the provinces so that families in need could grow vegetables and tubers to help themselves during the lean months. In localities with food shortages (such as Nghe Tinh Province), the party committees, mass organizations, and people's committees have tried to urge rural inhabitants to engage in mutual assistance, cultivate vegetables, coordinate the fall and spring harvests, and use food banks. They have encouraged cadres and workers to practice thrift in providing food assistance to the hungry, conduct effective educational campaigns, thoroughly assess the situation at hand, and provide timely assistance to the neediest areas. Unfortunately, the people's committees of the districts and province of Thanh Hoa have not been very diligent in their leadership and have failed to identify and resolve in time their urgent local hunger cases.

The recent situation reflects, first, the immediate and long-term difficulties in the relationship between the supply and demand of food in our country, particularly in the north. Over the past five years, food production has stagnated or risen only slightly while the population has grown very quickly, resulting in a steady drop in the per capita food supply, which has become increasingly severe in the north. From Binh Tri Thien Province north, the average annual per capita food production has fallen steadily from 264 kg (1982 [1 kilogram is 2.2 pounds]) to 247 kg (1985) and 230 kg (1987).[36]

Obviously, so long as there is no fundamental solution to the slow growth in food production, rapid population growth, and an excessive number of government employees and workers for whom food must be supplied by the state, periodic difficulties in the food supply cannot be avoided. Even in normal years, about 5 to 10 percent of peasants in the north (approximately 2 million to 3 million people) face food shortages because of local crop failures and inadequate labor in those families.

Unusually widespread and severe food shortages in recent months are due to the following factors:

• Food reserves in the countryside have dwindled. The severe failure of the 1987 spring/summer crop forced peasants affected by food shortages to borrow food and money. The 1987 harvest was comparatively better, but the newly

---

36. The average per-capita rice requirement is 240 kg of paddy a year.

harvested crop was consumed immediately after the early harvest (beginning in September and October 1987) and was used for repaying old debts. Food reserves in the agricultural cooperatives and the districts also were quite low.

• The state has been unable to provide adequate food supplies to state cadres, officials, and workers. As a result, many of them sought their own food from the rural areas or bought it on the open market. This reduced supplies in the rural areas and caused the price of paddy and rice to rise, in turn affecting the lives of peasants who faced food shortages and lacked the money to buy grain on the open market.

• Large-scale grain shortages have had a strong psychological impact on society, making it more difficult to regulate the rural food supply. Faced with inflation and a rapid rise in food prices, some people with surplus rice have hoarded their rice supplies instead of selling them. People with available cash, in both urban and rural areas, have tried to buy and hoard rice, further disrupting the food supply.

The principal shortcoming in the leadership of the Council of Ministers was its failure to foresee the operative factors and to correctly anticipate the amount of the grain shortage in late 1987 and early 1988, both in the state sector and among the population. This led to its lack of initiative in adopting special policies and measures for promptly checking the shortages and limiting their consequences. The Council of Ministers also failed to closely monitor the collection and transport of grain in late 1987, as well as food shortages and hunger in some places. The council was indecisive in its policy to import grain, and it failed to determine early the need to import the necessary grain to compensate for the shortfall in grain and to ensure adequate grain reserves.

If the Council of Ministers had predicted the situation earlier and if the administration at all levels had directed the food relief drive in an urgent manner and a spirit of full responsibility, we could have entirely avoided the regrettable events that occurred in a number of localities. The Council of Ministers accepts its responsibility for this situation before the National Assembly.

In reviewing the food situation over the past few months, we have determined that it will be necessary to firmly and uniformly carry out production, storage, processing, distribution, consumption, reserves, and food import measures. We also will need to reduce the population growth rate, relocate the population, and readjust state plans in keeping with resolution 10 of the Politburo on the renovation of agricultural economic management.[37] We also need to change and amend our economic policies in order to fundamentally resolve the food problem in our country. At the same time, we must always be mindful to monitor and to

---

37. Resolution 10 dismantled the agricultural cooperatives and returned land to individual peasant proprietors.

correctly predict the overall situation in each region in order to apply timely measures for dealing with urgent issues.

At present, along with strengthening the leadership of the summer/fall production and harvest and preparing for the winter crop, the Council of Ministers will see to it that production inputs and money are sent to rural areas at harvest time for people to buy food, initially through economic contracts, in order to mobilize peasants to cultivate the winter/spring crop and summer crop and to quickly collect all current taxes in paddy as well as unpaid taxes in paddy from previous crops.

Abruptly soaring prices of grain, food staples, and gold have led to rapidly increasing prices of production inputs and other goods. These increases have spread from region to region. Even in the regulated [state-controlled] market, prices have risen under the influence of the free market. In many cases, inflation in the regulated market has even surpassed that of the free market, triggering even stronger and more chaotic inflation in the free market.

The competition among state enterprises in purchasing commodities for export in region 2 [central Vietnam to the south] and in forcing up prices has continued at a very alarming pace: the purchase price of coffee for export has increased from the usual level of 1,300 to 1,500 *dong*/kg (January 1988) to 3,500 *dong*/kg and that of best-quality prawns, from 5,000 *dong*/kg to 20,000 *dong*/kg. The same situation applies to many other export commodities.

From the beginning of this year, provinces have purchased paddy with or without contracts based on market prices. But the price of paddy rose rapidly at the start of the summer harvest because the state and peasants faced food shortages in many areas. For example, the price of paddy in the Hau Giang River [southern branch of the Mekong River] Delta increased from 90 to 100 *dong*/kg in January 1988 to 220 to 240 *dong*/kg currently, and, in the Red River Delta, from 180 *dong*/kg to 400 *dong*/kg. The prices of pork and ocean fish continue to rise, with the trend of further increases.

The rapid rise in paddy prices has pushed up the wholesale prices of grain, food, and industrial consumer goods. Provincial authorities have had to continuously readjust the retail prices of goods sold by state trading organizations, including items that are rationed and on which wages are based, necessitating a monthly readjustment of the compensation of wages indexed by prices.[38] In Hanoi, pork prices increased from 900 *dong*/kg in January 1988 to 4,500 *dong*/kg in mid-June, and in Ho Chi Minh City the price of rice rose from 175 *dong*/kg to 470 *dong*/kg, and pork from 950 *dong*/kg to 2850 *dong*/kg. The retail prices of industrial consumer goods increased by one and a half to more than three times.

---

38. In the 1970s and 1980s, the salaries and wages of Vietnamese government officials and workers in state enterprises were indexed to the prices of a number of essential goods, including rice, sugar, kerosene, fish sauce, and meat.

The government's policy has been to maintain a very low wholesale price of production materials compared with production costs and import prices, and this has been slow to change. Yet, determining the state price of production materials continues to be poorly managed, with many loopholes. As a result, selling, buying, and reselling materials is a widespread practice, with many units using the pretense of "joint ventures and enterprises" to sell materials supplied by the state to reap a profit from the difference in price. This unjustified behavior by many state enterprises and cooperatives has given rise to a serious leakage of materials and price increases, with a concomitant deterioration in ethics among many officials.

Skyrocketing and fluctuating prices and the rapid devaluation of our currency have had serious consequences for the economy and have become a cause of anxiety for the entire society.

• The circulation of goods has been disrupted, and disparities in income distribution and difficulties in living conditions have worsened. Honest workers, particularly those who depend on salaries, have been the most adversely affected. Yet the bulk of traders, particularly wealthy trading households, have enjoyed unreasonably high incomes, while dishonest elements in state business and production enterprises and in society at large have availed themselves of the opportunities to reap profits for their units and for themselves, to the detriment of state property and the interests of laboring people.

• Price fluctuations have caused the relative price index between industrial goods and agricultural products to change rapidly, compared with [the prices of] industrial goods. The prices of paddy and agricultural products purchased by the state have increased very quickly, while the prices of construction materials and industrial goods have risen more slowly (such as the price ratio between fertilizer and paddy which in 1985, was one [unit of] urea for three units of paddy; in 1987, two and a half; after that, two units). As a result, the state has had to spend much more money to purchase paddy, which has become an important factor leading to overexpenditures in the state's budget and cash outlays. Although the prices for agricultural products have rapidly increased, peasants have not benefited fully from these increases. In a number of cases, price increases have filled only the pockets of intermediaries who benefited from the price differentials through their convoluted deals.

• With continually fluctuating prices, the central government, its administrative agencies, and the provincial and local authorities have faced great difficulties in economic planning. Economic organizations have faced insuperable difficulties in capital and sales and have been unable to perform honest and correct business accounting, with a clear picture of profits, losses, and productivity. There has been a widespread tendency in business and production enterprises to keep their goods in stock while waiting for the right price, while confusion, unease, and small-scale hoarding prevail among various strata of the population.

• Price volatility also is a major opportunity for enemies, speculators, and smugglers to undermine our economy.

Faced with such a situation in prices, the party and state have several times analyzed the causes and established policies and measures to deal with the problem. First, rapid price increases are the direct consequence of inflation. For many years now, our economy has been facing serious and widespread imbalances between production and consumption and between supply and demand. The mistakes and shortcomings of the 1981 and 1985 price readjustments have further exacerbated these imbalances, causing greater budget overspending, greater cash outlays, and higher inflation, with the growth in the volume of money in circulation largely surpassing the growth in the volume of goods.[39]

Serious food shortages in the north at the beginning of this year and soaring food prices in the whole country are important factors that have caused a rapid rise in the prices of all goods.

Price increases have also been associated with shortcomings in the process of implementing the new management system. We carried out several measures to vigorously promote the spirit of initiative of government agencies and provincial and local authorities in economic activities, but we have been slow to rectify and develop the institutions for macroeconomic management, particularly in finance, currency, prices and market circulation of materials and goods, export/import, and so on. We allowed erroneous tendencies in management to reduce the state's efficiency in regulating and controlling the material resources at its disposal (inputs, [consumer] goods, capital, foreign currency). As a result, the central government has not been able to focus on undertaking emergency measures to alleviate sudden and dangerous price fluctuations.

The chaotic price situation over the past six months is also due to shortcomings of the Council of Ministers in its leadership over price policies, particularly the exchange rate and the wholesale price of production inputs: there were endless meetings, but haphazard and slow decisions regarding implementation. This led to a wait-and-see attitude and created confusion among producers and traders, which resulted in a standstill in the production and consumption of goods. It also triggered expedient measures and drained budgetary resources, creating opportunities that bad elements were able to exploit.

The loose management of prices and the market by the central government and local authorities was a major shortcoming. On the local level, this was the direct responsibility of the people's committees.

In the near future, in order to reduce the rate of price increases and stabilize prices, we must apply uniform measures to gradually reduce and then end the excessive printing of money, as party and government resolutions have pointed

---

39. In 1985, the government devalued the *dong*, causing its purchasing power to drop sharply and contribute to inflation.

out, and narrow the imbalance between budget revenues and expenditures and between goods and money. In particular, we must satisfactorily resolve the food problem.

With respect to prices, we must focus on uniformly achieving two important objectives: a rational price system that supports the reforms of the economic management system in active and steady steps, and effective measures for price management in order to gradually stabilize prices. . . .

We would like to report further on implementing the one-price system. We believe that the one-price system has many advantages, and this is what our government needs to achieve. But, as mentioned in many party resolutions, shifting from the two-price to the one-price system requires steps consistent with the economic situation, with the necessary material conditions, especially with the volume of goods. Resolution 11 of the Politburo on urgent anti-inflation measures states that currently we must temporarily apply the two-price policy to certain basic production materials—indigenous or imported—such as coal, electricity, petroleum and oil, iron and steel, cement, wood, and newsprint.

- Stable prices will be applied to materials supplied to all branches of economic activity and to production and sales units in accordance with state plans and through economic contracts with the state.
- Market prices will be applied to materials supplied to other production units and the population.

Market prices will also be applied to other materials in keeping with state production and consumption policies.

In view of the severe shortages in production inputs and continuously fluctuating prices, we cannot rely solely on price control measures to overcome speculation and the sale and resale of production inputs for price advantage. It is more important to rectify the management of materials, to intensify the inspection of production input reserves subject to quotas, to efficiently monitor and evaluate the inventory of production inputs, to prevent and severely punish the illicit sale of materials on the free market, and to abolish the selling and reselling of strategic materials exclusively produced or imported by the state.

In view of the very large fluctuations in the market prices of paddy and rice, the sale, purchase, and payment of paddy and rice between the state and the peasants must be handled mainly through economic contracts, contract-like rational means, and a reasonable relative price index between agricultural and industrial prices.

For a number of important export items such as prawns, cuttlefish, pepper, coffee, and cinnamon—which are subject to sales competition [among state enterprises], resulting in excessive price increases, the state must specify the maximum price commensurate with production and market conditions in each area. In the near future, the state will promulgate import and export regulations, as well as measures for managing and using foreign currency, determining reasonable exchange rates, and so on. These are important conditions to restore order and discipline in the purchase of goods for export.

Noncontract agricultural products can be purchased directly from the producer at prices close to the market price, and this will be coordinated with the effort to eliminate negative factors such as speculation and competition in purchases and sales.

For now, retail sales will have two prices for a small number of essential consumer goods: stable retail prices during specific periods will be applied to wage earners and beneficiaries of state programs, and commercial prices will be applied to other groups of people.

This retail pricing policy should not be applied uniformly in all areas. Wherever there are adequate conditions [in goods and cash], stable retail prices can continue to be applied to persons whose wages are indexed to prices and to goods that are rationed and constitute part of their wages, but care should be taken so that indexing ensures balanced budgets. Other goods will be sold at one commercial price, while luxury goods and high-grade consumer goods also are sold at market prices.

Prices directly affect the lives of the people. Therefore, faced with rampant inflation, the state must control the prices of goods essential to production and livelihoods. Depending on the progress in stabilizing the economy and achieving reforms in the management system, the state will actively extend, in an orderly manner, the rights and responsibilities of grassroots economic units to determine and manage prices and will perfect state tools for managing prices and the market. The Council of Ministers has issued a new list of goods for the management of prices, which specifies which prices are to be determined by the Council of Ministers or by the chairman of the people's committees of the provinces and the cities. It is the responsibility of the relevant agencies to supervise and inspect the implementation of these regulations on price management, to help restore order, and to gradually stabilize prices.

[N. D., "Luong thuc va gia ca, tien te," 1, 4; trans. Jayne Werner]

DINH THU CUC

THE PEASANTS AND COUNTRYSIDE IN
VIETNAM TODAY (1988)

Written by historian Dinh Thu Cuc, this article was published in *Tap Chi Cong San*, the Communist Party's theoretical journal, in May 1988, two years after Doi Moi was officially launched. He describes how "village bullies," some of whom were associated with the local Communist Party, had managed to insinuate themselves as local power bosses inside the agricultural cooperatives, undermining farmers' interests and national party policies. These new village bullies gained a new lease on life as Vietnam began to decollectivize its agricultural land, by levying exorbitant fees on farmers and other corrupt practices, which led to revolts and other mass actions. Tran Do also mentioned this problem in 1998,[40] referring to Thai Binh Province. At the same time, this text echoes Nguyen Cu Trinh's memorial to the Nguyen ruler (1751) decrying oppressive local officials and their exorbitant taxes and fees.[41]

As the ally of the working class and the largest and most powerful force among the masses led by our party, the peasant class has played a very large role in the nation's revolutionary undertaking. History records enormous contributions by the peasant class to the success of the August Revolution and the victories over the French colonialists and U.S. imperialists. In addition, history has also witnessed profound social changes in the rural areas of our country in less than three decades. A feudal countryside in which the peasant class existed as tenant farmers or individual, small-scale producers, has become a new countryside in which the means of production has turned into collective ownership, and the peasant is the master of the countryside. Indeed, our country's peasant class has taken a long stride forward in the struggle to abolish the feudal countryside in order to build the new, socialist countryside.

The victory of the national, democratic revolution has made Vietnamese peasants the true owners of their land. The special relationship of the party, the working class, and the peasant class has also helped peasants voluntarily follow the party, with their lofty dream of building a new, civilized, and happy society in the countryside where they work and live.

In productive labor, peasants gradually began earning their living collectively by increasingly highly developed forms of production. Today, large numbers of peasants nationwide are the members of 16,331 agricultural cooperatives, 39,380 agricultural production collectives, 4,000 forestry cooperatives, 961 marine products cooperatives, and 2,571 marine products production collectives.

Our country's agriculture has undergone [many] changes in the level of development of production forces. Many scientific-technical advances have been applied to agriculture. A number of socioeconomic bases for transforming the psychology of small-scale production have emerged and are being nurtured.

These facts demonstrate that the socialist revolution has begun to establish a foundation in agriculture, the most backward economic field in our country, and that socialist production relations can gain a foothold in the countryside under certain conditions in the development of production forces.

Besides the preceding, we have, over the past several decades, placed too much emphasis on the collective ownership of the means of production and paid little attention to the factors of management and socialist distribution in the socialist

---

40. See Tran Do, "Letter to the Communist Party Urging Democratic Reform" (this chap.)
41. See Nguyen Cu Trinh, "Memorial Describing the Economic Crisis in the Nguyen Realm" (chap. 4).

transformation and construction of the agricultural economy. For this reason, the production forces in agriculture are underdeveloped and not only are unable to carry out expanded reproduction but also find it difficult to carry out simple reproduction.

The mechanism based on bureaucratic administrative management and state subsidies and the backwardness of many of the economic policies of the party and state concerning peasants have also severely constrained and exerted a negative influence on the countryside. Instead of being consolidated and improved, the initial bases of socialist production relations in the countryside have been weakened in many respects. There is a significant percentage of weak and deficient cooperatives and production collectives in nearly all provinces.

A search for an appropriate management mechanism for cooperatives and production collectives to open the way for the development of agriculture was launched in the early 1980s. When the "final product contract with groups of laborers and individual laborers" mechanism was officially established (secretariat directive 100 [January 1981]), it made a difference in agricultural production, particularly in the production of grains and foodstuffs.

But reality demands that we closely tie efforts to refine the contract mechanism to efforts to strengthen cooperatives and socialist production relations and to correctly use the various segments of the economy based on a comprehensive and coordinated renovation of the policies that apply to agriculture and peasant farmers. Many different kinds of work in the countryside (such as planning, financial and credit work, the trading of materials, pricing, marketing, agricultural taxes, and labor obligations) must be changed to be compatible with the ownership prevailing in the different segments of the economy.

The pressing needs of today are renovating the management mechanism within agriculture in order to liberate production capacity; develop the potential of labor, arable land, the trades, and material-technical bases; and develop the existing scientific potential in order to rapidly increase the supply of agricultural products to society and raise peasants' incomes.

The situation of the peasant class in the Vietnamese countryside at the present time also raises social problems that must be resolved right away. These problems are no less pressing than the economic problems we face.

First is the need to constantly struggle against *the negative vestiges of the past that linger in the countryside*. These vestiges are persistent and have directly affected the life of the countryside, especially in recent years.

As just mentioned, Vietnamese peasants have taken a long stride forward in the struggle to abolish the feudal countryside in order to build the new, socialist, countryside. Peasants' cultural standards have been raised gradually, giving them a new philosophy of life and worldview. But their traditional way of life is still quite deeply ingrained in their psychology, their habits, and the way they think and act.

Commendable expressions of the countryside's traditional way of life, such as the spirit of solidarity and of helping one another in work, production, and everyday life, as well as in the struggle against oppression and exploitation and the closeness of each person to the common ideals of the village and the country, have been maintained. But the limitations imposed by the traditional way of life are also very large and have impeded efforts to build the new countryside. The feudal laws, ethics, rituals, and ceremonies that bound peasants in the old society continue to slow their progress today. Patriarchy, gerontocracy, and bureaucratism [local feudal despots], the last being the most salient, have left deep marks in the countryside. In the local bureaucratic order, [jockeying for] position gave rise to bitter disputes within the ranks of the feudalists, causing them to form factions and slander and overthrow one another.

The bureaucratic feudal system and private ownership gave birth to an evil product: village bullies. These persons exploited and oppressed peasants through embezzlement, pilfering, misappropriation, repression, and the appropriation of public property.[42] In the past, these village bullies had many ways to exploit peasants using the public rice land. Today, the use of public funds and the rice land owned by collectives leads to many negative outcomes. Numerous investigations have shown that in more than a few localities, the party chapter, administration, and cooperative management board have actually been reincarnated as the old stratum of village bullies. From their positions as representatives of the people and the village, they have turned into people who oppress, exploit, and suppress farmers, becoming parasites who extort peasants. These "new village bullies" have been using their public positions and lineage ties—a problem that has become a grave concern in recent years—to control people, form factions, and oppress honest and legitimate laborers, resulting in the loss of internal unity. The community psychology of the village, a positive feature of peasants' spiritual life, is slowly disappearing. In the past, peasants united to oppose the village bullies and wicked landlords. Today, many persons see injustice but do not dare to struggle against it for fear of being accused of opposing the party or the administration! In many places, a new class structure has formed, whose backbone is the people who hold public office and their supporters. This structure controls the socioeconomic system in the countryside and creates serious inequities in the distribution of grain and other foodstuffs, industrial goods, and agricultural materials; the allocation of land to build houses; the distribution of contract fields; and the appointment of local officials. These [officials] have established many unreasonable "funds" and "laws" to squeeze money from the peasants' labor, resulting in an acute lack of democracy in the countryside.

In the past, the villages, with their strength as close-knit communities, used self-management and autonomy to struggle against oppression by landowners, officials, and the dictatorial monarchy and against intervention by the state in

---

42. In the old village, public property included public rice paddies and village funds [note in the original text]. See Le Code, "Public and Private Lands" (chap. 3).

village affairs, and to protect the rights of laborers. Today, many people in public office have distorted this tradition of "the edict of the king stops at the village gate." They violate the positions and policies of the party and state and have turned the locality they lead into their own "private space" in order to further their personal interests. In many places in the countryside, the division and the differences between rich and poor are becoming increasingly clear. Honest, hardworking laborers receive only a fraction of whatever they produce, which is not enough for them to live on. This is partly due to unreasonable state policies. It is due more to the local leaders taking the peasants' output for themselves or using it carelessly. Clearly, illegitimate economic interests are what is behind the bureaucratic system and the "new village bullies." The only way to get rid of them is for party cadres and working peasants to wage a forthright and determined struggle against them while combining economic policies with social policies in a correct and appropriate manner.

There is one other matter concerning those who make socioeconomic policies regarding peasants and the countryside and who guide agricultural production and the work of the peasant association. During the past ten years, *the countryside's overall cultural standard has been declining*. Peasants pay little attention to cultural life or to raising their cultural standards, partly because of the leadership's lack of concern. The basic cultural and social needs of farmers are not being met, particularly those in the border areas and on the islands. Shortages of teachers and schools, medical facilities, medicine, and doctors in rural areas are widespread. In contrast, economic difficulties and worries about contract land and private land (almost every farm family must farm with only crude implements and techniques and cope by themselves with the vagaries of the weather) have prevented peasants from broadening their knowledge, even though they have always wanted to learn and make technical improvements to produce higher yields. Many of the biological revolution's achievements have been applied very effectively in the countryside, but they have received little attention in recent years. The activities of science-technology teams, libraries, clubs, and local artistic troupes have markedly declined [as well]. The "semi-illiteracy" and illiteracy in the countryside are alarming. More than a few peasant families have had to take their children out of school so that they can stay home and work.

During the past several years, *many old customs have reappeared in the countryside* (such as lavish and costly funeral and wedding ceremonies, and superstitious beliefs). The main reasons for this are the near absence of economic and cultural development and socioeconomic policies in the countryside, and those that do exist are inappropriate or have not been thoroughly implemented. Propaganda and efforts to educate peasants, especially rural youths, regarding politics, ideology, culture, and a new worldview and philosophy of life have been somewhat lacking. In the past, members of the village were pleased to be recognized and praised when they contributed to the community, and they considered building and strengthening the village to be their duty, with each generation being responsible for setting an example for the next [generation]. Today, even though their worldview and philosophy of life have been broadened, many people remain isolated [from the community], withdrawing into their families and looking out for only their own interests.

To rid ourselves of this selfish and individualistic way of life that has trampled on all the moral and cultural values accumulated by our people over the generations and to reestablish a new system in the countryside (as manifested in economic, political, and cultural-spiritual life), it will be necessary, first, to consolidate and strengthen the ranks of cadres at the basic level, including party chapters, people's committees, cooperative and production collective management boards, the Peasant Association, the Communist Youth Union, the Women's Union, and so on. This is the most important way of guaranteeing the success of the policies of renovation in the countryside today.

[Dinh Thu Cuc, "Nong dan va nong thon Viet Nam hien nay,"
43–46; trans. Jayne Werner]

SOCIETY AND CULTURE

TRUONG CHINH

MARXISM AND VIETNAMESE CULTURE (1948)

Truong Chinh, the Communist Party's chief theoretician, issued a major statement in 1948 on culture and the arts as the party prepared to wage an all-out resistance war against the French. Breaking with the previous decade's literary focus on individualism and romanticism and the convention of "art for art's sake," Truong Chinh argued that culture must serve the national cause and contribute to the defense of the country. He had declared in 1943 that Vietnamese culture should be national, scientific, and mass based, which he expands on here. Now that Vietnam was at war, artists and writers could no longer indulge in their personal aesthetic pursuits. The Communist Party would monitor all artistic and cultural production for their adherence to these principles. This cultural policy, which set the parameters for cultural production in the Democratic Republic of Vietnam until 1986, aimed to cleanse Vietnamese culture of French colonial and Chinese influence, instill socialist realist principles, and uplift the quality of a pure Vietnamese culture, viewing culture as a key component in an ideological struggle. The Communist state's use of ideology and culture for political purposes reflected a time-honored practice in Vietnamese governance, as seen, for example, in the *Book of Good Government of the Hong Duc Era* (1540s), which issued moral and philosophical guidelines to the emperor's officials.[43] This selection is from a longer report.

---

43. See "Rules of Behavior" (chap. 3).

The Character and Mission of New-Democracy Culture

Vietnamese new-democracy culture must have the following three characteristics: it must be national, scientific, and popular. Opposed as it is to the enslaving colonial feature that characterizes the old Vietnamese culture, Vietnamese new-democracy culture fights against all oppressive and aggressive forces wherever they come from, for the independence and freedom of the people, and respects the independence and freedom of the peoples of the world. It also seeks to banish all ideas that smack of weakness and manifest a lack of independence and self-reliance. New-democracy culture has all the characteristics and traditional marks of our people and must grow by developing what is good and beautiful and rejecting what is bad and ugly. It represents what is best in the national heritage, and at the same time, it stands ready to absorb the good, the beautiful, and the progressive in a foreign culture. It is neither xenophobic nor racist. It denounces hybridism and rootlessness and opposes the gulping down raw of other people's cultures, parrot-fashion learning, or the mechanical introduction of a foreign culture into our own without taking into account the particularities and concrete conditions of the country and its people.

So that the national element in our culture may blossom, we must make vigorous propaganda for resisting the French colonialists and combine the offensive by pen and speech with the offensive by the gun. In paint and in ink, in each embroidered thread, in each cut of the sculptor, and in each sequence of thought lies a way to strengthen patriotism and intensify hatred for the enemy. We distinguish what constitutes the enslaving side of French imperialist culture from what represents the beneficent influence of French democratic culture, in order to eliminate the former and keep the latter. We learn from the advanced cultures of the world yet take a critical view of and censure its reactionary cultures.

We search for and study literary and art works bequeathed to us by our forefathers, but we put them under the microscope, criticize them, and pick out only the positive traditions of our national culture.

Vietnamese new-democracy culture must be scientific in character, as opposed to the backward, corrupt, and feudal character that still lingers in the old Vietnamese culture. It upholds freedom of faith but condemns superstition, idealism, mysticism, clumsiness, and carelessness, all those habits that are irrational or retrograde. It speeds up the campaign for a new life and opposes lax discipline and obsolete customs. It brings elementary science and information about preventive medicine to the masses. It propagates scientific thought and Marxist philosophy in order to counter prejudices and antiquated and fallacious viewpoints. A prominent feature of this new-democracy culture is that it takes practice seriously and seeks to combine it with theory. It rebels against the French policy of deceit and obscurantism and upholds the truth. It promotes progress and pushes aside what stands in the way of the people's advancement. Not progress that is divorced from the past of the nation, but progress that is not hybrid, uprooted, imitative, or mechanical. [Not progress] in favor of the "primacy of science," which claims that it is only with modern science that foreign aggressors equipped with high technology can be defeated and that we, for our part, must accept frustration because we are inferior in science and technology. With regard to artistic creation, new-democracy culture approves of socialist realism. . . .

Since new-democracy culture opposes the estrangement and antipopular character of the ruling cultures in former times and in the present French-occupied areas, it must be popular. It serves the masses, the overwhelming majority of the people. It rejects any idea of culture's being ethereal, that the higher it is, the more precious it will be, and the more complicated it is, the better it will be. On the contrary, it holds culture to be close to the masses so as to lead and educate them, to raise their cultural level, to single out and nurture the talents that blossom among them, and not to pander to them while learning from them. The joys and sorrows of the masses should be the joys and sorrows of the cultural fighters who, if they wish to fulfill the mission of enlightening them in thought and feelings and of solving their misapprehensions in time, ought to understand these joys and sorrows. A culture in service of the masses must faithfully reflect the aspirations and hopes of the people who are involved in fighting and production and make them conscious and enthusiastic, fortified by faith and will.

To that end, we, as vanguard cultural workers, are bound, on the one hand, to strive to completely liberate the masses from illiteracy and to awaken them politically, and, on the other, to eradicate with determination the erroneous tendencies in literature and art and the ailments that afflict our national culture or were passed on by the French colonialists' decadent culture. Examples that can be cited are individualism, fence-sitting, escapism, neutralism, aestheticism, and the like.[44]

While the ruling culture in our country for almost a century of French domination was antinational, antiscientific, and antipopular, its present new-democracy culture must be national, scientific, and popular. The three traits coexist and are interwoven, inseparable one from the other. . . .

As combatants on the cultural front, we can, in the light of these characteristics of new-democracy culture, advance three principles to guide our task

---

44. *Individualism* refers to being solely concerned with one's own interests, with big sales of one's works, no matter whether they benefit or harm the masses.

Fence-sitting refers to the shirking of responsibility to the nation and the war of resistance, and aloofness from the people so as to enjoy life and pass the time.

Escapism refers to burying one's head in distractions, in "pure art," and not caring for the material and moral conditions of the people.

Neutralism refers to the doctrine according to which culture is set above social classes and strata, ignorant of the struggle of the people, not caring to serve it, and unmindful of politics.

Aestheticism aims at so embellishing the form that it becomes overrefined and likely to attract only a very few "aristocratic intellectuals" and the group of exploiters and parasites [note in original text].

to promote the new culture: to render it national, scientific, and popular. What is antinational, antiscientific, and antipopular will be vigorously rejected; what is compatible with the nation, science, and the people, we will work hard to strengthen, maintain, and improve. At the same time, we will adopt a proper attitude on the basis of these principles:

1. To be absolutely loyal to the fatherland and the resistance, neither to accept compromise with reactionary thought and culture nor to adopt either neutralism or the attitude of fence-sitters.
2. To strive to conduct scientific and technological research and to apply the results to benefit production, the struggle, and human life; to rely on Marxist theory as the compass for action; to combine knowledge with action and theory with practice.
3. To serve the people wholeheartedly; to remain close to the workers, peasants, and soldiers; to be in sympathy with the masses; and to learn from but at the same time to educate and lead the people.

This should be the proper attitude for us fighters on the cultural front, and the key to our success. Such an attitude is essential to carry out the mission ahead as President Ho has directed us:

Culture aims not only at boosting our people's moral and material forces for resistance and nation building, but also at highlighting our people's great achievements for the whole world to know. Our cultural workers must create deserving works, not only to glorify our present efforts, but also to bequeath to future generations shining examples of resistance and national building.[45]

Some Concrete Problems in Our Country's Present Literature and Art

Those writers and artists who have the requisite conditions or feel inspired to work long and carefully on their creations to render their art "eternal" should by all means do so. It is certain that if they are faithful to their time and keep close to the struggle of the nation and the lives of their people, when their works reach the highest level of art, they will also have the highest propaganda value.

Another opinion is that during the war of resistance, because the people's level of culture was limited, they [now] are interested only in prosaic and easy works; that acceding to their wishes would result in lowering the quality of art; and that if we keep doing this, what will be left of culture?

---

45. Ho Chi Minh, "Message to the Second National Cultural Congress," July 1948 [note in the original text].

This is our answer: it is only natural, that after having been subjected to the exploitative, oppressive, and obscurantist regime of the French colonialists for so many years, the cultural level of the masses of our people would have limitations. But it would be wrong of us to think that they are not capable of artistic appreciation. They are bound to understand, feel for, enjoy, and love our works if they offer a lively description of reality.

The feelings of the masses are pure, sincere, and exceedingly warm. They are indifferent only to insincere, recondite, recherché, evasive, and preposterous works of art and hate the monsters of imagination.

The second problem that confronts a good number of our men of letters and art is, What is socialist realism?

As we understand it, socialist realism is a method of artistic creation that portrays the truth in a society evolving toward socialism according to objective laws. From objective reality, we must concentrate on "the typical features in typical situations"[46] and reveal the inexorable motive force driving society forward and the objective process of evolution.

Alexis Tolstoy writes: "The task of the artist . . . is to draw from reality what is typical, what people can see at first glance, gather facts, ideas, and contradictions into a lively picture and indicate the right direction leading to the correct future."[47]

The attitude of socialist realism is objective. Some objective truths are unfavorable to us. For example, shall we report truthfully a battle we have lost? We can, of course, describe a lost battle, but in doing so, we must see to it that people realize how heroically our combatants accepted sacrifices, why the battle was lost, what our gains were, and, notwithstanding the defeat, that our combatants never felt demoralized because all were eager to learn and draw the appropriate lessons in order to secure victories in future battles. We can describe a local defeat while showing that the war is going our way. It should be kept in mind that some truths are worth mentioning, but other truths are better left unmentioned, at least temporarily, and if mentioned at all, the question is where and how they should be revealed.

Another thing of note in socialist realist literature is that writers should let the facts speak for the opinions they wish to convey or propagandize. Engels says that "tendencies should spring from situations and actions, not be bared too candidly." Nothing is worse than a drama in which the playwright uses the words of a character to argue interminably.

Another question asked is, Should we have criticism and controversy now? It is our opinion that we definitely should. It is well known that the cultural life of our people is too tranquil. Generally, we have no way of knowing whether new

---

46. Friedrich Engels, "Letter to Miss Harkness," in *Marx and Engels on Literature and Art*, ed. Lee Baxandell and Stefan Marawski (St. Louis: Teleo Press, 1973), 114–16.

47. Alexis Tolstoy, *Creative Freedom* [note in the original text].

works of art are good or bad, are welcomed or rejected by the public. There is no one to criticize or appraise them! As soon as a policy, a point of view, is put forward, it falls straight into oblivion or is coldly received. As a result, Vietnamese authors have little chance to be patronized and encouraged, or criticized and helped to improve. Without criticism and controversy, our cultural movement is too placid, too uneventful! It is just like a horse trotting along with his head dropping, who needs the whip of criticism to set him galloping.

Some people fear that criticism may damage unity. What really matters is the manner in which criticism is made: this and not the criticism itself may damage unity. Criticism that is harmful to unity is criticism that is without tact and sincerity. On the contrary, criticism offered in a responsible spirit, with good intentions and in modest terms, not only does no harm but also helps us make progress and bring about mutual understanding. Facing the enemy of the nation, unity undoubtedly is necessary, but it does not require that we never raise any objection. Such unity is one-way unity. True unity must be founded on criticism motivated by unity and aimed at strengthening unity.

We sincerely await the appearance of conscientious critics in Vietnamese literature and art. Some friends object to criticism as tantamount to "washing our dirty linen in public" and thereby displaying our weaknesses for the enemy to seize and beat us with. [But] the criticism we have in mind is criticism that abides by principles and democratic discipline and not "free criticism." Some people may wish to use criticism to sow dissension and doubt in the ranks of our people and supply the enemy with documents to be used against us. They are not critics but troublemakers, who seek not progress but provocation. Their place is not on the public debating platform of a democratic country but in the prisons of the people's state.

The targets of our criticism should not be confined to fallacious tendencies in our own ideology, scholarship, and art; we must criticize and devote ourselves mainly to assailing the enemy's reactionary thoughts, literature, and art. The ideological and cultural struggle cannot be divorced from the political, armed, and economic struggle. The enemy uses its pessimistic and hedonistic theories to indoctrinate the youth in the areas it controls; it stultifies the masses with egoistical and idealistic points of view; it propagates decadent and rotten art; it poisons the spirit of our people in the most wicked manner. Have we exposed the enemy yet? Duhamel[48] came to Indochina to speak in defense of the colonialists' policy of plundering. Who among the cultural circles answered him as he deserved? In the war against the imperialist aggressors, we must also join the ideological battle!

We eagerly await the master critics of imperialist culture in general and French colonialist culture in particular. We should not forget that decadent French literary

---

48. This presumably refers to Georges Duhamel, a French author and political activist in the 1930s.

and artistic ideas and their dangerous theories have more or less penetrated the minds of our young people, intellectuals and the current generation of writers and artists. Criticizing the decadent literature and art of the French colonialists is another way of changing the thinking of our intellectual and cultural circles.

For creating works of good art, we would like to offer the following opinions. A number of writers and artists feel that they are running in circles, left behind by the war of resistance, which is moving ahead at great speed, with everyone taking an active part in it and in the task of national reconstruction. Time flies, but they themselves are at a loss what to do or what to create or have created only little, with negligible results. The prevailing mood among them is a feeling of perplexity as to the "right path" to take. Our friend Nguyen Dinh Thi, writing in the *Van Nghe* [*Art and Literature*] periodical,[49] has rightfully echoed the bewilderment, anguish, and anxiety that beset a whole generation of our country's writers and artists who are trying to break out of the trammels of the past in order to surge ahead and remain abreast of the movement.[50]

Artistic creation is an important matter. Its process, as we see it, includes a series of tasks:

1. Choosing the topic.
2. Determining the audience for one's creation.
3. Acquiring conditions necessary for realization.
4. Testing works by the reaction of the masses.

Topics are not really lacking. The war is being fought in a thousand and one forms and situations, which are reflected in our minds and stir our souls.

What is essential is to live among the masses of the people, that is, to live a worthy life, the militant life of our people. To investigate, research, collect information, study, be in sympathy with the masses, and commit oneself wholly to the movement; to let one's heart beat in harmony with the heart of the nation; to share in its joys and sorrows; to labor and fight with the people; and to share their faith and hatred. If we do this, why [would we] fear that life will not be rich in ideas and emotions?

The audience for our artistic creation is the people. For any creation we should ask, Who is to enjoy and watch what we are creating? If our real purpose is to create for the people, then we should determine who the people are, of what sections they are composed, what their current cultural level is, what their aspirations are, and so forth. Only when the answers to these questions are clear in our minds can we produce realistic and worthwhile works. Many works are expensive cakes offered to the masses when they are crying out for bread. We must

---

49. *Van Nghe* was published by the Vietnamese Writers Association [note in the original text].
50. "Nhan Duong" (Recognizing the Path), *Van Nghe*, no. 1 [note in the original text].

oppose subjectivity in artistic creation, that is, taking one's own level as the general level. To thoroughly understand the cultural level of the people is not to lower one's art to the lowest artistic level of the people but to use the average level of the majority of the people as the standard and to use one's works to raise their cultural level.

The conditions for artistic realization consist of what is directly necessary to complete a work of art. Any writer or artist who wishes to create as he should requires the three following conditions:

1. To have the opportunity to hear, look, feel, and see; to get in touch with the masses; to work in the movement; or to keep close to the movement. On-the-spot observation has always been profitable to artistic creation (condition of place).
2. To have the time to polish, perfect, and revise one's work (the time condition). Having time here does not imply abandoning action or seeking refuge in one's ivory tower. The French writer Henri Barbusse wrote and acted at the same time without ever easing up.
3. To have the means necessary for subsistence and creation (the material condition).

Some other, secondary, conditions also are important: a propitious climate for artistic creation and the publication of creative works. Favorable circumstances drive and encourage people to create. The war has supplied writers and artists with such an atmosphere, and cultural organizations can complement this condition. The publication of works of art also is a necessary condition. Without being able to print and publish, those engaged in producing art would lose enthusiasm for it.

To be a good finished product, a work of art must be born of the movement and the masses and return to where it originated. If one does not live with the army or is not a member of an army unit, one cannot write a play about the army. Even a play written by someone in the army still must be performed in front of the army and the people and be revised on the basis of criticism from various army units and the people in order to ensure its artistic worth. The masses are the most impartial and perspicacious judge of art. When once created, if works of art are devoured, admired, enjoyed, adopted, applied, and chosen by the people as their daily spiritual nourishment, they must have value. In contrast, those works whose birth is heeded and cared for by no one will die an early death.

Do the masses have to learn about art before they are capable of criticizing art? No. They are the most expert art critics of all, precisely because they have the many ears and eyes, the sound judgment and feelings, of large numbers of people. In this respect, no art critic can compare with the masses. It is quite possible that the majority in the masses are not knowledgeable about some technical aspects, but the masses include both experts and nonexperts; what some cannot see, others can.

So, to my knowledge, eminent writers never feel condescension, complacency, and contempt for the masses; instead, they usually go to them for final control of their works and to listen attentively to their opinions with a view to improving and completing their creations.

The method of artistic creation outlined here, together with the right ideological stand and some definite aptitude or talent, will produce good works of art. Let our writers and artists use these suggestions when participating actively in the current movement for patriotic emulation that is sweeping over the country. . . .

Let us hope that this cultural congress will provide an impetus for the movement of patriotic emulation by writers and artists.

[Adapted from Truong Chinh, "Marxism and the
Issue of Vietnamese Culture," 264–68, 270–71, 284–92, 294]

TRAN DAN

WE MUST WIN (1956)

Despite most writers' acceptance of the party's political line on culture during the first resistance war,[51] some writers struggled to retain their own artistic and creative freedom apart from the party's strictures. One such figure was Tran Dan (1926–1997), who, as a political commissar, had written about the heroes on the ramparts at Dien Bien Phu. In early 1956, Tran Dan's poem "We Must Win" appeared in a new journal, *Masterpieces of Spring*, which a group of prominent writers and poets in Hanoi started during a brief "hundred flowers" opening of the arts. This poem crystallizes and encapsulates the conflicts between intellectual and artistic freedom and the party's control of art and literature in the so-called Nhan Van Giai Pham affair (1956/1957). The party charged that writers associated with this group were remote from everyday life, in effect acting as agents of the capitalist class, lacked the correct ideological position, and opposed the state. "We Must Win" expresses the poet's ambivalence about the costs of war, especially the prospect of the renewal of war in the south, as well as disillusionment with the postwar society in the north. The sorrow and isolation of the poet and his lover are offset by a sense of the desolation of the city of Hanoi. At the end of this excerpt from the poem, these doubts move toward a cautious note of hope.

> *I live on Sinh Tu Street:*
> *Two people*
> *A small house*
> *Full of love, but why was life not joyful?*

---

51. See Truong Chinh, "Marxism and Vietnamese Culture" (this chap.).

Our country today
        although at peace
Is only in its first year
We have so many worries . . .
. . .
I was living with frayed nerves
A time dense with conversations about going south
The rain kept falling darkly
People kept dragging themselves away in groups
I became one who carried anger
I turned my body to block their way
—Stop!
        Where are you going?
                What are you doing?
They complained of lack of money, of rice
Of priests, of God, of this and that
Men and women even complained of sadness
—Here
        They longed for the wind, for the clouds . . .
                Oh!
Our sky faces a cloudy day
But why abandon it when it is our sky?
. . .
Who led them away?
        Who?
                Led them to where? And they kept crying
The sky still lashes down heavy wind
North and south, heartbreaking division
Kneeling down, I ask the rainstorm
Not to continue falling upon their heads
                —enough hardship!
It is their bad fate—don't punish them further
Neglected gardens and fields, empty houses
People are gone but they leave behind their hearts
Oh northern land! Let's safeguard for them
I live on Sinh Tu Street

Those sorrowful days
I walk on
        seeing no street
                seeing no house
Only the rain falling
        upon the red flag

I meet you in the rain
You were out looking for work
Returning each day with bowed head
—My beloved!
They still say to wait
I do not ask more, what can be said?
It rains, it rains
Three months gone
You waited
Living by the future
Days and nights like orphans
Sadly leading each other on
You walk
      in the rain
           head bowed
A young woman of nineteen
. . .

The rain keeps dragging on
I have yet to write about north south
I still believe Poetry has to generate storm and wind
But today
      I bow my head
Where did Poetry go?
Why do poetic lines
Not move the earth and sky?
It keeps raining
I want to abandon Poetry
      to do something else
But today while it is raining I am a man absorbed
A little talent
      I write political poetry
Those sorrowful days
I walk on
      seeing no street
           seeing no house
Only the rain falling
Upon the red flag
. . .

I am walking under the rainy sky of the north
My ears are filled with whispers
People talking and people shouting
—They're violating the agreement!
—Will there be an agreement?

—*Will there be elections?*
—*Will it be general elections or not?*
—*Will the elections be on time? Or a few years later?*
These questions in a midst of a disorderly life
Human beings have always distrusted their own kind
People are often frightened by the future
People forget that America is a paper tiger
People are still in a hurry, little patience
Their courage is not yet that of workers and peasants
They do not yet have hearts steely as iron
People should open their eyes wide to see!
A trumpet sounds
The heroic army
A sea of guns
A mountain of bayonets
Thousands of eyes
Our army is practicing in the streets
Fluttering flags redden the streets, redden the houses
That flag is ever victorious
That army is courageous in all battles
Rising from the earth
To be the proletarian army
Maturing with each step
. . .
Today
The whole country cries out: UNIFICATION
We believe in the demand of our slogan
—*Return the south*
                    I turn my face to the sky
Crying out—suddenly a piece of the sky falls down
A few drops of red blood fall upon me
My people!
The words we shout
Have the power to pierce the sky bloody
No enemy can hinder our desire
We walk on—like the giant earth
Very gentle, but with a determined walk
Today
The lines of poetry I have written are
Like a bayonet: pierce
Like a bullet: tear
Like a thunderstorm: scream
Like love: saturate

I believe in this struggle
The whole country has elected me unanimously
I am the champion of faith
But why is it that tonight
I lower my face before the light?
Empty room, the night rat nests
So many worries appear
They become the rocks
            blocking our path!
My love, it turns out
A believer like me
            still has moments of doubt
Who has REASON? Who has FORCE?

. . .

Today
It has stopped raining, no more wind
The rising sun reddens the streets, reddens the houses
Reddens all hearts and lungs
My love, try counting how many rainy days!
Now
As you bring things out to air
Don't forget
To also air out our hearts and souls
Look high into the sky
The streets below full of red flags!
You have found work
Low salary—Life is still hard
But blessed
The government has many concerns
But we would be worse off without its ability to dispel the storm
You hang the red flag above the house
The flag dispels the ghosts
Dispels their dark shadows!
The red wounds of the resistance
Have closed their dark shadows!
The red wounds of the resistance
Have closed their mouths, have began to heal

. . .

The flag flutters
            reddens the streets
                        reddens the houses
The color of the flag is the medicine for my ailment
Who wins and who loses?

Who has REASON? And who has FORCE?
My love
> *Today*
>> *the sky is blue*
>>> *dark blue*

The rising sun
> *reddens the streets*
>> *reddens the flags*

Demonstration after demonstration
Sorrowful days have passed
Peace
> *is more consolidated*

I walk on
> *seeing the streets*
>> *seeing the houses*

Not the falling rain
Only the sun rising
Upon the red flag
We live on Sinh Tu Street
My love
Today
Let's close the door
And go out
> *to join the demonstration*

Raise the red flag
> *and sing*
>> *until our lungs burst*

Of everyone
> *in cities*
>> *and countryside*

The hungry, the sated, the rich, the poor
Those who are happy
Those living in sadness
Everyone!
> *Out to the streets!*

Let's go!
> *in large groups*
> *in large groups*

Demanding the future:
PEACE
> *UNIFICATION*
>> *INDEPENDENCE*
>>> *DEMOCRACY*

> *That is the heart*
> > *the blood of our life*
> *Livelihood! Love!*
> *We must win!*
> > [Tran Dan, "Nhat dinh thang," in *Ghi*, 151–64; trans. Kim N. B. Ninh]

DEMOCRATIC REPUBLIC OF VIETNAM

LAW ON MARRIAGE AND THE FAMILY (1959)

The innovative Marriage and Family Law, passed by the Democratic Republic of Vietnam's National Assembly on December 29, 1959, and signed by Ho Chi Minh on January 13, 1960, was designed to reform such patriarchal marriage customs as child marriage, arranged marriage, and polygamy and to improve the status of women. Monogamy, marriage based on free will and mutual consent, as well as the protection of women's and children's rights in the family were among the guiding principles of the new matrimonial regime instituted by this law. In addition, women were given the right to divorce, along with the division of common property and the prospect of custody of their children. As in the Le Code, the regulation of marriage by the state was a standard practice in Vietnamese governance, similar to eighteenth- and nineteenth-century state guidelines on proper marriage rituals and social behavior.[52]

Chapter I: General Principles

ARTICLE 1

The state guarantees the implementation of a free and progressive matrimonial regime based on monogamy, equality between men and women, and protection of the interests of women and children, which is designed to promote a happy, democratic, and harmonious family whose members shall unanimously support and love one another and help one another so they can advance.

ARTICLE 2

The remnants of the feudalistic matrimonial regime based on the arbitrary superiority of men over women and the neglect of children's interests are abolished.

---

52. See Le Code, "Marriage" (chap. 3), and, for example, Trinh Cuong, "Edict Regarding Local Customs," and Pham Dinh Ho, "On Marriage" (both in chap. 4); and Minh Mang Emperor, "Ten Moral Precepts," and Gia Long Emperor, "Edict Outlining Propriety and Ritual" (both in chap. 5).

ARTICLE 3

Contracting for a premature marriage, concluding a marriage using force, hindering marriages based on free consent, requiring goods by reason of marriage or betrothal are prohibited. Violence toward and the ill treatment of women are prohibited, as are second-rank marriages.

Chapter II: Marriage

ARTICLE 4

Men and women who have attained the legal age shall have the full right to freely decide their marriage; neither party can impose constraints on the other; and no third person is allowed to use force or to cause hindrances.

ARTICLE 5

Married persons are prohibited from taking another wife or husband.

ARTICLE 6

A woman may marry only after reaching eighteen years of age; a man, only after twenty years.

ARTICLE 7

The period of mourning does not constitute a barrier to marriage.

ARTICLE 8

Widows have the right to remarry; in the case of remarriage, their rights and interests concerning their children and property are guaranteed.

ARTICLE 9

Marriage between relatives of lineal descent or between adoptive parents and adopted children is prohibited. Marriage between full brothers and sisters and between half brothers and half sisters on the father's side or between half brothers and half sisters on the mother's side is prohibited. Marriage between collateral relatives up to the fifth degree or between persons related by blood shall be regulated by custom.

ARTICLE 10

Those persons completely incapacitated by sexual impotence and those affected by diseases such as leprosy, venereal disease, and mental illness shall not marry for the duration of these conditions.

ARTICLE 11

Marriages must be approved by the local administrative committee where the bride or the groom reside and must be entered into the register of marriage. No other marriage formalities have legal effect.

Chapter III: Obligations and Rights of Spouses

ARTICLE 12

Husband and wife are equal within the family in all respects.

ARTICLE 13

Spouses have the obligation to love, esteem, and care for each other; provide each other with assistance so they can advance; bring up their children; participate in productive labor; and establish a harmonious and happy family.

ARTICLE 14

Each spouse shall have the right to freely choose an appropriate profession and to freely engage in political, cultural, and social activities.

ARTICLE 15

Spouses have equal rights with respect to the ownership, use, and disposal of property acquired before and during the marriage.

ARTICLE 16

If one spouse dies and distribution of the property becomes an issue, the distribution shall be carried out in accordance with the provisions in article 29. Each spouse shall have the right to inherit property from the other.

Chapter IV: Relations Between Parents and Children

ARTICLE 17

Parents have the obligation to love, raise, and educate their children. Children have the duty to love and respect their parents, take care of them, and provide for their needs.

ARTICLE 18

Parents shall not mistreat their children or ill treat their daughters-in-law, adopted children, or children born of a previous marriage. Abandoning a newborn child or making an attempt on its life is strictly prohibited. Any person who abandons a newborn child or makes an attempt on its life, or anyone who is responsible for these crimes shall be criminally liable.

ARTICLE 19

Boys and girls have equal rights and duties in the family.

ARTICLE 20

After attaining majority age, those children still living with their parents are free to choose their profession, to engage in political and social activities, and to possess and own property. They also, however, shall be obligated to care for the overall life of their family.

ARTICLE 21

The acknowledgment by the father or the mother of a child born out of wedlock must be certified by the local administrative committee. In case of litigation, the people's court shall resolve [the identification of the child].

ARTICLE 22

A child born out of wedlock shall have the right to ask the people's court for the father's or mother's acknowledgment [of his or her identity].

The mother shall have the equal right to request the identification of the father of a minor child born out of wedlock. The guardian of a minor child shall also have the right, in the name of the child, to request the identification of the father or mother of a child born out of wedlock.

ARTICLE 23

A child born out of wedlock who has been acknowledged by his or her father or mother or authorized by the people's court to acknowledge his or her parents has all the rights and duties of a legitimate child.

ARTICLE 24

Adopted children shall have the same rights and duties as biological children. The adoption must be approved by the local administrative committee of the domicile of the adoptive parent or that of the adopted child and must be entered into the civil register. The people's court can terminate an adoption at the request of the adopted child or other persons or organizations. This request must be made to protect the interests of the adopted child.

Chapter V: Divorce

ARTICLE 25

If an investigation is [undertaken] on petition for divorce filed by both spouses and is satisfied that both parties freely and fully consent to the divorce, the people's court will approve the divorce.

ARTICLE 26

On petition for divorce filed by one of the spouses, the appropriate organs shall initiate an investigation and make an effort at reconciliation. If the reconciliation fails, the people's court shall resolve the matter. If the situation between the spouses is grave, in which they cannot resume a life together and the purpose of the marriage is impossible to reach, the people's court shall decree a divorce.

ARTICLE 27

During pregnancy of the wife or within one year after she has given birth to a child, the husband does not have the right to file a petition for divorce. The inadmissibility of a petition does not apply if the wife has filed for divorce.

ARTICLE 28

In case of divorce, all claims for the restitution of gifts and the cost of nuptials are prohibited.

ARTICLE 29

In case of divorce, common property shall be divided, paying due consideration to the contributions made by each party, the state of the property, and the actual situation of the family. Household labor is considered equivalent to productive labor. In the distribution of property, the interests of women, children, and production are to be protected.

ARTICLE 30

In a divorce case, if one of the two parties in need requests support, the other party shall be obligated to pay alimony to the needy party within the limits of his or her own means. The amount and duration of alimony shall be fixed by mutual agreement of the two parties. If the parties disagree, the people's court shall resolve the matter. If the spouse who is receiving alimony remarries, he or she will relinquish their right to further alimony.

ARTICLE 31

A divorced couple reserves all their duties and rights toward the children common to their marriage.

ARTICLE 32

In a divorce case, the guardianship, maintenance, and education of minor children shall be determined in every respect in the children's interest. As a rule, a nursing infant is to be entrusted to the mother. The parent who is not awarded custody of the children has visitation rights and the right to give the children care and attention.

A divorced couple must, each according to his or her own ability, contribute to the cost of the upbringing and education of their children. If necessary, alternations in the guardianship of the children and the amount of contributions to their upbringing and education may be ordered in the best interests of the children.

ARTICLE 33

The parties shall agree on the guardianship, maintenance, and education of the children and the contribution to the cost of their maintenance and education. If they cannot agree or their agreement contains illegal elements, the people's court shall resolve the matter.

Chapter VI: Implementation

ARTICLE 34

All acts that violate the current law shall be punished according to existing legislation.

ARTICLE 35

The current law goes into effect on the date of its promulgation.

Depending on the specific situation, in regions where ethnic minorities reside, provisions may be enacted to adjust the current law. These provisions must be approved by the Standing Committee of the National Assembly.

[Democratic Republic of Vietnam,
Luat hon nhan va gia dinh Nam 1959;
trans. Jayne Werner]

NORTHERN AND SOUTHERN POETRY AND SONG
DURING THE VIETNAM WAR

When the American war divided Vietnam into two warring halves, writers, poets, and other artists tried to make sense of the intensity of the violence and its human costs. In the north, literature tended to hew to the principle of "serving the people," but sometimes a poem struck a tender note about innocence, heartbreak, and loss.

"Secret Scent" (1969), by Phan Thi Thanh Nhan, is a subtle lament by a young woman unable to directly express her love to her young man, a soldier about to go off to war. She leaves him a bouquet of grapefruit blossoms, a scent with which they both grew up, to tell him of her love. This poem, a muted statement of loss during war, greatly affected urban audiences in the north during the massive mobilization of troops sent to the south.

In the south, poetry and songs were based on the traditions of the 1930s New Poetry movement, with their emphasis on individual freedom and passionate disengagements and concerns. Although sometimes seemingly unaffected by the war, the most powerful works captured the sense of dread and futility of war. One of the southern republic's most important poets, Thanh Tam Tuyen, expresses in his poem "Resurrection" (1956) a sense of foreboding about the regime's ultimate fate. His poems marked a departure from the 1930s New Poets but, at the same time, echoed those of Han Mac Tu by plumbing the depths of consciousness through mystical and surrealistic means.[53] Often described as an existentialist, Thanh Tam Tuyen relied on intuition, imagination, and feeling to achieve his poetic effects.

---

53. See Han Mac Tu, "This Is Vi Gia Village" (chap. 6).

The south's preeminent folksinger, Trinh Cong Son, composed haunting melodies about death and destruction. "A Lullaby of Cannons for the Night" (1967) was written from the perspective of a city dweller, in the form of a lullaby. After the Tet Offensive of 1968, cities in South Vietnam no longer were safe. This song, with its cascading rhythms and chantlike cadences, reflected the quickening pace of the war and its increasing proximity to the cities, like a noose being tightened around them. Instead of a lullaby, cannons sound in the night, signaling an impending doom. Women poets in the republican south also became important interpreters of the wartime malaise, capturing both the mournful losses and the horrors of the war. One of the most distinguished poets, Nha Ca, wrote in a classical but distinctly modern mode. Her poems are known for their musicality and balance of form. Nha Ca's poem "The Bell of Thien Mu" (1964) describes how the sound of the bell of the Thien Mu pagoda on the Perfume River in her birthplace of Hue, like other bells throughout Vietnamese history, drew her into memories about life's journey and its vagaries.[54]

PHAN THI THANH NHAN

SECRET SCENT

The windows of the two houses at the end of the street
Always stayed open for no reason.
Two old friends who used to be classmates.
A grapefruit tree behind one house floats its scent to the other.

She hid a bunch of flowers in her handkerchief
    And, hesitantly, crossed to her neighbor's house.
Someone there would leave the next day for the front.

In silence they sat, lost for words.
Their eyes met, then turned away.
Who could dare say the first words?
The scent of grapefruit blossoms made them more shy.
The young man didn't dare ask for the blossoms;
The young girl didn't dare give them,
But the warm and refined fragrance
Could not hide itself . . .
And floated faintly by.

Like the blossoms, the young girl was silent.
She let their fragrance speak for her love:

---

54. For other bells in Vietnamese history, see Nguyen Binh Khiem, "The Three Teachings" (chap. 3).

How distant you seem; you still don't know.
Don't you see I come to you?
The fragrance will fill your chest.
When you leave
The fragrance will follow you, everywhere.

Leaving each other
They still didn't speak,
Yet the fragrance sweetens the young man's journey.

[Bowen, Nguyen, and Weigl, eds. and trans., *Mountain River*, 117]

THANH TAM TUYEN

RESURRECTION

I want to cry like I want to throw up
on the street
crystal sunlight
I call my own name to soothe my longing
Thanh Tam Tuyen
evening a star breaks against a church bell
I need a secret place to kneel
for a little boy's soul
fearful of a fierce dog
a hungry dog without colors

I want to die like I want to sleep
although I'm standing on a river bank
the deep dark water is restless
I scream my own name to slake my rage
Thanh Tam Tuyen
night falls onto a sinful whispering realm
O child wearing a red kerchief
Hey there wolf
a wandering sort of wolf

I crave suicide
an eternal sort of murderer
I scream my own name in distress
Thanh Tam Tuyen
strangle myself into collapsing
so I could be resurrected
into an ongoing string of life

mankind doesn't forgive the crime of murder
the executioners kneel
the time of resurrection

a shout is a prayer
for the waiting centuries
I want to live like I want to die
among intersecting breaths
a flaming chest
I call softly
dear
open the door to your heart
my living spirit has turned into a child
as pure as the truth one time.

> [Thanh Tam Tuyen, "Phuc sinh," in *Toi khong con co doc*,
> 2; trans. Linh Dinh]

TRINH CONG SON

A LULLABY OF CANNONS FOR THE NIGHT

Every night cannons resound in the town
A street cleaner stops sweeping and listens
The cannons wake up a mother
The cannons disturb a young child
At midnight a flare shines in the mountains

Every night cannons resound in the town
A street cleaner stops sweeping and listens
Each flight of the planes frightens the child
Destroying the shelter, tearing golden skin
Each night the native land's eyes stay open wide

Thousands of bombs rain down on the village
Thousands of bombs rain down on the field
And Vietnamese homes burn bright in the hamlet
Thousands of trucks with claymores and grenades
Thousands of trucks enter the cities
Carrying the remains of mothers, sisters, brothers

Every night cannons resound in the town
A street cleaner stops sweeping and listens
Every night cannon shells create a future without life

Cannons like a chant without a prayer
Children forget to live and anxiously wait

Every night cannons resound in the town
A street cleaner stops sweeping and listens
Every night the cannons sing a lullaby for golden skin
The cannons become like a familiar refrain
And children are gone before they see their native land

> [Trinh Cong Son, "Dai bac ru dem," in *Ca khuc da vang*, 10–11;
> trans. John C. Schafer and Cao Thi Nhu-Quynh]

NHA CA

THE BELL OF THIEN MU

I grew up on this side of the Huong River
The river that defines patches of memory,
The fruits of Kim Long, the steel of Bach Ho bridge,
The pagoda gate welcomes the quickening pace of the river flow.
Clear water flowed through my untroubled childhood,
Ancient stupa, old bell, gentle river, inconsequential waves.
The nights were vast, the days laden with importance
Morning birds, evening crickets, cockcrows at the break of dawn
The sounds of the bell permeated deep under my skin,
The bell and I were intimate like evening and night.
I left home at the age of nineteen,
The night before I lay waiting for the bell to toll,
The end of madness, the beginning of sad slumber.
The sounds of the bell came and gently woke me up,
The sounds of the bell came and went as only I could see
Only I could see the sounds of the bell dissolve
The sounds of the bell dissolve, regular like the breaths of siblings
The sounds of the bell dissolve into fragments like a mother's tears
The sounds of the bell dissolve yet linger on like the rain in the street
The sounds of the bell dissolve but take forever like a sleepless night
The sounds of the bell dissolve into pieces like the fragments of my heart
From the time when I parted way with my bell
I changed my name, took up writing and journalism
Life's needs taught me to lie, to bend the truth
The pagoda gate lost touch with the wayward child
Ancient stupa, old bell, minor river in morning mist
Water flows through opaque misty eyes
Grass grows on the old roads in my heart

The old bell now sunken deep under my skin
My childhood fell in and drowned a long time ago
Times of the past receded like long gone floods
But somehow memories return tonight
The sounds of the bell suddenly come alive
The sounds of the bell of my childhood
Break into thousands of voices inside me
Into fragments of bronze, dark like the skin of the night
fragments of bronze, dark like the stirrings of the body
fragments of bronze dark like the blood of restoration
fragments of dark bronze advancing in uniform steps
I have woken up, my bell, oh my bell
I have woken up, I already am awake
I have truly woken up
Woken up with storms and devastations
woken up with history
Dear mother, this afternoon in the old city
The sounds of the bell came to me, like tears falling on my hand
on the water, on the people's faces, on the road's surface
let me return, to stand here with my gaze fixed in a daze.

[Nha Ca, "Tieng chuong Thien Mu," in *Tho Nha Ca*, 25;
trans. Ton That Quynh Du]

NGUYEN THI THAP

RETURNING TO MY HOME VILLAGE (1986)

This excerpt from Nguyen Thi Thap's memoir, *From the Land of Tien Giang*, follows the standard format of a revolutionary narrative. Nguyen Thi Thap (1908–1996) was a founding member of the Viet Minh liberation committee in My Tho Province in southern Vietnam in 1945 and was a Communist militant during both the French and American wars. During the American war, she left for the north, where she became head of the Women's Union, among other posts. In 1975, after the end of the war, she returned to South Vietnam. This translation captures what it was like to return home after forty years and her observations of the changes the war had wrought in her homeland.

The small car taking us from Ho Chi Minh City to the Mekong Delta rolled along at a good speed along National Highway 4. About five kilometers [a little more than three miles] from the provincial capital, it began to slow down, crossed the Trung Luong intersection, and headed toward my home village.

My heart began to race. I had kept calm up to now, despite my rising excitement. Soon I would be home. It had been forty years—since I left to join the revolution. Tam Canh, my comrade and brother, was traveling with me. He was happy and excited and could not sit still in the car, his head turning right and left to take in the scene along the road.

It was a day in mid-June 1975, after the liberation of Saigon and all of South Vietnam. We had flown from Hanoi to Saigon, where Mrs. Nguyen Thi Dinh and other members of the Liberation Women's Association met us and took us to the association's guest house. I was going to stay in Ho Chi Minh City for a few days to meet and chat with friends and acquaintances whom I had not seen since the signing of the 1954 Geneva Agreements and the regroupment of Viet Minh cadres to the north. But my brother was impatient to get home, so I arranged for us to make the trip the next day.

It was the beginning of summer, and the sun was shining brightly. From the paddy fields and fruit orchards lining the road, a mass of dragonflies of different varieties and hues rushed toward our car and hovered over the highway, rising in the air to avoid the windshield and then descending again. They seemed to make way for our car and brought back memories of my childhood when my friends and I used to chase them in the hope of catching a few. Other children would chant, "Dragonflies, dragonflies, fly away; watch out for the hands that try to nab you." I would hold my breath and stealthily approach one, only to see it fly away just as I was about to catch it. Could it have heard the chant of the other children? It made a circle and then, when the danger seemed to have passed, landed at the exact same spot.

Later, after I joined the revolution, I left my village for Saigon to operate [as a militant] because my underground activities had been uncovered and I was about to be arrested. After a few years, however, I returned to my village—like the dragonfly that came back to the spot where it had landed. I came back because of the close ties I had to my home village—ties I felt unable to sever. But I would have to leave again, and this time it would be years before I could return—like the dragonfly that had to make numerous circles before it could come to rest.

But things had changed a lot. From the moment I could see Saigon from the air, I knew that things were different. It was as if I had never been here before. Houses crowded against one another. Tall buildings rose up in the air. Cars and motorcycles filled the streets, moving to and fro like the shuttle of a loom. It would be hard for me to recognize the areas where my comrades and I tried to lead the life of proletarians in order to penetrate the working class. The first time I traveled to Saigon from my village, I took the train. But now, the railway was gone—torn up and removed to be replaced by a wide asphalt road. In the old days, when we passed Phu Lam, we could see rolling paddy fields stretching to the horizon. Now, houses and shops lined both sides of the road all the way to Binh Dien and Binh Chanh. Gone were the small thatched peasant huts, with their wells, buffalo sheds, and bamboo hedges. In their places were brick houses with metal roofs, blue and red walls plastered with lurid advertisements, gas stations, administrative compounds, and old enemy outposts. I could not recognize anything. We sped past an unending succession of houses and orchards—particularly from Luong Phu to Ben Chua, and Trung Luong where the orchards formed a green mass of vegetation with their trees laden with mangoes and guava, and their heavy branches hanging over the irrigation ditches and creeks filled with water. I scrutinized the faces of people I passed, trying to see whether I could recognize someone I knew. But everything was unfamiliar. The baskets they carried, their hats, and their clothes had changed. Even the women peddlers carrying baskets suspended from bamboo poles were dressed differently from before.

After the long circle of the dragonfly, I was almost home. Mixed with the joy of home coming and the happiness over our great victory was a feeling of sadness. Almost all my comrades had perished. This day came at the cost of countless separations and losses. Ahead of us, we saw the Long Dinh bridge. Its white curve looked like the bleached half shell of a turtle. It was here that Ton Duc Thang directed the destruction of the bridge after he was released from the Con Dao penal island following the August 1945 Revolution, to block the French advance into Cai Lay and Cai Be.

We stopped about a kilometer from the village, left our car with a family living next to the road, and walked the rest of the way. I could hardly believe my eyes. Could this be my village? A few years before the Final Great Victory, some comrades who had been released by the enemy [that is, the Saigon government] as part of a POW exchange over the Thach Han River [separating North and South Vietnam], had come to visit me in Hanoi and told me about what Long Hung had become. But things had changed even more since then. We wanted to find the house of Mrs. Hau, my niece and the daughter of my brother Tam Canh. She was about forty years old by now. We had just finished asking some villagers, "Where is Mrs. Hau's house?" when we saw comrade Sau Danh approaching. He was a member of the Province Military Committee, a native of Long Dinh. He was fifty years old, but he was agile and quick like a man in his prime. He shouted with joy when he saw us, "You are back! Let me take you there."

But where was the road that led to our village? The old red laterite road, large enough for cars to pass through—the road that led to the Long Hung temple and that people from nearby villages had taken to participate in the 1940 uprising—was now just a narrow path. The comfortable houses that used to line the road had disappeared, replaced here and there by dilapidated, low, thatched huts. The trees had been cut down, and thorny underbrush spread along the path. I smelled the damp earth, the wild vegetation in the sunlight, the field crabs in their hollows, and the burned straw that the villagers had used to smoke out the field rats. These smells, which defy description, were the only things that had not changed since my childhood days in the village.

The news spread quickly. The whole village was now aware of our return. My brother Tam could not recognize his own wife. She was beautiful in her youth, and I was surprised to find her looking so old and weak, with a bent back—like an old woman. She embraced me and wept. Hau wrapped her arms around her father, and wailed, "Father, you have come back, but everyone has died; no one is left." I had never seen my brother cry before—except at our parents' funeral—but now he also shed tears. I had to turn away so that no one could see that I was doing the same.

Many visitors crowded in. A crippled neighbor also came, brought by his children. The thatched-roof house was too small to accommodate everyone. Some would enter and then leave to make room for those waiting in the court-yard to come in. Everyone cried—hosts and visitors, children, adults and old folks alike. No one could hold back tears, brought on by sadness and also by joy. I cried because I was overwhelmed by the emotion of homecoming. The visitors cried because they were happy to witness our family reunion but also be-cause they grieved over their own losses. Since the 1930s, their family members had left one by one, but none had come back. So tears of joy mingled with tears of sorrow.

Mr. Hai Ty, who lived in a nearby hamlet, was passing by our house just as we arrived. He was on his way back from visiting a granddaughter who had just given birth. He stayed to visit with us until we departed. He was over eighty years old, but he was still mentally fit and of good humor. He sat on the edge of the bed, his feet dangling, and let the tears stream down his face. He said, "Hau, don't tell your father that everyone has died. This is simply not true. During the nine-year war against the French, they swore they would exterminate the people in Long Hung. Then the U.S.-Diem regime swore they would bury the people of Long Hung. But, you see, your house is overflowing with people." Then he laughed heartily and wiped off his tears with the sleeve of his shirt.

Yes, I still remember when a UMDC detachment [Catholic militia unit] set up a military outpost in Vam Xang in 1950. They swore to exterminate the people of Long Hung. They all were Catholics. The people nicknamed them the "drinkers of the people's blood."[55] They were hooligans—abandoned illegitimate children who had been raised by reactionary Catholic priests. Men from Long Hung—whether revolutionary activists, guerrilla fighters, or inno-cent civilians—caught by the UMDC were invariably beaten and tortured to death. Their preferred method was to smash their victims' genital organs with a hammer or wooden club, or burn them with a rag soaked with gasoline until they dropped off. They proclaimed that their goal was to exterminate the Com-munists in Long Hung and to nip off all revolutionary offshoots. But they could never achieve their objective. It did not occur to them that the red flag with the

55. This play on the abbreviation UMDC turns it into Uong mau dan chung: "drinkers of the people's blood."

yellow star—now the glorious emblem of our fatherland—was unfurled for the first time in Long Hung and My Tho Province during the 1940 uprising. In the darkest years, when the enemy drowned the people of Long Hung and South Vietnam in a sea of blood, this flag was embedded in the hearts of the people, like red-hot embers that no force could extinguish.

Then, during the anti-French war, the first attack that set ablaze a whole enemy convoy took place on Giong Dua road in My Tho Province. It was followed by battles in Ham Vo, Hau My, and by the attack against enemy paratroopers in Gay Co. These attacks have become part of our nation's history— forever. During the American war, it was no accident that the U.S. and Saigon army set up Binh Duc military sector near Long Hung. With their river flotilla and artillery units, they subjected Long Hung day and night to shelling and bombing, and used helicopters to catch cadres and guerrillas by surprise. They intended to exterminate all living things—from the grass to the trees to the insects and worms—hoping to destroy the fighting spirit of the people lucky enough to survive in this tiny land raked with shells and bombs day and night. Yet they could not prevent the people of My Tho from inflicting a staggering blow on the Americans and their Saigon puppets at the battle of Ap Bac. Nor could they prevent the emergence in Long Hung of Le Thi Hong Gam, the national heroine.

Who doesn't fear death? But one also has to ask oneself: what kind of life is worth living? In February 1962, when I was in Hanoi, I heard that Vinh Kim had been liberated for the third time. The day before that battle, the inhabitants of Long Hung and the neighboring villages of Kim Son, Song Thuan, and Thanh Phu held a banquet for seventy-two fighters who had sworn to fight to the death. They sat under durian trees, talking and laughing. In front of them, sandalwood and incense was burning at the martyrs' memorial monument that had been set up, with a banner bearing the words "The Fatherland Honors Your Sacrifice" written in bright golden letters, and a coffin painted in red symbolizing the spirit of sacrifice of the soldiers willing to give their lives so that the fatherland could live. Weeping, women were serving food to the soldiers. The next night, the troops attacked and liberated Vinh Kim in a fierce, fiery battle. Three of them were killed. Their toughness reminded me of the heroes of Rach Gam under the Quang Trung emperor and of the courage of the comrades who took part in the 1940 uprising—people who did not fear death. All these heroes seemed to have coalesced in these seventy-two fighters—they are perhaps one and the same, the past and the present merged together. No one can wipe out all the heroes of our land because they keep on appearing generation after generation.

We were determined to continue on the path of our struggle. If we kept forging ahead, we would overcome whatever difficulties were lying in our way, and eventually we would reach our goal. The poet To Huu once said, "In the south, wherever there is verdant vegetation, the people wither; and wherever the vegetation withers, the people thrive." Looking down from the plane window, we could see green expanses and clusters of houses with red-tile roofs. These were formerly enemy-occupied areas, where the vegetation was luxuriant but the people were miserable because they were in the enemy's grip like fish lying on a chopping board, subjected to repression and their children forced into military conscription to meet the demands of "changing the color of corpses."[56] Some people in the occupied areas could not fully share the national joy of final victory because they had committed mistakes under enemy pressure or had given in to enemy enticements. But in areas where the vegetation, animals, and inhabitants were subjected to the abundant spraying of noxious chemicals and had to live in makeshift thatched-roof houses, the people were jubilant. Their revolutionary optimism, which had persistently illuminated their hearts throughout the dark years since the Ngo Dinh Diem regime, was finally rewarded—expressed today in boundless exuberance and even exultation.

We stayed from 9 A.M. until late in the afternoon. Half the inhabitants of Long Thanh A hamlet had come to see us. Everyone wanted to tell us about the situation in the hamlet since we left for the north—about the struggles and the events, and about those who had died and those who were still alive. Many recounted their own close brushes with death—with gestures and laughter, as though they were telling mythological tales, proud that they had survived while others would have perished in similar circumstances.

All the visitors brought food—bananas, custard apples, ducks, chickens, and fish from their ponds—and then went into the kitchen to cook it. They prepared a sumptuous lunch in our honor. I was not dreaming. I was really back in my home village, eating the native dishes of deep-fried fish and sour soup. As we clinked glasses, Sau Danh exclaimed, "If I had only known you were coming, I would have asked a photographer to come and film this occasion."

The smell of incense wafting from the altar gave the occasion the air of a festive ritual honoring ancestors. We wondered whether their souls were present to witness our happy reunion.

My brother Tam asked about Tamarind mound, where a group of comrades had killed themselves as the 1940 uprising was being repressed, in order to avoid capture by the enemy. We were told that the tamarind tree had grown to an enormous size. Tears welled up in my eyes as I looked at the altar. Now that the revolution had returned in triumph, these old comrades were no longer with us—they all had passed away.

At about 5 P.M., we heard gunshots. Sau Danh whispered to me, "You'd better go to My Tho or Saigon to spend the night. Not all the enemy troops have

---

56. This phrase refers to part of the demands of the "Vietnamization" policy to replace American combat troops with Vietnamese soldiers.

surrendered. Some of them remain in hiding and come out at night to look for food. We're searching for them, but you'd better take precautions."

I left when the sun was about to set behind the *so* tree. This tree had sprouted in the old foundation of my grandparents' and parents' house. The tree had shed all its leaves, but its branches were heavy with yellow fruit. A few early white flowers had appeared. A couple of birds flew in and landed softly on its curved branches. I could see the bases of the columns among the vines and wild vegetation. The old armoire made of hard wood that had been hidden in the bamboo grove since the days of the resistance against French domination was still there. Its glass panes had been broken, and most of the bamboo had died, but it was still standing at its old spot. The garden surrounding the house, once luxuriant, had become a wasteland, dotted here and there with the huts of people who had recently moved in. When we reached a canal that had been dug in recent times across my family's paddy fields to block American tanks, I was seized with emotion and felt I could not go on.

In the evening breeze that carried the smell of the alluvial soil in the Mekong River and was blowing over the rice fields, I thought I heard the shouts of Quang Trung's troops as they rushed over the waves in their boats to rout the ten thousand Thai troops in this section of the river. And I thought I could see faintly the gnarled tamarind tree that still stood erect on the mound near the edge of Phuoc Thanh village. So, our nation's and party's tradition of fighting against foreign intruders had continued uninterrupted from generation to generation in this part of the country.

In the 1930s and 1940s, the peasants in this region, under the leadership of the proletariat, rose up to demand the right to live. The waves after waves of people who marched to demand the reduction of taxes and land rents stimulated and influenced the movement in practically all the provinces of the south. After the French colonialists repressed the 1940 uprising and plunged it into a sea of blood, they were buoyed by the belief that the revolution would never be able to rise up again. But in August 1945, although we were still bearing the scars of the repression, we rose up again and joined the rest of the nation in a massive uprising to take back political power. Then during the nine years of fighting against the French and twenty-one years of fighting the Americans—the two wars during which we had to face much stronger enemies—we refused to let hardships and difficulties deter us, and the party poured all its political and military capabilities into defeating the French and then the Americans in succession. Waves after waves of people fell on the battlefield, but we kept rushing forward, determined not to cede an inch of the land that had been bequeathed by our heroic ancestors.

Someone said quite rightly, "It takes myriad blood drops to hold on to a bit of soil, and it takes several pieces of bone to hold on to a section of a bridge." This sentimental recollection, this giving in to emotions, was perhaps inevitable for me as I returned to my home village after decades of absence.

All the vestiges—and even the sounds—of my childhood were gone. I could no longer hear the sound of mangosteens falling on the ground in the quiet garden. I could no longer smell the fragrant ripe durian in the moonlight. I could no longer hear the bats beating their wings as they flew back and forth over the orchard all night long.

All that tied me to this historic land infused with the long-standing tradition of struggle seemed to have disappeared. But at the same time, my feelings for the revolution were never as intense as they were now. And I felt excited at the prospect of reconstructing my home village and my country and at the plans to rebuild them and make them better, more magnificent, and more beautiful. Many unforeseen difficulties lay ahead on the road to this future; therefore my unbreachable faith had to be tempered with realism.

[Nguyen Thi Thap, "Xom cu lang xa," in *Tu dat Tien Giang*, 11–22; trans. Mai Elliott]

RELIGION

THICH NHAT HANH

THE MIRACLE OF MINDFULNESS (1975)

Thich Nhat Hanh (b. 1926) is known as the founder of "engaged Buddhism," which views one's personal awakening as tied to social activism. Seeking an end to the violence of the Vietnam War and based on the foundation of the Buddhist revival movement of the 1930s, Buddhist social activists in South Vietnam in the 1960s developed a philosophy of nonviolence to forge a middle way between dogmatic Marxist doctrine and the right-wing military dictatorships sponsored by the United States. Thich Nhat Hanh's writings point to the interrelatedness of existence, practice, and action, and inner and outer worlds. Meditation or mindfulness is seen as the means to become aware of others' suffering and the oneness of things. Liberation and other basic Buddhist tenets are redefined by Thich Nhat Hanh's aphorisms: The raft is not the shore, and the finger pointing to the moon is not the moon. In other words, the journey is more important than the goal, and Buddhism must adapt to and confront the modern world's problems. Engaged Buddhism grows out of the Mahayana tradition, and the enlightened being is a bodhisattva. The two attributes of enlightenment, compassion and wisdom, are regarded as inseparable and are expressed in action. Everyone is capable of enlightenment; hence, Thich Nhat Hanh's precepts were written not just for monks but for laypeople as well. Nonetheless, Thich Nhat Hanh's text resembles Ngo Thi Nham's 1796 contemplative reflection on Buddhist principles.[57] Thich Nhat Hanh wrote the following as a letter to his young practitioners in the School of

---

57. See Ngo Thi Nham, "The Sound of Emptiness" (chap. 4).

Youth for Social Service, which he founded in 1964 as a branch of the Unified Buddhist Congregation of Vietnam (UBCV),[58] so they could learn how to discipline and fortify their minds for nonviolent action under dangerous conditions, as they often were in the line of fire.

One Is All, All Is One: The Five Aggregates

Let me devote a few lines here to talk about the methods you might use in order to arrive at liberation from narrow views and to obtain fearlessness and great compassion. These are the contemplations on interdependence, impermanency, and compassion.

While you sit in meditation, after having taken hold of your mind, you can direct your concentration to contemplate the interdependent nature of certain objects. This meditation is not a discursive reflection on a philosophy of interdependence. It is a penetration of mind into mind itself, using one's concentrative power to reveal the real nature of the object being contemplated.

Recall a simple and ancient truth: the subject of knowledge cannot exist independently from the object of knowledge. To see is to see something. To hear is to hear something. To be angry is to be angry over something. Hope is hope for something. Thinking is thinking about something. When the object of knowledge [the something] is not present, there can be no subject of knowledge. The practitioner meditates on mind and, by so doing, is able to see the interdependence of the subject of knowledge and the object of knowledge. When we practice mindfulness of breath, the knowledge of breath is mind. When we practice mindfulness of the body, the knowledge of body is mind. When we practice mindfulness of objects outside ourselves, the knowledge of these objects also is mind. Therefore the contemplation of the nature of interdependence of all objects also is the contemplation of the mind.

Every object of the mind is itself mind. In Buddhism, we call the objects of mind the dharmas. Dharmas are usually grouped into five categories:

Bodily and physical forms
Feelings
Perceptions
Mental functioning
Consciousness

---

58. The UBCV was part of the "third force" under the Republican regimes, and after Vietnam was reunified under Communist rule in 1976, the UBCV continued its independent posture vis-à-vis the new government. The Communist authorities still do not recognize the UBCV as a legitimate religious organization.

These five categories are called the five aggregates. The fifth category, consciousness, however, contains all the other categories and is the basis of their existence.

Contemplation on interdependence is a deep looking into all dharmas in order to pierce through to their real nature, in order to see them as part of the great body of reality and in order to see that the great body of reality is indivisible. It cannot be cut into pieces with separate existences of their own.

The first object of contemplation is our own person, the assembly of the five aggregates in ourselves. You contemplate right here and now on the five aggregates that make up your self.

You are conscious of the presence of bodily form, feeling, perception, mental functioning, and consciousness. You observe these "objects" until you see that each of them has intimate connection with the world outside yourself: if the world did not exist, then the assembly of the five aggregates could not exist either.

Consider the example of a table. The table's existence is possible because of the existence of things that we might call "the non-table world": the forest where the wood grew and was cut; the carpenter; the iron ore that became the nails and screws; and countless other things related to the table, the parents and ancestors of the carpenter, [and] the sun and rain that made it possible for the trees to grow.

If you grasp the table's reality, you will see that in the table itself are present all those things that we normally think of as the non-table world. If you took away any of these non-table elements and returned them to their sources—the nails back to the iron ore, the wood to the forest, the carpenter to his parents—the table would no longer exist.

A person who looks at the table and can see the universe is a person who can see the Way. You meditate on the assembly of the five aggregates in yourself in the same manner. You meditate on them until you are able to see the presence of the reality of one-ness in your own self and can see that your own life and the life of the universe are one. If the five aggregates return to their sources, the self no longer exists. Each second, the world nourishes the five aggregates. The self is no different from the assembly of the five aggregates themselves. The assembly of the five aggregates plays, as well, a crucial role in the formation, creation, and destruction of all things in the universe.

Liberation from Suffering

People normally divide reality into compartments and so are unable to see the interdependence of all phenomena. To see one in all and all in one is to break through the great barrier that narrows one's perception of reality, a barrier that Buddhism calls the attachment to the false view of self.

Attachment to the false view of self means belief in the presence of unchanging entities that exist on their own. To break through this false view is to be liberated from every sort of fear, pain, and anxiety. When the bodhisattva Quan Am,[59] who has been such a source of inspiration for peace workers in Vietnam, looked into the reality of the five aggregates giving rise to the emptiness of self, she was liberated from every suffering, pain, doubt, and anger. The same would apply to everyone. If we contemplate the five aggregates in a stubborn and diligent way, we, too, will be liberated from suffering, fear, and dread.

We have to strip away all the barriers in order to live as part of the universal life. A person isn't some private entity traveling unaffected through time and space as if sealed off from the rest of the world by a thick shell. Living for one hundred or one hundred thousand lives sealed off like that not only isn't living, but it also isn't possible. In our lives a multitude of phenomena are present, just as we ourselves are present in many different phenomena. We are life, and life is limitless. Perhaps one can say that we are alive only when we live the life of the world and so live the sufferings and joys of others. The suffering of others is our own suffering, and the happiness of others is our own happiness. If our lives have no limits, the assembly of the five aggregates that makes up our self, also has no limits. The impermanent character of the universe, the successes and failures of life, can no longer manipulate us. After having seen the reality of interdependence and entered deeply into its reality, nothing can oppress you any longer. You are liberated. Sit in the lotus position, observe your breath, and ask someone who has died for others.

Meditation on interdependence is to be practiced constantly, not only while sitting, but as an integral part of our involvement in all ordinary tasks. We must learn to see that the person in front of us is our self and that we are that person. We must be able to see the process of interorigination and interdependence of all events, both those that are happening and those that will happen.

A Ride on the Waves of Birth and Death

I cannot leave out the problem of life and death. Many young people and others have come out to serve others and to labor for peace, through their love for all who are suffering. They are always mindful of the fact that the most important question is the question of life and death, often not realizing that life and death are but two faces of one reality. Once we realize that, we will have the courage to encounter both of them.

When I was only nineteen years old, I was assigned by an older monk to meditate on the image of a corpse in the cemetery. But I found it very hard to

---

59. Quan Am (Guanyin) is the goddess of compassion and mercy.

take and resisted the meditation. Now I no longer feel that way. Then I thought that such a meditation should be reserved for older monks. But since then, I have seen many young soldiers lying motionless beside one another, some only thirteen, fourteen, and fifteen years old. They had no preparation or readiness for death. Now I see that if one doesn't know how to die, one can hardly know how to live—because death is a part of life. Just two days ago Mobi told me that she thought at twenty, one was old enough to meditate on the corpse. She has turned only twenty-one herself.

We must look death in the face, recognize and accept it, just as we look at and accept life.

The Buddhist Sutra on Mindfulness speaks about the meditation on the corpse: meditate on the decomposition of the body, how the body bloats and turns violet, how it is eaten by worms until only bits of blood and flesh still cling to the bones, meditate up to the point that only white bones remain, which in turn are slowly worn away and turned into dust. Meditate like that, knowing that your own body will undergo the same process. Meditate on the corpse until you are calm and at peace, until your mind and heart are light and tranquil, and a smile appears on your face. Thus, by overcoming revulsion and fear, life will be seen as infinitely precious, every second of it worth living. And it is not just our own lives that are recognized as precious, but also the lives of every other person, every other person, every other being, every other reality. We can no longer be deluded by the notion that the destruction of others' lives is necessary for our own survival. We see that life and death are but two faces of life and that without both, life is not possible, just as two sides of a coin are needed for the coin to exist. Only now is it possible to rise above birth and death and to know how to live and how to die. The sutra says that the bodhisattvas who have seen into the reality of interdependence have broken through all narrow views and have been able to enter birth and death as a person takes a ride in a small boat without being submerged or drowned by the waves of birth and death.

Some people have said that if you look at reality with the eyes of a Buddhist, you will become pessimistic. But to think in terms of either pessimism or optimism oversimplifies the truth. The problem is seeing reality as it is. A pessimistic attitude can never create the calm and serene smile that blossoms on the lips of the bodhisattvas and all others who obtain the Way.

The Almond Tree in Your Front Yard

[I spoke earlier] . . . about the contemplation on interdependence. Of course, all the methods in the search for truth should be regarded as means rather than as ends in themselves or as absolute truth. The meditation on interdependence is intended to remove the false barriers of discrimination so that one can enter into the universal harmony of life. It is not intended to produce a philosophical system, a philosophy of interdependence. In his novel *Siddartha*, Herman Hesse did not yet see this, and so his Siddhartha speaks about the philosophy of interdependence in words that strike us as somewhat naïve. The author offers us a picture of interdependence in which everything is interrelated, a system in which no fault can be found: everything must fit into the foolproof system of mutual dependence, a system in which one cannot consider the problem of liberation in this world.

According to an insight of our tradition, reality has three natures: imagination, interdependence, and ultimate perfection. One first considers interdependence. Because of forgetfulness and prejudices, we generally cloak reality with a veil of false views and opinions. This is seeing reality through imagination. Imagination is an illusion of reality that conceives of reality as an assembly of small pieces of separate entities and selves. In order to break through, the practitioner meditates on the nature of interdependence or the interrelatedness of phenomena in the processes of creation and destruction. The consideration is a way of contemplation, not the basis of a philosophical doctrine. If one clings merely to a system of concepts, one only becomes stuck. The meditation on interdependence is to help one penetrate reality in order to be one with it, not to become caught up in philosophical opinion or meditation methods. The raft is used to cross the river. It isn't to be carried around on your shoulders. The finger that points at the moon isn't the moon itself.

Finally, one proceeds to the nature of ultimate perfection—reality freed from all false views produced by the imagination. Reality is reality. It transcends every concept. There is no concept that can adequately describe it, not even the concept of interdependence. To ensure that one doesn't become attached to a philosophical concept, our teaching speaks of the three nonnatures to prevent the individual from becoming caught up in the doctrine of the three natures. The essence of Mahayana Buddhist teaching lies in this.

When reality is perceived in its nature of ultimate perfection, the practitioner has reached a level of wisdom called nondiscrimination mind—a wondrous communion that no longer distinguishes between subject and object. This isn't some far-off, unattainable state. Any one of us—by persisting in practicing even a little—can at least have a taste of it. I have on my desk a pile of applications to sponsor an orphan. I translate a few each day. Before I begin to translate a page, I look into the eyes of the child in the photograph and look closely at the child's expression and features. I feel a deep link between myself and each child, which allows me to enter a special communion with them. While writing this to you, I see that during those moments and hours the communion I have experienced while translating the simple lines in the applications has been a kind of nondiscrimination mind. I no longer see an "I" who translates the pages to help each child; I no longer see a child who received love and help. The child and I are one: no one pities; no one asks for help; no one helps. There is no task, no social work to be done, no compassion, no special wisdom. These are moments of non-discrimination mind.

When reality is experienced in its nature of ultimate perfection, an almond tree that may be in your front yard reveals its nature in perfect wholeness. The almond tree is itself truth, reality, your own self. Of all the people who have passed by your yard, how many have really seen the almond tree? The heart of an artist may be more sensitive; one hopes that he or she will be able to see the tree in a deeper way than many others. Because of the artist's more open heart, a certain communion already exists between him and the tree. What counts is your own heart. If your heart is not clouded by false views, you will be able to enter into a natural communion with the tree. The almond tree will be ready to reveal itself to you in complete wholeness. To see the almond tree is to see the way. When asked to explain the wonder of reality, one Zen master pointed to a cypress tree and said, "Look at the cypress tree over there."

The Voice of the Rising Tide

When your mind is liberated, your heart floods with compassion: compassion for yourself for having undergone countless sufferings because you were not yet able to relieve yourself of false views, hatred, ignorance, and anger; and compassion for others because they do not yet see and so are still imprisoned by false views, hatred, and ignorance and continue to create suffering for themselves and for others. Now you look at yourself and at others with the eyes of compassion, like a saint who hears the cry of every creature in the universe and whose voice is the voice of every person who has seen reality in perfect wholeness, just as a Buddhist sutra hears the voice of the bodhisattva of compassion:

> The wondrous voice, the voice of the one
> who attends to the cries of the world
> The noble voice, the voice of the rising
> tide surpassing all the sounds, of the world
> Let our mind be attuned to that voice.

> Put aside all doubts and meditate on the
> pure and holy nature of the regarder
> of the cries of the world
> Because that is our reliance in situations of pain, distress, calamity, death.
> Perfect in all merits, beholding all sentient
> beings with compassionate eyes, making the ocean of blessings limitless,
> Before this one, we should incline.

Practice looking at all beings with the eyes of compassion: this is the meditation called "the meditation on compassion."

The meditation on compassion must be realized during the hours you sit and during every moment you carry out service for others. No matter where you go or where you sit, remember the sacred call: "Look at all beings with the eyes of compassion."

There are many subjects and methods for meditation, so many that I could never hope to write them all down for our friends. I've mentioned only a few simple but basic methods here. A peace worker is like any one else. She or he must live her own life. Work is only a part of life. But work is life only when done in mindfulness. Otherwise, one becomes like the person "who lives as though dead." We need to light our own torch in order to carry on. But the life of each one of us is connected with the life of those around us. If we know how to live in mindfulness, if we know how to preserve and care for our own mind and heart, then thanks to that, our brothers and sisters will also know how to live in mindfulness.

[Thich Nhat Hanh, *Miracle of Mindfulness*, 45–60]

NGUYEN VAN BINH

VIETNAMESE CATHOLICS, MARXISM, AND THE PROBLEMS OF CATECHISTIC INSTRUCTION (1977)

After the end of the Vietnam War in 1975 and the reunification of the country as the Socialist Republic of Vietnam in 1976, Vietnamese Catholics were faced with an uncertain future under Communist rule. But in 1975, Monsignor Nguyen Van Binh, the archbishop of Ho Chi Minh City, immediately announced that he welcomed the return of peace, and he appealed to his fellow Catholics to participate in the new society and help reconstruct the country after years of war. This approach was further developed in Archbishop Nguyen Van Binh's letter to his fellow bishops, written in October 1977, in which he charted a new course, claiming that Catholicism could coexist with Vietnamese Marxism because they had common goals. Nguyen Van Binh was able to adopt this stance because of the reforms stemming from Vatican II, stressing the Vatican's dialogue and efforts to accommodate non-Western cultures. Thus the Catholic church itself had moved closer to the concept of "liberation" and respect for the customs and political integrity of developing countries, thereby facilitating the archbishop's conciliatory stance. In his letter, the archbishop recommended to his bishops a specific approach to catechistic instruction, including questions and answers. This text was translated from the French version of his letter.

Vietnamese Catholics live in a socialist republic ruled by the Vietnamese Communist Party.

To define the sociocultural environment of Vietnamese Catholics, one need only analyze the preceding statement, since that analysis will enable us to discover the elements that constitute this milieu. Reflection on these foundations will permit us to identify the problems relating to catechistic instruction. Under the direction of the Vietnamese Communist Party, Vietnam is in the process of taking the socialist path. This fact with which you are all familiar is composed of three elements: (1) The Vietnam that is currently under construction is a Vietnam modeled on the Communist ideal. (2) The road toward it, the course to be followed, [and] the policy to be adopted all must conform to Marxist-Leninist doctrine, applied in an intelligent way that adheres to the Vietnamese creative spirit. (3) Above all, it is necessary to remodel the social structure and produce a man who conforms to the new pattern, namely, a Marxist-Leninist man. Catholic Vietnamese are therefore acting in a Marxist setting.

In this Marxist milieu, the Marxist Vietnamese approach religion in general and Christianity in particular from a Marxist point of view. This is clearly evident in both the courses of instruction and the public lectures that are reproduced in the official press.

Vietnamese Communists view the Vietnamese Catholic Church through the entire history of the evangelization of Vietnam, from its origin down to the present day. In turn, all the historic, political, economic, and social conditions exerted through evangelization and by the church in Vietnam are analyzed and evaluated through the light of Marxism-Leninism. Consequently, the picture of Vietnamese Christianity as painted by Vietnamese Marxists leaves much to be desired. According to them, the case of Vietnam shows the theory of Christianity as conceived by Marx to be true, the most salient feature being the collusion between the church and imperialism. We state this fact, not through any guilt complex but in order to demonstrate its seriousness as far as the church is concerned. Communists want only concrete facts, not theoretical arguments. Christians must therefore project a fresh image—an authentic image of Christ and the church.

The attitude of Vietnamese Catholics is cooperation in the spirit of the encyclical *Gaudium et Spes*.[60] In a country where the established regime makes the unification of all its citizens an essential objective in order to build up the state, Catholics refuse to live in a "ghetto" and remain on the fringes of society.

In July 1976, at the Episcopal conference in the two ecclesiastical provinces of Hue and Saigon, we bishops unanimously and unambiguously launched an appeal to Catholics, inviting them to follow a life of commitment—in other words, to contribute to the construction of society. We do not consider that we have made a revolution in the church by adopting this attitude; we are merely conforming to the encyclical *Gaudium et Spes* of Vatican II. Indeed for us, cooperation with atheists in the spirit of this encyclical means, in concrete terms, living in the environment created by the Communists and building a new society with them.

---

60. The church's new pastoral constitution issued by Vatican II stressed dialogue between Catholics and non-Catholics in order to create a better world.

We have taken a definite position, but the fundamental problem remains: how do we coexist with the Communists, how do we cooperate with them in the construction of the country while at the same time remaining Catholic and thereby making our specific contribution to the common task? On the pastoral level, the problems arising out of this new situation are really beyond the scope of our human strength. At the present time in Vietnam, the faithful, like those responsible for pastoral work, have had no preparation for life in a Marxist society. The Holy Spirit is still at work, but we, for our part, must work together with Him.

Problems Concerning Catechistic Instruction

In order to emphasize the fundamental points, we formulate the following four questions: Who is listening to me? What must I say? What objective must I aim at? and How shall I express myself?

Who is listening to me? Those who listen to me are members of Marxist-Leninist society; they were born into it and are growing up in it; they were initiated into Marxist-Leninist doctrine in their earliest school days. (It is worth noting that in our socialist republic, all the schools are administered by the state and the educational curriculum is designed to produce socialists.) Thus in the very near future, we shall have to give catechistic instruction to Catholics imbued with Leninist Marxism. This brings us to the second question.

What must I say? The answer will be determined by two elements: what I must say and what I am expected to say. What I must say: I must speak of the gospel of the Kingdom of Heaven, of God, the universe, and man within the framework of creation and redemption. I must say everything and omit nothing.

What am I expected to say? To succeed in my task, I must start with what is expected, with what people wish to hear. That means that the content of my teachings must take into account the questioning and the worries of the young people of tomorrow. Thus, and only thus, shall I be able to help them overcome these difficulties so that they may progress further. In the Marxist environment, the young will be perplexed by the human condition, by the question of the presence of God in the universe and in their own existence. Is this presence a cause of conflict? Is it an obstacle in the path of human progress? Do Christ and salvation, the Holy Spirit and the church, add something to the faith and the hope of Marxists? Does Christian eschatological hope neglect Marxist hope? Does it greatly exceed it? All these questions oblige me to give special emphasis to certain features in the contents of the catechism in order to satisfy my listeners yet without distorting the word of God through any flattery toward them.

What objective should I aim at? To be consistent with the position adopted and explained earlier, I must help my listeners understand and live out their faith in this Marxist environment. This means that I must lead them to view a faith in which they can place God, the universe, and mankind. I do not seek merely to dispel transitory objections and difficulties, but I also will help the young themselves face up to fresh problems that may arise.

This is why it will not be permissible for me to hide the differences between Marxism and Christianity. On the contrary, I shall have to set these out honestly—not in any spirit of antagonism but in one of openness and dialogue. I shall have to help the young live and converse with the Marxists. We believe that this exchange of views must begin and that we must produce a new generation equipped to pursue a dialogue with the Marxists. But the key to the solution of the problem lies under the fourth heading, which follows.

How am I going to express myself? In order for my listeners to understand me, I must use their language. God himself respected this necessity. To address mankind, he spoke through the prophets and, ultimately, he spoke to us "as his Beloved son": "The word was made flesh and dwelt among us." The young who were born and have been brought up in the Marxist environment will speak a Marxist language. Can the position of St. Paul, " to be a Jew to the Jew and Greek to the Greeks," be applied to Christians living in a Marxist environment?

To present the Catholic faith today through the medium of Marxist language certainly does not signify the "Marxification" of Christianity. Indeed, when Aristotelian or existentialist vocabularies were used to present the Catholic faith, one did not thereby "Aristotelianize" or "existentialize" it—if I may be allowed to express myself thus. For God who had spoken to Israel did not consent to being identified with any other divinity, and neither did Jesus allow himself to be confused with any image of the Messiah conceived by the Jews of his time.

Conclusion

Such are the fundamental problems we face. We still have to answer more concrete questions, such as, Who is going to perform the catechism? Where, when, and how is it to be done? It must be added that all future activities of a religious character may take place only on church premises and also that priority is given to work and production.

Finally, allow me, my dear brothers in the episcopacy, to ask for the assistance of those among you who have some experience of these problems, and especially those who are proficient in the use of Marxist language.

[Nguyen Van Binh, "Le milieu socioculturel des catholiques
vietnamiens," 923–24; trans. C. Jon Delogu]

SOCIALIST REPUBLIC OF VIETNAM

DECREE ON RELIGIOUS ACTIVITIES (1991)

Beginning in 1990, Vietnam adopted a more conciliatory approach to religious belief and religious organizations, in line with the cultural changes occurring under Doi Moi (Renovation). For the first time, the Communist Party acknowledged that religion could serve a positive spiritual need and that religious organizations could be considered part of Vietnam's cultural heritage. The opprobrium associated with religion was finally lifted, although the state also sought to create a legal framework for the operation of religious organizations. While the government relaxed previous restrictions, it also required all religious organizations to register with the government and obtain prior authorization for most activities. This decree, passed on March 21, 1991, led to the official recognition and normalization of most religions organizations and activities in Vietnam in the 1990s, with the notable exception of the UBCV.[61] Since the early Le dynasty, the Vietnamese state had sought to regulate religious and ritual activity.[62]

Chapter I: General Provisions

ARTICLE 1

The state ensures the freedom of all citizens to adhere or not to adhere to a faith and prohibits any discrimination on account of religion or belief.

ARTICLE 2

Religious and nonreligious citizens are equal before the law, enjoy citizens' rights, and have the responsibility to discharge all the obligations of citizens.

ARTICLE 3

Religious activities must comply with the constitution and the laws of the Socialist Republic of Vietnam.

---

61. See note 58.
62. See also Gia Long Emperor, "Edict Outlining Propriety and Ritual" (chap. 5).

ARTICLE 4

Religious activities in the legitimate and lawful interests of the believers are assured. Religious activities in the interests of the fatherland and the people are encouraged.

ARTICLE 5

Religious activities based on superstition are prohibited. Activities that misuse religious belief to undermine the country's independence, oppose the Socialist Republic of Vietnam, undermine the solidarity of the entire people and harm the healthy culture of Vietnam, and prevent religious believers from carrying out their obligations as citizens shall be dealt with according to the law.

Chapter II: Specific Stipulations

ARTICLE 6

Every citizen has the freedom to follow or not to follow a religion and to relinquish or change his or her religion. All acts that violate this freedom shall be dealt with in accordance with the law.

ARTICLE 7

Religious believers have the right to carry out religious activities not contrary to the policies, positions, and laws of the state; to conduct worship ceremonies [and] prayers inside their homes; and to participate in religious activities held at places of worship. Believers are not allowed to disseminate superstitious beliefs [or] to impede productive or educational activities or the implementation of the obligations of citizens.

ARTICLE 8

Religious activities typically held at places of religious worship (prayer sessions, services, sermons, lectures on religious doctrine) that are registered annually and conducted in accordance with local religious customs need not receive prior permission from the authorities.

Religious activities that deviate [from this] or go beyond normal practices must receive prior permission from the authorities.

ARTICLE 9

Meditation sessions of priests in the diocese, or clergy from various establishments and orders of the Christian faith, study sessions for Protestant ministers and missionaries of the Protestant faith, purification sessions for Buddhist monks and nuns, and similar religious activities must apply for permission from the appropriate Provincial People's Committee or equivalent authority.

ARTICLE 10

Congresses and conferences of religious organizations at the national, regional, or local level must apply for permission from the Council of Ministers.

ARTICLE 11

The state protects the places of worship of religious organizations. Religious organizations are responsible for maintaining and safeguarding their places of worship. With respect to repairs and building extensions that change the architectural style of their buildings, approval from the Provincial People's Committee or an equivalent authority must be obtained.

ARTICLE 12

In new settlements or new economic zones, religious followers who wish to construct new places of worship must seek permission from the Provincial People's Committee or an equivalent authority.

ARTICLE 13

Religious dignitaries, clergy, and believers are permitted to use places of worship for regular activities that have been classified as such in accordance with the regulations of the [state] cultural authorities.

ARTICLE 14

Religious organizations are allowed to publish prayer books and religious books [and] to produce and import religious cultural items or instruments to be used for religious activities in accordance with state regulations relating to the publication, export, and import of cultural items.

The circulation and storage of books, newspapers and journals, and cultural items that contain propaganda and distortions against the Socialist Republic of Vietnam, violate its laws, and are designed to drive a wedge between various religious organizations [and] among the ethnic minorities and the people are prohibited.

ARTICLE 15

Religious dignitaries and clergy may conduct economic, cultural, and social activities as other citizens may. They are encouraged to engage in labor, production, and service activities in their places of worship in order to improve their living conditions and to build, maintain, and repair their places of worship, provided that they fully comply with state policies and laws.

ARTICLE 16

Religious dignitaries, clergy, and religious organizations are permitted to conduct charity work in fields permitted by the state. Existing charity organizations sponsored by religious organizations shall operate under the guidance of the appropriate state agencies.

ARTICLE 17

Religious organizations are permitted to establish schools for training dignitaries and clergy but must seek permission and approval from the Council of Ministers.

The organization and activities of the schools training religious dignitaries and clergy shall conform to the regulations issued by the Government Committee for Religious Affairs and other state agencies.

ARTICLE 18

Provincial People's Committees or the equivalent state authority shall, along with the Government Committee for Religious Affairs and the Ministry of Education and Training, examine the personnel, teaching, and instruction in schools for training dignitaries and clergy to see that the instruction is carried out in accordance with the approved program.

ARTICLE 19

The promotion of religious dignitaries and clergy must receive the approval of the Provincial People's Committee or an equivalent authority. The promotion of dignitaries such as senior Buddhist monks; Catholic bishops, archbishops, and cardinals, and equivalent dignitaries in other religions, must receive the approval of the Council of Ministers.

ARTICLE 20

The appointment and transfer of dignitaries and clergy and professional religious evangelists, including those elected by religious believers, must be approved by the government authorities in the area where they operate. These dignitaries, clergy, and religious officials can operate only after their appointment and transfer have been approved by the appropriate local authorities.

ARTICLE 21

Religious orders (or similar forms of collective religious practice) must seek the permission and obtain the approval of the Council of Ministers or an agency delegated by it to conduct their activities.

Religious orders are permitted to convert new adherents to their faiths. New adherents must fulfill the procedures relating to registration and administration with the local authorities where the monastery and/or the permanent residences of these members are located.

ARTICLE 22

International activities of religious organizations, dignitaries, and clergy must comply with the general regulations on foreign relations of the state.

ARTICLE 23

If foreign religious organizations appoint and promote religious dignitaries and practitioners, such appointments and promotions must receive the approval of the Council of Ministers of the Socialist Republic of Vietnam.

Before implementing a directive from a foreign religious organization, individual believers and religious organizations in Vietnam must seek the permission of the government authority.

ARTICLE 24

Religious organizations and individuals who wish to send their members abroad for religious purposes or to invite foreign dignitaries and clergy or representatives of foreign religious organizations to Vietnam must seek prior permission and approval from the Council of Ministers.

ARTICLE 25

Assistance activities from foreign religious organizations or related activities must conform with the current policies and regime regarding the management of aid and must be channeled through [state] agencies entrusted by the Council of Ministers for the management of aid.

Religious organizations or individuals in the country who wish to receive purely religious assistance must obtain permission from the Council of Ministers.

Apart from believers' voluntary and supportive financial contributions, religious organizations are not allowed to seek additional contributions that violate state regulations.

[Ban Ton Giao cua Chinh Phu, *Cac van ban cua nha nuoc ve hoat dong ton giao*, 8–13; trans. Jayne Werner]

ETHNIC AND INTERNATIONAL RELATIONS

CHU VAN TAN

THE FOUNDING OF THE PEOPLE'S LIBERATION ARMED FORCES (1971)

This text describes the founding of the People's Army of Vietnam, formerly called the People's Liberation Armed Forces, in May 1945 from the merger of two guerrilla units operating along the China–Vietnam border. The first unit, the Army for National Salvation, was led by Chu Van Tan, an ethnic Nung, who became a ranking military commander in the Viet Minh army, which fought the French from 1945 to 1954. The second unit was led by Vo Nguyen Giap, an ethnic Kinh (Vietnamese) from central Vietnam, and was called the Vietnam Propaganda and Liberation Army. In their struggle against the French colonialists, the Vietnamese Communists depended on the support and assistance of the ethnic minorities to establish secure base areas in the highlands from which to organize attacks on the coastal areas and the deltas. This text illustrates the close relationship between the Viet Minh and the ethnic minorities in the Viet Bac and is excerpted from *Reminiscences on the Army for National Salvation*, Chu Van Tan's memoir.

I will never forget that memorable last day of March 1945. A section of the Vietnam Propaganda and Liberation Army led by brother Vo Nguyen Giap arrived in Cho Chu. More than a year earlier, Vo Nguyen Giap and I had met on a high mountain peak, in a small Meo [Hmong] settlement and in a situation in which we had to keep our presence secret. This time, in this new situation of surging power and strength, we again met, on the soil of newly liberated Cho Chu, and this time around we were accompanied not just by a handful of cadres, but our meeting was also the meeting of two armies. What happiness it was for me to meet Vo Nguyen Giap again in broad daylight, right in the middle of a bustling and crowded market! There were so many things we wanted to tell each other!

Who could have guessed that what I had wished for at the end of last winter would come to pass within three months. So the Vietnam Propaganda and Liberation Army and the Army for National Salvation had met. And the two comrades who had met in the Lung Hoang conference[63] and had become attached to each other since then and who had been concerned about each other during the enemy wave of terrorism found themselves face to face again, each man now stronger and more enthusiastic than before. We clasped hands tightly, laughed happily, and looked at each other with eyes bright with joy.

At the end of the previous year, I had vaguely heard that the Vietnam Propaganda and Liberation Army had been set up. Now, meeting Vo Nguyen Giap in Cho Chu, I finally found out about the concrete instructions of comrade Ho Chi Minh on December 22, 1944, and about the expansion of this army and its combat activities during the past few months. . . .

Comrade Ho Chi Minh's instructions concerning the formation of the Vietnam Propaganda and Liberation Army made me think about the situation and the mission of the Army for National Salvation in the past and from now on. The principle that armed propaganda and political activities were more important than military activities, that propaganda was more important than combat, that military operations would be used to protect, consolidate, and expand our political base and, at the same time, to consolidate and expand armed units and paramilitary units not only applied to the Vietnam Propaganda and Liberation Army but also lit the way for the Army for National Salvation in all its activities. . . .

While on mission, I received a letter convoking a meeting of the Standing Committee of the Party Central Committee. The Standing Committee convened the North Vietnam Region Revolutionary Military Conference in Hiep Hoa (Bac Giang Province), which was presided over by comrade Truong Chinh,

---

63. Chu Van Tan and Vo Nguyen Giap met at a conference at Lung Hoang near the Vietnam–China border in January 1943 to coordinate and extend guerrilla activity from the border region southward toward Hanoi.

the party's secretary-general. The conference lasted six days, from April 15 to 20, 1945. This was the first important military conference of our party. . . .

Vo Nguyen Giap reported on the situation of the movement in Cao Bang-Bac Can and on the activities of the Vietnam Propaganda and Liberation Army there. I reported on the situation of the movement and the activities of the Army for National Salvation in Thai Nguyen-Tuyen Quang. This conference gave me an overall view of the situation everywhere in the country. It was only then that I understood that a high tide of anti-Japanese resistance was rising forcefully from north to south. Many armed demonstrations, each two thousand to three thousand strong, had moved to attack and seize rice depots in the plantations of French reactionaries and depots belonging to the Japanese to distribute rice to the poor people in Bac Ninh, Bac Giang, Ninh Binh, Thai Nguyen provinces, and so on. Many areas in the midlands had set up national minorities' liberation committees. Political prisoners in Nghia Lo (Yen Bai) rose up and smashed the jail. In addition to the party's armed forces in Viet Bac, there were many self-defense and combat self-defense units in the midlands, in the delta, and even in the big cities. In Quang Ngai Province, guerrillas also emerged; this was the guerrilla unit of Ba To. In the south, the Viet Minh were active in My Tho and in the lower Mekong Delta region (Hau Giang).

The conference pointed out the weaknesses and strengths of the anti-Japanese resistance for the national salvation of the Indochinese people. The conference affirmed that "the situation had placed the military task above all other important and urgent tasks at this juncture. Resolute efforts must be made to expand guerrilla warfare, build up the base areas to resist the Japanese, in order to make preparations for the general uprising and seize this opportunity in time." With regard to this military task, we all felt that it was necessary to define clearly and assign specific tasks to each war zone; to clear communication and liaison corridors linking up the war zones of north, central, and south Vietnam; to build up base areas to resist the Japanese; unify, consolidate, and expand the various armed forces; unify [the] military command; organize special armed units, and so forth. In accordance with the resolution of April 1945, the Vietnam Propaganda and Liberation Army and the Army for National Salvation were merged. The conference designated the North Vietnam Revolutionary Military Committee to command the war zones of north Indochina, and at the same time this committee also had the task of providing military assistance to the entire country. The Central Committee appointed comrades Vo Nguyen Giap, Van Tien Dung, Le Thanh Nghi, Trang Dang Ninh, and Chu Van Tan to this committee. With regard to the question of cadres, a number of outstanding members of the various armed forces would be selected and trained to become unit commanders and political officers; anti-Japanese military and political training schools would be established; people of talent would be recruited; students would be recruited to go to the war zones for military training; and the cadres would [receive military training].

A new atmosphere full of enthusiasm and confidence pervaded everywhere. There were so many things to do. We had the impression that time was fleeing too rapidly.

After attending the North Vietnam Region Revolutionary Military Conference, Vo Nguyen Giap returned to Cho Chu (Dinh Hoa) exactly on International Labor Day of May 1. Carrying out the resolution of April 1945, he convened a conference in Dinh Bien Thuong to officially announce the merger of all armed forces and clarify the brothers' ideological understanding concerning their immediate and long-term tasks. Besides Vo Nguyen Giap, the other key cadres included comrades Hien Mai, Mon, and Khanh Phuong.

After that, we heard the news that Uncle Ho was coming down from Cao Bang to the lowlands, and Vo Nguyen Giap galloped off on a horse toward Re pass to welcome him.

We continued to operate in the Cho Chu area. A few days later, a letter arrived from Vo Nguyen Giap saying, "Make preparations to welcome the Old Man." Brother Quang Trung and we moved our troops to Deo So and deployed them to protect the route that Uncle Ho would take and to welcome him. Later on, however, another letter from Vo Nguyen Giap arrived, reporting that "Uncle Ho had taken the route farther inland. He would go to Son Duong." We turned around and went back, passing Deo Re pass, going down to Dinh Hoa, into Thanh Dieu and Luc Ra, and then on to Hong Thai to welcome Uncle Ho. . . .

Uncle Ho chose Tan Trao as his living and working headquarters to guide the movement in the entire country and to make preparations for the National Congress.

After listening to the reports on the general situation in the country and on the North Vietnam Region Revolutionary Military Conference, he issued the following instructions. Since the liberated area in the North Vietnam Region included almost all the provinces of Cao Bang, Bac Can, Lang Son, Ha Giang, Tuyen Quang and Thai Nguyen, and a number of adjacent areas in the provinces of Bac Giang, Phu Tho, Yen Bai and Vinh Yen, and since all these areas were linked together, a large revolutionary base should be set up and designated the Liberated Zone.[64] It had been correct to unify all the armed forces and place them under the direct command of the Central Committee. This army should be called the Liberation Army because the term "liberation" was both simple and easy to understand, precise and penetrating—it denoted clearly the goal of fighting the French, driving out the Japanese, liberating the country, and aspiring to national independence.

To carry out these instructions, on June 4, 1945, the Viet Minh General Headquarters convoked a conference to officially announce the formation of the Liberated Zone, which was put under the leadership of the Provisional

---

64. Tan Trao was chosen as the capital of the Liberated Zone.

Command Committee and which should be firmly consolidated from the political, military, economic, and cultural points of view to become the springboard for the March Southward and the liberation of the whole country.

At that time, the concrete situation in the war zones and the areas within the Liberated Zone was very serious. Comrade Vo Nguyen Giap was designated as the permanent officer of this committee to maintain a liaison with the Central Committee in the [Red River] delta and also with comrades Le Thanh Nghi and Tran Dang Ninh in Bac Giang, on the one hand, and to maintain a liaison with the provinces of Cao Bang and Bac Son, on the other hand.

In the Liberated Zone, the People's Revolutionary Committees elected by the masses were carrying out the ten big programs. These were

1. Liquidating the Japanese forces, eliminating traitors, and punishing criminals.
2. Seizing the properties of the traitors and of the lackeys of the foreigners, and—depending in each situation—using them as the common property of the people or distributing them to the poor.
3. Instituting universal suffrage and other free and democratic rights.
4. Arming the masses, motivating the people to support the guerrillas and join the Liberation Army to resist the Japanese.
5. Organizing the clearing of land, encouraging production, and creating a self-sufficient economy for the Liberated Zone.
6. Restricting the number of workdays and carrying out social security laws and the relief of people afflicted by calamities.
7. Redistributing communal rice fields, reducing land rents and interest rates, and postponing the repayment of debts.
8. Abolishing taxes and labor conscription and making plans for a light and unique progressive taxation.
9. Fighting against illiteracy and organizing popular military and political training classes for the masses.
10. [Assuring] equality among all ethnic groups and equal rights for men and women.

A new Vietnam was born. A section of North Vietnam was placed under the revolutionary government. More than one million people began to enjoy a new life brought about by the revolution.

With the merging of all armed forces, the Liberation Army became fairly large and was split up into detachments. Almost all the former members of the Vietnam Propaganda and Liberation Army and of the Army for National Salvation became command cadres.

The problem of forming and training cadres became very urgent. At the beginning of July 1945, in accordance with the resolution by the North Vietnam Region Military Conference, the Resist-Japan Military Academy was established under the direction of Hoang Van Thai in order to train platoon leaders and platoon political officers. The school was set up in Khuoi Kich, on the bank of the stream where the ceremony establishing the Army for National Salvation's Third Platoon [had taken place]. The students were selected from the ranks of the Liberation Army and the youths from the delta who had been introduced by the National Salvation Associations.

The popular government in the Liberated Zone was reorganized by elections, with universal suffrage. Each village had a National Salvation Council Hall where the people frequently came to attend meetings, to listen to reports on the situation, and to discuss affairs of public interest.

Right after learning of the complete disintegration of the Japanese aggressors and their surrender to the Soviet Union and the Allies, on August 12, 1945, the Provisional Command Committee of the Liberated Zone issued the order for a general uprising to the Liberation Army, to the self-defense units, to the People's Revolutionary Committees and to the entire population in the region.

On August 13, 1945, the National Party Congress opened in Tan Trao. Attending the congress were representatives of party headquarters in all three regions of Vietnam—north, center, and south—and also a number of representatives operating abroad.

In this extremely urgent situation, the congress worked for three days. In order to provide correct leadership to ensure the success of the general insurrection, the congress set forth three principles:

1. *Concentration*: concentration of our forces on major tasks.
2. *Unification*: unification of all military and political means, and unification of leadership and command.
3. *Timely action*: acting in a timely manner and not losing any opportunities.

The congress emphasized that "we must concentrate our forces in critical areas to attack" and "we must attack and immediately seize the areas where we were sure of success, whether urban areas or the countryside."

Right in the night of August 13, 1945, the Insurrection Committee, set up by the Viet Minh General Headquarters, issued its military order no. 1, ordering the launching of the general insurrection.

Right after the National Congress broke up, the People's National Congress also convened in Tan Trao on August 16. This congress chose the national flag and national anthem and designated the Vietnam National Liberation Committee, that is, the Provisional Government, with comrade Ho Chi Minh as president.

Implementing the order of the Liberated Zone's Provisional Command Committee issued on August 12 and [the order] of the Insurrection Committee, units of the Liberation Army captured one after another the Japanese posts still remaining in the provinces of Cao Bang, Bac Can, Thai Nguyen, Yen Bai, and so on, and then advanced to liberate the towns and cities.

On August 16, a unit of the Liberation Army under the command of comrade Vo Nguyen Giap coming from Tan Trao, advanced and attacked the Thai Nguyen provincial capital to open the route to Hanoi.

On August 17, the Liberation Army attacked Tuyen Quang province town. The Japanese fascists returned fire, but in the face of the overwhelming force of the revolution, they were forced to offer to negotiate, and on August 21, the Viet Minh seized power in the province.

The Liberation Army was advancing in the surging revolutionary storm. Every Communist Party member, every Viet Minh fighter, and the population in the whole country showed their determination and their firm spirits in heroically fighting for the cause of national liberation, in accordance with President Ho's instructions: "At this moment, the favorable opportunity has arrived. No matter what the sacrifices, even if the entire Annamese Chain [Truong Son] has to go up in flames, we must maintain our determination in order to win back our national independence."

[Chu Van Tan, *Reminiscences on the Army for National Salvation*, 199–205]

REPUBLIC OF VIETNAM

LAWS ON VIETNAMESE NATIONALITY (1956)

In the mid-1950s, at the close of the French colonial period, the new states of northern Vietnam and southern Vietnam undertook measures to integrate non-Vietnamese minorities into their national collectivities. In the north, the Democratic Republic of Vietnam adopted an approach based on "one nation, many ethnic groups," which tended to give priority to the majoritarian Kinh (Vietnamese), notwithstanding the Communist Party's wartime collaboration with and reliance on the ethnic tribes in mountainous base areas. In the south, Ngo Dinh Diem's Republic of Vietnam took measures to compel the Chinese community, the largest and most powerful ethnic minority, to take Vietnamese citizenship and names (as Chams were required to do in the fifteenth century after their conquest by Emperor Le Thanh Tong).[65]

The Chinese controlled the southern rice trade and much of banking and commerce in the region. Children born of Chinese–Vietnamese parentage were declared to be Vietnamese, and all ethnic Chinese born in South Vietnam after 1956 were deemed to be Vietnamese. Others were considered to be "foreigners." In 1955, foreigners engaged in eleven trades were given up to a year to liquidate or transfer their businesses to Vietnamese citizens. Citizenship status for ethnic Chinese did not become a salient issue in the Communist part of Vietnam until 1975. After that date, however, the Chinese community was caught in the crossfire of increasingly hostile relations between

---

65. See "Ordering Ethnic Groups to Conform" (chap. 3).

Vietnam and the People's Republic of China. In 1978, the Socialist Republic of Vietnam confiscated or outlawed large-scale private trade in the country, while China attempted to strengthen its influence among Chinese living as boat people in Vietnam, moves that contributed to the large-scale exodus of Chinese from Vietnam and the 1979 border war between the two countries. The Republic of Vietnam's new laws regarding Vietnamese nationality and commercial activity took effect on August 21 and September 6, 1956.

ARTICLE 1

Article 16 of the decree dated December 7, 1955, regarding Vietnamese nationality, is hereby repealed and is now changed as follows:

NEW ARTICLE 16

A person born in Vietnam of a father and mother of Chinese descent is Vietnamese.

Children born in Vietnam before the issuance of the present decree of fathers and mothers of Chinese descent have Vietnamese nationality, except for the following:

1. Persons who have been expelled in accordance with edicts that have not yet been repealed in accordance with the forms with which they were initially promulgated.
2. Persons who have been convicted or sentenced for a crime or those who have been acquitted on grounds of insanity, except for offenses committed because of carelessness or unintentional acts without dishonest intentions.
3. Persons who have been put under surveillance or house arrest and the measure for whom has not yet been repealed.

[Republic of Vietnam, *Cong Bao Viet Nam Cong Hoa*,
August 23, 1956; trans. Jayne Werner]

Restrictions of Commercial Activity by Foreign Residents in the Republic of Vietnam

ARTICLE 1

Foreign residents, foreign societies and companies are not allowed to engage in the following occupations throughout Vietnam:[66]

---

66. These restrictions refer to edict no. 53 (*Cong Bao Viet Nam Cong Hoa*, December 8, 1955).

1. Buying and selling fish and meat.
2. Operating grocery stores.
3. Buying and selling coal, charcoal, or firewood.
4. Buying and selling gasoline, kerosene, and lubricants (except for imported items).
5. Pawnshops and mortgage companies.
6. Buying and selling coarse fabric and silk (up to a total of less than ten thousand meters [almost thirty-three thousand feet] for all these items), yarn, thread, and the like.
7. Buying and selling iron, copper, or bronze scraps.
8. Milling rice.
9. Buying and selling [other] grains.
10. Transporting goods and passengers by car, boat, or ship.
11. Serving as middlemen who charge commissions.

ARTICLE 2

Foreign residents engaged in the preceding occupations must cease their activities in accordance with the following schedules:

- For occupations numbered 1 to 7 within six months.
- For occupations numbered 8 to 11 within one year.

ARTICLE 3

All contracts concluded by foreign residents in the preceding activities that contradict this edict will be regarded as null and void.

ARTICLE 4

Foreign residents who violate this edict will be fined from 50,000 to 5 million piastres, not including other administrative measures such as expulsion.

ARTICLE 5

Any Vietnamese who colludes with foreign residents in violating this edict will receive a prison sentence from six months to three years and a fine of 50,000 to 5 million piastres, or both.

ARTICLE 6

Existing laws and regulations that do not contradict the preceding articles will continue to apply.

[Republic of Vietnam, *Cong Bao Viet Nam Cong Hoa*,
September 8, 1956; trans. Jayne Werner]

PHAN DOAN NAM

ALIGNING THE STRENGTH OF THE NATION WITH THE POWER OF THE AGE (1987)

With the adoption of market-oriented policies in 1986, Vietnam started to shift its foreign policy from socialist internationalism to a broader engagement with the world capitalist system. This was in line with its "new thinking" in foreign policy, which stressed economic interdependence, multilateralism, and peaceful relations with all countries. Theoretically, the Communist Party of Vietnam moved away from a class-based and anti-imperialist approach to international relations to integrating its economy into the global capitalist economy in order to fulfill its national development plans. This new approach also led to a shift in Vietnam's relations with China. In the following article, published in May 1987 in *Tap Chi Cong San* (*Communist Review*), the Communist Party's theoretical journal, Phan Doan Nam, a senior adviser to Foreign Minister Nguyen Co Thach, identified the theoretical basis for the new thinking in foreign policy, arguing that the world had fundamentally changed since the 1970s, particularly in the scientific technological revolution and the world economy's interdependence. These changes required Vietnam to renovate its concepts of national security and to promote international cooperation and integration into the global economy. This article looks at the Vietnamese state's historic concerns with international commerce and trade and how to achieve the correct balance between North and South.

The political report of the Central Committee of the Communist Party of Vietnam to the Sixth Party Congress pointed out: "In all our revolutionary work, we must attach special importance to developing our nation's interests in international factors, enhancing our traditions in accordance with current trends, and efficiently using every opportunity to expand trade, economic cooperation, and cooperation in science and technology with the outside world in order to build socialism [in our country] while always fulfilling our international obligations toward fraternal and friendly countries."[67]

This is the lesson drawn by our party from the realities of the Vietnamese revolution during the past fifty years: aligning the strength of the nation with

---

67. Quoted in *Tap Chi Cong San*, no. 1 (1987): 30 [note in the original text].

the power of the age. This also is a guideline for us in applying these experiences to the next stage of the revolution.

How has our party succeeded in aligning the strength of the nation with the power of the age, thus augmenting the comprehensive strength of our people and taking the Vietnamese revolution from one victory to the next? [We have been able to do so] because our party has had a good grasp of Marxism-Leninism and has firmly adhered to the working class in aligning our national interests with the interests of the world's people and in harmonizing the patriotism of our people with international proletarianism.

The combination of the national and the international, of the traditional and the modern in our party's revolutionary line [political position] is derived from two basic principles: First, the revolution in Vietnam is a part of the world revolution, and second, the revolution in Vietnam is taking place during the global transition from capitalism to socialism.

These two basic principles show the organic relationship between Vietnam and the world. This relationship is part of a whole that, although multifaceted, complicated, and fraught with contradictions, is also marked by interlinkages and interdependence. This relationship also demonstrates the laws and trends of development of the current age, whose power stems from these laws and trends. This power is the comprehensive strength of the forces of peace, national independence, democracy, and social progress, with the world's socialist system serving as the pillar of these forces and the main factor determining the current content, direction, and major characteristics of the development of human society. The victory of revolution in each country results from the alignment of that country's own strengths with the power of the age. It can be achieved when a country directs its development in accordance with the world's common trends to mobilize a comprehensive and invincible strength. This has become a law-like phenomenon.

Following the full victory of the war of resistance and national salvation against U.S. aggression, Vietnam's revolution entered a new period of development. This new revolutionary step is taking place when the world revolution finds itself in what many call the "post-Vietnam era," in which the world situation and international relations are qualitatively different from those of the previous era. As a result of these profound changes, new trends have emerged in the world economy and international politics and are creating new opportunities and challenges for the development of all nations.

First, starting in the early 1970s, the world's balance of forces underwent a fundamental change. This change resulted from the strategic-military parity between the Soviet Union and the United States, between the Warsaw Pact and NATO, and between the two sociopolitical systems in general.[68] This is a historic achievement of the forces of peace and revolution. It definitively ended the

---

68. The "two sociopolitical systems" refers to the socialist countries and the Western, primarily capitalist, nations.

period when [the forces of] imperialism could rely on their military supremacy to threaten the world's people and crush the forces of peace and revolution. For the first time in history, the world's people have the real capability to prevent a new world war, gradually enforce disarmament, and create peaceful coexistence among countries with different social systems. [As a result,] the major form of the worldwide class struggle between this era's two opposing forces has gradually changed from political-military confrontation to peaceful political-economic emulation and competition.

Second, a new cycle of the second scientific-technological revolution that started in the mid-1970s has had a profound impact on all aspects of humankind's social life. It has "shortened" the distance between countries, changed not only the relations between humanity and nature but also international relations and has fundamentally changed the world economy. As a direct force on production, today's science and technology have rapidly increased global material wealth on an unprecedented scale. At the same time, it has given humankind the capacity to destroy itself and all its material wealth in a heartbeat. On the one hand, today's science and technology have created an opportunity for underdeveloped countries to catch up with the developed ones. On the other hand, they can be instrumental in upsetting the balance or widening the development gap, even among the most advanced countries. The science and technology race toward the twenty-first century is taking place not only among countries with different social systems but also among the imperialist countries.

Third, also beginning in the early 1970s, the world economy has undergone profound changes and moved into [a new stage of development characterized by] in-depth expansion [rather than horizontal expansion]. The world economy in general and each system [socialist and capitalist blocs] in particular are undergoing a vigorous process of internationalization and integration, resulting in a new international division of labor within each system as well as in the entire world. National economies are interconnected with the entire world economy, becoming both complementary and interdependent. The success of each country's type of development depends on whether that country can create an optimal position for itself in the global economic chain. This is an objective phenomenon and thus a lawlike one.

The new characteristics of the global political and economic situation require us to adopt new ways of thinking and new methods of action in applying the lessons for aligning [our] national strengths with the power of the age. This means that we must not hesitate to change our thinking on the global political-economic situation and on our economic cooperation with other countries.

On the political and security front, we must take full advantage of the peaceful international environment over the next ten to fifteen years to focus on rebuilding our country after many years of war. This environment requires us to renovate our concepts of national security and the methods for protecting it. For in the current international context, no country, however powerful, can effectively defend its security if it tries to do so by itself, apart from the common security of the world and the region in which it is located. No country, however large, can be more secure than another. Today, the security of all nations must be even and equal within the common totality of world security. Today, the security of our nation is not merely military security but also must be comprehensive security, in which economic security is emerging as predominant. Therefore, at present, the best way to defend our national security is to incorporate it into the shared international security system, especially in the Asia-Pacific region and Southeast Asia. How can we do this? We can do this by increasing our contribution to the shared struggle of the Soviet Union, the socialist countries, the nonaligned countries, and other progressive forces for peace, disarmament, and the gradual elimination of nuclear weapons from the earth. We must continue to strive, along with the fraternal peoples of Laos and Cambodia, and other countries in Southeast Asia, to transform Southeast Asia into a zone of peace, friendship, and cooperation, first, by transforming it into a nuclear weapons–free zone. Only in the context of shared international and regional security can we ensure for ourselves rock-solid security. Only this can allow us to focus the bulk of our human and material resources on national construction. The new thinking on security and methods of protecting security in the new global situation will help us resolve the issue of development.

[For our economy], the alignment of national strengths with the power of the age under the new conditions also requires us to renovate our views on numerous issues relating to the line [official position] and policies of national development.

First, we must renovate our views on independence and sovereignty in planning economic strategy. Building an independent and sovereign economy does not mean building an autarkic economy that produces everything by itself and does not need anything from the outside world. In working out an economic strategy, we must take into account new factors such as the level of internationalization of the world economy, the tendency toward interlinkage in the international division of labor, and the interdependence of the national economies. In view of the current development of global productive forces and of science and technology, no single country, however strong and rich in resources, can develop its economy independently from the global economy and without relying on other countries. This is a matter of mutual dependence and not merely one-way dependence. It is this "interdependence" that gives rise to equality in countries' economic relations. In the capitalist world, Japan imports 90 percent of its oil, but that does not mean that it is dependent on the oil-producing countries because Japan has other strengths vis-à-vis these countries. The United States is less dependent on raw materials and fuel imports than Japan is, but this does not mean Japan should have a slower growth rate than the United States. On the contrary, Japan is currently the most formidable economic competitor of the United States. Interdependence is also a solid basis for the struggle of the nonaligned countries against the developed capitalist countries for establishing a new, equitable, and rational world economic order.

Second, it is necessary to correctly perceive the relationship between protecting national security and expanding international cooperation. We cannot expand economic cooperation without playing host to foreign experts, businessmen, and visitors. We must study how to safeguard our national security while promoting cooperation with foreign countries and settle this question correctly in order to expand, rather than restrict, international economic cooperation. Far from being the responsibility of security agencies alone, it is the responsibility of the entire party, all the people, and particularly all the officials handling foreign relations.

Third, we need to decide between diversifying our foreign economic relations, on the one hand, and consolidating and intensifying our cooperation and integration with the socialist countries in the Council for Mutual Economic Assistance (CMEA), on the other. Vietnam is a developing country that is advancing toward socialism without going through the stage of capitalist development. Therefore, in our foreign economic relations, we must rely mainly on the socialist countries. This is a law [a generalization based on a recurring fact]. The socialist countries also regard their assistance in economic development for Vietnam and the elimination of the development gap among CMEA members as their international responsibilities.

Yet at the same time, Vietnam is part of the world economy. Therefore, it is natural for Vietnam to develop economic relations with countries [other than socialist ones]. But we should see this diversification as complementing and enriching our cooperation with the socialist countries. In contrast, the better and the more effective Vietnam's cooperation with socialist countries is, the greater the possibility that Vietnam will be able to diversify its relations with other countries. This will both benefit Vietnam and promote cooperation among the CMEA countries. These relations are mutually complementary and not mutually exclusive.

Fourth, it is necessary to have a good grasp of the principles of equality and mutual benefit in foreign economic relations. Cooperation must be mutually beneficial and based on equality if it is to be lasting and fruitful, and this applies to cooperation among socialist countries as well as among capitalist countries. Of course, in our cooperation with the socialist countries, our friends will refrain from causing losses for us, but we should not abuse their goodwill and cause them losses. If we have only our own interests in mind and neglect the interests of our partners, this will lead to consequences detrimental to cooperation.

In regard to capitalist countries or capitalist companies, some people believe that "the capitalists will never 'help' us build socialism." We argue that this view is not completely accurate because its proponents forget that the basic law of capitalism is [the law of] profit. As [Karl] Marx said, Capitalists will do anything to make a profit; they are not even afraid of selling us "the rope to hang them with." Therefore, if they see a benefit in their business with us, they will not refuse it. [Thus, the question is] how to ensure our interests while making sure that our partners also benefit from the cooperation. To this end, we need experts, and we must change the way we manage [our] economy. Only by so doing can we make the most of the world's scientific-technological knowledge and capital in order to serve our socialist construction.

In the future, the economic alignment of our national strengths with the power of the age can be focused on three main directions:

First, [we must] continue to solicit assistance from friendly countries, first and foremost the socialist countries. This is a lawlike issue and will last for a long time. To be able to secure further assistance from our friends, we must first and foremost make effective use of such aid and turn the fruit of labor of our friends into material and spiritual strengths that will fortify us. Binding political conditions are not attached to socialist countries' assistance to Vietnam. But Vietnam must make it a rule to use this assistance effectively in order to increase our own strength and the strength of the socialist community, not to overburden and weaken us.

Second, [we must] identify the optimal position of Vietnam in the socialist economic system in particular and in the world economy in general. This is not simple, as it requires a deep knowledge of the world's economic issues, science, and technology, the development strategies of the countries as well as about our own economic problems, our strengths and weaknesses, and our capacity to utilize scientific-technological achievements for the rapid advancement of our role in the international division of labor. Our participation in the program on reviewing the scientific-technological advances of the CMEA countries and the issuance by the Sixth Party Congress of three focus programs for our current five-year plan, especially the export program, are indeed the first steps in this direction.

Third, we must learn from the outside world's experiences in using the achievements of the scientific-technological revolution in order to find the shortest and least costly path for Vietnam's industrialization and to work out a long-term economic development strategy. In this regard, we must pay attention to the experiences of those countries whose initial development level was similar to Vietnam, in particular those in East Asia and South Asia. . . .

The evolution of the global economic and political situation and the scientific-technological revolution are creating very favorable conditions for the Vietnamese people to fulfill their strategic tasks in the new revolutionary period. But as before, if we are to successfully align our national strengths with the power of the age, we first must develop our own strengths. In the past, our strengths were mainly political and military. At present, what is needed is political and economic strength, of which economic strength plays the decisive role. *Without economic strength of our own, our nation cannot effectively absorb assistance from friends or the scientific and technological advances from the world, and in-*

deed, we cannot actively and effectively participate in the international division of labor. The resolutions of the Sixth National Congress of the Communist Party of Vietnam have charted the path forward for our people. We have only one path: renovation and advance in accordance with common world trends.

[(Phan) Doan Nam, "Ket hop suc manh dan toc voi suc manh thoi dai," 53–57; trans. Luu Doan Huynh and Alexander Vu Ving]

BIBLIOGRAPHY

Anderson, James A. *The Rebel Den of Nung Tri Cao: Loyalty and Identity Along the Sino-Vietnamese Border*. Seattle: University of Washington Press, 2007.

Ban Ton Giao cua Chinh Phu. *Cac van ban cua nha nuoc ve hoat dong ton giao (State Documents on Religious Activities)*. Hanoi: Ban Ton Giao Cua Chinh Phu, 1992.

Bento Thien. "Lich su nuoc Annam" (History of the Country of Annam). In *Lich su chu quoc ngu, 1620–1659 (History of Quoc Ngu Writing, 1620–1659)*, by Do Quang Chinh. Saigon: Ra Khoi, 1972.

Bowen, Kevin, Nguyen Ba Chung, and Bruce Weigl, eds. and trans. *Mountain River: Vietnamese Poetry from the Wars, 1948–1993*. Amherst: University of Massachusetts Press, 1998.

Bui Huy Bich. *Hoang Viet van tuyen (Selected Writings of the Imperial Viet)*. Vol. 3. Saigon: Phu Quoc Vu Khanh Dac Trach Van Hoa Xuat Ban, 1972.

Callison, Charles Stuart. *Land-to-the-Tiller in the Mekong Delta: Economic, Social, and Political Effects of Land Reform in Four Villages of South Vietnam*. Monograph Series no. 23. Berkeley: Center for South and South East Asia Studies, University of California, 1983.

Chu Van Tan. *Reminiscences on the Army for National Salvation: Memoir of General Chu Van Tan*. Translated by Mai Elliott. Data Paper 97. Ithaca, N.Y.: Cornell University, Southeast Asia Program, 1974.

Dai Dao Tam Ky Pho Do. *Tan Luat (The New Code)*. Tay Ninh: Toa Thanh Tay Ninh, 1966.

——. *Thanh Ngon Hiep Tuyen: Quyen thu nhut* (*Collection of Spirit Messages*). Vol. 1. Tay Ninh: Toa Thanh Tay Ninh, 1969.

Dai Nam nhat thong chi (*The Unification Records of Dai Nam*). Edited by Dao Duy Anh. Translated by Pham Trong Diem. Hue: Nha Xuat Ban Thuan Hoa, 1996.

Dai Nam nhat thong chi (*The Unification Records of Dai Nam*). Tōyō bunko Library, Tokyo. [Photocopy of woodblock-printed version]

Dai Nam thuc luc (*The Veritable Records of Dai Nam*). 9 vols. Tokyo: Keio Institute of Linguistic Studies, 1961–.

Dai Nam thuc luc (*The Veritable Records of Dai Nam*). 10 vols. Translated by Nguyen Ngoc Tinh. Hanoi: Nha Xuat Ban Khoa Hoc Xa Hoi, 2004–2007.

Dai Nam thuc luc (*The Veritable Records of Dai Nam*). Vol. 29, *Chinh bien*. Hanoi: Nha Xuat Ban Khoa Hoc Xa Hoi, 1974.

Dai Viet su ky tuc bien (*A Continuation of the Chronicle of Dai Viet*). A.1415. Han Nom Institute Library, Hanoi.

Dai Viet su ky tuc bien (*A Continuation of the Chronicle of Dai Viet*). Translated by Ngo The Long and Nguyen Kim Hung. Edited by Nguyen Dong Chi. Hanoi: Nha Xuat Ban Khoa Hoc Xa Hoi, 1991.

Dang Thai Mai. *Van tho cach mang Viet Nam dau the ky XX* (*Vietnamese Revolutionary Poetry and Prose in the Early 20th Century*). Hanoi: Nha Xuat Ban Van Hoc, 1974.

Dao Duy Anh. *Viet Nam van hoa su cuong* (*An Outline of Vietnamese Culture*). Saigon: Xuat Ban Bon Phuong, 1938.

Democratic Republic of Vietnam. Luat hon nhan va gia dinh Nam 1959 (1959 Law on Marriage and the Family). Available at http://www.na.gov.vn/sach_qh/vkqhtoantap_1/nam1959/1959_18.html (accessed October 8, 2009).

Dinh Thu Cuc. "Nong dan va nong thon Viet Nam hien nay: Nhung van de can quan tam" (The Peasants and Countryside in Vietnam Today: Matters in Need of Attention). *Tap Chi Cong San*, no. 5 (1988): 43–46.

Do Quang Chinh. *Lich su chu quoc ngu, 1620–1659* (*History of Quoc Ngu Writing, 1620–1659*). Saigon: Ra Khoi, 1972.

Do Van Ninh. *Van Bia Quoc Tu Giam Ha Noi* (*Steles of the Royal Academy*). Hanoi: Nha Xuat Ban Van Hoa Thong Tin, 2001.

Dong Kinh Nghia Thuc. "Van minh tan hoc sinh" (A Civilization of New Learning). In *Van tho cach mang Viet Nam dau the ky XX* (*Vietnamese Revolutionary Poetry and Prose in the Early 20th Century*), by Dang Thai Mai. Hanoi: Nha Xuat Ban Van Hoc, 1974.

Duong Van An. *O Chau can luc* (*A Recent Record of O Chau*). Hanoi: Nha Xuat Ban Khoa Hoc Xa Hoi, 1997.

Épigraphie en chinois de Viet Nam. Vol. 1. Paris: École française d'extrême orient, 1998.

Gaspardone, Émile. "L'inscription du Ma Nhai." *Bulletin de la Société des études indochinoises*, n.s., 46, no. 1 (1971): 73–84.

Giao-Hoi Phat-Giao Hoa Hao. *Tieu-su va giao-ly cua Duc Huynh Giao-Chu* (*Biography and Teachings of Prophet Huynh Phu So*). Saigon: Giao-Hoi Phat Giao Hoa Hao, 1966.

Ha Van Tan. "Inscriptions from the Tenth to the Fourteenth Centuries Recently Discovered in Viet Nam." In *Essays into Vietnamese Pasts*, edited by K. W. Taylor and

John K. Whitmore, 51–58. Ithaca, N.Y.: Cornell University, Southeast Asia Program, 1995.

Han Mac Tu. *Tho Han Mac Tu: Che Lan Vien tuyen chon va gioi thieu* (*The Poems of Han Mac Tu: Selections and Introduction by Che Lan Vien*). Hanoi: Nha Xuat Ban Van Hoc, 1991.

Ho Chi Minh. "Appeal to Compatriots and Fighters Throughout the Country." In *Selected Writings, 1920–1969*, 307–10. Hanoi: Foreign Languages Printing House, 1973.

——. "Declaration of Independence of the Democratic Republic of Viet Nam." In *Selected Writings, 1920–1969*, 53–56. Hanoi: Foreign Languages Publishing House, 1973.

——. "Sua doi loi lam viec" (Reforming the Way We Work). In *Toan tap* (*Collected Works*). Vol. 5, 1947–1949. Hanoi: Nha Xuat Ban Chinh Tri Quoc Gia, 2000.

——. "Thu cua Ho Chu Tich gui dong bao nong thon va can bo nhan dip cai cach ruong dat o mien bac can ban thanh cong" (Letter Sent by President Ho to Peasant and Cadre Compatriots on the Basic Completion of the Land Reform in the North). *Nhan Dan*, August 18, 1956.

——. "Tu cach mot nguoi cach menh" (The Revolutionary's Code of Conduct), in "Duong cach meng" (The Road to Revolution). In *Tuyen tap* (*Selected Writings*). Vol. 1, 1920–1954, 231. Hanoi: Nha Xuat Ban Su That, 1980.

——. "Tuyen ngon doc lap" (Declaration of Independence). In *Tuyen tap* (*Selected Writings*). Vol. 1, 1920–1954. Hanoi: Nha Xuat Ban Su That, 1980.

Hoang Cam. *Ben kia song Duong: Tho chon loc 1942–1992* (*On the Other Side of the Duong River: Selected Poems from 1942 to 1992*). Hanoi: Nha Xuat Ban Van Hoa, 1993.

Hoang Dao. "Theo moi hoan toan theo moi khong chut do du" (Modernize Completely and Without Hesitation). In "Muoi dieu tam niem" (Ten Precepts). Manuscript, 1973.

Hoang Xuan Han. *La Son Phu Tu* (*The Master of La Son*). Paris: Minh Tan, 1952.

Holmgren, Jennifer. *Chinese Colonisation of Northern Vietnam: Administrative Geography and Political Development in the Tongking Delta, First to Sixth Centuries A.D.* Canberra: Australian National University Press, 1980.

Hong Duc thien chinh thu (*Book of Good Government of the Hong Duc Era*). EFEO A.330. Saigon: Nam Ha An Quan, 1959.

Huy Can. *Tuyen tap Huy Can* (*Selected Works of Huy Can*). Hanoi: Nha Xuat Ban Van Hoc, 1986.

Huynh Phu So. *Sam giang thi van: Toan bo cua Duc Huynh Giao-Chu* (*Complete Edition of Prophecies and Sermons of Prophet Huynh Phu So*). An Hanh: Ban Pho Thong Giao Ly Trung Uong, 1966.

Huynh Sanh Thong, ed. and trans. *An Anthology of Vietnamese Poems, from the Eleventh Through the Twentieth Centuries*. New Haven, Conn.: Yale University Press, 1996.

I Ching—Book of Changes. Translated by James Legge. Secaucus, N.J.: Citadel Press, 1964.

Kelley, Liam. *Beyond the Bronze Pillars: Envoy Poetry and the Sino-Vietnamese Relationship*. Honolulu: University of Hawai'i Press, 2005.

Kham dinh Viet su thong giam cuong muc (*The Imperially Ordered Mirror and Commentary on the History of the Viet*). 1884. R.524. National Library, Hanoi.

Kham dinh Viet su thong giam cuong muc (*The Imperially Ordered Mirror and Commentary on the History of the Viet*). 2 vols. Translated by Hoa Bang, Pham Trong Diem, and Tran Van Giap. Hanoi: Nha Xuat Ban Giao Duc, 1998.

La Son Yen Ho Hoang Xuan Han (*Hoang Xuan Han of La Son District, Yen Ho Village*). Vol. 2. Hanoi: Nha Xuat Ban Giao Duc, 1998.

Langlet, Philippe. *L'ancienne historiographie d'état au Vietnam*. Vol. 1, *Raisons d'être, conditions d'élaboration et caractères au siècle des Nguyen*. Paris: École française d'extrême orient, 1990.

The Le Code. Vols. 1 and 2. Translated and annotated by Nguyen Ngoc Huy and Ta Van Tai. Athens: Ohio University Press, 1987.

Le Huu Trac. *Hai Thuong Lan Ong y tong tam linh* (*The Medical Practices of the Lazy Master of Hai Thuong*). Hanoi: Y Hoc, 2001.

———. "Y huan cach ngon" (Discourse on Medical Training). Introduction to *Hai Thuong y tong tam linh* (*The Medical Practices of the Lazy Master of Hai Thuong*). 1783. A.902/1. Han Nom Institute Library, Hanoi.

Le Quang Dinh. *Hoang Viet nhat thong du dia chi* (*The Geographical Records of the Unified Imperial South*). Hue: Nha Xuat Ban Thuan Hoa, 2005.

Le Quy Don. *Dai Viet thong su* (*General History of Great Viet*). 1749. EFEO microfilm A.1389.

———. *Kien van tieu luc* (*Small Chronicle of Things Seen and Heard*). 2 vols. Saigon: Bo Giao Duc Quoc Gia, 1964.

———. *Phu bien tap luc* (*Chronicles of the Prefectural Borders*). EFEO microfilm A.1175. Cornell University, Ithaca, N.Y.

———. *Phu bien tap luc* (*Chronicles of the Prefectural Borders*). Saigon: Phu Quoc Vu Khanh Dac Trach Van Hoa Xuat Ban, 1972.

———. *Phu bien tap luc* (*Chronicles of the Prefectural Borders*). Translated by Do Mong Khuong et al. Hanoi: Nha Xuat Ban Khoa Hoc Xa Hoi, 1977.

———. *Toan Viet thi luc* (*Anthology of Vietnamese Poetry*). HM 2139. Société asiatique, Paris.

———. *Van dai loai ngu* (*Categorized Sayings from the Van Terrace*). Saigon: Phu Quoc Vu Khanh Dac Trach Van Hoa Xuat Ban, 1972.

Le Tac. *An Nam chi luoc* (*Short Record of Annan*). Hue: University of Hue Press, 1961.

Le trieu chieu linh thien chinh (*Royal Edicts of the Le Court on Good Government*). Translated by Nguyen Si Giac. Saigon: Dai-Hoc Saigon, Truong Luat-Khoa Dai Hoc, 1961.

Le trieu lich khoa tien si de danh bi ky (*Records of the Steles of Names of the Advanced Scholars from the Examinations of the Le Court*). Saigon: Bo Quoc Gia Giao Duc, 1962.

Li Tana and Anthony Reid, eds. *Southern Vietnam Under the Nguyen: Documents on the Economic History of Cochinchina (Dang Trong), 1602–1777*. Sources for the Economic History of Southeast Asia, no. 3. Singapore: Institute of Southeast Asian Studies, 1993.

Liu Xu. *Jiu Tang Shu* (*Old History of the Tang Dynasty*). In *Bona Ben Ershisi Shi* (*One Hundred Patches Edition of the Twenty-Four Histories*). 36 vols. Shanghai: Shangwu, 1930–1937.

Luu Trong Lu. *Tieng thu* (*The Sounds of Autumn*). Glendale, Calif.: Nha Xuat Ban Dai Nam, 1984.

Ly Te Xuyen. *Departed Spirits of the Viet Realm* (*Viet dien u linh tap*). Translated by Brian E. Ostrowski and Brian A. Zottoli. Ithaca, N.Y.: Cornell University, Southeast Asia Program, 1999. [Online]

Manguin, Pierre-Yves. *Les Nguyen, Macau et le Portugal: Aspects politiques et commerciaux d'une relation privilégiée en mer de Chine, 1773–1802*. Paris: École française d'extrême orient, 1984.

Miller, Edward Garvey. "Grand Designs: Vision, Power and Nation Building in America's Alliance with Ngo Dinh Diem, 1954–1960." Ph.D. diss., Harvard University, 2004.

Minh Mang chinh yeu (*Essential Records of Minh Menh*). 3 vols. Hue: Nha Xuat Ban Thuan Hoa, 1994.

Minh Menh chinh yeu (*Essential Records of Minh Menh*). 6 vols. Saigon: Phu Quoc Vu Khanh Dac Trach Van Hoa Xuat Ban, 1972.

N. D. [Vo Van Kiet]. "Luong thuc va gia ca, tien te—Hai van de noi bat trong 6 thang dang nam" (Food, Prices, and Money—Two Problems That Have Emerged in the Past 6 Months). *Nhan Dan*, June 28, 1988.

Ngo Cao Lang. *Lich trieu tap ky* (*Miscellaneous Records of Successive Dynasties*). Vhv. 1321/1. Han Nom Institute Library, Hanoi.

——. *Lich trieu tap ky* (*Miscellaneous Records of Successive Dynasties*). Translated by Hoa Bang and Hoang Van Lau. Hanoi: Nha Xuat Ban Khoa Hoc Xa Hoi, 1995.

Ngo Dinh Diem. *Major Policy Speeches by President Ngo Dinh Diem*. 3rd ed. Saigon: Press Office of the Presidency of the Republic of Vietnam, July 1957.

Ngo Duc Tho, ed. *Cac nha khoa bang Viet Nam, 1075–1919* (*The Examination Laureates of Vietnam, 1075–1919*). Hanoi: Nha Xuat Ban Van Hoc, 1993.

——. *Nghien cuu chu huy Viet Nam qua cac trieu dai* (*Research into Forbidden Characters in Vietnam Throughout the Dynasties*). Hanoi: Nha Xuat Ban Van Hoa, 1997.

Ngo Gia Van Phai. *Hoang Le nhat thong chi* (*The Unification Records of the Imperial Le*). Translated by Nguyen Duc Van and Kieu Thu Hoach. Ho Chi Minh City: Nha Xuat Ban Van Hoc, 1998.

——. *Hoang Le nhat thong chi* (*The Unification Records of the Imperial Le*). Vol. 5 of *Collection romans et contes du Viet Nam écrits en Han*. Paris: École française d'extrême orient; Taipei: Student Book Company, 1986.

Ngo Si Lien. *Dai Viet su ky toan thu* (*Complete Chronicle of Dai Viet*). 4 vols. Hanoi: Nha Xuat Ban Khoa Hoc Xa Hoi, 1998.

Ngo Thi Nham. *Ngo Thi Nham toan tap* (*The Complete Writings of Ngo Thi Nham*). Vol. 1, edited by Lam Giang. Hanoi: Nha Xuat Ban Khoa Hoc Xa Hoi, 2003.

——. *Ngo Thi Nham toan tap* (*The Complete Writings of Ngo Thi Nham*). Vol. 2, edited by Lam Giang and Nguyen Cong Viet. Hanoi: Nha Xuat Ban Khoa Hoc Xa Hoi, 2004.

——. *Tho van Ngo Thi Nham: Truc Lam dai vien giac thanh* (*The Writings of Ngo Thi Nham: The Sound of the True Great and Perfect Enlightenment from the Bamboo Grove*). Hanoi: Nha Xuat Ban Khoa Hoc Xa Hoi, 1978.

——. *Tuyen tap tho van Ngo Thi Nham* (*The Collected Writings of Ngo Thi Nham*). Vol. 2, translated by Mai Quoc Lien et al.; edited by Ngoc Hy. Hanoi: Nha Xuat Ban Khoa Hoc Xa Hoi, 1978.

Nguyen An Ninh. "L'idéal de la jeunesse annamite" (The Ideal of Annamese Youth). *La cloche fêlée*, January 7, 1924.

Nguyen Cam Thuy and Nguyen Pham Hung. *Van tho nom thoi Tay Son (Nom Literature of the Tay Son Period)*. Hanoi: Nha Xuat Ban Khoa Hoc Xa Hoi, 1997.

Nguyen Khac Vien and Huu Ngoc, eds. *Vietnamese Literature*. Hanoi: Red River, n.d.

Nguyen Khoa Chiem. *Viet Nam khai quoc chi truyen (Recorded Tales of the Founding of the Country of Vietnam)*. A.24. Han Nom Institute Library, Hanoi.

Nguyen Nam. "Being Confucian in Sixteenth Century Vietnam: Reading Stele Inscriptions from the Mac Dynasty." In *Confucianism in Vietnam*, 139–57. Ho Chi Minh City: Vietnam National University, 2002.

Nguyen Q. Thang and Nguyen Ba The. *Tu dien nhan vat lich su Viet Nam (Dictionary of Historical Figures of Vietnam)*. Ho Chi Minh City: Nha Xuat Ban Van Hoa, 1993.

Nguyen Thai Hoc. "Thu gui Ha Nghi Vien Phap" (Letter Addressed to the French Chambre des Députés). In *Tong tap van hoc Viet Nam*. Vol. 18, compiled by Chuong Thau. Hanoi: Nha Xuat Ban Khoa Hoc Xa Hoi, 2000.

Nguyen Thanh-Nha. *Tableau économique du Vietnam aux XVIIe et XVIIIe siècles*. Paris: Éditions Cujas, 1970.

Nguyen Thi Dinh. *No Other Road to Take: Memoir of Mrs. Nguyen Thi Dinh*. Translated by Mai Elliott. Data Paper 102. Ithaca, N.Y.: Cornell University, Southeast Asia Program, 1976.

Nguyen Thi Thap. *Tu dat Tien Giang (From the Land of Tien Giang)*. Ho Chi Minh City: Nha Xuat Ban Van Nghe, 1986.

Nguyen Trai. "Binh Ngo dai cao" (Great Proclamation on the Defeat of the Ming). In *Uc-Trai tap (Collected Writings of Nguyen Trai)*. Vol. 1. Saigon: Phu Quoc-Vu-Khanh Dac-Trach Van-Hoa, 1972.

——. *Du dia chi (Geography)*. In *Nguyen Trai toan tap (The Complete Works of Nguyen Trai)*. Hanoi: Nha Xuan Ban Van Hoa Thong Tin, 2001.

——. *Lam Son thuc luc (True Record of Mount Lam)*. EFEO A.26. Saigon: Tan Viet, 1956.

Nguyen Tu Cuong. *Zen in Medieval Vietnam: A Study and Translation of the Thien Uyen Tap Anh*. Honolulu: University of Hawai'i Press, 1997.

Nguyen Van Binh. "Le milieu socioculturel des catholiques vietnamiens et les problèmes de l'enseignement catéchetique" (The Sociocultural Milieu of Vietnamese Catholics and the Problems Teaching Catechism). *La documentation catholique*, November 6, 1977.

Nguyen Van Sieu. *Dai Viet dia du toan bien (The Complete Compilation of the Geography of Dai Viet)*. EFEO microfilm A.72, no. 53. Cornell University, Ithaca, N.Y.

——. *Dai Viet dia du toan bien (The Complete Compilation of the Geography of Dai Viet)*. Hanoi: Vien Su Hoc, 1997.

Nha Ca. *Tho Nha Ca (The Poems of Nha Ca)*. Westminster, Calif.: Vietbook, 1999.

O'Harrow, Stephen. "Men of Hu, Men of Han, Men of the Hundred Man." *Bulletin de l'École française d'Extrême-Orient* 75 (1981): 249–66.

Pham Dinh Ho. *Vu trung tuy but (Following the Brush Amid the Rains)*. Translated by Nguyen Huu Tien. Ho Chi Minh City: Nha Xuat Ban Van Nghe Thanh Pho Ho Chi Minh, 1998.

———. *Vu trung tuy but* (*Following the Brush Amid the Rains*). Translated by Tran Thi Kim Anh. Hanoi: Nha Xuat Ban Khoa Hoc Xa Hoi, 2003.

Pham Quynh. "Bai dien thuyet bang Phap van cua ong Pham Quynh" (Speech in French Given by Pham Quynh). *Nam Phong*, August 1924, 94–96.

———. "Réforme intellectuelle et morale" (Intellectual and Moral Reform). *Nam Phong*, November 1930, 36–38.

Phan Boi Chau. "Hai ngoai huyet thu" (A Letter from Abroad Written in Blood). In *Phan Boi Chau toan tap* (*Complete Works of Phan Boi Chau*). Vol. 2, edited by Chuong Thau. Hue: Nha Xuat Ban Thuan Hoa Trung Tam Van Hoa Ngon Ngu Dong Tay, 2001.

———. "Viet Nam vong quoc su" (The History of the Loss of the Country). In *Phan Boi Chau toan tap* (*Complete Works of Phan Boi Chau*). Vol. 2, edited by Chuong Thau. Hue: Nha Xuat Ban Thuan Hoa Trung Tam Van Hoa Ngon Ngu Dong Tay, 2001.

Phan Chau Trinh. *Phan Chau Trinh and His Political Writings*. Translated and edited by Vinh Sinh. Ithaca, N.Y.: Cornell University, Southeast Asia Program, 2009.

[Phan] Doan Nam. "Ket hop suc manh dan toc voi suc manh thoi dai trong giai doan cach mang moi" (Aligning the Strength of the Nation with the Power of the Age in the New Revolutionary Stage). *Tap Chi Cong San*, no. 1 (1987).

Phan Huy Chu. *Hai trinh chi luoc* (*Summary Record of an Overseas Voyage*). In "Récit sommaire d'un voyage en mer." Edited by Phan Huy Le. *Cahier d'archipel* 25 (1994).

———. *Hoang Viet dia du chi* (*Records of the Imperial Viet Territories*). EFEO microfilm A.71. Cornell University, Ithaca, N.Y.

———. *Hoang Viet dia du chi* (*Records of the Imperial Viet Territories*). Hue: Nha Xuat Ban Thuan Hoa, 1997.

———. *Lich trieu hien chuong loai chi* (*Categorized Records of the Institutions of Successive Dynasties*). 3 vols. Saigon: Bo Van Hoa Giai Duc va Thanh Nien Xuat Ban, 1973.

Phan Thuc Truc. *Quoc su di bien* (*Lost Records of the National History*). Saigon: Phu Quoc Vu Khanh Dac Trach Van Hoa Xuat Ban, 1973.

Reid, Anthony, ed. *The Last Stand of Asian Autonomies: Responses to Modernity in the Diverse States of Southeast Asia and Korea, 1750–1900*. New York: St. Martin's Press, 1997.

Reid, Anthony, and David G. Marr, eds. *Perceptions of the Past in Southeast Asia*. Singapore: Heinemann Educational Books, 1979.

Republic of Vietnam. *Cong Bao Viet Nam Cong Hoa* (*Official Gazette of the Republic of Vietnam*). August 23 and September 8, 1956.

Socialist Republic of Vietnam. *Sixth National Congress of the Communist Party of Vietnam*. Hanoi: Foreign Languages Publishing House, 1987.

Taboulet, Georges. *La geste française en Indochine: Histoire par les textes de la France en Indochine des origines a 1914*. Vol. 1. Paris: Librarie d'Amerique et d'Orient, 1956.

"Tai lieu tham khao: Hich cua Le Duy Mat ke toi ho Trinh" (Documentary Research: The Proclamation of Le Duy Mat Detailing the Crimes of the Trinh Clan). *Nghien Cuu Lich Su*, no. 108 (1968): 58–59.

Taylor, Keith W. "Authority and Legitimacy in 11th Century Vietnam." In *Southeast Asia in the 9th to 14th Centuries,* edited by David G. Marr and A. C. Milner, 139–76. Singapore: Institute for Southeast Asian Studies, 1986.

——. *The Birth of Vietnam.* Berkeley: University of California Press, 1983.

——. "The Literati Revival in Seventeenth-Century Vietnam." *Journal of Southeast Asia Studies* 18 (1987): 1–23.

——. "Looking Behind the Viet Annals: Ly Phat Ma and Ly Nhat Ton in the *Viet Su Luoc* and the *Dai Viet Su Ky Toan Thu.*" *Vietnam Forum* 7 (1986): 47–68.

——. "The Rise of Dai Viet and the Establishment of Thang-Long." In *Explorations in Early Southeast Asian History: The Origins of Southeast Asian Statecraft,* edited by Kenneth R. Hall and John K. Whitmore, 149–91. Ann Arbor: University of Michigan, Center for South and Southeast Asian Studies, 1976.

——. "Voices Within and Without: Tales from Stone and Paper About Do Anh Vu." In *Essays into Vietnamese Pasts,* edited by K. W. Taylor and John K. Whitmore, 59–80. Ithaca, N.Y.: Cornell University, Southeast Asia Program, 1995.

Taylor, K. W., and John K. Whitmore, eds. *Essays into Vietnamese Pasts.* Ithaca, N.Y.: Cornell University, Southeast Asia Program, 1995.

Thanh Tam Tuyen. *Toi khong con co doc (I No Longer Am Desolate).* Saigon: Nguoi Viet, 1956.

Thich Nhat Hanh. *The Miracle of Mindfulness: An Introduction to the Practice of Meditation.* Boston: Beacon Press, 1987.

Thien nam du ha tap (Record of Government Institutes of the South of Heaven). EFEO microfilm A.334.

Tho van Ly Tran (Ly and Tran Poetry and Prose). Vols. 1 and 2. Hanoi: Nha Xuat Ban Khoa Hoc Xa Hoi, 1978, 1989.

Thuong Si. *Thuong Si ngu luc (Collected Sayings of Thuong Si).* Hanoi: Association bouddhique du Tonkin, 1943.

Tran Dam Trai. *Hai Duong phong vat chi (Records of the Customs and People of Hai Duong).* Saigon: Nha Van Hoa Bo Van Hoa Giao Duc va Thanh Nien Xuat Ban, 1968.

Tran Dan. *Ghi, 1954–1960.* Edited by Pham Thi Hoai. Paris: Td memoire 2001.

Tran Do. "Thu cua Tran Do gui Dang, Quoc Hoi, Chinh Phu" (Letter Sent by Tran Do to the Party, National Assembly, and Government). 1998. Kroch Collection. Cornell University Library, Ithaca, N.Y.

Tran Nghia and François Gros, eds. *Di san Han Nom Viet Nam thu muc de yeu (Catalog of the Han Nom Heritage of Vietnam).* Vol. 1. Hanoi: Nha Xuat Ban Khoa Hoc Xa Hoi, 1993.

Tran Quoc Vuong. "The Legend of Ong Giong from the Text to the Field." In *Essays into Vietnamese Pasts,* edited by K. W. Taylor and John K. Whitmore, 13–41. Ithaca, N.Y.: Cornell University, Southeast Asia Program, 1995.

——, ed. *Viet su luoc (Short History of Dai Viet).* 1960. Reprint, Hue: Nha Xuat Ban Thuan Hoa, 2005.

Tran Thai Tong. "Thien ton chi nam" (A Guide to Thien). In *Ngu khoa hu (Exhortations on Resolution).* Reprinted in *Viet Nam phat dien tung khan (A General Collection of Buddhist Books in Vietnam).* Hanoi, 1943.

Tran Trong Kim. *Nho giao (Confucianism).* Bo Giao Duc: Trung Tam Hoc Lieu Xuat Ban, 1971.

Tran Van Giap. *Tim hieu kho sach Han Nom, nguon tu lieu van hoc su hoc Viet Nam* (*Investigating the Han Nom Treasury: The Foundational Documents of the Literary and Historical Study of Vietnam*). Hanoi: Nha Xuat Ban Khoa Hoc Xa Hoi, 1990.

Tran Van Tra. "Tet: The 1968 General Offensive and General Uprising." In *The Vietnam War: Vietnamese and American Perspectives*, edited by Jayne S. Werner and Luu Doan Huynh, 37–65. Armonk, N.Y.: Sharpe, 1991.

Tri Hai. "Vi sao ma phai chan hung Phat Giao" (Why We Must Revive Buddhism). *Duoc Tue*, February 20, 1938.

Trinh Cong Son. *Ca khuc da vang* (*Songs of Golden Skin*). 5th ed. Saigon: Nhan Ban, 1967.

Trinh Hoai Duc. *Gia Dinh thanh thong chi* (*Gia Dinh Citadel Records*). Ho Chi Minh City: Nha Xuat Ban Giao Duc, 1998.

Truong Ba Can. *Nguyen Truong To: Con nguoi va di thao* (*Nguyen Truong To: The Person and His Written Legacy*). Ho Chi Minh City: Nha Xuat Ban Thanh Pho Ho Chi Minh, 2002.

Truong Buu Lam. *Patterns of Vietnamese Response to Foreign Intervention, 1858–1900*. Monograph Series no. 11. New Haven, Conn.: Yale University, Southeast Asia Studies, 1967.

Truong Chinh. "Marxism and the Issue of Vietnamese Culture." In *Selected Writings*. Hanoi: Foreign Languages Publishing House, 1977.

——. "Political Report to the Conference on National Unification." In *Selected Writings*. Hanoi: Foreign Languages Publishing House, 1977.

Truong Vinh Ky. *Voyage au Tonking en 1876* (*Chuyen di Bac-Ki Nam At-Hoi [1876]*). Saigon: Guilland et Martinon, 1881. In *Voyage to Tonking in the Year At-Hoi* (*Truyen di Bac Ky*), translated and edited by P. J. Honey, 14–16. London: University of London, School of Oriental and African Studies, 1982.

——. *Voyage to Tonking in the Year At-Hoi* (*Truyen di Bac Ky*). Translated and edited by P. J. Honey. London: University of London, School of Oriental and African Studies, 1982.

Ung Qua. "Le *Binh Ngo Dai Cao*, une texte vietnamienne du XVe s." *Bulletin de l'école française d'extrême orient* 46 (1954): 283–95.

Ungar, Esta Serne. "Vietnamese Leadership and Order: Dai Viet Under the Le Dynasty (1428–59)." Ph.D. diss., Cornell University, 1983.

Vo Nguyen Giap. "People's War, People's Army." In *The Military Art of People's War: Selected Writings of General Vo Nguyen Giap*, edited by Russell Stetler, 101–16. New York: Monthly Review Press, 1970.

——. "The War of Liberation, 1945–1954." In *The Military Art of People's War: Selected Writings of General Vo Nguyen Giap*, edited by Russell Stetler, 79–100. New York: Monthly Review Press, 1970.

Werner, Jayne. "The Cao Dai: The Politics of a Vietnamese Syncretic Religious Movement." Ph.D. diss., Cornell University, 1976.

Wheeler, Charles. "Buddhism in the Re-ordering of an Early Modern World: Chinese Missions to Cochinchina in the Seventeenth Century." *Journal of Global History* 2 (2007): 303–24.

Whitmore, John K. "Chung-Hsing and Cheng-T'ung in Texts of and on the Sixteenth Century." In *Essays into Vietnamese Pasts*, edited by K. W. Taylor and

John K. Whitmore, 116–36. Ithaca, N.Y.: Cornell University, Southeast Asia Program, 1995.

——. "The Establishment of Le Government in 15th Century Vietnam." Ph.D. diss., Cornell University, 1968.

——. "Literati Culture in Dai Viet, c. 1430–1840." In *Beyond Binary Histories: Reimagining Eurasia to c. 1830*, edited by Victor Lieberman, 221–44. Ann Arbor: University of Michigan Press, 1999.

——. "Text and Thought in the Hong-Duc Era (1470–97)." In *Confucianism in Vietnam*, 255–66. Ho Chi Minh City: Vietnam National University, 2002.

——. *Vietnam, Ho Quy Ly, and the Ming, 1371–1421*. Lac-Viet Series no. 2. New Haven, Conn.: Yale University, Council on Southeast Asian Studies, 1985.

Wolters, O. W. "Historians and Emperors in Vietnam and China: Comments Arising out of Le Van Huu's History, Presented to the Tran Court in 1272." In *Perceptions of the Past in Southeast Asia*, edited by Anthony Reid and David G. Marr, 69–89. Singapore: Heinemann Educational Books, 1979.

——. "Possibilities for a Reading of the 1293–1357 Period in the Vietnamese Annals." In *Southeast Asia in the 9th to 14th Centuries*, edited by David G. Marr and A. C. Milner, 369–410. Singapore: Institute for Southeast Asian Studies, 1986.

——. *Two Essays on Dai-Viet in the Fourteenth Century*. Lac-Viet Series no. 9. New Haven, Conn.: Yale University, Council on Southeast Asian Studies, 1988.

Woodside, Alexander. "Conceptions of Change and of Human Responsibility for Change in Late Traditional Vietnam." In *Moral Order and the Question of Change: Essays on Southeast Asian Thought*, edited by David K. Wyatt and Alexander Woodside, 104–50. New Haven, Conn.: Yale University Press, 1982.

——. "The Political Relationship Between Political Theory and Economic Growth in Vietnam, 1750–1840." In *The Last Stand of Asian Autonomies: Responses to Modernity in the Diverse States of Southeast Asia and Korea, 1750–1900*, edited by Anthony Reid, 245–68. New York: St. Martin's Press, 1997.

——. *Vietnam and the Chinese Model: A Comparative Study of Nguyen and Ch'ing Civil Government in the First Half of the Nineteenth Century*. Cambridge, Mass.: Harvard University Press, 1988.

Xuan Dieu. *Tuyen tap Xuan Dieu (Collected Works of Xuan Dieu)*. Hanoi: Nha Xuat Ban Van Hoc, 1983.

Yamamoto Tatsurō. "Van-Don: A Trade Port in Vietnam." *Memoirs of the Research Department of the Tōyō Bunko* 39 (1981): 1–28.

PERMISSIONS

The editors and publisher acknowledge with thanks permission granted to reprint in this volume the following material.

James A. Anderson, *The Rebel Den of Nung Tri Cao: Loyalty and Identity Along the Sino-Vietnamese Frontier*. Copyright © 2007 by University of Washington Press. Reprinted by permission of the publisher.

Charles Stuart Callison, *Land-to-the-Tiller in the Mekong Delta*. Monograph Series no. 23. Berkeley: Center for South and South East Asia Studies, University of California, 1983. Reprinted by permission of University Press of America.

Chu Van Tan, *Reminiscence on the Army of National Salvation: Memoir of Chu Van Tan*. Translated by Mai Elliot. Ithaca, N.Y.: Cornell University, Southeast Asia Program, 1995. Reprinted by permission of Cornell University, Southeast Asia Program.

Cuong Tu Nguyen, *Zen in Medieval Vietnam: A Study and Translation of Thien Uyen Tap Anh*. Copyright © 1997 by University of Hawai'i Press. Reprinted by permission of the publisher.

Ho Xuan Huong, "On Being a Concubine," "Ode to the Fan," and "Poking Fun at a Bonze," in *An Anthology of Vietnamese Poems: From the Eleventh Through the Twentieth Centuries*, edited and translated by Huynh Sanh Thong. New Haven, Conn.: Yale University Press, 1996. Reprinted by permission of the publisher.

Liam C. Kelley, *Beyond the Bronze Pillars: Envoy Poetry and the Sino-Vietnamese Relationship*. Copyright © 2005 by University of Hawai'i Press. Reprinted by permission of the publisher.

Le Quy Don, "Miscellaneous Nguyen Records Seized in 1775–6 [Miscellaneous Records of Pacification in the Border Area]." Excerpts translated by Li Tana in *Southern Vietnam Under the Nguyen: Documents on the Economic History of Cochinchina (Dang Trong), 1602–1777*, edited by Li Tana and Anthony Reid (1993), pp. 124–5 (2 pages). Reproduced here with the kind permission of the publisher, Institute of Southeast Asian Studies, Singapore, http://bookshop.iseas.edu.sg.

Ly Te Xuyen, *Departed Spirits of the Viet Realm*, translated by Brian E. Ostrowski and Brian A. Zottoli. Ithaca, N.Y.: Cornell University, Southeast Asia Program, 1999. Reprinted by permission of Cornell University, Southeast Asia Program.

Nguyen Du, "A Dirge for All Ten Classes of Beings," in *An Anthology of Vietnamese Poems: From the Eleventh Through the Twentieth Centuries*, edited and translated by Huynh Sanh Thong. New Haven, Conn.: Yale University Press, 1996. Reprinted by permission of the publisher

Nguyen Nam, "Being Confucian in Sixteenth Century Vietnam: Reading Stele Inscriptions from the Mac Dynasty," in *Confucianism in Vietnam*. Ho Chi Minh City: Vietnam National University, 2002. Reprinted by permission of the author.

From the book *The Le Code: Law in Traditional Vietnam* by Nguyen Ngoc Huy and Tan Van Tai with the cooperation of Tran Van Liem. Reprinted with permission of Ohio University Press, Athens, Ohio (www.ohioswallow.com).

Nguyen Thi Dinh, *No Other Road to Take: Memoir of Mrs. Nguyen Thi Dinh*. Translated by Mai Elliot. Ithaca, N.Y.: Cornell University, Southeast Asia Program, 2000; first published 1976. Reprinted by permission of Cornell University, Southeast Asia Program.

Nguyen Van Binh, "Le milieu socioculturel des catholiques vietnamiens et les problèmes de l'enseignement catéchetique," *La documentation catholique*, November 6, 1977. Reprinted by permission of La documentation catholique.

Nha Ca, "The Bell of Thien Mu." Translated by Ton That Quynh Du. Reprinted by permission of the author.

Stephen O'Harrow, "Men of Hu, Men of Han, Men of the Hundred Man," *Bulletin de l'École française d'Extrême-Orient* 75 (1986): 249–266. Reprinted by permission of the publisher and the author.

Phan Chau Trinh, *Phan Chau Trinh and His Political Writings*. Translated and edited by Vinh Sinh. Ithaca, N.Y.: Cornell University, Southeast Asia Program, 2009. Reprinted by permission of Cornell University, Southeast Asia Program.

Phan Thi Thanh Nhan, "Secret Scent," in *Mountain River: Vietnamese Poetry from the Wars, 1948–1993*, edited by Kevin Bowen, Nguyen Ba Chung, and Bruce Weigl. Amherst: University of Massachusetts Press, 1998. Reprinted by permission of the publisher.

Keith W. Taylor, "Authority and Legitimacy in 11th Century Vietnam," in *Southeast Asia in the 9th to 14th Centuries*, edited by David Marr and A. C. Milner (Singapore: Institute of Southeast Asian Studies, 1986), pp. 162–3 (2 pages). Reproduced here with the kind permission of the publisher, Institute of Southeast Asian Studies, Singapore, http://bookshop.iseas.edu.sg.

Keith W. Taylor, *The Birth of Vietnam*. Berkeley: University of California Press, 1983. Reprinted by permission of University of California Press and the author.

Keith W. Taylor. "Looking Behind the Viet Annals: Ly Phat Ma and Ly Nhat Ton in the *Viet Su Luoc* and the *Dai Viet Su Ky Toan Thu*," *Vietnam Forum* 7 (1986): 47–68. Reprinted by permission of Council on Southeast Asia Studies.

Keith W. Taylor, "Voices Within and Without: Tales from Stone and Paper About Do Anh Vu," in *Essays into Vietnamese Pasts*, edited by K. W. Taylor and John K. Whitmore. Ithaca, N.Y.: Cornell University, Southeast Asia Program, 1995. Reprinted by permission of Cornell University, Southeast Asia Program.

The Miracle of Mindfulness by Thich Nhat Hanh. Copyright © 1975, 1976 by Thich Nhat Hanh. Preface and English translation Copyright © 1975, 1976, 1987 by Mobi Ho. Reprinted by permission of Beacon Press, Boston.

To Huu, "Prison Thoughts," in *An Anthology of Vietnamese Poems: From the Eleventh Through the Twentieth Centuries*, edited and translated by Huynh Sanh Thong. New Haven, Conn.: Yale University Press, 1996. Reprinted by permission of the publisher.

Originally published as General Tran Van Tra, "Tet: The 1968 General Offensive," in *The Vietnamese War: Vietnamese and American Perspectives*, ed. Jayne S. Werner and Luu Doan Huynh (Armonk, N.Y.: M. E. Sharpe, 1993): 37–65. English translation copyright © 1993 by M. E. Sharpe, Inc. Used by permission.

Truong Bu Lam, *Patterns of Vietnamese Response to Foreign Intervention, 1858–1900*. New Haven, Conn.: Council on Southeast Asia Studies, Yale Center for International and Area Studies, 1967. Reprinted by permission of Council on Southeast Asia Studies.

Esta Serne Ungar, "Vietnamese Leadership and Order: Dai Viet Under the Le Dynasty (1428–59)" (Ph.D. diss., Cornell University, 1983). Reprinted by permission of the author.

Vo Nguyen Giap, "People's War, People's Army," and "The War of Liberation, 1945–1954," in *The Military Art of People's War: Selected Writings of General Vo Nguyen Giap*, edited by Russell Stetler. Reprinted by permission of Monthly Review Press.

John K. Whitmore, "The Establishment of Le Government in 15th Century Vietnam" (Ph.D. diss., Cornell University, 1968). Reprinted by permission of the author.

John K. Whitmore, "Text and Thought in the Hong Duc Era (1470–97)," in *Confucianism in Vietnam*. Ho Chi Minh City: Vietnam National University, 2002. Reprinted by permission of the author.

John K. Whitmore, *Vietnam, Ho Quy Ly, and the Ming, 1371–1421*. New Haven, Conn.: Council on Southeast Asia Studies, Yale Center for International and Area Studies, 1985. Reprinted by permission of Council on Southeast Asia Studies.

O. W. Wolters, "Historians and Emperors in Vietnam and China: Comments Arising Out of Le Van Huu's History, Presented to the Tran Court in 1272," from *Perceptions of the Past in Southeast Asia*, edited by A. Reid and D. G. Marr. Singapore: Published for the Asian Studies Association of Australia by Heinemann Educational Books (Asia), 1979. Reprinted by permission of the Asian Studies Association of Australia.

O. W. Wolters, "Possibilities for a Reading of the 1293–1357 Period in the Vietnamese Annals," in *Southeast Asia in the 9th to 14th Centuries*, edited by David Marr and A. C. Milner (Singapore: Institute of Southeast Asian Studies, 1986), pp. 388–91 and p. 395 (5 pages). Reproduced here with the kind permission of the publisher, Institute of Southeast Asian Studies, Singapore, http://bookshop.iseas.edu.sg.

O. W. Wolters, *Two Essays on Dai-Viet in the Fourteenth Century*. New Haven, Conn.: Council on Southeast Asia Studies, Yale Center for International and Area Studies, 1988. Reprinted by permission of Council on Southeast Asia Studies.

Tatsurō Yamamoto, "Van-don: A Trade Port in Vietnam," *Memoirs of the Research Department of the Toyo Bunko* 39 (1981): 1–28.

INDEX

acupuncture, 52, 64, 74

"Against the Rhapsody in Praise of West Lake" (poem; Pham Thai), 242

Agrarian Reform Law (1953), 496

agriculture: Chinese introduction of, 25, 26; collectivization of, 448–49, 496–99, 518; in French colonial period, 348, 352–53, 370, 373, 417, 428–29; in independence period, 448–49, 488, 496–99, 504, 506, 517–22; in Le dynasty, 91, 103–5, 123–24, 166–67, 496; in Ly-Tran-Ho period, 29, 30, 41, 42, 71; in Mac dynasty, 92; in Nguyen dynasty, 273, 274; reforms of, 370, 373, 504, 506, 518–19; taxation of, 273–74, 352–53; in Tay Son dynasty, 166–68; in Trinh-Nguyen period, 175n.18, 199; and war against France, 462; and Westernization, 428–29

Ai Lao, 1, 87, 154

Aleni, Giulio, 173

American war (1960–1975): bombing in, 454, 469; and Cambodia, 467; and Catholicism, 550; and Geneva Agreements, 455; Ho Chi Minh on, 454–57; and Japan, 471; and Laos, 465, 467; literature on, 542–47; and NLF, 454, 455, 478, 484–85, 550; opposition to, in U.S., 456, 468–69, 472; and Paris peace talks, 467, 468, 469, 470; Phoenix program in, 467; and reunification, 487, 489; Tet Offensive in, 448, 463–73, 543; Vietnamese military in, 448, 570–76; Vietnamization policy in, 466, 469, 470, 552n.56; women in, 472, 478, 482–83, 547, 551, 553

An Duong (Thuc Phan; king of Au Lac), 13–14, 243n.101, 314

An Lushan, 207, 339n.3, 340n.7

Analects (Confucius), 59, 191n.35, 296n.21, 321n.44

Annam (Annan), 1, 12, 16, 72, 154, 258, 259, 260; French protectorate of, 337, 348, 382. *See also* Vietnam: names for

ancestor worship, 26, 74, 92, 107, 111, 130, 136, 439, 442–43, 500, 552

Angkor, kingdom of (Cambodia), 29, 33, 46, 54, 83–84

animals, draft, 41, 92, 103–4

aristocracy, 20, 426; in Le dynasty, 89, 91–93, 116, 118, 127–28; vs. literati, 119–20; in Ly-Tran-Ho period, 29, 31, 46, 51, 54, 63, 73, 75, 78–79, 83, 87–88, 226; in Mac dynasty, 92. *See also* elites

Cao Van Vien, 464

Cao Zhi, 362n.29

capitalism, 488, 530; and democracy, 495; and global economy, 337, 449, 579–83; and imperialism, 487; and Marxism, 488; and reform, 494–95, 507

Castro, Guilhem de, 403

Categorized Records of the Institutions of Successive Dynasties (*Lich trieu hien chuong loai chi*; Phan Huy Chu), 4, 112, 265, 273–74, 277–80, 315–17

Categorized Sayings from the Van Terrace (*Van dai loai ngu*; Le Quy Don), 170–74

Catholicism, 223, 329; in American war, 482, 550; vs. Buddhism, 329; in French colonial period, 360, 363; and Marxism, 561–64; in Nguyen dynasty, 256, 284, 325–26; in Republic of Vietnam, 447–48, 476, 482; in reunified Vietnam, 449, 569

Celestial South's [Records Made] at Leisure (*Thien Nam du ha tap*), 130, 132, 241

Chaisson, John, 466

Champa, 1, 263–64; Buddhism in, 10, 30; and China, 10–11, 27, 140–41; culture of, 43, 82–83; in French colonial period, 357; in independence period, 576; and Le dynasty, 91–92, 94, 138, 139–42, 143; in Ly-Tran-Ho period, 29, 31, 33, 40, 47–48, 68, 82–84, 87, 89; and Nguyen dynasty, 261–63, 316; in Trinh-Nguyen period, 148–50, 154, 241

Chat Da Tu Na, 264

Che Bong Nga, 141

Chen dynasty (China), 154

Chen Shi, 178

Chen Shou, 10–12, 15, 17, 21–22, 26

Cheng (Chinese ruler of antiquity), 32

Cheng Hao, 59

Cheng Tang, 246n.124

Cheng Yi, 59

Chi Dam (prince). *See* Minh Mang emperor

Chi Thanh (Cam Thanh; Buddhist monk), 62

Chieu Linh Queen Mother (Ly dynasty), 84–85

"Child-Giving Guanyin, The," 180–86

children: Le Code on, 133–34; in Marriage and Family Law, 539–40

China: and Buddhism, 18–19, 49–50, 180; bureaucracy of, 89–90, 92, 94; calendar of, 313–14; and Champa, 10–11, 27, 140–41; culture of, 10, 17, 232, 235, 241, 245nn.120–21, 383; dominance of, 9–28, 153–55;

envoys to, 263, 270, 300; and European colonialism, 255, 275–76, 284, 320; in French colonial period, 373–75, 404; geography of, 4, 96–97; influence of, 25–26, 81, 84, 116, 295, 297–98, 306–7, 407–8, 522; and Le dynasty, 93, 121–22, 138–39, 202, 217; literature of, 95, 239–41, 403, 405; in Ly-Tran-Ho period, 32, 36, 40, 67, 93; and names for Vietnam, 258–60; and Nguyen dynasty, 254, 277, 286, 288, 290; People's Republic of (PRC), 577, 579; and Tay Son, 148, 167–69; trade with, 43, 150, 162–64, 167, 210, 370; in Trinh-Nguyen period, 149–50, 154, 217. *See also* classics, Chinese; poetry, Chinese; *specific dynasties*

Chinese, ethnic, 152, 230n.86, 269, 314–15; in north, 308, 576–77; and PRC, 577; and rebellions, 148, 282; in south, 448, 576

Chinese language, written, 11, 369, 403, 418, 429; in south, 298–99; vs. Vietnamese script, 3, 336, 374

Christianity: and Cao Dai, 429; vs. Confucianism, 256; vs. filial piety, 256, 326, 328; in French colonial period, 257, 318, 320, 363; and Le Van Khoi rebellion, 281–82, 327n.50; opposition to, 254, 256, 321, 324–28; Protestant, 449, 567; restrictions on, 162, 256–57, 325–28, 567; in reunified Vietnam, 449, 562, 567, 569. *See also* Catholicism

Chronicle of Dai Viet (*Dai Viet su ky*; Le Van Huu), 27, 103, 122; on Ly-Tran-Ho period, 32–33, 41, 44, 46, 53, 67, 80, 82–83, 84–86

Chronicle of Dai Viet, Continued (*Dai Viet su ky*; Phan Phu Tien), xxxvi, 108, 118–19

Chronicle of the Three Kingdoms (*San guo zhi*; Chen Shou), 11, 15, 26

Chronicle of the Wu Dynasty (Chen Shou), 11, 15, 17, 21

Chronicles of the Prefectural Borders (*Phu bien tap luc*; Le Quy Don), 163–64

Chu Cong. *See* Zhou, Duke of

chu nom (Vietnamese script), 3, 153, 205, 242

Chu Van An, 31, 57–58, 70, 109, 266

Chu Van Tan, 570–76

Churchill, Winston, 475n.23

Cid, Le (Corneille), 403

civilization, discourses on, 48–51, 112, 342, 370, 375

"Civilization of New Learning, A" (Tonkin Free School), 369–75

Council for Mutual Economic Assistance
(CMEA), 507, 583–84
"Courtesan" (poem; Xuan Dieu), 409–11
criticism, self-criticism, 397, 401–2
culture: of Champa, 43, 82–83; Chinese, 10,
17, 232, 235, 241, 245nn.120–21, 383; and
colonialism, 522–24, 526; Confucian,
383, 415; and ethnic relations, 138–39;
European, 313–15, 382, 388, 425; foreign,
82–83, 87–88, 91, 523; French, 336, 402–3,
407–8, 522–24, 526; in independence
period, 522–54; Indian, 383–84; Japanese,
383, 425; in Le dynasty, 126–37; in
Ly-Tran-Ho period, 73–81; Marxism on,
522–30; in modern Vietnam, 521–22;
and modernization, 336, 415–24; and
nationalism, 384, 389, 523–25; in Nguyen
dynasty, 255, 257, 266, 292–310, 320; of
north, 308–10; in period of Northern
empire, 25–27; reform of, 374, 382–89;
in reunified Vietnam, 449, 521; socialist,
487–88; of south, 281, 294–99; in
Trinh-Nguyen period, 223–51; and
Vatican II, 561; Western, 403, 406–9,
417, 424–29, 450
currency: in Le dynasty, 97–98, 165; in modern
Vietnam, 510, 514, 516; in Nguyen dynasty,
274; in Trinh-Nguyen period, 150, 165–66
Cuu Chi, 45

Da Bao, 62–63
Da Bia Mountains, 155
Da Nang, xxvii, xxix, 320
Da Shan, 151
Dai (king of Zhou), 340
Dai Hanh empress, 187
Dai Kaizhi, 173
Dai La, xxiii, 13, 28, 32, 35, 268. See also
Hanoi
Dai Nam, 1, 258–60, 370
Dai Viet, 1, 72, 258, 260. See also Vietnam:
names for
Dam Di Mong, 77
Dame aux camélias, La (Dumas), 393
Dang Trung marquis, 213
Dao Duy Anh, 424–29
Dao Huang, 27
Daoism, 16, 54, 175nn.17–18, 295; and
Buddhism, 114–15; and Cao Dai, 429–30;
and Confucianism, 174
Dat Khuat, 264
Declaration of Independence (U.S.), 473–74,
495

Declaration of Independence (Vietnam),
473–76, 495
democracy: in French colonial period, 336,
353, 375–82; and Mencius, 375, 376; vs.
monarchy, 376–78, 381; new socialist,
522–24; in Republic of Vietnam, 476–78;
in reunified Vietnam, 449, 490–91,
493–96, 580; and war against France,
462–63, 574
Democratic Republic of Vietnam. See
Vietnam, Democratic Republic of
Departed Spirits of the Viet Realm (Viet dien
u linh tap; Ly Te Xuyen), 19, 23, 33, 37, 47,
56, 68, 242, 324
Di people, 23, 69
Di Renjie, 323
Diao Gan of Qin, 341n.11
Dien Bien Phu, battle of (1954), 447, 457, 460,
481, 530
Dieu Nhan, 46
dikes, 30, 42, 91, 197, 303, 329
Dinh Bo Linh, 28, 32, 44, 60
Dinh Dat, 326
Dinh dynasty, 93, 156, 218, 261, 277, 316
Dinh Hang Lang, 44
Dinh Khuong Lien, 44
Dinh Thu Cuc, 517–22
"Dirge for All Ten Classes of Beings, A"
(poem; Nguyen Du), 299–304
Do Anh Vu, 51–52, 63–65, 67, 73–75, 83–84,
122–23
Do Thien, 13, 56
Do Tu Binh, 109
Doi Moi (Renovation), 449, 490, 504–9, 517,
565. See also reform
Dong Ho paintings, 450–51
Dong Kinh Nghia Thuc. See Tonkin Free
School
Dong Nai, 169, 296
Duhamel, Georges, 527
Duong Duc Nhan, 238
Duong Thanh, 154
Duong Thi Bi, 118
Duong Van An, 92, 96–97, 125–26, 189, 279

economy: and foreign relations, 507, 579–85;
in French colonial period, 337, 387;
global, 337, 449, 579–85; in independence
period, 496–522; inflation in, 510, 513–17;
of Le dynasty, 91, 97–106; of Liberated
Zone, 574; in Ly-Tran-Ho period, 29,
41–43, 97; of Nguyen dynasty, 253, 273–76;
in period of Northern empire, 15–16;

Han Guangwu (Chinese emperor, Eastern
Han dynasty), 56, 208n.59, 312
Han Lam (Hanlin) Academy, 79
Han Mac Tu, 409, 412, 542
Han Wudi (Chinese emperor, Western Han
dynasty), 142, 173, 236
Han Yu, 58–59, 176
Hanoi, xxii, xxiv, xxx, xxxii, 3, 13, 20n.8, 26,
34n.3, 40, 61, 232, 257, 263, 308–9, 329,
337n.4, 373, 426–27, 455, 469, 473, 478,
486, 513, 530, 548–49, 551, 571n.63, 576.
See also Thang Long
Hepu, 22, 56, 80
heroes, heroines, 72, 112, 346, 361–68, 398,
459, 470, 472, 476. *See also* Le Thai To;
Quang Trung (emperor); Tran Quoc
Tuan; Trung sisters
Hesse, Herman, 559
Hien Chi Queen Mother (Ly dynasty), 64
Hien Mai, 573
Hieu Vu emperor. *See* Nguyen The Tong
History (Do Thien), 13, 56
"History of the Country of Annam" (Lich su
nuoc Annam; Bento Thien), 123, 223–26
History of the Han Dynasty (Hanshu; Ban
Gu), 245n.121
*History of the Later Han Dynasty (Hou Han
shu;* Fan Ye), 21, 25
"History of the Loss of the Country, The"
(Viet Nam vong quoc su; Phan Boi
Chau), 342–53
Ho Chi Minh (Nguyen Ai Quoc), 396–402,
447, 470–71; on American war, 454–57;
and August Revolution, 575, 576; on
culture, 525; Declaration of
Independence of, 473–76; and democratic
reform, 495; on land reform, 496–99;
and Marriage and Family Law, 536; on
reunification, 486–87; and Viet Minh,
571, 573
Ho Chi Minh Trail (Truong Son trail), 467,
576
Ho dynasty, 31, 40, 89, 97, 118, 241
Ho Hao Nghia, 485
Ho Quy Ly (Le Quy Ly; emperor, Ho
dynasty), 31, 72, 90, 165; and literati,
58–60, 81, 111–12
Ho Xuan Huong, 305–6
Hoa Hao (Peace and Harmony; Buddhist
sect), 337, 438–44, 449
Hoan Kiem (lake), 265, 268
Hoang Cam, 450–54
Hoang Cao Khai, 346

Hoang Dao, 406–9
Hoang Dieu, 337–39
Hoang Duc Luong, 94–95, 238
Hoang Quang, 152, 229–31
Hoang To, 204
Hoang Van Thai, 575
Hoanh, Mount, 140, 155, 165, 312, 358
Hoi Luong, 282
Hon Dien, 263
Hong Kong, 396
Hongwu. *See* Ming Taizu
Hou Chi (Hau Tac), 51
household registers. *See* village registers
Huang Fu, 267
Huang Gai, 365
Hue, xxxvi, 40, 92, 96, 125, 253–55, 280, 306,
340, 372, 543, 562. *See also* Phu Xuan
Hue Lam, 47–48
Huineng, 53
Huizong Tangxiu, 239
Hung kings, xxi, 31, 39–40, 59, 156, 436
hunger, 73, 117, 123–24, 474, 510
Huong Hai, 239
huong hoa (incense and fire) ritual land, 130,
136, 137, 500
Huy Can, 409, 411–12
Huy Quan, 210
Huyen Quang, 176n.20, 239
Huyen Thien, 267
Huynh Cong Ly, 281
Huynh Phu So, 438–44

"Ideal of Annamese Youth, The" (L'idéal de
la jeunesse annamite; Nguyen An Ninh),
382–89
Imperial Rescript on Education (Japan),
391–92
imperialism, 518, 526–28, 581; war against,
457–59, 474. *See also* Britain: colonialism
of; France: colonialism of
*Imperially Ordered Mirror and Commentary
on the History of the Viet, The (Kham
dinh Viet su thong giam cuong muc),*
290–92
India, 264, 286; in Ly-Tran-Ho period, 48, 49,
50; trade with, 15, 18; vs. Vietnamese
culture, 383–84, 405
individualism, 390, 406–9, 426, 524, 542; vs.
collectivism, 398–402, 522, 524
Indra (god), 29–30, 46–47
industrialization, 373, 417, 493, 584; and new
working class, 427–28; and reform, 374,
394, 504–6; and socialism, 487–88